Excel® 2016 Formulas

Excel® 2016 Formulas

Michael Alexander
Dick Kusleika

WILEY

Excel® 2016 Formulas

Published by
John Wiley & Sons, Inc.
10475 Crosspoint Boulevard
Indianapolis, IN 46256
www.wiley.com

Published simultaneously in Canada

ISBN: 978-1-119-06786-3

ISBN: 978-1-119-06792-4 (ebk)

ISBN: 978-1-119-06798-6 (ebk)

Manufactured in the United States of America

10 9 8 7 6 5 4 3 2 1

For general information on our other products and services please contact our Customer Care Department within the United States at (877) 762-2974, outside the United States at (317) 572-3993 or fax (317) 572-4002.

Wiley publishes in a variety of print and electronic formats and by print-on-demand. Some material included with standard print versions of this book may not be included in e-books or in print-on-demand. If this book refers to media such as a CD or DVD that is not included in the version you purchased, you may download this material at http://booksupport.wiley.com. For more information about Wiley products, visit www.wiley.com.

Library of Congress Control Number: 2015958259

About the Authors

Michael Alexander is a Microsoft Certified Application Developer (MCAD) and author of several books on advanced business analysis with Microsoft Access and Microsoft Excel. He has more than 15 years of experience consulting and developing Microsoft Office solutions. Mike has been named a Microsoft MVP for his ongoing contributions to the Excel community. In his spare time, he runs a free tutorial site, `www.datapigtechnologies.com`, where he shares Excel and Access tips.

Dick Kusleika has been awarded as a Microsoft MVP for 12 consecutive years and has been working with Microsoft Office for more than 20. Dick develops Access- and Excel-based solutions for his clients and has conducted training seminars on Office products in the United States and Australia. Dick also writes a popular Excel-related blog at `www.dailydoseofexcel.com`.

About the Technical Editor

Niek Otten lives in the Netherlands. He started in data processing in 1967 in an insurance company. He ran into Visicalc in 1980 and has been addicted to spreadsheets ever since. His first encounter with Excel (version 1!) was in 1985 on a Macintosh. Since 2005, Niek has been self-employed—reviewing books, writing articles, and developing Excel-related software, such as a high-performance actuarial add-in.

Credits

Acquisitions Editor
Stephanie McComb

Project Editor
Kelly Talbot

Technical Editor
Niek Otten

Production Editor
Rebecca Anderson

Copy Editor
Karen Gill

Manager of Content Development and Assembly
Mary Beth Wakefield

Marketing Director
David Mayhew

Marketing Manager
Carrie Sherrill

Professional Technology & Strategy Director
Barry Pruett

Business Manager
Amy Knies

Executive Editor
Jody Lefevere

Project Coordinator, Cover
Patrick Redmond

Proofreader
Rebecca Rider

Indexer
Johnna VanHoose Dinse

Cover Designer
Wiley

Contents at a Glance

Part VII: Appendixes

Table of Contents

Part II: Leveraging Excel Functions

Part III: Financial Formulas

Part IV: Array Formulas

Part V: Miscellaneous Formula Techniques

Part VI: Developing Custom Worksheet Functions

Part VII: Appendixes

INTRODUCTION

There's no arguing that formulas are the true engines of Excel. Employing various Excel functions, formulas enable Excel analysts to create aggregated reporting, complex calculation engines, clever dashboard models, and much more. Indeed, Excel analysts become more productive as their proficiency with Excel functions and formulas improves.

But building proficiency with Excel functions and formulas takes time. Given that Excel contains more than 400 functions, you could spend months, even years, learning which functions are best for certain tasks and which functions can be combined with others functions.

This is where this book comes in. Here, we will introduce you to the world of Excel formulas by guiding you through the various built-in functions Excel has to offer. Each chapter builds on the last, taking you from basic math functions to actually building your own custom functions.

As you'll discover, leveraging Excel functions will not only make you more productive, but it will allow you to accomplish tasks that you didn't know could be handled with Excel formulas.

What You Need to Know

This is *not* a book for beginning Excel users. If you have absolutely no experience with Excel, this is probably not the best book for you unless you're one of a rare breed who can learn a new software product almost instantaneously.

To get the most out of this book, you should have some background using Excel. Specifically, we assume that you know how to

- Create workbooks, insert sheets, save files, and complete other basic tasks.
- Navigate a workbook.
- Use the Excel Ribbon and dialog boxes.
- Use basic Windows features, such as file management and copy-and-paste techniques.

What You Need to Have

This book was written with Excel 2016 as a base, but most of the material also applies to Excel 2007–2013. If you're using a version prior to Excel 2016, you may find that a handful of functions (such as the new Forecasting functions introduced in Excel 2016) will not be available to you. Any function not available in all four versions of Excel will be called out in each chapter.

If you are using a version of Excel prior to 2007, we highly recommend you pick up a previous edition of this book. The changes introduced in Excel 2007 are so extensive that you might be hopelessly confused if you try to follow along using an earlier version of Excel.

To download the examples for this book, you need to access the Internet. The examples are discussed further in the "About This Book's Website" section, later in this Introduction.

Note

Note that the examples for this book were created on the Windows platform. For you MAC users, we can't guarantee that all examples will work with Excel for Mac. Excel's cross-platform compatibility is pretty good, but it's definitely not perfect.

As far as hardware goes, the faster the better. And, of course, the more memory in your system, the happier you'll be.

Conventions in This Book

Take a minute to skim this section and learn some of the typographic conventions used throughout this book.

Keyboard conventions

You use the keyboard to enter formulas. In addition, you can work with menus and dialog boxes directly from the keyboard—a method you may find easier if your hands are already positioned over the keys.

Formula listings

Formulas usually appear on a separate line in `monospace font`. For example, we may list the following formula:

```
=VLOOKUP(StockNumber,PriceList,2,False)
```

Excel supports a special type of formula known as an *array formula*. When you enter an array formula, press Ctrl+Shift+Enter (not just Enter). Excel encloses an array formula in brackets in order to remind you that it's an array formula. When we list an array formula, we include the brackets to make it clear that it is, in fact, an array formula. For example:

```
{=SUM(LEN(A1:A10))}
```

Note

Do not type the brackets for an array formula. Excel will put them in automatically.

VBA code listings

This book also contains examples of VBA code. Each listing appears in a `monospace font`; each line of code occupies a separate line. To make the code easier to read, we usually use one or more tabs to create indentations. Indentation is optional, but it does help to delineate statements that go together.

If a line of code doesn't fit on a single line in this book, we use the standard VBA line continuation sequence: a space followed by an underscore character. This indicates that the line of code extends to the next line. For example, the following two lines comprise a single VBA statement:

```
If Right(cell.Value, 1) = "!" Then cell.Value _
   = Left(cell.Value, Len(cell.Value) - 1)
```

You can enter this code either exactly as shown on two lines or on a single line without the trailing underscore character.

Key names

Names of keys on the keyboard appear in normal type: for example, Alt, Home, PgDn, and Ctrl. When you should press two keys simultaneously, the keys are connected with a plus sign: "Press Ctrl+G to display the Go To dialog box."

Functions, procedures, and named ranges

Excel's worksheet functions appear in all uppercase, like so: "Use the SUM function to add the values in column A."

Macro and procedure names appear in normal type: "Execute the InsertTotals procedure." We often use mixed upper- and lowercase to make these names easier to read. Named ranges appear in italic: "Select the *InputArea* range."

Unless you're dealing with text inside of quotation marks, Excel is not sensitive to case. In other words, both of the following formulas produce the same result:

```
=SUM(A1:A50)
=sum(a1:a50)
```

Excel, however, will convert the characters in the second formula to uppercase.

Mouse conventions

The mouse terminology in this book is all standard fare: pointing, clicking, right-clicking, dragging, and so on. You know the drill.

What the icons mean

Throughout the book, icons appear to call your attention to points that are particularly important.

Note

We use Note icons to tell you that something is important—perhaps a concept that may help you master the task at hand or something fundamental for understanding subsequent material.

Tip

Tip icons indicate a more efficient way of doing something or a technique that may not be obvious. These will often impress your officemates.

On the Web

These icons indicate that an example file is on this book's website. (See the upcoming "About This Book's Website" section.)

Warning

We use Warning icons when the operation that we are describing can cause problems if you're not careful.

Cross-Ref

We use the Cross Reference icon to refer you to other chapters that have more to say on a particular topic.

How This Book Is Organized

This book is divided into seven parts with each part focusing on a key aspect of Excel functions.

Part I: Understanding Formula Basics

This part is introductory in nature; it consists of Chapters 1–3. Chapter 1 sets the stage with a quick and dirty overview of Excel. This chapter is designed for readers who are new to Excel but have used other spreadsheet products. In Chapter 2, we cover the basics of formulas. This chapter is absolutely essential reading to get the most out of this book. Chapter 3 deals with names. If you thought names were just for cells and ranges, you'll see that you're missing out on quite a bit.

Part II: Leveraging Excel Functions

This part consists of Chapters 4–10. Chapter 4 covers the basics of using worksheet functions in your formulas. We get more specific in subsequent chapters. Chapter 5 deals with manipulating text, Chapter 6 covers dates and times, and Chapter 7 explores counting techniques. In Chapter 8, we discuss various types of lookup formulas. Chapter 9 deals with tables and worksheet databases; and Chapter 10 covers a variety of miscellaneous calculations, such as unit conversions and rounding.

Part III: Financial Formulas

Part III consists of three chapters (Chapters 11–13) that deal with creating financial formulas. You'll find lots of useful formulas that you can adapt to your needs.

Part IV: Array Formulas

This part consists of Chapters 14 and 15. The majority of Excel users know little or nothing about array formulas—a topic that happens to be dear to us. Therefore, we devote an entire part to this little-used yet extremely powerful feature.

Part V: Miscellaneous Formula Techniques

This part consists of Chapters 16–22. They cover a variety of topics—some of which, on the surface, may appear to have nothing to do with formulas. Chapter 16 provides lots of useful information about cleaning up data. In Chapter 17, you'll see why formulas can be important when you work with charts, and Chapter 18 covers formulas as they relate to pivot tables. Chapter 19 contains some very interesting (and useful) formulas that you can use in conjunction with Excel's conditional formatting feature. Chapter 20 covers the data validation feature. Chapter 21 covers "megaformulas," which are huge formulas that take the place of several intermediary formulas. And what do you do when your formulas don't work correctly? Consult Chapter 22 for some debugging techniques.

Part VI: Developing Custom Worksheet Functions

This part consists of Chapters 23–26. This is the part that explores Visual Basic for Applications (VBA), the key to creating custom worksheet functions. Chapter 23 introduces VBA and the VB Editor, and Chapter 24 covers programming concepts. Chapter 25 provides some necessary background on custom worksheet functions, and Chapter 26 provides a slew of custom worksheet function examples that you can use as-is or customize for your own needs.

Part VII: Appendixes

This book has two appendixes: Appendix A is a quick reference guide to Excel worksheet functions, and Appendix B contains tips on using custom number formats.

About This Book's Website

This book contains many examples, and the workbooks for those examples are available at this URL:

www.wiley.com/go/excel2016formulas

Files that have an *.xlsm extension contain VBA macros. To use the macros, you must enable the macros when you open the file (or put the files in a trusted location).

About the Power Utility Pak Offer

Toward the back of the book, you'll find a coupon that you can redeem for a discounted copy of John Walkenbach's award-winning Power Utility Pak, which comprises a collection of useful Excel utilities, plus many worksheet functions.

You can also use this coupon to purchase the complete VBA source code for a nominal fee. Studying the code is an excellent way to pick up some useful programming techniques.

You can download a 30-day trial version of the most recent version of the Power Utility Pak from John's website:

http://spreadsheetpage.com

If you find it useful, use the coupon to purchase a licensed copy at a discount.

PART I

Understanding Formula Basics

The Excel User Interface in a Nutshell

In This Chapter

- The workings of Excel workbooks
- The Excel user interface
- Protection options

In this chapter, you'll gain a foundational understanding of the various components in the Excel user interface that you'll encounter as you move through this book. You'll get a primer on some of the ways you can protect your formulas and data models before distributing your Excel files.

If you're already familiar with the basic workings of Excel, you can safely skip to the next chapter. If it has been a while since you've worked with Excel, it may be worth your time to scan this chapter to set the stage for the subsequent chapters in the book.

The Workings of Workbooks

When you think about the different components of Excel, it helps to consider a hierarchy of objects. Excel objects include the following:

- The Excel application itself
- An Excel workbook
- A worksheet in a workbook
- A range in a worksheet
- A cell in a range

Notice the existence of an *object hierarchy:* the Excel application contains workbook objects, which contain worksheet objects, which contain range objects, which contain cells. Indeed, Microsoft actually has a name for this inherent hierarchy: the *Excel object model.*

The core object in the Excel object model is the workbook. Everything that you do in Excel takes place in a workbook.

In Excel 2003 and prior versions, Excel workbook files had the default .xls extension. Excel .xls files are binary files that can be read and manipulated with any version of Excel.

Since the release of Excel 2007, Excel workbooks have been saved as .xlsx files. These .xslsx files are actually compressed folders that can be read and manipulated with Excel 2007 and higher versions.

Inside the compressed folders are a number of files that hold all the information about your workbook, including charts, macros, formatting, and the data in its cells.

Tip

If you're the curious type, make a copy of an XLSX workbook file and add a .zip extension to the filename. Then unzip the file to see what's inside.

An Excel workbook can hold any number of sheets. The four types of sheets follow:

- Worksheets
- Chart sheets
- MS Excel 4.0 macro sheets (obsolete, but still supported)
- MS Excel 5.0 dialog sheets (obsolete, but still supported)

You can open or create as many workbooks as you want (each in its own window), but only one workbook is the active workbook at any given time. Similarly, only one sheet in a workbook is the active sheet. To activate a different sheet, click its corresponding tab at the bottom of the window, or press Ctrl+PgUp (for the previous sheet) or Ctrl+PgDn (for the next sheet). To change a sheet's name, double-click its Sheet tab and type the new text for the name. Right-clicking a tab brings up a shortcut menu with some additional sheet-manipulation options.

You can also hide the window that contains a workbook by using the View ➜ Window ➜ Hide command. A hidden workbook window remains open but not visible. Use the View ➜ Window ➜ Unhide command to make the window visible again. A single workbook can display in multiple windows (choose View ➜ Window ➜ New Window). Each window can display a different sheet or a different area of the same sheet.

Worksheets

The most common type of sheet is a worksheet, which you normally think of when you think of a spreadsheet. Excel 2016 worksheets have 16,384 columns and 1,048,576 rows.

Note

Versions prior to Excel 2007 support only 256 columns and 65,536 rows. If you open such a file, Excel enters compatibility mode to work with the smaller worksheet grid. To work with the larger grid, you must save the file in one of the newer Excel formats (XLSX or XLSM). Then close the workbook and reopen it. XLSM files can contain macros; XLSX files cannot.

Having access to more cells isn't the *real* value of using multiple worksheets in a workbook. Rather, multiple worksheets are valuable because they enable you to organize your work better. Back in the old days, when a spreadsheet file consisted of a single worksheet, developers wasted a lot of time trying to organize the worksheet to hold their information efficiently. Now you can store information on any number of worksheets and still access it instantly.

You have complete control over the column widths and row heights, and you can even hide rows and columns (as well as entire worksheets). You can display the contents of a cell vertically (or at an angle) and even wrap around to occupy multiple lines. In addition, you can *merge* cells to form a larger cell.

Chart sheets

A chart sheet holds a single chart. Many users ignore chart sheets, preferring to use embedded charts, which are stored on the worksheet's drawing layer. Using chart sheets is optional, but they make it a bit easier to locate a particular chart, and they prove especially useful for presentations.

Macro sheets and dialog sheets

This section discusses two obsolete Excel features that continue to be supported.

An Excel 4.0 macro sheet, whose purpose is to hold XLM macros, is a worksheet that has some different defaults. XLM is the macro system used in Excel version 4.0 and earlier. This macro system was replaced by VBA in Excel 5.0 and is not discussed in this book.

An Excel 5.0 dialog sheet is a drawing grid that can hold text and controls. In Excel 5.0 and Excel 95, dialog sheets were used to make custom dialog boxes. UserForms were introduced in Excel 97 to replace these sheets.

The Excel User Interface

A *user interface* (UI) is the means by which an end user communicates with a computer program. The UI for Excel consists of the following components:

- Tabs and the Ribbon
- The Quick Access toolbar
- Right-click (shortcut) menus
- The mini-toolbar
- Dialog boxes
- Keyboard shortcuts
- Task panes

The Ribbon

The Ribbon is the primary UI component in Excel. The Ribbon provides the user with a single place to conveniently find every commonly used command and dialog box

Note

Before the Ribbon was introduced in Office 2007, almost every Windows program included a more convoluted system of menu bars and toolbars, each of which contained assorted commands and shortcuts.

Tip

A few commands do not appear on the Ribbon but are still available if you know where to look for them. Right-click the Quick Access toolbar and choose Customize Quick Access Toolbar. Excel displays a dialog box with a list of commands that you can add to your Quick Access toolbar. Some of these commands aren't available elsewhere in the UI. You can also add new commands to the Ribbon; just right-click the Ribbon and select Customize the Ribbon.

Tabs, groups, and tools

The Ribbon is a band of tools that stretches across the top of the Excel window. The Ribbon sports a number of tabs, including Home, Insert, Page Layout, and others. On each tab are groups that contain related tools. On the Home tab, for example, you find the Clipboard group, the Font group, the Alignment group, and others. Within the groups, you'll find command buttons that activate their respective features.

The Ribbon and all its components resize dynamically as you resize the Excel window horizontally. Smaller Excel windows collapse the tools on compressed tabs and groups, and maximized Excel windows on large monitors show everything that's available. Even in a small window, all Ribbon commands remain available. You just may need to click a few extra clicks to access them.

Navigation

Using the Ribbon is fairly easy with a mouse or touchscreen. You click a tab and then click a tool. If you prefer to use the keyboard, Microsoft has a feature just for you. Pressing Alt displays tiny squares with shortcut letters in them that hover over their respective tab or tool. Each shortcut letter that you press either executes its command or drills down to another level of shortcut letters. Pressing Esc cancels the letters or moves up to the previous level.

For example, a keystroke sequence of Alt+HBB adds a double border to the bottom of the selection. The Alt key activates the shortcut letters, the H shortcut activates the Home tab, the B shortcut activates the Borders tool menu, and the second B shortcut executes the Bottom Double Border command. Note that you don't have to keep the Alt key depressed while you press the other keys.

Contextual tabs

The Ribbon contains tabs that are visible only when they are needed. Generally, when a hidden tab appears, it's because you selected an object or a range with special characteristics (like a chart or a pivot table). A typical example is the Drawing Tools contextual tab. When you select a shape or

WordArt object, the Drawing Tools tab is made visible and active. It contains many tools that are applicable only to shapes, such as shape-formatting tools.

Dialog box launchers

At the bottom of many of the Ribbon groups is a small box icon (a dialog box launcher) that opens a dialog box related to that group. Some of the icons open the same dialog boxes but to different areas. For instance, the Font group icon opens the Format Cells dialog box with the Font tab activated. The Alignment group opens the same dialog box but activates the Alignment tab. The Ribbon makes using dialog boxes a far less frequent activity than in the past because most of the commonly used operations can be done directly from the Ribbon.

Galleries and Live Preview

A *gallery* is a large collection of tools that look like the choice they represent. The Styles gallery, for example, does not just list the name of the style but also displays it in the same formatting that will be applied to the cell.

Although galleries help to give you an idea of what your object will look like when an option is selected, Live Preview takes it to the next level. Live Preview displays your selected object or data as it will look right on the worksheet when you hover over the gallery tool. By hovering over the various tools in the Format Table gallery, you can see exactly what your selected table will look like before you commit to a format.

Backstage View

The File tab is unlike the other tabs. Clicking the File tab doesn't change the Ribbon but takes you to the Backstage View. This is where you perform most of the document-related activities: creating new workbooks, opening files, saving files, printing, and so on.

The Backstage View also gives you access to the Options dialog button, which opens a dialog box containing dozens of settings for customizing Excel.

Shortcut menus and the mini toolbar

Excel also features dozens of shortcut menus. These menus appear when you right-click after selecting one or more objects. The shortcut menus are context sensitive. In other words, the menu that appears depends on the location of the mouse pointer when you right-click. You can right-click just about anything—a cell, a row or column border, a workbook title bar, and so on.

Right-clicking items often displays the shortcut menu as well as a mini toolbar, which is a floating toolbar that contains a dozen or so of the most popular formatting commands.

Dialog boxes

Some Ribbon commands display a dialog box, from which you can specify options or issue other commands. You'll find two general classes of dialog boxes in Excel:

- **Modal dialog boxes:** When a modal dialog box is displayed, it must be closed to execute the commands. An example is the Format Cells dialog box. None of the options you specify is executed until you click OK. Or click the Cancel button to close the dialog box without making any changes.
- **Modeless dialog boxes:** These are stay-on-top dialog boxes. An example is the Find and Replace dialog box. Modeless dialog boxes usually have a Close button rather than OK and Cancel buttons.

Customizing the UI

The *Quick Access toolbar* is a set of tools that the user can customize. By default, the Quick Access toolbar contains three tools: Save, Undo, and Redo. If you find that you use a particular Ribbon command frequently, right-click the command and choose Add to Quick Access Toolbar. You can make other changes to the Quick Access toolbar from the Quick Access Toolbar tab of the Excel Options dialog box. To access this dialog box, right-click the Quick Access toolbar and choose Customize Quick Access Toolbar.

You can also customize the Ribbon by using the Customize Ribbon tab of the Excel Options dialog box. Choose File ➜ Options to display the Excel Options dialog box.

You can customize the Ribbon in these ways:

- Add a new tab.
- Add a new group to a tab.
- Add commands to a group.
- Remove groups from a tab.
- Remove commands from custom groups.
- Change the order of the tabs.
- Change the order of the groups within a tab.
- Change the name of a tab.
- Change the name of a group.
- Move a group to a different tab.
- Reset the Ribbon to remove all customizations.

That's a fairly comprehensive list of customization options, but there are some actions that you *cannot* do:

- You cannot remove built-in tabs, but you *can* hide them.
- You cannot remove commands from built-in groups.
- You cannot change the order of commands in a built-in group.

Task panes

Yet another user interface element is the task pane. Task panes appear automatically in response to several commands. For example, when working with a picture, you can right-click the image and choose Format Picture. Excel responds by displaying the Format Picture task pane. A task pane is similar to a dialog box except that you can keep it visible as long as it's needed.

By default, the task panes are docked on the right side of the Excel window, but you can move them anywhere you like by clicking the title text and dragging. Excel remembers the last position, so the next time you use a particular task pane, it will be where you left it. There's no OK button in a task pane. When you're finished using a task pane, click the Close button (X) in the upper-right corner.

Customizing onscreen display

Excel offers some flexibility regarding onscreen display (status bar, Formula bar, the Ribbon, and so on). For example, click the Ribbon Display Options control (in the title bar), and you can choose how to display the Ribbon. You can hide everything except the title bar, thereby maximizing the amount of visible information.

You can customize the status bar at the bottom of the screen. Right-click the status bar, and you see lots of options that allow you to control what information is displayed.

Many other customizations can be made by choosing File ➜ Options and clicking the Advanced tab. On this tab are several sections that deal with what displays onscreen.

Numeric formatting

Numeric formatting refers to how a value appears in the cell. In addition to choosing from an extensive list of predefined formats, you can create your own custom number formats in the Number tab of the Format Cells dialog box. (Choose the dialog box launcher at the bottom of the Home ➜ Number group.)

Excel applies some numeric formatting automatically, based on the entry. For example, if you precede a value with your local currency symbol (such as a dollar sign), Excel applies Currency number formatting. If you append a percent symbol, Excel applies Percent formatting.

Cross-Ref

Refer to Appendix B, "Using Custom Number Formats," for additional information about creating custom number formats.

The number format doesn't affect the actual value stored in the cell. For example, suppose that a cell contains the value 3.14159. If you apply a format to display two decimal places, the number appears as 3.14. When you use the cell in a formula, however, the actual value (3.14159)—not the displayed value—is used.

Stylistic formatting

Stylistic formatting refers to the cosmetic formatting (colors, shading, fonts, borders, and so on) that you apply to make your work look good. The Home ➜ Font and Home ➜ Styles groups contain commands to format your cells and ranges.

Document themes allow you to set many formatting options at once, such as font, colors, and cell styles. The formatting options contained in a theme are designed to work well together. If you're not feeling particularly artistic, you can apply a theme and know the colors won't clash. All the commands for themes are in the Themes group of the Page Layout tab.

Don't overlook Excel's conditional formatting feature. This handy tool enables you to specify formatting that appears only when certain conditions are met. For example, you can make the cell's interior red if the cell contains a negative number.

Cross-Ref

See Chapter 19, "Conditional Formatting," for more information on conditional formatting.

Protection Options

Excel offers a number of different protection options. For example, you can protect formulas from being overwritten or modified, protect a workbook's structure, and protect your VBA code.

Before distributing any Excel-based work, you should always consider protecting your file using the protection capabilities native to Excel. Although none of Excel's protection methods are hacker-proof, they do serve to avoid accidental corruption of formulas and to protect sensitive information from unauthorized users.

Securing access to the entire workbook

Perhaps the best way to protect your Excel file is to use Excel's protection options for file sharing. These options enable you to apply security at the workbook level, requiring a password to view or make changes to the file. This method is by far the easiest to apply and manage because there's no need to protect each worksheet one at a time. You can apply a blanket protection to guard against unauthorized access and edits. Take a moment to review the file-sharing options, which are as follows:

- Forcing read-only access to a file until a password is given
- Requiring a password to open an Excel file
- Removing workbook-level protection

The next few sections discuss these options in detail.

Permitting read-only access unless a password is given

You can force your workbook to go into read-only mode until the user types the password. This way, you can keep your file safe from unauthorized changes yet still allow authorized users to edit the file.

Here are the steps to force read-only mode:

1. With your file open, click the File tab.
2. To open the Save As dialog box, select Save As and then double-click the This PC icon.
3. In the Save As dialog box, click the Tools button and select General Options (see Figure 1-1). The General Options dialog box appears.
4. Type an appropriate password in the Password to Modify input box (see Figure 1-2), and click OK.
5. Excel asks you to reenter your password, so reenter your chosen password.
6. Save your file to a new name.

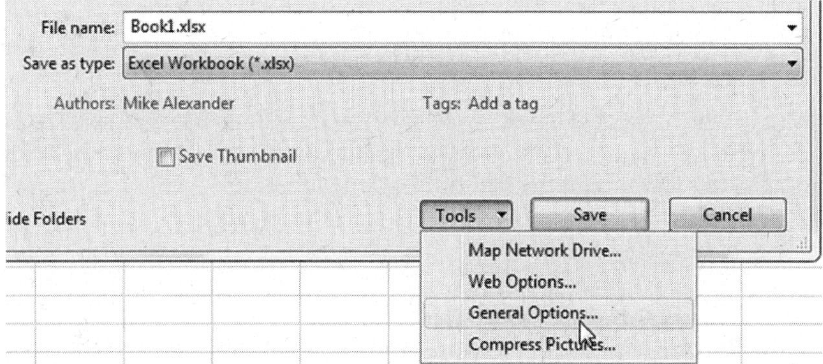

Figure 1-1: The File Sharing options are well hidden away in the Save As dialog box under General Options.

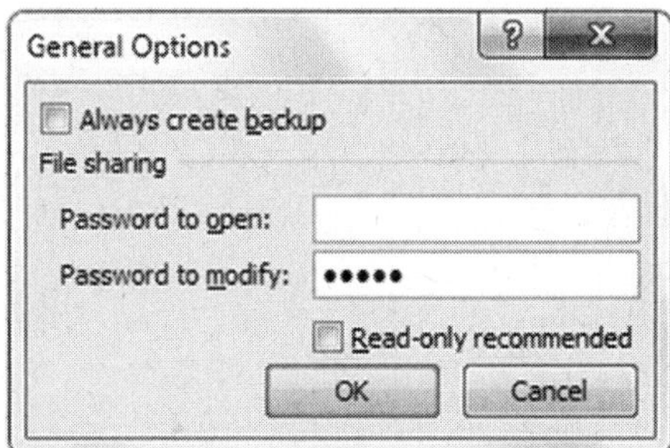

Figure 1-2: Type the password needed to modify the file.

At this point, your file is password protected from unauthorized changes. If you were to open your file, you'd see something similar to Figure 1-3. Failing to type the correct password causes the file to go into read-only mode.

Figure 1-3: A password is now needed to make changes to the file.

Note that Excel passwords are case sensitive, so make sure Caps Lock on your keyboard is in the off position when you're entering your password.

Requiring a password to open an Excel file

You may have instances in which the data in your Excel files is so sensitive that only certain users are authorized to see it. In these cases, you can require your workbook to receive a password to open it. Here are the steps to set up a password for the file:

1. With your file open, click the File tab.
2. To open the Save As dialog box, select Save As and then double-click the Computer icon.
3. In the Save As dialog box, click the Tools button and select General Options (refer to Figure 1-1). The General Options dialog box opens.
4. Type an appropriate password in the Password to Open text box (as shown in Figure 1-4), and click OK.
5. Excel asks you to reenter your password.
6. Save your file to a new name.

At this point, your file is password protected from unauthorized viewing.

Figure 1-4: Type the password needed to modify the file.

Removing workbook-level protection

Removing workbook-level protection is as easy as clearing the passwords from the General Options dialog box. Here's how you do it:

1. With your file open, click the File tab.
2. To open the Save As dialog box, select Save As.
3. In the Save As dialog box, click the Tools button and select General Options (refer to Figure 1-1). The General Options dialog box opens.
4. Clear the Password to Open input box as well as the Password to Modify input box, and click OK.
5. Save your file.

Note

When you select the Read-Only Recommended check box in the General Options dialog box (refer to Figure 1-4), you get a message recommending read-only access upon opening the file. This message is only a recommendation and doesn't prevent anyone from opening the file as read/write.

Limiting access to specific worksheet ranges

You may find that you need to lock specific worksheet ranges, preventing users from taking certain actions. For example, you may not want users to break your formulas inserting or deleting columns and rows. You can prevent this by locking those columns and rows.

Unlocking editable ranges

By default, all cells in a worksheet are set to be locked when you apply worksheet-level protection. You can't alter the cells on that worksheet in any way. That being said, you may find that you need certain cells or ranges to be editable even in a locked state, as in the example shown in Figure 1-5.

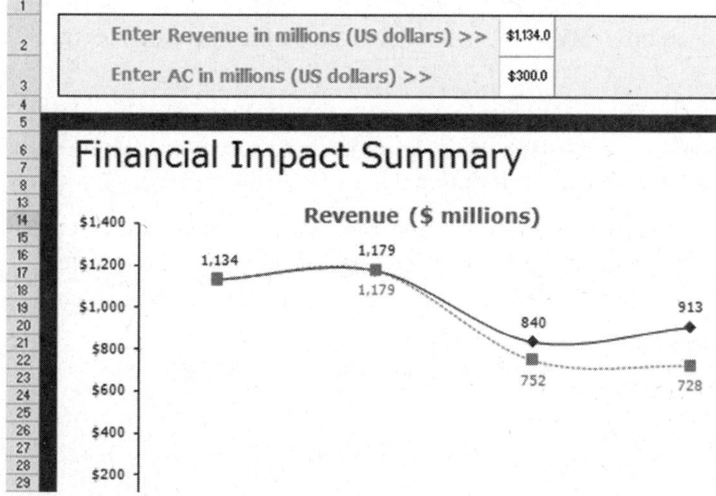

Figure 1-5: Although this sheet is protected, users can enter data into the input cells provided.

Before you protect your worksheet, you can unlock the cell or range of cells that you want users to be able to edit. (The next section shows you how to protect your entire worksheet.) Here's how to do it:

1. Select the cells you need to unlock.
2. Right-click and select Format Cells.
3. On the Protection tab, as shown in Figure 1-6, deselect the Locked check box.
4. Click OK to apply the change.

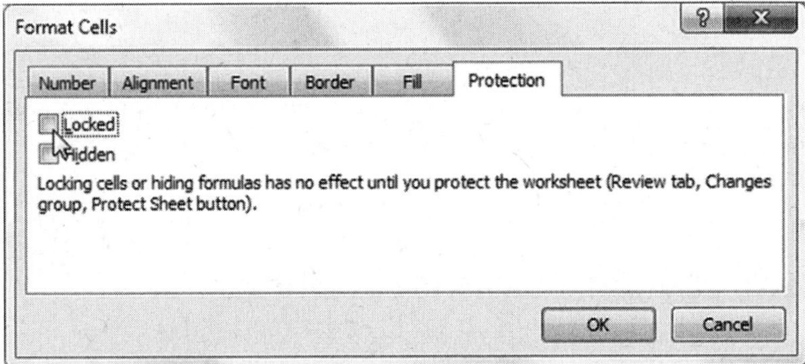

Figure 1-6: To ensure that a cell remains unlocked when the worksheet is protected, deselect the Locked check box.

Applying worksheet protection

After you've selectively unlocked the necessary cells, you can begin to apply worksheet protection. Just follow these steps:

1. To open the Protect Sheet dialog box, click the Protect Sheet icon on the Review tab of the Ribbon (see Figure 1-7).
2. Type a password into the text box (see Figure 1-8) and then click OK. This is the password that removes worksheet protection. Note that because you can apply and remove worksheet protection without a password, specifying one is optional.
3. In the list box (see Figure 1-8), select which elements users can change after you protect the worksheet. When a check box is checked for a particular action, Excel prevents users from taking that action.
4. If you provided a password, reenter it.
5. Click OK to apply the worksheet protection.

Figure 1-7: Select Protect Sheet in the Review tab.

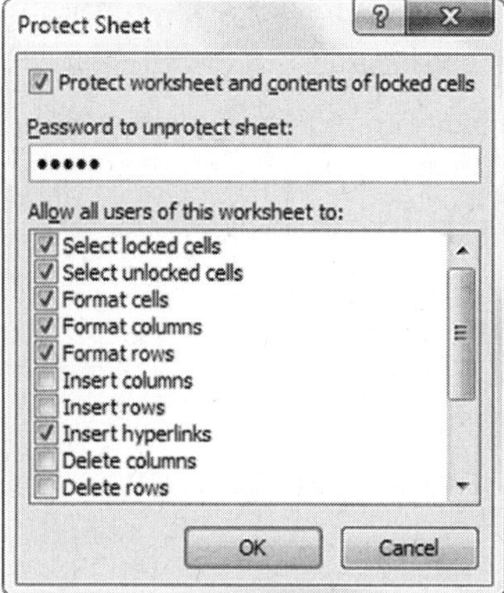

Figure 1-8: Specify a password that removes worksheet protection.

Protecting sheet elements and actions

Take a moment to familiarize yourself with some of the other actions you can limit when protecting a worksheet (refer to Figure 1-8). They are as follows:

- **Select Locked Cells:** Allows or prevents the selection of locked cells.
- **Select Unlocked Cells:** Allows or prevents the selection of unlocked cells.
- **Format Cells:** Allows or prevents the formatting of cells.
- **Format Columns:** Allows or prevents the use of column formatting commands, including changing column width or hiding columns.
- **Format Rows:** Allows or prevents the use of row formatting commands, including changing row height or hiding rows.
- **Insert Columns:** Allows or prevents the inserting of columns.
- **Insert Rows:** Allows or prevents the inserting of rows.

- **Insert Hyperlinks:** Allows or prevents the inserting of hyperlinks.
- **Delete Columns:** Allows or prevents the deleting of columns. Note that if Delete Columns is protected and Insert Columns is not, you can technically insert columns you can't delete.
- **Delete Rows:** Allows or prevents the deleting of rows. Note that if Delete Rows is protected and Insert Rows is not, you can technically insert columns you can't delete.
- **Sort:** Allows or prevents the use of Sort commands. Note that this doesn't apply to locked ranges. Users can't sort ranges that contain locked cells on a protected worksheet, regardless of this setting.
- **Use AutoFilter:** Allows or prevents use of Excel's AutoFilter functionality. Users can't create or remove AutoFiltered ranges on a protected worksheet, regardless of this setting.
- **Use PivotTable Reports:** Allows or prevents the modifying, refreshing, or formatting of pivot tables found on the protected sheet.
- **Edit Objects:** Allows or prevents the formatting and altering of shapes, charts, text boxes, controls, or other graphics objects.
- **Edit Scenarios:** Allows or prevents the viewing of scenarios.

Removing worksheet protection

Just follow these steps to remove any worksheet protection you may have applied:

1. Click the Unprotect Sheet icon on the Review tab.
2. If you specified a password while protecting the worksheet, Excel asks you for that password (see Figure 1-9). Type the password and click OK to immediately remove protection.

Figure 1-9: The Unprotect Sheet icon removes worksheet protection.

Protecting the workbook structure

If you look under the Review tab in the Ribbon, you see the Protect Workbook icon next to the Protect Sheet icon. Protecting the workbook enables you to prevent users from taking any action that affects the structure of your workbook, such as adding/deleting worksheets, hiding/unhiding worksheets, and naming or moving worksheets. Just follow these steps to protect a workbook:

1. Click the Protect Workbook icon on the Review tab of the Ribbon, which opens the Protect Structure and Windows dialog box as shown in Figure 1-10.
2. Choose which elements you want to protect: workbook structure, windows, or both. When a check box is cleared for a particular action, Excel prevents users from taking that action.
3. If you provided a password, reenter it.
4. Click OK to apply the worksheet protection.

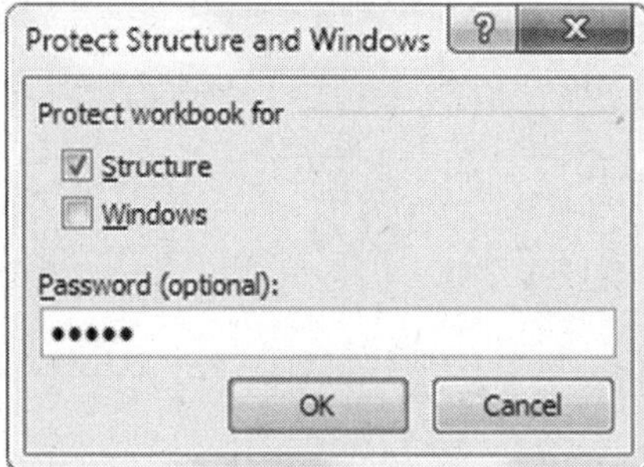

Figure 1-10: The Protect Structure and Windows dialog box.

Selecting Structure prevents users from doing the following:

- Viewing worksheets that you've hidden
- Moving, deleting, hiding, or changing the names of worksheets
- Inserting new worksheets or chart sheets
- Moving or copying worksheets to another workbook
- Displaying the source data for a cell in a pivot table Values area or displaying pivot table Filter pages on separate worksheets
- Creating a scenario summary report
- Using an Analysis ToolPak utility that requires results to be placed on a new worksheet
- Recording new macros

Choosing Windows prevents users from changing, moving, or sizing the workbook windows while the workbook is opened.

2

Basic Facts About Formulas

In This Chapter

- How to enter, edit, and paste names into formulas
- The various operators used in formulas
- How Excel calculates formulas
- Cell and range references used in formulas
- Copying and moving cells and ranges
- How to make an exact copy of a formula
- How to convert formulas to values
- How to prevent formulas from being viewed
- The types of formula errors
- Circular reference messages and correction techniques
- Excel's goal seeking feature

This chapter serves as a basic introduction to using formulas in Excel. Although it's intended primarily for newcomers to Excel, even veteran Excel users may find some new information here.

Entering and Editing Formulas

This section describes the basic elements of a formula. It also explains various ways of entering and editing your formulas.

Formula elements

A formula entered into a cell can consist of five elements:

- **Operators:** These include symbols such as + (for addition) and * (for multiplication).
- **Cell references:** These include named cells and ranges that can refer to cells in the current worksheet, cells in another worksheet in the same workbook, or even cells in a worksheet in another workbook.
- **Values or text strings:** Examples include 7.5 (a value) and *"Year-End Results"* (a string, enclosed in quotes).
- **Worksheet functions and their arguments:** These include functions such as SUM or AVERAGE and their arguments. Function arguments appear in parentheses and provide input for the function's calculations.
- **Parentheses:** These control the order in which expressions within a formula are evaluated.

Entering a formula

When you type an equal sign into an empty cell, Excel assumes that you are entering a formula because a formula always begins with an equal sign. Excel's accommodating nature also permits you to begin your formula with a minus sign or a plus sign. However, Excel always inserts the leading equal sign after you enter the formula.

As a concession to former Lotus 1-2-3 users, Excel also allows you to use an "at" symbol (@) to begin a formula that starts with a function. For example, Excel accepts either of the following formulas:

```
=SUM(A1:A200)
@SUM(A1:A200)
```

However, after you enter the second formula, Excel replaces the @ symbol with an equal sign.

If your formula uses a cell reference, you can enter the cell reference in one of two ways: enter it manually, or enter it by pointing to cells that are used in the formula. We discuss each method in the following sections.

Entering a formula manually

Entering a formula manually involves, well, entering a formula manually. You simply activate a cell and type an equal sign (=) followed by the formula. As you type, the characters appear in the cell as well as in the Formula bar. You can, of course, use all the normal editing keys when typing a formula. After you insert the formula, press Enter.

Note

When you type an array formula, you must press Ctrl+Shift+Enter rather than just Enter. An array formula is a special type of formula, which we discuss in Part IV, "Array Formulas."

After you press Enter, the cell displays the result of the formula. The formula itself appears in the Formula bar when the cell is activated.

Entering a formula by pointing

The other method of entering a formula that contains cell references still involves some manual typing, but you can simply point to the cell references instead of typing them manually. For example, to enter the formula =A1+A2 into cell A3, follow these steps:

1. Move the cell pointer to cell A3.
2. Type an equal sign (=) to begin the formula.
   Notice that Excel displays *Enter* in the left side of the status bar.
3. Press the up arrow twice.
   As you press this key, notice that Excel displays a moving border around the cell and that the cell reference (A1) appears in cell A3 and in the Formula bar. Also notice that Excel displays *Point* on the status bar.
   If you prefer, you can use your mouse and click cell A1.
4. Type a plus sign (+).
   The moving border becomes a solid blue border around A1, and *Enter* reappears in the status bar. The cell cursor also returns to the original cell (A3).
5. Press the up arrow one more time. If you prefer, you can use your mouse and click cell A2.
   A2 is appended to the formula.
6. Press Enter to end the formula.
   As with typing the formula manually, the cell displays the result of the formula, and the formula appears in the Formula bar when the cell is activated.
   If you prefer, you can use your mouse and click the check mark icon next to the Formula bar instead of pressing Enter. And if, at any time, you change your mind about entering the formula, just press Esc or click the X icon next to the Formula bar.

This method might sound a bit tedious, but it's actually very efficient after you get the hang of it. Pointing to cell addresses rather than entering them manually is almost always faster and more accurate.

Tip

Excel color-codes the range addresses and ranges when you are entering or editing a formula. This helps you quickly spot the cells that are used in a formula.

Cross-Ref

When you're working with a table of data (created by using Insert → Tables → Table), you can use a different type of formula—a self-propagating formula that takes advantage of column names. We cover this topic in Chapter 9, "Working with Tables and Lists."

Pasting names

As we discuss in Chapter 3, "Working with Names," you can assign a name to a cell or range. If your formula uses named cells or ranges, you can type the name in place of the address or choose the name from a list and have Excel insert the name for you automatically.

To insert a name into a formula, position your cursor in the formula where you want the name entered and use one of these two methods:

- Press F3 to display the Paste Name dialog box. Select the name and click OK.
- Take advantage of the Formula AutoComplete feature. When you type a letter while constructing a formula, Excel displays a list of matching options. These options include functions and names.

Figure 2-1 shows Formula AutoComplete in use. In this case, SalesData is a defined range name. This name appears in the drop-down list, along with worksheet function names.

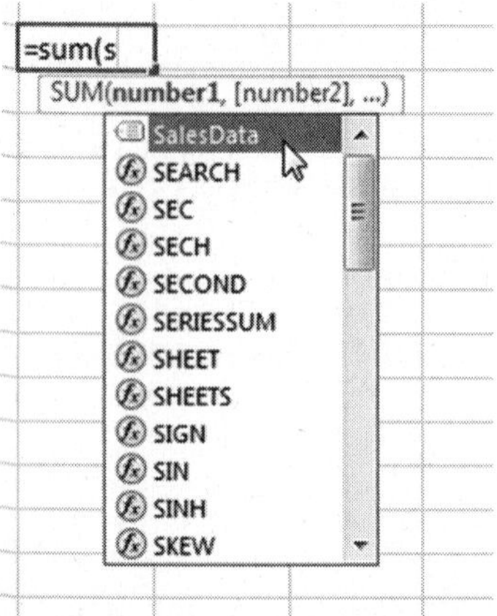

Figure 2-1: Using Formula AutoComplete to enter a range name into a formula.

Spaces and line breaks

Normally, you enter a formula without using spaces. However, you can use spaces (and even line breaks) within your formulas. Doing so has no effect on the formula's result but can make the formula easier to read. To enter a line break in a formula, press Alt+Enter. Figure 2-2 shows a formula that contains spaces (indentions) and line breaks.

Tip

To make the Formula bar display more than one line, drag the border below the Formula bar downward. Or click the downward-pointing icon at the extreme right of the Formula bar.

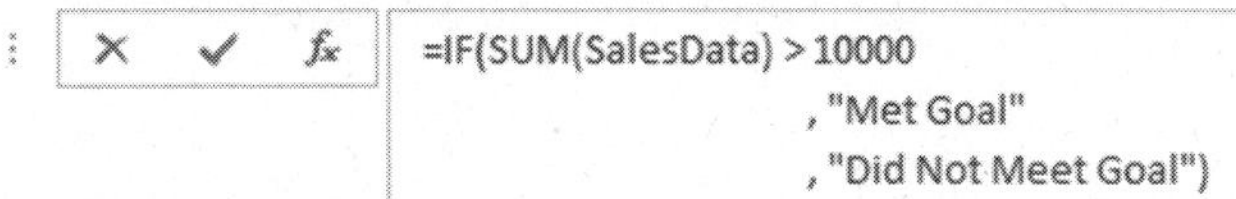

Figure 2-2: This formula contains spaces and line breaks.

Formula limits

A formula can consist of up to about 8,000 characters. In the unlikely event that you need to create a formula that exceeds this limit, you must break the formula into multiple formulas. You also can opt to create a custom function by using Visual Basic for Applications (VBA).

Cross-Ref

Part VI, "Developing Custom Worksheet Functions," focuses on creating custom functions.

Sample formulas

If you follow the preceding instructions for entering formulas, you can create a variety of them. This section looks at some sample formulas.

- The following formula multiplies 150 × .01, returning 1.5. This formula uses only literal values, so it doesn't seem very useful. However, it may be useful to show your work when you review your spreadsheet later:

```
=150*.01
```

- This formula adds the values in cells A1 and A2:

```
=A1+A2
```

- The next formula subtracts the value in the cell named *Expenses* from the value in the cell named *Income*:

```
=Income-Expenses
```

- The following formula uses the SUM function to add the values in the range A1:A12:

```
=SUM(A1:A12)
```

- The next formula compares cell A1 with cell C12 by using the = operator. If the values in the two cells are identical, the formula returns *TRUE*; otherwise, it returns *FALSE*:

```
=A1=C12
```

- This final formula subtracts the value in cell B3 from the value in cell B2 and then multiplies the result by the value in cell B4:

```
=(B2-B3)*B4
```

Editing formulas

If you make changes to your worksheet, you may need to edit formulas. Or if a formula returns one of the error values described later in this chapter, you might need to edit the formula to correct the error. You can edit your formulas just as you edit any other cell.

Here are several ways to get into cell edit mode:

- **Double-click the cell.** This enables you to edit the cell contents directly in the cell. This technique works only if the Double-click Allow Editing Directly in Cells check box is selected on the Advanced tab in the Excel Options dialog box.
- **Press F2.** This enables you to edit the cell contents directly in the cell. If the Double-Click Allow Editing Directly in Cells check box is not selected, the editing occurs in the Formula bar.
- **Select the formula cell that you want to edit and then click in the Formula bar.** This enables you to edit the cell contents in the Formula bar.

When you edit a formula, you can select multiple characters by dragging the mouse over them or by holding down Shift while you use the arrow keys. You can also press Home or End to select from the cursor position to the beginning or end of the current line of the formula.

Tip

Suppose you have a lengthy formula that contains an error, and Excel won't let you enter it because of the error. In this case, you can convert the formula to text and tackle it again later. To convert a formula to text, just remove the initial equal sign (=). When you're ready to return to editing the formula, insert the initial equal sign to convert the cell contents back to a formula.

Using the Formula bar as a calculator

If you simply need to perform a calculation, you can use the Formula bar as a calculator. For example, enter the following formula into any cell:

```
=(145*1.05)/12
```

Because this formula always returns the same result, you may prefer to store the formula's result rather than the formula. To do so, press F2 to edit the cell. Then press F9, followed by Enter. Excel stores the formula's result (12.6875) rather than the formula. This technique also works if the formula uses cell references.

This technique is most useful when you use worksheet functions. For example, to enter the square root of 221 into a cell, type **=SQRT(221)**, press F9, and then press Enter. Excel enters the result: *14.8660687473185*. You also can use this technique to evaluate just part of a formula. Consider this formula:

```
=(145*1.05)/A1
```

If you want to convert just the expression within the parentheses to a value, get into cell edit mode and select the part that you want to evaluate. In this example, select 145*1.05. Then press F9 followed by Enter. Excel converts the formula to the following:

```
=(152.25)/A1
```

Using Operators in Formulas

As previously discussed, an operator is one of the basic elements of a formula. An *operator* is a symbol that represents an operation. Table 2-1 shows the Excel-supported operators.

Table 2-1: Excel-Supported Operators

Symbol	Operator
+	Addition
–	Subtraction
/	Division
*	Multiplication
%	Percent*
&	Text concatenation
^	Exponentiation
=	Logical comparison (equal to)
>	Logical comparison (greater than)
<	Logical comparison (less than)
>=	Logical comparison (greater than or equal to)
<=	Logical comparison (less than or equal to)
<>	Logical comparison (not equal to)

**Percent isn't really an operator, but it functions similarly to one in Excel. Entering a percent sign after a number divides the number by 100. If the value is not part of a formula, Excel also formats the cell as percent.*

Reference operators

Excel supports another class of operators known as *reference operators*; see Table 2-2. Reference operators work with cell references.

Table 2-2: Reference Operators

Symbol	Operator
: (colon)	Range. Produces one reference to all the cells between two references.
, (comma)	Union. Combines multiple cell or range references into one reference.
(single space)	Intersection. Produces one reference to cells common to two references.

Sample formulas that use operators

These examples of formulas use various operators:

- The following formula joins *(concatenates)* the two literal text strings (each enclosed in quotes) to produce a new text string: *Part-23A:*

```
="Part-"&"23A"
```

- The next formula concatenates the contents of cell A1 with cell A2:

```
=A1&A2
```

- Usually, concatenation is used with text, but concatenation works with values as well. For example, if cell A1 contains 123, and cell A2 contains 456, the preceding formula would return the value *123456*. Note that, technically, the result is a text string. However, if you use this string in a mathematical formula, Excel treats it as a number. Some Excel functions ignore this "number" because they are designed to ignore text.
- The following formula uses the exponentiation (^) operator to raise 6 to the third power to produce a result of *216*:

```
=6^3
```

- A more useful form of the preceding formula uses a cell reference instead of the literal value. Note this example that raises the value in cell A1 to the third power:

```
=A1^3
```

- This formula returns the cube root of 216 (which is 6):

```
=216^(1/3)
```

- The next formula returns *TRUE* if the value in cell A1 is less than the value in cell A2. Otherwise, it returns *FALSE*:

```
=A1<A2
```

- Logical comparison operators also work with text. If A1 contains Alpha and A2 contains Gamma, the formula returns *TRUE* because Alpha comes before Gamma in alphabetical order.
- The following formula returns *TRUE* if the value in cell A1 is less than or equal to the value in cell A2. Otherwise, it returns *FALSE*:

```
=A1<=A2
```

- The next formula returns *TRUE* if the value in cell A1 does not equal the value in cell A2. Otherwise, it returns *FALSE*:

```
=A1<>A2
```

- Excel doesn't have logical AND and OR operators. Rather, you use functions to specify these types of logical operators. For example, this formula returns *TRUE* if cell A1 contains either 100 or 1000:

```
=OR(A1=100,A1=1000)
```

- This last formula returns *TRUE* only if both cell A1 and cell A2 contain values less than 100:

```
=AND(A1<100,A2<100)
```

Operator precedence

You can (and should) use parentheses in your formulas to control the order in which the calculations occur. As an example, consider the following formula that uses references to named cells:

```
=Income-Expenses*TaxRate
```

The goal is to subtract expenses from income and then multiply the result by the tax rate. If you enter the preceding formula, though, you discover that Excel computes the wrong answer. The formula multiplies expenses by the tax rate and then subtracts the result from the income. In other words, Excel does not necessarily perform calculations from left to right (as you might expect).

The correct way to write this formula is

```
=(Income-Expenses)*TaxRate
```

To understand how this works, you need to be familiar with *operator precedence*—the set of rules that Excel uses to perform its calculations. Upcoming Table 2-3 lists Excel's operator precedence. Operations are performed in the order listed in the table. For example, multiplication is performed before subtraction.

Subtraction or negation?

One operator that can cause confusion is the minus sign (–), which you use for subtraction. However, a minus sign can also be a negation operator, which indicates a negative number.

Consider this formula:

```
=-3^2
```

Excel returns the value 9 (not –9). The minus sign serves as a negation operator and has a higher precedence than all other operators. The formula is evaluated as "negative 3, squared." Using parentheses clarifies it:

```
=(-3)^2
```

The formula is *not* evaluated like this:

```
=-(3^2)
```

This is another example of why using parentheses, even if they are not necessary, is a good idea.

Use parentheses to override Excel's built-in order of precedence. Returning to the previous example, the formula without parentheses is evaluated using Excel's standard operator precedence. Because multiplication has a higher precedence, the *Expenses* cell multiplies by the *TaxRate* cell. Then this result is subtracted from Income—producing an incorrect calculation.

The correct formula uses parentheses to control the order of operations. Expressions within parentheses are always evaluated first. In this case, *Expenses* is subtracted from *Income,* and the result is multiplied by *TaxRate.*

Table 2-3: Operator Precedence in Excel Formulas

Symbol	Operator
Colon (:), comma (,), space( )	Reference
–	Negation
%	Percent
^	Exponentiation
* and /	Multiplication and division
+ and –	Addition and subtraction
&	Text concatenation
=, <, >, <=, >=, and <>	Comparison

Nested parentheses

You can also *nest* parentheses in formulas—that is, put parentheses inside parentheses. When a formula contains nested parentheses, Excel evaluates the most deeply nested expressions first and works its way out. The following example of a formula uses nested parentheses:

```
=((B2*C2)+(B3*C3)+(B4*C4))*B6
```

The preceding formula has four sets of parentheses. Three sets are nested inside the fourth set. Excel evaluates each nested set of parentheses and then sums the three results. This sum is then multiplied by the value in B6.

Make liberal use of parentheses in your formulas even when they aren't necessary. Using parentheses clarifies the order of operations and makes the formula easier to read. For example, if you want to add 1 to the product of two cells, the following formula does the job:

```
=A1*A2+1
```

Because of Excel's operator precedence rules, the multiplication will be performed before the addition. Therefore, parentheses are not necessary. You may find it much clearer, however, to use the following formula even though it contains superfluous parentheses:

```
=(A1*A2)+1
```

Tip

Every left parenthesis, of course, must have a matching right parenthesis. If you have many levels of nested parentheses, you may find it difficult to keep them straight. Fortunately, Excel lends a hand in helping you match parentheses. When editing a formula, matching parentheses are colored the same, although the colors can be difficult to distinguish if you have a lot of parentheses. Also, when the cursor moves over a parenthesis, Excel momentarily displays the parenthesis and its matching parenthesis in bold. This lasts for less than a second, so watch carefully.

Don't hard-code values

When you create a formula, think twice before using a literal value in the formula. For example, if your formula calculates a 7.5 percent sales tax, you may be tempted to enter a formula such as this:

```
=A1*.075
```

A better approach is to insert the sales tax rate into a cell and use the cell reference in place of the literal value. This makes it easier to modify and maintain your worksheet. For example, if the sales tax range changes to 7.75 percent, you need to modify every formula that uses the old value. If the tax rate is stored in a cell, you simply change one cell, and all the formulas recalculate using the new value.

Calculating Formulas

You've probably noticed that the formulas in your worksheet are calculated immediately. If you change any cells that the formula uses, the formula displays a new result with no effort on your part. This occurs when Excel's Calculation mode is set to Automatic. In this mode (the default mode), Excel follows certain rules when calculating your worksheet:

- When you make a change (enter or edit data or formulas, for example), Excel calculates immediately those formulas that depend on new or edited data.
- If working on a lengthy calculation, Excel temporarily suspends calculation when you need to perform other worksheet tasks; it resumes when you finish.
- Formulas are evaluated in a natural sequence. For instance, if a formula in cell D12 depends on the result of a formula in cell F12, cell F12 is calculated before D12.

Sometimes, however, you may want to control when Excel calculates formulas. For example, if you create a worksheet with thousands of complex formulas, you may find that things can slow to a snail's pace while Excel does its thing. In this case, you can set Excel's Calculation mode to Manual. Do this by choosing Formulas ➜ Calculation ➜ Calculation Options ➜ Manual.

When you work in manual Calculation mode, Excel displays *Calculate* in the status bar when you have any uncalculated formulas.

The Formulas ➜ Calculation group contains two controls that, when clicked, perform a calculation: Calculate Now and Calculate Sheet. In addition to these controls, you can click the *Calculate* word on the status bar or use the following shortcut keys to recalculate the formulas:

- **F9:** Calculates the formulas in all open workbooks (same as the Calculate Now control).
- **Shift+F9:** Calculates only the formulas in the active worksheet. It does not calculate other worksheets in the same workbook (same as the Calculate Sheet control).
- **Ctrl+Alt+F9:** Forces a complete recalculation of all open workbooks. Use it if Excel (for some reason) doesn't seem to return correct calculations.
- **Ctrl+Shift+Alt+F9:** Rechecks all the dependent formulas and then forces a recalculation of all open workbooks.

Caution

Contrary to what you might expect, Excel's Calculation mode isn't specific to a particular workbook. When you change Excel's Calculation mode, it affects all open workbooks—not just the active workbook. Also, the initial Calculation mode is set by the Calculation mode saved with the first workbook that you open.

Cell and Range References

Most formulas reference one or more cells by using the cell or range address (or the name if it has one). Cell references come in four styles; the use of the dollar sign symbol differentiates them:

- **Relative:** The reference is fully relative. When you copy the formula, the cell reference adjusts to its new location.

  Example: A1

- **Absolute:** The reference is fully absolute. When you copy the formula, the cell reference does not change.

  Example: $A$1

- **Row Absolute:** The reference is partially absolute. When you copy the formula, the column part adjusts, but the row part does not change.

  Example: A$1

- **Column Absolute:** The reference is partially absolute. When you copy the formula, the row part adjusts, but the column part does not change.

  Example: $A1

Creating an absolute or a mixed reference

When you create a formula by pointing to cells, all cell and range references are relative. To change a reference to an absolute reference or a mixed reference, you must do so manually by adding the dollar signs. Or when you're entering a cell or range address, you can press the F4 key to cycle among all possible reference modes.

If you think about it, you may realize that the only reason you would ever need to change a reference is if you plan to copy the formula.

Figure 2-3 demonstrates an absolute reference in a formula. Cell D2 contains a formula that calculates a final sales price based on the quantity (cell B2), price (cell C2) and the sales tax (cell B7):

```
=(B2*C2)*(1+$B$7)
```

	A	B	C	D
1		Quantity	Price	
2		50	$30	=(B2*C2)*(1+$B$7)
3		23	$45	$1,118
4		65	$15	$1,053
5				
6		Sales Tax		
7		8%		
8				

Figure 2-3: This worksheet demonstrates the use of an absolute reference.

The reference to cell B7 is an absolute reference. When you copy the formula in cell D2 to the cells below, the $B$7 reference always points to the sales tax cell. Using a relative reference (B7) results in incorrect results in the copied formulas.

Figure 2-4 demonstrates the use of mixed references. Note the formula in cell J3:

```
=SUM($I$2:I3)
```

This formula calculates a running total for Units Sold. Because the formula uses absolute references to row 2 and column I, each copied formula sums all Units Sold starting from cell I2. If the formula used relative references, copying the formula would cause that reference to adjust and produce the wrong results.

	H	I	J
1	Month	Units Sold	Running Total
2	January	99	99
3	February	37	=SUM($I$2:I3)
4	March	53	189
5	April	97	286
6	May	74	360
7	June	29	389
8	July	56	445
9	August	75	520
10	September	98	618
11	October	56	674
12	November	59	733
13	December	80	813

Figure 2-4: An example of using mixed references in a formula.

A1 versus R1C1 notation

Normally, Excel uses *A1 notation.* Each cell address consists of a column letter and a row number. However, Excel also supports *R1C1 notation.* In this system, cell A1 is referred to as cell R1C1, cell A2 as R2C1, and so on.

To change to R1C1 notation, choose File ➜ Options to open the Excel Options dialog box, click the Formulas tab, and place a check mark next to the R1C1 Reference Style option. Notice that all the column letters change to numbers. And all the cell and range references in your formulas adjust.

Look at the following examples of formulas using standard notation and R1C1 notation. The formula is assumed to be in cell B1 (also known as R1C2).

Standard	R1C1
=A1+1	=RC[–1]+1
=$A$1+1	=R1C1+1
=$A1+1	=RC1+1
=A$1+1	=R1C[–1]+1
=SUM(A1:A10)	=SUM(RC[–1]:R[9]C[–1])
=SUM($A$1:$A$10)	=SUM(R1C1:R10C1)

If you find R1C1 notation confusing, you're not alone. R1C1 notation isn't too bad when you're dealing with absolute references. When relative references are involved, though, the brackets can drive you nuts.

The numbers in brackets refer to the relative position of the references. For example, R[–5]C[–3] specifies the cell that appears five rows above and three columns to the left. Conversely, R[5]C[3] references the cell that appears five rows below and three columns to the right. If you omit the brackets (or the numbers), it specifies the same row or column. For example, R[5]C refers to the cell five rows below in the same column.

Although you probably won't use R1C1 notation as your standard system, it *does* have at least one good use. R1C1 notation makes it easy to spot an erroneous formula. When you copy a formula, every copied formula is the same in R1C1 notation. This remains true regardless of the types of cell references you use (relative, absolute, or mixed). Therefore, you can switch to R1C1 notation and check your copied formulas. If one looks different from its surrounding formulas, it's probably incorrect.

However, you can take advantage of the background formula auditing feature, which can flag potentially incorrect formulas. We discuss this feature in Chapter 22, "Tools and Methods for Debugging Formulas."

Referencing other sheets or workbooks

A formula can use references to cells and ranges that are in a different worksheet. To refer to a cell in a different worksheet, precede the cell reference with the sheet name followed by an exclamation point. Note this example of a formula that uses a cell reference in a different worksheet (Sheet2):

```
=Sheet2!A1+1
```

You can also create link formulas that refer to a cell in a different workbook. To do so, precede the cell reference with the workbook name (in square brackets), the worksheet name, and an exclamation point (!), like this:

```
=[Budget.xlsx]Sheet1!A1+1
```

If the workbook name or sheet name in the reference includes one or more spaces, you must enclose it (and the sheet name) in single quotation marks. For example:

```
='[Budget Analysis.xlsx]Sheet1'!A1+A1
```

If the linked workbook is closed, you must add the complete path to the workbook reference. For example:

```
='C:\MSOffice\Excel\[Budget Analysis.xlsx]Sheet1'!A1+A1
```

A linked file can also reside on another system that's accessible on your corporate network. The following formula refers to a cell in a workbook in the files directory of a computer named DataServer:

```
='\\DataServer\files\[Budget Analysis.xlsx]Sheet1'!A1
```

If the linked workbook is stored on the Internet, the formula also includes the uniform resource locator (URL). For example:

```
='https://d.docs.live.net/86a61fd208/files/[Annual Budget.xlsx]Sheet1'!A1
```

Opening a workbook with external reference formulas

When you open a workbook that contains links, Excel displays a dialog box that asks whether you want to do the following:

- **Update:** The links are updated with the current information in the source file(s).
- **Don't Update:** The links are not updated, and the workbook displays the previous values returned by the link formulas.
- **Help:** The Excel Help screen displays so you can read about links.

What if you choose to update the links, but the source workbook is no longer available? If Excel can't locate a source workbook that's referred to in a link formula, it displays its Edit Links dialog box. Click the Change Source button to specify a different workbook or click the Break Link to destroy the link.

Although you can enter link formulas directly, you can also create the reference by using the normal pointing methods discussed earlier. To do so, make sure the source file is open. Normally, you can create a formula by pointing to results in relative cell references. But when you create a reference to another workbook by pointing, Excel always creates *absolute* cell references. If you plan to copy the formula to other cells, you must edit the formula to make the references relative.

Caution

Working with links can be tricky and may cause some unexpected problems. For example, if you use the File ➜ Save As command to make a backup copy of the source workbook, you automatically change the link formulas to refer to the new file (not usually what you want). You can also mess up your links by renaming the source workbook file.

Copying or Moving Formulas

As you create a worksheet, you may find it necessary to copy or move information from one location to another. Excel makes copying or moving ranges of cells easy. Here are some common things you might do:

- **Copy a cell to another location.** Contents of the source cell are duplicated in the destination cell.
- **Copy a cell to a range of cells.** The source cell is copied to every cell in the destination range.
- **Copy a range to another range.** Both ranges must be the same size.
- **Move a range of cells to another location.** Contents are removed from the source cell and relocated to the destination.

The primary difference between copying and moving a range is the effect of the operation on the source range. When you copy a range, the source range is unaffected. When you move a range, the contents are removed from the source range.

Note

Copying a cell normally copies the cell's contents, any formatting that is applied to the original cell (including conditional formatting and data validation), and the cell comment (if it has one). When you copy a cell that contains a formula, the cell references in the copied formulas are changed automatically to be relative to their new destination.

Copying or moving consists of two steps (although shortcut methods are available):

1. Select the cell or range to copy (the source range) and copy it to the Clipboard. To move the range instead of copying it, cut the range rather than copying it.
2. Move the cell pointer to the range that will hold the copy (the destination range), and paste the Clipboard contents.

Caution

When you paste information, Excel overwrites any cells that get in the way without warning you. If you find that pasting overwrote some essential cells, choose Undo from the Quick Access toolbar (or press Ctrl+Z).

Note

When you copy a cell or range, Excel surrounds the copied area with an animated border. As long as that border remains animated, the copied information is available for pasting. If you press Esc to cancel the animated border, Excel removes the information from the Clipboard.

When you copy a range that contains formulas, the cell references in the formulas are adjusted. When you move a range that contains formulas, the cell references in the formulas are not adjusted. This is almost always what you want.

About the Office Clipboard

Whenever you cut or copy information from a Windows program, Windows stores the information on the *Windows Clipboard,* which is an area of your computer's memory. Each time that you cut or copy information, Windows replaces the information previously stored on the Clipboard with the new information that you cut or copied. The Windows Clipboard can store data in a variety of formats. Because Windows manages information on the Clipboard, it can be pasted to other Windows applications, regardless of where it originated.

Microsoft Office has its own Clipboard (the Office Clipboard), which is available only in Office programs. To view or hide the Office Clipboard, click the dialog launcher icon in the bottom-right corner of the Home ➜ Clipboard group.

Whenever you cut or copy information in an Office program, such as Excel or Word, the program places the information on both the Windows Clipboard and the Office Clipboard. However, the program treats information on the Office Clipboard differently than it treats information on the Windows Clipboard. Instead of replacing information on the Office Clipboard, the program appends the information to the Office Clipboard. With multiple items stored on the Clipboard, you can then paste the items individually or as a group.

The Office Clipboard has a serious problem that makes it virtually worthless for Excel users: if you copy a range that contains formulas, the formulas are not transferred when you paste to a different range. Only the values are pasted. Furthermore, Excel doesn't even warn you about this fact.

Making an Exact Copy of a Formula

When you copy a formula, Excel adjusts the formula's cell references when you paste it to a different location. Usually, adjusting the cell references is exactly what you want. Sometimes, however, you may want to make an exact copy of the formula. You can do this by converting the cell references to absolute references, as discussed earlier—but this isn't always desirable.

A better approach is to select the formula while in edit mode and then copy it to the Clipboard as text. There are several ways to do this. Here we present a step-by-step example of how to make an exact copy of the formula in A1 and copy it to A2:

1. Select cell A1 and press F2 to activate edit mode.
2. Press Ctrl+Home to move the cursor to the start of the formula, followed by Ctrl+Shift+End to select all the formula text.

Or you can drag the mouse to select the entire formula.

Note that holding down the Ctrl key is necessary when the formula is more than one line long, but it's optional for formulas that are a single line.

3. Choose Home ➜ Clipboard ➜ Copy (or press Ctrl+C).

   This copies the selected text to the Clipboard.

4. Press Esc to end edit mode.
5. Activate cell A2.
6. Press F2 for edit mode.
7. Choose Home ➜ Clipboard ➜ Paste (or press Ctrl+V), followed by Enter.

   This operation pastes an exact copy of the formula text into cell A2.

You can also use this technique to copy just part of a formula to use in another formula. Just select the part of the formula that you want to copy by dragging the mouse or by pressing the Shift+arrow keys. Then use any of the available techniques to copy the selection to the Clipboard. After that, you can paste the text to another cell.

Formulas (or parts of formulas) copied in this manner won't have their cell references adjusted when you paste them to a new cell. This is because you copy the formulas as text, not as actual formulas.

Another technique for making an exact copy of a formula is to edit the formula and remove its initial equal sign. This converts the formula to text. Then copy the "nonformula" to a new location. Finally, edit both the original formula and the copied formula by inserting the initial equal sign.

Converting Formulas to Values

If you have a range of formulas that always produce the same result (that is, dead formulas), you may want to convert them to values. You can use the Home ➜ Clipboard ➜ Paste ➜ Values command to do this.

Suppose that range A1:A10 contains formulas that calculate results that never change. To convert these formulas to values, do the following:

1. Select A1:A10.
2. Choose Home ➜ Clipboard ➜ Copy (or press Ctrl+C).
3. Choose Home ➜ Clipboard ➜ Paste ➜ Values (V).
4. Press Enter or Esc to cancel paste mode.

You can also take advantage of a drop-down control that shows paste options. In step 3 in the preceding list, press Ctrl+V to paste. A drop-down list appears at the lower-right corner of the range. Click and select one of the Paste Values icons (see Figure 2-5).

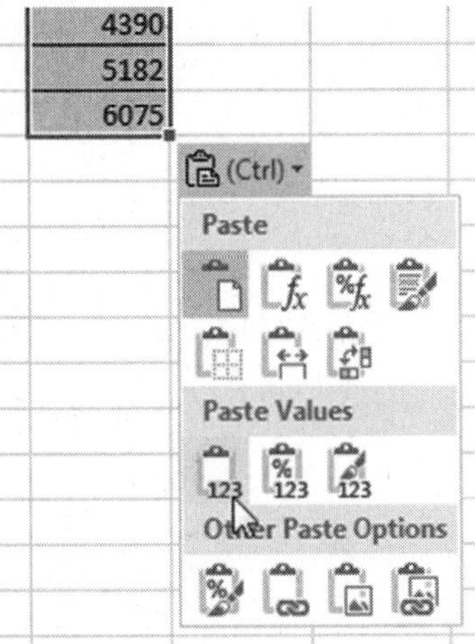

Figure 2-5: Choosing a paste option after pasting data.

Converting formulas to values is useful when you use formulas as a means to convert cells. For example, assume that you have a list of names (in uppercase) in column A. You want to convert these names to proper case. To do so, you need to create formulas in a separate column; then convert the formulas to values and replace the original values in column A. The following steps illustrate how to do this:

1. Insert a new column after column A.
2. Insert the following formula into cell B1:

```
=PROPER(A1)
```

3. Copy the formula down column B to accommodate the number of entries in column A.

   Column B then displays the values in column A, but in proper case.

4. Select all the names in column B.
5. Choose Home ➜ Clipboard ➜ Copy.
6. Select cell A1.
7. Choose Home ➜ Clipboard ➜ Paste ➜ Values.
8. Press Enter or Esc to cancel paste mode.
9. Delete column B.

When to use AutoFill rather than formulas

Excel's AutoFill feature provides a quick way to copy a cell to adjacent cells. AutoFill also has some other uses that may substitute for formulas in some cases. Many experienced Excel users don't take advantage of the AutoFill feature, which can save a lot of time.

For example, if you need values from 1 to 100 to appear in A1:A100, you can do it with formulas. You type **1** into cell A1, type the formula **=A1+1** into cell A2, and then copy the formula to the 98 cells below.

You can also use AutoFill to create the series for you without using a formula. To do so, type **1** into cell A1 and **2** into cell A2. Select A1:A2 and drag the fill handle down to cell A100. (The *fill handle* is the small square at the lower-right corner of the active cell.) When you use AutoFill in this manner, Excel analyzes the selected cells and uses this information to complete the series. If cell A1 contains 1 and cell A2 contains 3, Excel recognizes this pattern and fills in 5, 7, 9, and so on. This also works with decreasing series (10, 9, 8, and so on) and dates. If there is no discernible pattern in the selected cells, Excel performs a linear regression and fills in values on the calculated trend line.

Excel also recognizes common series names such as months and days of the week. If you type **Monday** into a cell and then drag its fill handle, Excel fills in the successive days of the week. You also can create custom AutoFill lists using the Custom Lists panel in the Excel Options dialog box. Finally, if you drag the fill handle with the right mouse button, Excel displays a shortcut menu to enable you to select an AutoFill option.

Tip

Flash Fill can be an alternative to formulas. See Chapter 16, "Importing and Cleaning Data," for more information about Flash Fill.

Hiding Formulas

In some cases, you may not want others to see your formulas. For example, you may have a special formula you developed that performs a calculation proprietary to your company. You can use the Format Cells dialog box to hide the formulas contained in these cells.

To prevent one or more formulas from being viewed:

1. Select the formula or formulas.
2. Right-click and choose Format Cells to show the Format Cells dialog box (or press Ctrl+1).
3. In the Format Cells dialog box, click the Protection tab.
4. Place a check mark in the Hidden check box, as shown in Figure 2-6.
5. Use the Review ➜ Changes ➜ Protect command to protect the worksheet.

   To prevent others from unprotecting the sheet, specify a password in the Protect Sheet dialog box.

By default, all cells are locked. Protecting a sheet prevents any locked cells from being changed. So you should unlock any cells that require user input before protecting your sheet.

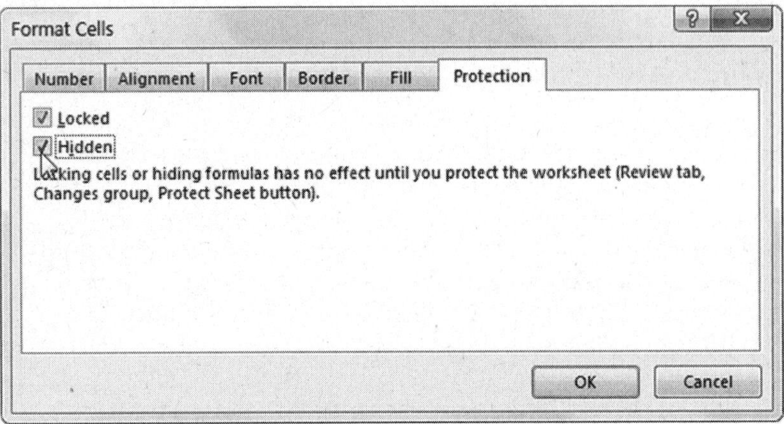

Figure 2-6: Use the Format Cells dialog box to change the Hidden and Locked status of a cell or range.

Caution

Be aware that it's easy to crack the password for a worksheet. So this technique of hiding your formulas does not ensure that no one can view them.

Errors in Formulas

It's not uncommon to enter a formula only to find that the formula returns an error. Table 2.4 lists the types of error values that may appear in a cell that has a formula.

Formulas may return an error value if a cell that they refer to has an error value. This is known as the ripple effect: a single error value can make its way to lots of other cells that contain formulas that depend on that cell.

Table 2-4: Excel Error Values

Error Value	Explanation
#DIV/0!	The formula attempts to divide by zero (an operation not allowed on this planet). This also occurs when the formula attempts to divide by an empty cell.
#NAME?	The formula uses a name that Excel doesn't recognize. This can happen if you delete a name used in the formula or if you misspell a function.
#N/A	The formula refers (directly or indirectly) to a cell that uses the NA function to signal unavailable data. This error also occurs if a lookup function does not find a match.
#NULL!	The formula uses an intersection of two ranges that don't intersect. (We describe range intersection in Chapter 3.)
#NUM!	A problem occurs with a value; for example, you specify a negative number where a positive number is expected.
#REF!	The formula refers to an invalid cell. This happens if the cell has been deleted from the worksheet.
#VALUE!	The formula includes an argument or operand of the wrong type. An operand refers to a value or cell reference that a formula uses to calculate a result.

Note

If the entire cell fills with hash marks (#########), this usually means that the column isn't wide enough to display the value. You can either widen the column or change the number format of the cell. The cell also fills with hash marks if it contains a formula that returns an invalid date or time.

Caution

Refer to Chapter 22 for more information about identifying and tracing errors.

Dealing with Circular References

When you enter formulas, you may occasionally see a message from Excel like the one shown in Figure 2-7. This indicates that the formula you just entered will result in a *circular reference.*

A circular reference occurs when a formula refers to its own value, either directly or indirectly. For example, if you type **=A1** into cell A3, =**A3** into cell B3, and =**B3** into cell A1, it produces a circular reference because the formulas create a circle in which each formula depends on the one before it. Every time the formula in A3 is calculated, it affects the formula in B3, which in turn affects the formula in A1. The result of the formula in A1 then causes A3 to recalculate, and the calculation circle starts all over again.

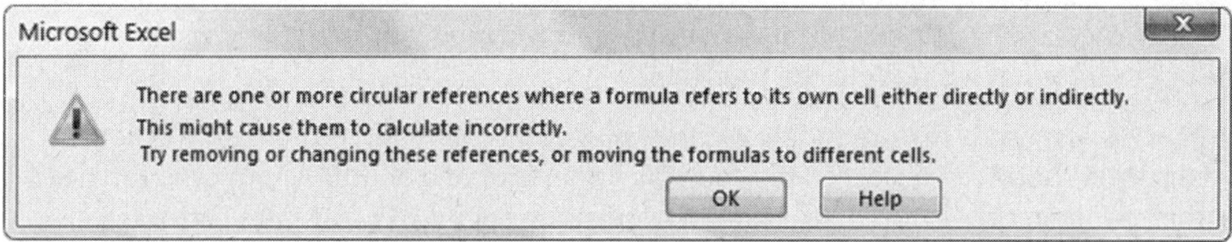

Figure 2-7: Excel's way of telling you that your formula contains a circular reference.

When you enter a formula that contains a circular reference, Excel displays a dialog box with two options: OK and Help.

Normally, you'll want to correct any circular references, so you should click OK. After you do so, Excel inserts tracing arrows. Clicking the Help option displays the Excel Help topic for circular references.

The status bar displays *Circular References: A3,* in this case. To resolve the circular reference, choose Formulas ➜ Formula Auditing ➜ Error Checking ➜ Circular References to see a list of the cells involved in the circular reference. Click each cell in turn and try to locate the error. If you cannot determine whether the cell is the cause of the circular reference, navigate to the next cell on the Circular References submenu. Continue reviewing each cell on the Circular References submenu until the status bar no longer reads *Circular References.*

Tip

Instead of navigating to each cell using the Circular References submenu, you can click the tracer arrows to quickly jump between cells.

After you enter a formula that contains a circular reference, Excel displays a message in the status bar reminding you that a circular reference exists. In this case, the message reads *Circular References: A3*. If you activate a different worksheet or workbook, the message simply displays *Circular References* (without the cell reference).

Caution

Excel doesn't warn you about a circular reference if you have the Enable Iterative Calculation setting turned on. You can check this in the Excel Options dialog box (in the Calculation section of the Formulas tab). If this option is checked, Excel performs the circular calculation the number of times specified in the Maximum Iterations field (or until the value changes by less than .001—or whatever other value appears in the Maximum Change field). You should, however, keep the Enable Iterative Calculation setting off so that you'll be warned of circular references. Generally, a circular reference indicates an error that you must correct.

When the formula in a cell refers to that cell, the cause of the circular reference is quite obvious and is, therefore, easy to identify and correct. For this type of circular reference, Excel does not show tracer arrows. For an indirect circular reference, as in the preceding example, the tracer arrows can help you identify the problem.

Goal Seeking

Many spreadsheets contain formulas that enable you to ask questions such as, "What would be the total profit if sales increase by 20 percent?" If you set up your worksheet properly, you can change the value in one cell to see what happens to the profit cell.

Goal seeking serves as a useful feature that works in conjunction with your formulas. If you know what a formula result should be, Excel can tell you which values of one or more input cells you need to produce that result. In other words, you can ask a question such as, "What sales increase is needed to produce a profit of $1.2 million?"

Single–cell goal seeking (also known as *backsolving*) represents a rather simple concept. Excel determines what value in an input cell produces a desired result in a formula cell. You can best understand how this works by walking through an example.

A goal seeking example

Figure 2-8 shows a loan payment calculator that shows the expected monthly payment based on a given loan amount, number of payment months, and interest rate.

	M	N
1	Loan Amount	$ 50,000
2	# Months	60
3	Annual Interest	7%
4		
5	Payment	$990.06

Figure 2-8: This worksheet presents a simple demonstration of goal seeking.

Imagine that you know you can afford a payment of $500 per month. Knowing you can get a fixed-rate of 7 percent over 60 payment months, what is the maximum loan you can take and still have a payment of $500?

In other words, what value in cell N1 causes the formula in cell N5 to yield $500? You can plug values into cell N1 until N5 displays $500. Or you can let Excel determine the answer.

To answer this question, choose Data ➜ Data Tools ➜ What-If Analysis ➜ Goal Seek. Excel displays the Goal Seek dialog box, as shown in Figure 2-9. Completing this dialog box resembles forming the following sentence: set cell N5 to 500 by changing cell N1. Clicking OK begins the goal seeking process.

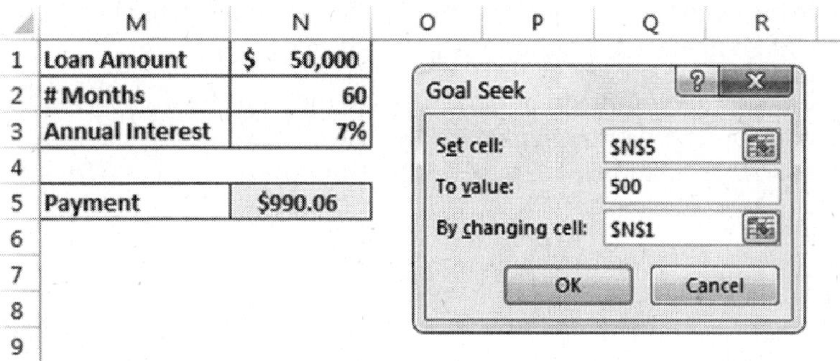

Figure 2-9: The Goal Seek dialog box.

Almost immediately, Excel announces that it has found the solution and displays the Goal Seek status box (see Figure 2-10). This box tells you the target value and what Excel came up with. In this case, Excel found that a loan amount of $25,251 would yield $500 monthly payments.

You can click OK to replace the original value with the found value, or you can click Cancel to restore your worksheet to its original form before you chose Goal Seek.

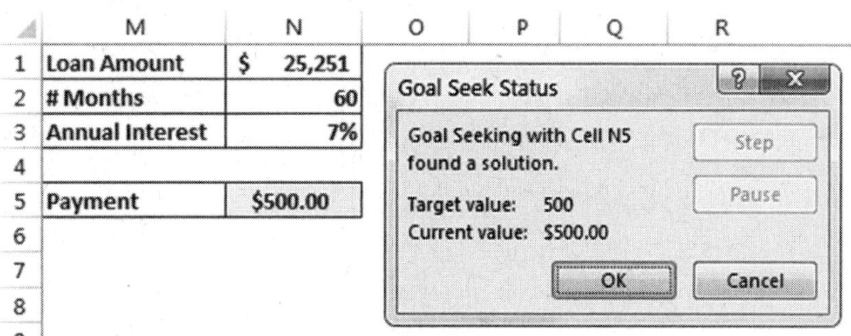

Figure 2-10: The Goal Seek Status dialog box.

More about goal seeking

If you think about it, you may realize that Excel can't always find a value that produces the result you're looking for—sometimes a solution doesn't exist. In such a case, the Goal Seek Status box informs you of that fact. Other times, however, Excel may report that it can't find a solution even though you believe one exists. In this case, you can adjust the current value of the changing cell to a value closer to the solution and then reissue the command. If that fails, double-check your logic and make sure that the formula cell does indeed depend on the specified changing cell.

Like all computer programs, Excel has limited precision. To demonstrate this, enter **=A1^2** into cell A2. Then choose Data ➜ Data Tools ➜ What-If Analysis ➜ Goal Seek to find the value in cell A1 that causes the formula to return 16. Excel returns a value of 4.00002269—close to the square root of 16, but certainly not exact. You can adjust the precision in the Calculation section of the Formulas tab in the Excel Options dialog box (make the Maximum change value smaller).

In some cases, multiple values of the input cell produce the same desired result. For example, the formula =A1^2 returns 16 if cell A1 contains either –4 or +4. If you use goal seeking when two solutions exist, Excel gives you the solution that is nearest to the current value in the cell.

Perhaps the main limitation of the Goal Seek command is that it can find the value for only one input cell. For example, it can't tell you what purchase price *and* what down payment percent result in a particular monthly payment. If you want to change more than one variable at a time, use the Solver add-in.

3

Working with Names

In This Chapter

- An overview and the advantages of using names in Excel
- The difference between workbook- and worksheet-level names
- Working with the Name Manager dialog box
- Shortcuts for creating cell and range names
- How to create names that extend across multiple worksheets
- How to perform common operations with range and cell names
- How Excel maintains cell and range names
- Potential problems that may crop up when you use names
- The secret behind names, and examples of named constants and named formulas
- Examples of advanced techniques that use names

Most intermediate and advanced Excel users are familiar with the concept of named cells or ranges. Naming cells and ranges is an excellent practice and offers several important advantages. As you see in this chapter, Excel supports other types of names—and the power of this concept may surprise you.

What's in a Name?

You can think of a *name* as an identifier for something in a workbook. This "something" can consist of a cell, a range, a chart, a shape, and so on.

Note

Although you can give a name to any object in Excel, this chapter focuses exclusively on cell and range names (which are handled differently than other types of names).

If you provide a name for a range, you can then use that name in your formulas. For example, suppose your worksheet contains daily sales information stored in the range B2:B200. Further, assume that cell C1 contains a sales commission rate. The following formula returns the sum of the sales, multiplied by the commission rate:

```
=SUM(B2:B200)*C1
```

This formula works fine, but its purpose is not at all clear. To help clarify the formula, you can define a descriptive name for the daily sales range and another descriptive name for cell C1. Assume, for this example, that the range B2:B200 is named *DailySales* and cell C1 is named *CommissionRate*. You can then rewrite the formula to use the names instead of the actual range addresses:

```
=SUM(DailySales)*CommissionRate
```

As you can see, using names instead of cell references makes the formula self-documenting and much easier to understand.

Using named cells and ranges offers a number of advantages:

- Names make your formulas more understandable and easier to use, especially for people who didn't create the worksheet. Obviously, a formula such as =Income-Taxes is more intuitive than =D20-D40.
- When entering formulas, keep in mind that a descriptive range name (such as *Total_Income*) is easier to remember than a cell address (such as AC21). And typing a name is less likely to result in an error than entering a cell or range address.
- You can quickly navigate to areas of your worksheet either by using the Name box located at the left side of the Formula bar (click the arrow for a drop-down list of defined names) or by choosing Home ➜ Editing ➜ Find & Select ➜ Go To (or press F5) and specifying the range name.
- When you select a named cell or range, its name appears in the Name box. This is a good way to verify that your names refer to the correct cells.
- You may find that creating formulas is easier if you use named cells. You can easily insert a name into a formula by using the drop-down list that's displayed when you enter a formula. Or press F3 to get a list of defined names.
- Macros are easier to create and maintain when you use range names rather than cell addresses.

A Name's Scope

Before we explain how to create and work with names, it's important to understand that all names have a scope. A name's *scope* defines where you can use the name. Names are scoped at either of two levels:

- **Workbook-level names:** Can be used in any worksheet in the workbook. This is the default type of range name.
- **Worksheet-level names:** Can be used only in the worksheet in which they are defined unless they are preceded with the worksheet's name. A workbook may contain multiple worksheet-level names that are identical. For example, three sheets can have a cell named *Region_Total.*

Most of the time, you will use workbook-level names. For some situations, though, using worksheet-level names makes sense. For example, you might use a workbook to store monthly data, one worksheet per month. You start out with a worksheet named January, and you create worksheet-level names on that sheet. Then, rather than create a new sheet called February, you copy the January sheet and name it February. All the worksheet-level names from the January sheet are reproduced as worksheet-level names on the February sheet.

Referencing names

You can refer to a workbook-level name just by using its name from any sheet in the workbook. For worksheet-level names, you must precede the name with the name of the worksheet unless you're using it on its own worksheet.

For example, assume that you have a workbook with two sheets: Sheet1 and Sheet2. In this workbook, you have *Total_Sales* (a workbook-level name), *North_Sales* (a worksheet-level name on Sheet1), and *South_Sales* (a worksheet-level name on Sheet2). On Sheet1 or Sheet2, you can refer to *Total_Sales* by simply using this name:

```
=Total_Sales
```

If you're on Sheet1 and you want to refer to *North_Sales,* you can use a similar formula because *North_Sales* is defined on Sheet1:

```
=North_Sales
```

However, if you want to refer to *South_Sales* on Sheet1, you need to do a little more work. Sheet1 can't "see" the name *South_Sales* because it's defined on another sheet. Sheet1 can see workbook-level names and worksheet-level names only as defined on Sheet1. To refer to *South_Sales* on Sheet1, prefix the name with the worksheet name and an exclamation point:

```
=Sheet2!South_Sales
```

Tip

If your worksheet name contains a space, enclose the worksheet name in single quotes when referring to a name defined on that sheet:

```
='My Sheet'!My_Name
```

Note

Only the worksheet-level names on the current sheet appear in the Name box. Similarly, only worksheet-level names on the current sheet appear in the list under Formulas ➜ Defined Names ➜ Use in Formulas.

Referencing names from another workbook

Chapter 2, "Basic Facts About Formulas," describes how to use links to reference cells or ranges in other workbooks. The same rules apply when using names defined in another workbook.

For example, the following formula uses a range named *MonthlySales,* a workbook-level name defined in a workbook named Annual Budget.xlsx (which is assumed to be open):

```
=AVERAGE('Annual Budget.xlsx'!MonthlySales)
```

If the name *MonthlySales* is a worksheet-level name on Sheet1, the formula looks like this:

```
=AVERAGE('[Annual Budget.xlsx]Sheet1'!MonthlySales)
```

If you use the pointing method to create such formulas, Excel takes care of the details automatically.

Conflicting names

Using worksheet-level names can be a bit confusing because Excel lets you define worksheet-level names even if the workbook contains the same name as a workbook-level name. In such a case, the worksheet-level name takes precedence over the workbook-level name, but only in the worksheet in which you defined the sheet-level name.

For example, you can define a workbook-level name of *Total* for a cell on Sheet1. You can also define a worksheet-level name of *Sheet2!Total.* When Sheet2 is active, *Total* refers to the worksheet-level name. When any other sheet is active, *Total* refers to the workbook-level name. Confusing? Probably. To make your life easier, we recommend that you simply avoid using the same name at the workbook and worksheet levels.

One way you can avoid this type of conflict is to adopt a naming convention when you create names. By using a naming convention, your names tell you more about themselves. For instance, you can prefix all your workbook-level names with *wb* and your worksheet-level names with *ws.* With this method, you never confuse *wbTotal* with *wsTotal.*

The Name Manager

Now that you understand the concept of scope, you can start creating and using names. Excel has a handy feature for maintaining names called the Name Manager, shown in Figure 3-1.

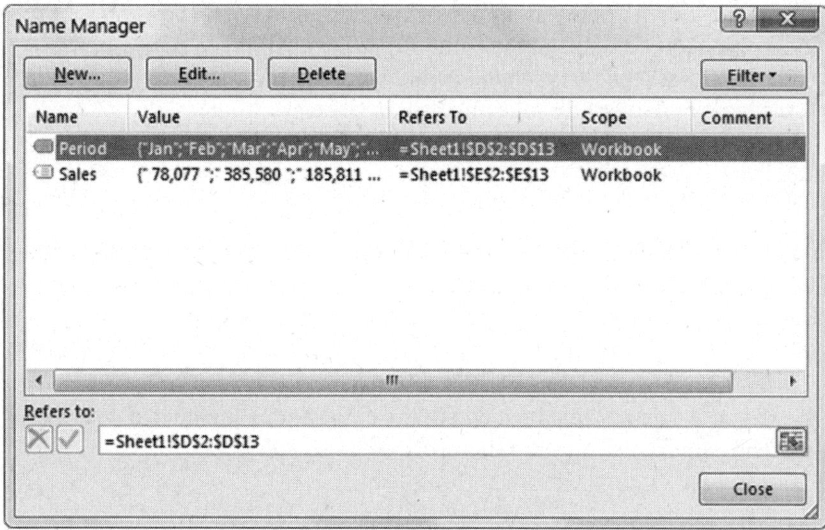

Figure 3-1: The Name Manager dialog box.

To display the Name Manager, choose Formulas ➜ Defined Names ➜ Name Manager. Within this dialog box, you can view, create, edit, and delete names. In the Name Manager main window, you can see the current value of the name, what the name refers to, the scope of the name, and any comments that you've written to describe the name. The names are sortable, and the columns are resizable, allowing you to see your names in many different ways. If you use a lot of names, you can also apply some predefined filters to view only the names that interest you.

Note that the Name Manager dialog box is resizable. Drag the lower-right corner to make it wider or taller.

Creating names

The Name Manager contains a New button for creating new names. The New button displays the New Name dialog box, as shown in Figure 3-2.

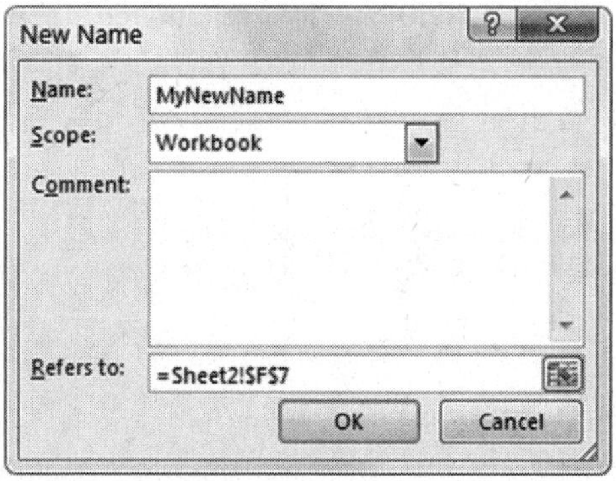

Figure 3-2: The New Name dialog box.

In the New Name dialog box, you name the name, define its scope and what it refers to, and (optionally) add any comments about the name to help yourself and others understand its purpose. The Refers To field displays the range address that was selected when you invoked the dialog box. You can change the address displayed by typing or by selecting cells in the worksheet.

Editing names

Clicking the Edit button in the Name Manager displays the Edit Name dialog box, which looks strikingly similar to the New Name dialog box. You can change any property of your name except the scope. If you change the Name field, all the formulas in your workbook that use that name are updated.

Tip

To change the scope of a name, you must delete the name and re-create it. If you're careful to use the same name, your formulas that use that name still work.

The Edit Name dialog box isn't the only way to edit a name. If the only property that you want to change is the Refers To property, you can do it right in the Name Manager dialog box. At the bottom of the dialog box is the field labeled Refers To. Simply select the name that you'd like to edit in the main window and change the reference in the Refers To field.

Tip

If you edit the contents of the Refers To field manually, the status bar displays *Point*, indicating that you're in point mode. If you try to use keys such as the arrows, Home, or End, you find that you're navigating around the worksheet rather than editing the Refers To text. This is a constant source of frustration to many Excel users. But there's a simple solution. To switch from point mode to edit mode, press F2 and note that the status bar changes to show *Edit*.

Deleting names

Clicking the Delete button in the Name Manager permanently removes the selected name from your workbook. Excel warns you first because this action cannot be undone.

Caution

Unfortunately, Excel does *not* replace deleted names with the original cell references. Any formulas that use a name you delete display the #NAME? error.

Shortcuts for Creating Cell and Range Names

Excel provides a few additional ways to create names for cells and ranges other than the Name Manager. We discuss these methods in this section, along with some other relevant information that pertains to names.

The New Name dialog box

You can access the New Name dialog box directly by choosing Formulas ➜ Defined Names ➜ Define Name. The New Name dialog box that's displayed is identical in form and function to the one from the New button on the Name Manager dialog box.

Note

A single cell or range can have any number of names. We can't think of a good reason to use more than one name, but Excel does permit it. If a cell or range has multiple names, the Name box always displays the name that's first alphabetically when you select the cell or range.

A name can also refer to a noncontiguous range of cells. You can select a noncontiguous range by pressing Ctrl while you select various cells or ranges with the mouse.

Rules for naming names

Although Excel is quite flexible about the names you can define, it does have some rules:

- **Names can't contain spaces.** You might want to use an underscore or a period character to simulate a space (such as *Annual_Total* or *Annual.Total*).
- **You can use any combination of letters and numbers, but the name must begin with a letter or underscore.** A name can't begin with a number (such as *3rdQuarter*).
- **A name cannot look like a cell reference.** This excludes names such as *Q3* and *TAX2012*.
- **You cannot use symbols, except for underscores and periods.** Although not documented, we've found that Excel also permits a backslash (\) and question mark (?) as long as they don't appear as the first character in a name.
- **Names cannot exceed 255 characters in length.**
- **You can use single letters (except for R or C).** However, it is not recommended because it also defeats the purpose of using meaningful names.
- **Names are not case sensitive.** The name *AnnualTotal* is the same as *annualtotal.* Excel stores the name exactly as you type it when you define it, but it doesn't matter how you capitalize the name when you use it in a formula.

Although periods are allowed, you can't use a period if the resulting name can be construed as a range address. For example *A1.A12* is not a valid name because it's equivalent to the address A1:A12.

Excel also uses a few names internally for its own use. Although you can create names that override Excel's internal names, you should avoid doing so unless you know what you're doing. Generally, avoid using the following names: *Print_Area, Print_Titles, Consolidate_Area, Database, Criteria, Extract, FilterDatabase,* and *Sheet_Title.*

Creating names using the Name box

A faster way to create a name for a cell or range is to use the Name box. The Name box is the drop-down list box to the left of the Formula bar. Select the cell or range to name, click the Name box, type the name, and then press Enter to create the name. If a name already exists, you can't use the Name box to change the range to which that name refers. Attempting to do so simply selects the original range. You must use the Name Manager dialog box to change the reference for a name.

Caution

When you type a name in the Name box, you *must* press Enter to actually record the name. If you type a name and then click in the worksheet, Excel doesn't create the name.

To create a worksheet-level name using the Name box, precede the name with the active worksheet's name, followed by an exclamation point. For example, to create the name *Total* as a worksheet-level name for Sheet1, type this into the Name box and press Enter:

```
Sheet1!Total
```

If the worksheet name contains spaces, enclose the sheet name in single quotes, like this:

```
'Summary Sheet'!Total
```

Because the Name box works only on the currently selected range, typing a worksheet name other than the active worksheet results in an error.

If you type an invalid name (such as *May21*, which is a cell address), Excel activates that address (and doesn't warn you that the name is not valid). If the name you type includes an invalid character, Excel displays an error message.

The Name box serves double duty by also providing a quick way to activate a named cell or range. To select a named cell or range, click the Name box and choose the name, as shown in Figure 3-3. This selects the named cell or range. Oddly, the Name box does not have a keyboard shortcut. In other words, you can't access the Name box by using the keyboard; you must use the mouse. After you click the Name box, however, you can use the direction keys and Enter to choose a name.

Notice that the Name box is resizable. To make the Name box wider, just click the three vertical dots icon to the right of the Name box, and drag it to the right. The Name box shares space with the Formula bar, so if you make the Name box wider, the Formula bar gets narrower.

Creating names from text in cells

You may have a worksheet containing text that you want to use for names of adjacent cells or ranges. Figure 3-4 shows an example of such a worksheet. In this case, you might want to use the text in column R to create names for the corresponding values in columns S through AD. Excel makes this easy to do.

Running_Total

Month
Running_Total
Units_Sold

		I	J
		Units Sold	Running Total
		99	99
3	February	37	136
4	April	97	233
5	May	74	307
6	June	29	336
7	July	56	392
8	August	75	467
9	September	98	565
10	October	56	621
11	November	59	680
12	December	80	760

Figure 3-3: The Name box provides a quick way to select a named cell or range.

R	S	T	U	V	W	X	Y	Z	AA	AB	AC	AD
Months	J	F	M	A	M	J	J	A	S	O	N	D

Figure 3-4: Excel makes it easy to create names by using text in adjacent cells.

To create names by using adjacent text, start by selecting the name text and the cells that you want to name. (These can consist of individual cells or ranges of cells.) The names must be adjacent to the cells that you're naming. (A multiple selection is allowed.) Then choose Formulas ➜ Defined Names ➜ Create from Selection (or Ctrl+Shift+F3). Excel displays the Create Names from Selection dialog box, as shown in Figure 3-5.

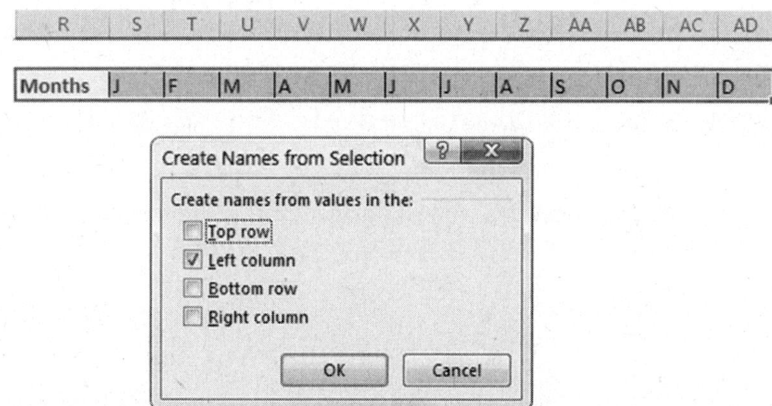

Figure 3-5: The Create Names from Selection dialog box.

The check marks in this dialog box are based on Excel's analysis of the selected range. For example, if Excel finds text in the first row of the selection, it proposes that you create names based on the top row. If it finds text in the first column, it proposes to create names based on those cells. If Excel doesn't guess correctly, you can change the check boxes. Click OK, and Excel creates the names.

Note that when Excel creates names using text in cells, it does not include those text cells in the named range.

If the text in a cell would result in an invalid name, Excel modifies the name to make it valid. For example, if a cell contains the text *Net Income* (which is invalid for a name because it contains a space), Excel converts the space to an underscore character and creates the name *Net_Income.* If Excel encounters a value or a formula instead of text, however, it doesn't convert it to a valid name. It simply doesn't create a name.

Naming entire rows and columns

Sometimes it makes sense to name an entire row or column. Often, a worksheet is used to store information that you enter over a period of time. The sheet in Figure 3-6 is an example of such a worksheet. If you create a name for the data in column I, you need to modify the name's reference each day you add new data. The solution is to name the entire column.

H	I	J
Month	Units Sold	Running Total
1/1/2015	99	99
1/2/2015	37	136
1/3/2015	97	233
1/4/2015	74	307
1/5/2015	29	336
1/6/2015	56	392
1/7/2015	75	467
1/8/2015	98	565
1/9/2015	56	621
1/10/2015	59	680
1/11/2015	80	760

Figure 3-6: This worksheet, which tracks daily sales, uses a named range that consists of an entire column.

For example, you might name column I as *DailySales.* This range is on Sheet3; its reference would appear like this:

```
=Sheet3!$I:$I
```

To define a name for an entire column, select the column by clicking the column letter. Then type the name in the Name box and press Enter (or use the New Name dialog box to create the name).

After defining the name, you can use it in a formula. The following formula, for example, returns the sum of all values in column I:

```
=SUM(DailySales)
```

Names created by Excel

Excel creates some names on its own. For example, if you set a print area for a sheet, Excel creates the name *Print_Area*. If you set repeating rows or columns for printing, you also have a worksheet-level name called *Print_Titles*. When you execute a query that returns data to a worksheet, Excel assigns a name to the data that is returned. Also, many of the add-ins that ship with Excel create hidden names. (See the "Hidden names" sidebar.)

You can modify the reference for any of the names that Excel creates automatically, but make sure you understand the consequences.

Hidden names

Some Excel macros and add-ins create hidden names. These names exist in a workbook but don't appear in the Name Manager dialog box or the Name box. For example, the Solver add-in creates a number of hidden names. Normally, you can just ignore these hidden names. However, sometimes these hidden names create problems. If you copy a sheet to another workbook, the hidden names are also copied, and they may create a link that is difficult to track down.

Although Excel's Name Manager is versatile, it doesn't have an option to display hidden names. Here's a simple VBA procedure that lists all hidden names in the active workbook. The macro adds a new worksheet, and the list is written to that worksheet:

```
Sub ListHiddenNames()
    Dim n As Name, r As Long
    Worksheets.Add
    r = 1
    For Each n In ActiveWorkbook.Names
       If Not n.Visible Then
        Cells(r, 1) = n.Name
        Cells(r, 2) = "'" & n.RefersTo
        r = r + 1
       End If
    Next n
End Sub
```

Creating Multisheet Names

Names can extend into the third dimension; in other words, they can extend across multiple worksheets in a workbook. You can't simply select the multisheet range and type a name in the Name box, however. You must use the New Name dialog box to create a multisheet name. The syntax for a multi-sheet reference is the following:

```
FirstSheet:LastSheet!RangeReference
```

In Figure 3-7, a multisheet name, *DataCube*, defined for A1:E5, extends across Sheet1, Sheet2, and Sheet3.

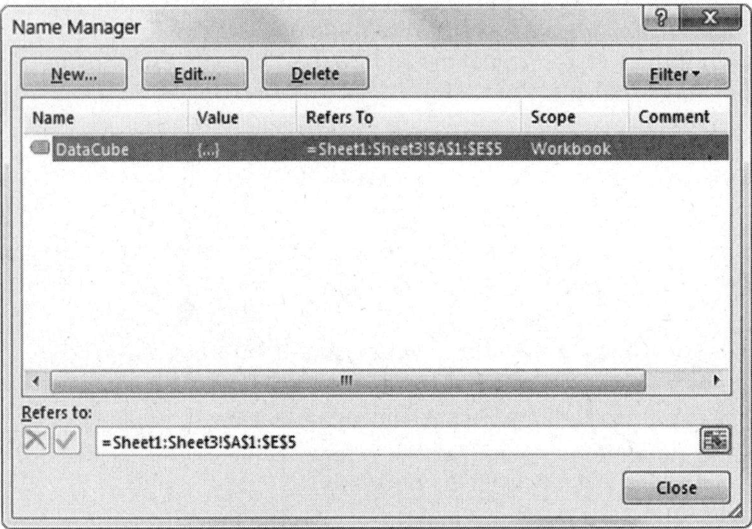

Figure 3-7: Create a multisheet name.

You can, of course, simply type the multisheet range reference in the Refers To field. If you want to create the name by pointing to the range, though, it's a bit tricky. Even if you begin by selecting a multisheet range, Excel does not use this selected range address in the New Name dialog box.

Follow this step-by-step procedure to create a name called *DataCube* that refers to the range A1:E5 across three worksheets (Sheet1, Sheet2, and Sheet3):

1. Activate Sheet1.
2. Choose Formulas ➜ Defined Names ➜ Define Name to display the New Name dialog box.
3. Type **DataCube** into the Name field.
4. Highlight the range reference in the Refers To field and press Delete to delete the range reference.
5. Click the sheet tab for Sheet1.
6. Press Shift and click the sheet tab for Sheet3.

At this point, the Refers To field contains the following:

```
='Sheet1!Sheet3'!
```

7. Select the range A1:E5 in Sheet1 (which is still the active sheet).

   The following appears in the Refers To field:

```
='Sheet1:Sheet3'!$A$1:$E$5
```

8. Because the Refers To field now has the correct multisheet range address, click OK to close the New Name dialog box.

After you define the name, you can use it in your formulas. For example, the following formula returns the sum of the values in the range named *DataCube*:

```
=SUM(DataCube)
```

Note

Multisheet names do not appear in the Name box or in the Go To dialog box (which appears when you choose Home ➜ Editing ➜ Find & Select & Go To). In other words, Excel enables you to define the name, but it doesn't give you a way to automatically select the cells to which the name refers. However, multisheet names *do* appear in the Formula AutoComplete drop-down list that appears when you type a formula.

If you insert a new worksheet into a workbook that uses multisheet names, the multisheet names include the new worksheet—as long as the sheet resides between the first and last sheet in the name's definition. In the preceding example, a worksheet inserted between Sheet1 and Sheet2 is included in the *DataCube* range. However, a worksheet inserted before Sheet1 or after Sheet3 is not included.

If you delete the first or the last sheet included in a multisheet name, Excel changes the name's range in the Refers To field automatically. In the preceding example, deleting Sheet1 causes the Refers To range of *DataCube* to change to this:

```
='Sheet2:Sheet3'!$A$1:$E$5
```

Multisheet names can be scoped at the workbook level or worksheet level. If it's a worksheet-level name, the name is valid only on the sheet that it's scoped to.

Working with Range and Cell Names

After you create range or cell names, you can work with them in a variety of ways. This section describes how to perform common operations with range and cell names.

Creating a list of names

If you create a large number of names, you may need to know the ranges that each name refers to, particularly if you're trying to track down errors or document your work. You might want to create a list of all names (and their corresponding addresses) in the workbook. The Name Manager dialog box doesn't provide this option, but there's a way to do it.

To create a list of names, first move the cell pointer to an empty area of your worksheet. (The two-column name list, created at the active cell position, overwrites any information at that location.) Use the Formulas ➜ Defined Names ➜ Use in Formula ➜ Paste Names command (or press F3). Excel displays the Paste Name dialog box that lists all the defined names. To paste a list of names, click the Paste List button. Figure 3-8 shows the Paste Name dialog box.

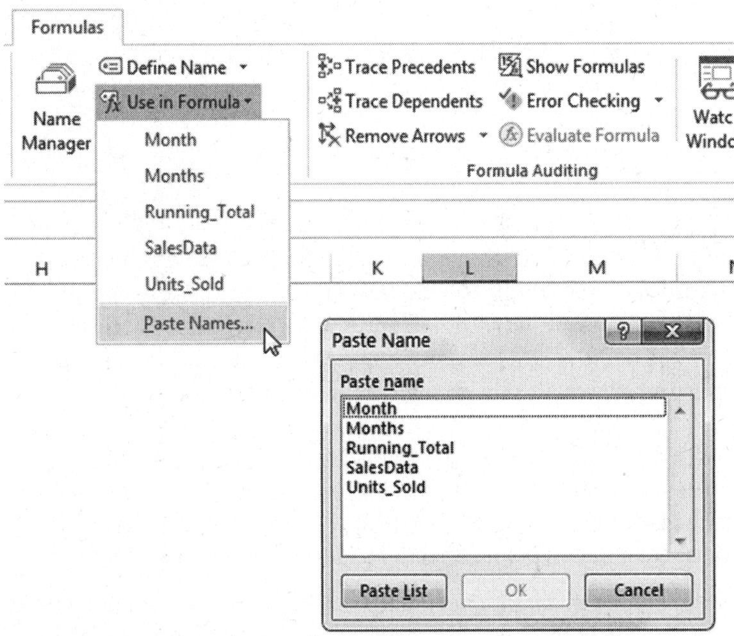

Figure 3-8: Use the Paste Name dialog box to create a list of names.

Caution

The list of names does not include hidden names or worksheet-level names that appear in sheets other than the active sheet.

The list of names pasted to your worksheet occupies two columns. The first column contains the names, and the second column contains the corresponding range addresses. The range addresses in the second column consist of text strings that look like formulas. You can convert such a string to an actual formula by editing the cell. Press F2 and then press Enter. The string then converts to a formula. If the name refers to a single cell, the formula displays the cell's current value. If the name refers to a range, the formula may return a *#VALUE!* error, or, in the case of multisheet names, a *#REF!* error.

Cross-Ref

We discuss formula errors such as *#VALUE!* and *#REF!* in Chapter 22, "Tools and Methods for Debugging Formulas."

Using names in formulas

After you define a name for a cell or range, you can use it in a formula. For example, the following formula calculates the sum of the values in the range named *UnitsSold:*

```
=SUM(UnitsSold)
```

Recall from the earlier section on scope ("A Name's Scope") that when you write a formula that uses a worksheet-level name on the sheet in which it's defined, you don't need to include the worksheet name in the range name. If you use the name in a formula on a different worksheet, however, you must use the entire name (sheet name, exclamation point, and name). For example, if the name *UnitsSold* represents a worksheet-level name defined on Sheet1, the following formula (on a sheet other than Sheet1) calculates the total of the *UnitsSold* range:

```
=SUM(Sheet1!UnitsSold)
```

When you're composing a formula and you need to insert a name, you have three options:

- Start typing the name, and it appears in the Formula AutoComplete drop-down list, along with a list of worksheet functions. To use Formula AutoComplete, begin typing the defined name until it is highlighted on the list, and then press Tab to complete the entry. Or use the down arrow key and press Tab to select a name from the list.
- Press F3 to display the Paste Name dialog box. This dialog box displays a list of defined names. Just select the name and click OK, and it's inserted into your formula.
- Choose Formulas ➜ Defined Names ➜ Use in Formula. This command also displays a list of defined names. Click a name, and it's inserted into your formula.

If you use a nonexistent name (or a name that's scoped to a different worksheet) in a formula, Excel displays a #NAME? error, indicating that it cannot find the name you are trying to use. Often, this means that you misspelled the name or that the name was deleted.

Using the intersection operators with names

Excel's range intersection operator is a single space character. The following formula, for example, displays the sum of the cells at the intersection of two ranges: B1:C20 and A8:D8:

```
=SUM(B1:C20 A8:D8)
```

The intersection of these two ranges consists of two cells: B8 and C8.

The intersection operator also works with named ranges. Figure 3-9 shows a worksheet containing named ranges that correspond to the row and column labels. For example, *January* refers to B2:E2, and *Region3* refers to D2:D13. The following formula returns the contents of the cell at the intersection of the *January* range and the *Region3* range:

```
=January Region3
```

	A	B	C	D	E
1		Region1	Region2	Region3	Region4
2	January	183	310	242	46
3	February	359	133	482	38
4	March	297	231	124	53
5	April	289	346	186	39
6	May	294	304	446	44
7	June	251	188	313	50
8	July	355	151	231	34
9	August	433	323	151	49
10	September	255	160	253	51
11	October	436	328	412	37
12	November	294	440	469	22
13	December	221	377	371	36
14					
15		242	=January Region3		

Figure 3-9: The formula in cell B15 uses the intersection operator.

Using a space character to separate two range references or names is known as *explicit intersection* because you explicitly tell Excel to determine the intersection of the ranges.

Excel can also perform *implicit intersections,* which occur when Excel chooses a value from a multicell range based on the row or column of the formula that contains the reference. An example should clear this up. Figure 3-10 shows a worksheet that contains a range (A2:A13) named *MonthNames.* Cell G5 contains the simple formula shown here:

```
=MonthNames
```

	A	F	G
1			
2	January		
3	February		
4	March		
5	April		April
6	May		
7	June		
8	July		
9	August		
10	September		
11	October		
12	November		
13	December		

Figure 3-10: Range A2:A13 in this worksheet is named MonthNames. Cell G5 demonstrates an implicit intersection.

Notice that cell G5 displays the value from *MonthNames* that corresponds to the formula's row. Similarly, if you enter the same formula into any other cell in rows 3 through 14, the formula displays the corresponding value from *MonthNames*. Excel performs an implicit intersection using the *MonthNames* range and the row that contains the formula.

If you enter the formula into a cell that's in a row not occupied by *MonthNames*, the formula returns an error because the implicit intersection returns nothing.

By the way, implicit intersections are not limited to named ranges. In the preceding example, you get the same result if cell G5 contains the following formula (which doesn't use a named range):

```
=$A$2:$A$13
```

If you use *MonthNames* as an argument for a function, implicit intersection applies only if the function argument is interpreted as a single value. For example, if you enter this formula into cell G5, implicit intersection works, and the formula returns *5* (the number of characters in *April*):

```
=LEN(MonthNames)
```

But if you enter this formula, implicit intersection does not apply, and the formula returns *12*, the number of cells in the *MonthNames* range:

```
=COUNTA(MonthNames)
```

Using the range operator with names

You can also use the range operator, which is a colon (:), to work with named ranges. Refer to Figure 3-9. For example, this formula returns the sum of the values in the 12-cell range that extends from Region1 January (cell B2) through Region4 March (cell E4):

```
=SUM((Region1 January):(Region4 March))
```

Referencing a single cell in a multicell named range

You can use Excel's INDEX function to return a single cell from a multicell named range. Assume that range A1:A10 is named *DataRange*. The following formula displays the fourth value (the value in A4) in *DataRange:*

```
=INDEX(DataRange,4)
```

The second and third arguments for the INDEX function are optional—although at least one of them must always be specified. The second argument (used in the preceding formula) specifies the row offset within the *DataRange* range.

If *DataRange* consists of multiple cells in a single row (for example, A1:J1), use a formula like the following one to return the fourth element in the range. This formula omits the second argument for the INDEX function but uses the third argument that specifies the column offset with the *DataRange* range:

```
=INDEX(DataRange,,4)
```

If the range consists of multiple rows and columns, use both the second and the third arguments for the INDEX function. For example, if *DataRange* is defined as A1:J10, this formula returns the value in the fourth row and fifth column of the named range:

```
=INDEX(DataRange,4,5)
```

Applying names to existing formulas

When you create a name for a cell or range, Excel does not scan your formulas automatically and replace the cell references with your new name. You can, however, tell Excel to "apply" names to a range of formulas.

Select the range that contains the formulas you want to modify so they will use names rather than cell references. Then choose Formulas ➜ Defined Names ➜ Define Name ➜ Apply Names. The Apply Names dialog box appears, as shown in Figure 3-11. In the Apply Names dialog box, select which names you want applied to the formulas. Only those names you select are applied to the formulas.

Figure 3-11: The Apply Names dialog box.

Tip

To apply names to all the formulas in the worksheet, select a single cell before you display the Apply Names dialog box.

The Ignore Relative/Absolute check box controls how Excel substitutes the range name for the actual address. A cell or range name is usually defined as an absolute reference. If the Ignore Relative/Absolute check box is selected, Excel applies the name only if the reference in the formula matches exactly. In most cases, you will want Excel to apply names whether the formulas are a relative or absolute reference. So leave the Ignore Relative/Absolute check box selected.

If the Use Row and Column Names check box is selected, Excel takes advantage of the intersection operator when applying names. Excel uses the names of row and column ranges that refer to the cells if it cannot find the exact names for the cells. Excel uses the intersection operator to join the names. Clicking the Options button displays some additional options that are available only when you select the Use Row and Column Names check box.

Applying names automatically when creating a formula

When you insert a cell or range reference into a formula by *pointing,* Excel automatically substitutes the cell or range name if it has one.

In some cases, this feature can be useful. In other cases, it can be annoying; you may prefer to use an actual cell or range reference instead of the name. For example, if you plan to copy the formula, the range references don't adjust if the reference is a name rather than an address. Unfortunately, you cannot turn off this feature. If you prefer to use a regular cell or range address, you need to type the cell or range reference manually. (Don't use the pointing technique.)

Unapplying names

Excel does not provide a direct method for unapplying names. In other words, you cannot replace a name in a formula with the name's actual cell reference automatically. However, you can take advantage of a trick described here (which works only for workbook-level names). You need to (temporarily) change Excel's Transition Formula Entry option so that it emulates Lotus 1-2-3.

1. Choose File ➜ Options and then click the Advanced tab in the Excel Options dialog box.
2. Under the Lotus Compatibility Settings section, place a check mark next to Transition Formula Entry and then click OK.
3. Select a cell that contains a formula that uses one or more cell or range names.
4. Press F2 and then press Enter.

   In other words, edit the cell but don't change anything.
5. Repeat steps 3 and 4 for other cells that use range names.
6. Go back to the Options dialog box and remove the check mark from the Transition Formula Entry check box.

The edited cells use relative range references rather than names.

Note

This trick is not documented, and it might not work in all cases, so make sure that you check the results carefully.

Names with errors

If you delete the rows or columns that contain named cells or ranges, the names are not deleted (as you might expect). Rather, each name contains an invalid reference. For example, if cell A1 on Sheet1 is named *Interest* and you delete row 1 or column A, *Interest* then refers to *=Sheet1!#REF!* (that is, an erroneous reference). If you use *Interest* in a formula, the formula displays *#REF*.

To get rid of this erroneous name, you must delete the name manually using the Delete button in the Name Manager dialog box. Or you can redefine the name so it refers to a valid cell or range.

Tip

The Name Manager allows you to filter the names that it displays using predefined filters. One of the filters provided, Names with Errors, shows only those names that contain errors, which enables you to quickly locate problematic names.

Viewing named ranges

As you probably know, you can change the zoom factor of a worksheet by using the slider on the right side of the status bar (or, use commands in the View ➜ Zoom group). When you zoom a worksheet to 39 percent or smaller, you see a border around the named ranges with the name displayed in blue letters, as shown in Figure 3-12. The border and name do not print; they simply help you visualize the named ranges on your sheet.

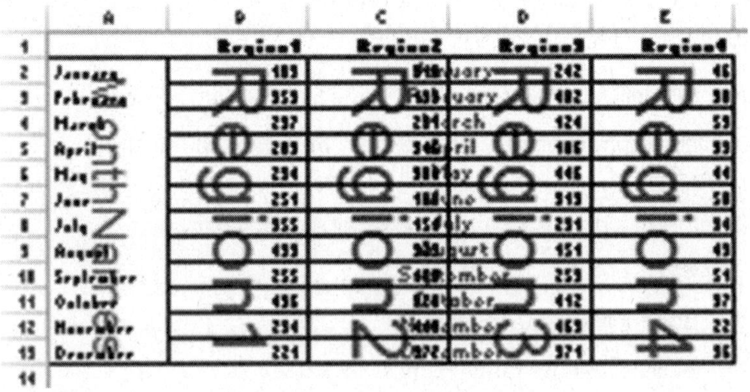

Figure 3-12: Excel displays range names when you zoom a sheet to 39 percent or less.

Using names in charts

When you create a chart, each data series has an associated SERIES formula. The SERIES formula contains references to the ranges used in the chart. If you have a defined range name, you can edit a chart's SERIES formula and replace the range reference with the name. After doing so, the chart series adjusts if you change the definition for the name.

Cross-Ref

See Chapter 17, "Charting Techniques," for additional information about charts.

How Excel Maintains Cell and Range Names

After you create a name for a cell or range, Excel automatically maintains the name as you edit or modify the worksheet. The following examples assume that Sheet1 contains a workbook-level name *(MyRange)* that refers to the following nine-cell range:

```
=Sheet1!$C$3:$E$5
```

Inserting a row or column

When you insert a row above the named range or insert a column to the left of the named range, Excel changes the range reference to reflect its new address. For example, if you insert a new row 1, *MyRange* then refers to =Sheet1!$C$4:$E$6.

If you insert a new row or column within the named range, the named range expands to include the new row or column. For example, if you insert a new column to the left of column E, *MyRange* then refers to =Sheet1!$C$3:$F$5.

Deleting a row or a column

When you delete a row above the named range or delete a column to the left of the named range, Excel adjusts the range reference to reflect its new address. For example, if you delete row 1, *MyRange* refers to =Sheet1!$C$2:$E$4.

If you delete a row or a column within the named range, the named range adjusts accordingly. For example, if you delete column D, *MyRange* then refers to =Sheet1!$C$3:$D$5.

If you delete all rows or all columns that make up a named range, the named range continues to exist, but it contains an error reference. For example, if you delete columns C, D, and E, *MyRange* then refers to =Sheet1!#REF!. Any formulas that use the name also return errors.

Cutting and pasting

When you cut and paste an entire named range, Excel changes the reference accordingly. For example, if you move *MyRange* to a new location beginning at cell A1, *MyRange* then refers to =Sheet1!$A$1:$C$3. Cutting and pasting only a part of a named range does not affect the name's reference.

Potential Problems with Names

Names are great, but they can also cause some problems. This section contains information that you should remember when you use names in a workbook.

Name problems when copying sheets

Excel lets you copy a worksheet within the same workbook or to a different workbook. Focus first on copying a sheet within the same workbook. If the copied sheet contains worksheet-level names, those names are also present on the copy of the sheet, adjusted to use the new sheet name. Usually, this is exactly what you want to happen. However, if the workbook contains a workbook-level name that refers to a cell or range on the sheet that's copied, that name is also present on the copied sheet. However, it is converted to a worksheet-level name. That is usually *not* what you want to happen.

Consider a workbook that contains one sheet (Sheet1). This workbook has a workbook-level name (*BookLevel*) for cell A1 and a worksheet-level name (*Sheet1!SheetLevel*) for cell A2. If you make a copy of Sheet1 within the workbook, the new sheet is named Sheet1 (2). After copying the sheet, the workbook contains four names. The new sheet has two worksheet-level names.

Not only is this proliferation of names when copying a sheet confusing, but it can result in errors that can be difficult to identify. In this case, typing the following formula on the copied sheet displays the contents of cell A1 in the copied sheet:

```
=BookLevel
```

In other words, the newly created worksheet-level name (not the original workbook-level name) is being used. This is probably *not* what you want.

If you copy the worksheet from a workbook containing a name that refers to a multisheet range, you also copy this name. A #REF! error appears in its Refers To field.

When you copy a sheet to a new workbook, all the names in the original workbook that refer to cells on the copied sheet are also copied to the new workbook. These include both workbook-level and worksheet-level names.

Note

Copying and pasting cells from one sheet to another does not copy names, even if the copied range contains named cells.

Bottom line? You must use caution when copying sheets from a workbook that uses names. After copying the sheet, check the names and delete those that you didn't intend to copy.

Name problems when deleting sheets

When you delete a worksheet that contains cells used in a workbook-level name, the name is not deleted. The name remains with the workbook, but it contains an erroneous reference in its Refers To definition.

For instance, imagine your workbook contained a sheet named Sheet2, which has a workbook-level name (*MyRange*). After deleting Sheet2, the name *MyRange* still exists in the workbook, but the Refers To column displays a #Ref error for the sheet name. You might see something like this:

```
=#REF!$A$1:$E$12
```

Keeping erroneous names in a workbook doesn't cause harm, but it's still good practice to delete or correct all names that contain an erroneous reference.

Naming objects

When you add an object to a worksheet (such as a shape, an image, or a chart), the object has a default name that reflects the type of object (for example, *Rectangle 3* or *Text Box 1*).

To change the name of an object, select it, type the new name in the Name box, and press Enter.

Excel is a bit inconsistent with regard to the Name box. Although you can use the Name box to rename an object, the Name box does not display a list of objects, so you can't use the Name box to select an object. However, you can use the Selection Pane to list all objects and make them easy to select. To display the Selection Pane, choose Home ➜ Editing ➜ Find & Select ➜ Selection Pane.

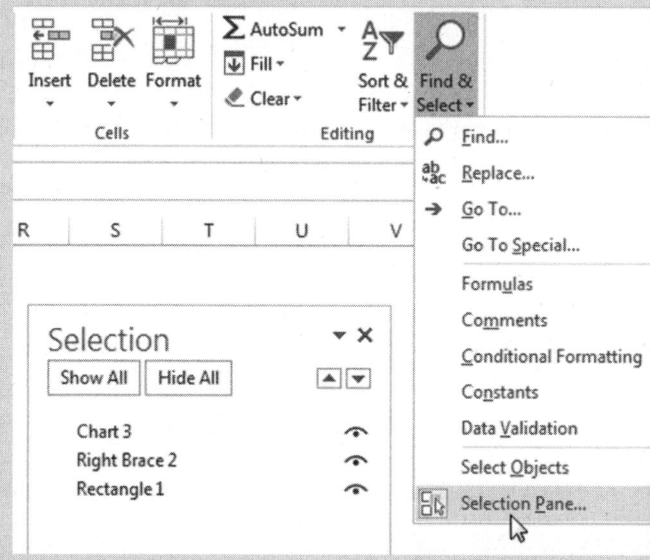

Excel also allows you to define a name with the same name as an object; two or more objects can even have the same name. The Name Manager dialog box does not list the names of objects.

The Secret to Understanding Names

Excel users often refer to *named ranges* and *named cells*. In fact, we use these terms frequently throughout this chapter. Technically, this terminology is not quite accurate.

Here's the secret to understanding names: when you create a name, you're actually creating a named formula. Unlike a normal formula, a named formula doesn't exist in a cell. Rather, it exists in Excel's memory.

This is not exactly an earth-shaking revelation, but keeping this "secret" in mind can help you understand the advanced naming techniques that follow.

When you work with the Name Manager dialog box, the Refers To field contains the formula, and the Name field contains the formula's name. The content of the Refers To field always begins with an equal sign, which makes it a formula.

For example, if your workbook contains a name (*InterestRate*) referring to cell B1, that name is technically a named formula, not a named cell. Whenever you use the name *InterestRate*, Excel actually evaluates the formula with that name and returns the result. For example, you might type this formula into a cell:

```
=InterestRate*1.05
```

When Excel evaluates this formula, it first evaluates the formula named *InterestRate* (which exists only in memory, not in a cell). It then multiplies the result of this named formula by 1.05 and displays the result. This cell formula, of course, is equivalent to the following formula, which uses the actual cell reference instead of the name:

```
=Sheet1!$B$1*1.05
```

At this point, you may be wondering whether it's possible to create a named formula that doesn't contain cell references. The answer comes in the next section.

Naming constants

Consider a worksheet that generates an invoice and calculates sales tax for a sales amount. The common approach is to insert the sales tax rate value into a cell and then use this cell reference in your formulas. To make things easier, you probably would name this cell something like *SalesTax*.

You can handle this situation another way. Figure 3-13 demonstrates the following steps:

1. Choose Formulas ➜ Defined Names ➜ Define Name to bring up the New Name dialog box.
2. Type the name (in this case, **SalesTax**) into the Name field.
3. Click in the Refers To field, delete its contents, and replace it with a simple formula, such as **=.075**.
4. Click OK to close the New Name dialog box.

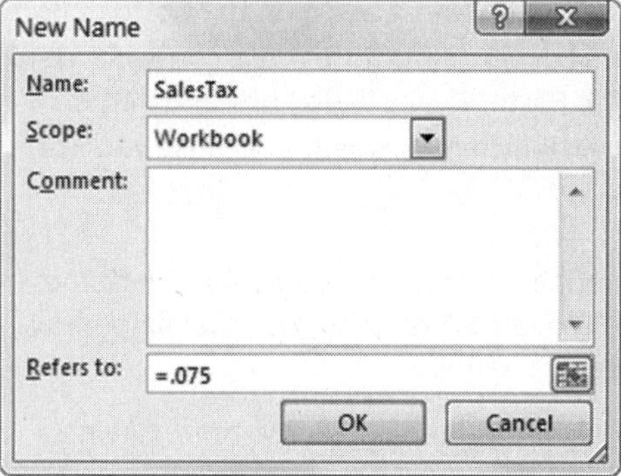

Figure 3-13: Defining a name that refers to a constant.

The preceding steps create a named formula that doesn't use cell references. To try it out, enter the following formula into any cell:

```
=SalesTax
```

This simple formula returns .075, the result of the formula named *SalesTax*. Because this named formula always returns the same result, you can think of it as a named constant. And you can use this constant in a more complex formula, such as the following:

```
=A1*SalesTax
```

If you didn't change the scope from the default of Workbook, you can use *SalesTax* in any worksheet in the workbook.

Naming text constants

In the preceding example, the constant consisted of a numeric value. A constant can also consist of text. For example, you can define a constant for a company's name. You can use the New Name dialog box to create the following formula named *MS:*

```
="Microsoft Corporation"
```

Then you can use a cell formula, such as the following:

```
="Annual Report: "&MS
```

This formula returns the text *Annual Report: Microsoft Corporation.*

Note

Names that do not refer to ranges do not appear in the Name box or in the Go To dialog box (which appears when you press F5). This makes sense because these constants don't reside anywhere tangible. They *do* appear in the Paste Names dialog box and in the Formula AutoComplete drop-down list, however, which makes sense because you use these names in formulas.

As you might expect, you can change the value of the constant at any time by accessing the Name Manager dialog box and changing the formula in the Refers To field. When you close the dialog box, Excel uses the new value to recalculate the formulas that use this name.

Although this technique is useful in many situations, changing the value takes some time. Having a constant located in a cell makes it much easier to modify.

Using worksheet functions in named formulas

Figure 3-14 shows another example of a named formula. In this case, the formula is named *ThisMonth,* and the actual formula is this:

```
=MONTH(TODAY())
```

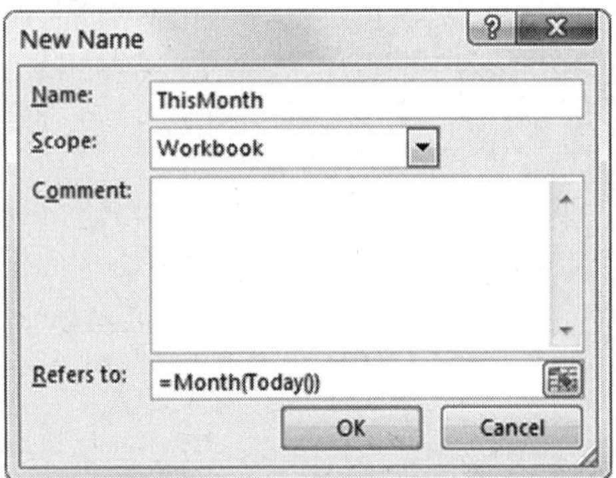

Figure 3-14: Defining a named formula that uses worksheet functions.

The formula in Figure 3-14 uses two worksheet functions. The TODAY function returns the current date, and the MONTH function returns the month number of its date argument. Therefore, you can enter a formula such as the following into a cell, and it returns the number of the current month. For example, if the current month is April, the formula returns 4:

```
=ThisMonth
```

A more useful named formula would return the actual month name as text. To do so, create a formula named *MonthName,* defined as follows:

```
=TEXT(TODAY(),"mmmm")
```

Cross-Ref

See Chapter 5, "Manipulating Text," for more information about Excel's TEXT function.

Now enter the following formula into a cell, and it returns the current month name as text. In the month of April, the formula returns the text *April*:

```
=MonthName
```

Using cell and range references in named formulas

Figure 3-15 shows yet another example of creating a named formula, this time with a cell reference. This formula, named *FirstChar,* returns the first character of the contents of cell A1 on Sheet1. This formula uses the LEFT function, which returns characters from the left part of a text string. The named formula is the following:

```
=LEFT(Sheet1!$A$1,1)
```

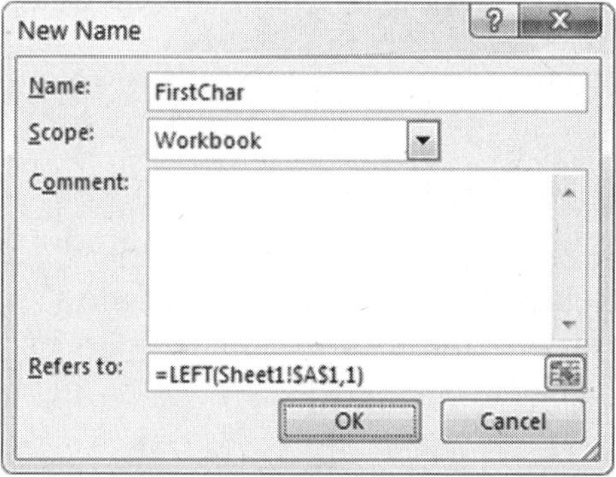

Figure 3-15: Defining a named formula that uses a cell reference.

After creating this named formula, you can enter the following formula into a cell. The formula always returns the first character of cell A1 on Sheet1:

```
=FirstChar
```

Note that if you insert a new row above row 1, the reference in the *FirstChar* name adjusts so it shows the first character in cell A2. It's possible to create a name that always refers to a specific cell or range, even if you insert new rows or columns. For example, suppose you want the name *FirstChar* to always refer to cell A1. You need to modify the formula for *FirstChar* so that it users the INDIRECT function:

```
=LEFT(INDIRECT("$A$1"),1)
```

After creating this named formula, *FirstChar* always returns the first character in cell A1, even if you insert new rows or columns. The INDIRECT function, in the preceding formula, lets you specify a cell address indirectly by using a text argument. Because the argument appears in quotation marks, it never changes.

Here's an example that uses a range reference in a named formula. The formula named *ColumnACount* returns the number of nonempty cells in column A of Sheet1. The formula is this:

```
=COUNTA(Sheet1!$A:$A)
```

You can display this count in a cell by using this formula:

```
=ColumnACount
```

Note, however, that entering this formula in column A of Sheet1 results in a circular reference error—just what you would expect.

Notice that the cell references in the preceding named formulas are absolute references. By default, all cell and range references in named formulas use an absolute reference, with the worksheet qualifier. But, as you can see in the next section, overriding this default behavior by using a relative cell reference can result in some interesting named formulas.

Using named formulas with relative references

As we noted previously, when you use the New Name dialog box to create a named formula that refers to cells or ranges, the Refers To field always uses absolute cell references, and the references include the sheet name qualifier. In this section, we describe how to use relative cell and range references in named formulas.

Using a relative cell reference

Begin by following these steps to create a named formula that uses a relative reference:

1. Start with an empty worksheet.
2. Select cell A1.

   This step is important.
3. Choose Formulas ➜ Defined Names ➜ Define Name.

   This brings up the New Name dialog box.
4. Type **CellToRight** in the Name field.

5. Delete the contents of the Refers To field and type the following formula. (Don't point to the cell in the sheet.)

```
=Sheet1!B1
```

6. Click OK to close the New Name dialog box.
7. Type something (anything) into cell B1.
8. Enter this formula into cell A1:

```
=CellToRight
```

The formula in A1 simply returns the contents of cell B1.

Next, copy the formula in cell A1 down a few rows. Then enter some values in column B. The formula in column A returns the contents of the cell to the right. In other words, the named formula (*CellToRight*) acts in a relative manner.

You can use the *CellToRight* name in any cell (not just cells in column A). For example, if you enter **=CellToRight** into cell D12, it returns the contents of cell E12.

To demonstrate that the formula named *CellToRight* truly uses a relative cell reference, activate any cell other than cell A1 and display the Name Manager dialog box. You see that the Refers To field contains a formula that points one cell to the right of the active cell, not A1. For example, if cell B7 is selected when the Name Manager is displayed, the formula for *CellToRight* appears as follows:

```
=Sheet1!C7
```

If you use the *CellToRight* name on a different worksheet, you find that it continues to reference the cell to the right—but it's the cell with the same address on Sheet1. This happens because the named formula includes a sheet reference. To modify the named formula so it works on any sheet, follow these steps:

1. Activate cell A1 on Sheet1.
2. Choose Formulas ➜ Defined Names ➜ Name Manager to bring up the Name Manager dialog box.
3. In the Name Manager dialog box, select the CellToRight item in the list box.
4. In the Refers To field, delete the sheet name (but keep the exclamation point). The formula should look like this:

```
=!B1
```

5. Click Close to close the Name Manager dialog box.

After making this change, you find that the *CellToRight* named formula works correctly on any worksheet in the workbook.

Note

Interestingly, the *CellToRight* named formula works even if you use it in column XFD (the last column, which has no column to its right). The formula displays the value in column A. In other words, it's as if the worksheet wraps around, and column A comes after column XFD.

Using a relative range reference

This example expands upon the previous example and demonstrates how to create a named formula that sums the values in 12 cells directly above a particular cell. To create this named formula, follow these steps:

1. Activate cell A13 (very important).
2. Choose Formulas ➜ Defined Names ➜ Define Name to bring up the New Name dialog box.
3. Type **Sum12Cells** into the Name field.
4. Type this formula into the Refers To field:

```
=SUM(!A1:!A12)
```

After creating this named formula, you can insert the following formula into any cell in row 13 or higher to return the sum of the 12 cells directly above that cell:

```
=Sum12Cells
```

For example, if you enter this formula into cell D40, it returns the sum of the values in the 12-cell range D28:D39.

Note that because cell A1 was the active cell when you defined the named formula, the relative references used in the formula definition are relative to cell A1. Also note that the sheet name was not used in the formula. Omitting the sheet name (but including the exclamation point) causes the named formula to work in any sheet.

If you select cell D40 and then bring up the Name Manager dialog box, you see that the Refers To field for the *Sum12Cells* name displays the following:

```
=SUM(!D28:!D39)
```

Note

If you use the *Sum12Cells* named formula in rows 1:12, it causes a circular reference error because of the "wrap-around" effect we noted earlier. For example, if you enter the named formula in cell D3, it's attempting to sum the values in the range D1048567:D2, and that range includes cell D3.

Using a mixed range reference

As we discussed in Chapter 2, a cell reference can be absolute, relative, or mixed. A mixed cell reference consists of either of the following:

- An absolute column reference and a relative row reference (for example, $A1)
- A relative column reference and an absolute row reference (for example, A$1)

As you might expect, a named formula can use mixed cell references. To demonstrate, activate cell B1. Use the New Name dialog box to create a formula named *FirstInRow,* using this formula definition:

```
=!$A1
```

This formula uses an absolute column reference and a relative row reference. Therefore, it always returns a value in column A. The row depends on the row in which you use the formula. For example, if you enter the following formula into cell F12, it displays the contents of cell A12:

```
=FirstInRow
```

And, of course, you can create in *FirstInColumn* a named formula. Activate cell A2 and create a *FirstInColumn* name using this formula:

```
=!A$1
```

Note

You can't use the *FirstInRow* formula in column A, and you can't use the *FirstInColumn* formula in row 1. In either case, it generates a *circular reference*—a formula that refers to itself.

Advanced Techniques That Use Names

This section presents several examples of advanced techniques that use names. The examples assume that you're familiar with the naming techniques described earlier in this chapter.

Using the INDIRECT function with a named range

Excel's INDIRECT function lets you specify a cell address indirectly. For example, if cell A1 contains the text C45, this formula returns the *contents* of cell C45:

```
=INDIRECT(A1)
```

Figure 3-16 shows a worksheet with 12 range names that correspond to the month names. For example, *January* refers to the range B2:E2. Cell B16 contains the following formula:

```
=SUM(INDIRECT(A16))
```

This formula returns the sum of the named range entered as text in cell A16.

B16 =SUM(INDIRECT(A16))

	A	B	C	D	E
1		Region 1	Region 2	Region 3	Region 4
2	January	183	310	242	45
3	February	359	133	482	47
4	March	297	231	124	51
5	April	289	346	186	32
6	May	294	304	446	30
7	June	251	188	313	37
8	July	355	151	231	20
9	August	433	323	151	24
10	September	255	160	253	40
11	October	436	328	412	33
12	November	294	440	469	38
13	December	221	377	371	32
14					
15					
16	September	708			

Figure 3-16: Using the INDIRECT function with a named range.

Tip

You can use the Data → Data Tools → Data Validation command to insert a drop-down list box into cell A16. (Use the List option in the Data Validation dialog box and specify A2:A13 as the list source.) This allows the user to select a month name from a list; the total for the selected month then displays in B16.

On the Web

The workbook with this example is available at this book's website. The filename is indirect functions.xlsx.

You can also reference worksheet-level names with the INDIRECT function. For example, suppose you have a number of worksheets named Region1, Region2, and so on. Each sheet contains a worksheet-level name called *TotalSales*. This formula retrieves the value from the appropriate sheet using the sheet name typed in cell A1:

```
=INDIRECT(A1&"!TotalSales")
```

If cell A1 contains the text Region2, the formula evaluates to the following:

```
=Region2!TotalSales
```

Using arrays in named formulas

An *array* is a collection of items. You can visualize an array as a single-column vertical collection, a single-row horizontal collection, or a multirow and multicolumn collection.

Cross-Ref

Part IV of this book, "Array Formulas," discusses arrays and array formulas, but this topic is also relevant when discussing names.

You specify an array by using curly brackets. A comma or semicolon separates each item in the array. Use a comma to separate items arranged horizontally, and use a semicolon to separate items arranged vertically.

Use the New Name dialog box to create a formula named *MonthNames* that consists of the following formula definition:

```
={"Jan","Feb","Mar","Apr","May","Jun","Jul","Aug","Sep","Oct","Nov","Dec"}
```

This formula defines a 12-item array of text strings, arranged horizontally.

Note

When you type this formula, make sure that you include the brackets. Entering an array formula into the New Name dialog box is different from entering an array formula into a cell.

After you define the *MonthNames* formula, you can use it in a formula. However, your formula needs to specify which array item to use. The INDEX function is perfect for this. For example, the following formula returns *Aug*:

```
=INDEX(MonthNames,8)
```

You can also display the entire 12-item array, but it requires 12 adjacent cells to do so. For example, to enter the 12 items of the array into A3:L3, follow these steps (which assume that you used the New Name dialog box to create the formula named *MonthNames*):

1. Select the range A3:L3.
2. Type **=MonthNames** into the Formula bar.
3. Press Ctrl+Shift+Enter.

Pressing Ctrl+Shift+Enter tells Excel to insert an array formula into the selected cells. In this case, the single formula is entered into the selected adjacent cell. Excel places brackets around an array formula to remind you that it's a special type of formula. If you examine any cell in A3:L3, you see its formula listed as follows:

```
{=MonthNames}
```

Notice that you can't delete any of the months because the 12 cells make up a multicell array formula—a single formula that occupies multiple cells.

To insert the month names into A1:A12 (a vertical range), do the following:

1. Select the range A1:A12.
2. Type **=TRANSPOSE(MonthNames)** into the Formula bar.
3. Press Ctrl+Shift+Enter.

Creating a dynamic named formula

A *dynamic* named formula is a named formula that refers to a range not fixed in size. You may find this concept difficult to grasp, so a quick example is in order.

Examine the worksheet shown in Figure 3-17. This sheet contains a listing of sales by month, through the month of June.

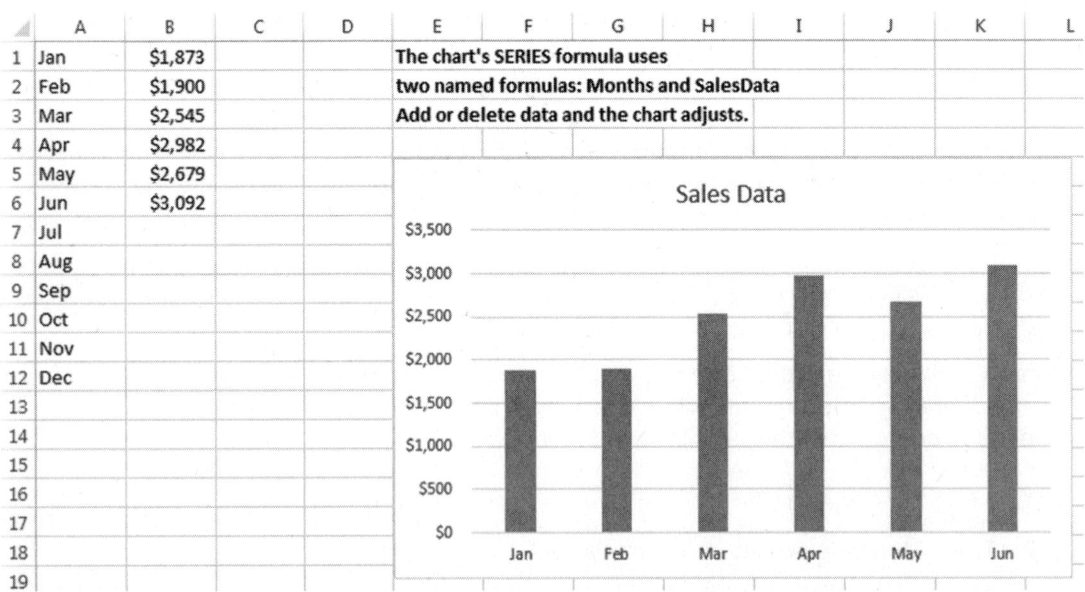

Figure 3-17: You can use a dynamic named formula to represent the sales data in column B.

Suppose you want to create a name (*SalesData*) for the data in column B, but you don't want this name to refer to empty cells. In other words, the reference for the *SalesData* range would change each month as you add a new sales figure. You could, of course, use the Name Manager dialog box to change the range name definition each month. Or you could create a dynamic named formula that changes automatically as you enter new data.

To create a dynamic named formula, start by re-creating the worksheet shown in Figure 3-17. Then follow these steps:

1. Bring up the New Name dialog box.
2. Type **SalesData** into the Name field.
3. Type the following formula into the Refers To field:

```
=OFFSET(Sheet1!$B$1,0,0,COUNTA(Sheet1!$B:$B),1)
```

4. Click OK to close the New Name dialog box.

The preceding steps create a named formula that uses Excel's OFFSET and COUNTA functions to return a range that changes, based on the number of nonempty cells in column B.

Note

This formula assumes that the range doesn't contain blank cells. For example, if cell B2 is empty, the COUNTA function does not count that cell, and the OFFSET function returns an incorrect range.

To try out this formula, enter the following formula into any cell not in column B:

```
=SUM(SalesData)
```

This formula returns the sum of the values in column B. Note that *SalesData* does not display in the Name box and does not appear in the Go To dialog box. You can, however, type **SalesData** into the Name box to select the range. Or bring up the Go To dialog box and type **SalesData** to select the range.

At this point, you may be wondering about the value of this exercise. After all, a simple formula such as the following does the same job, without the need to define a formula:

```
=SUM(B:B)
```

Or you could just enter this formula directly into a cell without creating a named formula:

```
=SUM(OFFSET($B$1,0,0,COUNTA($B:$B),1))
```

The truth is, dynamic named formulas were more important in older versions of Excel. Dynamic named formulas used to be the only way to create a chart that adjusted automatically as you added new data. However, with the introduction of tables (created by using Insert ➜ Tables ➜ Table), dynamic named formulas are rarely necessary. If you create a chart from data in a table, the chart adjusts automatically.

Cross-Ref

Refer to Chapter 9, "Working with Tables and Lists," for more information about tables.

On the Web

The workbook with this example is available at this book's website. The filename is dynamic named formula.xlsx. The named formula is also used in a chart's SERIES formula, creating a self-expanding chart.

Using an XLM macro in a named formula

The final example is both interesting—because it uses an Excel 4 XLM macro function in a named formula—and useful—because it's a relatively simple way of getting a list of filenames into a worksheet.

Start with an empty workbook, and create a formula named *FileList*, defined as

```
=FILES(Sheet1!$A$1)
```

The FILES function is not a normal worksheet function. Rather, it's an old XLM style macro function that is intended to be used on a special macro sheet. This function takes one argument (a directory path and file specification) and returns an array of filenames in that directory that match the file specification.

A normal worksheet formula cannot use these old XLM functions, but named formulas can.

After defining the named formula, enter a directory path and file specification into cell A1. For example:

```
E:\Backup\Excel\*.xl*
```

Then this formula displays the first file found:

```
=INDEX(FileList, 1)
```

If you change the second argument to 2, it displays the second file found, and so on.

Figure 3-18 shows an example. The path and filespec is in cell A1. Cell A2 contains this formula, copied down the column:

```
=INDEX(FileList,ROW()-1)
```

The ROW function, as used here, generates a series of consecutive integers: 1, 2, 3, and so on. These integers are used as the second argument for the INDEX function. Note that cell A22 displays an error because the directory has only 20 files, and it's attempting to display the twenty-first file.

When you change the directory or filespec in cell A1, the formulas update to display the new filenames.

	A
1	C:\windows*.*
2	ativpsrm.bin
3	bfsvc.exe
4	DirectX.log
5	DtcInstall.log
6	DXError.log
7	explorer.exe
8	fveupdate.exe
9	HelpPane.exe
10	hh.exe
11	IE11_main.log

Figure 3-18: Using an XLM macro in a named formula can generate a list of file names in a worksheet.

On the Web

This workbook is available at this book's website. The filename is file list.xlsm. You must enable macros when you open this workbook.

Leveraging Excel Functions

4

Introducing Worksheet Functions

In This Chapter

- The advantages of using functions in your formulas
- The types of arguments used by functions
- How to enter a function into a formula

A thorough knowledge of Excel's worksheet functions is essential for anyone who wants to master the art of formulas. This chapter provides an overview of the functions available for use in formulas.

What Is a Function?

A *worksheet function* is a built-in tool that you use in a formula. Worksheet functions allow you to perform calculations or operations that would otherwise be impossible. A typical function (such as SUM) takes one or more arguments and then returns a result. The SUM function, for example, accepts a range argument and then returns the sum of the values in that range.

You'll find functions useful because they

- Simplify your formulas
- Permit formulas to perform otherwise impossible calculations
- Speed up some editing tasks
- Allow *conditional* execution of formulas—giving them rudimentary decision-making capability

The examples in the sections that follow demonstrate each of these points.

Simplify your formulas

Using a built-in function can simplify a formula significantly. For example, you might need to calculate the average of the values in 10 cells (A1:A10). Without the help of any functions, you would need to construct a formula like this:

```
=(A1+A2+A3+A4+A5+A6+A7+A8+A9+A10)/10
```

Not very pretty, is it? Even worse, you would need to edit this formula if you inserted a new row in the A1:A10 range and needed the new value to be included in the average. However, you can replace this formula with a much simpler one that uses the AVERAGE function:

```
=AVERAGE(A1:A10)
```

Perform otherwise impossible calculations

Functions permit formulas to perform calculations that go beyond the standard mathematical operations. Perhaps you need to determine the largest value in a range. A formula can't tell you the answer without using a function. This formula uses the MAX function to return the largest value in the range A1:D100:

```
=MAX(A1:D100)
```

Speed up editing tasks

Functions can sometimes eliminate manual editing. Assume that you have a worksheet that contains 1,000 names in cells A1:A1000 and that all the names appear in all-uppercase letters. Your boss sees the listing and informs you that you need to mail-merge the names with a form letter and that the use of all uppercase is not acceptable. For example, JOHN F. CRANE must appear as John F. Crane. You *could* spend the rest of the afternoon reentering the list—or you could use a formula such as the following, which uses the PROPER function to convert the text in cell A1 to proper case:

```
=PROPER(A1)
```

1. Type this formula in cell B1 and then copy it down to the next 999 rows.
2. Select B1:B1000 and choose Home ➜ Clipboard ➜ Copy to copy the range to the Clipboard (or press Ctrl+C).

3. Activate cell A1 and choose Home ➜ Clipboard ➜ Paste ➜ Paste Values to convert the formulas to values.
4. Delete column B.

   You're finished! With the help of a function, you just eliminated several hours of tedious work in less than a minute.

Note

Excel 2013 introduced Flash Fill, which can sometimes take the place of formulas for text-conversion tasks like the one described here. See Chapter 16, "Importing and Cleaning Data," for details.

Provide decision-making capability

You can use the Excel IF function to give your formulas decision-making capabilities. Suppose that you have a worksheet that calculates sales commissions. If a salesperson sells at least $100,000 of product, the commission rate reaches 7.5 percent; otherwise, the commission rate remains at 5.0 percent. Without using a function, you would need to create two different formulas and make sure that you use the correct formula for each sales amount. This formula uses the IF function to check the value in cell A1 and make the appropriate commission calculation:

```
=IF(A1<100000,A1*5%,A1*7.5%)
```

The IF function takes three arguments, each separated by a comma. These arguments provide input to the function. The formula is making a decision: if the value in cell A1 is less than 100,000, then return the value in cell A1 multiplied by 5 percent. Otherwise, return the value in cell A1 multiplied by 7.5 percent.

More about functions

All told, Excel 2016 includes more than 400 functions. And if that's not enough, you can purchase additional specialized functions from third-party suppliers. You can even create your own custom functions using VBA.

Cross-Ref

If you're ready to create your own custom functions by using VBA, check out Part VI, "Developing Custom Worksheet Functions."

The sheer number of available worksheet functions may overwhelm you, but you'll probably find that you use only a dozen or so of the functions on a regular basis. And as you'll see, the Function Library group on the Formulas tab (described later in this chapter) makes it easy to locate and insert a function, even if you use it only rarely.

Cross-Ref

Appendix A, "Excel Function Reference," contains a complete listing of Excel's worksheet functions, with a brief description of each.

Function Argument Types

If you examine the preceding examples in this chapter, you'll notice that all the functions use a set of parentheses. The information within the parentheses is the function's *arguments*. Functions vary in the way they use arguments. A function may use

- No arguments
- A fixed number of arguments
- An indeterminate number of arguments
- Optional arguments

For example, the RAND function, which returns a random number between 0 and 1, doesn't use an argument. Even if a function doesn't require an argument, you must provide a set of empty parentheses when you use the function in a formula, like this:

```
=RAND()
```

If a function uses more than one argument, a comma separates the arguments. For example, the LARGE function, which returns the *n*th largest value in a range, uses two arguments. The first argument represents the range; the second argument represents the value for *n*. The formula that follows returns the third-largest value in the range A1:A100:

```
=LARGE(A1:A100,3)
```

Note

In some non-English versions of Excel, the character used to separate function arguments can be something other than a comma—for example, a semicolon. The examples in this book use a comma as the argument separator character.

The examples at the beginning of the chapter use cell or range references for arguments. Excel proves quite flexible when it comes to function arguments, however. The following sections demonstrate additional argument types for functions.

Accommodating former Lotus 1-2-3 users

If you've ever used any of the Lotus 1-2-3 spreadsheets (or any version of Corel's Quattro Pro), you may recall that these products require you to type an "at" sign (@) before a function name. Excel is smart enough to distinguish functions without your having to flag them with a symbol.

Because old habits die hard, however, Excel accepts @ symbols when you type functions in your formulas, but it removes them as soon as you enter the formula.

These other spreadsheet programs also use two dots (..) as a range reference operator—for example, A1..A10. Excel allows you to use this notation when you type formulas, but it replaces the dots with its own range reference operator: a colon (:). In fact, you can use any number of dots as a range reference operator, even something like this: A1..........A10.

This accommodation goes only so far, however. Excel still insists that you use the standard Excel function names, and it doesn't recognize or translate the function names used in other spreadsheets. For example, if you enter the 1-2-3 @AVG function, Excel flags it as an error. (Excel's name for this function is AVERAGE.)

Names as arguments

As you've seen, functions can use cell or range references for their arguments. When Excel calculates the formula, it uses the current contents of the cell or range to perform its calculations. The SUM function returns the sum of its argument(s). To calculate the sum of the values in A1:A20, you can use this:

```
=SUM(A1:A20)
```

And, not surprisingly, if you've defined a name for A1:A20 (such as *Sales*), you can use the name in place of the reference:

```
=SUM(Sales)
```

Cross-Ref

For more information about defining and using names, refer to Chapter 3, "Working with Names."

Full-column or full-row as arguments

In some cases, you may find it useful to use an entire column or row as an argument. For example, the following formula sums all values in column B:

```
=SUM(B:B)
```

Using full-column and full-row references is particularly useful if the range that you're summing changes—if you continually add new sales figures, for instance. If you do use an entire row or column, just make sure that the row or column doesn't contain extraneous information that you don't want to include in the sum.

And, make sure your formula isn't in the column that's being referenced. If the preceding SUM formula is in column B, it will generate a circular reference error.

You may think that using such a large range (a column consists of 1,048,576 cells) might slow down calculation time. Not true. Excel keeps track of the last-used row and last-used column and does not use cells beyond them when computing a formula result that references an entire column or row.

Literal values as arguments

A *literal argument* refers to a value or text string that you enter directly. For example, the SQRT function, which calculates the square root of a number, takes one argument. In the following example, the formula uses a literal value for the function's argument:

```
=SQRT(225)
```

Using a literal argument with a simple function like this one usually defeats the purpose of using a formula. This formula always returns the same value, so you could just as easily replace it with the value 15. You may want to make an exception to this rule in the interest of clarity. For example, you may want to make it perfectly clear that the value in the cell is the square root of 225.

Using literal arguments makes more sense with formulas that use more than one argument. For example, the LEFT function (which takes two arguments) returns characters from the beginning of its first argument; the second argument specifies the number of characters. If cell A1 contains the text *Budget*, the following formula returns the first three letters (*Bud*):

```
=LEFT(A1,3)
```

Expressions as arguments

You can also use expressions as arguments. Think of an *expression* as a formula within a formula (but without the leading equal sign). When Excel encounters an expression as a function's argument, it evaluates the expression and then uses the result as the argument's value. Here's an example:

```
=SQRT((A1^2)+(A2^2))
```

This formula uses the SQRT function, and its single argument consists of the following expression:

```
(A1^2)+(A2^2)
```

When Excel evaluates the formula, it first evaluates the expression in the argument and then computes the square root of the result. This expression squares the value in cell A1 and adds it to the square of the value in cell A2.

Other functions as arguments

Because Excel can evaluate expressions as arguments, it shouldn't surprise you that these expressions can include other functions. Writing formulas that have functions within functions is sometimes known as *nesting* functions. Excel starts by evaluating the most deeply nested expression and works its way out.

Here's an example of a nested function:

```
=SIN(RADIANS(B9))
```

The RADIANS function converts degrees to *radians,* the unit that all Excel trigonometric functions use. If cell B9 contains an angle in degrees, the RADIANS function converts it to radians, and then the SIN function computes the sine of the angle.

A formula can contain up to 64 levels of nested functions—a limit that will probably never be a factor.

Arrays as arguments

A function can also use an array as an argument. An *array* is a series of values separated by a comma and enclosed in curly brackets. The formula that follows uses the OR function with an array as an argument. The formula returns *TRUE* if cell A1 contains 1, 3, or 5.

```
=OR(A1={1,3,5})
```

Cross-Ref

See Part IV, "Array Formulas," for more information about working with arrays.

Often, using arrays can help simplify your formula. The following formula, for example, returns the same result as the previous formula but uses nested IF functions instead of an array:

```
=IF(A1=1,TRUE,IF(A1=3,TRUE,IF(A1=5,TRUE,FALSE)))
```

Ways to Enter a Function into a Formula

You can enter a function into a formula by typing it manually, by using the Function Library commands, or by using the Insert Function dialog box.

Entering a function manually

If you're familiar with a particular function—that is, you know its correct spelling and the types of arguments that it takes—you may choose to simply type the function and its arguments into your formula. Often, this method is the most efficient.

However, you can also use the handy Formula AutoComplete feature. When you type an equal sign and the first letter of a function in a cell, Excel displays a drop-down list box of all the functions that begin with that letter and a ScreenTip with a brief description for the function (see Figure 4-1). You can continue typing the function to limit the list or use the arrow keys to select the function from the list. After you select the desired function, press Tab to insert the function and its opening parenthesis into the formula.

=in
INDEX
INDIRECT
INFO
INT
INTERCEPT
INTRATE
Returns a value or reference of the cell at the intersection of a particular row and column, in a given range

Figure 4-1: When you begin to type a function, Excel lists available functions that begin with the typed letters.

Cross-Ref

In addition to displaying function names, the Formula AutoComplete feature lists cell and range names and table references. See Chapter 3 for information on names and Chapter 9, "Working with Tables and Lists," for information about tables.

After you press Tab to insert the function and its opening parenthesis, Excel displays another ScreenTip that shows the arguments for the function (see Figure 4-2). The bold argument is the argument that you are entering. Arguments shown in square brackets are optional. Notice that the text in the ScreenTip contains a hyperlink for each argument that you've entered. Click a hyperlink to select the corresponding argument. If that ScreenTip gets in your way, you can drag it to a different location.

=VLOOKUP(
VLOOKUP(**lookup_value**, table_array, col_index_num, [range_lookup])

Figure 4-2: Excel displays a list of the function's arguments.

If you don't like using Formula AutoComplete, you can disable this feature. Choose File ➜ Options to display the Excel Options dialog box. On the Formulas tab, remove the check mark from the Formula AutoComplete option.

Tip

When you type a built-in function, Excel always converts the function's name to uppercase. Therefore, it's a good idea to use lowercase when you type function names manually. If Excel doesn't convert your text to uppercase after you press Enter, your entry isn't recognized as a function, which means that you spelled it incorrectly or that the function isn't available.

Using the Function Library commands

Another way to insert a function into a formula is to use the icons in the Formulas ➜ Function Library group. Figure 4-3 shows these icons, each of which is a drop-down control.

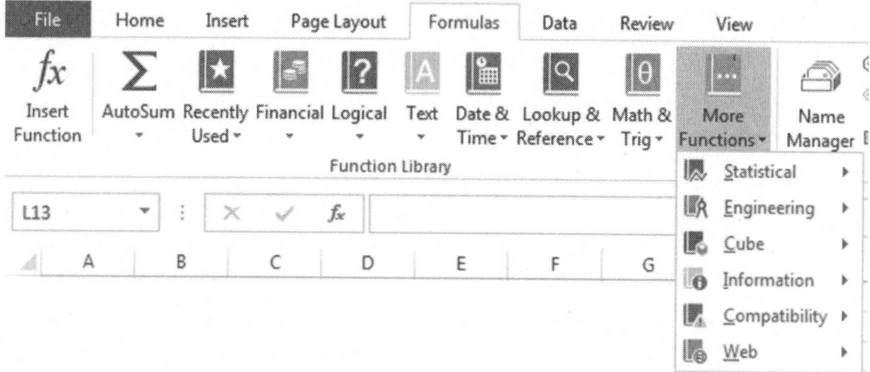

Figure 4-3: The icons in the Function Library group on the Formulas tab.

Each Function category is dedicated to a specific topic area.

Financial functions: The financial functions enable you to perform common business calculations that deal with money. For example, you can use the PMT function to calculate the monthly payment for a car loan. You need to provide the loan amount, interest rate, and loan term as arguments.

Date & Time functions: The functions in this category enable you to analyze and work with date and time values in formulas. For example, the TODAY function returns the current date (as stored in the system clock).

Lookup & Reference functions: Functions in this category are used to find (look up) values in lists or tables. A common example is a tax table. For example, you can use the VLOOKUP function to determine a tax rate for a particular income level.

Math & Trig functions: This category contains a variety of functions that perform mathematical and trigonometric calculations.

Statistical functions: The functions in this category perform statistical analysis on ranges of data. For example, you can calculate statistics such as mean, mode, standard deviation, and variance.

Text functions: Text functions enable you to manipulate text strings in formulas. For example, you can use the MID function to extract any number of characters beginning at any character position. Other functions enable you to change the case of text: convert to uppercase, for example.

Logical functions: This category consists of only seven functions that enable you to test a condition, for logical *TRUE* or *FALSE*. You will find the IF function useful because it gives your formulas simple decision-making capabilities.

Information functions: The functions in this category help you determine the type of data stored within a cell. For example, the ISTEXT function returns *TRUE* if a cell reference contains text. Or you can use the ISBLANK function to determine whether a cell is empty. The CELL function returns lots of potentially useful information about a particular cell.

Engineering functions: The functions in this category can prove useful for engineering applications. They enable you to work with complex numbers and to perform conversions between various numbering and measurement systems.

Cube functions: The functions in this category allow you to manipulate data that is part of an OLAP data cube.

Compatibility functions: The Compatibility category was introduced in Excel 2010. Functions in this category are statistical functions that have been replaced with improved versions of themselves. These older functions are retained in Excel for the purpose of backward compatibility with Excel 2007 and prior versions.

Web functions: The Web category was introduced in Excel 2013 and includes three functions that deal with Internet-related tasks like encoding URL addresses and parsing web services.

When you select a function from one of these lists, Excel displays its Function Arguments dialog box to help you enter the arguments. See the section, "Using the Insert Function dialog box" for more information about the Function Arguments dialog box.

In addition to the function categories described previously, Excel includes other categories that will not appear on the Excel Ribbon. These are Database functions, Commands, Customizing, Macro Control, and DDE/External. Although many of the functions found in these categories are holdovers from older versions of Excel, some of the functions still prove to be useful in some scenarios. For example, the Database functions come in handy when you need to summarize data in a table that meets specific criteria. See Chapter 9 for more information on Database functions.

Using the Insert Function dialog box

The Insert Function dialog box is another way to enter a function into a formula. Using the Insert Function dialog box ensures that you spell the function correctly and that it contains the proper number of arguments in the correct order.

To insert a function, select the function from the Insert Function dialog box, as shown in Figure 4-4. You access this dialog box in several ways:

- Choose Formulas ➜ Function Library ➜ Insert Function.
- Choose any icon category in the Formulas ➜ Function Library group, and select Insert Function from the drop-down list.
- Click the *fx* icon to the left of the Formula bar.
- Press Shift+F3.

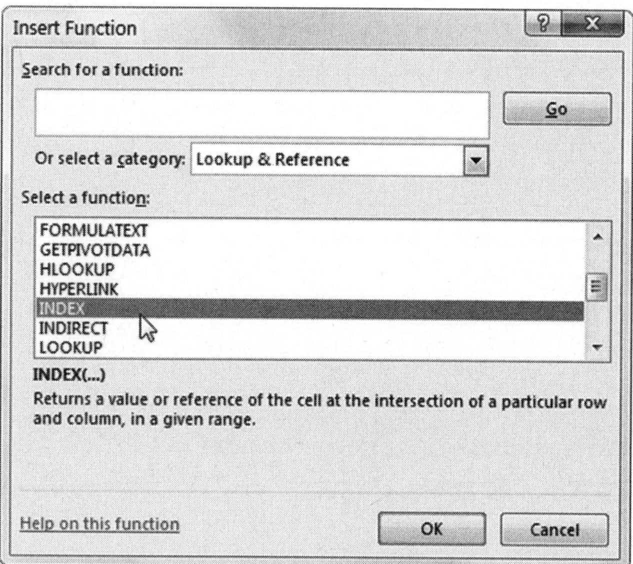

Figure 4-4: The Insert Function dialog box.

The Insert Function dialog box contains a drop-down list of categories. When you select a category from the list, the list box displays the functions in the selected category. The Most Recently Used category lists the functions that you've used most recently. The All category lists all the functions available across all categories. Access this category if you know a function's name but not its category.

If you're not sure which function to use, you can search for a function. Use the field at the top of the Insert Function dialog box. Type one or more keywords and click Go. Excel then displays a list of functions that match your search criteria. For example, if you're looking for functions to calculate a loan payment, type **loan** as the search term.

When you select a function from the Select a Function list box, notice that Excel displays the function (and its argument names) in the dialog box, along with a brief description of what the function does. Also, you can click Help on This Function to read about the selected function in Excel's Help system.

When you locate the function that you want to use, click OK. Excel's Function Arguments dialog box appears, as shown in Figure 4-5, where you can specify the arguments for the function. To specify a cell or range as an argument, just click in the worksheet and point to the cell or range. Note that each argument is described.

When you choose Formulas ➜ Function Library ➜ AutoSum (or Home ➜ Editing ➜ AutoSum), Excel does a quick check of the surrounding cells. It then proposes a formula that uses the SUM function. If Excel guessed your intentions correctly, just press Enter to accept the proposed formula(s). If Excel guessed incorrectly, you can simply select the range with your mouse to override Excel's suggestion (or press Esc to cancel the AutoSum).

You can preselect the cells to be included in an AutoSum rather than let Excel guess which cells you want. To insert a SUM function into cell A11 that sums A1:A10, select A1:A11 and then click the AutoSum button.

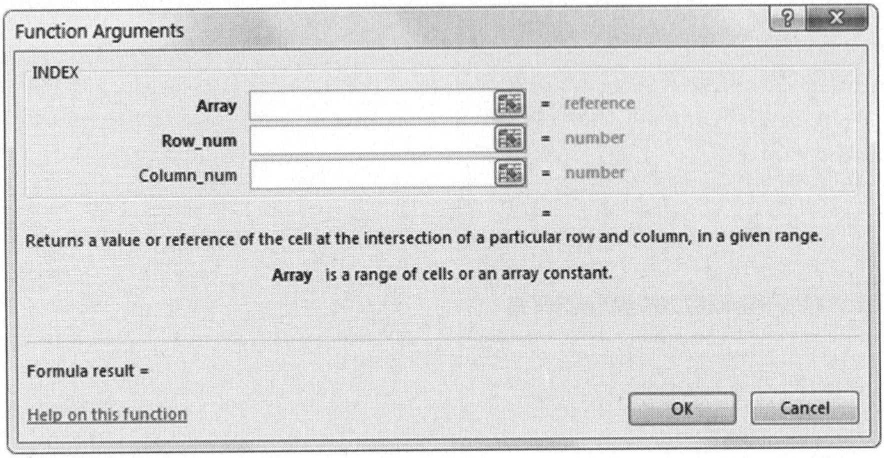

Figure 4-5: The Function Arguments dialog box.

The AutoSum button displays an arrow that, when clicked, displays additional functions. For example, you can use this button to insert a formula that uses the AVERAGE function.

When you're working with a table (created by using Insert ➜ Tables ➜ Table), you can choose Table Tools ➜ Design ➜ Total Row, and Excel displays a new row at the bottom of the table that contains summary formulas for the columns. See Chapter 9 for more information about tables.

When you choose Data ➜ Data Tools ➜ Outline ➜ Subtotal, Excel displays a dialog box that enables you to specify some options. Then it proceeds to insert rows and enter some formulas automatically. These formulas use the SUBTOTAL function.

More tips for entering functions

The following list contains some additional tips to keep in mind when you use the Insert Function dialog box to enter functions:

- Click the Help on This Function link (lower left, Figure 4-5) to get help (see Figure 4-6) about the function that you selected.
- If the active cell already contains a formula that uses a function, clicking the Insert Function button displays the Function Arguments dialog box.
- You can use the Insert Function dialog box to insert a function into an existing formula. Just edit the formula and move the insertion point to the location where you want to insert the function. Then open the Insert Function dialog box and select the function.
- If you change your mind about entering a function, click Cancel.
- The number of arguments used by the function that you select determines the number of boxes that you see in the Function Arguments dialog box. If a function uses no arguments, you won't see any boxes. If the function uses a variable number of arguments (as with the AVERAGE function), Excel adds a new box every time you enter an optional argument.

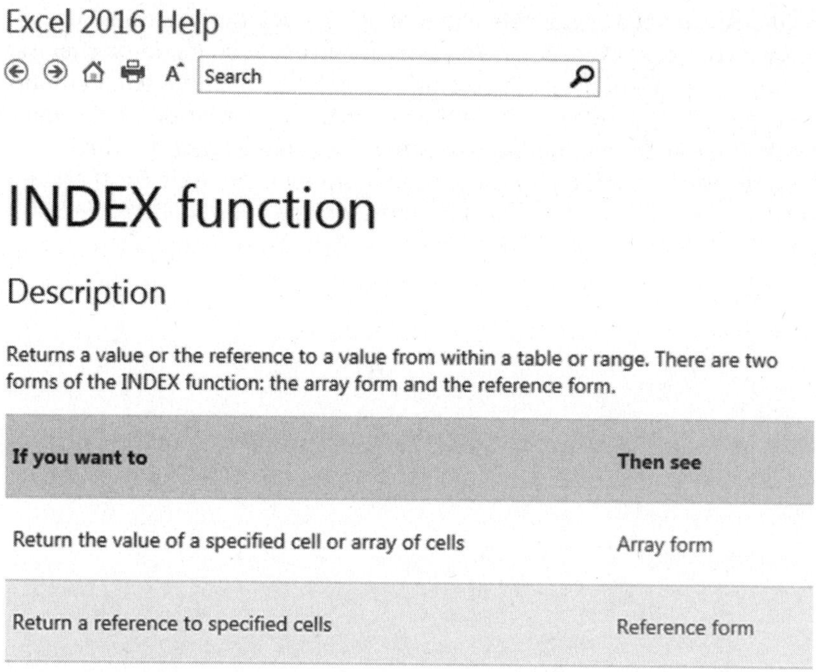

Excel 2016 Help

Search

INDEX function

Description

Returns a value or the reference to a value from within a table or range. There are two forms of the INDEX function: the array form and the reference form.

If you want to	Then see
Return the value of a specified cell or array of cells	Array form
Return a reference to specified cells	Reference form

Figure 4-6: Don't forget about Excel's Help system. It's the most comprehensive function reference source available.

- On the right side of each box in the Function Arguments dialog box, you'll see the current value for each argument that's entered or the type of argument (such as text or number) for arguments yet to be entered.
- A few functions, such as INDEX, have more than one form. If you choose such a function, Excel displays the Select Arguments dialog box that enables you to choose which form you want to use.
- To locate a function quickly in the Function Name list that appears in the Insert Function dialog box, open the list box, type the first letter of the function name, and then scroll to the desired function. For example, if you select the All category and want to insert the SIN function, click anywhere on the Select a Function list box and type **S**. Excel selects the first function that begins with *S*. Keep typing **S** (or press the down arrow key) until you reach the SIN function.
- If the active cell contains a formula that uses one or more functions, the Function Arguments dialog box enables you to edit each function. In the Formula bar, click the function that you want to edit and then click the Insert Function button.
- Some Excel functions are considered to be volatile. Volatile functions are those that recalculate whenever Excel recalculates the workbook, even if the formula that contains the function is not involved in the recalculation. It is by no means a bad thing to use functions that are volatile. Many of them are quite important to many data models.

However, you should be aware of a minor side effect of using a volatile function: Excel will prompt you to save your workbook when you close it—even if you made no changes to it. For example, if you open a workbook that contains a volatile function, scroll around a bit (but don't change anything) and then close the file, Excel will ask whether you want to save the workbook. The RAND function is an example of a volatile function. Think about how the RAND function generates a new random number every time Excel calculates the worksheet. Other examples of volatile functions include NOW, TODAY, OFFSET, INDIRECT, and CELL.

5

Manipulating Text

In This Chapter

- How Excel handles text entered into cells
- Excel worksheet functions that handle text
- Examples of advanced text formulas

Excel, of course, is best known for its ability to crunch numbers. However, it is also quite versatile when it comes to handling text. As you know, Excel enables you to enter text for items such as row and column headings, customer names and addresses, part numbers, and just about anything else. And, as you might expect, you can use formulas to manipulate the text contained in cells.

This chapter contains many examples of formulas that use functions to manipulate text. Some of these formulas perform feats that you may not have thought possible.

A Few Words About Text

When you type data into a cell, Excel immediately goes to work and determines whether you're entering a formula, a number (including a date or time), or anything else. Anything else is considered text.

Note

You may hear the term *string* used instead of *text*. You can use these terms interchangeably. Sometimes they even appear together, as in *text string*.

How many characters in a cell?

A single cell can hold up to 32,000 characters. To put things into perspective, this chapter contains about 30,000 characters. We certainly don't recommend using a cell in lieu of a word processor, but you really don't have to lose much sleep worrying about filling up a cell with text.

Numbers as text

As we mentioned, Excel distinguishes between numbers and text. In some cases, such as part numbers and credit card numbers, you don't need a number to be numerical. If you want to "force" a number to be considered as text, you can do one of the following:

- Apply the Text number format to the cell before you enter the number. Select Text from the Number Format drop-down list, which can be found in the Home ➜ Number group. If you haven't applied other horizontal alignment formatting, the value will appear left aligned in the cell (like normal text), and functions like SUM will not treat it as a value. Note, however, that it doesn't work in the opposite direction. If you enter a number and then format it as text, the number will be left aligned, but functions will continue to treat the entry as a value.
- Precede the number with an apostrophe. The apostrophe isn't displayed, but the cell entry will be treated as if it were text. Functions like SUM will not treat the cell as a number.

Even though a cell is formatted as text (or uses an apostrophe), you can still perform some mathematical operations on the cell if the entry looks like a number. For example, assume cell A1 contains a numeric value preceded by an apostrophe. This formula displays the value in A1, incremented by 1:

```
=A1+1
```

This formula, however, treats the contents of cell A1 as 0:

```
=SUM(A1:A10)
```

To confuse things even more, if you format cell A1 as text, the preceding SUM formula treats it as 0.

In some cases, treating text as a number can be useful. In other cases, it can cause problems. Bottom line? Just be aware of Excel's inconsistency in how it treats a number formatted as text.

Note

If background error checking is turned on, Excel flags numbers preceded by an apostrophe (and numbers in cells formatted as text before the number was entered) with a small triangle indicator in the cell's upper-left corner. Activate a cell that displays such an indicator, and Excel displays an icon. Click the icon, and you have several options on how to handle that potential error. Figure 5-1 shows an example. Background error checking is controlled from the Excel Options dialog box. Choose File ➜ Options and navigate to the Error Checking section of the Formulas tab.

Figure 5-1: Excel's background error checking flags numbers that are formatted as text.

When a number isn't treated as a number

If you import data into Excel, you may be aware of a common problem: sometimes the imported values are treated as text. Here's a quick way to convert these nonnumbers to actual values. Activate any empty cell and choose Home ➔ Clipboard ➔ Copy. Then select the range that contains the values you need to fix. Choose Home ➔ Clipboard ➔ Paste ➔ Paste Special. In the Paste Special dialog box, select the Add option, and then click OK. By "adding zero" to the text, you force Excel to treat the nonnumbers as actual values.

If background error checking is enabled, Excel will usually identity such nonnumber cells and give you an opportunity to convert them.

Text Functions

Excel has an excellent assortment of worksheet functions that can handle text. For your convenience, the Function Library group on the Formulas tab includes a Text drop-down list that provides access to most of these functions. A few other functions that are relevant to text manipulation appear in other function categories. For example, the ISTEXT function is in the Information category (Formulas ➔ Function Library ➔ More Functions ➔ Information).

Refer to Appendix A, "Excel Function Reference," for a complete list of the functions in the Text category.

Most of the functions in the Text category are not limited for use with text. In other words, these functions can also operate with cells that contain values. Excel is very accommodating when it comes to treating numbers as text and text as numbers.

The examples in this section demonstrate some common (and useful) things that you can do with text. You may need to adapt some of these examples for your own use.

Determining whether a cell contains text

In some situations, you may need a formula that determines the type of data contained in a particular cell. For example, you can use an IF function to return a result only if a cell contains text. The easiest way to make this determination is to use the ISTEXT function.

The ISTEXT function takes a single argument, returning *TRUE* if the argument contains text and *FALSE* if it doesn't contain text. The formula that follows returns *TRUE* if A1 contains a string:

```
=ISTEXT(A1)
```

You can also use the TYPE function. The TYPE function takes a single argument and returns a value that indicates the type of data in a cell. If cell A1 contains a text string, the formula that follows returns *2* (the code number for text):

```
=TYPE(A1)
```

Both the ISTEXT function and the TYPE function consider a numeric value that's preceded by an apostrophe to be text. However, these functions do *not* consider a number formatted as Text to be text unless the Text formatting is applied before you enter the number in the cell.

This sounds very confusing (and it is), but in actual practice, it's rare to need to identify the contents of a cell as numeric or text.

Working with character codes

Every character that you see on your screen has an associated code number. For Windows systems, Excel uses the standard American National Standards Institute (ANSI) character set. The ANSI character set consists of 255 characters, numbered from 1 to 255. An ANSI character requires one byte of storage. Excel also supports an extended character set known as *Unicode,* in which each character requires two bytes of storage.

Figure 5-2 shows an Excel worksheet that displays all 255 ANSI characters. This example uses the Calibri font. (Other fonts may have different characters.)

	A	B	C	D	E	F	G	H	I	J	K	L
1		Font:	Calibri					Size:	11		☐ Bold	
2		Sample text:									Type your sample text here	
3		1		33	!	65	A	97	a	129		161
4		2	┐	34	"	66	B	98	b	130	‚	162
5		3	└	35	#	67	C	99	c	131	ƒ	163
6		4	┘	36	$	68	D	100	d	132	„	164
7		5	│	37	%	69	E	101	e	133	…	165
8		6	─	38	&	70	F	102	f	134	†	166
9		7	•	39	'	71	G	103	g	135	‡	167
10		8	◘	40	(	72	H	104	h	136	ˆ	168
11		9		41	)	73	I	105	i	137	‰	169
12		10		42	*	74	J	106	j	138	Š	170
13		11	♂	43	+	75	K	107	k	139	‹	171
14		12	⍰	44	,	76	L	108	l	140	Œ	172
15		13		45	-	77	M	109	m	141		173
16		14	♫	46	.	78	N	110	n	142	Ž	174
17		15	☼	47	/	79	O	111	o	143		175
18		16	┼	48	0	80	P	112	p	144		176
19		17	◄	49	1	81	Q	113	q	145	‘	177
20		18	↕	50	2	82	R	114	r	146	’	178
21		19	‼	51	3	83	S	115	s	147	“	179
22		20	¶	52	4	84	T	116	t	148	”	180
23		21	┴	53	5	85	U	117	u	149	•	181
24		22	┬	54	6	86	V	118	v	150	–	182
25		23	┤	55	7	87	W	119	w	151	—	183
26		24	↑	56	8	88	X	120	x	152	˜	184
27		25	├	57	9	89	Y	121	y	153	™	185
28		26	→	58	:	90	Z	122	z	154	š	186

Figure 5-2: The ANSI character set (for the Calibri font).

On the Web

This book's website includes a copy of the workbook character set.xlsm. It has some simple macros that enable you to display the character set for any font installed on your system.

Two functions come into play when dealing with character codes: CODE and CHAR. These functions aren't very useful by themselves. However, they can prove quite useful in conjunction with other functions. We discuss these functions in the following sections.

Note

The CODE and CHAR functions work only with ANSI strings. Excel 2013 introduced two functions that are similar to CODE and CHAR but work with double-byte Unicode characters. These functions are UNICODE and UNICHAR.

The CODE function

Excel's CODE function returns the ANSI character code for its argument. The formula that follows returns *65,* the character code for uppercase *A*:

```
=CODE("A")
```

If the argument for CODE consists of more than one character, the function uses only the first character. Therefore, this formula also returns *65*:

```
=CODE("Abbey Road")
```

The CHAR function

The CHAR function is essentially the opposite of the CODE function. Its argument is a value between 1 and 255; the function returns the corresponding character. The following formula, for example, returns the letter *A:*

```
=CHAR(65)
```

To demonstrate the opposing nature of the CODE and CHAR functions, try entering this formula:

```
=CHAR(CODE("A"))
```

This formula (illustrative rather than useful) returns the letter *A*. First it converts the character to its code value (65), and then it converts this code back to the corresponding character.

Assume that cell A1 contains the letter A (uppercase). The following formula returns the letter *a* (lowercase):

```
=CHAR(CODE(A1)+32)
```

This formula takes advantage of the facts that the alphabetic characters in most fonts appear in alphabetical order within the character set, and the lowercase letters follow the uppercase letters (with a few other characters tossed in between). Each lowercase letter lies exactly 32 character positions higher than its corresponding uppercase letter.

How to find special characters

Don't overlook the handy Symbol dialog box (which appears when you choose Insert ➜ Symbols ➜ Symbol). This dialog box makes it easy to insert special characters (including Unicode characters) into cells. For example, you might (for some strange reason) want to include a smiley face character in your spreadsheet. From the Symbol dialog box, select the Wingdings font (see the accompanying figure). Examine the characters, locate the smiley face, click Insert, and then click Cancel. You'll also find out that this character has a code of 74.

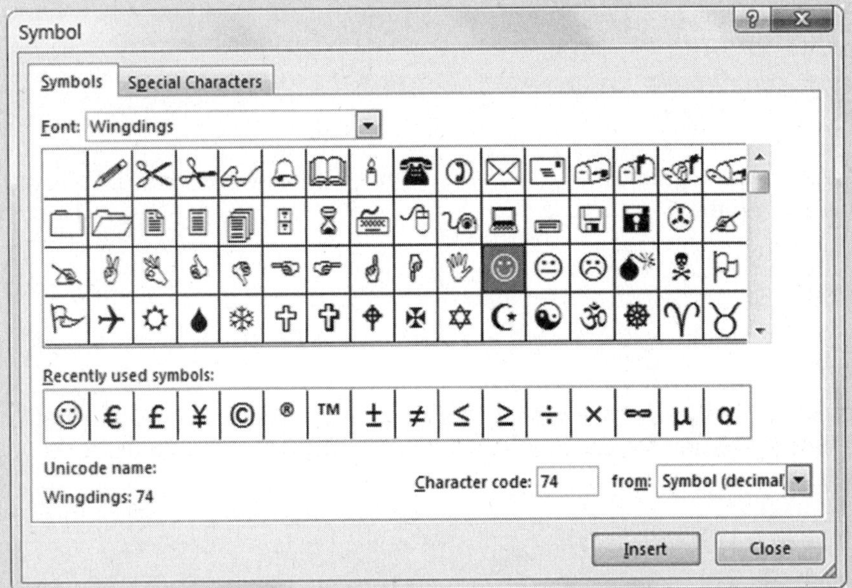

In addition, Excel has several built-in AutoCorrect symbols. For example, if you type **(c)** followed by a space or the Enter key, Excel converts the (c) to a copyright symbol.

To see the other symbols that you can enter this way, display the AutoCorrect dialog box by choosing File ➜ Options. On the Proofing tab in the Excel Options dialog box, click the AutoCorrect Options button. You can then scroll through the list to see which autocorrections are enabled (and delete those that you don't want).

If you find that Excel makes an autocorrection that you don't want, press Ctrl+Z immediately to undo it.

Determining whether two strings are identical

You can enter a simple logical formula to determine whether two cells contain the same entry. For example, use this formula to determine whether cell A1 has the same contents as cell A2:

```
=A1=A2
```

Excel acts a bit lax in its comparisons when text is involved. Consider the case in which A1 contains the word *January* (initial capitalization), and A2 contains *JANUARY* (all uppercase). You'll find that the previous formula returns *TRUE* even though the contents of the two cells are not really the same. In other words, the comparison is not case sensitive.

In many cases, you don't need to worry about the case of the text. However, if you need to make an exact, case-sensitive comparison, you can use Excel's EXACT function. The formula that follows returns *TRUE* only if cells A1 and A2 contain exactly the same entry:

```
=EXACT(A1,A2)
```

The following formula returns *FALSE* because the two strings do not match exactly with respect to case:

```
=EXACT("California","california")
```

Joining two or more cells

Excel uses an ampersand (&) as its concatenation operator. *Concatenation* is simply a fancy term that describes what happens when you join the contents of two or more cells. For example, if cell A1 contains the text *Tucson*, and cell A2 contains the text *Arizona,* the following formula then returns *TucsonArizona:*

```
=A1&A2
```

Notice that the two strings are joined without an intervening space. To add a space between the two entries (to get *Tucson Arizona*), use a formula like this one:

```
=A1&" "&A2
```

Or, even better, use a comma and a space to produce *Tucson, Arizona:*

```
=A1&", "&A2
```

Another option is to eliminate the quote characters and use the CHAR function with an appropriate argument. Note this example of using the CHAR function to represent a comma (44) and a space (32):

```
=A1&CHAR(44)&CHAR(32)&A2
```

If you'd like to force a line break between strings, concatenate the strings by using CHAR(10), which inserts a line break character. Also, make sure that you apply the wrap text format to the cell. (Choose Home ➜ Alignment ➜ Wrap Text.) The following example joins the text in cell A1 and the text in cell B1 with a line break in between:

```
=A1&CHAR(10)&B1
```

The following formula returns the string *Stop* by concatenating four characters returned by the CHAR function:

```
=CHAR(83)&CHAR(116)&CHAR(111)&CHAR(112)
```

Here's a final example of using the & operator. In this case, the formula combines text with the result of an expression that returns the maximum value in column C:

```
="The largest value in Column C is " &MAX(C:C)
```

Note

Excel also has a CONCATENATE function, which takes up to 255 arguments. This function simply combines the arguments into a single string. You can use this function if you like, but using the & operator is usually simpler and results in shorter formulas.

Cross-Ref

In some cases, the Flash Fill feature can substitute for creating formulas that concatenate text. See Chapter 16, "Importing and Cleaning Data," for more information.

Displaying formatted values as text

The Excel TEXT function enables you to display a value in a specific number format. Although this function may appear to have dubious value, it does serve some useful purposes, as the examples in this section demonstrate. Figure 5-3 shows a simple worksheet. The formula in cell D2 is

```
="The net profit is " & B2
```

D2 | ="The net profit is " & B2

	A	B	C	D
1				
2	The net profit is	$171,653		The net profit is 171653
3				
4				

Figure 5-3: The formula in cell D2 doesn't display the formatted number.

This formula essentially combines a text string with the contents of cell B2 and displays the result. Note, however, that the value from cell B2 is not formatted in any way. You might want to display the contents in cell B2 using a currency number format.

Note

Contrary to what you might expect, applying a number format to the cell that contains the formula has no effect. This is because the formula returns a string, not a value.

We can use the TEXT function to simulate the number formatting shown in cell D2:

```
="The net profit is " & TEXT(B2,"$#,##0.00")
```

This formula displays the text along with a nicely formatted value: *The net profit is $171,653.*

The second argument for the TEXT function consists of a standard Excel number format string. You can enter any valid number format string for this argument. Note, however, that color codes in number format strings are ignored.

The preceding example uses a simple cell reference (B2). You can, of course, use an expression instead. Here's an example that combines text with a number resulting from a computation:

```
="Average Expenditure: "& TEXT(AVERAGE(A:A),"$#,##0.00")
```

This formula might return a string such as *Average Expenditure: $7,794.57.*

Here's another example that uses the NOW function (which returns the current date and time). The TEXT function displays the date and time, nicely formatted:

```
="Report printed on "&TEXT(NOW(),"mmmm d, yyyy, at h:mm AM/PM")
```

Cross-Ref

In Chapter 6, "Working with Dates and Times," we discuss how Excel handles dates and times.

The formula might display the following: *Report printed on July 22, 2015 at 3:23 PM.*

Refer to Appendix B, "Using Custom Number Formats," for details on Excel number formats.

Displaying formatted currency values as text

Excel's DOLLAR function converts a number to text using the currency format. It takes two arguments: the number to convert, and the number of decimal places to display. The DOLLAR function uses the regional currency symbol (for example, $).

You can sometimes use the DOLLAR function in place of the TEXT function. The TEXT function, however, is much more flexible because it doesn't limit you to a specific number format. The second argument for the DOLLAR function specifies the number of decimal places.

The following formula returns *Total: $1,287.37*:

```
="Total: " & DOLLAR(1287.367, 2)
```

If you're looking for a function that converts a number into spelled-out text (such as *One hundred twelve and 32/100 dollars*), you won't find such a function. Well, Excel does have a function—BAHTTEXT—but it converts the number into the Thai language. Why Excel doesn't include an English language version of this function remains a mystery. VBA can often be used to overcome Excel's deficiencies, though. In Chapter 26, "VBA Custom Function Examples," you'll find a custom VBA worksheet function called SPELLDOLLARS, which displays dollar amounts as English text.

Removing excess spaces and nonprinting characters

Often, data imported into an Excel worksheet contains excess spaces or strange (often unprintable) characters. Excel provides you with two functions to help whip your data into shape: TRIM and CLEAN:

- TRIM removes all leading and trailing spaces, and it replaces internal strings of multiple spaces with a single space.
- CLEAN removes all nonprinting characters from a string. These "garbage" characters often appear when you import certain types of data.

This example uses the TRIM function. The formula returns *Fourth Quarter Earnings* (with no excess spaces):

```
=TRIM("   Fourth    Quarter    Earnings    ")
```

Cross-Ref

See Chapter 16 for detailed coverage of cleaning up data.

Counting characters in a string

The LEN function takes one argument and returns the number of characters in the argument. For example, assume that cell A1 contains the string *September Sales*. The following formula returns *15*:

```
=LEN(A1)
```

Notice that space characters are included in the character count. The LEN function can be useful for identifying strings with extraneous spaces, which can cause problems in some situations, such as in lookup formulas. The following formula returns *FALSE* if cell A1 contains any leading spaces, trailing spaces, or multiple spaces.

```
=LEN(A1)=LEN(TRIM(A1))
```

The following formula shortens text that is too long. If the text in A1 is more than ten characters in length, this formula returns the first nine characters plus an ellipsis (133 on the ANSI chart) as a continuation character. If cell A1 contains ten or fewer characters, the entire string is returned:

```
=IF(LEN(A1)>10,LEFT(A1,9)&CHAR(133),A1)
```

Cross-Ref

Later in this chapter, you'll see sample formulas that demonstrate how to count the number of a specific character within a string. (See the "Advanced Text Formulas" section.) Also, Chapter 7, "Counting and Summing Techniques," contains additional counting techniques. Still more counting examples are provided in Chapter 15, "Performing Magic with Array Formulas," which deals with array formulas.

Repeating a character or string

The REPT function repeats a text string (first argument) any number of times you specify (second argument). For example, this formula returns *HoHoHo:*

```
=REPT("Ho",3)
```

You can also use this function to create a crude horizontal divider between cells. This example displays a squiggly line, 20 characters in length:

```
=REPT("~",20)
```

Creating a text histogram

A clever use for the REPT function is to create a simple histogram (also known as a *frequency distribution*) directly in a worksheet (chart not required). Figure 5-4 shows an example of such a histogram. You'll find this type of graphical display especially useful when you need to visually summarize many values. In such a case, a standard chart may be unwieldy.

	A	B	C	D
1	Month	Units Sold		Chart
2	January	834		■■■■■■■■
3	February	1,132		■■■■■■■■■■■
4	March	1,243		■■■■■■■■■■■■
5	April	1,094		■■■■■■■■■■
6	May	902		■■■■■■■■■
7	June	1,543		■■■■■■■■■■■■■■■
8	July	1,654		■■■■■■■■■■■■■■■■
9	August	2,123		■■■■■■■■■■■■■■■■■■■■■
10	September	1,566		■■■■■■■■■■■■■■■
11	October	1,434		■■■■■■■■■■■■■■
12	November	1,321		■■■■■■■■■■■■■
13	December	1,654		■■■■■■■■■■■■■■■■
14				

Figure 5-4: Using the REPT function to create a histogram in a worksheet range.

Tip

The data bars conditional formatting feature is a much better way to display a simple histogram directly in cells. See Chapter 19, "Conditional Formatting," for more information about data bars.

The formulas in column D graphically depict the values in column B by displaying a series of characters in the Wingdings 2 font. This example uses character code 162, which displays as a solid rectangle in the Wingdings 2 font. A formula using the REPT function determines the number of characters displayed. Cell D2 contains this formula:

```
=REPT(CHAR(162),B2/100)
```

Assign the Wingdings 2 font to cell D2 and then copy the formulas down the column to accommodate all the data. Depending on the numerical range of your data, you may need to change the scaling. Experiment by replacing the 100 value in the formulas. You can substitute any character you like to produce a different character in the chart.

On the Web

The workbook shown in Figure 5-4, text histogram.xlsx, is available at this book's website and contains another example of this technique.

Padding a number

You're probably familiar with a common security measure (frequently used on printed checks) in which numbers are padded with asterisks on the right. The following formula displays the value in cell A1, along with enough asterisks to make 24 characters total:

```
=(A1 & REPT("*",24-LEN(A1)))
```

Or if you'd prefer to pad the number with asterisks on the left, use this formula:

```
=REPT("*",24-LEN(A1))&A1
```

The following formula displays asterisk padding on both sides of the number. It returns 24 characters when the number in cell A1 contains an even number of characters; otherwise, it returns 23 characters:

```
=REPT("*",12-LEN(A1)/2)&A1&REPT("*",12-LEN(A1)/2)
```

The preceding formulas are a bit deficient because they don't show any number formatting. Note this revised version that displays the value in A1 (formatted), along with the asterisk padding on the left:

```
=REPT("*",24-LEN(TEXT(A1,"$#,##0.00")))&TEXT(A1,"$#,##0.00")
```

Figure 5-5 shows these formulas in action.

	A	B	C
1	1234.56	1234.56*****************	=(A1 & REPT("*",24-LEN(A1)))
2		*****************1234.56	=REPT("*",24-LEN(A1))&A1
3		********1234.56********	=REPT("*",12-LEN(A1)/2)&A1&REPT("*",12-LEN(A1)/2)
4		***************$1,234.56	=REPT("*",24-LEN(TEXT(A1,"$#,##0.00")))&TEXT(A1,"$#,##0.00")

Figure 5-5: Using a formula to pad a number with asterisks.

You can also pad a number by using a custom number format. To repeat the next character in the format to fill the column width, include an asterisk (*) in the custom number format code. For example, use this number format to pad the number with dashes:

```
$#,##0.00*-
```

To pad the number with asterisks, use two asterisks, like this:

```
$#,##0.00**
```

Cross-Ref

See Appendix B for more information about custom number formats, including additional examples using the asterisk format code.

Changing the case of text

Excel provides three handy functions to change the case of text:

- **UPPER:** Converts the text to ALL UPPERCASE.
- **LOWER:** Converts the text to all lowercase.
- **PROPER:** Converts the text to Proper Case. (The First Letter In Each Word Is Capitalized.)

These functions are quite straightforward. The formula that follows, for example, converts the text in cell A1 to proper case. If cell A1 contained the text *MR. JOHN Q. PUBLIC,* the formula would return *Mr. John Q. Public:*

```
=PROPER(A1)
```

These functions operate only on alphabetic characters; they ignore all other characters and return them unchanged.

Caution

The PROPER function capitalizes the first letter of every word, which isn't always desirable. Applying the PROPER function to *a tale of two cities* results in *A Tale Of Two Cities.* Normally, the preposition *of* wouldn't be capitalized. In addition, applying the PROPER function to a name such as *ED MCMAHON* results in *Ed Mcmahon* (not *Ed McMahon*). And, apparently, the function is programmed to capitalize the letter following an apostrophe. Using the function with an argument of *don't* results in *Don'T.* But if the argument is *o'reilly*, it works perfectly.

Transforming data with formulas

Many of the examples in this chapter describe how to use functions to transform data in some way. For example, you can use the UPPER function to transform text into uppercase. Often, you'll want to replace the original data with the transformed data. To do so, paste values over the original text. Here's how:

1. Create your formulas to transform the original data.
2. Select the formula cells.
3. Choose Home ➜ Clipboard ➜ Copy (or press Ctrl+C).
4. Select the original data cells.
5. Choose Home ➜ Clipboard ➜ Paste ➜ Values (V).

After performing these steps, you can delete the formulas.

Extracting characters from a string

Excel users often need to extract characters from a string. For example, you may have a list of employee names (first and last names) and need to extract the last name from each cell. Excel provides several useful functions for extracting characters:

- **LEFT:** Returns a specified number of characters from the beginning of a string
- **RIGHT:** Returns a specified number of characters from the end of a string
- **MID:** Returns a specified number of characters beginning at any specified position within a string

The formula that follows returns the last 10 characters from cell A1. If A1 contains fewer than 10 characters, the formula returns all the text in the cell:

```
=RIGHT(A1,10)
```

This next formula uses the MID function to return five characters from cell A1, beginning at character position 2. In other words, it returns characters *2* through *6*:

```
=MID(A1,2,5)
```

The following example returns the text in cell A1, with only the first letter in uppercase (sometimes referred to as *sentence case*). It uses the LEFT function to extract the first character and convert it to uppercase. This character then concatenates to another string that uses the RIGHT function to extract all but the first character (converted to lowercase):

```
=UPPER(LEFT(A1))&LOWER(RIGHT(A1,LEN(A1)-1))
```

If cell A1 contained the text *FIRST QUARTER,* the formula would return *First quarter.*

Replacing text with other text

In some situations, you may need a formula to replace a part of a text string with some other text. For example, you may import data that contains asterisks, and you may need to convert the asterisks to some other character. You could use Excel's Home ➜ Editing ➜ Find & Select ➜ Replace command to make the replacement. If you prefer a formula-based solution, you can take advantage of either of two functions:

- **SUBSTITUTE** replaces specific text in a string. Use this function when you know the character(s) that you want to replace but not the position.
- **REPLACE** replaces text that occurs in a specific location within a string. Use this function when you know the position of the text that you want to replace but not the actual text.

The following formula uses the SUBSTITUTE function to replace 2012 with 2013 in the string *2012 Budget*. The formula returns *2013 Budget*:

```
=SUBSTITUTE("2012 Budget","2012","2013")
```

The following formula uses the SUBSTITUTE function to remove all spaces from a string. In other words, it replaces all space characters with an empty string. The formula returns *2013OperatingBudget*:

```
=SUBSTITUTE("2013 Operating Budget"," ","")
```

The following formula uses the REPLACE function to replace one character beginning at position 5 with nothing. In other words, it removes the fifth character (a hyphen) and returns *Part544*:

```
=REPLACE("Part-544",5,1,"")
```

You can, of course, nest these functions to perform multiple replacements in a single formula. The formula that follows demonstrates the power of nested SUBSTITUTE functions. The formula essentially strips out any of the following seven characters in cell A1: space, hyphen, colon, asterisk, underscore, left parenthesis, and right parenthesis:

```
=SUBSTITUTE(SUBSTITUTE(SUBSTITUTE(SUBSTITUTE(SUBSTITUTE(SUBSTITUTE((A1," ",""),"-
 ",""),":",""),"*",""),"_",""),"(",""),")","")
```

Therefore, if cell A1 contains the string *Part-2A - Z(4M1)_A**, the formula returns *Part2AZ4M1A*.

Finding and searching within a string

The Excel FIND and SEARCH functions enable you to locate the starting position of a particular substring within a string:

- **FIND:** Finds a substring within another text string and returns the starting position of the substring. You can specify the character position at which to begin searching. Use this function for case-sensitive text comparisons. Wildcard comparisons are not supported.
- **SEARCH:** Finds a substring within another text string and returns the starting position of the substring. You can specify the character position at which to begin searching. Use this function for non–case-sensitive text or when you need to use wildcard characters.

The following formula uses the FIND function and returns *7*, the position of the first *m* in the string. Notice that this formula is case sensitive:

```
=FIND("m","Big Mamma Thornton",1)
```

The formula that follows, which uses the SEARCH function, returns *5,* the position of the first *m* (either uppercase or lowercase):

```
=SEARCH("m","Big Mamma Thornton",1)
```

You can use the following wildcard characters within the first argument for the SEARCH function:

- **Question mark (?):** Matches any single character
- **Asterisk (*):** Matches any sequence of characters

Tip

If you want to find an actual question mark or asterisk character, type a tilde (~) before the question mark or asterisk. If you want to find a tilde, type two tildes.

The next formula examines the text in cell A1 and returns the position of the first three-character sequence that has a hyphen in the middle of it. In other words, it looks for any character followed by a hyphen and any other character. If cell A1 contains the text *Part-A90,* the formula returns *4:*

```
=SEARCH("?-?",A1,1)
```

Searching and replacing within a string

You can use the REPLACE function in conjunction with the SEARCH function to create a new string that replaces part of the original text string with another string. In effect, you use the SEARCH function to find the starting location used by the REPLACE function.

For example, assume cell A1 contains the text *Annual Profit Figures.* The following formula searches for the word *Profit* and replaces those six characters with the word *Loss:*

```
=REPLACE(A1,SEARCH("Profit",A1),6,"Loss")
```

This next formula uses the SUBSTITUTE function to accomplish the same effect in a more efficient manner:

```
=SUBSTITUTE(A1,"Profit","Loss")
```

Advanced Text Formulas

The examples in this section are more complex than the examples in the previous section, but as you'll see, these formulas can perform some useful text manipulations.

All of the examples in this section are available at this book's website. The filename is text formula examples.xlsx file.

Counting specific characters in a cell

This formula counts the number of *B*s (uppercase only) in the string in cell A1:

```
=LEN(A1)-LEN(SUBSTITUTE(A1,"B",""))
```

This formula uses the SUBSTITUTE function to create a new string (in memory) that has all the *B*s removed. Then the length of this string is subtracted from the length of the original string. The result reveals the number of *B*s in the original string.

The following formula is a bit more versatile. It counts the number of *B*s (both upper- and lowercase) in the string in cell A1:

```
=LEN(A1)-LEN(SUBSTITUTE(SUBSTITUTE(A1,"B",""),"b",""))
```

Counting the occurrences of a substring in a cell

The formulas in the preceding section count the number of occurrences of a particular character in a string. The following formula works with more than one character. It returns the number of occurrences of a particular substring (contained in cell B1) within a string (contained in cell A1). The substring can consist of any number of characters:

```
=(LEN(A1)-LEN(SUBSTITUTE(A1,B1,"")))/LEN(B1)
```

For example, if cell A1 contains the text *Blonde On Blonde* and B1 contains the text *Blonde,* the formula returns *2*.

The comparison is case sensitive, so if B1 contains the text *blonde,* the formula returns *0*. The following formula is a modified version that performs a case-insensitive comparison:

```
=(LEN(A1)-LEN(SUBSTITUTE(UPPER(A1),UPPER(B1),"")))/LEN(B1)
```

Removing trailing minus signs

Some accounting systems use a trailing minus sign to indicate negative values. If you import such a report into Excel, the values with trailing minus signs are interpreted as text.

The formula that follows checks for a trailing minus sign. If found, it removes the minus sign and returns a negative number. If cell A1 contains *198.43–*, the formula returns *–198.43*:

```
=IF(RIGHT(A1,1)="-",LEFT(A1,LEN(A1)-1)*-1,A1)
```

Expressing a number as an ordinal

You may need to express a value as an ordinal number: for example, *Today is the 21st day of the month.* In this case, the number 21 converts to an ordinal number by appending the characters *st* to the number. Keep in mind that the result of this formula is a string, not a value. Therefore, it can't be used in numerical formulas.

The characters appended to a number depend on the number. There is no clear pattern, making the construction of a formula more difficult. Most numbers will use the *th* suffix. Exceptions occur for numbers that end with 1, 2, or 3 *except* if the preceding number is a 1: that is, numbers that end with 11, 12, or 13. These may seem like fairly complex rules, but you can translate them into an Excel formula.

The formula that follows converts the number in cell A1 (assumed to be an integer) to an ordinal number:

```
=A1&IF(OR(VALUE(RIGHT(A1,2))={11,12,13}),"th",IF(OR(VALUE(RIGHT(A1))={1,2,3}),
CHOOSE(RIGHT(A1),"st","nd","rd"),"th"))
```

This is a rather complicated formula, so it may help to examine its components. Basically, the formula works as follows:

- **Rule #1:** If the last two digits of the number are 11, 12, or 13, use *th.*
- **Rule #2:** If Rule #1 does not apply, check the last digit.
  - If the last digit is 1, use *st.*
  - If the last digit is 2, use *nd.*
  - If the last digit is 3, use *rd.*
- **Rule #3:** If neither Rule #1 nor Rule #2 apply, use *th.*

Cross-Ref

The formula uses two arrays, specified by brackets. See Chapter 14, "Introducing Arrays," for more information about using arrays in formulas.

Figure 5-6 shows the formula in use.

	A	B
18	Creating an ordinal number	
19	1	1st
20	3	3rd
21	45	45th
22	122	122nd

Figure 5-6: Using a formula to express a number as an ordinal.

Determining a column letter for a column number

This next formula returns a worksheet column letter (ranging from A to XFD) for the value contained in cell A1. For example, if A1 contains *29*, the formula returns *AC* (the 29th column letter in a worksheet):

```
=LEFT(ADDRESS(1,A1,4),FIND(1,ADDRESS(1,A1,4))-1)
```

Note that the formula doesn't check for a valid column number. In other words, if A1 contains a value less than 1 or greater than 16,384, the formula then returns an error. The following modification uses the IFERROR function to display text (*Invalid Column*) instead of an error value:

```
=IFERROR(LEFT(ADDRESS(1,A1,4),FIND(1,ADDRESS(1,A1,4))-1),"Invalid Column")
```

The IFERROR function was introduced in Excel 2007. For compatibility with versions prior to Excel 2007, use this formula:

```
=IF(ISERR(LEFT(ADDRESS(1,A1,4),FIND(1,ADDRESS(1,A1,4))-1)),
"Invalid Column",LEFT(ADDRESS(1,A1,4),FIND(1,ADDRESS(1,A1,4))-1))
```

Extracting a filename from a path specification

The following formula returns the filename from a full path specification. For example, if cell A1 contains *c:\files\excel\myfile.xlsx*, the formula returns *myfile.xlsx*:

```
=MID(A1,FIND("*",SUBSTITUTE(A1,"\","*",LEN(A1)-LEN(SUBSTITUTE(A1,"\",""))))+1,LE
  N(A1))
```

The preceding formula assumes that the system path separator is a backslash (\). It essentially returns all the text following the last backslash character. If cell A1 doesn't contain a backslash character, the formula returns an error.

Note

In some cases, the Flash Fill feature can substitute for creating formulas that extract text from cells. See Chapter 16 for more information.

Extracting the first word of a string

To extract the first word of a string, a formula must locate the position of the first space character and then use this information as an argument for the LEFT function. The following formula does just that:

```
=LEFT(A1,FIND(" ",A1)-1)
```

This formula returns all the text prior to the first space in cell A1. However, the formula has a slight problem: it returns an error if cell A1 consists of a single word. A simple modification solves the problem by using an IFERROR function to check for the error:

```
=IFERROR(LEFT(A1,FIND(" ",A1)-1),A1)
```

For compatibility with versions prior to Excel 2007, use this formula:

```
=IF(ISERR(FIND(" ",A1)),A1,LEFT(A1,FIND(" ",A1)-1))
```

Extracting the last word of a string

Extracting the last word of a string is more complicated because the FIND function works from left to right only. Therefore, the problem rests with locating the *last* space character. The formula that follows, however, solves this problem. It returns the last word of a string (all the text following the last space character):

```
=RIGHT(A1,LEN(A1)-FIND("*",SUBSTITUTE(A1," ","*",LEN(A1)-LEN(SUBSTITUTE(A1," ","")))))
```

This formula, however, has the same problem as the first formula in the preceding section: it fails if the string does not contain at least one space character. The following modified formula uses the IFERROR function to avoid the error value:

```
=IFERROR(RIGHT(A1,LEN(A1)-FIND("*",SUBSTITUTE(A1," ","*",
LEN(A1)-LEN(SUBSTITUTE(A1," ",""))))),A1)
```

For compatibility with versions prior to Excel 2007, use this formula:

```
=IF(ISERR(FIND(" ",A1)),A1,
RIGHT(A1,LEN(A1)-FIND("*",SUBSTITUTE(A1," ","*",LEN(A1)-LEN(SUBSTITUTE(A1," ",""))))))
```

Extracting all but the first word of a string

The following formula returns the contents of cell A1, except for the first word:

```
=RIGHT(A1,LEN(A1)-FIND(" ",A1,1))
```

If cell A1 contains *2013 Operating Budget,* the formula then returns *Operating Budget.*

This formula returns an error if the cell contains only one word. The following formula solves this problem and returns an empty string if the cell does not contain multiple words:

```
=IFERROR(RIGHT(A1,LEN(A1)-FIND(" ",A1,1)),"")
```

For compatibility with versions prior to Excel 2007, use this formula:

```
=IF(ISERR(FIND(" ",A1)),"",RIGHT(A1,LEN(A1)-FIND(" ",A1,1)))
```

Extracting first names, middle names, and last names

Suppose you have a list consisting of people's names in a single column. You have to separate these names into three columns: one for the first name, one for the middle name or initial, and one for the last name. This task is more complicated than you may initially think because not every name in the column has a middle name or middle initial. However, you can still do it.

Note

The task becomes a *lot* more complicated if the list contains names with titles (such as Mrs. or Dr.) or names followed by additional details (such as Jr. or III). In fact, the following formulas will *not* handle these complex cases. However, they still give you a significant head start if you're willing to do a bit of manual editing to handle the special cases.

All the formulas that follow assume that the name appears in cell A1.

You can easily construct a formula to return the first name:

```
=IFERROR(LEFT(A1,FIND(" ",A1)-1),A1)
```

Returning the middle name or initial is much more complicated because not all names have a middle initial. This formula returns the middle name or initial (if it exists); otherwise, it returns nothing:

```
=IF(LEN(A1)-LEN(SUBSTITUTE(A1," ",""))>1,
MID(A1,FIND(" ",A1)+1,FIND(" ",A1,FIND(" ",A1)+1)-(FIND(" ",A1)+1)),"")
```

Finally, this formula returns the last name:

```
=IFERROR(RIGHT(A1,LEN(A1)-FIND("*",SUBSTITUTE(A1," ","*",LEN(A1)-LEN(SUBSTITUTE
    (A1," ",""))))),"")
```

The formula that follows is a much shorter way to extract the middle name. This formula is useful if you use the other formulas to extract the first name and the last name. It assumes that the first name is in B1 and that the last name is in D1:

```
=IF(LEN(B1&D1)+2>=LEN(A1),"",MID(A1,LEN(B1)+2,LEN(A1)-LEN(B1&D1)-2)
```

As you can see in Figure 5-7, the formulas work fairly well. There are a few problems, however: notably, names that contain four "words." But, as we mentioned earlier, you can clean up these cases.

If you want to know how we created these complex formulas, see Chapter 21, "Creating Megaformulas."

	A	B	C	D	E
42					
43	**Extracting first name, middle names, last names**				
44	John Q. Public	John	Q.	Public	
45	Lisa Smith	Lisa		Smith	
46	J. R. Robins	J.	R.	Robins	
47	Cher	Cher			

Figure 5-7: This worksheet uses formulas to extract the first name, middle name (or initial), and last name from a list of names in column A.

Splitting text strings without using formulas

In many cases, you can eliminate the use of formulas and use Excel's Data ➜ Data Tools ➜ Convert Text to Columns command to parse strings into their component parts. Selecting this command displays Excel's Convert Text to Columns Wizard (see the accompanying figure), which consists of a series of dialog boxes that walk you through converting a single column of data into multiple columns. Generally, you'll want to select the Delimited option (in step 1) and use Space as the delimiter (in step 2).

continued

continued

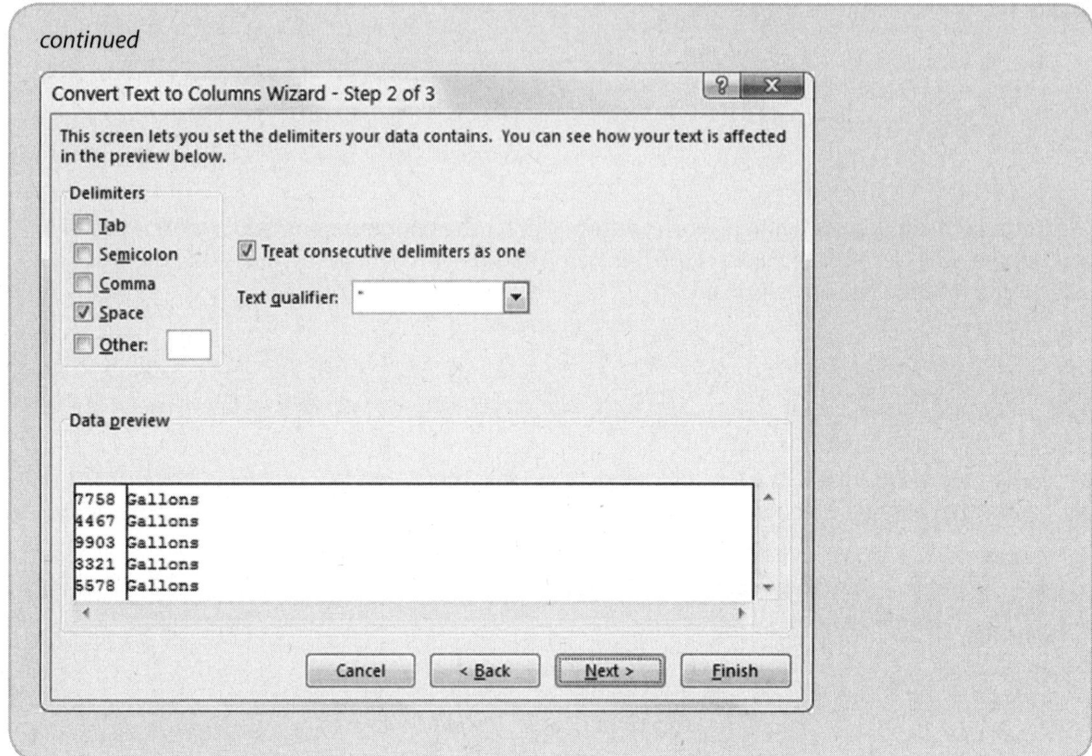

Another string-splitting option is to use the Flash Fill feature.

Removing titles from names

You can use the formula that follows to remove four common titles (Mr., Dr., Ms., and Mrs.) from a name. For example, if cell A1 contains *Mr. Fred Munster,* the following formula would return *Fred Munster:*

```
=IF(OR(LEFT(A1,2)={"Mr","Dr","Ms"}),RIGHT(A1,LEN(A1)-(FIND(".",A1)+1)),A1)
```

Counting the number of words in a cell

The following formula returns the number of words in cell A1:

```
=LEN(TRIM(A1))-LEN(SUBSTITUTE((A1)," ",""))+1
```

The formula uses the TRIM function to remove excess spaces. It then uses the SUBSTITUTE function to create a new string (in memory) that has all the space characters removed. The length of this string is subtracted from the length of the original (trimmed) string to get the number of spaces. This value is then incremented by 1 to get the number of words.

Note that this formula returns *1* if the cell is empty. The following modification solves that problem:

```
=IF(LEN(A1)=0,0,LEN(TRIM(A1))-LEN(SUBSTITUTE(TRIM(A1)," ",""))+1)
```

Cross-Ref

Excel has many functions that work with text, but you're likely to run into a situation in which the appropriate function just doesn't exist. In such a case, you can often create your own worksheet function using VBA. Chapter 26 also contains a number of custom text functions written in VBA.

6

Working with Dates and Times

In This Chapter

- An overview of using dates and times in Excel
- Excel's date-related functions
- Excel's time-related functions

Beginners often find working with dates and times in Excel to be frustrating. To help avoid this frustration, you'll need a good understanding of how Excel handles time-based information. This chapter provides the information you need to create powerful formulas that manipulate dates and times.

Note

The dates in this chapter correspond to the U.S. English date format: month/day/year. For example, 3/1/1952 refers to March 1, 1952—not January 3, 1952. We know this may seem illogical to those of you who are accustomed to seeing dates in the day/month/year format, but that's how we Americans have been trained. We trust you can make the adjustment while reading this chapter.

How Excel Handles Dates and Times

This section presents a quick overview of how Excel deals with dates and times. It includes coverage of Excel's date and time serial number system and offers tips for entering and formatting dates and times.

Cross-Ref

Other chapters in this book contain additional date-related information. For example, see Chapter 7, "Counting and Summing Techniques," for counting examples that use dates. Also, Chapter 26, "VBA Custom Function Examples," contains some VBA functions that work with dates.

Understanding date serial numbers

To Excel, a date is simply a number. More precisely, a date is a serial number that represents the number of days since January 0, 1900. A serial number of 1 corresponds to January 1, 1900; a serial number of 2 corresponds to January 2, 1900; and so on. This system makes it possible to create formulas that perform calculations with dates. For example, you can create a formula to calculate the number of days between two dates or to determine the date of the third Friday of January in 2020.

You may wonder about January 0, 1900. This nondate (which corresponds to date serial number 0) is actually used to represent times that are not associated with a particular day. This will become clear later in this chapter.

To view a date serial number as a date, you must format the cell as a date. Use the Format Cells dialog box (Number tab) to apply a date format.

Note

Excel 2000 and later versions support dates from January 1, 1900, through December 31, 9999 (serial number = 2,958,465). Versions prior to Excel 2000 support a much smaller range of dates: from January 1, 1900, through December 31, 2078 (serial number = 65,380).

Choose your date system: 1900 or 1904

Excel actually supports two date systems: the 1900 date system and the 1904 date system. Which system you use in a workbook determines what date serves as the basis for dates. The 1900 date system uses January 1, 1900, as the day assigned to date serial number 1. The 1904 date system uses January 1, 1904, as the base date. By default, Excel for Windows uses the 1900 date system, and Excel for Mac uses the 1904 date system—or, at least, it used to. Microsoft made a change, and now Excel 2011 for Mac (and presumably subsequent Mac versions) uses the 1900 date system by default.

Excel for Windows supports the 1904 date system for compatibility with Mac files. You can choose to use the 1904 date system from the Excel Options dialog box. (Choose File ➜ Options and navigate to the When Calculating This Workbook section of the Advanced tab.)

Generally, you should use the default 1900 date system. And you should exercise caution if you use two different date systems in workbooks that are linked. For example, assume that Book1 uses the 1904 date system and contains the date 1/15/1999 in cell A1. Further assume that Book2 uses the 1900 date system and contains a link to cell A1 in Book1. Book2 will display the date as 1/14/1995. Both workbooks use the same date serial number (34713), but they are interpreted differently.

One advantage to using the 1904 date system is that it enables you to display negative time values. With the 1900 date system, a calculation that results in a negative time (for example, 4:00 PM–5:30 PM) cannot be displayed. When using the 1904 date system, the negative time displays as 1:30 (a difference of one hour and 30 minutes).

Entering dates

You can enter a date directly as a serial number (if you know it), but more often, you'll enter a date using any of several recognized date formats. Excel automatically converts your entry into the corresponding date serial number (which it uses for calculations) and applies a date format to the cell so that it displays as an easily readable date rather than a cryptic serial number.

For example, if you need to enter June 18, 2015, you can simply enter the date by typing **June 18, 2015** (or use any of several different date formats). Excel interprets your entry and stores the value 42173, which is the date serial number for that date. Excel also applies one of several date formats depending on how the date is originally entered, so the cell contents may not appear exactly as you typed them.

Note

Depending on your regional settings, entering a date in a format such as *June 18, 2015* may be interpreted as a text string. In such a case, you would need to enter the date in a format that corresponds to your regional settings, such as *18 June, 2015*.

When you activate a cell that contains a date, the Formula bar shows the cell contents formatted using the default date format, which corresponds to your system's short date style. The Formula bar does *not* display the date's serial number, which is inconsistent with other types of number formatting. If you need to find out the serial number for a particular date, format the cell by using the General format.

Tip

To change the default date format, you need to change a system-wide setting. Access the Windows Control Panel and choose Regional and Language Options. Then click the Customize button to display the Customize Regional Options dialog box. Select the Date tab. The selected item for the Short date style format determines the default date format that Excel uses.

Table 6-1 shows a sampling of the date formats that Excel recognizes (using the U.S. settings). Results will vary if you use a different regional setting. The displayed data assumes that the cell contains no numeric formatting.

Table 6-1: Date Entry Formats Recognized by Excel

Entry	Excel's Interpretation (U.S. Settings)	What Excel Displays
6-18-15	June 18, 2015	Windows short date
6-18-2015	June 18, 2015	Windows short date
6/18/15	June 18, 2015	Windows short date
6/18/2015	June 18, 2015	Windows short date
6-18/15	June 18, 2015	Windows short date
June 18, 2015	June 18, 2015	18-Jun-15
Jun 18	June 18 of the current year	18-Jun
Jun18	June 18 of the current year	18-Jun

continued

Table 6-1: Date Entry Formats Recognized by Excel *(continued)*

Entry	Excel's Interpretation (U.S. Settings)	What Excel Displays
June 18	June 18 of the current year	18-Jun
June18	June 18 of the current year	18-Jun
6/18	June 18 of the current year	18-Jun
6-18	June 18 of the current year	18-Jun
18-Jun-2015	June 18, 2015	18-Jun-15
2015/6/18	June 18, 2015	Windows short date

As you can see in Table 6-1, Excel is pretty good at recognizing dates entered into a cell. It's not perfect, however. For example, Excel does *not* recognize any of the following entries as dates:

- June 18 2015
- Jun-18 2015
- Jun-18/2015

Rather, it interprets these entries as text. If you plan to use dates in formulas, make sure that Excel can recognize the date you enter as a date; otherwise, the formulas that refer to these dates will produce incorrect results.

If you attempt to enter a date that lies outside the supported date range, Excel interprets it as text. If you attempt to format a serial number that lies outside the supported range as a date, the value displays as a series of hash marks (#########).

Tip

If you want to be absolutely sure that a valid date is entered into a particular cell, you can use Excel's data validation feature. Just set it up so the validation criteria allow only dates. You can also specify a valid range of dates. See Chapter 20, "Using Data Validation," for more about data validation.

Searching for dates

If your worksheet uses many dates, you may need to search for a particular date by using the Find and Replace dialog box (Home ➜ Editing ➜ Find & Select ➜ Find, or press Ctrl+F). Excel is rather picky when it comes to finding dates. You must enter the date as it appears in the Formula bar. For example, if a cell contains a date formatted to display as June 18, 2015, the date appears in the Formula bar using your system's short date format (for example, 6/18/2015). Therefore, if you search for the date as it appears in the cell, Excel won't find it, but it will find the cell if you search for the date in the format that appears in the Formula bar.

Understanding time serial numbers

When you need to work with time values, you simply extend Excel's date serial number system to include decimals. In other words, Excel works with times by using fractional days. For example, the date serial number for June 18, 2015, is 42173. Noon (halfway through the day) is represented internally as 42173.5.

The serial number equivalent of 1 minute is approximately 0.00069444. The formula that follows calculates this number by multiplying 24 hours by 60 minutes and then dividing the result into 1. The denominator consists of the number of minutes in a day (1,440).

```
=1/(24*60)
```

Similarly, the serial number equivalent of 1 second is approximately 0.00001157, obtained by the following formula (1 divided by 24 hours times 60 minutes times 60 seconds). In this case, the denominator represents the number of seconds in a day (86,400).

```
=1/(24*60*60)
```

In Excel, the smallest unit of time is one one-thousandth of a second. The time serial number shown here represents 23:59:59.999, or one one-thousandth of a second before midnight:

```
0.99999999
```

Table 6-2 shows various times of day, along with each associated time serial number.

Table 6-2: Times of Day and Their Corresponding Serial Numbers

Time of Day	Time Serial Number
12:00:00 AM (midnight)	0.0000
1:30:00 AM	0.0625
3:00:00 AM	0.1250
4:30:00 AM	0.1875
6:00:00 AM	0.2500
7:30:00 AM	0.3125
9:00:00 AM	0.3750
10:30:00 AM	0.4375
12:00:00 PM (noon)	0.5000
1:30:00 PM	0.5625
3:00:00 PM	0.6250

continued

Table 6-2: Times of Day and Their Corresponding Serial Numbers *(continued)*

Time of Day	Time Serial Number
4:30:00 PM	0.6875
6:00:00 PM	0.7500
7:30:00 PM	0.8125
9:00:00 PM	0.8750
10:30:00 PM	0.9375

Entering times

As with entering dates, you normally don't have to worry about the actual time serial numbers. Just enter the time into a cell using a recognized format. Table 6-3 shows some examples of time formats that Excel recognizes.

Table 6-3: Time Entry Formats Recognized by Excel

Entry	Excel's Interpretation	What Excel Displays
11:30:00 am	11:30 AM	11:30:00 AM
11:30:00 AM	11:30 AM	11:30:00 AM
11:30 pm	11:30 PM	11:30 PM
11:30	11:30 AM	11:30
13:30	1:30 PM	13:30
11 AM	11:00 AM	11:00 AM

Because the preceding samples don't have a specific day associated with them, Excel uses a date serial number of 0, which corresponds to the nondate January 0, 1900.

Note

If you're using the 1904 date system, time values without an explicit date use January 1, 1904, as the date. The discussion that follows assumes that you are using the default 1900 date system.

Often, you'll want to combine a date and time. Do so by using a recognized date entry format, followed by a space and then a recognized time-entry format. For example, if you enter the following text in a cell, Excel interprets it as 11:30 AM on June 18, 2015. Its date/time serial number is 42163.4791666667.

```
6/18/2015 11:30
```

When you enter a time that exceeds 24 hours, the associated date for the time increments accordingly. For example, if you enter the following time into a cell, it is interpreted as 1:00 AM on January 1, 1900.

The day part of the entry increments because the time exceeds 24 hours. (Keep in mind that a time value entered without a date uses January 0, 1900, as the date.)

```
25:00:00
```

Similarly, if you enter a date *and* a time (and the time exceeds 24 hours), the date that you entered is adjusted. The following entry, for example, is interpreted as 9/2/2015 1:00:00 AM:

```
9/1/2015 25:00:00
```

If you enter a time only (without an associated date), you'll find that the maximum time that you can enter into a cell is 9999:59:59 (just under 10,000 hours). Excel adds the appropriate number of days. In this case, 9999:59:59 is interpreted as 3:59:59 PM on 02/19/1901. If you enter a time that exceeds 10,000 hours, the time appears as a text string.

Formatting dates and times

You have a great deal of flexibility in formatting cells that contain dates and times. For example, you can format the cell to display the date part only, the time part only, or both the date and the time parts.

One way to format dates and times is by selecting the cells and then using the Number Format control from the Home ➜ Number group (see Figure 6-1). This control offers two date formats and one time format. The date formats are those specified as your Windows Short Date and Long Date formats.

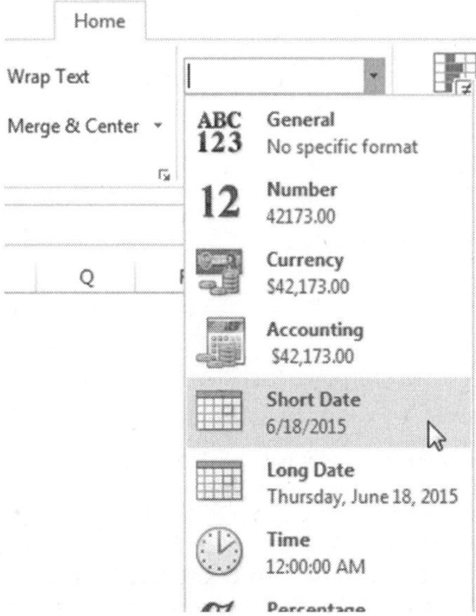

Figure 6-1: Use the Number Format drop-down list to change the appearance of dates and times.

Tip

When you create a formula that refers to a cell containing a date or a time, Excel may automatically format the formula cell as a date or a time. Sometimes, this is helpful; other times, it's completely inappropriate and downright annoying. Unfortunately, you cannot turn off this automatic date formatting. You can, however, use a shortcut key combination to remove all number formatting from the cell and return to the default General format. Just select the cell and press Ctrl+Shift+~.

For more control over date and time formatting, select the cells and then use the Number tab of the Format Cells dialog box, as shown in Figure 6-2. Here are ways to display this dialog box:

- Click the dialog box launcher icon of the Number group of the Home tab.
- Click the Number Format control and choose More Number Formats from the list that appears.
- Press Ctrl+1.

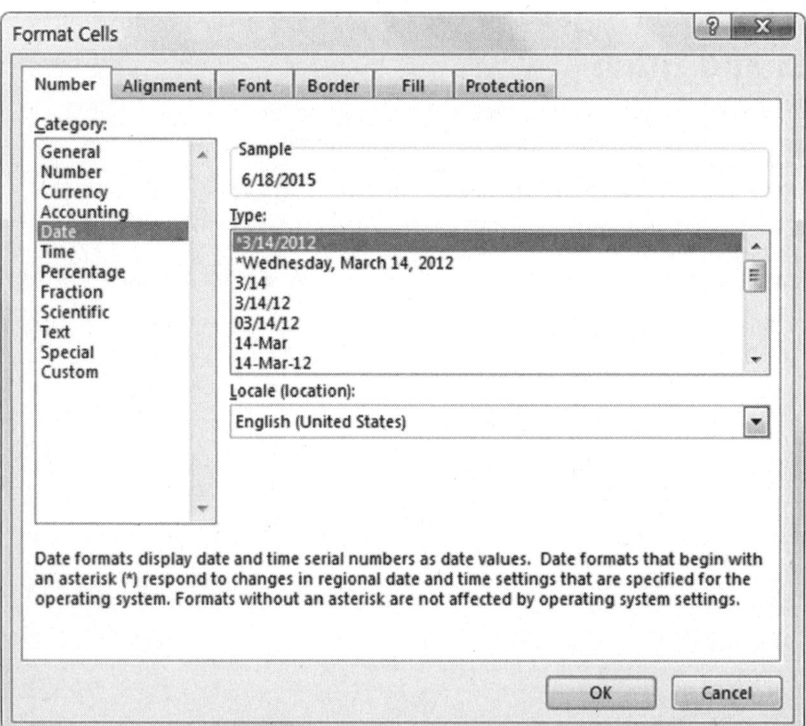

Figure 6-2: Use the Number tab of the Format Cells dialog box to change the appearance of dates and times.

The Date category shows built-in date formats, and the Time category shows built-in time formats. Additional date and time formats are available from the Custom category. Some formats include both date and time displays. Just select the desired format from the Type list and then click OK.

Note that the first two date formats in the Date category and the first time format in the Time category correspond to your Windows date and time settings.

If none of the built-in formats meets your needs, you can create a custom number format. Select the Custom category and type the custom format codes into the Type box. (See Appendix B, "Using Custom Number Formats," for information on creating custom number formats.)

Problems with dates

Excel has some problems when it comes to dates. Many of these problems stem from the fact that Excel was designed many years ago, before the acronym Y2K became a household term. And, as we describe, the Excel designers basically emulated the Lotus 1-2-3 limited date and time features, which contain a nasty bug duplicated intentionally in Excel (described later). In addition, versions of Excel show inconsistency in how they interpret a cell entry that has a two-digit year. Finally, the way Excel interprets a date entry depends on your regional date settings.

If Excel were being designed from scratch today, I'm sure it would be much more versatile in dealing with dates. Unfortunately, we're currently stuck with a product that leaves much to be desired in the area of dates.

The Excel leap year bug

A *leap year,* which occurs every four years, contains an additional day (February 29). Specifically, years that are evenly divisible by 100 are not leap years unless they are also evenly divisible by 400. Although the year 1900 was not a leap year, Excel treats it as such. In other words, when you type the following into a cell, Excel does not complain. It interprets this as a valid date and assigns a serial number of 60:

```
2/29/1900
```

If you type the following invalid date, Excel correctly interprets it as a mistake and *doesn't* convert it to a date. Rather, it simply makes the cell entry a text string:

```
2/29/1901
```

How can a product used daily by millions of people contain such an obvious bug? The answer is historical. The original version of Lotus 1-2-3 contained a bug that caused it to consider 1900 as a leap year. When Excel was released some time later, the designers knew of this bug and chose to reproduce it in Excel to maintain compatibility with Lotus worksheet files.

Why does this bug still exist in later versions of Excel? Microsoft asserts that the disadvantages of correcting this bug outweigh the advantages. If the bug were eliminated, it would mess up hundreds of thousands of existing workbooks. In addition, correcting this problem would affect compatibility between Excel and other programs that use dates. As it stands, this bug really causes very few problems because most users do not use dates before March 1, 1900.

Pre-1900 dates

The world, of course, didn't begin on January 1, 1900. People who work with historical information using Excel often need to work with dates before January 1, 1900. Unfortunately, the only way to work with pre-1900 dates is to enter the date into a cell as text. For example, you can type the following into a cell, and Excel won't complain:

```
July 4, 1776
```

Tip

If you plan to sort information by old dates entered as text, you should enter your text dates with a four-digit year, followed by a two-digit month, and then a two-digit day, like this: 1776-07-04. This format will enable accurate sorting.

You can't, however, perform manipulation on dates recognized as text. For example, you can't change its numeric formatting, you can't determine which day of the week this date occurred on, and you can't calculate the date that occurs seven days later.

Cross-Ref

In Chapter 26, we present some custom VBA functions that enable you to work with any date in the years 0100 through 9999.

Inconsistent date entries

You need to be careful when entering dates by using two digits for the year. When you do so, Excel has some rules that kick in to determine which century to use. And those rules vary, depending on the version of Excel that you use.

Two-digit years between 00 and 29 are interpreted as 21st Century dates, and two-digit years between 30 and 99 are interpreted as 20th Century dates. For example, if you enter 12/15/28, Excel interprets your entry as December 15, 2028. However, if you enter 12/15/30, Excel sees it as December 15, 1930, because Windows uses a default boundary year of 2029. You can keep the default as is or change it by using the Windows Control Panel. Display the Regional and Language Options dialog box. Then click the Customize button to display the Customize Regional Options dialog box. Select the Date tab and then specify a different year.

Tip

The best way to avoid any surprises is to simply enter *all* years using *all* four digits for the year.

Date-Related Functions

Excel has quite a few functions that work with dates. They are all listed under the Date & Time drop-down list in the Formulas ➜ Function Library group.

Table 6-4 summarizes the date-related functions available in Excel.

Table 6-4: Date-Related Functions

Function	Description
DATE	Returns the serial number of a date given the year, month, and day
DATEDIF	Calculates the number of days, months, or years between two dates
DATEVALUE	Converts a date in the form of text to an actual date
DAY	Returns the day of the month for a given date
DAYS***	Returns the number of days between two dates
DAYS360	Calculates the number of days between two dates based on a 360-day year
EDATE*	Returns the date that represents the indicated number of months before or after the start date
EOMONTH*	Returns the date of the last day of the month before or after a specified number of months
ISOWEEKNUM***	Returns the ISO week number for a date
MONTH	Returns the month for a given date
NETWORKDAYS*	Returns the number of whole work days between two dates
NETWORKDAYS.INTL**	Returns an international version of the NETWORKDAYS function
NOW	Returns the current date and time
TODAY	Returns today's date
WEEKDAY	Returns the day of the week (expressed as a number) for a date
WEEKNUM*	Returns the week number of the year for a date
WORKDAY*	Returns the date before or after a specified number of workdays
WORKDAY.INTL**	Returns an international version of the WORKDAY function
YEAR	Returns the year for a given date
YEARFRAC*	Returns the year fraction representing the number of whole days between two dates

** In versions prior to Excel 2007, this function is available only when the Analysis ToolPak add-in is installed.*
*** A function introduced in Excel 2010*
**** A function introduced in Excel 2013*

Displaying the current date

The following function displays the current date in a cell:

```
=TODAY()
```

You can also display the date, combined with text. The formula that follows, for example, displays text such as *Today is Tuesday, April 9, 2015:*

```
="Today is "&TEXT(TODAY(),"dddd, mmmm d, yyyy")
```

It's important to understand that the TODAY function is updated whenever the worksheet is calculated. For example, if you enter either of the preceding formulas into a worksheet, the formula displays the current date. When you open the workbook tomorrow, though, it will display the current date for that day (not the date when you entered the formula).

Tip

To enter a date stamp into a cell, press Ctrl+; (semicolon). This enters the date directly into the cell and does not use a formula. Therefore, the date does not change.

Displaying any date with a function

As explained earlier in this chapter, you can easily enter a date into a cell by typing it using any of the date formats that Excel recognizes. You can also create a date by using the DATE function, which takes three arguments: the year, the month, and the day. The following formula, for example, returns a date comprising the year in cell A1, the month in cell B1, and the day in cell C1:

```
=DATE(A1,B1,C1)
```

Tip

The DATE function accepts invalid arguments and adjusts the result accordingly. For example, this next formula uses 13 as the month argument and returns *January 1, 2015*. The month argument is automatically translated as month 1 of the following year:

```
=DATE(2014,13,1)
```

Often, you'll use the DATE function with other functions as arguments. For example, the formula that follows uses the YEAR and TODAY functions to return the date for Independence Day (July 4th) of the current year:

```
=DATE(YEAR(TODAY()),7,4)
```

The DATEVALUE function converts a text string that looks like a date into a date serial number. The following formula returns *42238*, the date serial number for August 22, 2015:

```
=DATEVALUE("8/22/2015")
```

To view the result of this formula as a date, you need to apply a date number format to the cell.

Warning

Be careful when using the DATEVALUE function. A text string that looks like a date in your country may not look like a date in another country. The preceding example works fine if your system is set for U.S. date formats, but it returns an error for other regional date formats because Excel is looking for the eighth day of the 22nd month!

Generating a series of dates

Often, you want to insert a series of dates into a worksheet. For example, in tracking weekly sales, you may want to enter a series of dates, each separated by seven days. These dates will serve to identify the sales figures.

In some cases, you can use the Excel AutoFill feature to insert a series of dates. Enter the first date and drag the cell's fill handle while holding the right mouse button. Release the mouse button and select an option from the shortcut menu (see Figure 6-3)—Fill Days, Fill Weekdays, Fill Months, or Fill Years. Notice that Excel does not provide a Fill Weeks option.

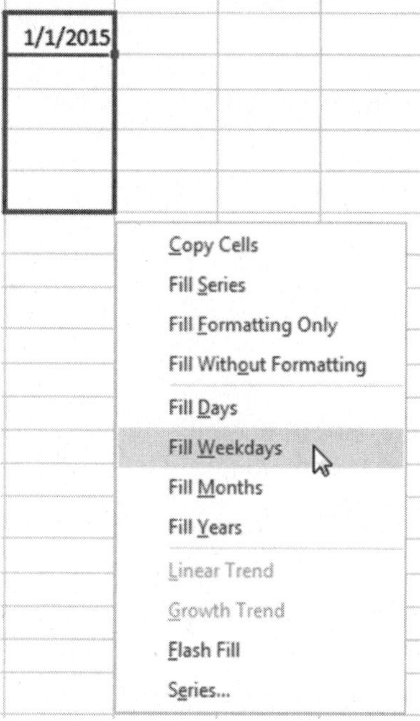

Figure 6-3: Using Excel's AutoFill feature to create a series of dates.

For more flexibility, enter the first *two* dates in the series—for example, the starting day for week 1 and the starting day for week 2. Then select both cells and drag the fill handle down the column. Excel will complete the date series, with each date separated by the interval represented by the first two dates.

The advantage of using formulas (rather than the AutoFill feature) to create a series of dates is that you can change the first date, and the others will then update automatically. You need to enter the starting date into a cell and then use formulas (copied down the column) to generate the additional dates.

The following examples assume that you entered the first date of the series into cell A1 and the formula into cell A2. You can then copy this formula down the column as many times as needed.

To generate a series of dates separated by seven days, use this formula:

```
=A1+7
```

To generate a series of dates separated by one month, you need a more complicated formula because months don't all have the same number of days. This formula creates a series of dates, separated by one month:

```
=DATE(YEAR(A1),MONTH(A1)+1,DAY(A1))
```

To generate a series of dates separated by one year, use this formula:

```
=DATE(YEAR(A1)+1,MONTH(A1),DAY(A1))
```

To generate a series of weekdays only (no Saturdays or Sundays), use the formula that follows. This formula assumes that the date in cell A1 is not a weekend day:

```
=IF(WEEKDAY(A1)=6,A1+3,A1+1)
```

Converting a nondate string to a date

You may import data that contains dates coded as text strings. For example, the following text represents August 21, 2013 (a four-digit year followed by a two-digit month, followed by a two-digit day):

```
20130821
```

To convert this string to an actual date, you can use a formula such as this one, which assumes the coded date is in cell A1:

```
=DATE(LEFT(A1,4),MID(A1,5,2),RIGHT(A1,2))
```

This formula uses text functions (LEFT, MID, and RIGHT) to extract the digits and then uses these extracted digits as arguments for the DATE function.

Cross-Ref

See Chapter 5, "Manipulating Text," for more information about using formulas to manipulate text.

Calculating the number of days between two dates

A common type of date calculation determines the number of days between two dates. For example, you may have a financial worksheet that calculates interest earned on a deposit account. The interest earned depends on how many days the account is open. If your sheet contains the open date and the close date for the account, you can calculate the number of days the account was open.

Because dates store as consecutive serial numbers, you can use simple subtraction to calculate the number of days between two dates. For example, if cells A1 and B1 both contain a date, the following formula returns the number of days between these dates:

```
=A1-B1
```

If cell B1 contains a more recent date than the date in cell A1, the result will be negative. If you don't care about which date is earlier and want to avoid displaying a negative value, use this formula:

```
=ABS(A1-B1)
```

Note

You can also use the DAYS worksheet function, introduced in Excel 2013. Here is an example of how to use it to calculate the number of days between two dates:

```
=DAYS(A1,B1)
```

Sometimes, calculating the difference between two days is more difficult. To demonstrate, consider the common "fence post" analogy. If somebody asks you how many units make up a fence, you can respond with either of two answers: the number of fence posts or the number of gaps between the fence posts. The number of fence posts is always one more than the number of gaps between the posts.

To bring this analogy into the realm of dates, suppose you start a sales promotion on February 1 and end the promotion on February 9. How many days was the promotion in effect? Subtracting February 1 from February 9 produces an answer of eight days. However, the promotion actually lasted nine days. In this case, the correct answer involves counting the fence posts, as it were, and not the gaps. The formula to calculate the length of the promotion (assuming you have appropriately named cells) appears like this:

```
=EndDay-StartDay+1
```

Calculating the number of work days between two dates

When calculating the difference between two dates, you may want to exclude weekends and holidays. For example, you may need to know how many business days fall in the month of November. This calculation should exclude Saturdays, Sundays, and holidays. Using the NETWORKDAYS function can help.

Note

The NETWORKDAYS function has a misleading name. This function has nothing to do with networks or networking. Rather, it calculates the net number of workdays between two dates.

The NETWORKDAYS function calculates the difference between two dates, excluding weekend days (Saturdays and Sundays). As an option, you can specify a range of cells that contain the dates of holidays, which are also excluded. Excel has absolutely no way of determining which days are holidays, so you must provide this information in a range.

Figure 6-4 shows a worksheet that calculates the workdays between two dates. The range A2:A11 contains a list of holiday dates. The formulas in column C calculate the workdays between the dates in column A and column B. For example, the formula in cell C15 is

```
=NETWORKDAYS(A15,B15,A2:A11)
```

	A	B	C	D
1	Date	Holiday		
2	1/1/15	New Year's Day		
3	1/19/15	Martin Luther King Day		
4	2/16/15	Presidents' Day		
5	5/25/15	Memorial Day		
6	7/4/15	Independence Day		
7	9/7/15	Labor Day		
8	10/12/15	Columbus Day		
9	11/11/15	Veterans Day		
10	11/26/15	Thanksgiving Day		
11	12/25/15	Christmas Day		
12				
13				
14	First Day	Last Day	Working Days	
15	Thursday 1/1/2015	Wednesday 1/7/2015	4	=NETWORKDAYS(A15,B15,$A$2:$A$11)
16	Thursday 1/1/2015	Thursday 12/31/2015	252	=NETWORKDAYS(A16,B16,$A$2:$A$11)

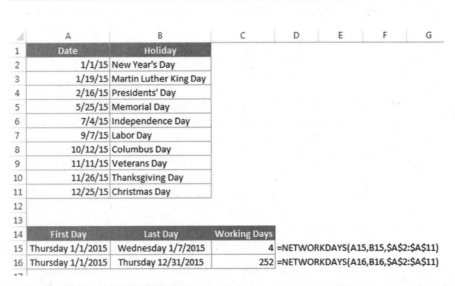

Figure 6-4: Using the NETWORKDAYS function to calculate the number of working days between two dates.

This formula returns *4*, which means that the seven-day period beginning with January 1 contains four workdays. In other words, the calculation excludes one holiday, one Saturday, and one Sunday. The formula in cell C16 calculates the total number of workdays in the year.

Note

Excel 2010 introduced an updated version of the NETWORKDAYS function, named NETWORKDAYS.INTL. This version is useful if you consider weekend days to be days other than Saturday and Sunday.

On the Web

This workbook, work days.xlsx, is available at this book's website.

Offsetting a date using only work days

The WORKDAY function is the opposite of the NETWORKDAYS function. For example, if you start a project on January 4, and the project requires 10 working days to complete, the WORKDAY function can calculate the date that you will finish the project.

The following formula uses the WORKDAY function to determine the date 10 working days from January 4, 2015. A *working day* is a weekday (Monday through Friday).

```
=WORKDAY("1/4/2015",10)
```

The formula returns a date serial number, which must be formatted as a date. The result is January 16, 2015. (Two weekend dates fall between January 4 and January 16.)

Warning

The preceding formula may return a different result, depending on your regional date setting. (The hard-coded date may be interpreted as April 1, 2015.) A better formula is

```
=WORKDAY(DATE(2015,1,4),10)
```

The second argument for the WORKDAY function can be negative. And, as with the NETWORKDAYS function, the WORKDAY function accepts an optional third argument (a reference to a range that contains a list of holiday dates).

Note

Excel 2010 introduced an updated version of the WORKDAY function, named WORKDAY .INTL. This version of the function is useful if you consider weekend days to be days other than Saturday and Sunday.

Calculating the number of years between two dates

The following formula calculates the number of years between two dates. This formula assumes that cells A1 and B1 both contain dates:

```
=YEAR(A1)-YEAR(B1)
```

This formula uses the YEAR function to extract the year from each date and then subtracts one year from the other. If cell B1 contains a more recent date than the date in cell A1, the result is negative.

Note that this function doesn't calculate *full* years. For example, if cell A1 contains 12/31/2014, and cell B1 contains 01/01/2015, the formula returns a difference of one year even though the dates differ by only one day.

You can also use the YEARFRAC function to calculate the number of years between two dates. This function returns the number of years, including partial years. For example:

```
=YEARFRAC(A1,B1,1)
```

Because the YEARFRAC function is often used for financial applications, it uses an optional third argument that represents the "basis" for the year (for example, a 360-day year). A third argument of 1 indicates an actual year.

Calculating a person's age

A person's age indicates the number of full years that the person has been alive. The formula in the previous section (for calculating the number of years between two dates) won't calculate this value correctly. You can use two other formulas, however, to calculate a person's age.

The following formula returns the age of the person whose date of birth you enter into cell A1. This formula uses the YEARFRAC function:

```
=INT(YEARFRAC(TODAY(),A1,1))
```

The following formula uses the DATEDIF function to calculate an age. (See the sidebar "Where's the DATEDIF function?")

```
=DATEDIF(A1,TODAY(),"y")
```

Where's the DATEDIF function?

In several places throughout this chapter, we refer to the DATEDIF function. You may notice that this function does not appear in the Insert Function dialog box, is not listed in the Date & Time drop-down list, and does not appear in the Formula AutoComplete list. Therefore, to use this function, you must always enter it manually.

The DATEDIF function has its origins in Lotus 1-2-3, and apparently Excel provides it for compatibility purposes. For some reason, Microsoft wants to keep this function a secret. You won't even find the DATEDIF function in the Help files, although it's available in all Excel versions. Strangely, DATEDIF made an appearance in the Excel 2000 Help files but hasn't been seen since.

DATEDIF is a handy function that calculates the number of days, months, or years between two dates. The function takes three arguments: start_date, end_date, and a code that represents the time unit of interest. Here's an example of a formula that uses the DATEDIF function. (It assumes cells A1 and A2 contain a date.) The formula returns the number of complete years between those two dates:

```
=DATEDIF(A1,A2,"y")
```

The following table displays valid codes for the third argument. You must enclose the codes in quotation marks.

Unit Code	Returns
"y"	The number of complete years in the period.
"m"	The number of complete months in the period.
"d"	The number of days in the period.
"md"	The difference between the days in start_date and end_date. The months and years of the dates are ignored.
"ym"	The difference between the months in start_date and end_date. The days and years of the dates are ignored.
"yd"	The difference between the days of start_date and end_date. The years of the dates are ignored.

The start_date argument must be earlier than the end_date argument, or the function returns an error.

Determining the day of the year

January 1 is the first day of the year, and December 31 is the last day. So, what about all those days in between? The following formula returns the day of the year for a date stored in cell A1:

```
=A1-DATE(YEAR(A1),1,0)
```

The day argument supplied is 0 (zero), calling for the "0th" day of the first month. The DATE function interprets this as the day before the first day, or December 31 of the previous year in this example. Similarly, negative numbers can be supplied for the day argument.

Here's a similar formula that returns the day of the year for the current date:

```
=TODAY()-DATE(YEAR(TODAY()),1,0)
```

The following formula returns the number of days remaining in the year from a particular date (assumed to be in cell A1):

```
=DATE(YEAR(A1),12,31)-A1
```

When you enter this formula, Excel applies date formatting to the cell. You need to apply a nondate number format to view the result as a number.

To convert a particular day of the year (for example, the 90th day of the year) to an actual date in a specified year, use the formula that follows. This formula assumes that the year is stored in cell A1 and that the day of the year is stored in cell B1:

```
=DATE(A1,1,B1)
```

Determining the day of the week

The WEEKDAY function accepts a date argument and returns an integer between 1 and 7 that corresponds to the day of the week. The following formula, for example, returns *3* because the first day of the year 2015 falls on a Thursday:

```
=WEEKDAY(DATE(2015,1,1))
```

The WEEKDAY function uses an optional second argument that specifies the day numbering system for the result. If you specify 2 as the second argument, the function returns *1* for Monday, *2* for Tuesday, and so on. If you specify 3 as the second argument, the function returns 0 for Monday, 1 for Tuesday, and so on.

Tip

You can also determine the day of the week for a cell that contains a date by applying a custom number format. A cell that uses the following custom number format displays the day of the week, spelled out:

```
dddd
```

Determining the week of the year

To determine the week of the year for a date, use the WEEKNUM function. The following formula returns the week number for the data in cell A1:

```
=WEEKNUM(A1)
```

When you use WEEKNUM function, you can specify a second optional argument to indicate the type of week numbering system you prefer. The second argument can be one of ten values, which are described in the Help system.

Note

Excel includes the ISOWEEKNUM function. This function returns the same result as WEEKNUM with a second argument of 21.

Determining the date of the most recent Sunday

You can use the following formula to return the date for the previous Sunday. If the current day is a Sunday, the formula returns the current date. (You will need to format the cell to display as a date.)

```
=TODAY()-MOD(TODAY()-1,7)
```

To modify this formula to find the date of a day other than Sunday, change the 1 to a different number between 2 (for Monday) and 7 (for Saturday).

Determining the first day of the week after a date

This next formula returns the specified day of the week that occurs after a particular date. For example, use this formula to determine the date of the first Monday after a particular date. The formula assumes that cell A1 contains a date and that cell A2 contains a number between 1 and 7 (1 for Sunday, 2 for Monday, and so on).

```
=A1+A2-WEEKDAY(A1)+(A2<WEEKDAY(A1))*7
```

If cell A1 contains June 1, 2014 (a Sunday) and cell A2 contains 2 (for Monday), the formula returns *June 2, 2014*. This is the first Monday following June 1, 2014.

Determining the *n*th occurrence of a day of the week in a month

You may need a formula to determine the date for a particular occurrence of a weekday. For example, suppose your company payday falls on the second Friday of each month, and you need to determine the paydays for each month of the year. The following formula makes this type of calculation:

```
=DATE(A1,A2,1)+A3-WEEKDAY(DATE(A1,A2,1))+(A4-(A3>=WEEKDAY(DATE(A1,A2,1))))*7
```

The formula in this section assumes the following:

- Cell A1 contains a year.
- Cell A2 contains a month.
- Cell A3 contains a day number (1 for Sunday, 2 for Monday, and so on).
- Cell A4 contains the occurrence number (for example, 2 to select the second occurrence of the weekday specified in cell A3).

If you use this formula to determine the date of the second Tuesday in November 2015, it returns *November 10, 2015*.

Note

If the value in cell A4 exceeds the number of the specified day in the month, the formula returns a date from a subsequent month. For example, if you attempt to determine the date of the fifth Friday in November 2015 (there is no such date), the formula returns the first Friday in December.

Counting the occurrences of a day of the week

You can use the following formula to count the number of occurrences of a particular day of the week for a specified month. It assumes that cell A1 contains a date and that cell B1 contains a day number (1 for Sunday, 2 for Monday, and so on). The formula is an array formula, so you must enter it by pressing Ctrl+Shift+Enter.

```
{=SUM((WEEKDAY(DATE(YEAR(A1),MONTH(A1),ROW(INDIRECT("1:"&DAY
(DATE(YEAR(A1),MONTH(A1)+1,0)))))=B1)*1)}
```

If cell A1 contains the date January 6, 2015 and cell B1 contains the value 3 (for Tuesday), the formula returns *4*, which reveals that January 2015 contains four Tuesdays.

The preceding array formula calculates the year and month by using the YEAR and MONTH functions. You can simplify the formula a bit if you store the year and month in separate cells. The following formula (also an array formula) assumes that the year appears in cell A1, the month in cell A2, and the day number in cell B1:

```
{=SUM((WEEKDAY(DATE(A1,A2,ROW(INDIRECT("1:"&DAY(DATE(A1,A2+1,0)))))=B1)*1)}
```

Cross-Ref

See Chapters 14, "Introducing Arrays," and 15, "Performing Magic with Array Formulas," for more information about array formulas.

Figure 6-5 shows this formula used in a worksheet. In this case, the formula uses mixed cell references so that you can copy it. For example, the formula in cell C3 is

```
{=SUM((WEEKDAY(DATE($B$2,$A3,ROW(INDIRECT("1:"&DAY(DATE($B$2,$A3+1,0)))))=C$1)*1)}
```

	A	B	C	D	E	F	G	H	I	J
1			1	2	3	4	5	6	7	
2	YEAR ->	2015	Sun	Mon	Tue	Wed	Thu	Fri	Sat	Month
3	1	January	4	4	4	4	5	5	5	31
4	2	February	4	4	4	4	4	4	4	28
5	3	March	5	5	5	4	4	4	4	31
6	4	April	4	4	4	5	5	4	4	30
7	5	May	5	4	4	4	4	5	5	31
8	6	June	4	5	5	4	4	4	4	30
9	7	July	4	4	4	5	5	5	4	31
10	8	August	5	5	4	4	4	4	5	31
11	9	September	4	4	5	5	4	4	4	30
12	10	October	4	4	4	4	5	5	5	31
13	11	November	5	5	4	4	4	4	4	30
14	12	December	4	4	5	5	5	4	4	31
15		Total Days:	52	52	52	52	53	52	52	365

Figure 6-5: Calculating the number of each weekday in each month of a year.

Additional formulas use the SUM function to calculate the number of days per month (column J) and the number of each weekday in the year (row 15).

On the Web

The workbook shown in Figure 6-5, day of the week count.xlsx, is available at this book's website.

Expressing a date as an ordinal number

You may want to express the day portion of a date as an ordinal number. For example, you can display 4/16/2015 as *April 16th, 2015.* The following formula expresses the date in cell A1 as an ordinal date:

```
=TEXT(A1,"mmmm ")&DAY(A1)&IF(INT(MOD(DAY(A1),100)/10)=1, "th",IF(MOD(DAY(A1),10)=1,
   "st",IF(MOD(DAY(A1),10)=2,"nd",IF(MOD(DAY(A1),10)=3, "rd","th"))))&TEXT(A1,", yyyy")
```

Warning

The result of this formula is text, not an actual date.

The following formula shows a variation that expresses the date in cell A1 in day-month-year format. For example, 4/16/2015 would appear as *16th April, 2015.* Again, the result of this formula represents text, not an actual date:

```
=DAY(A1)&IF(INT(MOD(DAY(A1),100)/10)=1, "th",IF(MOD(DAY(A1),10)=1, "st",
IF(MOD(DAY(A1),10)=2,"nd", IF(MOD(DAY(A1),10)=3, "rd","th"))))& " " &TEXT(A1,"mmmm,
  yyyy")
```

On the Web

This book's website contains the workbook ordinal dates.xlsx that demonstrates the formulas for expressing dates as ordinal numbers.

Calculating dates of holidays

Determining the date for a particular holiday can be tricky. Some, such as New Year's Day and U.S. Independence Day, are no-brainers because they always occur on the same date. For these kinds of holidays, you can simply use the DATE function, which we covered earlier in this chapter. To enter New Year's Day (which always falls on January 1) for a specific year in cell A1, you can enter this function:

```
=DATE(A1,1,1)
```

Other holidays are defined in terms of a particular occurrence on a particular weekday in a particular month. For example, Labor Day in the United States falls on the first Monday in September.

Figure 6-6 shows a workbook with formulas to calculate the date for 11 U.S. holidays. The formulas reference the year in cell A1. Notice that because New Year's Day, Independence Day, Veterans Day, and Christmas Day all fall on the same days each year, their dates can be calculated by using the simple DATE function.

2015 ← Enter the year

U.S. Holiday Calculations

Holiday	Description	Date	Weekday
New Year's Day	1st Day in January	January 1, 2015	Thursday
Martin Luther King Jr. Day	3rd Monday in January	January 19, 2015	Monday
Presidents' Day	3rd Monday in February	February 16, 2015	Monday
Memorial Day	Last Monday in May	May 25, 2015	Monday
Independence Day	4th Day of July	July 4, 2015	Saturday
Labor Day	1st Monday in September	September 7, 2015	Monday
Columbus Day	2nd Monday in October	October 12, 2015	Monday
Veterans Day	11th Day of November	November 11, 2015	Wednesday
Thanksgiving Day	4th Thursday in November	November 26, 2015	Thursday
Christmas Day	25th Day of December	December 25, 2015	Friday

Figure 6-6: Using formulas to determine the date for various holidays.

On the Web

The workbook shown in Figure 6-6, holidays.xlsx, is available at this book's website.

New Year's Day

This holiday always falls on January 1:

```
=DATE(A1,1,1)
```

Martin Luther King, Jr. Day

This holiday occurs on the third Monday in January. This formula calculates Martin Luther King, Jr., Day for the year in cell A1:

```
=DATE(A1,1,1)+IF(2<WEEKDAY(DATE(A1,1,1)),7-WEEKDAY
(DATE(A1,1,1))+2,2-WEEKDAY(DATE(A1,1,1)))+((3-1)*7)
```

Presidents' Day

Presidents' Day occurs on the third Monday in February. This formula calculates Presidents' Day for the year in cell A1:

```
=DATE(A1,2,1)+IF(2<WEEKDAY(DATE(A1,2,1)),7-WEEKDAY
(DATE(A1,2,1))+2,2-WEEKDAY(DATE(A1,2,1)))+((3-1)*7)
```

Easter

Calculating the date for Easter is difficult because of the complicated manner in which Easter is determined. Easter Day is the first Sunday after the next full moon occurs after the vernal equinox. These formulas were taken from the Internet and utilize a curious string of functions. We have found these formulas to be reliable, although they do not seem to work if your workbook uses the 1904 date system:

```
=DOLLAR(("4/"&A1)/7+MOD(19*MOD(A1,19)-7,30)*14%,)*7-6
```

This one is slightly shorter but equally obtuse:

```
=FLOOR("5/"&DAY(MINUTE(A1/38)/2+56)&"/"&A1,7)-34
```

Memorial Day

The last Monday in May is Memorial Day. This formula calculates Memorial Day for the year in cell A1:

```
=DATE(A1,6,1)+IF(2<WEEKDAY(DATE(A1,6,1)),7-WEEKDAY
(DATE(A1,6,1))+2,2-WEEKDAY(DATE(A1,6,1)))+((1-1)*7)-7
```

Notice that this formula actually calculates the first Monday in June and then subtracts 7 from the result to return the last Monday in May.

Independence Day

This holiday always falls on July 4:

```
=DATE(A1,7,4)
```

Labor Day

Labor Day occurs on the first Monday in September. This formula calculates Labor Day for the year in cell A1:

```
=DATE(A1,9,1)+IF(2<WEEKDAY(DATE(A1,9,1)),7-WEEKDAY
(DATE(A1,9,1))+2,2-WEEKDAY(DATE(A1,9,1)))+((1-1)*7)
```

Columbus Day

This holiday occurs on the second Monday in October. This formula calculates Columbus Day for the year in cell A1:

```
=DATE(A1,10,1)+IF(2<WEEKDAY(DATE(A1,10,1)),7-WEEKDAY
(DATE(A1,10,1))+2,2-WEEKDAY(DATE(A1,10,1)))+((2-1)*7)
```

Veterans Day

This holiday always falls on November 11:

```
=DATE(A1,11,11)
```

Thanksgiving Day

Thanksgiving Day is celebrated on the fourth Thursday in November. This formula calculates Thanksgiving Day for the year in cell A1:

```
=DATE(A1,11,1)+IF(5<WEEKDAY(DATE(A1,11,1)),7-WEEKDAY
(DATE(A1,11,1))+5,5-WEEKDAY(DATE(A1,11,1)))+((4-1)*7)
```

Christmas Day

This holiday always falls on December 25:

```
=DATE(A1,12,25)
```

Determining the last day of a month

To determine the date that corresponds to the last day of a month, you can use the DATE function. However, you need to increment the month by 1 and use a day value of 0 (zero). In other words, the 0th day of the next month is the last day of the current month.

The following formula assumes that a date is stored in cell A1. The formula returns the date that corresponds to the last day of the month:

```
=DATE(YEAR(A1),MONTH(A1)+1,0)
```

You can use a variation of this formula to determine how many days make up a specified month. The formula that follows returns an integer that corresponds to the number of days in the month for the date in cell A1.

```
=DAY(DATE(YEAR(A1),MONTH(A1)+1,0))
```

Determining whether a year is a leap year

To determine whether a particular year is a leap year, you can write a formula that determines whether the 29th day of February occurs in February or March. You can take advantage of the fact that Excel's DATE function adjusts the result when you supply an invalid argument—for example, a day of 29 when February contains only 28 days.

The following formula returns *TRUE* if the year in cell A1 is a leap year; otherwise, it returns *FALSE*:

```
=IF(MONTH(DATE(A1,2,29))=2,TRUE,FALSE)
```

Warning

This function returns the wrong result (*TRUE*) if the year is 1900. See the section "The Excel leap year bug," earlier in this chapter.

The following formula is a bit more complicated, but it correctly identifies 1900 as a nonleap year. This formula assumes that cell A1 contains a year:

```
=IF(OR(MOD(A1,400)=0,AND(MOD(A1,4)=0,MOD(A1,100)<>0)),TRUE, FALSE)
```

Determining a date's quarter

For financial reports, you might find it useful to present information in terms of quarters. The following formula returns an integer between 1 and 4 that corresponds to the calendar quarter for the date in cell A1:

```
=ROUNDUP(MONTH(A1)/3,0)
```

This formula divides the month number by 3 and then rounds up the result.

Converting a year to roman numerals

Fans of old movies will like this one. The following formula converts the year 1945 to the Roman numerals MCMXLV:

```
=ROMAN(1945)
```

This function returns a text string, so you can't perform calculations using the result.

Note

Use the ARABIC function to convert a Roman numeral to a value. Here's an example, which returns *1945*:

```
=ARABIC("MCMXLV")
```

Time-Related Functions

Excel includes a number of functions that enable you to work with time values in your formulas. This section contains examples that demonstrate the use of these functions.

Table 6-5 summarizes the time-related functions available in Excel. Like the date functions discussed earlier, time-related functions can be found under the Date & Time drop-down list via Formulas ➜ Function Library.

Table 6-5: Time-Related Functions

Function	Description
HOUR	Returns the hour of a time value
MINUTE	Returns the minute of a time value
NOW	Returns the current date and time
SECOND	Returns the second of a time
TIME	Returns a time for a specified hour, minute, and second
TIMEVALUE	Converts a time in the form of text to an actual time value

Displaying the current time

This formula displays the current time as a time serial number (or a serial number without an associated date):

```
=NOW()-TODAY()
```

You need to format the cell with a time format to view the result as a recognizable time. The quickest way is to choose Home ➜ Number ➜ Format Number and then select Time from the drop-down list.

You can also display the time, combined with text. The formula that follows displays this text: *The current time is 6:28 PM.*

```
="The current time is "&TEXT(NOW(),"h:mm AM/PM")
```

Note

These formulas are updated only when the worksheet is calculated. The time comes from your computer's clock, so if the clock is wrong, the formulas will return an incorrect time.

Tip

To enter a time stamp into a cell, press Ctrl+Shift+: (colon). Excel inserts the time as a *static value*. (It does not change.)

Displaying any time using a function

Earlier in this chapter, we described how to enter a time value into a cell: just type it into a cell, making sure that you include at least one colon (:). You can also create a time by using the TIME function. For example, the following formula returns a time comprising the hour in cell A1, the minute in cell B1, and the second in cell C1:

```
=TIME(A1,B1,C1)
```

Like the DATE function, the TIME function accepts invalid arguments and adjusts the result accordingly. For example, the following formula uses 80 as the minute argument and returns *10:20:15 AM*. The 80 minutes are simply added to the hour, with 20 minutes remaining:

```
=TIME(9,80,15)
```

Warning

If you enter a value greater than 24 as the first argument for the TIME function, the result may not be what you expect. Logically, a formula such as the one that follows should produce a date/time serial number of 1.041667 (that is, one day and one hour):

```
=TIME(25,0,0)
```

In fact, this formula is equivalent to the following:

```
=TIME(1,0,0)
```

You can also use the DATE function along with the TIME function in a single cell. The formula that follows generates a date and time with a serial number of 41612.7708333333—which represents 6:30 PM on December 4, 2013:

```
=DATE(2013,12,4)+TIME(18,30,0)
```

Note

When you enter the preceding formula, Excel formats the cell to display the date only. To see the time, you'll need to change the number format to one that displays a date and a time.

Tip

To enter the current date and time into a cell that doesn't change when the worksheet recalculates, press Ctrl+; (semicolon), space, Ctrl+Shift+: (colon), and then press Enter.

The TIMEVALUE function converts a text string that looks like a time into a time serial number. This formula returns *0.2395833333*, which is the time serial number for 5:45 AM:

```
=TIMEVALUE("5:45 am")
```

To view the result of this formula as a time, you need to apply number formatting to the cell. The TIMEVALUE function doesn't recognize all common time *formats*. For example, the following formula returns an error because Excel doesn't like the periods in *a.m.*

```
=TIMEVALUE("5:45 a.m.")
```

Calculating the difference between two times

Because times are represented as serial numbers, you can subtract the earlier time from the later time to get the difference. For example, if cell A2 contains 5:30:00 and cell B2 contains 14:00:00, the following formula returns 08:30:00 (a difference of eight hours and 30 minutes):

```
=B2-A2
```

If the subtraction results in a negative value, however, it becomes an invalid time; Excel displays a series of hash marks (#######) because a time without a date has a date serial number of 0. A negative time results in a negative serial number, which cannot be displayed—although you can still use the calculated value in other formulas.

If the direction of the time difference doesn't matter, you can use the ABS function to return the absolute value of the difference:

```
=ABS(B2-A2)
```

This "negative time" problem often occurs when calculating an elapsed time—for example, calculating the number of hours worked given a start time and an end time. This presents no problem if the two times fall in the same day. If the work shift spans midnight, though, the result is an invalid negative time. For example, you may start work at 10:00 PM and end work at 6:00 AM the next day. Figure 6-7 shows a worksheet that calculates the hours worked. As you can see, the shift that spans midnight presents a problem if you are simply subtracting the end time from the start time.

	A	B	C	D
1	Start Time	End Time	Hours Worked	
2	10:00 PM	6:00 AM	####################	=B2-A2
3				
4	Start Time	End Time	Hours Worked	
5	10:00 PM	6:00 AM	8:00:00	=IF(B5<A5,B5+1,B5)-A5
6				
7	Start Time	End Time	Hours Worked	
8	10:00 PM	6:00 AM	8:00:00	=MOD(B2-A2,1)

Figure 6-7: Calculating the number of hours worked returns an error if the shift spans midnight.

Using the ABS function (to calculate the absolute value) isn't an option in this case because it will also return a wrong answer.

The following formula, however, *does* work:

```
=IF(B2<A2,B2+1,B2)-A2
```

Another (even simpler) formula will also do the job:

```
=MOD(B2-A2,1)
```

Tip

Negative times *are* permitted if the workbook uses the 1904 date system. To switch to the 1904 date system, choose Office ➜ Excel Options and then navigate to the When Calculating This Workbook section of the Advanced tab. Place a check mark next to the Use 1904 Date System option. But beware! When changing the workbook's date system, if the workbook uses dates, the dates will be off by four years.

Summing times that exceed 24 hours

Many people are surprised to discover that when you sum a series of times that exceed 24 hours, Excel doesn't display the correct total. Figure 6-8 shows an example. The range C1:C11 contains times that represent the hours and minutes worked each day. The formula in cell C12 follows:

```
=SUM(C1:C11)
```

	A	B	C
1			04:23:33
2			03:10:28
3			02:31:06
4			02:10:32
5			02:20:17
6			07:57:30
7			04:17:06
8			01:52:12
9			01:28:22
10			01:12:18
11			01:08:30
12			8:31

Figure 6-8: Incorrect cell formatting makes the total appear incorrectly.

As you can see, the formula returns a seemingly incorrect total (8 hours, 31 minutes). The total should read 32 hours, 31 minutes. The problem is that the formula is displaying the total as a date/time serial number of 1.35549, but the cell formatting is not displaying the *date* part of the date/time. The answer is incorrect because cell C12 has the wrong number format.

To view a time that exceeds 24 hours, you need to change the number format for the cell so square brackets surround the *hour* part of the format string. Applying the number format here to cell C12 displays the sum correctly:

```
[h]:mm
```

Figure 6-9 shows another example of a worksheet that manipulates times. This worksheet keeps track of hours worked during a week (regular hours and overtime hours).

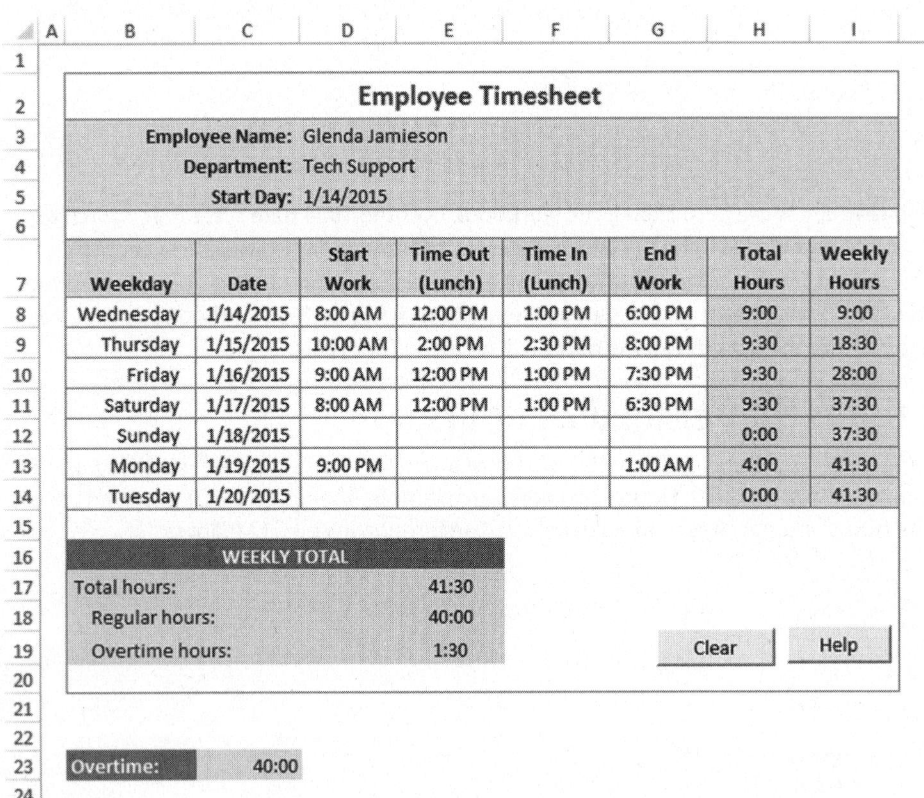

Employee Timesheet

Employee Name: Glenda Jamieson
Department: Tech Support
Start Day: 1/14/2015

Weekday	Date	Start Work	Time Out (Lunch)	Time In (Lunch)	End Work	Total Hours	Weekly Hours
Wednesday	1/14/2015	8:00 AM	12:00 PM	1:00 PM	6:00 PM	9:00	9:00
Thursday	1/15/2015	10:00 AM	2:00 PM	2:30 PM	8:00 PM	9:30	18:30
Friday	1/16/2015	9:00 AM	12:00 PM	1:00 PM	7:30 PM	9:30	28:00
Saturday	1/17/2015	8:00 AM	12:00 PM	1:00 PM	6:30 PM	9:30	37:30
Sunday	1/18/2015					0:00	37:30
Monday	1/19/2015	9:00 PM			1:00 AM	4:00	41:30
Tuesday	1/20/2015					0:00	41:30

WEEKLY TOTAL	
Total hours:	41:30
Regular hours:	40:00
Overtime hours:	1:30

Clear Help

Overtime: 40:00

Figure 6-9: An employee timesheet workbook.

The week's starting date appears in cell D5, and the formulas in column C fill in the dates for the days of the week. Times appear in the range D8:G14, and formulas in column H calculate the number of hours worked each day. For example, the formula in cell H8 is

```
=IF(E8<D8,E8+1-D8,E8-D8)+IF(G8<F8,G8+1-G8,G8-F8)
```

The first part of this formula subtracts the time in column D from the time in column E to get the total hours worked before lunch. The second part subtracts the time in column F from the time in column G to get the total hours worked after lunch. We use IF functions to accommodate graveyard shift cases that span midnight—for example, an employee may start work at 10:00 PM and begin lunch at 2:00 AM. Without the IF function, the formula returns a negative result.

The following formula in cell H17 calculates the weekly total by summing the daily totals in column H:

```
=SUM(H8:H14)
```

This worksheet assumes that hours that exceed 40 hours in a week are considered overtime hours. The worksheet contains a cell named *Overtime* (cell C23) that contains 40:00. If your standard workweek consists of something other than 40 hours, you can change the *Overtime* cell.

The following formula (in cell E18) calculates regular (nonovertime) hours. This formula returns the smaller of two values: the total hours, or the overtime hours:

```
=MIN(E17,Overtime)
```

The final formula, in cell E19, simply subtracts the regular hours from the total hours to yield the overtime hours:

```
=E17-E18
```

The times in H17:H19 may display time values that exceed 24 hours, so these cells use a custom number format:

```
[h]:mm
```

On the Web

The workbook shown in Figure 6-9, time sheet.xlsm, is available at this book's website.

Converting from military time

Military time is expressed as a four-digit number from 0000 to 2359. For example, 1:00 AM is expressed as 0100 hours, and 3:30 PM is expressed as 1530 hours. The following formula converts such a number (assumed to appear in cell A1) to a standard time:

```
=TIMEVALUE(LEFT(A1,2)&":"&RIGHT(A1,2))
```

The formula returns an incorrect result if the contents of cell A1 do not contain four digits. The following formula corrects the problem and returns a valid time for any military time value from 0 to 2359:

```
=TIMEVALUE(LEFT(TEXT(A1,"0000"),2)&":"&RIGHT(A1,2))
```

The following is a simpler formula that uses the TEXT function to return a formatted string and then uses the TIMEVALUE function to express the result in terms of a time:

```
=TIMEVALUE(TEXT(A1,"00\:00"))
```

Converting decimal hours, minutes, or seconds to a time

To convert decimal hours to a time, divide the decimal hours by 24. For example, if cell A1 contains 9.25 (representing hours), this formula returns *09:15:00* (9 hours, 15 minutes):

```
=A1/24
```

To convert decimal minutes to a time, divide the decimal minutes by 1,440 (the number of minutes in a day). For example, if cell A1 contains 500 (representing minutes), the following formula returns *08:20:00* (8 hours, 20 minutes):

```
=A1/1440
```

To convert decimal seconds to a time, divide the decimal seconds by 86,400 (the number of seconds in a day). For example, if cell A1 contains 65,000 (representing seconds), the following formula returns *18:03:20* (18 hours, 3 minutes, and 20 seconds):

```
=A1/86400
```

Adding hours, minutes, or seconds to a time

You can use the TIME function to add any number of hours, minutes, or seconds to a time. For example, assume that cell A1 contains a time. The following formula adds two hours and 30 minutes to that time and displays the result:

```
=A1+TIME(2,30,0)
```

You can use the TIME function to fill a range of cells with incremental times. Figure 6-10 shows a worksheet with a series of times in ten-minute increments. Cell A1 contains a time that was entered directly. Cell A2 contains the following formula, which was copied down the column:

```
=A1+TIME(0,10,0)
```

A2 =A1+TIME(0,10,0)

	A	B	C	D	E
1	8:00 AM				
2	8:10 AM				
3	8:20 AM				
4	8:30 AM				
5	8:40 AM				
6	8:50 AM				
7	9:00 AM				
8	9:10 AM				
9	9:20 AM				
10	9:30 AM				
11	9:40 AM				
12	9:50 AM				

Figure 6-10: Using a formula to create a series of incremental times.

You can also use the Excel AutoFill feature to fill a range with times. For example, to create a series of times with 10-minute increments, type 8:00 AM in cell A1 and 8:10 AM in cell A2. Select both cells and then drag the fill handle (in the lower-right corner of cell A2) down the column to create the series.

Converting between time zones

You may receive a worksheet that contains dates and times in Greenwich Mean Time (GMT, sometimes referred to as *Zulu time*), and you may need to convert these values to local time. To convert dates and times into local times, you need to determine the difference in hours between the two time zones. For example, to convert GMT times to U.S. Central Standard Time (CST), the hour conversion factor is –6.

You can't use the TIME function with a negative argument, so you need to take a different approach. One hour equals 1/24 of a day, so you can divide the time conversion factor by 24 and then add it to the time.

Figure 6-11 shows a worksheet set up to convert dates and times (expressed in GMT) to local times. Cell B1 contains the hour conversion factor (–5 hours for U.S. Eastern Standard Time; EST). The formula in B4, which copies down the column, is this:

```
=A4+($B$1/24)
```

	A	B	C
1	**Conversion Factor:**	**-5**	**hours**
2			
3	GMT	Local Time	
4	01/08/2015 01:00 AM	01/07/2015 08:00 PM	
5	01/08/2015 03:30 AM	01/07/2015 10:30 PM	
6	01/08/2015 06:00 AM	01/08/2015 01:00 AM	
7	01/08/2015 08:30 AM	01/08/2015 03:30 AM	
8	01/08/2015 11:00 AM	01/08/2015 06:00 AM	
9	01/08/2015 01:30 PM	01/08/2015 08:30 AM	
10	01/08/2015 04:00 PM	01/08/2015 11:00 AM	
11	01/08/2015 06:30 PM	01/08/2015 01:30 PM	
12	01/08/2015 09:00 PM	01/08/2015 04:00 PM	
13	01/08/2015 11:30 PM	01/08/2015 06:30 PM	
14	01/09/2015 02:00 AM	01/08/2015 09:00 PM	
15	01/09/2015 04:30 AM	01/08/2015 11:30 PM	
16	01/09/2015 07:00 AM	01/09/2015 02:00 AM	
17	01/09/2015 09:30 AM	01/09/2015 04:30 AM	
18	01/09/2015 12:00 PM	01/09/2015 07:00 AM	
19			

Figure 6-11: This worksheet converts dates and times between time zones.

On the Web

You can download the workbook shown in Figure 6-11, gmt conversion.xlsx, from this book's website.

This formula effectively adds *x* hours to the date and time in column A. If cell B1 contains a negative hour value, the value subtracts from the date and time in column A. Note that, in some cases, this also affects the date.

Rounding time values

You may need to create a formula that rounds a time to a particular value. For example, you may need to enter your company's time records rounded to the nearest 15 minutes. This section presents examples of various ways to round a time value.

The following formula rounds the time in cell A1 to the nearest minute:

```
=ROUND(A1*1440,0)/1440
```

The formula works by multiplying the time by 1440 (to get total minutes). This value is passed to the ROUND function, and the result is divided by 1440. For example, if cell A1 contains 11:52:34, the formula returns *11:53:00*.

The following formula resembles this example, except that it rounds the time in cell A1 to the nearest hour:

```
=ROUND(A1*24,0)/24
```

If cell A1 contains 5:21:31, the formula returns *5:00:00*.

The following formula rounds the time in cell A1 to the nearest 15 minutes (quarter of an hour):

```
=ROUND(A1*24/0.25,0)*(0.25/24)
```

In this formula, 0.25 represents the fractional hour. To round a time to the nearest 30 minutes, change 0.25 to 0.5, as in the following formula:

```
=ROUND(A1*24/0.5,0)*(0.5/24)
```

Calculating Durations

Sometimes, you may want to work with time values that don't represent an actual time of day. For example, you might want to create a list of the finish times for a race or record the time you spend jogging each day. Such times don't represent a time of day. Rather, a value represents the time for an event (in hours, minutes, and seconds). The time to complete a test, for instance, might be 35 minutes and 45 seconds. You can enter that value into a cell as follows:

```
00:35:45
```

Excel interprets such an entry as 12:35:45 AM, which works fine (just make sure that you format the cell so it appears as you like). When you enter such times that do not have an hour component, you must include at least one zero for the hour. If you omit a leading zero for a missing hour, Excel interprets your entry as 35 hours and 45 minutes.

Figure 6-12 shows an example of a worksheet set up to keep track of someone's jogging activity. Column A contains simple dates. Column B contains the distance, in miles. Column C contains the time it took to run the distance. Column D contains formulas to calculate the speed, in miles per hour. For example, the formula in cell D2 is this:

```
=B2/(C2*24)
```

	A	B	C	D	E	F	G
1	Date	Distance	Time	Speed (mph)	Pace (min/mile)	YTD Distance	Cumulative Time
2	1/1/2015	1.50	00:18:45	4.80	12.50	1.50	00:18:45
3	1/2/2015	1.50	00:17:40	5.09	11.78	3.00	00:36:25
4	1/3/2015	2.00	00:21:30	5.58	10.75	5.00	00:57:55
5	1/4/2015	1.50	00:15:20	5.87	10.22	6.50	01:13:15
6	1/5/2015	2.40	00:25:05	5.74	10.45	8.90	01:38:20
7	1/6/2015	3.00	00:31:06	5.79	10.37	11.90	02:09:26
8	1/7/2015	3.80	00:41:06	5.55	10.82	15.70	02:50:32
9	1/8/2015	5.00	01:09:00	4.35	13.80	20.70	03:59:32
10	1/9/2015	4.00	00:45:10	5.31	11.29	24.70	04:44:42
11	1/10/2015	3.00	00:29:06	6.19	9.70	27.70	05:13:48
12	1/11/2015	5.50	01:08:30	4.82	12.45	33.20	06:22:18
13							

Figure 6-12: This worksheet uses times not associated with a time of day.

Column E contains formulas to calculate the pace, in minutes per mile. For example, the formula in cell E2 is this:

```
=(C2*60*24)/B2
```

Columns F and G contain formulas that calculate the year-to-date distance (using column B) and the cumulative time (using column C). The cells in column G are formatted using the following number format (which permits time displays that exceed 24 hours):

```
[hh]:mm:ss
```

On the Web

You can access the workbook shown in Figure 6-12, jogging log.xlsx, at this book's website.

7

Counting and Summing Techniques

In This Chapter

- Counting and summing cells
- Counting and summing records in databases and pivot tables
- Basic counting formulas
- Advanced counting formulas
- Formulas for common summing tasks
- Conditional summing formulas using a single criterion
- Conditional summing formulas using multiple criteria
- Using VBA for counting and summing tasks

Many of the most frequently asked spreadsheet questions involve counting and summing values and other worksheet elements. It seems that people are always looking for formulas to count or sum various items in a worksheet. This chapter will answer the majority of such questions.

Counting and Summing Worksheet Cells

Generally, a *counting formula* returns the number of cells in a specified range that meet certain criteria. A *summing formula* returns the sum of the values of the cells in a range that meet certain criteria. The range that you want counted or summed may or may not consist of a worksheet database or a table.

Table 7-1 lists the worksheet functions that come into play when you are creating counting and summing formulas. If none of the functions in Table 7-1 can solve your problem, an array formula can likely come to the rescue.

Table 7-1: Excel Counting and Summing Functions

Function	Description
AGGREGATE	Can be used for counting and summing, with options to ignore hidden cells, error values, and nested SUBTOTAL or AGGREGATE functions.
COUNT	Returns the number of cells in a range that contain a numeric value.
COUNTA	Returns the number of nonblank cells in a range.
COUNTBLANK	Returns the number of blank cells in a range.
COUNTIF	Returns the number of cells in a range that meet a single specified criterion.
COUNTIFS*	Returns the number of cells in a range that meet one or more specified criteria.
DCOUNT	Counts the number of records in a worksheet database that meet specified criteria.
DCOUNTA	Counts the number of nonblank records in a worksheet database that meet specified criteria.
DEVSQ	Returns the sum of squares of deviations of data points from the sample mean; used primarily in statistical formulas.
DSUM	Returns the sum of a column of values in a worksheet database that meet specified criteria.
FREQUENCY	Calculates how often values occur within a range of values and returns a vertical array of numbers; used only in a multicell array formula.
SUBTOTAL	When used with a first argument of 2 or 3, returns a count of cells that make up a subtotal; when used with a first argument of 9, returns the sum of cells that make up a subtotal. Ignores other nested SUBTOTAL functions.
SUM	Returns the sum of its arguments.
SUMIF	Returns the sum of cells in a range that meet a specified criterion.
SUMIFS*	Returns the sum of the cells in a range that meet one or more specified criteria.
SUMPRODUCT	Multiplies corresponding cells in two or more ranges and returns the sum of those products.

** These functions were introduced in Excel 2007.*

Getting a quick count or sum

The Excel status bar can display useful information about the currently selected cells—no formulas required. Normally, the status bar displays the sum and count of the values in the selected range. You can, however, right-click the status bar to bring up a menu with other options. You can choose any or all the following: Average, Count, Numerical Count, Minimum, Maximum, and Sum.

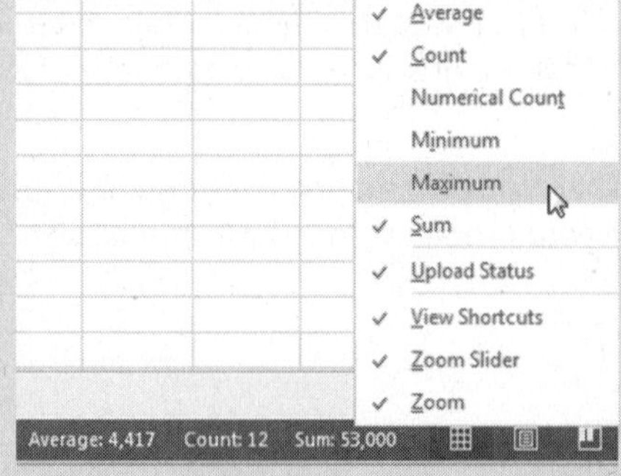

Other Counting Methods

As is often the case, Excel provides more than one way to accomplish a task. This chapter deals with standard formulas to count and sum cells.

Other parts of this book cover additional methods that are used for counting and summing:

- **Filtering:** If your data is in the form of a table, you can use AutoFilter to accomplish many counting and summing operations. Just set the AutoFilter criteria, and the table displays only the rows that match your criteria: The nonqualifying rows in the table are hidden. Then you can select formulas to display counts or sums in the table's total row. See Chapter 9, "Working with Tables and Lists," for more information on using tables.
- **Advanced filtering:** Special database functions provide additional ways to achieve counting and summing. Excel's DCOUNT and DSUM functions are database functions. They work in conjunction with a worksheet database and require a special criterion range that holds the counting or summing criteria. See Chapter 9 for more information.
- **Pivot tables:** Creating a pivot table is a quick way to get a count or sum of items without using formulas. Using a pivot table is appropriate when your data is in the form of a worksheet database or table. See Chapter 18, "Pivot Tables," for information about pivot tables.

Basic Counting Formulas

The basic counting formulas presented here are all straightforward and relatively simple. They demonstrate how to count the number of cells in a range that meet specific criteria. Figure 7-1 shows a worksheet that uses formulas (in column E) to summarize the contents of range A1:B10—a 20-cell range named *Data*.

	A	B	C	D	E	F
1	Jan	Feb		Total cells:	20	=ROWS(data)*COLUMNS(data)
2	525	718		Blank cells:	6	=COUNTBLANK(data)
3				Nonblank cells:	14	=COUNTA(data)
4	3			Numeric values:	7	=COUNT(data)
5	552	911		Non-text cells:	17	{=SUM(IF(ISNONTEXT(data),1))}
6	250	98		Text cells:	3	{=SUM(IF(ISTEXT(data),1))}
7				Logical values:	2	{=SUM(IF(ISLOGICAL(data),1))}
8	TRUE	FALSE		Error values:	2	{=SUM(IF(ISERROR(data),1))}
9		#DIV/0!		#N/A errors:	0	=COUNTIF(data,"#N/A")
10	Total	#NAME?		#NULL! errors:	0	=COUNTIF(data,"#NULL!")
11				#DIV/0! errors:	1	=COUNTIF(data,"#DIV/0!")
12				#VALUE! errors:	0	=COUNTIF(data,"#VALUE!")
13				#REF! errors:	0	=COUNTIF(data,"#REF!")
14				#NAME? errors:	1	=COUNTIF(data,"#NAME?")
15				#NUM! errors:	0	=COUNTIF(data,"#NUM!")

Figure 7-1: Formulas provide various counts of the data in A1:B10.

On the Web

You can access the basic counting.xlsx workbook shown in Figure 7-1 at this book's website.

About this chapter's examples

Most of the examples in this chapter use named ranges for function arguments. When you adapt these formulas for your own use, you'll need to substitute either the actual range address or a range name defined in your workbook.

Also, some examples are array formulas. An *array formula,* as explained in Chapter 14, "Introducing Arrays," is a special type of formula. You can spot an array formula because it is enclosed in brackets when it is displayed in the Formula bar. For example:

```
{=Data*2}
```

When you enter an array formula, press Ctrl+Shift+Enter (not just Enter). You don't need to type the brackets—Excel inserts the brackets for you. And if you need to edit an array formula, don't forget to press Ctrl+Shift+Enter after you finish editing. Otherwise, the array formula will revert to a normal formula, and it will return an incorrect result.

Counting the total number of cells

To get a count of the total number of cells in a range, use the following formula. This formula returns the number of cells in a range named *Data.* It simply multiplies the number of rows (returned by the ROWS function) by the number of columns (returned by the COLUMNS function).

```
=ROWS(Data)*COLUMNS(Data)
```

Counting blank cells

The following formula returns the number of blank (empty) cells in a range named *Data:*

```
=COUNTBLANK(Data)
```

This function works only with a contiguous range of cells. If *Data* is defined as a noncontiguous range, the function returns a *#VALUE!* error.

The COUNTBLANK function also counts cells containing a formula that returns an empty string. For example, the formula that follows returns an empty string if the value in cell A1 is greater than 5. If the cell meets this condition, the COUNTBLANK function counts that cell:

```
=IF(A1>5,"",A1)
```

Note

The COUNTBLANK function does not count cells that contain a zero value, even if you clear the Show a Zero in Cells That Have Zero Value option in the Excel Options dialog box. (Choose File ➜ Options and navigate to the Display Options for This Worksheet section of the Advanced tab.)

You can use the COUNTBLANK function with an argument that consists of entire rows or columns. For example, this next formula returns the number of blank cells in column A:

```
=COUNTBLANK(A:A)
```

The following formula returns the number of empty cells on the entire worksheet named Sheet1. You must enter this formula on a sheet other than Sheet1, or it will create a circular reference.

```
=COUNTBLANK(Sheet1!1:1048576)
```

Counting nonblank cells

The following formula uses the COUNTA function to return the number of nonblank cells in a range named *Data:*

```
=COUNTA(Data)
```

The COUNTA function counts cells that contain values, text, or logical values (*TRUE* or *FALSE*).

Note

If a cell contains a formula that returns an empty string, that cell is included in the count returned by COUNTA even though the cell appears to be blank.

Counting numeric cells

To count only the numeric cells in a range, use the following formula, which assumes that the range is named *Data:*

```
=COUNT(Data)
```

Cells that contain a date or a time are considered to be numeric cells. Cells that contain a logical value (*TRUE* or *FALSE*) are not considered to be numeric cells.

Counting text cells

To count the number of text cells in a range, you need to use an array formula. The array formula that follows returns the number of text cells in a range named *Data*:

```
{=SUM(IF(ISTEXT(Data),1))}
```

Counting nontext cells

The following array formula uses Excel's ISNONTEXT function, which returns *TRUE* if its argument refers to any nontext cell (including a blank cell). This formula returns the count of the number of cells not containing text (including blank cells):

```
{=SUM(IF(ISNONTEXT(Data),1))}
```

Counting logical values

The following array formula returns the number of logical values (*TRUE* or *FALSE*) in a range named *Data:*

```
{=SUM(IF(ISLOGICAL(Data),1))}
```

Counting error values in a range

Excel has three functions that help you determine whether a cell contains an error value:

- **ISERROR:** Returns *TRUE* if the cell contains any error value (#N/A, #VALUE!, #REF!, #DIV/0!, #NUM!, #NAME?, or #NULL!)
- **ISERR:** Returns *TRUE* if the cell contains any error value except #N/A
- **ISNA:** Returns *TRUE* if the cell contains the #N/A error value

Note

Notice that the #N/A error value is treated separately. In most cases, #N/A is not a "real" error. #N/A is often used as a placeholder for missing data. You can enter the #N/A error value directly or use the NA function:

```
=NA()
```

You can use these functions in an array formula to count the number of error values in a range. The following array formula, for example, returns the total number of error values in a range named *Data*:

```
{=SUM(IF(ISERROR(Data),1))}
```

Depending on your needs, you can use the ISERR or ISNA function in place of ISERROR.

If you need to count specific types of errors, you can use the COUNTIF function. The following formula, for example, returns the number of #DIV/0! error values in the range named *Data*:

```
=COUNTIF(Data,"#DIV/0!")
```

Note that the COUNTIF function works only with a contiguous range argument. If *Data* is defined a noncontiguous range, the formula returns a *#VALUE!* error.

Advanced Counting Formulas

Most of the basic examples we presented previously use functions or formulas that perform conditional counting. The advanced counting formulas that we present here represent more complex examples for counting worksheet cells based on various types of selection criteria.

Counting cells with the COUNTIF function

Excel's COUNTIF function is useful for single-criterion counting formulas. The COUNTIF function takes two arguments:

- **range:** The range that contains the values that determine whether to include a particular cell in the count
- **criteria:** The logical criteria that determine whether to include a particular cell in the count

Table 7-2 contains several examples of formulas that use the COUNTIF function. All these formulas work with a range named *Data*. As you can see, the *criteria* argument is quite flexible. You can use constants, expressions, functions, cell references, and even wildcard characters (* and ?).

Table 7-2: Examples of Formulas Using the COUNTIF Function

Function	Description
=COUNTIF(Data,12)	Returns the number of cells containing the value 12
=COUNTIF(Data,"<0")	Returns the number of cells containing a negative value
=COUNTIF(Data,"<>0")	Returns the number of cells not equal to 0
=COUNTIF(Data,">5")	Returns the number of cells greater than 5
=COUNTIF(Data,A1)	Returns the number of cells equal to the contents of cell A1
=COUNTIF(Data,">"&A1)	Returns the number of cells greater than the value in cell A1

continued

Table 7-2: Examples of Formulas Using the COUNTIF Function *(continued)*

Function	Description
=COUNTIF(Data,"*")	Returns the number of cells containing text
=COUNTIF(Data,"???")	Returns the number of text cells containing exactly three characters
=COUNTIF(Data,"budget")	Returns the number of cells containing the single word *budget* and nothing else (not case sensitive)
=COUNTIF(Data,"*budget*")	Returns the number of cells containing the text *budget* anywhere within the text (not case sensitive)
=COUNTIF(Data,"A*")	Returns the number of cells containing text that begins with the letter A (not case sensitive)
=COUNTIF(Data,TODAY())	Returns the number of cells containing only the current date
=COUNTIF(Data,">"&AVERAGE(Data))	Returns the number of cells with a value greater than the average
=COUNTIF(Data,">"&AVERAGE(Data)+ STDEV(Data)*3)	Returns the number of values exceeding three standard deviations above the mean
=COUNTIF(Data,3)+COUNTIF(Data,-3)	Returns the number of cells containing the value 3 or –3
=COUNTIF(Data,TRUE)	Returns the number of cells containing or returning logical *TRUE*
=COUNTIF(Data,TRUE)+COUNTIF (Data,FALSE)	Returns the number of cells containing or returning a logical value (*TRUE* or *FALSE*)
=COUNTIF(Data,"#N/A")	Returns the number of cells containing the #N/A error value

Counting cells that meet multiple criteria

In many cases, your counting formula will need to count cells only if two or more criteria are met. These criteria can be based on the cells that are being counted or based on a range of corresponding cells.

Figure 7-2 shows a simple worksheet that we use for the examples in this section. This sheet shows sales figures (Amount) categorized by Month, SalesRep, and Type. The worksheet contains named ranges that correspond to the labels in row 1.

On the Web

The workbook multiple criteria counting.xlsx is available at this book's website.

Note

Several of the examples in this section use the COUNTIFS function, which was introduced in Excel 2007. We also present alternative versions of the formulas, which you should use if you plan to share your workbook with others who use a version prior to Excel 2007.

	A	B	C	D	E	F	G	H	I
1	Month	SalesRep	Type	Amount		COUNTIFS (Excel 2007+)	Array Formula	Alternate Formula	Description
2	January	Albert	New	85		4	4	4	Amount >100 and <=200
3	January	Albert	New	675		2	2	2	January sales for Brooks >1000
4	January	Brooks	New	130			17	17	January and February sales
5	January	Cook	New	1350			16		January OR Brooks OR Amount > 1000
6	January	Cook	Existing	685			6		January sales for Brook or Cook
7	January	Brooks	New	1350					
8	January	Cook	New	475					
9	January	Brooks	New	1205					
10	February	Brooks	Existing	450					
11	February	Albert	New	495					
12	February	Cook	New	210					
13	February	Cook	Existing	1050					
14	February	Albert	New	140					
15	February	Brooks	New	900					
16	February	Brooks	New	900					
17	February	Cook	New	95					
18	February	Cook	New	780					
19	March	Brooks	New	900					
20	March	Albert	Existing	875					
21	March	Brooks	New	50					
22	March	Brooks	New	875					
23	March	Cook	Existing	225					
24	March	Cook	New	175					
25	March	Brooks	Existing	400					
26	March	Albert	New	840					
27	March	Cook	New	132					

Figure 7-2: This worksheet demonstrates various counting techniques that use multiple criteria.

Using And criteria

An And criterion counts cells if all specified conditions are met. A common example is a formula that counts the number of values that fall within a numerical range. For example, you may want to count cells that contain a value greater than 100 *and* less than or equal to 200. For this example, the COUNTIFS function will do the job:

```
=COUNTIFS(Amount,">100",Amount,"<=200")
```

The COUNTIFS function accepts any number of paired arguments. The first member of the pair is the range to be counted (in this case, the range named *Amount*); the second member of the pair is the criterion. The preceding example contains two sets of paired arguments and returns the number of cells in which *Amount* is greater than 100 and less than or equal to 200.

Prior to Excel 2007, you would need to use a formula like this:

```
=COUNTIF(Amount,">100")-COUNTIF(Amount,">200")
```

The preceding formula counts the number of values that are greater than 100 and then subtracts the number of values that are greater than 200. The result is the number of cells that contain a value greater than 100 and less than or equal to 200.

Creating this type of formula can be confusing because the formula refers to a condition ">200" even though the goal is to count values that are less than or equal to 200. An alternate technique is to use an array formula, such as the one that follows. You may find creating this type of formula easier:

```
{=SUM((Amount>100)*(Amount<=200))}
```

Note

When you enter an array formula, remember to use Ctrl+Shift+Enter—and don't type the curly brackets.

Sometimes, the counting criteria will be based on cells other than ones being counted. You may, for example, want to count the number of sales that meet the following criteria:

- *Month* is January, *and*
- SalesRep is Brooks, *and*
- *Amount* is greater than 1,000

The following formula returns the number of items that meet all three criteria. Note that the COUNTIFS function uses three sets of pairs of arguments:

```
=COUNTIFS(Month,"January",SalesRep,"Brooks",Amount,">1000")
```

An alternative formula, which works with versions prior to Excel 2007, uses the SUMPRODUCT function. The following formula returns the same result as the previous formula:

```
=SUMPRODUCT((Month="January")*(SalesRep="Brooks")*(Amount>1000))
```

Yet another way to perform this count is to use an array formula:

```
{=SUM((Month="January")*(SalesRep="Brooks")*(Amount>1000))}
```

Using Or criteria

To count cells by using an Or criterion, you can sometimes use multiple COUNTIF functions. The following formula, for example, counts the number of sales made in January or February:

```
=COUNTIF(Month,"January")+COUNTIF(Month,"February")
```

You can also use the COUNTIF function in an array formula. The following array formula, for example, returns the same result as the previous formula:

```
{=SUM(COUNTIF(Month,{"January","February"}))}
```

But if you base your Or criteria on cells other than the ones being counted, the COUNTIF function won't work. Referring to Figure 7-2, suppose that you want to count the number of sales that meet at least one of the following criteria:

- *Month* is January, *or*
- *SalesRep* is Brooks, *or*
- *Amount* is greater than 1,000

If you attempt to create a formula that uses COUNTIF, some double counting will occur. The solution is to use an array formula like this:

```
{=SUM(IF((Month="January")+(SalesRep="Brooks")+(Amount>1000),1))}
```

Combining And and Or criteria

In some cases, you may need to combine And and Or criteria when counting. For example, perhaps you want to count sales that meet both of the following criteria:

- *Month* is January, *and*
- *SalesRep* is Brooks, *or SalesRep* is Cook

You can add two COUNTIFS functions to get the desired result:

```
=COUNTIFS(Month,"January",SalesRep,"Brooks")+
COUNTIFS(Month,"January",SalesRep,"Cook")
```

Because you have to repeat the And portion of the criteria in each function's arguments, using COUNTIFS can produce long formulas with more criteria. When you have a lot of criteria, it makes sense to use an array formula, like this one that produces the same result:

```
{=SUM((Month="January")*((SalesRep="Brooks")+(SalesRep="Cook")))}
```

Counting the most frequently occurring entry

Excel's MODE function returns the most frequently occurring value in a range. Figure 7-3 shows a worksheet with values in range A1:A9 (named *Data*). The formula that follows returns *10* because that value appears most frequently in the *Data* range:

```
=MODE(Data)
```

The formula returns an #N/A error if the *Data* range contains no duplicated values.

To count the number of times the most frequently occurring value appears in the range—in other words, the frequency of the mode—use the following formula:

```
=COUNTIF(Data,MODE(Data))
```

This formula returns *3* because the modal value (10) appears three times in the *Data* range.

	A	B
1	4	
2	10	
3	12	
4	10	
5	44	
6	31	
7	10	
8	11	
9	5	
10	10	=MODE(Data)

Figure 7-3: The MODE function returns the most frequently occurring value in a range.

The MODE function works only for numeric values, and it ignores cells that contain text. To find the most frequently occurring text entry in a range, you need to use an array formula.

To count the number of times the most frequently occurring item (text or values) appears in a range named *Data,* use the following array formula:

```
{=MAX(COUNTIF(Data,Data))}
```

This next array formula operates like the MODE function except that it works with both text and values:

```
{=INDEX(Data,MATCH(MAX(COUNTIF(Data,Data)),COUNTIF(Data,Data),0))}
```

Warning

If there is a tie for the most frequent value, the preceding formula returns only the first in the list.

Counting the occurrences of specific text

The examples in this section demonstrate various ways to count the occurrences of a character or text string in a range of cells. Figure 7-4 shows a worksheet that demonstrates these examples. Various text appears in the range A1:A10 (named *Data*); cell B1 is named *Text.*

	A	B	C	D	E
1	aa	Alpha		2	Entire cell (not case-sensitive)
2	Alpha			1	Entire cell (case-sensitive)
3	AAA				
4	aaa			3	Part of cell (not case-sensitive)
5	Beta			2	Part of cell (case-sensitive)
6	B				
7	BBB			3	Total occurrences in range (not case-sensitive)
8	Alpha Beta			2	Total occurrences in range (case-sensitive)
9	AB				
10	alpha				
11					

Figure 7-4: This worksheet demonstrates various ways to count characters in a range.

On the Web

This book's website contains a workbook named counting text in a range.xlsx that demonstrates the formulas in this section.

Entire cell contents

To count the number of cells containing the contents of the *Text* cell (and nothing else), you can use the COUNTIF function. The following formula demonstrates:

```
=COUNTIF(Data,Text)
```

For example, if the *Text* cell contains the string *Alpha*, the formula returns *2* because two cells in the Data range contain this text. This formula is not case sensitive, so it counts both *Alpha* (cell A2) and *alpha* (cell A10). Note, however, that it does not count the cell that contains *Alpha Beta* (cell A8).

The following array formula is similar to the preceding formula, but this one is case sensitive:

```
{=SUM(IF(EXACT(Data,Text),1))}
```

Partial cell contents

To count the number of cells that contain a string that includes the contents of the *Text* cell, use this formula:

```
=COUNTIF(Data,"*"&Text&"*")
```

For example, if the *Text* cell contains the text *Alpha*, the formula returns *3* because three cells in the *Data* range contain the text *alpha* (cells A2, A8, and A10). Note that the comparison is not case sensitive.

An alternative is a longer array formula that uses the SEARCH function:

```
{=SUM(IF(NOT(ISERROR(SEARCH(text,data))),1))}
```

The SEARCH function returns an error if *Text* is not found in *Data*. The preceding formula counts one for every cell where SEARCH does not find an error. Because SEARCH is not case sensitive, neither is this formula.

If you need a case-sensitive count, you can use the following array formula:

```
{=SUM(IF(LEN(Data)-LEN(SUBSTITUTE(Data,Text,""))>0,1))}
```

If the *Text* cell contains the text *Alpha*, the preceding formula returns *2* because the string appears in two cells (A2 and A8).

Like the SEARCH function, the FIND function returns an error if *Text* is not found in *Data*, as in this alternative array formula:

```
{=SUM(IF(NOT(ISERROR(FIND(text,data))),1))}
```

Unlike SEARCH, the FIND function is case sensitive.

Total occurrences in a range

To count the total number of occurrences of a string within a range of cells, use the following array formula:

```
{=(SUM(LEN(Data))-SUM(LEN(SUBSTITUTE(Data,Text,""))))/LEN(Text)}
```

If the *Text* cell contains the character *B*, the formula returns *7* because the range contains seven instances of the string. This formula is case sensitive.

The following array formula is a modified version that is not case sensitive:

```
{=(SUM(LEN(Data))-SUM(LEN(SUBSTITUTE(UPPER(Data),UPPER(Text),""))))/
  LEN(Text)}
```

Counting the number of unique values

The following array formula returns the number of unique values in a range named *Data*:

```
{=SUM(1/COUNTIF(Data,Data))}
```

To understand how this formula works, you need a basic understanding of array formulas. (See Chapter 14 for an introduction to this topic.) In Figure 7-5, range A1:A12 is named *Data*. Range C1:C12 contains the following multicell array formula. A single formula was entered into all 12 cells in the range:

```
{=COUNTIF(Data,Data)}
```

	A	B	C	D	E	F	G	H
1	125		3	0.333333				
2	125		3	0.333333				
3	125		3	0.333333				
4	200		2	0.5				
5	200		2	0.5				
6	350		1	1				
7	400		2	0.5				
8	400		2	0.5				
9	550		4	0.25				
10	550		4	0.25				
11	550		4	0.25				
12	550		4	0.25				
13				5	<-- Unique items in Column A			
14								
15				5	<-- Single formula			
16				5	<-- Array formula, handles blank cells			

Figure 7-5: Using an array formula to count the number of unique values in a range.

On the Web

You can access the workbook count unique.xlsx shown in Figure 7-5 at this book's website.

The array in range C1:C12 consists of the count of each value in *Data*. For example, the number 125 appears three times, so each array element that corresponds to a value of 125 in the *Data* range has a value of 3.

Range D1:D12 contains the following array formula:

```
{=1/C1:C12}
```

This array consists of each value in the array in range C1:C12, divided into 1. For example, each cell in the original *Data* range that contains a 200 has a value of 0.5 in the corresponding cell in D1:D12.

Summing the range D1:D12 gives the number of unique items in *Data*. The array formula presented at the beginning of this section essentially creates the array that occupies D1:D12 and sums the values.

This formula has a serious limitation: if the range contains any blank cells, it returns an error. The following array formula solves this problem:

```
{=SUM(IF(COUNTIF(Data,Data)=0,"",1/COUNTIF(Data,Data)))}
```

Cross-Ref

To create an array formula that returns a list of unique items in a range, see Chapter 15, "Performing Magic with Array Formulas."

Creating a frequency distribution

A *frequency distribution* basically comprises a summary table that shows the frequency of each value in a range. For example, an instructor may create a frequency distribution of test scores. The table would show the count of As, Bs, Cs, and so on. Excel provides a number of ways to create frequency distributions. You can

- Use the FREQUENCY function.
- Create your own formulas.
- Use the Analysis ToolPak add-in.
- Use a pivot table.

On the Web

The frequency distribution.xlsx workbook that demonstrates these four techniques is available at this book's website.

The FREQUENCY function

The first method that we discuss uses the FREQUENCY function. This function always returns an array, so you must use it in an array formula entered into a multicell range.

Figure 7-6 shows some data in range A1:E25 (named *Data*). These values range from 1 to 500. The range G2:G11 contains the bins used for the frequency distribution. Each cell in this bin range contains the upper limit for the bin. In this case, the bins consist of <=50, 51–100, 101–150, and so on. See the sidebar, "Creating bins for a frequency distribution," to discover an easy way to create a bin range.

To create the frequency distribution, select a range of cells that corresponds to the number of cells in the bin range. Then enter the following array formula in H2:H11:

```
{=FREQUENCY(Data,G2:G11)}
```

The array formula enters the count of values in the *Data* range that fall into each bin. To create a frequency distribution that consists of percentages, use the following array formula:

```
{=FREQUENCY(Data,G2:G11)/COUNT(Data)}
```

Figure 7-7 shows two frequency distributions—one in terms of counts, and one in terms of percentages. The figure also shows a chart (histogram) created from the frequency distribution.

	A	B	C	D	E	F	G	H
1	55	316	223	185	124		Bins	Count
2	124	93	163	213	314		50	12
3	211	41	231	241	212		100	11
4	118	113	400	205	254		150	19
5	262	1	201	12	101		200	19
6	167	479	205	337	118		250	21
7	489	15	89	362	148		300	10
8	179	248	125	197	177		350	15
9	456	153	269	49	127		400	8
10	289	500	198	317	300		450	4
11	126	114	303	314	270		500	6
12	151	279	347	314	170			
13	250	175	93	209	61			
14	166	113	356	124	242			
15	152	384	157	233	99			
16	277	195	436	6	240			
17	147	80	173	211	244			
18	386	93	330	400	141			
19	332	173	129	323	188			
20	338	263	444	84	220			
21	221	402	498	98	2			
22	201	400	3	190	105			
23	35	225	12	265	329			
24	43	302	125	301	444			
25	56	9	135	500	398			

Figure 7-6: Creating a frequency distribution for the data in A1:E25.

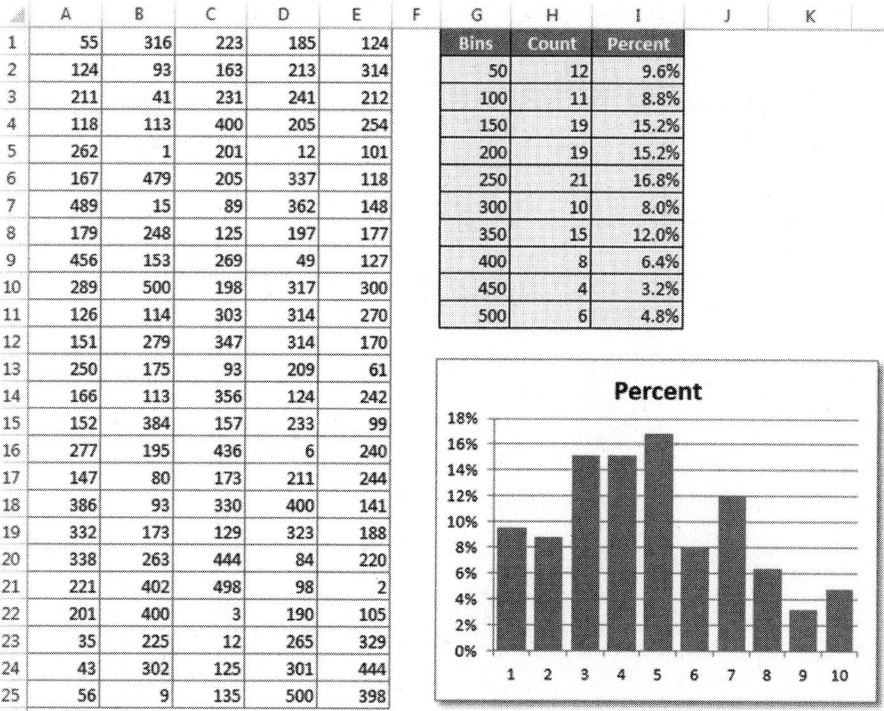

	A	B	C	D	E	F	G	H	I	J	K
1	55	316	223	185	124		Bins	Count	Percent		
2	124	93	163	213	314		50	12	9.6%		
3	211	41	231	241	212		100	11	8.8%		
4	118	113	400	205	254		150	19	15.2%		
5	262	1	201	12	101		200	19	15.2%		
6	167	479	205	337	118		250	21	16.8%		
7	489	15	89	362	148		300	10	8.0%		
8	179	248	125	197	177		350	15	12.0%		
9	456	153	269	49	127		400	8	6.4%		
10	289	500	198	317	300		450	4	3.2%		
11	126	114	303	314	270		500	6	4.8%		
12	151	279	347	314	170						
13	250	175	93	209	61						
14	166	113	356	124	242						
15	152	384	157	233	99						
16	277	195	436	6	240						
17	147	80	173	211	244						
18	386	93	330	400	141						
19	332	173	129	323	188						
20	338	263	444	84	220						
21	221	402	498	98	2						
22	201	400	3	190	105						
23	35	225	12	265	329						
24	43	302	125	301	444						
25	56	9	135	500	398						

Figure 7-7: Frequency distributions created using the FREQUENCY function.

Creating bins for a frequency distribution

When creating a frequency distribution, you must first enter the values into the bin range. The number of bins determines the number of categories in the distribution. Most of the time, each of these bins will represent an equal range of values.

To create 10 evenly spaced bins for values in a range named *Data,* enter the following array formula into a range of 10 cells in a column:

```
{=MIN(Data)+(ROW(INDIRECT("1:10"))*(MAX(Data)-MIN(Data)+1)/10)-1}
```

This formula creates 10 bins, based on the values in the *Data* range. The upper bin will always equal the maximum value in the range.

To create more or fewer bins, use a value other than 10 and enter the array formula into a range that contains the same number of cells. For example, to create 5 bins, enter the following array formula into a 5-cell vertical range:

```
{=MIN(Data)+(ROW(INDIRECT("1:5"))*(MAX(Data)-MIN(Data)+1)/5)-1}
```

Using formulas to create a frequency distribution

Figure 7-8 shows a worksheet that contains test scores for 50 students in column B. (The range is named *Grades.*) Formulas in columns G and H calculate a frequency distribution for letter grades. The minimum and maximum values for each letter grade appear in columns D and E. For example, a test score between 80 and 89 (inclusive) qualifies for a B.

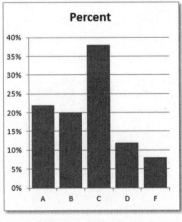

	A	B
1	Student	Grades
2	Student 1	62
3	Student 2	92
4	Student 3	52
5	Student 4	60
6	Student 5	81
7	Student 6	66
8	Student 7	63
9	Student 8	100
10	Student 9	46
11	Student 10	87
12	Student 11	93
13	Student 12	84
14	Student 13	44
15	Student 14	71
16	Student 15	100
17	Student 16	40
18	Student 17	35
19	Student 18	73
20	Student 19	99
21	Student 20	88
22	Student 21	90
23	Student 22	90
24	Student 23	44
25	Student 24	74

	D	E	F	G	H
1	Min	Max	Grade	Frequency	Pct.
2	90	100	A	11	22.0%
3	80	89	B	10	20.0%
4	51	79	C	19	38.0%
5	41	50	D	6	12.0%
6	0	40	F	4	8.0%

Percent

40%, 35%, 30%, 25%, 20%, 15%, 10%, 5%, 0%

A B C D F

Figure 7-8: Creating a frequency distribution of test scores.

The formula in cell G2 that follows is an array formula that counts the number of scores that qualify for an A:

```
{=SUM((Grades>=D2)*(Grades<=E2))}
```

You may recognize this formula from a previous section in this chapter. (See "Counting cells that meet multiple criteria.") This formula was copied to the four cells below G2.

The formulas in column H calculate the percentage of scores for each letter grade. The formula in H2, which was copied to the four cells below H2, is

```
=G2/SUM($G$2:$G$6)
```

Using the Analysis ToolPak to create a frequency distribution

After you install the Analysis ToolPak add-in, you can use the Histogram option to create a frequency distribution. Start by entering your bin values in a range. Then choose Data ➜ Analysis ➜ Data Analysis to display the Data Analysis dialog box. Next, select Histogram and click OK. You should see the Histogram dialog box shown in Figure 7-9.

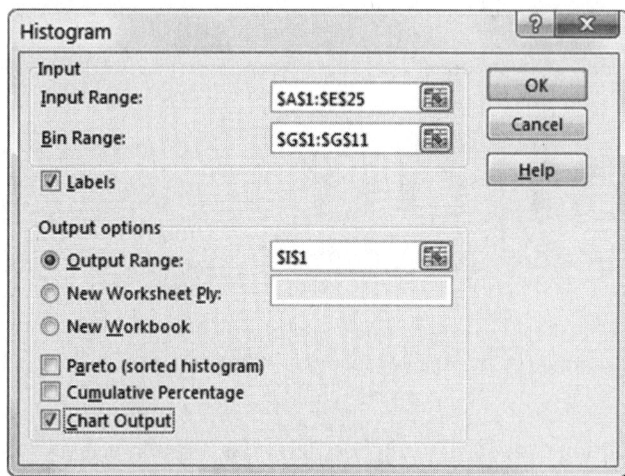

Figure 7-9: The Analysis ToolPak's Histogram dialog box.

Is the Analysis ToolPak installed?

To make sure that the Analysis ToolPak add-in is installed, click the Data tab. If the Ribbon displays the Data Analysis command in the Analysis group, you're all set. If not, you'll need to install the add-in:

1. Choose File ➜ Options to display the Excel Options dialog box.
2. Click the Add-Ins tab on the left.

continued

continued

3. Select Excel Add-Ins from the Manage drop-down list.
4. Click Go to display the Add-Ins dialog box.
5. Place a check mark next to Analysis ToolPak.
6. Click OK.

Note: In the Add-Ins dialog box, you see an additional add-in, Analysis ToolPak - VBA. This add-in is for a programmer, and you don't need to install it.

Specify the ranges for your data *(Input Range)*, bins *(Bin Range)*, and results *(Output Range)*, and then select any options. Figure 7-10 shows a frequency distribution (and chart) created with the Histogram option.

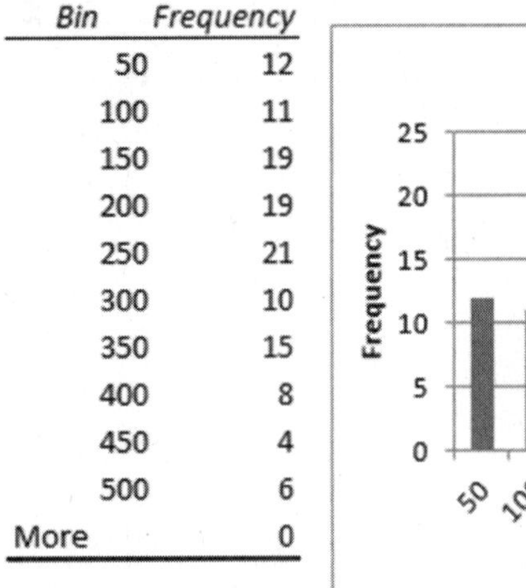

Bin	*Frequency*
50	12
100	11
150	19
200	19
250	21
300	10
350	15
400	8
450	4
500	6
More	0

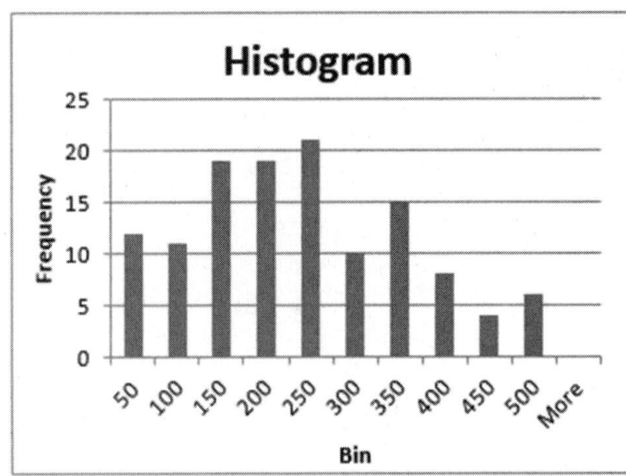

Figure 7-10: A frequency distribution and chart generated by the Analysis ToolPak's Histogram option.

Warning

Note that the frequency distribution consists of values, not formulas. Therefore, if you make any changes to your input data, you need to rerun the Histogram procedure to update the results.

Using a pivot table to create a frequency distribution

If your data is in the form of a table, you may prefer to use a pivot table to create a histogram. Figure 7-11 shows the student grade data summarized in a pivot table and a pivot chart.

Cross-Ref

We cover pivot tables in Chapter 18.

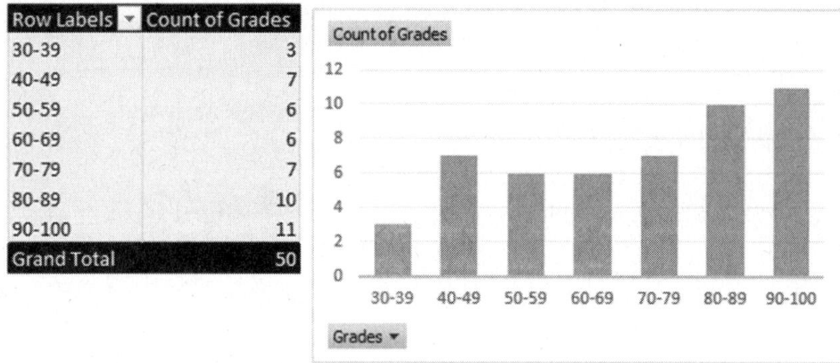

Row Labels	Count of Grades
30-39	3
40-49	7
50-59	6
60-69	6
70-79	7
80-89	10
90-100	11
Grand Total	50

Figure 7-11: Summarizing grades with a pivot table and pivot chart.

Using adjustable bins to create a histogram

Figure 7-12 shows a worksheet with student grades listed in column B (67 students total). Columns D and E contain formulas that calculate the upper and lower limits for bins, based on the entry in cell E1 (named *BinSize*). For example, if *BinSize* is 12 (as in the figure), then each bin contains 12 scores (1–12, 13–24, and so on).

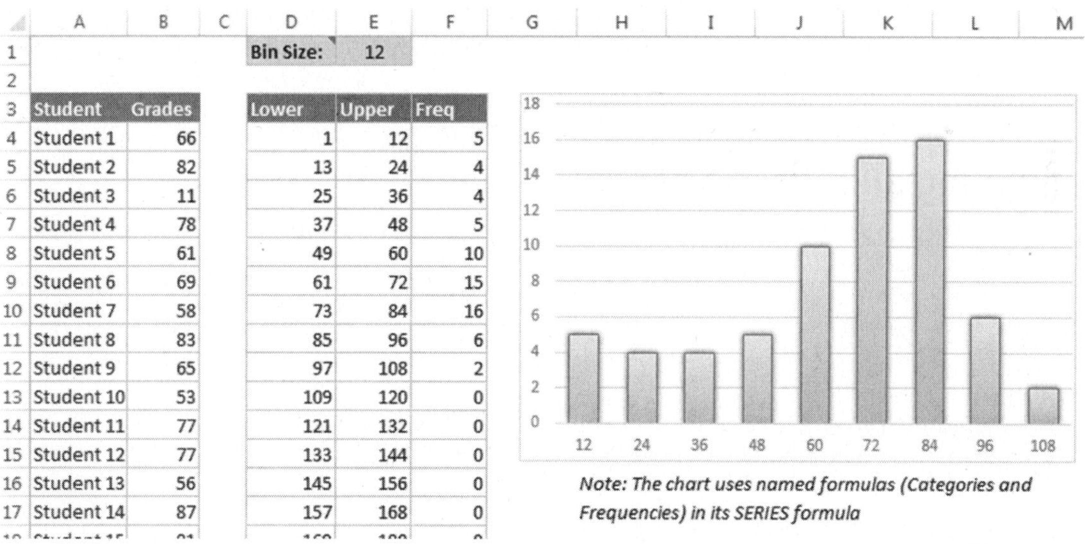

	A	B	C	D	E	F
1				Bin Size:	12	
2						
3	Student	Grades		Lower	Upper	Freq
4	Student 1	66		1	12	5
5	Student 2	82		13	24	4
6	Student 3	11		25	36	4
7	Student 4	78		37	48	5
8	Student 5	61		49	60	10
9	Student 6	69		61	72	15
10	Student 7	58		73	84	16
11	Student 8	83		85	96	6
12	Student 9	65		97	108	2
13	Student 10	53		109	120	0
14	Student 11	77		121	132	0
15	Student 12	77		133	144	0
16	Student 13	56		145	156	0
17	Student 14	87		157	168	0

Figure 7-12: The chart displays a histogram; the contents of cell E1 determine the number of categories.

On the Web

The workbook adjustable bins.xlsx, shown in Figure 7-12, is available at this book's website.

The chart uses two dynamic names in its SERIES formula. You can define the name *Categories* with the following formula:

```
=OFFSET(Sheet1!$E$4,0,0,ROUNDUP(100/BinSize,0))
```

You can define the name *Frequencies* with this formula:

```
=OFFSET(Sheet1!$F$4,0,0,ROUNDUP(100/BinSize,0))
```

The net effect is that the chart adjusts automatically when you change the *BinSize* cell.

Cross-Ref

See Chapter 17, "Charting Techniques," for more about creating a chart that uses dynamic names in its SERIES formula.

Summing Formulas

The examples in this section demonstrate how to perform common summing tasks by using formulas. The formulas range from very simple to relatively complex array formulas that compute sums of cells that match multiple criteria.

Summing all cells in a range

It doesn't get much simpler than this. The following formula returns the sum of all values in a range named *Data*:

```
=SUM(Data)
```

The SUM function can take up to 255 arguments. The following formula, for example, returns the sum of the values in five noncontiguous ranges:

```
=SUM(A1:A9,C1:C9,E1:E9,G1:G9,I1:I9)
```

You can use complete rows or columns as an argument for the SUM function. The formula that follows, for example, returns the sum of all values in column A. If this formula appears in a cell in column A, it generates a circular reference error.

```
=SUM(A:A)
```

The following formula returns the sum of all values on Sheet1. To avoid a circular reference error, this formula must appear on a sheet other than Sheet1.

```
=SUM(Sheet1!1:1048576)
```

The SUM function is versatile. The arguments can be numerical values, cells, ranges, text representations of numbers (which are interpreted as values), logical values, array constants, and even embedded functions. For example, consider the following formula:

```
=SUM(B1,5,"6",,SQRT(4),{1,2,3},A1:A5,TRUE)
```

This formula, which is a perfectly valid formula, contains all the following types of arguments, listed here in the order of their presentation:

- A single cell reference
- A literal value
- A string that looks like a value
- A missing argument
- An expression that uses another function
- An array constant
- A range reference
- A logical *TRUE* value

Warning

The SUM function is versatile, but it's also inconsistent when you use logical values (*TRUE* or *FALSE*). Logical values stored in cells are always treated as 0. But logical *TRUE*, when used as an argument in the SUM function, is treated as 1.

Summing a range that contains errors

The SUM function does not work if the range to be summed includes errors. For example, if one of the cells to be summed displays *#N/A*, the SUM function will also return *#N/A*.

To add the values in a range and ignore the error cells, use the AGGREGATE function. For example, to sum a range named *Data* (which may have error values), use this formula:

```
=AGGREGATE(9,6,Data)
```

The AGGREGATE function is versatile and can do a lot more than just add values. In this example, the first argument (9) specifies SUM. The second argument (6) means to ignore error values.

The arguments are described in the Excel Help. Excel also provides good autocomplete assistance when you enter a formula that uses this function.

Note

The AGGREGATE function was introduced in Excel 2010. For compatibility with earlier versions, use this array formula:

```
{=SUM(IF(ISERROR(Data),"",Data))}
```

Computing a cumulative sum

You may want to display a cumulative sum of values in a range—sometimes known as a *running total.* Figure 7-13 illustrates a cumulative sum. Column B shows the monthly amounts, and column C displays the cumulative (year-to-date) totals.

C2 | =SUM(B$2:B2)

	A	B	C	D
1	Month	Amount	Year-to-Date	
2	January	850	850	
3	February	900	1,750	
4	March	750	2,500	
5	April	1,100	3,600	
6	May	600	4,200	
7	June	500	4,700	
8	July	1,200	5,900	
9	August		5,900	
10	September		5,900	
11	October		5,900	
12	November		5,900	
13	December		5,900	
14	TOTAL	5,900		

Figure 7-13: Simple formulas in column C display a cumulative sum of the values in column B.

The formula in cell C2 is

```
=SUM(B$2:B2)
```

Notice that this formula uses a *mixed reference.* The first cell in the range reference always refers to the same row: in this case, row 2. When this formula is copied down the column, the range argument adjusts so that the sum always starts with row 2 and ends with the current row. For example, after copying this formula down column C, the formula in cell C8 is

```
=SUM(B$2:B8)
```

You can use an IF function to hide the cumulative sums for rows in which data hasn't been entered. The following formula, entered in cell C2 and copied down the column, is

```
=IF(ISBLANK(B2),"",SUM(B$2:B2))
```

Figure 7-14 shows this formula at work.

C2 `=IF(B2<>"",SUM(B$2:B2),"")`

	A	B	C	D
1	**Month**	**Amount**	**Year-to-Date**	
2	January	850	850	
3	February	900	1,750	
4	March	750	2,500	
5	April	1,100	3,600	
6	May	600	4,200	
7	June	500	4,700	
8	July	1,200	5,900	
9	August			
10	September			
11	October			
12	November			
13	December			
14	**TOTAL**	**5,900**		

Figure 7-14: Using an IF function to hide cumulative sums for missing data.

On the Web

The workbook cumulative sum.xlsx is available at this book's website.

Summing the "top *n*" values

In some situations, you may need to sum the *n* largest values in a range—for example, the top 10 values. If your data resides in a table, you can use AutoFilter to hide all but the top *n* rows and then display the sum of the visible data in the table's Total row.

Another approach is to sort the range in descending order and then use the SUM function with an argument consisting of the first *n* values in the sorted range.

A better solution—which doesn't require a table or sorting—uses an array formula like this one:

```
{=SUM(LARGE(Data,{1,2,3,4,5,6,7,8,9,10}))}
```

This formula sums the 10 largest values in a range named *Data*. To sum the 10 smallest values, use the SMALL function instead of the LARGE function:

```
{=SUM(SMALL(Data,{1,2,3,4,5,6,7,8,9,10}))}
```

These formulas use an array constant comprising the arguments for the LARGE or SMALL function. If the value of *n* for your top-*n* calculation is large, you may prefer to use the following variation. This formula returns the sum of the top 30 values in the *Data* range. You can, of course, substitute a different value for 30. Figure 7-15 shows this array formula in use:

```
{=SUM(LARGE(Data,ROW(INDIRECT("1:30"))))}
```

Cross-Ref

See Chapter 14 for more information about array constants.

	A	B	C	D	E	F	G
1	Sum of Top 30 Values						
2	11,645	{=SUM(LARGE(data,ROW(INDIRECT("1:30"))))}					
3							
4	55	316	223	185	124		
5	124	93	163	213	314		
6	211	41	231	241	212		
7	118	113	400	205	254		
8	262	1	201	12	101		
9	167	479	205	337	118		
10	489	15	89	362	148		
11	179	248	125	197	177		
12	456	153	269	49	127		
13	289	500	198	317	300		
14	126	114	303	314	270		
15	151	279	347	314	170		
16	250	175	93	209	61		

Figure 7-15: Using an array formula to calculate the sum of the 30 largest values in a range.

Conditional Sums Using a Single Criterion

Often, you need to calculate a conditional sum. With a *conditional sum,* values in a range that meet one or more conditions are included in the sum. This section presents examples of conditional summing using a single criterion.

The SUMIF function is useful for single-criterion sum formulas. The SUMIF function takes three arguments:

- **range:** The range containing the values that determine whether to include a particular cell in the sum.
- **criteria:** An expression that determines whether to include a particular cell in the sum.
- **sum_range:** (Optional) The range that contains the cells you want to sum. If you omit this argument, the function uses the range specified in the first argument.

The examples that follow demonstrate the use of the SUMIF function. These formulas are based on the worksheet shown in Figure 7-16, set up to track invoices. Column F contains a formula that subtracts the date in column E from the date in column D. A negative number in column F indicates a past-due payment. The worksheet uses named ranges that correspond to the labels in row 1. Various summing formulas begin in row 15.

	A	B	C	D	E	F
1	InvoiceNum	Office	Amount	DateDue	Today	Difference
2	AG-0145	Oregon	$5,000.00	4/1/2013	5/5/2013	-34
3	AG-0189	California	$450.00	4/19/2013	5/5/2013	-16
4	AG-0220	Washington	$3,211.56	4/28/2013	5/5/2013	-7
5	AG-0310	Oregon	$250.00	4/30/2013	5/5/2013	-5
6	AG-0355	Washington	$125.50	5/4/2013	5/5/2013	-1
7	AG-0409	Washington	$3,000.00	5/10/2013	5/5/2013	5
8	AG-0581	Oregon	$2,100.00	5/24/2013	5/5/2013	19
9	AG-0600	Oregon	$335.39	5/24/2013	5/5/2013	19
10	AG-0602	Washington	$65.00	5/28/2013	5/5/2013	23
11	AG-0633	California	$250.00	5/31/2013	5/5/2013	26
12	TOTAL		$14,787.45			29

Figure 7-16: A negative value in column F indicates a past-due payment.

On the Web

All the examples in this section also appear at this book's website in the file named conditional summing.xlsx.

Summing only negative values

The following formula returns the sum of the negative values in column F. In other words, it returns the total number of past-due days for all invoices. For this worksheet, the formula returns –63:

```
=SUMIF(Difference,"<0")
```

Because you omit the third argument, the second argument ("<0") applies to the values in the *Difference* range.

You do not need to hard-code the arguments for the SUMIF function into your formula. For example, you can create a formula such as the following, which gets the criteria argument from the contents of cell G2:

```
=SUMIF(Difference,G2)
```

This formula returns a new result if you change the criteria in cell G2.

Note

You can also use the following array formula to sum the negative values in the *Difference* range:

```
{=SUM(IF(Difference<0,Difference))}
```

Summing values based on a different range

The following formula returns the sum of the past-due invoice amounts (see column C in Figure 7-16):

```
=SUMIF(Difference,"<0",Amount)
```

This formula uses the values in the *Difference* range to determine whether the corresponding values in the *Amount* range contribute to the sum.

Note

You can also use the following array formula to return the sum of the values in the *Amount* range, where the corresponding value in the *Difference* range is negative:

```
{=SUM(IF(Difference<0,Amount))}
```

Summing values based on a text comparison

The following formula returns the total invoice amounts for the Oregon office:

```
=SUMIF(Office,"=Oregon",Amount)
```

Using the equal sign is optional. The following formula has the same result:

```
=SUMIF(Office,"Oregon",Amount)
```

To sum the invoice amounts for all offices *except* Oregon, use this formula:

```
=SUMIF(Office,"<>Oregon",Amount)
```

Text comparisons are not case sensitive.

Summing values based on a date comparison

The following formula returns the total invoice amounts that have a due date after May 1, 2013:

```
=SUMIF(DateDue,">="&DATE(2013,5,1),Amount)
```

Notice that the second argument for the SUMIF function is an expression. The expression uses the DATE function, which returns a date. Also, the comparison operator, enclosed in quotation marks, is concatenated (using the & operator) with the result of the DATE function.

The formula that follows returns the total invoice amounts that have a future due date (including today):

```
=SUMIF(DateDue,">="&TODAY(),Amount)
```

Conditional Sums Using Multiple Criteria

All the examples in the preceding section use a single comparison criterion. The examples in this section involve summing cells based on multiple criteria.

Figure 7-17 shows the sample worksheet again, for your reference. The worksheet also shows the result of several formulas that demonstrate summing by using multiple criteria.

	A	B	C	D	E	F
1	InvoiceNum	Office	Amount	DateDue	Today	Difference
2	AG-0145	Oregon	$5,000.00	4/1/2013	5/5/2013	-34
3	AG-0189	California	$450.00	4/19/2013	5/5/2013	-16
4	AG-0220	Washington	$3,211.56	4/28/2013	5/5/2013	-7
5	AG-0310	Oregon	$250.00	4/30/2013	5/5/2013	-5
6	AG-0355	Washington	$125.50	5/4/2013	5/5/2013	-1
7	AG-0409	Washington	$3,000.00	5/10/2013	5/5/2013	5
8	AG-0581	Oregon	$2,100.00	5/24/2013	5/5/2013	19
9	AG-0600	Oregon	$335.39	5/24/2013	5/5/2013	19
10	AG-0602	Washington	$65.00	5/28/2013	5/5/2013	23
11	AG-0633	California	$250.00	5/31/2013	5/5/2013	26
12	TOTAL		$14,787.45			29

Figure 7-17: This worksheet demonstrates summing based on multiple criteria.

The SUMIFS function (introduced in Excel 2007) can be used to sum a range when multiple conditions are met. The first argument of SUMIFS is the range to be summed. The remaining arguments are 1 to 127 range/criterion pairs that determine which values in the sum range are included. In the following examples, alternatives to SUMIFS are presented for those workbooks that are required to work in versions prior to 2007.

Using And criteria

Suppose you want to get a sum of both the invoice amounts that are past due as well as associated with the Oregon office. In other words, the value in the *Amount* range will be summed only if both of the following criteria are met:

- The corresponding value in the *Difference* range is negative.
- The corresponding text in the *Office* range is *Oregon*.

The SUMIFS function was designed for just this task:

```
=SUMIFS(Amount,Difference,"<0",Office,"Oregon")
```

For use with versions prior to Excel 2007, the following array formula also does the job:

```
{=SUM((Difference<0)*(Office="Oregon")*Amount)}
```

This formula creates two new arrays (in memory):

- A Boolean array that consists of *TRUE* if the corresponding *Difference* value is less than zero; *FALSE* otherwise
- A Boolean array that consists of *TRUE* if the corresponding *Office* value equals *Oregon; FALSE* otherwise

Multiplying Boolean values result in the following:

- TRUE * TRUE = 1
- TRUE * FALSE = 0
- FALSE * FALSE = 0

Therefore, the corresponding *Amount* value returns nonzero only if both the corresponding values in the memory arrays are *TRUE*. The result produces a sum of the *Amount* values that meet the specified criteria.

Note

You may think that you can rewrite the previous array function as follows, using the SUMPRODUCT function to perform the multiplication and addition:

```
=SUMPRODUCT((Difference<0),(Office="Oregon"),Amount)
```

For some reason, the SUMPRODUCT function does not handle Boolean values properly, so the formula does not work. The following formula, which multiplies the Boolean values by 1, *does* work:

```
=SUMPRODUCT(1*(Difference<0),1*(Office="Oregon"),Amount)
```

Using Or criteria

Suppose you want to get a sum of past-due invoice amounts, *or* ones associated with the Oregon office. In other words, the value in the *Amount* range will be summed if either of the following criteria is met:

- The corresponding value in the *Difference* range is negative.
- The corresponding text in the *Office* range is *Oregon.*

The following array formula does the job:

```
{=SUM(IF((Office="Oregon")+(Difference<0),1,0)*Amount)}
```

A plus sign (+) joins the conditions; you can include more than two conditions.

Using And and Or criteria

As you might expect, things get a bit tricky when your criteria consists of both And and Or operations. For example, you may want to sum the values in the *Amount* range when both of the following conditions are met:

- The corresponding value in the *Difference* range is negative.
- The corresponding text in the *Office* range is *Oregon* or *California.*

Notice that the second condition actually consists of two conditions, joined with Or. Using multiple SUMIFS can accomplish this:

```
=SUMIFS(Amount,Difference,"<0",Office,"Oregon")
+SUMIFS(Amount,Difference,"<0",Office,"California")
```

The following array formula also does the trick:

```
{=SUM((Difference<0)*((Office="Oregon")+(Office="California"))*(Amount))}
```

8

Using Lookup Functions

In This Chapter

- An introduction to formulas that look up values in a table
- An overview of the worksheet functions used to perform lookups
- Basic lookup formulas
- More sophisticated lookup formulas

This chapter discusses various techniques that you can use to look up a value in a table. Microsoft Excel has three functions (LOOKUP, VLOOKUP, and HLOOKUP) designed for this task, but you may find that these functions don't quite cut it. This chapter provides many lookup examples, including alternative techniques that go well beyond Excel's normal lookup capabilities.

What Is a Lookup Formula?

A *lookup formula* essentially returns a value from a table (in a range) by looking up another related value. A common telephone directory (remember those?) provides a good analogy: if you want to find a person's telephone number, you first locate the name (look it up) and then retrieve the corresponding number.

Note

Note that the term *table* is used here to describe a range of data. The range does not necessarily need to be an "official" table, as created by the Excel Insert ➜ Tables ➜ Table command.

Figure 8-1 shows a simple worksheet that uses several lookup formulas. This worksheet contains a table of employee data (named *EmpData*). When you enter a last name into cell C2, lookup formulas in D2:G2 retrieve the matching information from the table. The lookup formulas in the following table use the VLOOKUP function.

Cell	Formula
D2	=VLOOKUP(C2,EmpData,2,FALSE)
E2	=VLOOKUP(C2,EmpData,3,FALSE)
F2	=VLOOKUP(C2,EmpData,4,FALSE)
G2	=VLOOKUP(C2,EmpData,5,FALSE)

		First Name	Department	Extension	Date Hired
Last Name -->	Cramden	Moe	Administration	1231	3/12/2011

Last Name	First Name	Department	Extension	Date Hired
Allen	Yolanda	Sales	4466	3/5/1998
Baker	Nancy	Operations	3432	4/16/2003
Bunnel	Ken	Marketing	4422	12/1/2010
Charles	Larry	Administration	2822	9/16/1999
Cramden	Moe	Administration	1231	3/12/2011
Davis	Rita	Administration	2604	4/15/2009
Dunwell	James	Operations	3983	2/9/2012
Ellis	Pamela	Data Processing	2144	3/24/2004
Endow	Ed	Data Processing	1102	11/12/2003

Figure 8-1: Lookup formulas in row 2 look up the information for the last name in cell C2.

This particular example uses four formulas to return information from the *EmpData* range. In many cases, you'll want only a single value from the table, so use only one formula.

Functions Relevant to Lookups

Several Excel functions are useful when writing formulas to look up information in a table. Table 8-1 lists and describes each of these functions.

Table 8-1: Functions Used in Lookup Formulas

Function	Description
CHOOSE	Returns a specific value from a list of values supplied as arguments.
HLOOKUP	Horizontal lookup. Searches for a value in the top row of a table and returns a value in the same column from a row you specify in the table.
IF	Returns one value if a condition you specify is *TRUE*, and returns another value if the condition is *FALSE*.
IFERROR*	If the first argument returns an error, the second argument is evaluated and returned. If the first argument does not return an error, then it is evaluated and returned.

continued

Table 8-1: Functions Used in Lookup Formulas *(continued)*

Function	Description
INDEX	Returns a value (or the reference to a value) from within a table or range.
LOOKUP	Returns a value either from a one-row or one-column range. Another form of the LOOKUP function works like VLOOKUP (or HLOOKUP) but is restricted to returning a value from the last column (or row) of a range.
MATCH	Returns the relative position of an item in a range that matches a specified value.
OFFSET	Returns a reference to a range that is a specified number of rows and columns from a cell or range of cells.
VLOOKUP	Vertical lookup. Searches for a value in the first column of a table and returns a value in the same row from a column you specify in the table.

** Introduced in Excel 2007.*

The examples in this chapter use the functions listed in Table 8-1.

Using the IF function for simple lookups

The IF function is versatile and is often suitable for simple decision-making problems. The accompanying figure shows a worksheet with student grades in column B. Formulas in column C use the IF function to return text: either Pass (a score of 65 or higher) or Fail (a score below 65). For example, the formula in cell C2 is

```
=IF(B2>=65,"Pass","Fail")
```

C2 =IF(B2>=65,"Pass","Fail")

	A	B	C	D	E	F
1	Student	Grades				
2	Student 1	62	Fail			
3	Student 2	92	Pass			
4	Student 3	52	Fail			
5	Student 4	60	Fail			
6	Student 5	81	Pass			
7	Student 6	66	Pass			
8	Student 7	63	Fail			
9	Student 8	100	Pass			
10	Student 9	46	Fail			
11	Student 10	87	Pass			
12	Student 11	93	Pass			
13	Student 12	84	Pass			
14	Student 13	44	Fail			
15	Student 14	71	Pass			

continued

continued

You can "nest" IF functions to provide even more decision-making ability. This formula, for example, returns one of four strings: Excellent, Very Good, Fair, or Poor:

```
=IF(B2>=90,"Excellent",IF(B2>=70,"Very Good",IF(B2>=50,"Fair","Poor")))
```

This technique is fine for situations that involve only a few choices. However, using nested IF functions can quickly become complicated and unwieldy. The lookup techniques described in this chapter usually provide a much better solution.

Basic Lookup Formulas

You can use Excel's basic lookup functions to search a column or row for a lookup value to return another value as a result. Excel provides three basic lookup functions: HLOOKUP, VLOOKUP, and LOOKUP. The MATCH and INDEX functions are often used together to return a cell or relative cell reference for a lookup value.

Note

The examples in this section (plus the example in Figure 8-1) are available at this book's website. The filename is basic lookup examples.xlsx.

The VLOOKUP function

The VLOOKUP function looks up the value in the first column of the lookup table and returns the corresponding value in a specified table column. The lookup table is arranged vertically. The syntax for the VLOOKUP function is

```
VLOOKUP(lookup_value,table_array,col_index_num,range_lookup)
```

The VLOOKUP function's arguments are as follows:

- **lookup_value:** The value that you want to look up in the first column of the lookup table.
- **table_array:** The range that contains the lookup table.
- **col_index_num:** The column number within the table from which the matching value is returned.
- **range_lookup:** (Optional) If *TRUE* or omitted, an approximate match is returned. (If an exact match is not found, the next largest value that is less than *lookup_value* is used.) If *FALSE*, VLOOKUP searches for an exact match. If VLOOKUP cannot find an exact match, the function returns *#N/A*.

Note

If the *range_lookup* argument is *TRUE* or omitted, the first column of the lookup table must be in ascending order. If *lookup_value* is smaller than the smallest value in the first column of *table_array*, VLOOKUP returns #N/A. If the *range_lookup* argument is *FALSE*, the first column of the lookup table need not be in ascending order. If an exact match is not found, the function returns #N/A.

Tip

If the *lookup_value* argument is text (and the fourth argument, *range_lookup*, is *FALSE*), you can include the wildcard characters * and ?. An asterisk matches any group of characters, and a question mark matches any single character.

The classic example of a lookup formula involves an income tax rate schedule (see Figure 8-2). The tax rate schedule shows the income tax rates for various income levels. The following formula (in cell B3) returns the tax rate for the income in cell B2:

```
=VLOOKUP(B2,D2:F7,3)
```

B3 =VLOOKUP(B2,D2:F7,3)

	A	B	C	D	E	F
1				Income is Greater Than or Equal To...	But Less Than or Equal To...	Tax Rate
2	Enter Income:	$32,650		$0	$2,650	15.00%
3	The Tax Rate is:	31.00%		$2,651	$27,300	28.00%
4				$27,301	$58,500	31.00%
5				$58,501	$131,800	36.00%
6				$131,801	$284,700	39.60%
7				$284,701		45.25%
8						
9	*Note: This is set up to work with whole numbers only (no decimals).*					
10						

Figure 8-2: Using VLOOKUP to look up a tax rate.

The lookup table resides in a range that consists of three columns (D2:F7). Because the third argument for the VLOOKUP function is 3, the formula returns the corresponding value in the third column of the lookup table.

Note that an exact match is not required. If an exact match is not found in the first column of the lookup table, the VLOOKUP function uses the next largest value that is less than the lookup value. In other words, the function uses the row in which the value you want to look up is greater than or equal to the row value but less than the value in the next row. In the case of a tax table, this is exactly what you want to happen.

The HLOOKUP function

The HLOOKUP function works just like the VLOOKUP function except that the lookup table is arranged horizontally instead of vertically. The HLOOKUP function looks up the value in the first row of the lookup table and returns the corresponding value in a specified table row.

The syntax for the HLOOKUP function is

```
HLOOKUP(lookup_value,table_array,row_index_num,range_lookup)
```

The HLOOKUP function's arguments are as follows:

- **lookup_value:** The value that you want to look up in the first row of the lookup table.
- **table_array:** The range that contains the lookup table.
- **row_index_num:** The row number within the table from which the matching value is returned.
- **range_lookup:** (Optional) If *TRUE* or omitted, an approximate match is returned. (If an exact match is not found, the next largest value less than *lookup_value* is used.) If *FALSE*, VLOOKUP searches for an exact match. If VLOOKUP cannot find an exact match, the function returns *#N/A*.

Tip

If the *lookup_value* argument is text (and the fourth argument is *FALSE*), you can use the wildcard characters * and ?. An asterisk matches any number of characters, and a question mark matches a single character.

Figure 8-3 shows the tax rate example with a horizontal lookup table (in the range E1:J3). The formula in cell B3 is

```
=HLOOKUP(B2,E1:J3,3)
```

	A	B	C	D	E	F	G	H	I	J
1				Income is Greater Than or Equal To...	$0	$2,651	$27,301	$58,501	$131,801	$284,701
2	Enter Income:	$21,566		But Less Than...	$2,650	$27,300	$58,500	$131,800	$284,700	
3	The Tax Rate is:	28.00%		Tax Rate	15.00%	28.00%	31.00%	36.00%	39.60%	45.25%
4										
5										

Figure 8-3: Using HLOOKUP to look up a tax rate.

The LOOKUP function

The LOOKUP function has the following syntax:

```
LOOKUP(lookup_value,lookup_vector,result_vector)
```

The function's arguments are as follows:

- **lookup_value:** The value that you want to look up in the *lookup_vector.*
- **lookup_vector:** A single-column or single-row range that contains the values to be looked up. These values must be in ascending order.
- **result_vector:** The single-column or single-row range that contains the values to be returned. It must be the same size as the *lookup_vector.*

The LOOKUP function looks in a one-row or one-column range (*lookup_vector*) for a value (*lookup_value*) and returns a value from the same position in a second one-row or one-column range (*result_vector*).

Warning

Values in the *lookup_vector* must be in ascending order. If *lookup_value* is smaller than the smallest value in *lookup_vector,* LOOKUP returns #N/A.

Note

The Help system also lists an "array" syntax for the LOOKUP function. This alternative syntax is included for compatibility with other spreadsheet products. In general, you can use the VLOOKUP or HLOOKUP functions rather than the array syntax.

Figure 8-4 shows the tax table again. This time, the formula in cell B3 uses the LOOKUP function to return the corresponding tax rate. The formula in B3 is

```
=LOOKUP(B2,D2:D7,F2:F7)
```

	A	B	C	D	E	F
1				Income is Greater Than or Equal To...	But Less Than...	Tax Rate
2	Enter Income:	$123,409		$0	$2,650	15.00%
3	The Tax Rate is:	36.00%		$2,651	$27,300	28.00%
4				$27,301	$58,500	31.00%
5				$58,501	$131,800	36.00%
6				$131,801	$284,700	39.60%
7				$284,701		45.25%
8						

Figure 8-4: Using LOOKUP to look up a tax rate.

Warning

If the values in the first column are not arranged in ascending order, the LOOKUP function may return an incorrect value.

Note that LOOKUP (as opposed to VLOOKUP) can return a value that's in a different row than the matched value. If your *lookup_vector* and your *result_vector* are not part of the same table, LOOKUP can be a useful function. If, however, they are part of the same table, VLOOKUP is usually a better choice if for no other reason than that LOOKUP will not work on unsorted data.

Combining the MATCH and INDEX functions

The MATCH and INDEX functions are often used together to perform lookups. The MATCH function returns the relative position of a cell in a range that matches a specified value. The syntax for MATCH is

```
MATCH(lookup_value,lookup_array,match_type)
```

The MATCH function's arguments are as follows:

- **lookup_value:** The value that you want to match in *lookup_array*. If *match_type* is 0 and the *lookup_value* is text, this argument can include the wildcard characters * and ?.
- **lookup_array:** The range that you want to search. This should be a one-column or one-row range.
- **match_type:** An integer (–1, 0, or 1) that specifies how the match is determined.

Note

If match_type is 1, MATCH finds the largest value less than or equal to *lookup_value* (*lookup_array* must be in ascending order). If *match_type* is 0, MATCH finds the first value exactly equal to *lookup_value*. If *match_type* is –1, MATCH finds the smallest value greater than or equal to *lookup_value* (*lookup_array* must be in descending order). If you omit the *match_type* argument, this argument is assumed to be 1.

The INDEX function returns a cell from a range. The syntax for the INDEX function is

```
INDEX(array,row_num,column_num)
```

The INDEX function's arguments are as follows:

- **array:** A range
- **row_num:** A row number within the array argument
- **column_num:** A column number within the array argument

Note

If an array contains only one row or column, the corresponding *row_num* or *column_num* argument is optional.

Figure 8-5 shows a worksheet with dates, day names, and amounts in columns D, E, and F. When you enter a date in cell B1, the following formula (in cell B2) searches the dates in column D and returns the corresponding amount from column F. The formula in B2 is

```
=INDEX(F2:F21,MATCH(B1,D2:D21,0))
```

B2 =INDEX(F2:F21,MATCH(B1,D2:D21,0))

	A	B	C	D	E	F
1	Date:	1/12/2013		Date	Weekday	Amount
2	Amount:	189		1/1/2013	Tuesday	23
3				1/2/2013	Wednesday	179
4				1/3/2013	Thursday	149
5				1/4/2013	Friday	196
6				1/5/2013	Saturday	131
7				1/6/2013	Sunday	179
8				1/7/2013	Monday	134
9				1/8/2013	Tuesday	179
10				1/9/2013	Wednesday	193
11				1/10/2013	Thursday	191
12				1/11/2013	Friday	176
13				1/12/2013	Saturday	189
14				1/13/2013	Sunday	163
15				1/14/2013	Monday	121
16				1/15/2013	Tuesday	100
17				1/16/2013	Wednesday	109
18				1/17/2013	Thursday	151
19				1/18/2013	Friday	138
20				1/19/2013	Saturday	114
21				1/20/2013	Sunday	156

Figure 8-5 Using the INDEX and MATCH functions to perform a lookup.

To understand how this formula works, start with the MATCH function. This function searches the range D2:D21 for the date in cell B1. It returns the relative row number where the date is found. This value is then used as the second argument for the INDEX function. The result is the corresponding value in F2:F21.

Specialized Lookup Formulas

You can use some additional types of lookup formulas to perform more specialized lookups. For instance, you can look up an exact value, search in another column besides the first in a lookup table, perform a case-sensitive lookup, return a value from among multiple lookup tables, and perform other specialized and complex lookups.

On the Web

The examples in this section are available at this book's website. The filename is specialized lookup examples.xlsx.

Looking up an exact value

As demonstrated in the previous examples, VLOOKUP and HLOOKUP don't necessarily require an exact match between the value to be looked up and the values in the lookup table. An example of an approximate match is looking up a tax rate in a tax table. In some cases, you may require a perfect match. For example, when looking up an employee number, you would probably require a perfect match for the number.

To look up an exact value only, use the VLOOKUP (or HLOOKUP) function with the optional fourth argument set to *FALSE*.

Figure 8-6 shows a worksheet with a lookup table that contains employee numbers (column A) and employee names (column B). The lookup table is named *EmpList*. The formula in cell B2, which follows, looks up the employee number entered into cell B1 and returns the corresponding employee name:

```
=VLOOKUP(B1,EmpList,2,FALSE)
```

B2 =VLOOKUP(B1,EmpList,2,FALSE)

	A	B	C	D
1	**Employee No.:**	972		
2	**Employee Name:**	Sally Rice		
3				
4	**Employee No.**	**Employee Name**		
5	873	Charles K. Barkley		
6	1109	Francis Jenikins		
7	1549	James Brackman		
8	1334	Linda Harper		
9	1643	Louise Victor		
10	1101	Melinda Hindquest		
11	1873	Michael Orenthal		
12	983	Peter Yates		
13	972	Sally Rice		
14	1398	Walter Franklin		

Figure 8-6 This lookup table requires an exact match.

Because the last argument for the VLOOKUP function is *FALSE*, the function returns an employee name only if an exact match is found. If the employee number is not found, the formula returns *#N/A*. This, of course, is exactly what you want to happen because returning an approximate match for an employee number makes no sense. Also, notice that the employee numbers in column A are not in ascending order. If the last argument for VLOOKUP is *FALSE*, the values need not be in ascending order.

Tip

If you prefer to see something other than #N/A when the employee number is not found, you can use the IFERROR function to test for the error result and substitute a different string. The following formula displays the text *Not Found* rather than *#N/A*:

```
=IFERROR(VLOOKUP(B1,EmpList,2,FALSE),"Not Found")
```

IFERROR works only with Excel 2007 and later. For compatibility with previous versions, use the following formula:

```
=IF(ISNA(VLOOKUP(B1,EmpList,2,FALSE)),"Not Found",
VLOOKUP(B1,EmpList,2,FALSE))
```

When a blank is not a zero

Excel's lookup functions treat empty cells in the result range as zeros. The worksheet in the accompanying figure contains a two-column lookup table, and the following formula looks up the name in cell B1 and returns the corresponding amount:

```
=VLOOKUP(E2,A2:B9,2,FALSE)
```

Note that the Amount cell for Charlie is blank, but the formula returns a 0.

	A	B	C	D	E	F
1	Student	Score				Score
2	Mike	62		Enter Name	Charlie	0
3	Max	92				
4	Joe	52				
5	Jim	60				
6	Charlie					
7	Nancy	66				
8	Dave	63				
9	Gina	100				
10						

If you need to distinguish zeros from blank cells, you must modify the lookup formula by adding an IF function to check whether the length of the returned value is 0. When the looked-up value is blank, the length of the return value is 0. In all other cases, the length of the returned value is nonzero. The following formula displays an empty string (a blank) whenever the length of the looked-up value is zero, and it displays the actual value whenever the length is anything but zero:

```
=IF(LEN(VLOOKUP(E2,A2:B9,2,FALSE))=0,"",(VLOOKUP(E2,A2:B9,2,FALSE)))
```

Alternatively, you can specifically check for an empty string, as in the following formula:

```
=IF(VLOOKUP(E2,A2:B9,2,FALSE)="","",(VLOOKUP(E2,A2:B9,2,FALSE)))
```

Looking up a value to the left

The VLOOKUP function always looks up a value in the first column of the lookup range. But what if you want to look up a value in a column other than the first column? It would be helpful if you could supply a negative value for the third argument for VLOOKUP—but you can't.

Figure 8-7 illustrates the problem. Suppose you want to look up the batting average (column B, in a range named *Average*) of a player in column C (in a range named *Player*). The player you want data for appears in a cell named *LookupValue*. The VLOOKUP function won't work because the data is not arranged correctly. One option is to rearrange your data, but sometimes that's not possible.

	A	B	C	D	E	F	G
1	At Bats	Average	Player	Player to lookup:		Gomez	
2	0	0.000	Henderson				
3	9	0.333	Mazden		Average	0.160	<-- LOOKUP
4	12	0.333	Albertson		At Bats:	25	<-- LOOKUP
5	14	0.286	Perez				
6	16	0.313	Mendez		Average	0.160	<-- INDEX and MATCH
7	23	0.217	Gonzolez		At Bats:	25	<-- INDEX and MATCH
8	24	0.333	Deerberg				
9	25	0.160	Gomez				
10	28	0.321	Talisman				
11	30	0.300	Hardy				
12	36	0.139	Klorber				
13	41	0.390	Darvin				
14	43	0.186	King				
15	44	0.341	Nester				
16	51	0.333	Jackson				

Figure 8-7: The VLOOKUP function can't look up a value in column B based on a value in column C.

Another solution is to use the LOOKUP function, which requires two range arguments. The following formula (in cell F3) returns the batting average from column B of the player name contained in the cell named *LookupValue*:

```
=LOOKUP(LookupValue,Players,Averages)
```

Using the LOOKUP function requires the lookup range (in this case, the *Players* range) to be in ascending order. In addition to this limitation, the formula suffers from a slight problem: if you enter a non-existentplayer—in other words, the *LookupValue* cell contains a value not found in the *Players* range—the formula returns an erroneous result.

A better solution uses the INDEX and MATCH functions. The formula that follows works just like the previous one except that it returns *#N/A* if the player is not found. Another advantage to using this formula is that the player names don't need to be sorted:

```
=INDEX(Averages,MATCH(LookupValue,Players,0))
```

Performing a case-sensitive lookup

Excel's lookup functions (LOOKUP, VLOOKUP, and HLOOKUP) are not case sensitive. For example, if you write a lookup formula to look up the text *budget,* the formula considers any of the following a match: *BUDGET, Budget,* or *BuDgEt.*

Figure 8-8 shows a simple example. Range D2:D9 is named *Range1,* and range E2:E9 is named *Range2.* The word to be looked up appears in cell B1 (named *Value*).

B2 | {=INDEX(Range2,MATCH(TRUE,EXACT(Value,Range1),0))}

	A	B	C	D	E	F	G	H	I
1	Word	DOG		Range1	Range2				
2	Result:	700		apple	100				
3				candy	200				
4				dog	300				
5				earth	400				
6				APPLE	500				
7				CANDY	600				
8				DOG	700				
9				EARTH	800				

Figure 8-8: Using an array formula to perform a case-sensitive lookup.

The array formula that follows is in cell B2. This formula does a case-sensitive lookup in *Range1* and returns the corresponding value in *Range2.*

```
{=INDEX(Range2,MATCH(TRUE,EXACT(Value,Range1),0))}
```

The formula looks up the word *DOG* (uppercase) and returns *700*. The following standard LOOKUP formula (which is not case sensitive) returns *300*:

```
=LOOKUP(Value,Range1,Range2)
```

Note

When entering an array formula, remember to use Ctrl+Shift+Enter, and do not type the curly brackets.

Choosing among multiple lookup tables

You can, of course, have any number of lookup tables in a worksheet. In some cases, your formula may need to decide which lookup table to use. Figure 8-9 shows an example.

D2 =VLOOKUP(C2,IF(B2<3,Table1,Table2),2)

	A	B	C	D	E	F	G	H	I	J	K
1	Sales Rep	Years	Sales	Comm. Rate	Commission		<3 Years Tenure			3+ Years Tenure	
2	Benson	2	120,000	7.00%	8,400		Amt Sold	Rate		Amt Sold	Rate
3	Davidson	1	210,921	7.00%	14,764		0	1.50%		0	2.00%
4	Ellison	1	100,000	7.00%	7,000		5,000	3.25%		50,000	6.25%
5	Gomez	2	87,401	6.00%	5,244		10,000	3.50%		100,000	7.25%
6	Hernandez	6	310,983	9.25%	28,766		20,000	5.00%		200,000	8.25%
7	Kelly	3	43,902	2.00%	878		50,000	6.00%		300,000	9.25%
8	Martin	2	121,021	7.00%	8,471		100,000	7.00%		500,000	10.00%
9	Oswald	3	908	2.00%	18		250,000	8.00%			
10	Reginald	1	0	1.50%	0						
11	Veras	4	359,832	9.25%	33,284						
12	Wilmington	4	502,983	10.00%	50,298						

Figure 8-9: This worksheet demonstrates the use of multiple lookup tables.

This workbook calculates sales commission and contains two lookup tables: G3:H9 (named *Table1*) and J3:K8 (named *Table2*). The commission rate for a particular sales representative depends on two factors: the sales rep's years of service (column B) and the amount sold (column C). Column D contains formulas that look up the commission rate from the appropriate table. For example, the formula in cell D2 is

```
=VLOOKUP(C2,IF(B2<3, Table1, Table2),2)
```

The second argument for the VLOOKUP function consists of an IF function that uses the value in column B to determine which lookup table to use.

The formula in column E simply multiplies the sales amount in column C by the commission rate in column D. The formula in cell E2, for example, is

```
=C2*D2
```

Determining letter grades for test scores

A common use of a lookup table is to assign letter grades for test scores. Figure 8-10 shows a worksheet with student test scores. The range E2:F6 (named *GradeList*) displays a lookup table used to assign a letter grade to a test score.

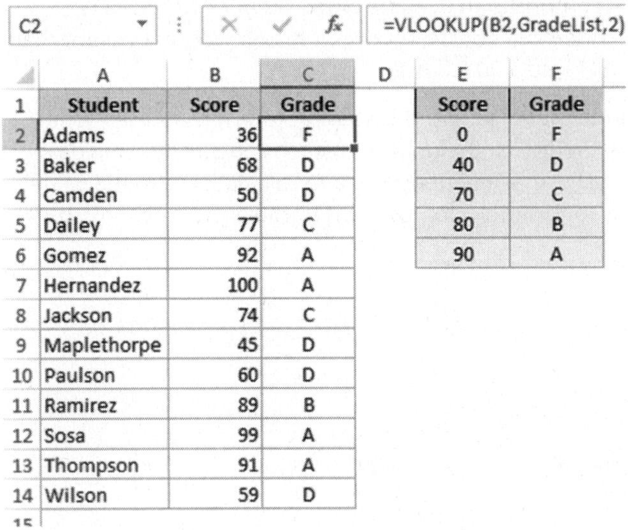

C2 =VLOOKUP(B2,GradeList,2)

	A	B	C	D	E	F
1	Student	Score	Grade		Score	Grade
2	Adams	36	F		0	F
3	Baker	68	D		40	D
4	Camden	50	D		70	C
5	Dailey	77	C		80	B
6	Gomez	92	A		90	A
7	Hernandez	100	A			
8	Jackson	74	C			
9	Maplethorpe	45	D			
10	Paulson	60	D			
11	Ramirez	89	B			
12	Sosa	99	A			
13	Thompson	91	A			
14	Wilson	59	D			
15						

Figure 8-10: Looking up letter grades for test scores.

Column C contains formulas that use the VLOOKUP function and the lookup table to assign a grade based on the score in column B. The formula in C2, for example, is

```
=VLOOKUP(B2,GradeList,2)
```

When the lookup table is small (as in the example shown in Figure 8-10), you can use a literal array in place of the lookup table. The formula that follows, for example, returns a letter grade without using a lookup table. Instead, the information in the lookup table is hard-coded into an array constant. See Chapter 14, "Introducing Arrays," for more information about array constants:

```
=VLOOKUP(B2,{0,"F";40,"D";70,"C";80,"B";90,"A"},2)
```

Another approach, which uses a more legible formula, is to use the LOOKUP function with two array arguments:

```
=LOOKUP(B2,{0,40,70,80,90},{"F","D","C","B","A"})
```

Calculating a grade point average

A student's *grade point average* (GPA) is a numerical measure of the average grade received for classes taken. This discussion assumes a letter grade system, in which each letter grade is assigned a numeric value (A=4, B=3, C=2, D=1, and F=0). The GPA comprises an average of the numeric grade values, weighted by the credit hours of the course. A one-hour course, for example, receives less weight than a three-hour course. The GPA ranges from 0 (all Fs) to 4.00 (all As).

Figure 8-11 shows a worksheet with information for a student. This student took five courses, for a total of 13 credit hours. Range B2:B6 is named *Credit Hrs.* The grades for each course appear in column C (Range C2:C6 is named *Grade*). Column D uses a lookup formula to calculate the grade value for each course. The lookup formula in cell D2, for example, follows. This formula uses the lookup table in G2:H6 (named *GradeTable*).

```
=VLOOKUP(C2,GradeTable,2,FALSE)
```

	A	B	C	D	E	F	G	H
1	Course	Credit Hrs	Grade	Grade Val	Weighted Val		GradeTable	
2	Psych 101	3	A	4	12		A	4
3	PhysEd	2	C	2	4		B	3
4	PoliSci 101	4	B	3	12		C	2
5	IndepStudy	1	A	4	4		D	1
6	IntroMath	3	A	4	12		F	0
7								
8	GPA:	3.38	<-- Requires multiple formulas and lookup table					
9								
10								
11		3.38	<--Array formula					

Figure 8-11: Using multiple formulas to calculate a GPA.

Formulas in column E calculate the weighted values. The formula in E2 is

```
=D2*B2
```

Cell B8 computes the GPA by using the following formula:

```
=SUM(E2:E6)/SUM(B2:B6)
```

The preceding formulas work fine, but you can streamline the GPA calculation quite a bit. In fact, you can use a single array formula to make this calculation and avoid using the lookup table and the formulas in columns D and E. This array formula does the job:

```
{=SUM((MATCH(Grades,{"F","D","C","B","A"},0)-1)*CreditHours)/
  SUM(CreditHours)}
```

Performing a two-way lookup

Figure 8-12 shows a worksheet with a table that displays product sales by month. To retrieve sales for a particular month and product, the user enters a month in cell B1 and a product name in cell B2.

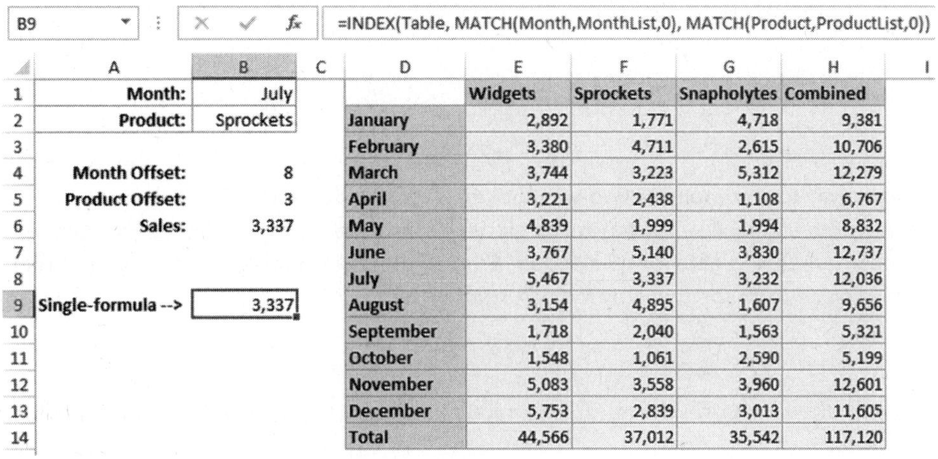

B9 =INDEX(Table, MATCH(Month,MonthList,0), MATCH(Product,ProductList,0))

	A	B	C	D	E	F	G	H
1	Month:	July			Widgets	Sprockets	Snapholytes	Combined
2	Product:	Sprockets		January	2,892	1,771	4,718	9,381
3				February	3,380	4,711	2,615	10,706
4	Month Offset:	8		March	3,744	3,223	5,312	12,279
5	Product Offset:	3		April	3,221	2,438	1,108	6,767
6	Sales:	3,337		May	4,839	1,999	1,994	8,832
7				June	3,767	5,140	3,830	12,737
8				July	5,467	3,337	3,232	12,036
9	Single-formula -->	3,337		August	3,154	4,895	1,607	9,656
10				September	1,718	2,040	1,563	5,321
11				October	1,548	1,061	2,590	5,199
12				November	5,083	3,558	3,960	12,601
13				December	5,753	2,839	3,013	11,605
14				Total	44,566	37,012	35,542	117,120

Figure 8-12: This table demonstrates a two-way lookup.

To simplify things, the worksheet uses the following named ranges:

Name	Refers To
Month	B1
Product	B2
Table	D1:H14
MonthList	D1:D14
ProductList	D1:H1

The following formula (in cell B4) uses the MATCH function to return the position of the month within the *MonthList* range. For example, if the month is January, the formula returns *2* because January is the second item in the *MonthList* range. (The first item is a blank cell, D1.)

```
=MATCH(Month,MonthList,0)
```

The formula in cell B5 works similarly but uses the *ProductList* range:

```
=MATCH(Product,ProductList,0)
```

The final formula, in cell B6, returns the corresponding sales amount. It uses the INDEX function with the results from cells B4 and B5:

```
=INDEX(Table,B4,B5)
```

You can combine these formulas into a single formula, as shown here:

```
=INDEX(Table,MATCH(Month,MonthList,0),MATCH(Product,ProductList,0))
```

Tip

Another way to accomplish a two-way lookup is to provide a name for each row and column of the table. A quick way to do this is to select the table and choose Formulas ➜ Defined Names ➜ Create from Selection. After creating the names, you can use a simple formula to perform the two-way lookup, such as this:

```
=Sprockets July
```

This formula, which uses the range intersection operator (a space), returns July sales for Sprockets.

See Chapter 3, "Working with Names," for details about the range intersection operator.

Performing a two-column lookup

Some situations may require a lookup based on the values in two columns. Figure 8-13 shows an example.

B3 | {=INDEX(Code, MATCH(Make&Model,Makes&Models,0))}

	A	B	C	D	E	F	G
1	Make:	Toyota		Make	Model	Code	
2	Model:	Sequoia		Chevy	Suburban	C-094	
3	Code:	T-871		Chevy	Tahoe	C-823	
4				Ford	Explorer	F-772	
5				Ford	Escape	F-229	
6				Honda	Pilot	I-897	
7				Honda	CR-V	I-900	
8				Jeep	Compass	J-983	
9				Jeep	Grand Cherokee	J-701	
10				Nissan	Suburban	N-231	
11				Toyota	Sequoia	T-871	
12				Toyota	Land Cruiser	T-981	
13							

Figure 8-13: This workbook performs a lookup by using information in two columns (D and E).

The lookup table contains automobile makes and models and a corresponding code for each. The worksheet uses named ranges, as shown here:

F2:F12	*Code*
B1	*Make*
B2	*Model*
D2:D12	*Makes*
E2:E12	*Models*

The following array formula displays the corresponding code for an automobile make and model:

```
{=INDEX(Code,MATCH(Make&Model,Makes&Models,0))}
```

This formula works by concatenating the contents of *Make* and *Model* and then searching for this text in an array consisting of the concatenated corresponding text in *Makes* and *Models*.

Determining the address of a value within a range

Most of the time, you want your lookup formula to return a value. You may, however, need to determine the cell address of a particular value within a range. For example, Figure 8-14 shows a worksheet with a range of numbers that occupy a single column (named *Data*). Cell B1, which contains the value to look up, is named *Target*.

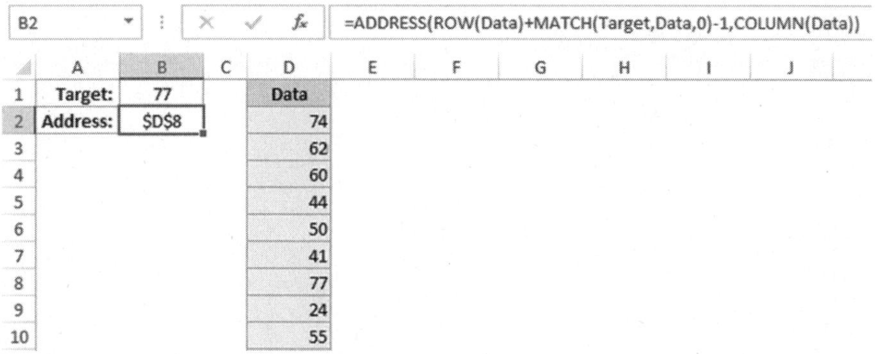

B2 =ADDRESS(ROW(Data)+MATCH(Target,Data,0)-1,COLUMN(Data))

	A	B	C	D	E	F	G	H	I	J
1	**Target:**	77		**Data**						
2	**Address:**	$D$8		74						
3				62						
4				60						
5				44						
6				50						
7				41						
8				77						
9				24						
10				55						

Figure 8-14: The formula in cell B2 returns the address in the Data range for the value in cell B1.

The formula in cell B2, which follows, returns the address of the cell in the *Data* range that contains the *Target* value:

```
=ADDRESS(ROW(Data)+MATCH(Target,Data,0)-1,COLUMN(Data))
```

If the *Data* range occupies a single row, use this formula to return the address of the *Target* value:

```
=ADDRESS(ROW(Data),COLUMN(Data)+MATCH(Target,Data,0)-1)
```

If the *Data* range contains more than one instance of the *Target* value, the address of the first occurrence is returned. If the *Target* value is not found in the *Data* range, the formula returns *#N/A*.

Looking up a value by using the closest match

The VLOOKUP and HLOOKUP functions are useful in the following situations:

- You need to identify an exact match for a target value. Use *FALSE* as the function's fourth argument.
- You need to locate an approximate match. If the function's fourth argument is *TRUE* or omitted, and an exact match is not found, the next largest value that is less than the lookup value is used.

But what if you need to look up a value based on the *closest* match? Neither VLOOKUP nor HLOOKUP can do the job.

Figure 8-15 shows a worksheet with student names in column A and data values in column B. Range B2:B20 is named *Data.* Cell E2, named *Target Value,* contains a value to search for in the *Data* range. Cell E3, named *Column Offset,* contains a value that represents the column offset from the *Data* range.

	A	B	C	D	E
1	Student	Data			
2	Ann	9,101		Target Value:	7200
3	Betsy	8,873		Column Offset :	-1
4	Chuck	6,000			
5	David	9,820		Student:	Paul
6	George	10,500			
7	Hilda	3,500			
8	James	12,873			
9	John	5,867			
10	Keith	8,989			
11	Leslie	8,000			
12	Michelle	1,124			
13	Nora	9,099			
14	Paul	6,800			
15	Peter	5,509			
16	Rasmusen	5,460			
17	Sally	8,400			
18	Theresa	7,777			
19	Violet	3,600			
20	Wendy	5,400			

Figure 8-15: This workbook demonstrates how to perform a lookup by using the closest match.

The array formula that follows identifies the closest match to the *Target Value* in the *Data* range and returns the names of the corresponding student in column A (that is, the column with an offset of –1). The formula returns *Paul* (with a corresponding value of 6,800, which is the one closest to the *Target Value* of 7,200).

```
{=INDIRECT(ADDRESS(ROW(Data)+MATCH(MIN(ABS(Target-Data)),ABS(Target-
  Data),0)-1,COLUMN(Data)+ColOffset))}
```

If two values in the *Data* range are equidistant from the *Target Value*, the formula uses the first one in the list.

The value in *Column Offset* can be negative (for a column to the left of *Data*), positive (for a column to the right of *Data*), or 0 (for the actual closest match value in the *Data* range).

To understand how this formula works, you need to understand the INDIRECT function. This function's first argument is a text string in the form of a cell reference (or a reference to a cell that contains a text string). In this example, the text string is created by the ADDRESS function, which accepts a row and column reference and returns a cell address.

Looking up a value using linear interpolation

Interpolation refers to the process of estimating a missing value by using existing values. For an illustration of this concept, see Figure 8-16. Column D contains a list of values (named *x*), and column E contains corresponding values (named *y*).

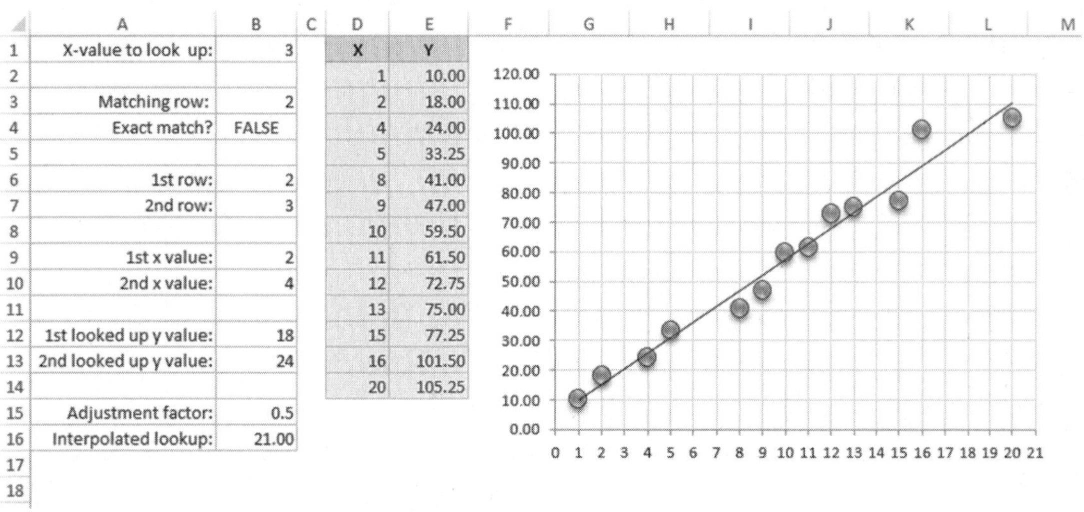

	A	B	C	D	E
1	X-value to look up:	3		X	Y
2				1	10.00
3	Matching row:	2		2	18.00
4	Exact match?	FALSE		4	24.00
5				5	33.25
6	1st row:	2		8	41.00
7	2nd row:	3		9	47.00
8				10	59.50
9	1st x value:	2		11	61.50
10	2nd x value:	4		12	72.75
11				13	75.00
12	1st looked up y value:	18		15	77.25
13	2nd looked up y value:	24		16	101.50
14				20	105.25
15	Adjustment factor:	0.5			
16	Interpolated lookup:	21.00			
17					
18					

Figure 8-16: This worksheet demonstrates a table lookup using linear interpolation.

The worksheet also contains a chart that depicts the relationship between the *x* range and the *y* range graphically, and it includes a linear trendline. As you can see, an approximate linear relationship exists between the corresponding values in the *x* and *y* ranges: as *x* increases, so does *y*. Notice that the values in the *x* range are not strictly consecutive. For example, the *x* range doesn't contain the following values: 3, 6, 7, 14, 17, 18, and 19.

You can create a lookup formula that looks up a value in the *x* range and returns the corresponding value from the *y* range. But what if you want to estimate the *y* value for a missing *x* value? A normal lookup formula does not return a very good result because it simply returns an existing *y* value (not an estimated *y* value). For example, the following formula looks up the value 3 and returns *18.00* (the value that corresponds to 2 in the *x* range):

```
=LOOKUP(3,x,y)
```

In such a case, you probably want to interpolate. In other words, because the lookup value (3) is halfway between existing *x* values (2 and 4), you want the formula to return a *y* value of *21.00*—a value halfway between the corresponding *y* values 18.00 and 24.00.

Formulas to perform a linear interpolation

Figure 8-17 shows a worksheet with formulas in column B. The value to be looked up is entered into cell B1. The final formula, in cell B16, returns the result. If the value in B3 is found in the *x* range, the corresponding *y* value is returned. If the value in B3 is not found, the formula in B16 returns an estimated *y* value, obtained using linear interpolation.

	A	B
1	X-value to look up:	3
2		
3	Matching row:	=LOOKUP(B1,x,x)
4	Exact match?	=B1=B3
5		
6	1st row:	=MATCH(B3,x,0)
7	2nd row:	=IF(B4,B6,B6+1)
8		
9	1st x value:	=INDEX(x,B6)
10	2nd x value:	=INDEX(x,B7)
11		
12	1st looked up y value:	=LOOKUP(B9,x,y)
13	2nd looked up y value:	=LOOKUP(B10,x,y)
14		
15	Adjustment factor:	=IF(B4,0,(B1-B3)/(B10-B9))
16	Interpolated lookup:	=B12+((B13-B12)*B15)

Figure 8-17: Column B contains formulas that perform a lookup using linear interpolation.

It's critical that the values in the *x* range appear in ascending order. If B1 contains a value less than the lowest value in *x* or greater than the largest value in *x*, the formula returns an error value. Table 8-2 lists and describes these formulas.

Table 8-2: Formulas for a Lookup Using Linear Interpolation

Cell	Formula	Description
B3	=LOOKUP(B1,x,x)	Performs a standard lookup on the *x* range and returns the looked-up value.
B4	=B1=B3	Returns *TRUE* if the looked-up value equals the value to be looked up.
B6	=MATCH(B3,x,0)	Returns the row number of the *x* range that contains the matching value.
B7	=IF(B4,B6,B6+1)	Returns the same row as the formula in B6 if an exact match is found. Otherwise, it adds 1 to the result in B6.
B9	=INDEX(x,B6)	Returns the *x* value that corresponds to the row in B6.
B10	=INDEX(x,B7)	Returns the *x* value that corresponds to the row in B7.
B12	=LOOKUP(B9,x,y)	Returns the *y* value that corresponds to the *x* value in B9.
B13	=LOOKUP(B10,x,y)	Returns the *y* value that corresponds to the *x* value in B10.
B15	=IF(B4,0,(B1-B3)/(B10-B9))	Calculates an adjustment factor based on the difference between the *x* values.
B16	=B12+((B13-B12)*B15)	Calculates the estimated *y* value using the adjustment factor in B15.

Combining the lookup and trend functions

Another slightly different approach, which you may find preferable to performing lookup using linear interpolation, uses the LOOKUP and TREND functions. One advantage is that it requires only one formula (see Figure 8-18).

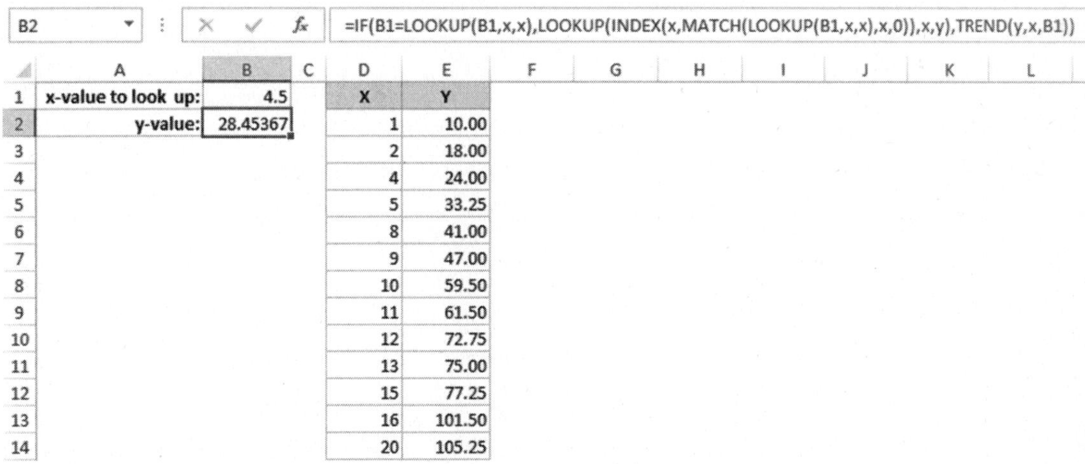

Figure 8-18: This worksheet uses a formula that uses the LOOKUP function and the TREND function.

The formula in cell B2 follows. This formula uses an IF function to make a decision. If an exact match is found in the *x* range, the formula returns the corresponding *y* value (using the LOOKUP function). If an exact match is not found, the formula uses the TREND function to return the calculated "best-fit" *y* value. (It does not perform a linear interpolation.)

```
=IF(B1=LOOKUP(B1,x,x),LOOKUP(INDEX(x,MATCH(LOOKUP(B1,x,x),x,0)),x,y),TREND(
   y,x,B1))
```

9

Working with Tables and Lists

In This Chapter

- Using Excel's table feature
- Basic information about using tables and lists
- Filtering data using simple criteria
- Using advanced filtering to filter data by specifying more complex criteria
- Understanding how to create a criteria range for use with advanced filtering or database functions
- Using the SUBTOTAL function to summarize data in a table

A *list* is a rectangular range of data that usually has a row of text headings to describe the contents of each column. Excel 2007 introduced a twist by letting you designate such a range as an "official" table, which makes common tasks much easier. More importantly, this table feature may eliminate some errors.

This chapter discusses Excel tables and covers what we refer to as *lists,* which are essentially tables of data that have not been converted to an official table.

Tables and Terminology

It seems that Microsoft can't quite make up its mind when it comes to naming some of Excel's features. Excel 2003 introduced a feature called *lists,* which is a way of working with what is sometimes called a *worksheet database.* In Excel 2007, the list features evolved into a much more useful feature called *tables,* and that feature was enhanced a bit in Excel 2010. To confuse the issue even more, Excel also has a feature called *data tables,* which has nothing at all to do with the table feature. And don't forget about *pivot tables,* which are not actual tables but can be created from a table.

In this chapter, we use these two terms:

- **List:** An organized collection of information contained in a rectangular range of cells. More specifically, a list comprises a row of *headers* (descriptive text), followed by additional rows of data holding values or text.
- **Table:** A list that has been converted to a special type of range by using the Insert ➜ Tables ➜ Table command. Converting a list into an official table offers several advantages (and a few disadvantages), as we explain in this chapter.

A list example

Figure 9-1 shows a small list that contains employee information. It consists of a Header row, seven columns, and several rows of data. Notice that the data consists of different data types: text, numerical values, dates, and logical values. Column E even contains a formula that calculates the monthly salary from the value in column D.

	A	B	C	D	E	F	G
1	Employee	Location	Sex	Salary	Monthly Salary	Date Hired	Exempt
2	Krista Orcutt	Pennsylvania	Female	54,176	4,515	10/22/1991	FALSE
3	Cora Soto	Massachusetts	Female	58,120	4,843	1/15/1992	TRUE
4	James Millen	Washington	Male	26,135	2,178	5/25/1992	FALSE
5	Tara Applewhite	California	Female	80,274	6,690	5/30/1992	TRUE
6	Devin Lear	Massachusetts	Male	43,532	3,628	6/29/1992	FALSE
7	Lucile Sexton	Washington	Female	68,637	5,720	7/18/1992	TRUE
8	Jarrod Faith	California	Male	53,478	4,457	8/21/1992	FALSE
9	Terry Gross	Massachusetts	Male	64,497	5,375	9/19/1992	TRUE
10	Jim Martin	Pennsylvania	Male	32,433	2,703	10/7/1992	FALSE

Figure 9-1: A typical list.

You can do lots of things with this list. You can sort it, filter it, create a chart from it, create subtotals, summarize it with a pivot table, and even remove duplicate rows (if it had any duplicate rows). A list like this is a common way to handle structured data.

A table example

Figure 9-2 shows the employee list after we converted it to a table, using Insert ➜ Tables ➜ Table. The table looks similar to a list, and the most obvious difference is the formatting (which was applied automatically).

	A	B	C	D	E	F	G
1	Employee	Location	Sex	Salary	Monthly Salary	Date Hired	Exempt
2	Krista Orcutt	Pennsylvania	Female	54,176	4,515	10/22/1991	FALSE
3	Cora Soto	Massachusetts	Female	58,120	4,843	1/15/1992	TRUE
4	James Millen	Washington	Male	26,135	2,178	5/25/1992	FALSE
5	Tara Applewhite	California	Female	80,274	6,690	5/30/1992	TRUE
6	Devin Lear	Massachusetts	Male	43,532	3,628	6/29/1992	FALSE
7	Lucile Sexton	Washington	Female	68,637	5,720	7/18/1992	TRUE
8	Jarrod Faith	California	Male	53,478	4,457	8/21/1992	FALSE
9	Terry Gross	Massachusetts	Male	64,497	5,375	9/19/1992	TRUE
10	Jim Martin	Pennsylvania	Male	32,433	2,703	10/7/1992	FALSE

Figure 9-2: A list, converted to a table.

Apart from cosmetics, what's the difference between a list and a table?

- Activating any cell in the table gives you access to the Table Tools contextual tab on the Ribbon.
- You can easily add a summary row at the bottom that summarizes the columns. When a summary row is present, Excel creates summary formulas automatically.
- The table is assigned a name automatically (for example, *Table1*), and the range name adjusts automatically when you add or remove rows. You can change the name of the table using Formulas ➜ Defined Names ➜ Name Manager, but you cannot delete the name or change its definition. Note that the range name definition does not include the Header row or Total row.
- The cells contain background color and text color formatting, applied automatically by Excel. This formatting is optional. The formatting is done by named table styles, which are customizable and tied to the workbook theme.
- Each column header contains a Filter button that, when clicked, displays a drop-down list with sorting and filtering options. You can get this same functionality in a list by choosing Data ➜ Sort & Filter ➜ Filter.
- You can add "Slicers" to make it easy for novices to filter the table. This feature was added with the release of Excel 2013.
- If you scroll the worksheet down so that the Header row disappears, the table headers replace the column letters in the worksheet header. In other words, you don't need to "freeze" the top row to keep the column labels visible when you scroll down.
- Tables support calculated columns. A single formula entered into a column is propagated automatically to all cells in the column.
- If you create a chart from data in a table, the chart series expands automatically after you add new data.
- Tables support structured references. Rather than using cell references, formulas can use table names and column headers.
- When you move your mouse pointer to the lower-right corner of the lower-right cell, you can click and drag to extend the table's size horizontally (add more columns) or vertically (add more rows).
- Excel is able to remove duplicate rows automatically. You can get this same functionality in a list by choosing Data ➜ Data Tools ➜ Remove Duplicates.
- If your company uses Microsoft's SharePoint service, you can easily publish a table to your SharePoint server. Choose Table Tools Design ➜ External Table Data ➜ Export ➜ Export Table to SharePoint List.
- Selecting rows and columns within the table is simplified.

Table limitations

Although an Excel table offers several advantages over a normal list, the Excel designers did impose some restrictions and limitations on tables. These limitations include the following:

- If a workbook contains a table, you cannot create or use custom views in that workbook (View ➜ Workbook Views ➜ Custom Views).
- A table cannot contain multicell array formulas.
- You cannot insert automatic subtotals (Data ➜ Outline ➜ Subtotal).
- You cannot share a workbook that contains a table (Review ➜ Changes ➜ Protect and Share Workbook).
- You cannot track changes in a workbook that contains a table (Review ➜ Changes ➜ Track Changes).
- You cannot use the Home ➜ Alignment ➜ Merge & Center command cells in a table (which makes sense because doing so would break up the rows or columns).
- You cannot use Flash Fill within a table.

If you encounter any of these limitations, just convert the table back to a list by using Table Tools ➜ Design ➜ Tools ➜ Convert to Range.

Working with Tables

It may take you a while to get used to working with tables, but you'll soon discover that a table offers many advantages over a standard list.

The sections that follow cover common operations that you perform with a table.

Creating a table

Although Excel allows you to create a table from an empty range, most of the time you'll create a table from an existing range of data (a list). The following instructions assume that you already have a range of data suitable for a table.

1. Make sure that the range doesn't contain any completely blank rows or columns.
2. Activate any cell within the range.
3. Choose Insert ➜ Tables ➜ Table (or press Ctrl+T).

   Excel responds with its Create Table dialog box. Excel tries to guess the range and whether the table has a Header row. Most of the time, it guesses correctly. If not, make your corrections before you click OK.
4. Click OK.

The table is automatically formatted, and Filter mode for the table is enabled. In addition, Excel displays its Table Tools contextual tab (as shown in Figure 9-3). The controls on this tab are relevant to working with a table.

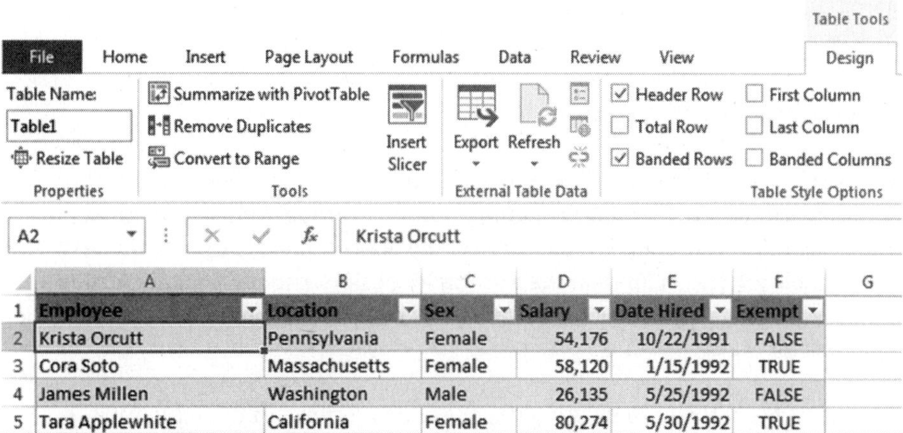

	A	B	C	D	E	F	G
1	Employee	Location	Sex	Salary	Date Hired	Exempt	
2	Krista Orcutt	Pennsylvania	Female	54,176	10/22/1991	FALSE	
3	Cora Soto	Massachusetts	Female	58,120	1/15/1992	TRUE	
4	James Millen	Washington	Male	26,135	5/25/1992	FALSE	
5	Tara Applewhite	California	Female	80,274	5/30/1992	TRUE	

Figure 9-3: When you select a cell in a table, you can use the commands on the Table Tools contextual tab.

Tip

Another method for converting a range into a table is Home ➜ Styles ➜ Format as Table. This command name is a bit misleading. Choosing this command not only *formats* a range as a table but *makes* the range a table.

In the Create Table dialog box, Excel may guess the table's dimensions incorrectly if the table isn't separated from other information by at least one empty row or column. If Excel guesses incorrectly, just specify the exact range for the table in the dialog box. Or, click Cancel and rearrange your worksheet such that the table is separated from your other data by at least one blank row or column.

To create a table from an empty range, just select the range and choose Insert ➜ Tables ➜ Table. Excel creates the table, adds generic column headers (such as Column1 and Column2), and applies table formatting to the range. Almost always, you'll want to replace the generic column headers with more meaningful text.

Changing the look of a table

When you create a table, Excel applies the default table style. The actual appearance depends on which document theme you use in the workbook. If you prefer a different look, you can easily change the entire look of the table.

Select any cell in the table and choose Table Tools ➜ Design ➜ Table Styles. The Ribbon shows one row of styles, but if you click the bottom of the vertical scrollbar, the Table Styles group expands, as shown in Figure 9-4. The styles are grouped into three categories: Light, Medium, and Dark. Notice that you get a live preview as you move your mouse among the styles. When you see one that you like, just click to make it permanent.

For a different set of color choices, choose Page Layout ➜ Themes ➜ Themes to select a different document theme.

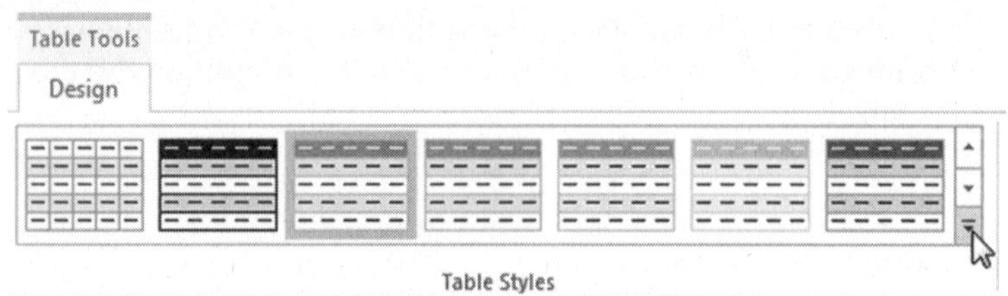

Figure 9-4: Excel offers many different table styles.

Tip

If applying table styles isn't working, the range was probably already formatted before you converted it to a table. (Table formatting doesn't override normal formatting.) To clear the existing background fill colors, select the entire table and choose Home ➜ Font ➜ Fill Color ➜ No Fill. To clear the existing font colors, choose Home ➜ Font ➜ Font Color ➜ Automatic. After you issue these commands, the table styles should work as expected.

You can change some elements of the style by using the check box controls of the Table Tools ➜ Design ➜ Table Style Options group. These controls determine whether various elements of the table are displayed and whether some formatting options are in effect:

- **Header Row:** Toggles the display of the Header Row.
- **Total Row:** Toggles the display of the Total Row.
- **First Column:** Toggles special formatting for the first column. Depending on the table style used, this command might have no effect.
- **Last Column:** Toggles special formatting for the last column. Depending on the table style used, this command might have no effect.
- **Banded Rows:** Toggles the display of *banded* (alternating color) rows.
- **Banded Columns:** Toggles the display of banded columns.
- **Filter Button:** Toggles the display of the drop-down buttons in the table's Header row.

Navigating and selecting in a table

Moving among cells in a table works just like moving among cells in a normal range. One difference is when you use the Tab key. When the active cell is in a table, pressing Tab moves to the cell to the right, as it normally does. But when you reach the last column, pressing Tab again moves to the first cell in the next row.

When you move your mouse around in a table, you may notice that the pointer changes shapes. These shapes help you select various parts of the table:

- **To select an entire column:** Move the mouse to the top of a cell in the Header row, and the mouse pointer changes to a down-pointing arrow. Click to select the data in the column.

Click a second time to select the entire table column (including the Header and Total row). You can also press Ctrl+spacebar (once or twice) to select a column.

- **To select an entire row:** Move the mouse to the left of a cell in the first column, and the mouse pointer changes to a right-pointing arrow. Click to select the entire table row. You can also press Shift+spacebar to select a table row.
- **To select the entire table:** Move the mouse to the upper-left part of the upper-left cell. When the mouse pointer turns into a diagonal arrow, click to select the data area of the table. Click a second time to select the entire table (including the Header row and the Total row). You can also press Ctrl+A (once or twice) to select the entire table.

Tip

Right-clicking a cell in a table displays several selection options in the shortcut menu.

Adding new rows or columns

To add a new column to the end of a table, just activate a cell in the column to the right of the table and start entering the data. Excel automatically extends the table horizontally.

Similarly, if you enter data in the row below a table, Excel extends the table vertically to include the new row. An exception to automatically extending tables is when the table is displaying a Total row. If you enter data below the Total row, the table will not be extended. To add a new row to a table that's displaying a Total row, activate the lower-right table cell and press Tab.

To add rows or columns within the table, right-click and choose Insert from the shortcut menu. The Insert shortcut menu command displays additional menu items that describe where to add the rows or columns.

Another way to extend a table is to drag its resize handle, which appears in the lower-right corner of the table (but only when the entire table is selected). When you move your mouse pointer to the resize handle, the mouse pointer turns into a diagonal line with two arrow heads. Click and drag down to add more rows to the table. Click and drag to the right to add more columns.

When you insert a new column, the Header row displays a generic description, such as Column 1, Column 2, and so on. Normally, you'll want to change these names to more descriptive labels.

Excel remembers

When you do something with a complete column in a table, Excel remembers that and extends that "something" to all new entries added to that column. For example, if you apply currency formatting to a column and then add a new row, Excel applies currency formatting to the new value in that column.

The same thing applies to other operations, such as conditional formatting, cell protection, data validation, and so on. And if you create a chart using the data in a table, the chart will be extended automatically if you add new data to the table.

Deleting rows or columns

To delete a row (or column) in a table, select any cell in the row (or column) that you want to delete. If you want to delete multiple rows or columns, select them all. Then right-click and choose Delete ➜ Table Rows (or Delete ➜ Table Columns).

Moving a table

To move a table to a new location in the same worksheet, move the mouse pointer to any of its borders. When the mouse pointer turns into a cross with four arrows, click and drag the table to its new location.

To move a table to a different worksheet (in the same workbook or in a different workbook), do the following:

1. Select any cell in the table and press Ctrl+A *twice* to select the entire table.
2. Press Ctrl+X to cut the selected cells.
3. Activate the new worksheet and select the upper-left cell for the table.
4. Press Ctrl+V to paste the table.

Using a Data form

Excel can display a dialog box to help you work with a list or table. This Data form enables you to enter new data, delete rows, and search for rows that match certain criteria; and it works with either a list or a range that has been designated as a table (choosing the Insert ➜ Tables ➜ Table command).

Unfortunately, the command to access the Data form is not on the Ribbon. To use the Data form, you must add it to your Quick Access toolbar:

1. Right-click the Quick Access toolbar and choose Customize Quick Access Toolbar from the menu that appears.

   Excel displays the Quick Access Toolbar tab of the Excel Options dialog box.
2. From the Choose Commands From drop-down list, select Commands Not in the Ribbon.
3. In the list box on the left, select Form.
4. Click the Add button to add the selected command to your Quick Access toolbar.
5. Click OK to close the Excel Options dialog box.

After performing these steps, a new icon appears on your Quick Access toolbar.

Excel's Data form can be handy (if you like that sort of thing) but is by no means ideal. If you like the idea of using a dialog box to work with data in a table, check out John Walkenbach's Enhanced Data Form add-in. It offers many advantages over Excel's Data form. You can download a free copy from the website `www.spreadsheetpage.com`.

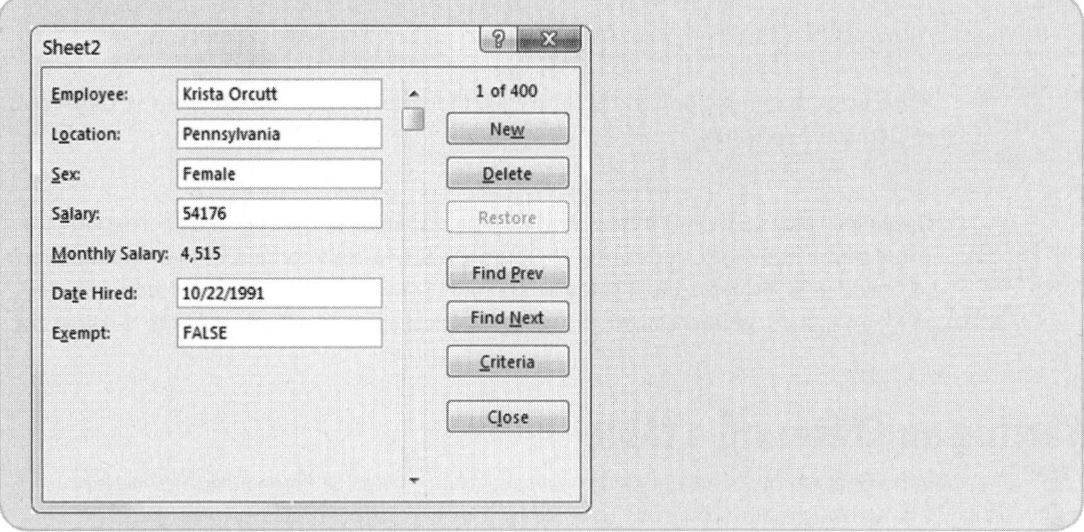

Removing duplicate rows from a table

If data in a table was compiled from multiple sources, the table may contain duplicate items. Most of the time, you want to eliminate the duplicates. In the past, removing duplicate data was essentially a manual task, but it's easy if the data is in a table.

Start by selecting any cell in your table and then choose Table Tools ➜ Design ➜ Tools ➜ Remove Duplicates. Excel responds with a dialog box like the one shown in Figure 9-5. The dialog box lists all the columns in your table. Place a check mark next to the columns that you want to include in the duplicate search. Most of the time, you'll want to select all the columns, which is the default. Click OK, and Excel weeds out the duplicate rows and displays a message that tells you how many duplicates it removed.

Figure 9-5: Removing duplicate rows from a table is easy.

Unfortunately, Excel does not provide a way for you to review the duplicate records before deleting them. You can, however, use Undo (or press Ctrl+Z) if the result isn't what you expect.

Tip

If you want to remove duplicates from a list that's not a table, choose Data ➜ Data Tools ➜ Remove Duplicates.

Warning

Duplicate values are determined by the value *displayed* in the cell—not necessarily the value *stored* in the cell. For example, assume that two cells contain the same date. One of the dates is formatted to display as 5/15/2015, and the other is formatted to display as May 15, 2015. When removing duplicates, Excel considers these dates to be different.

Sorting and filtering a table

Each column in the Header row of a table contains a clickable control (a Filter button), which normally displays a downward-pointing arrow. That control, when clicked, displays sorting and filtering options.

Note

You can toggle the display of Filter buttons in a table's Header row. Choose Table Tools ➜ Design ➜ Table Style Options ➜ Filter Button to display or hide the drop-down arrows.

Figure 9-6 shows a table of real estate listing information after clicking the control for the Date Listed column. If a column is filtered or sorted, the image on the control changes to remind you that the column was used in a filter or sort operation.

8	Agent	Date Listed	Area	List Price	Bed
16	Adams	5/30/2012	N. County	$379,900	
17	Adams	5/17/2012	N. County	$349,000	
18	Adams	4/21/2012	Central	$265,000	
19	Adams	4/14/2012	S. County	$208,750	
20	Adams	4/8/2012	N. County	$339,900	
25	Barnes	3/15/2012	N. County	$350,000	
26	Barnes	3/7/2012	N. County	$264,900	
27	Barnes	2/29/2012	N. County	$299,000	
30	Bennet	5/20/2012	N. County	$229,900	
31	Bennet	5/5/2012	Central	$229,500	

Figure 9-6: Each column in a table contains sorting and filtering options.

On the Web

This workbook, named real estate table.xlsx, is available at this book's website.

Tip

If you're working with a list (rather than a table), use Data ➜ Sort & Filter ➜ Filter to add Filter button controls to the top row of your list. This command is a toggle, so you can hide the drop-down arrows by selecting that command again. You can also use Data ➜ Sort & Filter ➜ Filter to hide the drop-down arrows in a table.

Sorting a table

Sorting a table rearranges the rows based on the contents of a particular column. You may want to sort a table to put names in alphabetical order. Or, maybe you want to sort your sales staff by the total sales made.

To sort a table by a particular column, click the drop-down arrow in the column header and choose one of the sort commands. The exact command varies, depending on the type of data in the column. Sort A to Z and Sort Z to A are the options that appear when the columns contain text. The options for columns that contain numeric data or True/False are Sort Smallest to Largest and Sort Largest to Smallest. Columns that contain dates change the options into Sort Oldest to Newest and Sort Newest to Oldest.

You can also select Sort by Color to sort the rows based on the background or text color of the data. This option is relevant only if you've overridden the table style colors with custom colors or you've used conditional formatting to apply colors based on the cell contents.

Tip

When a column is sorted, the drop-down control in the Header row displays a different graphic to remind you that the table is sorted by that column. If you sort by several columns, only the column most recently sorted displays the sort graphic.

You can sort on any number of columns. The trick is to sort the least significant column first and then proceed until the most significant column is sorted last.

For example, in the real estate listing table (refer to Figure 9-6), you may want the list to be sorted by agent. And within each agent's group, the rows should be sorted by area. And within each area, the rows should be sorted (descending) by list price. For this type of sort, first sort by the List Price column, then sort by the Area column, and then sort by the Agent column. Figure 9-7 shows the table sorted in this manner.

8	Agent	Date Listed	Area	List Price	B
9	Adams	6/8/2012	Central	$325,000	
10	Adams	7/25/2012	Central	$309,950	
11	Adams	11/29/2012	Central	$273,500	
12	Adams	7/12/2012	Central	$268,500	
13	Adams	4/21/2012	Central	$265,000	
14	Adams	8/12/2012	Central	$214,500	
15	Adams	10/2/2012	Central	$199,000	
16	Adams	5/30/2012	N. County	$379,900	
17	Adams	8/1/2012	N. County	$379,000	
18	Adams	5/17/2012	N. County	$349,000	
19	Adams	4/8/2012	N. County	$339,900	
20	Adams	4/14/2012	S. County	$208,750	
21	Barnes	6/19/2012	N. County	$355,000	
22	Barnes	3/15/2012	N. County	$350,000	
23	Barnes	8/3/2012	N. County	$345,000	
24	Barnes	2/29/2012	N. County	$299,000	

Figure 9-7: A table, after performing a three-column sort.

Another way of performing a multiple-column sort is to use the Sort dialog box. To display this dialog box, choose Home ➜ Editing ➜ Sort & Filter ➜ Custom Sort. Or right-click any cell in the table and choose Sort ➜ Custom Sort from the shortcut menu.

In the Sort dialog box, use the drop-down lists to specify the first search specifications. Note that the searching is opposite of what we described earlier. In this example, you start with Agent. Then click the Add Level button to insert another set of search controls. In this set of controls, specify the sort specifications for the Area column. Then add another level and enter the specifications for the List Price column. Figure 9-8 shows the dialog box after entering the specifications for the three-column sort. This technique produces the same sort as described previously.

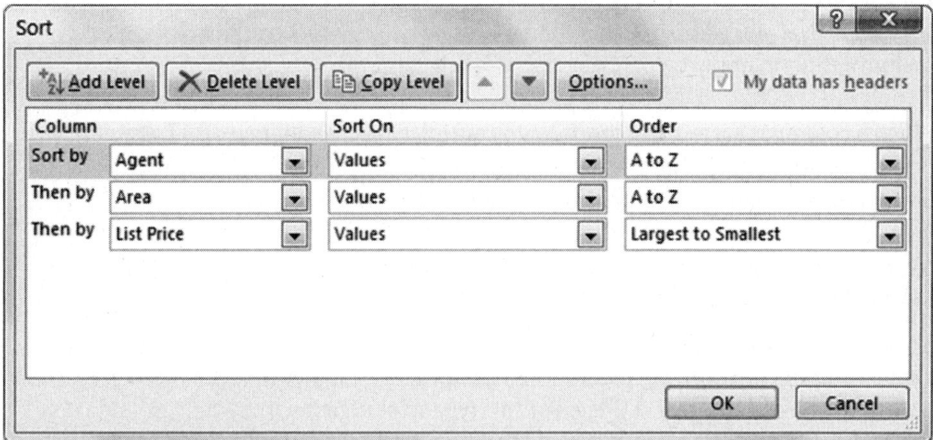

Figure 9-8: Using the Sort dialog box to specify a three-column sort.

Filtering a table

Filtering a table refers to displaying only the rows that meet certain conditions. After you apply a filter, rows that don't meet the conditions are hidden. Filtering a table lets you focus on a subset of interest.

Note

Excel provides two ways to filter a table. This section discusses standard filtering, which is adequate for most filtering requirements. For more complex filter criteria, you may need to use advanced filtering (discussed later in this chapter).

Using the real estate table, assume that you're only interested in the data for the N. County area. Click the drop-down control in the Area Row header and remove the check mark from Select All, which deselects everything. Then place a check mark next to N. County (see Figure 9-9). Click OK, and the table will be filtered to display only the listings in the N. County area. Rows for other areas are hidden.

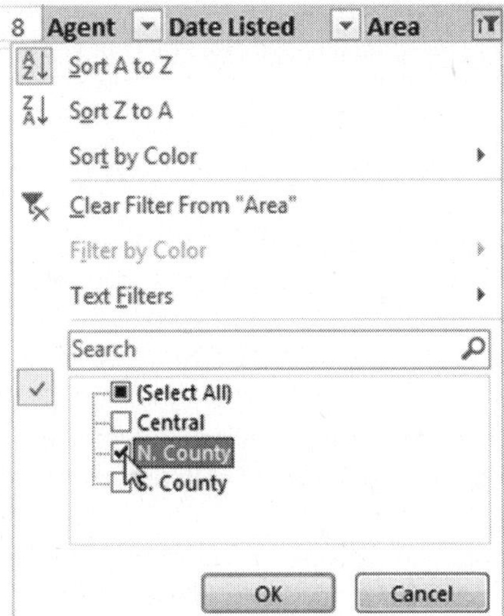

Figure 9-9: Filtering a table to show only the information for N. County.

You can filter by multiple values—for example, filter the table to show only N. County and Central.

You can filter a table using any number of columns. For example, you may want to see only the N. County listings in which the Type is Single Family. Just repeat the operation using the Type column. All tables then display only the rows in which the Area is N. County and the Type is Single Family.

For additional filtering options, select Text Filters (or Number Filters, if the column contains values). The options are fairly self-explanatory, and you have a great deal of flexibility in displaying only the rows that you're interested in.

In addition, you can right-click a cell and use the Filter command on the shortcut menu. This menu item leads to several additional filtering options. For example, you can filter the table to show only rows that contain the same value as the active cell.

Note

As you may expect, the Total row (if present) is updated to show the total for the visible rows only.

When you copy data in a filtered table, only the visible rows are copied. This filtering makes it easy to copy a subset of a larger table and paste it to another area of your worksheet. Keep in mind that the pasted data is not a table—it's just a normal range.

Similarly, you can select and delete the visible rows in the table, and the rows hidden by filtering will not be affected.

You cannot, however, unhide rows that are hidden by filtering. For example, if you select all the rows in a table, right-click, and choose Unhide, that command has no effect.

To remove filtering for a column, click the drop-down control in the row Header and select Clear Filter. If you've filtered using multiple columns, it may be faster to remove all filters by choosing Home ➜ Editing ➜ Sort & Filter ➜ Clear.

Filtering a table with Slicers

Another way to filter a table is to use one or more Slicers. This method is less flexible but more visually appealing. Slicers are particularly useful when the table will be viewed by novices or those who find the normal filtering techniques too complicated. Slicers are visual, and it's easy to see exactly what type of filtering is in effect. A disadvantage of Slicers is that they take up a lot of room onscreen.

Note

Slicers for tables was added as a feature in Excel 2013. Slicers for pivot tables were introduced in Excel 2010, but as you may have deduced, they only worked with pivot tables.

To add one or more Slicers, activate any cell in the table and choose Table Tools ➜ Design ➜ Tools ➜ Insert Slicer. Excel responds with a dialog box that displays each header in the table. Place a check mark next to the field(s) that you want to filter. You can create a Slicer for each column, but that's rarely needed. In most cases, you'll want to be able to filter the table by only a few fields. Click OK, and Excel creates a Slicer for each field you specified.

Figure 9-10 shows a table with two Slicers. The table is filtered to show only the records for Adams and Jenkins in the Central area.

Agent: Adams, Bennet, Chung, Daily, Hamilton, Jenkins

Area: Central, N. County, S. County

	Agent	Date Listed	Area	List Price	Bedroon	Baths
17	Adams	6/8/2012	Central	$325,000	3	
18	Adams	7/25/2012	Central	$309,950	4	
19	Adams	11/29/2012	Central	$273,500	2	
20	Adams	7/12/2012	Central	$268,500	4	
21	Adams	4/21/2012	Central	$265,000	4	
22	Adams	8/12/2012	Central	$214,500	4	
23	Adams	10/2/2012	Central	$199,000	3	
61	Jenkins	4/4/2012	Central	$319,000	4	

Figure 9-10: The table is filtered by two Slicers.

A Slicer contains a button for every unique item in the field. In the real estate listing example, the Slicer for the Agent field contains 14 buttons because the table has records for 14 different agents.

Note

Slicers may not be appropriate for columns that contain numeric data. For example, the real estate listing table has 78 different values in the List Price column. Therefore, a Slicer for this column would have 78 buttons.

To use a Slicer, just click one of the buttons. The table displays only the rows that correspond to the button. You can also press Ctrl to select multiple buttons and press Shift to select a continuous group of buttons, which would be useful for selecting a range of List Price values.

If your table has more than one Slicer, it's filtered by the selected buttons in each Slicer. To remove filtering for a particular Slicer, click the icon in the upper-right corner of the Slicer.

Use the tools from the Slicer Tools ➜ Options contextual menu to change the appearance or layout of a Slicer. You have quite a bit of flexibility.

Working with the Total row

The Total row is an optional table element that contains formulas that summarize the information in the columns. Normally, the Total row isn't displayed. To display the Total row, choose Table Tools ➜ Design ➜ Table Style Options ➜ Total Row. This command is a toggle that turns the Total row on and off.

By default, the Total row displays the sum of the values in a column of numbers. In many cases, you'll want a different type of summary formula. When you select a cell in the Total row, a drop-down arrow appears, and you can select from a number of other summary formulas (see Figure 9-11):

- **None:** No formula.
- **Average:** Displays the average of the numbers in the column.
- **Count:** Displays the number of entries in the column. (Blank cells are not counted.)
- **Count Numbers:** Displays the number of numeric values in the column. (Blank cells, text cells, and error cells are not counted.)
- **Max:** Displays the maximum value in the column.
- **Min:** Displays the minimum value in the column.
- **Sum:** Displays the sum of the values in the column.
- **StdDev:** Displays the standard deviation of the values in the column. *Standard deviation* is a statistical measure of how "spread out" the values are.
- **Var:** Displays the variance of the values in the column. Variance is another statistical measure of how "spread out" the values are.
- **More Functions:** Displays the Insert Function dialog box so that you can select a function that isn't in the list.

Figure 9-11: Several types of summary functions are available for the Total row.

Using the drop-down list, you can select a summary function for the column. Excel inserts a formula that uses the SUBTOTAL function and refers to the table's column using a special structured syntax (described later). The first argument of the SUBTOTAL function determines the type of summary displayed. For example, if the first argument is 109, the function displays the sum. You can override the formula inserted by Excel and enter any formula you like in the Total row cell. For more information, see the sidebar "About the SUBTOTAL function."

Warning

The SUBTOTAL function is one of two functions that ignore data hidden by filtering. (The other is the AGGREGATE function.) If you have other formulas that refer to data in a filtered table, these formulas don't adjust to use only the visible cells. For example, if you use the SUM function to add the values in column C and some rows are hidden because of filtering, the formula continues to show the sum for all the values in column C—not just those in the visible rows.

Warning

If you have a formula that refers to a value in the Total row of a table, the formula returns an error if you hide the Total row. However, if you make the Total row visible again, the formula works as it should.

About the SUBTOTAL function

The SUBTOTAL function is versatile, but it's also one of the most confusing functions in Excel's arsenal. First of all, it has a misleading name because it does a lot more than addition. The first argument for this function requires an arbitrary (and impossible to remember) number that determines the type of result that's returned. Fortunately, the Excel Formula AutoComplete feature helps you insert these numbers.

In addition, the SUBTOTAL function was enhanced in Excel 2003 with an increase in the number of choices for its first argument, which opens the door to compatibility problems if you share your workbook with someone who uses an earlier version of Excel.

The first argument for the SUBTOTAL function determines the actual function used. For example, when the first argument is 1, the SUBTOTAL function works like the AVERAGE function. When you enter a formula that uses the SUBTOTAL function, the Formula AutoComplete feature guides you through the arguments, so you never have to memorize the numbers.

When the first argument is greater than 100, the SUBTOTAL function behaves a bit differently. Specifically, it does not include data in rows that were hidden manually. When the first argument is less than 100, the SUBTOTAL function includes data in rows that were hidden manually but excludes data in rows that were hidden as a result of filtering or using an outline.

To add to the confusion, a manually hidden row is not always treated the same. If a row is manually hidden in a range that already contains rows hidden via a filter, Excel treats the manually hidden rows as filtered rows. After a filter is applied, Excel can't seem to tell the difference between filtered rows and manually hidden rows. The SUBTOTAL function with a first argument over 100 behaves the same as those with a first argument under 100, and removing the filter shows all rows—even the manually hidden ones.

Another interesting characteristic of the SUBTOTAL function is its ability to produce an accurate grand total. It does this by ignoring any cells that already contain a formula with SUBTOTAL in them. For a demonstration of this ability, see the "Inserting Subtotals" section later in this chapter.

Using formulas within a table

Adding a Total row to a table is an easy way to summarize the values in a table column. In many cases, you'll want to use formulas *within* a table. For example, in the table shown in Figure 9-12, you might want to add a column that shows the difference between the Actual and the Projected amounts. As you'll see, Excel makes this easy when the data is in a table.

	A	B	C	D	E
1					
2		Month	Projected	Actual	
3		Jan	40,000	32,783	
4		Feb	40,000	38,308	
5		Mar	40,000	46,725	
6		Apr	50,000	53,794	
7		May	50,000	51,544	
8		Jun	50,000	53,314	
9		Jul	50,000	53,906	
10		Aug	60,000	58,397	
11		Sep	60,000	65,639	
12		Oct	70,000	67,183	
13		Nov	80,000	68,247	
14		Dec	90,000	73,269	
15		**Total**	**680,000**	**663,109**	
16					

Figure 9-12: Adding a calculated column to this table is easy.

On the Web

This workbook, named table formulas.xlsx, is available at this book's website.

To add a column that calculates the difference between the Actual and Projected columns, follow these steps:

1. Activate cell E2 and type **Difference** for the column header.

   Excel automatically expands the table to include a new column.
2. Move to cell E3 and type an equal sign to signify the beginning of a formula.
3. Press the left arrow, and Excel displays =[@Actual], which is the column heading in the Formula bar.
4. Type a minus sign and then press the left arrow twice. Excel displays =[@Actual]-[@Projected] in your formula.
5. Press Enter to end the formula.

   Excel copies the formula to all rows in the table.

Figure 9-13 shows the table with the new calculated column.

E3 =[@Actual]-[@Projected]

	A	B	C	D	E
1					
2		Month	Projected	Actual	Differe
3		Jan	40,000	32,783	-7217
4		Feb	40,000	38,308	-1692
5		Mar	40,000	46,725	6725
6		Apr	50,000	53,794	3794
7		May	50,000	51,544	1544
8		Jun	50,000	53,314	3314
9		Jul	50,000	53,906	3906
10		Aug	60,000	58,397	-1603
11		Sep	60,000	65,639	5639
12		Oct	70,000	67,183	-2817
13		Nov	80,000	68,247	-11753
14		Dec	90,000	73,269	-16731
15		Total	680,000	663,109	

Figure 9-13: The Difference column contains a formula.

If you examine the table, you'll find this formula for all cells in the Difference column:

```
=[@Actual]-[@Projected]
```

Note

The @ symbol that precedes the column header represents "this row" (the row that contains the formula). So each formula in column E calculates "this row's Actual value minus this row's Projected value."

The syntax is a bit different if a column header contains spaces or nonalphanumeric characters such as a pound sign, an asterisk, and so on). In such a case, Excel encloses the column header text in brackets (not quote marks). For example, if the column C header was *Projected Income*, the formula would appear as follows:

```
=[@Actual]-[@[Projected Income]]
```

Some symbols in a column header (such as a square bracket) require the use of an apostrophe as an escape character. It is usually much simpler to create table formulas by pointing and let Excel handle the syntax details.

Keep in mind that we didn't define names in this worksheet. The formula uses table references that are based on the column names. If you change the text in a column header, any formulas that refer to that data update automatically. That's an example of how working with a table is easier than working with a regular list.

Although we entered the formula into the first data row of the table, that's not necessary. We could have put that formula in any cell in column D. Any time you enter a formula into any cell in an empty table column, it will automatically fill all the cells in that column. And if you need to edit the formula, edit the copy in any row, and Excel automatically copies the edited formula to the other cells in the column.

The preceding steps use the pointing technique to create the formula. Alternatively, you can enter the formula manually using standard cell references. For example, you can enter the following formula in cell E3:

```
=D3-C3
```

If you type the formulas using cell references, Excel still copies the formula to the other cells automatically; it just doesn't use the column headings.

Tip

When Excel inserts a calculated column formula, it also displays an icon. Click the icon to display some options, one of which is Stop Automatically Creating Calculated Columns. Select this option if you prefer to do your own copying within a column.

Referencing data in a table

The preceding section describes how to create a column of formulas within a table—often called a *calculated column*. What about formulas outside a table that refer to data inside a table? You can take advantage of the structured table referencing that uses the table name, column headers, and other table elements. You don't need to create names for these items.

The table itself has a name that was assigned automatically when you created the table (for example, *Table1*), and you can refer to data within the table by using the column header text.

You can, of course, use standard cell references to refer to data in a table, but the structured table referencing has a distinct advantage: the names adjust automatically if the table size changes by adding or deleting rows.

Figure 9-14 shows a simple table that contains regional sales information. Excel named this table *Table2* when it was created because it was the second table in the workbook. To calculate the sum of all the values in the table, use this formula:

```
=SUM(Table2)
```

F2 =SUM(Table2)

Month	Region	Sales
Jan	Region 1	789,345
Jan	Region 2	431,263
Feb	Region 1	812,302
Feb	Region 2	509,239
Mar	Region 1	871,902
Mar	Region 2	411,287
		3,825,338

F2: 3,825,338

Figure 9-14: This table shows sales by month and by region.

This formula always returns the sum of all the data, even if rows or columns are added or deleted. And if you change the name of the table, Excel adjusts all formulas that refer to that table automatically. For example, if you rename Table1 to be Q1Data, the preceding formula changes to this:

```
=SUM(Q1Data)
```

Tip

To change the name of a table, select any cell in the table and use the Table Name box of the Table Tools ➜ Design ➜ Properties group. Or you can use the Name Manager to change the name of a table (Formulas ➜ Defined Names ➜ Name Manager).

Most of the time, your formulas will refer to a specific column in the table rather than the entire table. The following formula returns the sum of the data in the Sales column:

```
=SUM(Table2[Sales])
```

Notice that the column name is enclosed in square brackets. Again, the formula adjusts automatically if you change the text in the column heading.

Warning

Keep in mind that the preceding formula does not adjust if table rows are hidden as a result of filtering. SUBTOTAL and AGGREGATE are the only functions that change their result to ignore hidden rows. To sum the Sales column and ignore filtered rows, use either of the following formulas:

```
=SUBTOTAL(109,Table2[Sales])
=AGGREGATE(9,1,Table2[Sales])
```

Excel provides some helpful assistance when you create a formula that refers to data within a table. Figure 9-15 shows the Formula AutoComplete feature helping create a formula by showing a list of the elements in the table. The list appeared after we typed the left square bracket.

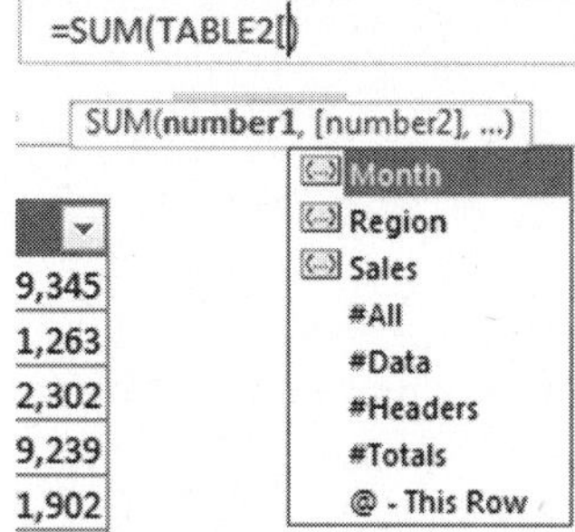

Figure 9-15: The Formula AutoComplete feature is useful when creating a formula that refers to data in a table.

Here's another example that returns the sum of the January sales:

```
=SUMIF(Table2[Month],"Jan",Table2[Sales])
```

For an explanation of the SUMIF worksheet function, refer to Chapter 7, "Counting and Summing Techniques."

Using this structured table syntax is optional—you can use actual range references if you like. For example, the following formula returns the same result as the preceding one:

```
=SUMIF(B3:B8,"Jan",D3:D8)
```

To refer to a cell in the Total row of a table, use a formula like this:

```
=Table2[[#Totals],[Sales]]
```

This formula returns the value in the Total row of the Sales column in Table2. If the Total row in Table2 is not displayed, the preceding formula returns a *#REF* error.

To count the total number of rows in Table2, use the following formula:

```
=ROWS(Table2[#All])
```

The preceding formula counts all rows, including the Header row, Total row, and hidden rows.

To count only the data rows (including hidden rows), use a formula like this:

```
=ROWS(Table2[#Data])
```

To count only the visible data rows, use the SUBTOTAL or AGGREGATE function. For example, you can use either of these formulas:

```
=SUBTOTAL(103,Table2[Region])
=AGGREGATE(3,5,Table2[Region])
```

Because the formula is counting visible rows, you can use any column header in the preceding formula.

A formula that's not in the table but is in the same *row* as a table can use an @ reference to refer to table data that is in the same row. For example, assume the following formula is in row 3, in a column outside Table2. The formula returns the value in row 3 of the Sales column in Table2:

```
= Table2[@Sales])
```

You can also combine row and column references by nesting brackets and including multiple references separated by commas. The following example returns Sales from the current row divided by the total sales:

```
=Table2[@Sales]/Table2[[#Totals],[Sales]]
```

A formula like the preceding one is much easier to create if you use the pointing method.

Table 9-1 summarizes the row identifiers for table references and describes which ranges they represent.

Table 9-1: Table Row References

Row Identifier	Description
#All	Returns the range that includes the Header row, all data rows, and the Total row.
#Data	Returns the range that includes the data rows but not the Header and Total rows.
#Headers	Returns the range that includes the Header row only. Returns a *#REF!* error if the table has no Header row.
#Totals	Returns the range that includes the Total row only. Returns a *#REF!* error if the table has no Total row.
@	Represents "this row." Returns the range that is the intersection of the formula's row and a table column. If the formula row does not intersect with the table (or is the same row as the Header or Total row) a *#VALUE!* error is returned.

Filling in the gaps

When you import data, you can end up with a worksheet that looks something like the one in the accompanying figure. In this example, an entry in column A applies to several rows of data. If you sort such a range, you can end up with a mess, and you won't be able to tell who sold what.

	A	B	C	D	E
1	Region	Month	State	Contacts	Sales
2	East	January	New York	25	107,600
3			New Jersey	47	391,600
4		February	New York	52	233,800
5			New Jersey	29	154,200
6		March	New York	36	134,300
7			New Jersey	14	162,200
8	West	January	California	58	283,800
9			Washington	35	507,200
10			Oregon	39	226,700
11		February	California	44	558,400
12			Washington	74	411,800
13			Oregon	46	350,400
14		March	California	30	353,100
15			Washington	57	258,400
16			Oregon	44	532,100

When you have a small range, you can type the missing cell values manually. If your list has hundreds of rows, though, you need a better way of filling in those cell values. Here's how:

1. Select the range (A1:A16 in this example).
2. Choose Home ➜ Editing ➜ Find & Select ➜ Go To Special to display the Go To Special dialog box.
3. In the Go To Special dialog box, select the Blanks option.
4. Click OK to close the Go To Special dialog box.
5. In the Formula bar, type =, followed by the address of the first cell with an entry in the column (=A2 in this example), and then press Ctrl+Enter to copy that formula to all selected cells.
6. Reselect the range from step 1 and press Ctrl+C.
7. Choose Home ➜ Clipboard ➜ Paste Values (V).

Each blank cell in the column is filled with data from above.

Converting a table to a list

In some cases, you may need to convert a table back to a normal list. For example, you may need to share your workbook with someone who uses an older version of Excel. Or, maybe you'd like the use the Custom Views feature (which is disabled when the workbook contains a table). To convert a table to a normal list, just select a cell in the table and choose Table Tools ➜ Design ➜ Tools ➜ Convert To Range. The table style formatting remains intact, but the range no longer functions as a table.

Formulas inside and outside the table that use structured table references are converted, so they use range addresses rather than table items.

Using Advanced Filtering

In many cases, standard filtering (as we described previously in this chapter) does the job just fine. If you run up against its limitations, you need to use advanced filtering. Advanced filtering is much more flexible than standard filtering, but it takes a bit of upfront work to use it. Advanced filtering provides you with the following capabilities:

- You can specify more complex filtering criteria.
- You can specify computed filtering criteria.
- You can automatically extract a copy of the rows that meet the criteria and place it in another location.

You can use advanced filtering with a list or with a table.

The examples in this section use a real estate listing list (shown in Figure 9-16), which has 125 rows and 10 columns. This list contains an assortment of data types: value, text string, logical, and date. The list occupies the range A8:J133. (Rows above the table are used for the criteria range.)

This workbook, named real estate list.xlsx, is available at this book's website.

	A	B	C	D	E	F	G	H	I	J
7										
8	Agent	Date Listed	Area	List Price	Bedrooms	Baths	SqFt	Type	Pool	Sold
9	Adams	11/29/2012	Central	$273,500	2	2	1,552	Single Family	TRUE	FALSE
10	Romero	11/21/2012	N. County	$369,900	4	3	1,988	Condo	FALSE	FALSE
11	Robinson	11/18/2012	Central	$375,000	4	3	2,368	Single Family	TRUE	TRUE
12	Chung	10/11/2012	S. County	$264,900	4	2.5	2,488	Condo	FALSE	FALSE
13	Lang	10/11/2012	S. County	$360,000	3	2.5	2,330	Single Family	FALSE	FALSE
14	Lang	10/7/2012	Central	$243,000	4	2.5	1,914	Single Family	FALSE	FALSE
15	Kelly	10/4/2012	Central	$345,000	3	2	2,694	Single Family	FALSE	FALSE
16	Adams	10/2/2012	Central	$199,000	3	2.5	1,510	Condo	FALSE	FALSE
17	Peterson	10/2/2012	Central	$227,500	4	3	1,990	Single Family	TRUE	FALSE
18	Peterson	10/2/2012	Central	$272,500	4	3	2,006	Single Family	FALSE	FALSE

Figure 9-16: This real estate listing table is used to demonstrate advanced filtering.

Setting up a criteria range

Before you can use the advanced filtering feature, you must set up a *criteria range*, which is a range on a worksheet that conforms to certain requirements. The criteria range holds the information that Excel uses to filter the table. The criteria range must conform to the following specifications:

- It must consist of at least two rows, and the first row must contain some or all of the column names from the table. An exception to this is when you use computed criteria. Computed criteria can use an empty Header cell. (See the "Specifying computed criteria" section later in this chapter.)
- The other rows of the criteria range contain your filtering criteria.

You can put the criteria range anywhere in the worksheet or even in a different worksheet. However, you should avoid putting the criteria range in rows that are occupied by the list or table. Because Excel may hide some of these rows when filtering, you may find that your criteria range is no longer visible after filtering. Therefore, you should generally place the criteria range above or below the table.

Figure 9-17 shows a criteria range in A1:B2, located above the list that it uses. Notice that the criteria range does not include all the field names from the table. You can include only the field names for fields that you use in the selection criteria.

	A	B
1	Pool	Bedrooms
2	TRUE	3
3		
4		

Figure 9-17: A criteria range for advanced filtering.

In this example, the criteria range has only one row of criteria. The fields in each row of the criteria range are joined with an AND operator. Therefore, after applying the advanced filter, the list shows only the rows in which the Bedrooms column is *3 and* the Pool column is *TRUE*. In other words, it shows only the listings for three-bedroom homes with a pool.

You may find specifying criteria in the criteria range a bit tricky. We discuss this topic in detail later in this chapter in the section "Specifying Advanced Filter Criteria."

Applying an advanced filter

To perform the advanced filtering:

1. Ensure that you've set up a criteria range.
2. Choose Data ➜ Sort & Filter ➜ Advanced.

   Excel displays the Advanced Filter dialog box, as shown in Figure 9-18.
3. Excel guesses your database range if the active cell is within or adjacent to a block of data, but you can change it if necessary.

Figure 9-18: The Advanced Filter dialog box.

4. Specify the criteria range.

   If you happen to have a named range with the name Criteria, Excel will insert that range in the Criteria Range field—you can also change this range if you like.

5. To filter the database in place (that is, to hide rows that don't qualify), select the option labeled Filter the List, In-Place.

   If you select Copy to Another Location, you need to specify a range in the Copy To field. Specifying the upper-left cell of an empty range will do.

6. Click OK, and Excel filters the table by the criteria that you specify.

Figure 9-19 shows the list after applying the advanced filter that displays three-bedroom homes with a pool.

	A	B	C	D	E	F	G
1	Pool	Bedrooms					
2	TRUE	3					
3							
4							
5							
6							
7							
8	Agent	Date Listed	Area	List Price	Bedrooms	Baths	SqFt
21	Shasta	9/25/2012	N. County	$349,000	3	2.5	1,7
29	Shasta	9/6/2012	N. County	$349,000	3	2	1,8
50	Shasta	7/29/2012	N. County	$349,000	3	2.5	2,0
52	Romero	7/27/2012	N. County	$359,900	3	2	2,1
58	Shasta	7/15/2012	S. County	$238,000	3	2.5	2,3
69	Bennet	6/19/2012	S. County	$229,900	3	2.5	1,5
84	Shasta	5/12/2012	Central	$335,000	3	2.5	2,0
90	Lang	4/26/2012	N. County	$369,900	3	2.5	2,0
98	Randolph	4/17/2012	N. County	$405,000	3	3	2,4
106	Adams	4/8/2012	N. County	$339,900	3	2	1,8
117	Shasta	3/17/2012	Central	$215,000	3	1.75	2,1
121	Chung	3/15/2012	S. County	$205,000	3	2.5	2,0
133	Shasta	2/4/2012	Central	$350,000	3	2	2,2

Figure 9-19: The result of applying an advanced filter.

Tip

When you select the Copy to Another Location option, you can specify which columns to include in the copy. Before displaying the Advanced Filter dialog box, copy the desired field labels to the first row of the area where you plan to paste the filtered rows. In the Advanced Filter dialog box, specify a reference to the copied column labels in the Copy To field. The copied rows then include only the columns for which you copied the labels.

Clearing an advanced filter

When you apply an advanced filter, Excel hides all rows that don't meet the criteria you specified. To clear the advanced filter and display all rows, choose Data ➜ Sort & Filter ➜ Clear.

Specifying Advanced Filter Criteria

The key to using advanced filtering is knowing how to set up the criteria range, which is the focus of the sections that follow. You have a great deal of flexibility, but some of the options are not exactly intuitive. Here, you'll find plenty of examples to help you understand how to create a criteria range that extracts the information you need.

Note

The use of a separate criteria range for advanced filtering originated with the first version of Lotus 1-2-3, more than 30 years ago. Excel adapted this method, and it has never been changed, despite the fact that specifying advanced filtering criteria remains one of the most confusing aspects of Excel. Fortunately, however, Excel's standard filtering is sufficient for most needs.

Specifying a single criterion

The examples in this section use a single-selection criterion. In other words, the contents of a single field determine the record selection.

Note

You also can use standard filtering to perform this type of filtering.

To select only the records that contain a specific value in a specific field, enter the field name in the first row of the criteria range and the value to match in the second row.

Note that the criteria range does not need to include all the fields from the database. If you work with different sets of criteria, you may find it more convenient to list all the field names in the first row of your criteria range.

Using comparison operators

You can use comparison operators to refine your record selection. For example, you can select records based on any of the following single criteria:

- Homes with at least four bedrooms
- Homes with square footage less than 2,000
- Homes with a list price of no more than $250,000

To select the records that describe homes that have at least four bedrooms, type **Bedrooms** in cell A1 and then type **>=4** in cell A2 of the criterion range.

Table 9-2 lists the comparison operators that you can use with text or value criteria. If you don't use a comparison operator, Excel assumes the equal sign operator (=).

Table 9-2: Comparison Operators

Operator	Comparison Type
=	Equal to
>	Greater than
>=	Greater than or equal to
<	Less than
<=	Less than or equal to
< >	Not equal to

Using wildcard characters

Criteria that use text also can make use of two wildcard characters: an asterisk (*) matches any number of characters; a question mark (?) matches any single character.

Table 9-3 shows examples of criteria that use text. Some of these are a bit counterintuitive. For example, to select records that match a single character, you must enter the criterion as a formula (refer to the last entry in the table).

Table 9-3: Examples of Text Criteria

Criteria	Selects
="=January"	Records that contain the text *January* (and nothing else). You enter this exactly as shown: as a formula, with an initial equal sign. Alternatively, you can use a leading apostrophe and omit the quotes: '=January
January	Records that begin with the text *January.*
C	Records that contain text that begins with the letter *C.*
<>C*	Records that contain any text, except text that begins with the letter *C.*
>=L	Records that contain text that begins with the letters *L* through *Z.*
County	Records that contain text that includes the word *county.*
Sm*	Records that contain text that begins with the letters *SM.*
s*s	Records that contain text that begins with *S* and has a subsequent occurrence of the letter *S.*
s?s	Records that contain text that begins with *S* and has another *S* as its third character. Note that this does *not* select only three-character words.
="=s*s"	Records that contain text that begins and ends with *S.* You enter this exactly as shown: as a formula, with an initial equal sign. Alternatively, you can use a leading apostrophe and omit the quotes: '=s*s
<>*c	Records that contain text that does not end with the letter *C.*

Criteria	Selects
=????	Records that contain exactly four characters.
<>?????	All records that don't contain exactly five characters.
<>*c*	Records that do not contain the letter *C*.
~?	Records that contain text that begins with a single question mark character. (The tilde character overrides the wildcard question mark character.)
=	Records of which the key is completely blank.
<>	Records that contain any nonblank entry.
="=c"	Records that contain the single character *C*. You enter this exactly as shown: as a formula, with an initial equal sign. Alternatively, you can use a leading apostrophe and omit the quotes: '=c

Note

The text comparisons are not case sensitive. For example, se* matches *Seligman, seller,* and *SEC*.

Specifying multiple criteria

Often, you may want to select records based on criteria that use more than one field or multiple values within a single field. These selection criteria involve logical OR or AND comparisons. Here are a few examples of the types of multiple criteria that you can apply to the real estate database:

- A list price less than $250,000, and square footage of at least 2,000
- A single-family home with a pool
- At least four bedrooms, at least three bathrooms, and square footage less than 3,000
- A home that has been listed for no more than two months, with a list price greater than $300,000
- A condominium with square footage between 1,000 and 1,500
- A single-family home listed in the month of March

To join criteria with an AND operator, use multiple columns in the criteria range. Figure 9-20 shows a criteria range that filters records to show those with at least four bedrooms, more than 3,000 square feet, a pool, and a list price of $390,000 or less.

	A	B	C	D	E	F	G
1	Pool	Bedrooms	SqFt	List Price			
2	TRUE	>=4	>3000	<=390000			
3							
4							
5							
6							
7							
8	Agent	Date Listed	Area	List Price	Bedrooms	Baths	SqFt
57	Lang	7/15/2012	N. County	$349,000	4	3	3,930

Figure 9-20: This criteria range uses multiple columns that select records using a logical AND operation.

Figure 9-21 shows another example. This criteria range displays listings from the month of August 2012. Notice that the column name (Date Listed) appears twice in the criteria range. The criteria selects the records in which the Date Listed date is greater than or equal to August 1, *and* the Date Listed date is less than or equal to August 31.

	A	B	C	D	E	F	G	
1	Date Listed	Date Listed						
2	>8/1/2012	<8/31/2012						
3								
4								
5								
6								
7								
8	Agent	Date Listed	Area	List Price	Bedrooms	Baths	SqFt	Ty
31	Robinson	8/28/2012	Central	$239,900	4	3	2,278	S
32	Randolph	8/27/2012	Central	$149,900	2	1	1,234	S
33	Chung	8/26/2012	S. County	$245,000	4	3	2,084	S
34	Peterson	8/25/2012	S. County	$365,000	5	3	3,938	S
35	Hamilton	8/22/2012	Central	$225,911	4	3	2,285	S
36	Jenkins	8/22/2012	N. County	$1,200,500	5	5	4,696	S
37	Robinson	8/21/2012	S. County	$300,000	4	3	2,650	C
38	Chung	8/20/2012	Central	$339,900	4	2	2,238	S
39	[illegible]	[illegible]	[illegible]	[illegible]	[illegible]	[illegible]	[illegible]	[illegible]

Figure 9-21: This criteria range selects records that describe properties that were listed in the month of August.

Warning

The date selection criteria may not work properly for systems that don't use the U.S. date formats. To ensure compatibility with different date systems, use the DATE function to define such criteria, as in the following formulas:

```
=">="&DATE(2012,8,1)
="<="&DATE(2012,8,31)
```

To join criteria with a logical OR operator, use more than one row in the criteria range. A criteria range can have any number of rows, each of which joins with the others via an OR operator. Figure 9-22 shows a criteria range (A1:D3) with two rows of criteria.

In this example, the filtered table shows the rows that meet either of the following conditions:

- A property with a square footage of at least 1,800, in the Central area

  or

- A single-family home of any size, priced at $220,000 or less, in any area

Note

This is an example of the type of filtering that you cannot perform by using standard (non-advanced) filtering.

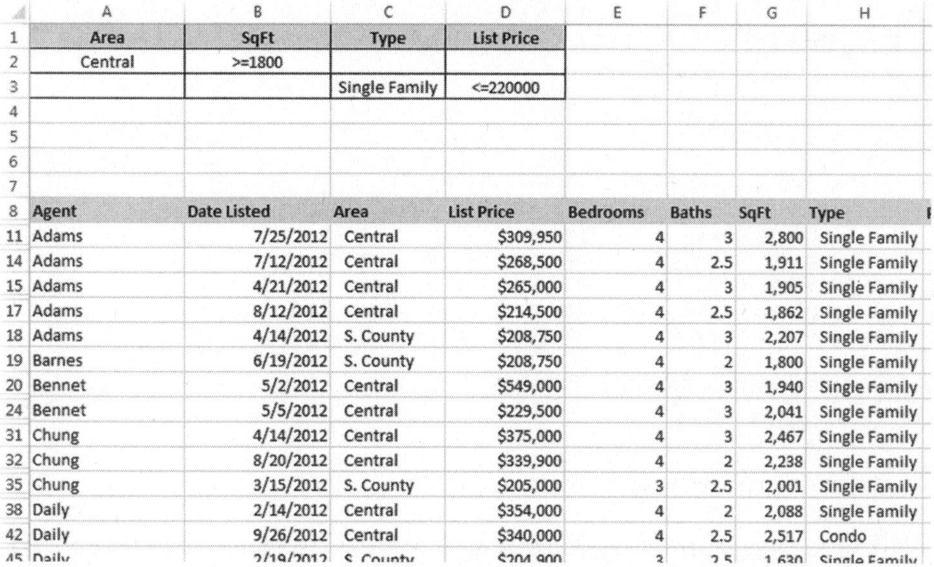

	A	B	C	D	E	F	G	H
1	Area	SqFt	Type	List Price				
2	Central	>=1800						
3			Single Family	<=220000				
4								
5								
6								
7								
8	Agent	Date Listed	Area	List Price	Bedrooms	Baths	SqFt	Type
11	Adams	7/25/2012	Central	$309,950	4	3	2,800	Single Family
14	Adams	7/12/2012	Central	$268,500	4	2.5	1,911	Single Family
15	Adams	4/21/2012	Central	$265,000	4	3	1,905	Single Family
17	Adams	8/12/2012	Central	$214,500	4	2.5	1,862	Single Family
18	Adams	4/14/2012	S. County	$208,750	4	3	2,207	Single Family
19	Barnes	6/19/2012	S. County	$208,750	4	2	1,800	Single Family
20	Bennet	5/2/2012	Central	$549,000	4	3	1,940	Single Family
24	Bennet	5/5/2012	Central	$229,500	4	3	2,041	Single Family
31	Chung	4/14/2012	Central	$375,000	4	3	2,467	Single Family
32	Chung	8/20/2012	Central	$339,900	4	2	2,238	Single Family
35	Chung	3/15/2012	S. County	$205,000	3	2.5	2,001	Single Family
38	Daily	2/14/2012	Central	$354,000	4	2	2,088	Single Family
42	Daily	9/26/2012	Central	$340,000	4	2.5	2,517	Condo
45	Daily	2/19/2012	S. County	$204,900	3	2.5	1,630	Single Family

Figure 9-22: This criteria range has two sets of criteria, each of which is in a separate row.

Specifying computed criteria

Using computed criteria can make filtering even more powerful. Computed criteria filter the table based on one or more calculations. For example, you can specify computed criteria that display only the rows in which the List Price (column D) is greater than average.

```
=D9>AVERAGE(D:D)
```

Notice that this formula uses a reference to cell D9, the first data cell in the List Price column. Also, when you use computed criteria, the cell above it must *not* contain a field name. You can leave that cell blank or provide a descriptive label, such as Above Average. The formula will return a value, but that value is meaningless.

By the way, you can also use a standard filter to display data that's above (or below) average.

The next example displays the rows in which the listing has a pool *and* the price per square foot is less than $100. Cell D9 is the first data cell in the List Price column, and cell G9 is the first data cell in the SqFt column. In Figure 9-23, the computed criteria formula is

```
=(D9/G9)<100
```

Here is another example of a computed criteria formula. This formula displays the records listed within the past 60 days:

```
=B9>TODAY()-60
```

	A	B	C	D	E	F	G
1	Pool	Under $100/sqft					
2	TRUE	FALSE					
3							
4							
5							
6							
7							
8	Agent	Date Listed	Area	List Price	Bedrooms	Baths	SqFt
35	Hamilton	8/22/2012	Central	$225,911	4	3	2,285
57	Lang	7/15/2012	N. County	$349,000	4	3	3,930
66	Bennet	6/24/2012	N. County	$229,500	6	3	2,700
100	Adams	4/14/2012	S. County	$208,750	4	3	2,207
117	Shasta	3/17/2012	Central	$215,000	3	1.75	2,157

Figure 9-23: Using computed criteria with advanced filtering.

Keep the following points in mind when using computed criteria:

- Computed criteria formulas are always logical formulas: they must return either *TRUE* or *FALSE*. However, the value that's returned is irrelevant.
- When referring to columns, use a reference to the cell in the first data row in the field of interest (not a reference to the cell that contains the field name).
- When you use computed criteria, do not use an existing field label in your criteria range. A computed criterion essentially computes a new field for the table. Therefore, you must supply a new field name in the first row of the criteria range. Or, if you prefer, you can simply leave the field name cell blank.
- You can use any number of computed criteria and mix and match them with noncomputed criteria.
- If your computed formula refers to a value outside the table, use an absolute reference rather than a relative reference. For example, use $C$1 rather than C1.
- In many cases, you may find it easier to add a new calculated column to your list or table and avoid using computed criteria.

Using Database Functions

To create formulas that return results based on a criteria range, use Excel's database worksheet functions. All these functions begin with the letter D, and they are listed in the Database category of the Insert Function dialog box.

Table 9-4 lists Excel's database functions. Each of these functions operates on a single field in the database.

Table 9-4: Excel Database Worksheet Functions

Function	Description
DAVERAGE	Returns the average of database entries that match the criteria
DCOUNT	Counts the cells containing numbers from the specified database and criteria
DCOUNTA	Counts nonblank cells from the specified database and criteria
DGET	Extracts from a database a single field from a single record that matches the specified criteria
DMAX	Returns the maximum value from selected database entries
DMIN	Returns the minimum value from selected database entries
DPRODUCT	Multiplies the values in a particular field of records that match the criteria in a database
DSTDEV	Estimates the standard deviation of the selected database entries (assumes that the data is a sample from a population)
DSTDEVP	Calculates the standard deviation of the selected database entries, based on the entire population of selected database entries
DSUM	Adds the numbers in the field column of records in the database that match the criteria
DVAR	Estimates the variance from selected database entries (assumes that the data is a sample from a population)
DVARP	Calculates the variance, based on the entire population of selected database entries

All the database functions require a separate criteria range, which is specified as the last argument for the function. The database functions use the same type of criteria range as discussed earlier in the "Specifying Advanced Filter Criteria" section (see Figure 9-24).

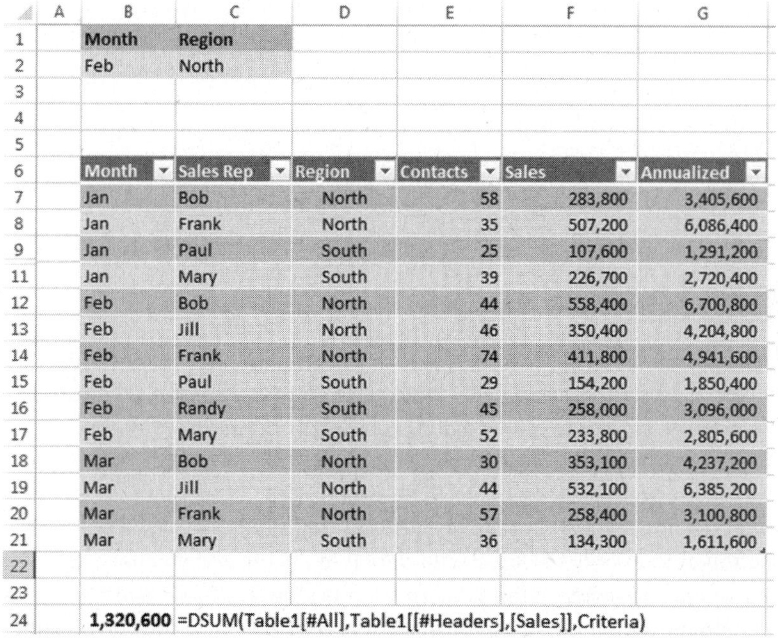

	A	B	C	D	E	F	G
1		Month	Region				
2		Feb	North				
3							
4							
5							
6		Month	Sales Rep	Region	Contacts	Sales	Annualized
7		Jan	Bob	North	58	283,800	3,405,600
8		Jan	Frank	North	35	507,200	6,086,400
9		Jan	Paul	South	25	107,600	1,291,200
11		Jan	Mary	South	39	226,700	2,720,400
12		Feb	Bob	North	44	558,400	6,700,800
13		Feb	Jill	North	46	350,400	4,204,800
14		Feb	Frank	North	74	411,800	4,941,600
15		Feb	Paul	South	29	154,200	1,850,400
16		Feb	Randy	South	45	258,000	3,096,000
17		Feb	Mary	South	52	233,800	2,805,600
18		Mar	Bob	North	30	353,100	4,237,200
19		Mar	Jill	North	44	532,100	6,385,200
20		Mar	Frank	North	57	258,400	3,100,800
21		Mar	Mary	South	36	134,300	1,611,600
22							
23							
24		1,320,600	=DSUM(Table1[#All],Table1[[#Headers],[Sales]],Criteria)				

Figure 9-24: Using the DSUM function to sum a table using a criteria range.

The formula in cell B24, which follows, uses the DSUM function to calculate the sum of values in a table that meet certain criteria. Specifically, the formula returns the sum of the Sales column for records in which the Month is Feb and the Region is North.

```
=DSUM(B6:G21,F6,B1:C2)
```

In this case, B6:G21 is the entire table, F6 is the column heading for Sales, and B1:C2 is the criteria range.

This alternative version of the formula uses structured table references:

```
=DSUM(Table1[#All],Table1[[#Headers],[Sales]],B1:C2)
```

On the Web

This workbook is available at this book's website. The filename is database formulas .xlsx.

Note

You may find it cumbersome to set up a criteria range every time you need to use a database function. Fortunately, Excel provides some alternative ways to perform conditional sums and counts. See Chapter 7 for examples that use SUMIF, COUNTIF, and various other techniques.

If you're an array formula aficionado, you might be tempted to use a literal array in place of the criteria range. In theory, the following array formula *should* work (and would eliminate the need for a separate criteria range). Unfortunately, the database functions do not support arrays, and this formula simply returns a *#VALUE!* error.

```
=DSUM(B6:G21,F6, {"Month","Region";"Feb","North"})
```

Inserting Subtotals

Excel's Data ➜ Outline ➜ Subtotal command is a handy tool that inserts formulas into a list automatically. These formulas use the SUBTOTAL function. To use this feature, your list must be sorted because the formulas are inserted whenever the value in a specified column changes. For more information about the SUBTOTAL function, refer to the sidebar, "About the SUBTOTAL function," earlier in this chapter.

Note

When a table is selected, the Data ➜ Outline ➜ Subtotal command is not available. Therefore, this section applies only to lists. If your data is in a table and you need to insert subtotals automatically, convert the table to a range by using Table Tools ➜ Design ➜ Tools ➜ Convert To Range. After you insert the subtotals, you can convert the range back to a table by using Insert ➜ Tables ➜ Table.

Figure 9-25 shows an example of a list that's appropriate for subtotals. This list is sorted by the Month field, and the Region field is sorted within months.

	A	B	C	D	E
1	**Month**	**Region**	**State**	**Contacts**	**Sales**
2	April	East	New Jersey	14	162,200
3	April	West	Oregon	46	350,400
4	April	West	Washington	57	258,400
5	February	East	New Jersey	47	391,600
6	February	East	New York	52	233,800
7	February	West	California	44	558,400
8	February	West	Washington	35	507,200
9	January	East	New York	25	107,600
10	January	West	California	58	283,800
11	March	East	New Jersey	29	154,200
12	March	East	New York	36	134,300
13	March	West	California	30	353,100
14	March	West	Oregon	39	226,700
15	March	West	Washington	74	411,800
16	May	West	Oregon	44	532,100

Figure 9-25: This list is a good candidate for subtotals, which are inserted at each change of the month.

On the Web

This workbook, named nested subtotals.xlsx, is available at this book's website.

To insert subtotal formulas into a list automatically, activate any cell in the range and choose Data ➜ Outline ➜ Subtotal. You will see the Subtotal dialog box, similar to the one shown in Figure 9-26.

Subtotal

At each change in:

Month

Use function:

Sum

Add subtotal to:

Month

Region

State

Contacts

Sales

Replace current subtotals

Page break between groups

Summary below data

Remove All | OK | Cancel

Figure 9-26: The Subtotal dialog box automatically inserts subtotal formulas into a sorted table.

The Subtotal dialog box offers the following choices:

- **At Each Change In:** This drop-down list displays all the fields in your table. You must have sorted the list by the field that you choose.
- **Use Function:** Choose from 11 functions. (Sum is the default.)
- **Add Subtotal To:** This list box shows all the fields in your table. Place a check mark next to the field or fields that you want to subtotal.
- **Replace Current Subtotals:** If checked, Excel removes any existing subtotal formulas and replaces them with the new subtotals.
- **Page Break Between Groups:** If checked, Excel inserts a manual page break after each subtotal.
- **Summary Below Data:** If checked, Excel places the subtotals below the data (the default). Otherwise, the subtotal formulas appear above the data.
- **Remove All:** This button removes all subtotal formulas in the list.

When you click OK, Excel analyzes the database and inserts formulas as specified—it even creates an outline for you. Figure 9-27 shows a worksheet after adding subtotals that summarize by month. You can, of course, use the SUBTOTAL function in formulas that you create manually. Using the Data ➜ Outline ➜ Subtotals command is usually easier.

	A	B	C	D	E
1	**Month**	**Region**	**State**	**Contacts**	**Sales**
2	April	East	New Jersey	14	162,200
3	April	West	Oregon	46	350,400
4	April	West	Washington	57	258,400
5	**April Total**				771,000
6	February	East	New Jersey	47	391,600
7	February	East	New York	52	233,800
8	February	West	California	44	558,400
9	February	West	Washington	35	507,200
10	**February Total**				1,691,000
11	January	East	New York	25	107,600
12	January	West	California	58	283,800
13	**January Total**				391,400
14	March	East	New Jersey	29	154,200
15	March	East	New York	36	134,300
16	March	West	California	30	353,100
17	March	West	Oregon	39	226,700
18	March	West	Washington	74	411,800
19	**March Total**				1,280,100
20	May	West	Oregon	44	532,100
21	**May Total**				532,100
22	**Grand Total**				4,665,600

Figure 9-27: Excel adds the subtotal formulas automatically and creates an outline.

All the formulas use the SUBTOTAL worksheet function. For example, the formula in cell E20 (Grand Total) is as follows:

```
=SUBTOTAL(9,E2:E18)
```

Although this formula refers to other cells that contain a SUBTOTAL formula, those cells are ignored, to avoid double-counting.

You can use the outline controls to adjust the level of detail shown. Figure 9-28, for example, shows only the summary rows from the subtotaled table. These rows contain the SUBTOTAL formulas.

	A	B	C	D	E
1	Month	Region	State	Contacts	Sales
5	April Total				771,000
10	February Total				1,691,000
13	January Total				391,400
19	March Total				1,280,100
21	May Total				532,100
22	Grand Total				4,665,600

Figure 9-28: Use the outline controls to hide the detail and display only the summary rows.

Note

In most cases, using a pivot table to summarize data is a better choice. Pivot tables are much more flexible, and formulas aren't required. Figure 9-29 shows a pivot table created from the data. See Chapter 18, "Pivot Tables," for more information about pivot tables.

Month	Region	State	Contacts	Sales
⊟January	⊟East	New Jersey	47	$391,600
		New York	25	$107,600
	East Total		72	$499,200
	⊟West	California	58	$283,800
		Oregon	39	$226,700
		Washington	35	$507,200
	West Total		132	$1,017,700
January Total			204	$1,516,900
⊟February	⊟East	New Jersey	29	$154,200
		New York	52	$233,800
	East Total		81	$388,000
	⊟West	California	44	$558,400
		Oregon	46	$350,400
		Washington	74	$411,800
	West Total		164	$1,320,600
February Total			245	$1,708,600
⊟March	⊟East	New Jersey	14	$162,200
		New York	36	$134,300
	East Total		50	$296,500
	⊟West	California	30	$353,100
		Oregon	44	$532,100
		Washington	57	$258,400
	West Total		131	$1,143,600
March Total			181	$1,440,100
Grand Total			630	$4,665,600

Figure 9-29: Use a pivot table to summarize data. Formulas are not required.

10

Miscellaneous Calculations

In This Chapter

- Converting between measurement units
- Formulas that demonstrate various ways to round numbers
- Formulas for calculating the various parts of a right triangle
- Calculations for area, surface, circumference, and volume
- Matrix functions to solve simultaneous equations
- Useful formulas for working with normal distributions

This chapter contains reference information that may be useful to you at some point. Consider it a cheat sheet to help you remember the stuff you may have learned but have long since forgotten.

Unit Conversions

You know the distance from New York to London in miles, but your European office needs the numbers in kilometers. What's the conversion factor?

Excel's CONVERT function can convert between a variety of measurements in the following categories:

- Area
- Distance
- Energy
- Force
- Information
- Magnetism

- Power
- Pressure
- Speed
- Temperature
- Time
- Volume (or liquid measure)
- Weight and mass

The CONVERT function requires three arguments: the value that you want to convert, the from-unit, and the to-unit. For example, if cell A1 contains a distance expressed in miles, use this formula to convert miles to kilometers:

```
=CONVERT(A1,"mi","km")
```

The second and third arguments are unit abbreviations, which are listed in the Excel Help system. Some of the abbreviations are commonly used, but others aren't. And, of course, you must use the *exact* abbreviation. Furthermore, the unit abbreviations are case sensitive, so the following formula returns an error:

```
=CONVERT(A1,"Mi","km")
```

The CONVERT function is even more versatile than it seems. When using metric units, you can apply a multiplier. In fact, the first example we presented uses a multiplier. The actual unit abbreviation for the third argument is *m* for meters. We added the kilo-multipler—*k*—to express the result in kilometers.

Sometimes you need to use a bit of creativity. For example, if you need to convert 100 km/hour into miles/sec, the formula requires two uses of the CONVERT function:

```
=CONVERT(100,"km","mi")/CONVERT(1,"hr","sec")
```

Figure 10-1 shows a conversion table for area measurements. The CONVERT argument codes are in column B and duplicated in row 3. Cell A1 contains a value. The formula in cell C4, which was copied down and across, is

```
=CONVERT($A$1,$B4,C$3)
```

The table shows, for example, that 1 square foot is equal to 144 square inches. It also shows that one square light year can hold a *lot* of acres.

By the way, this formula is also a good example of when to use an absolute reference and mixed references in a formula.

	A	B	C	D	E	F	G	H	I
1	1								
2			*International acre*	*U.S. survey/statute acre*	*Square angstrom*	*Are*	*Square feet*	*Hectare*	*Square inches*
3			**uk_acre**	**us_acre**	**ang2**	**ar**	**ft2**	**ha**	**in2**
4	*International acre*	uk_acre	1	0.999996	4.04686E+23	40.46856422	43560	0.404685642	6272640
5	*U.S. survey/statute acre*	us_acre	1.000004	1	4.04687E+23	40.4687261	43560.17424	0.404687261	6272665.091
6	*Square angstrom*	ang2	2.47105E-24	2.47104E-24	1	1E-22	1.07639E-19	1E-24	1.55E-17
7	*Are*	ar	0.024710538	0.024710439	1E+22	1	1076.391042	0.01	155000.31
8	*Square feet*	ft2	2.29568E-05	2.29567E-05	9.2903E+18	0.00092903	1	9.2903E-06	144
9	*Hectare*	ha	2.471053815	2.47104393	1E+24	100	107639.1042	1	15500031
10	*Square inches*	in2	1.59423E-07	1.59422E-07	6.4516E+16	6.4516E-06	0.006944444	6.4516E-08	1
11	*Square light-year*	ly2	2.21173E+28	2.21172E+28	8.95054E+51	8.95054E+29	9.63428E+32	8.95054E+27	1.38734E+35
12	*Square meters*	m2	0.000247105	0.000247104	1E+20	0.01	10.76391042	0.0001	1550.0031
13	*Morgen*	Morgen	0.617763454	0.617760983	2.5E+23	25	26909.77604	0.25	3875007.75
14	*Square miles*	mi2	640	639.99744	2.58999E+26	25899.8811	27878400	258.998811	4014489600
15	*Square nautical miles*	Nmi2	847.5477363	847.5443461	3.4299E+26	34299.04	36919179.39	342.9904	5316361833
16	*Square Pica*	Picapt2	3.07528E-11	3.07527E-11	1.24452E+13	1.24452E-09	1.33959E-06	1.24452E-11	0.000192901
17	*Square yards*	yd2	0.000206612	0.000206611	8.36127E+19	0.008361274	9	8.36127E-05	1296

Figure 10-1: A table that lists all the area units supported by the CONVERT function.

The workbook shown in Figure 10-1 is available at this book's website. The filename is area conversion table.xlsx.

Figure 10-2 shows part of a table that lists all the conversion units supported by the CONVERT function. The table can be sorted and filtered and indicates which of the units support the metric prefixes.

	Category	Unit	Abbreviation	Metric Prefixes?	For Excel 2013+
13	Area	Square nautical miles	"Nmi2" or "Nmi^2"	FALSE	TRUE
14	Area	Square Pica	"Picapt2", "Pica2", "I	FALSE	TRUE
15	Area	Square yards	"yd2" or "yd^2"	FALSE	TRUE
16	Distance	Meter	"m"	TRUE	FALSE
17	Distance	Statute mile	"mi"	FALSE	FALSE
18	Distance	Nautical mile	"Nmi"	FALSE	FALSE
19	Distance	Inch	"in"	FALSE	FALSE
20	Distance	Foot	"ft"	FALSE	FALSE
21	Distance	Yard	"yd"	FALSE	FALSE
22	Distance	Angstrom	"ang"	FALSE	FALSE
23	Distance	Ell	"ell"	FALSE	TRUE
24	Distance	Light-year	"ly"	FALSE	TRUE
25	Distance	Parsec	"parsec" or "pc"	FALSE	TRUE
26	Distance	Pica (1/72 inch)	"Picapt" or "Pica"	FALSE	TRUE
27	Distance	Pica (1/6 inch)	"pica"	FALSE	FALSE
28	Distance	U.S survey mile (statute mile)	"survey_mi"	FALSE	TRUE
29	Energy	Joule	"J"	TRUE	FALSE

Figure 10-2: A table that lists all the units supported by the CONVERT function.

On the Web

This workbook is available at this book's website. The filename is conversion units table.xlsx.

If you can't find a particular unit that works with the CONVERT function, perhaps Excel has another function that will do the job. Table 10-1 lists some other functions that convert between measurement units.

Table 10-1: Other Conversion Functions

Function	Description
ARABIC*	Converts an Arabic number to decimal
BASE*	Converts a decimal number to a specified base
BIN2DEC	Converts a binary number to decimal
BIN2OCT	Converts a binary number to octal
DEC2BIN	Converts a decimal number to binary
DEC2HEX	Converts a decimal number to hexadecimal
DEC2OCT	Converts a decimal number to octal
DEGREES	Converts an angle (in radians) to degrees
HEX2BIN	Converts a hexadecimal number to binary
HEX2DEC	Converts a hexadecimal number to decimal
HEX2OCT	Converts a hexadecimal number to octal
OCT2BIN	Converts an octal number to binary
OCT2DEC	Converts an octal number to decimal
OCT2HEX	Converts an octal number to hexadecimal
RADIANS	Converts an angle (in degrees) to radians

** Function available in Excel 2013 and higher versions.*

Need to convert other units?

The CONVERT function, of course, doesn't handle every possible unit conversion. To calculate other unit conversions, you need to find the appropriate conversion factor. The Internet is a good source for such information. Use any web search engine and enter search terms that correspond to the units you use. Likely, you'll find the information that you need.

Also, you can download a copy of Josh Madison's popular (and free) Convert software. This excellent program can handle just about any conceivable unit conversion that you throw at it. The URL is `http://joshmadison.com/convert-for-windows`.

You can use the program to find the conversion factor and then use that value in your formulas.

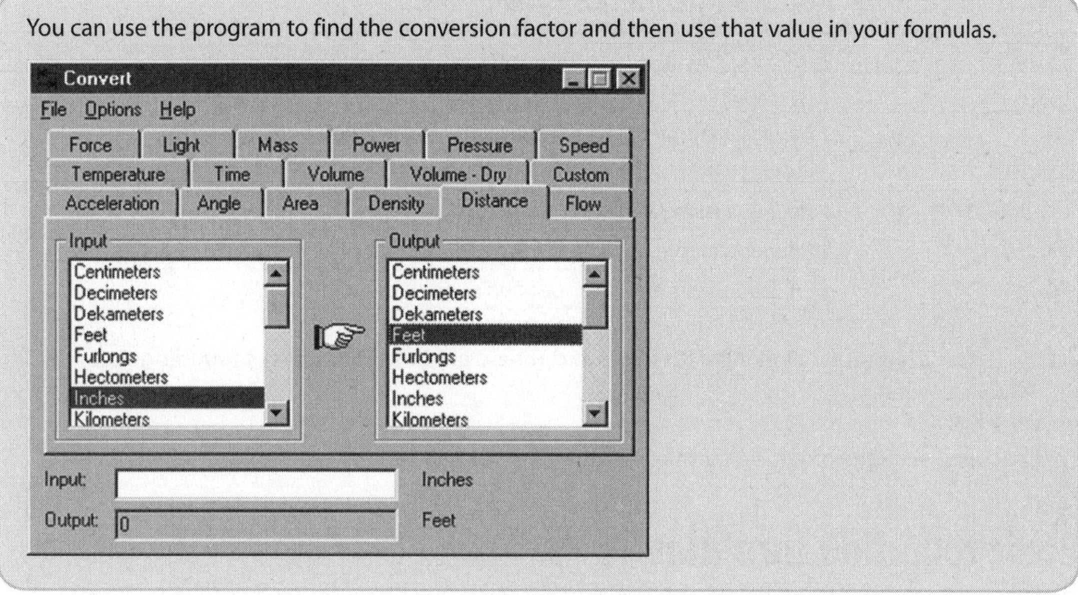

Rounding Numbers

Excel provides quite a few functions that round values in various ways. Table 10-2 summarizes these functions.

Warning

It's important to understand the difference between rounding a value and formatting a value. When you format a number to display a specific number of decimal places, formulas that refer to that number use the actual value, which may differ from the displayed value. When you round a number, formulas that refer to that value use the rounded number.

Table 10-2: Excel Rounding Functions

Function	Description
CEILING.MATH	Rounds a number up to the nearest specified multiple
DOLLARDE	Converts a dollar price expressed as a fraction into a decimal number
DOLLARFR	Converts a dollar price expressed as a decimal into a fractional number
EVEN	Rounds a number up (away from zero) to the nearest even integer
FLOOR.MATH	Rounds a number down to the nearest specified multiple
INT	Rounds a number down to make it an integer

continued

Table 10-2: Excel Rounding Functions *(continued)*

Function	Description
MROUND	Rounds a number to a specified multiple
ODD	Rounds a number up (away from zero) to the nearest odd integer
ROUND	Rounds a number to a specified number of digits
ROUNDDOWN	Rounds a number down (toward zero) to a specified number of digits
ROUNDUP	Rounds a number up (away from zero) to a specified number of digits
TRUNC	Truncates a number to a specified number of significant digits

Chapter 6, "Working with Dates and Times," contains examples of rounding time values.

The following sections provide examples of formulas that use various types of rounding.

Basic rounding formulas

The ROUND function is useful for basic rounding to a specified number of digits. You specify the number of digits in the second argument for the ROUND function. For example, the formula that follows returns *123.4*. (The value is rounded to one decimal place.)

```
=ROUND(123.37,1)
```

If the second argument for the ROUND function is zero, the value is rounded to the nearest integer. The formula that follows, for example, returns *123.00*:

```
=ROUND(123.37,0)
```

The second argument for the ROUND function can also be negative. In such a case, the number is rounded to the left of the decimal point. The following formula, for example, returns *120.00*:

```
=ROUND(123.37,-1)
```

The ROUND function rounds either up or down. But how does it handle a number such as 12.5, rounded to no decimal places? You'll find that the ROUND function rounds such numbers away from zero. The formula that follows, for instance, returns *13.0*:

```
=ROUND(12.5,0)
```

The next formula returns *–13.00*. (The rounding occurs away from zero.)

```
=ROUND(-12.5,0)
```

To force rounding to occur in a particular direction, use the ROUNDUP or ROUNDDOWN functions. The following formula, for example, returns *12.0*. The value rounds down:

```
=ROUNDDOWN(12.5,0)
```

The formula that follows returns *13.0*. The value rounds up to the nearest whole value:

```
=ROUNDUP(12.43,0)
```

Rounding to the nearest multiple

The MROUND function is useful for rounding values to the nearest multiple. For example, you can use this function to round a number to the nearest 5. The following formula returns *135*:

```
=MROUND(133,5)
```

The second argument for MROUND can be a fractional number. For example, this formula rounds the value in cell A1 to the nearest one-eighth:

```
=MROUND(A1,1/8)
```

Rounding currency values

Often, you need to round currency values. For example, you may need to round a dollar amount to the nearest penny. A calculated price may be something like $45.78923. In such a case, you'll want to round the calculated price to the nearest penny. This may sound simple, but there are actually three ways to round such a value:

- Round it up to the nearest penny.
- Round it down to the nearest penny.
- Round it to the nearest penny. (The rounding may be up or down.)

The following formula assumes that a dollar-and-cents value is in cell A1. The formula rounds the value to the nearest penny. For example, if cell A1 contains $12.421, the formula returns *$12.42*:

```
=ROUND(A1,2)
```

If you need to round the value *up* to the nearest penny, use the CEILING function. The following formula rounds the value in cell A1 up to the nearest penny. For example, if cell A1 contains $12.421, the formula returns *$12.43*:

```
=CEILING(A1,0.01)
```

To round a dollar value *down,* use the FLOOR function. The following formula, for example, rounds the dollar value in cell A1 down to the nearest penny. If cell A1 contains $12.421, the formula returns *$12.42*:

```
=FLOOR(A1,0.01)
```

To round a dollar value up to the nearest nickel, use this formula:

```
=CEILING(A1,0.05)
```

You've probably noticed that many retail prices end in $0.99. If you have an even-dollar price and you want it to end in $0.99, just subtract .01 from the price. Some higher-ticket items are always priced to end with $9.99. To round a price to the nearest $9.99, first round it to the nearest $10.00 and then subtract a penny. If cell A1 contains a price, use a formula like this to convert it to a price that ends in $9.99:

```
=(ROUND(A1/10,0)*10)-0.01
```

For example, if cell A1 contains $345.78, the formula returns *$349.99.*

A simpler approach uses the MROUND function:

```
=MROUND(A1,10)-0.01
```

Working with fractional dollars

The DOLLARFR and DOLLARDE functions are useful when working with fractional dollar values, as in stock market quotes.

Consider the value $9.25. You can express the decimal part as a fractional value ($9 1/4, $9 2/8, $9 4/16, and so on). The DOLLARFR function takes two arguments: the dollar amount and the denominator for the fractional part. The following formula, for example, returns *9.1* (and is interpreted as "nine and one-quarter"):

```
=DOLLARFR(9.25,4)
```

This formula returns *9.2* (interpreted as "nine and two-eighths"):

```
=DOLLARFR(9.25,8)
```

Warning

In most situations, you won't use the value returned by the DOLLARFR function in other calculations. To perform calculations on such a value, you need to convert it back to a decimal value by using the DOLLARDE function.

The DOLLARDE function converts a dollar value expressed as a fraction to a decimal amount. It also uses a second argument to specify the denominator of the fractional part. The following formula, for example, returns *9.25*:

```
=DOLLARDE(9.1,4)
```

Working with feet and inches

A problem that has always plagued Excel users is how to work with measurements that are in feet and inches. Excel doesn't have any special features to make it easy to work with this type of measurement units, but in some cases, you can use the DOLLARDE and DOLLARFR functions.

If you enter **5'9"** into a cell, Excel interprets it as a text string—not five feet, nine inches. But if you enter the value as 5.09, you can work with it as a value by using the DOLLARDE function. The following formula returns *5.75,* which is the decimal representation of five feet nine inches expressed as fractional feet:

```
=DOLLARDE(5.09,12)
```

If you don't work with fractional inches, you can even create a custom number format. Entering the following custom format will display values as feet and inches.

```
#" ft". 00" in."
```

On the Web

This workbook is available at this book's website. The filename is feet and inches.xlsx.

Using the INT and TRUNC functions

On the surface, the INT and TRUNC functions seem similar. Both convert a value to an integer. The TRUNC function simply removes the fractional part of a number. The INT function rounds a number down to the nearest integer, based on the value of the fractional part of the number.

In practice, INT and TRUNC return different results only when using negative numbers. For example, the following formula returns *–14.0*:

```
=TRUNC(-14.2)
```

The next formula returns *–15.0* because –14.3 is rounded down to the next lower integer:

```
=INT(-14.2)
```

The TRUNC function takes an additional (optional) argument that's useful for truncating decimal values. For example, the formula that follows returns *54.33* (the value truncated to two decimal places):

```
=TRUNC(54.3333333,2)
```

Rounding to an even or odd integer

The ODD and EVEN functions are provided when you need to round a number up to the nearest odd or even integer. These functions take a single argument and return an integer value. The EVEN function rounds its argument up to the nearest even integer. The ODD function rounds its argument up to the nearest odd integer. Table 10-3 shows some examples of these functions.

Table 10-3: Results Using the EVEN and ODD Functions

Number	EVEN Functiwon	ODD Function
–3.6	–4	–5
–3.0	–4	–3
–2.4	–4	–3
–1.8	–2	–3
–1.2	–2	–3
–0.6	–2	–1
0.0	0	1
0.6	2	1
1.2	2	3
1.8	2	3
2.4	4	3
3.0	4	3
3.6	4	5

Rounding to *n* significant digits

In some cases, you may need to round a value to a particular number of significant digits. For example, you might want to express the value 1,432,187 in terms of two significant digits: that is, as 1,400,000. The value 9,187,877 expressed in terms of three significant digits is 9,180,000.

If the value is a positive number with no decimal places, the following formula does the job. This formula rounds the number in cell A1 to two significant digits. To round to a different number of significant digits, replace the 2 in this formula with a different number:

```
=ROUNDDOWN(A1,2-LEN(A1))
```

For nonintegers and negative numbers, the solution gets a bit trickier. The formula that follows provides a more general solution that rounds the value in cell A1 to the number of significant digits specified in cell A2. This formula works for positive and negative integers and nonintegers:

```
=ROUND(A1,A2-1-INT(LOG10(ABS(A1))))
```

For example, if cell A1 contains 1.27845 and cell A2 contains 3, the formula returns *1.28000* (the value, rounded to three significant digits).

Note

Don't confuse this technique with significant decimal digits, which are the number of digits displayed to the right of the decimal points. It's an entirely different concept. Also, these formulas make the values less accurate.

Solving Right Triangles

A right triangle has six components: three sides and three angles. Figure 10-3 shows a right triangle with its various parts labeled. Angles are labeled A, B, and C; sides are labeled Hypotenuse, Base, and Height. Angle C is always 90 degrees (or PI/2 radians). If you know any two of these components (excluding Angle C, which is always known), you can use formulas to solve for the others.

The Pythagorean theorem states that

```
Height^2 + Base^2 = Hypotenuse^2
```

Therefore, if you know two sides of a right triangle, you can calculate the remaining side. The formula to calculate a right triangle's height (given the length of the hypotenuse and base) is as follows:

```
=SQRT((hypotenuse^2) - (base^2))
```

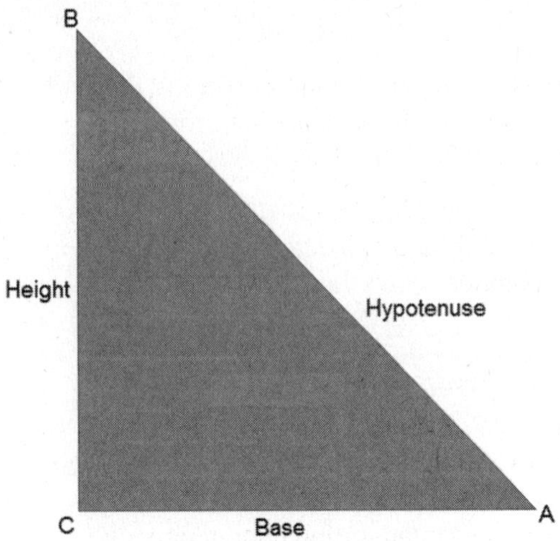

Figure 10-3: A right triangle's components.

The formula to calculate a right triangle's base (given the length of the hypotenuse and height) is as follows:

```
=SQRT((hypotenuse^2) - (height^2))
```

The formula to calculate a right triangle's hypotenuse (given the length of the base and height) is as follows:

```
=SQRT((height^2)+(base^2))
```

Other useful trigonometric identities are

```
SIN(A) = Height/Hypotenuse
SIN(B) = Base/Hypotenuse
COS(A) = Base/Hypotenuse
COS(B) = Height/Hypotenuse
TAN(A) = Height/Base
SIN(A) = Base/Height
```

Note

Excel's trigonometric functions assume that the angle arguments are in radians. To convert degrees to radians, use the RADIANS function. To convert radians to degrees, use the DEGREES function.

If you know the height and base, you can use the following formula to calculate the angle formed by the hypotenuse and base (angle A):

```
=ATAN(height/base)
```

The preceding formula returns radians. To convert to degrees, use this formula:

```
=DEGREES(ATAN(height/base))
```

If you know the height and base, you can use the following formula to calculate the angle formed by the hypotenuse and height (angle B):

```
=PI()/2-ATAN(height/base)
```

The preceding formula returns radians. To convert to degrees, use this formula:

```
=90-DEGREES(ATAN(height/base))
```

On the Web

This book's website contains a workbook —solve right triangle.xlsm— with formulas that calculate various parts of a right triangle, given two known parts. These formulas give you some insight on working with right triangles. The workbook uses a simple VBA macro to enable you to specify the known parts of the triangle.

Figure 10-4 shows a workbook containing formulas to calculate the various parts of a right triangle.

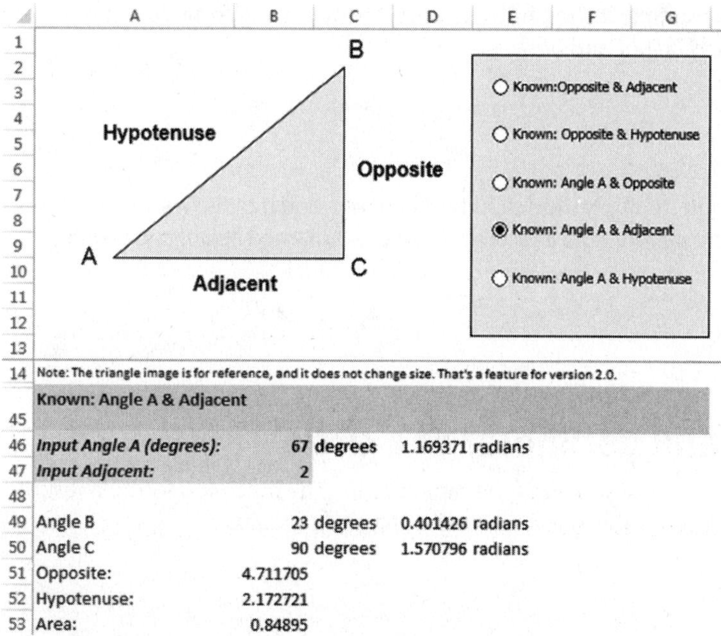

Figure 10-4: This workbook is useful for working with right triangles.

Area, Surface, Circumference, and Volume Calculations

This section contains formulas for calculating the area, surface, circumference, and volume for common two- and three-dimensional shapes.

Calculating the area and perimeter of a square

To calculate the area of a square, square the length of one side. The following formula calculates the area of a square for a cell named *side*:

```
=side^2
```

To calculate the perimeter of a square, multiply one side by 4. The following formula uses a cell named *side* to calculate the perimeter of a square:

```
=side*4
```

Calculating the area and perimeter of a rectangle

To calculate the area of a rectangle, multiply its height by its base. The following formula returns the area of a rectangle, using cells named *height* and *base*:

```
=height*base
```

To calculate the perimeter of a rectangle, multiply the height by 2 and then add it to the width multiplied by 2. The following formula returns the perimeter of a rectangle, using cells named *height* and *width*:

```
=(height*2)+(width*2)
```

Calculating the area and perimeter of a circle

To calculate the area of a circle, multiply the square of the radius by (π). The following formula returns the area of a circle. It assumes that a cell named *radius* contains the circle's radius:

```
=PI()*(radius^2)
```

The radius of a circle is equal to one-half of the diameter.

To calculate the circumference of a circle, multiply the diameter of the circle by (π). The following formula calculates the circumference of a circle using a cell named *diameter*:

```
=diameter*PI()
```

The diameter of a circle is the radius times 2.

Calculating the area of a trapezoid

To calculate the area of a trapezoid, add the two parallel sides, multiply by the height, and then divide by 2. The following formula calculates the area of a trapezoid, using cells named *parallel side 1, parallel side 2,* and *height*:

```
=((parallel side 1+parallel side 2)*height)/2
```

Calculating the area of a triangle

To calculate the area of a triangle, multiply the base by the height and then divide by 2. The following formula calculates the area of a triangle, using cells named *base* and *height*:

```
=(base*height)/2
```

Calculating the surface and volume of a sphere

To calculate the surface of a sphere, multiply the square of the radius by (π) and then multiply by 4. The following formula returns the surface of a sphere, the radius of which is in a cell named *radius*:

```
=PI()*(radius^2)*4
```

To calculate the volume of a sphere, multiply the cube of the radius by 4 times (π) and then divide by 3. The following formula calculates the volume of a sphere. The cell named *radius* contains the sphere's radius:

```
=((radius^3)*(4*PI()))/3
```

Calculating the surface and volume of a cube

To calculate the surface area of a cube, square one side and multiply by 6. The following formula calculates the surface of a cube using a cell named *side,* which contains the length of a side of the cube:

```
=(side^2)*6
```

To calculate the volume of a cube, raise the length of one side to the third power. The following formula returns the volume of a cube, using a cell named *side*:

```
=side^3
```

Calculating the surface and volume of a rectangular solid

The following formula calculates the surface of a rectangular solid using cells named *height, width,* and *length*:

```
=(length*height*2)+(length*width*2)+(width*height*2)
```

To calculate the volume of a rectangular solid, multiply the height by the width by the length:

```
=height*width*length
```

Calculating the surface and volume of a cone

The following formula calculates the surface of a cone (including the surface of the base). This formula uses cells named *radius* and *height*:

```
=PI()*radius*(SQRT(height^2+radius^2)+radius)
```

To calculate the volume of a cone, multiply the square of the radius of the base by (π), multiply by the height, and then divide by 3. The following formula returns the volume of a cone, using cells named *radius* and *height*:

```
=(PI()*(radius^2)*height)/3
```

Calculating the volume of a cylinder

To calculate the volume of a cylinder, multiply the square of the radius of the base by (π) and then multiply by the height. The following formula calculates the volume of a cylinder, using cells named *radius* and *height*:

```
=(PI()*(radius^2)*height)
```

Calculating the volume of a pyramid

Calculate the area of the base, multiply by the height, and then divide by 3. This formula calculates the volume of a pyramid. It assumes cells named *width* (the width of the base), *length* (the length of the base), and *height* (the height of the pyramid).

```
=(width*length*height)/3
```

Solving Simultaneous Equations

This section describes how to use formulas to solve simultaneous linear equations. The following is an example of a set of simultaneous linear equations:

```
3x + 4y = 8
4x + 8y = 1
```

Solving a set of simultaneous equations involves finding the values for x and y that satisfy both equations. For this set of equations, the solution is as follows:

```
x = 7.5
y = -3.625
```

The number of variables in the set of equations must be equal to the number of equations. The preceding example uses two equations with two variables. Three equations are required to solve for three variables (x, y, and z).

The general steps for solving a set of simultaneous equations follow. See Figure 10-5, which uses the equations presented at the beginning of this section.

1. **Express the equations in standard form.** If necessary, use simple algebra to rewrite the equations such that all the variables appear on the left side of the equal sign. The two equations that follow are identical, but the second one is in standard form:

   ```
   3x -8 = -4y
   3x + 4y = 8
   ```

2. **Place the coefficients in an $n \times n$ range of cells, where n represents the number of equations.** In Figure 10-5, the coefficients are in the range I2:J3.

3. **Place the constants (the numbers on the right side of the equal sign) in a vertical range of cells.** In Figure 10-5, the constants are in the range L2:L3.

4. Use an array formula to calculate the inverse of the coefficient matrix. In Figure 10-5, the following array formula is entered into the range I6:J7. (Remember to press Ctrl+Shift+Enter to enter an array formula, and omit the curly brackets.)

```
{=MINVERSE(I2:J3)}
```

5. Use an array formula to multiply the inverse of the coefficient matrix by the constant matrix. In Figure 10-5, the following array formula is entered into the range J10:J11. This range holds the solution:

```
{=MMULT(I6:J7,L2:L3)}
```

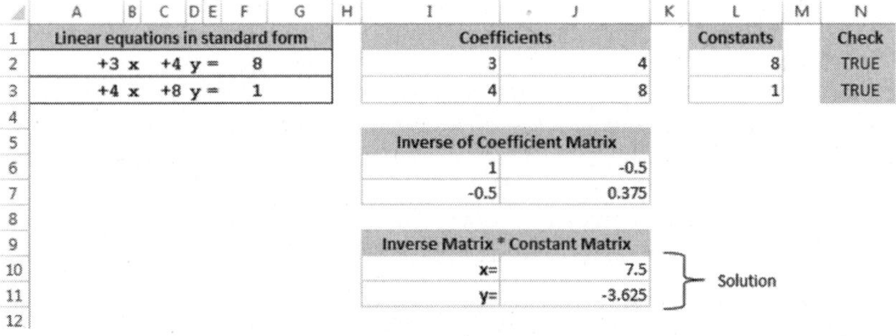

	A	B	C	D	E	F	G	H	I	J	K	L	M	N
1	Linear equations in standard form								Coefficients			Constants		Check
2		+3	x	+4	y =	8			3	4		8		TRUE
3		+4	x	+8	y =	1			4	8		1		TRUE
4														
5									Inverse of Coefficient Matrix					
6									1	-0.5				
7									-0.5	0.375				
8														
9									Inverse Matrix * Constant Matrix					
10									x=	7.5		Solution		
11									y=	-3.625				
12														

Figure 10-5: Using formulas to solve simultaneous equations.

Cross-Ref

See Chapter 14, "Introducing Arrays," for more information on array formulas.

On the Web

You can access the workbook, simultaneous equations.xlsx, shown in Figure 10-5, from this book's website. This workbook solves simultaneous equations with two or three variables.

Working with Normal Distributions

In statistics, a common topic is the normal distribution, also known as a *bell curve.* Excel has several functions designed to work with normal distributions. This is not a statistics book, so we assume that if you're reading this section, you're familiar with the concept.

On the Web

The examples in this section are available at this book's website. The filename is normal distribution.xlsx.

Figure 10-6 shows a workbook containing formulas that generate the two charts: a normal distribution and a cumulative normal distribution.

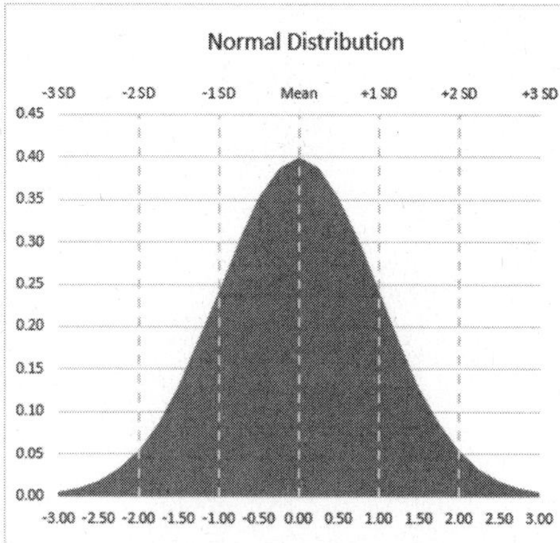

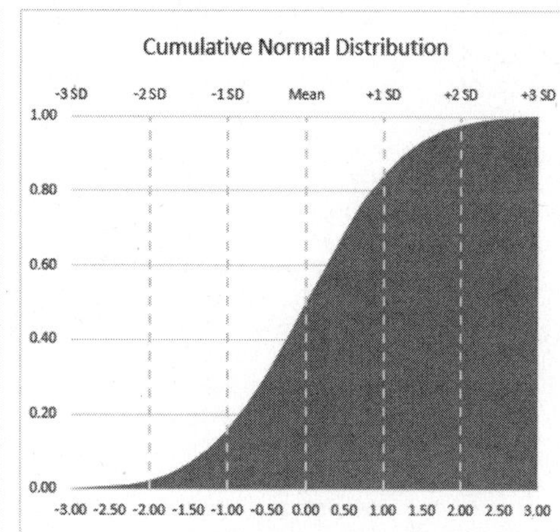

Figure 10-6: Using formulas to calculate a normal distribution and a cumulative normal distribution.

The formulas use the values entered into cell B1 (name *Mean*) and cell B2 (named *SD*, for *standard deviation*). The values calculated cover the mean plus/minus three standard deviations. Column A contains formulas that generate 25 equally spaced intervals, ranging from –3 standard deviations to +3 standard deviations.

A normal distribution with a mean of 0 and a standard deviation of 1 is known as the "standard normal distribution." The worksheet is set up to work with any mean and any standard deviation.

Formulas in column B calculate the height of the normal curve for each of the 25 values in column A. Cell B5 contains this formula, which is copied down the column:

```
=NORM.DIST(A5,Mean,SD,FALSE)
```

The formula in cell C5 is the same, except for the last argument. When that argument is *TRUE*, the function returns the cumulative probability:

```
=NORMDIST(A5,Mean,SD,TRUE)
```

Figure 10-7 shows a worksheet with 2,600 data points in column A (named *Data*) that is approximately normally distributed. Formulas in column D calculate some basic statistics for this data: N (the number of data points), the minimum, the maximum, the mean, and the standard deviation.

Column F contains an array formula that creates 25 equal-interval bins that cover the complete range of the data. It uses the technique described in Chapter 7, "Counting and Summing Techniques." The multicell array formula, entered in F2:F26 (named *Bins*), is

```
=MIN(Data)+(ROW(INDIRECT("1:25"))*(MAX(Data)-MIN(Data)+1)/25)-1
```

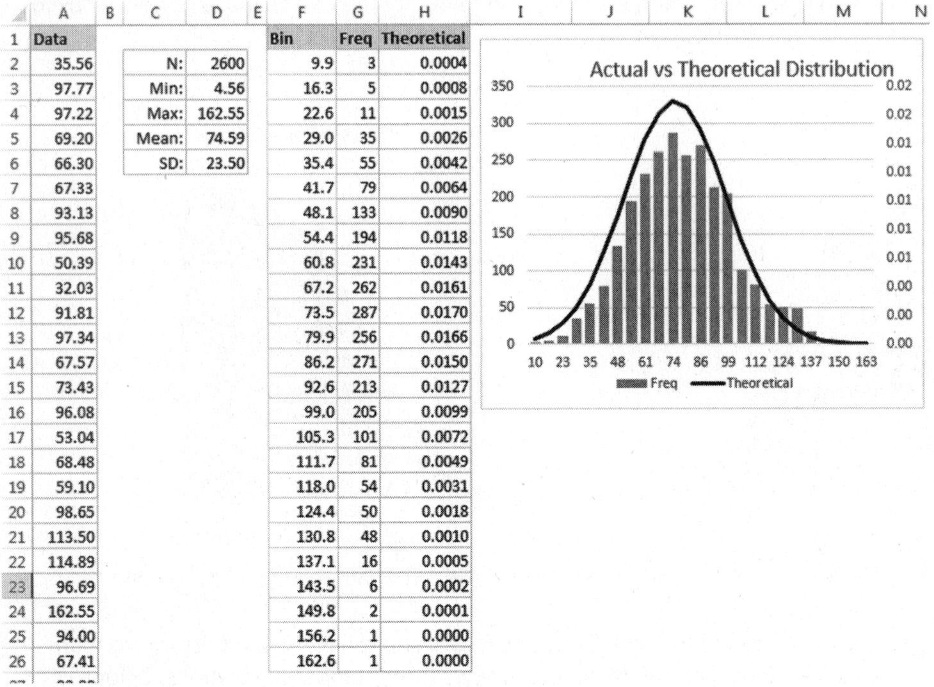

	A	C	D	F	G	H
1	Data			Bin	Freq	Theoretical
2	35.56	N:	2600	9.9	3	0.0004
3	97.77	Min:	4.56	16.3	5	0.0008
4	97.22	Max:	162.55	22.6	11	0.0015
5	69.20	Mean:	74.59	29.0	35	0.0026
6	66.30	SD:	23.50	35.4	55	0.0042
7	67.33			41.7	79	0.0064
8	93.13			48.1	133	0.0090
9	95.68			54.4	194	0.0118
10	50.39			60.8	231	0.0143
11	32.03			67.2	262	0.0161
12	91.81			73.5	287	0.0170
13	97.34			79.9	256	0.0166
14	67.57			86.2	271	0.0150
15	73.43			92.6	213	0.0127
16	96.08			99.0	205	0.0099
17	53.04			105.3	101	0.0072
18	68.48			111.7	81	0.0049
19	59.10			118.0	54	0.0031
20	98.65			124.4	50	0.0018
21	113.50			130.8	48	0.0010
22	114.89			137.1	16	0.0005
23	96.69			143.5	6	0.0002
24	162.55			149.8	2	0.0001
25	94.00			156.2	1	0.0000
26	67.41			162.6	1	0.0000

Figure 10-7: Comparing a set of data with a normal distribution.

Column G also contains a multicell array formula that calculates the frequency for each of the 25 bins:

```
=FREQUENCY(Data,Bins)
```

The data in column G is displayed in the chart as columns and uses the axis on the left.

Column H contains formulas that calculate the value of the theoretical normal distribution, using the mean and standard deviation of the *Data* range.

The formula in cell H2, which is copied down the column, is

```
=NORMDIST(F2,$D$5,$D$6,FALSE)
```

In the chart, the values in column H are plotted as a line and use the right axis. As you can see, the data conforms fairly well to the normal distribution. There are goodness-of-fit tests to determine the "normality" of a set of data samples, but that's beyond the scope of this book.

Financial Formulas

Borrowing and Investing Formulas

In This Chapter

- A brief overview of the Excel functions that deal with the time value of money
- Formulas that perform various types of loan calculations
- Formulas that perform various types of investment calculations

It's a safe bet that the most common use for Excel is to perform calculations involving money. Every day, people make hundreds of thousands of financial decisions based on the numbers that are calculated in a spreadsheet. These decisions range from simple (*Can I afford to buy a new car?*) to complex (*Will purchasing XYZ Corporation result in a positive cash flow in the next 18 months?*). This is the first of three chapters that discuss financial calculations you can perform with the assistance of Excel.

The Time Value of Money

The face value of money may not always be what it seems. A key consideration is the time value of money. This concept involves calculating the value of money in the past, present, or future. It's based on the premise that money increases in value over time because of interest earned by the money. In other words, a dollar invested today will be worth more tomorrow.

For example, imagine that your rich uncle decided to give away some money and asked you to choose one of the following options:

- Receive $8,000 today
- Receive $9,500 in one year
- Receive $12,000 in five years
- Receive $150 per month for five years

If your goal is to maximize the amount received, you need to take into account not only the face value of the money but also the *time value* of the money when it arrives in your hands.

The time value of money depends on your perspective. In other words, you're either a lender or a borrower. When you take out a loan to purchase an automobile, you're a borrower, and the institution that provides the funds to you is the lender. When you invest money in a bank savings account, you're a lender; you're lending your money to the bank, and the bank is borrowing it from you.

Several concepts contribute to the time value of money:

- **Present value (PV):** This is the principal amount. If you deposit $5,000 in a bank savings account, this amount represents the *principal,* or present value, of the money you invested. If you borrow $15,000 to purchase a car, this amount represents the principal, or present value, of the loan. The present value may be positive or negative.
- **Future value (FV):** This is the principal plus interest. If you invest $5,000 for five years and earn 3% annual interest, your investment is worth $5,796.37 at the end of the five-year term. This amount is the future value of your $5,000 investment. If you take out a three-year car loan for $15,000 and make monthly payments based on a 5.25% annual interest rate, you pay a total of $16,244.97. This amount represents the principal plus the interest you paid. The future value may be positive or negative, depending on the perspective (lender or borrower).
- **Payment (PMT):** This is either principal or principal plus interest. If you deposit $100 per month into a savings account, $100 is the payment. If you have a monthly mortgage payment of $1,025, this amount is made up of principal and interest.
- **Interest rate:** Interest is a percentage of the principal, usually expressed on an annual basis. For example, you may earn 2.5% annual interest on a bank CD (certificate of deposit). Or your mortgage loan may have a 6.75% interest rate.
- **Period:** This represents the point in time when interest is paid or earned, such as a bank CD that pays interest quarterly or an auto loan that requires monthly payments.
- **Term:** This is the amount of time of interest. A 12-month bank CD has a term of one year. A 30-year mortgage loan has a term of 360 months.

Loan Calculations

This section describes how to calculate various components of a loan. Think of a loan as consisting of the following components:

- The loan amount
- The interest rate
- The number of payment periods
- The periodic payment amount

If you know any three of these components, you can create a formula to calculate the unknown component.

Note

All the loan calculations in this section assume a fixed-rate loan with a fixed term.

Worksheet functions for calculating loan information

This section describes six commonly used financial functions: PMT, PPMT, IPMT, RATE, NPER, and PV. For information about the arguments used in these functions, see Table 11-1. In the sections that follow, you'll notice that many of the functions also serve as arguments of other functions. This is quite logical, as all of these terms are interconnected with each other in a variety of ways.

Table 11-1: Financial Function Arguments

Function Argument	Description
rate	The interest rate per period. If the rate is expressed as an annual interest rate, you must divide it by the number of periods in a year.
nper	The total number of payment periods.
per	A particular period. The period must be less than or equal to nper.
pmt	The payment made each period (a constant value that does not change).
fv	The future value after the last payment is made. If you omit fv, it is assumed to be 0. (The future value of a loan, for example, is 0.)
type	Indicates when payments are due—either 0 (due at the end of the period) or 1 (due at the beginning of the period). If you omit type, it is assumed to be 0.
guess	Used by the RATE function. An initial estimate of what the result will be. The RATE function is calculated by iteration. If the function doesn't converge on a result, changing the guess argument helps.

PMT

The PMT function answers the question, "How much will my payment be for a loan with constant payment amounts and a fixed interest rate?" The syntax for the PMT function follows:

```
PMT(rate,nper,pv,fv,type)
```

The following formula returns the monthly payment amount for a $5,000 loan with a 6% annual percentage rate. The loan has a term of four years (48 months).

```
=PMT(6&/12,48,5000)
```

This formula returns *($117.43)*, the monthly payment for the loan. The first argument, rate, is the annual rate divided by the number of months in a year to convert it to monthly rate. Also, notice that the third argument (pv, for present value) is positive because it's a cash inflow to you (the borrower), and the result is negative because the payments are cash outflows.

PPMT

The PPMT function answers the question, "How much of a particular payment is applied to the principal?" The syntax for the PPMT function follows:

```
PPMT(rate,per,nper,pv,fv,type)
```

The following formula returns the amount paid to principal for the first month of a $5,000 loan with a 6% annual percentage rate. The loan has a term of four years (48 months):

```
=PPMT(6&/12,1,48,5000)
```

The formula returns *($92.43)* for the principal, which is about 78.7% of the total loan payment. If we change the second argument to 48 (to calculate the principal amount for the last payment), the formula returns *($116.84),* or about 99.5% of the total loan payment.

Note

To calculate the cumulative principal paid between any two payment periods, use the CUMPRINC function. This function uses two additional arguments: start_period and end_period. In Excel versions prior to Excel 2007, CUMPRINC is available only when you install the Analysis ToolPak add-in.

IPMT

The IPMT function answers the question, "How much of a particular payment is for interest?" Here's the syntax for the IPMT function:

```
IPMT(rate,per,nper,pv,fv,type)
```

The following formula returns the amount paid to interest for the first month of a $5,000 loan with a 6% annual percentage rate. The loan has a term of four years (48 months):

```
=IPMT(6&/12,1,48,5000)
```

This formula returns an interest amount of $25.00. By the last payment period for the loan, the interest payment is only $0.58. If you add the result of IPMT to PPMT for the same payment, you get the result of PMT (the total payment amount).

Note

To calculate the cumulative interest paid between any two payment periods, use the CUMIPMT function. This function uses two additional arguments: start_period and end_period. In Excel versions prior to Excel 2007, CUMIPMT is available only when you install the Analysis ToolPak add-in.

RATE

The RATE function answers the question, "What is the interest rate of my loan given the number of payment periods, the payment amount, and the loan amount?" Here's the syntax for the RATE function:

```
RATE(nper,pmt,pv,fv,type,guess)
```

The following formula calculates the annual interest rate for a 48-month loan for $5,000 that has a monthly payment amount of $117.43:

```
=RATE(48,-117.43,5000)*12
```

This formula returns *6.00%*. Notice that the result of the function is multiplied by 12 to get the annual percentage rate.

NPER

The NPER function answers the question, "How many payments are needed to pay off my loan given the loan amount, interest rate, and periodic payment amount?" Here's the syntax for the NPER function:

```
NPER(rate,pmt,pv,fv,type)
```

The following formula calculates the number of payment periods for a $5,000 loan that has a monthly payment amount of $117.43. The loan has a 6% annual interest rate:

```
=NPER(6&/12,-117.43,5000)
```

This formula returns *47.997* (that is, 48 months). The monthly payment was rounded to the nearest penny, causing the minor discrepancy.

PV

The PV function answers the question, "How much can I borrow given the interest rate, the number of periods, and the payment amount?" The syntax for the PV function follows:

```
PV(rate,nper,pmt,fv,type)
```

The next formula calculates the amount of a loan that can be paid off with 48 monthly payments of $117.43 at an annual interest rate of 6%:

```
=PV(6&/12,48,-117.43)
```

This formula returns *$5,000.21*. The monthly payment was rounded to the nearest penny, causing the $0.21 discrepancy.

A loan calculation example

Figure 11-1 shows a worksheet set up to calculate the periodic payment amount for a loan.

	A	B	C
1	Loan Amount:	$25,000.00	
2	Annual Interest Rate:	6.25%	
3	Payment Period (months):	1	
4	Number of Periods:	36	
5			
6	Payment per Period:	$763.38	
7			
8			
9	Period	36	
10	Principal Amount	$759.43	
11	Interest Amount	$3.96	
12			

Figure 11-1: Using the PMT function to calculate a periodic loan payment amount.

On the Web

The workbook described in this section is available at this book's website. The file is named loan payment.xlsx.

The loan amount is in cell B1, and the annual interest rate is in cell B2. Cell B3 contains the payment period expressed in months. For example, if cell B3 is 1, the payment is due monthly. If cell B3 is 3, the payment is due every three months, or quarterly. Cell B4 contains the number of periods of the loan. The example shown in this figure calculates the payment for a $25,000 loan at 6.25% annual interest with monthly payments for 36 months. The formula in cell B6 follows:

```
=PMT(B2*(B3/12),B4,-B1)
```

Notice that the first argument is an expression that calculates the *periodic interest rate* by using the annual interest rate and the payment period. Therefore, if payments are made quarterly on a three-year loan, the payment period is 3, the number of periods is 12, and the periodic interest rate is calculated as the annual interest rate multiplied by three-twelfths.

The worksheet in Figure 11-1 is set up to calculate the principal and interest amount for a particular payment period. Cell B9 contains the payment period used by the formulas in B10:B11. (The payment period must be less than or equal to the value in cell B4.)

The formula in cell B10, shown here, calculates the amount of the payment that goes toward principal for the payment period in cell B9:

```
=PPMT(B2*(B3/12),B9,B4,-B1)
```

The following formula, in cell B11, calculates the amount of the payment that goes toward interest for the payment period in cell B9:

```
=IPMT(B2*(B3/12),B9,B4,-B1)
```

The sum of B10 and B11 is equal to the total loan payment calculated in cell B6. However, the relative proportion of principal and interest amounts varies with the payment period. (An increasingly larger proportion of the payment is applied toward principal as the loan progresses.) Figure 11-2 shows the principal and interest portions graphically.

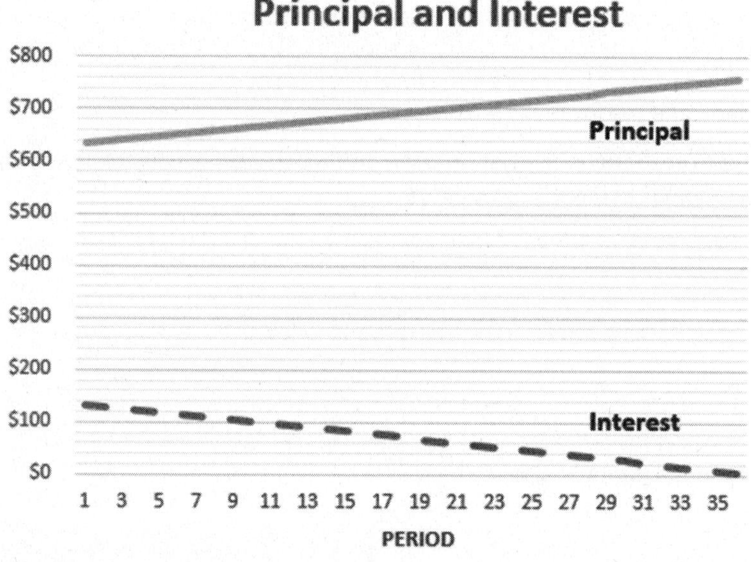

Figure 11-2: This chart shows how the interest and principal amounts vary during the payment periods of a loan.

Credit card payments

Do you ever wonder how long it takes to pay off a credit card balance if you make the minimum payment amount each month? Figure 11-3 shows a worksheet set up to make this type of calculation.

	A	B	C
1	Credit Card Balance	$1,000.00	
2	Annual Interest Rate:	21.25%	
3	Minimum Payment Pct:	2.00%	
4	Minimum Monthly Payment Amount:	$20.00	
5	Your Actual Monthly Payment:	$20.00	
6			
7	No. of Payments Required:	123.4	10.3 years
8	Total Amount Paid:	$2,468.42	
9	Total Interest Paid:	$1,468.42	
10			

Figure 11-3: This worksheet calculates the number of payments required to pay off a credit card balance by paying the minimum payment amount each month.

On the Web

The workbook shown in Figure 11-3 is available at this book's website. The file is named credit card payments.xlsx.

Range B1:B5 stores input values. In this example, the credit card has a balance of $1,000, and the lender charges a 21.25% annual percentage rate (APR). The minimum payment is 2.00% (typical of many credit card lenders). Therefore, the minimum payment amount for this example is $20. You can enter a different payment amount in cell B5, but it must be large enough to pay off the loan. For example, you may choose to pay $50 per month to pay off the balance more quickly. However, paying $10 per month isn't sufficient, and the formulas return an error.

Range B7:B9 holds formulas that perform various calculations. The formula in cell B7, which follows, calculates the number of months required to pay off the balance:

```
=NPER(B2/12,B5,-B1,0)
```

The formula in B8 calculates the total amount you will pay. This formula follows:

```
=B7*B5
```

The formula in cell B9 calculates the total interest paid:

```
=B8-B1
```

In this example, it would take about 123 months (more than 10 years) to pay off the credit card balance if the borrower made only the minimum monthly payment. The total interest paid on the $1,000 loan would be $1,468.42. This calculation assumes, of course, that no additional charges are made on the account. This example may help explain why you receive so many credit card solicitations in the mail.

Figure 11-4 shows some additional calculations for the credit card example. For example, if you want to pay off the credit card in 12 months, you need to make monthly payments of $93.23. (This amount results in total payments of $1,118.81 with total interest of $118.81.) The formula in B13 follows:

```
=PMT($B$2/12,A13,-$B$1)
```

11				
12	Other Payoff Periods (months)	Pmt Required	Total Pmts	Total Interest
13	2	$513.32	$1,026.64	$26.64
14	6	$177.15	$1,062.89	$62.89
15	12	$93.23	$1,118.81	$118.81
16	24	$51.51	$1,236.20	$236.20
17	36	$37.80	$1,360.93	$360.93
18	48	$31.10	$1,492.82	$492.82
19	60	$27.19	$1,631.65	$631.65
20	72	$24.68	$1,777.17	$777.17
21	84	$22.96	$1,929.06	$929.06
22	96	$21.74	$2,086.97	$1,086.97
23	108	$20.84	$2,250.54	$1,250.54
24	120	$20.16	$2,419.38	$1,419.38
25	132	$19.64	$2,593.09	$1,593.09
26				

Figure 11-4: The second column shows the payment required to pay off the credit card balance for various payoff periods.

Creating a loan amortization schedule

A *loan amortization schedule* is a table of values that shows various types of information for each payment period of a loan. Figure 11-5 shows a worksheet that uses formulas to calculate an amortization schedule.

	A	B	C	D	E	F	G	H
1	Loan Amount:		$18,500.00					
2	Annual Interest Rate:		7.25%					
3	Pmt. Period (months):		1					
4	Number of Periods:		36					
5								
6				Loan Amortization Schedule				
7	Payment Period	Payment Amount	Cumulative Payments	Interest	Cumulative Interest	Principal	Cumulative Principal	Principal Balance
8								$18,500.00
9	1	$573.34	$573.34	$111.77	$111.77	$461.57	$461.57	18,038.43
10	2	573.34	1,146.69	108.98	220.75	464.36	925.93	17,574.07
11	3	573.34	1,720.03	106.18	326.93	467.17	1,393.10	17,106.90
12	4	573.34	2,293.37	103.35	430.28	469.99	1,863.09	16,636.91
13	5	573.34	2,866.72	100.51	530.80	472.83	2,335.92	16,164.08
14	6	573.34	3,440.06	97.66	628.46	475.69	2,811.60	15,688.40
15	7	573.34	4,013.40	94.78	723.24	478.56	3,290.16	15,209.84
16	8	573.34	4,586.75	91.89	815.13	481.45	3,771.61	14,728.39
17	9	573.34	5,160.09	88.98	904.12	484.36	4,255.97	14,244.03
18	10	573.34	5,733.43	86.06	990.18	487.29	4,743.26	13,756.74
19	11	573.34	6,306.78	83.11	1,073.29	490.23	5,233.49	13,266.51
20	12	573.34	6,880.12	80.15	1,153.44	493.19	5,726.68	12,773.32
21	13	573.34	7,453.46	77.17	1,230.61	496.17	6,222.85	12,277.15
22	14	573.34	8,026.81	74.17	1,304.79	499.17	6,722.02	11,777.98
23	15	573.34	8,600.15	71.16	1,375.95	502.18	7,224.20	11,275.80
24	16	573.34	9,173.49	68.12	1,444.07	505.22	7,729.42	10,770.58
25	17	573.34	9,746.84	65.07	1,509.14	508.27	8,237.69	10,262.31

Figure 11-5: A loan amortization schedule.

On the Web

This workbook is available on this book's website. The file is named loan amortization schedule.xlsx.

The loan parameters are entered into C1:C4, and the formulas beginning in row 9 use these values for the calculations. Table 11-2 shows the formulas in row 9 of the schedule. These formulas were copied down to row 488. Therefore, the worksheet can calculate amortization schedules for a loan with as many as 480 payment periods (40 years of monthly payments).

Note

Formulas in the rows that extend beyond the number of payments return an error value. The worksheet uses conditional formatting to hide the data in these rows.

Cross-Ref

See Chapter 19, "Conditional Formatting," for more information about conditional formatting.

Table 11-2: Formulas Used to Calculate an Amortization Schedule

Cell	Formula	Description
A9	`=A8+1`	Returns the payment number
B9	`=PMT($C$2*($C$3/12),$C$4,-$C$1)`	Calculates the periodic payment amount
C9	`=C8+B9`	Calculates the cumulative payment amounts
D9	`=IPMT($C$2*($C$3/12),A9, $C$4,-$C$1)`	Calculates the interest portion of the periodic payment
E9	`=E8+D9`	Calculates the cumulative interest paid
F9	`=PPMT($C$2*($C$3/12),A9, $C$4,-$C$1)`	Calculates the principal portion of the periodic payment
G9	`=G8+F9`	Calculates the cumulative amount applied toward principal
H9	`=H8-F9`	Returns the principal balance at the end of the period

Calculating a loan with irregular payments

So far, the loan calculation examples in this chapter have involved loans with regular periodic payments. In some cases, loan payback is irregular. For example, you may loan some money to a friend without a formal agreement as to how he'll pay the money back. You still collect interest on the loan, so you need a way to perform the calculations based on the actual payment dates.

Figure 11-6 shows a worksheet set up to keep track of such a loan. The annual interest rate for the loan is stored in cell B1 (named *APR*). The original loan amount and loan date are stored in row 5.

Notice that the loan amount is entered as a negative value in cell B5. Formulas, beginning in row 6, track the irregular loan payments and perform calculations.

	A	B	C	D	E	F	G	H
1	Interest Rate (APR):	5.00%					Loan Payment History	
2								
3								
4	Payment Number	Payment Amount	Payment Date	Amount to Interest	Amount to Principal	Cumulative Payments	Cumulative Interest	Loan Balance
5	Original Loan	($7,500.00)	6/8/2011					$7,500.00
6	1	$200.00	7/25/2011	$48.29	$151.71	$200.00	$48.29	$7,348.29
7	2	$200.00	8/9/2011	$15.10	$184.90	$400.00	$63.39	$7,163.39
8	3	$200.00	9/24/2011	$45.14	$154.86	$600.00	$108.53	$7,008.53
9	4	$100.00	12/9/2011	$72.97	$27.03	$700.00	$181.49	$6,981.49
10	5	$250.00	1/19/2012	$39.21	$210.79	$950.00	$220.70	$6,770.70
11	Addition to Principal	($500.00)	2/1/2012	$12.06	($512.06)	$450.00	$232.76	$7,282.76
12	6	$100.00	2/21/2012	$19.95	$80.05	$550.00	$252.71	$7,202.71
13	7	$100.00	2/27/2012	$5.92	$94.08	$650.00	$258.63	$7,108.63
14	8	$1,000.00	3/7/2012	$8.76	$991.24	$1,650.00	$267.40	$6,117.40
15	9	$250.00	3/22/2012	$12.57	$237.43	$1,900.00	$279.97	$5,879.97
16	10	$200.00	4/8/2012	$13.69	$186.31	$2,100.00	$293.66	$5,693.66
17	11	$200.00	4/25/2012	$13.26	$186.74	$2,300.00	$306.92	$5,506.92
18	12	$1,000.00	5/10/2012	$11.32	$988.68	$3,300.00	$318.23	$4,518.23
19	13	$100.00	5/22/2012	$7.43	$92.57	$3,400.00	$325.66	$4,425.66
20	14	$200.00	6/8/2012	$10.31	$189.69	$3,600.00	$335.97	$4,235.97
21	15	$200.00	6/25/2012	$9.86	$190.14	$3,800.00	$345.83	$4,045.83
22	16	$100.00	7/11/2012	$8.87	$91.13	$3,900.00	$354.70	$3,954.70
23	17	$100.00	7/21/2012	$5.42	$94.58	$4,000.00	$360.12	$3,860.12
24	Addition to Principal	($500.00)	9/7/2012	$25.38	($525.38)	$3,500.00	$385.50	$4,385.50
25	18	$100.00	11/8/2012	$37.25	$62.75	$3,600.00	$422.75	$4,322.75
26	19	$100.00	11/21/2012	$7.70	$92.30	$3,700.00	$430.44	$4,230.44
27	20	$200.00	12/21/2012	$17.39	$182.61	$3,900.00	$447.83	$4,047.83
28	21	$750.00	1/11/2013	$11.64	$738.36	$4,650.00	$459.47	$3,309.47
29	22	$750.00	2/11/2013	$14.05	$735.95	$5,400.00	$473.53	$2,573.53
30	23	$750.00	3/11/2013	$9.87	$740.13	$6,150.00	$483.40	$1,833.40
31	24							
32	25							
33	26							

Figure 11-6: This worksheet tracks loan payments that are made on an irregular basis.

Column B stores the payment amount made on the date in column C. Notice that the payments are not made on a regular basis. Also, notice that in two cases (row 11 and row 24), the payment amount is negative. These entries represent additional borrowed money added to the loan balance. Formulas in columns D and E calculate the amount of the payment credited toward interest and principal. Columns F and G keep a running tally of the cumulative payments and interest amounts. Formulas in column H compute the new loan balance after each payment.

Table 11-3 lists and describes the formulas in row 6. Note that each formula uses an IF function to determine whether the payment date in column C is missing. If so, the formula returns an empty string, so no data appears in the cell.

Table 11-3: Formulas to Calculate a Loan with Irregular Payments

Cell	Formula	Description
D6	`=IF(C6<>"",(C6-C5)/365*H5*APR,"")`	Calculates the interest, based on the payment date
E6	`=IF(C6<>"",B6-D6,"")`	Subtracts the interest amount from the payment to calculate the amount credited to principal
F6	`=IF(C6<>"",F5+B6,"")`	Adds the payment amount to the running total
G6	`=IF(C6<>"",G5+D6,"")`	Adds the interest to the running total
H6	`=IF(C6<>"",H5-E6,"")`	Calculates the new loan balance by subtracting the principal amount from the previous loan balance

Note that the formula in cell D6 assumes that the year has 365 days. A more precise formula uses the YEARFRAC function, which calculates the fraction of a year when a leap year is involved:

```
=IF(C6<>"",YEARFRAC(C6,C5,1)*H5*APR,"")
```

On the Web

This workbook is available at this book's website. The filename is irregular payments.xlsx.

Investment Calculations

Investment calculations involve calculating interest on fixed-rate investments, such as bank savings accounts, CDs, and annuities. You can make these interest calculations for investments that consist of a single deposit or multiple deposits.

On the Web

This book's website contains a workbook with all the interest calculation examples in this section. The file is named investment calculations.xlsx.

Future value of a single deposit

Many investments consist of a single deposit that earns interest over the term of the investment. This section describes calculations for simple interest and compound interest.

Calculating simple interest

Simple interest refers to the fact that interest payments are not compounded. The basic formula for computing interest is this:

```
Interest=Principal*Rate*Term
```

For example, suppose that you deposit $1,000 into a bank CD that pays a 3% simple annual interest rate. After one year, the CD matures, and you withdraw your money. The bank adds $30, and you walk away with $1,030. In this case, the interest earned is calculated by multiplying the principal ($1,000) by the interest rate (0.03) by the term (one year).

If the investment term is less than one year, the simple interest rate is adjusted accordingly, based on the term. For example, $1,000 invested in a six-month CD that pays 3% simple annual interest earns $15.00 when the CD matures. In this case, the annual interest rate multiplies by six-twelfths.

Figure 11-7 shows a worksheet set up to make simple interest calculations. The formula in cell B7, shown here, calculates the interest due at the end of the term:

```
=B3*B4*B5
```

The formula in B8 simply adds the interest to the original investment amount.

	A	B	C
1	**Simple Interest Calculation**		
2			
3	Investment amount:	$1,000.00	
4	Annual interest rate:	3.00%	
5	Investment term (years):	1.00	
6			
7	Interest:	$30.00	
8	Investment at the end of the term:	$1,030.00	
9			

Figure 11-7: This worksheet calculates simple interest payments.

Calculating compound interest

Most fixed-term investments pay interest by using some type of compound interest calculation. *Compound interest* refers to interest credited to the investment balance, and the investment then earns interest on the interest.

For example, suppose that you deposit $1,000 into a bank CD that pays 3% annual interest rate, compounded monthly. Each month, the interest is calculated on the balance, and that amount is credited to your account. The next month's interest calculation is based on a higher amount because it also includes the previous month's interest payment. One way to calculate the final investment amount involves a series of formulas (see Figure 11-8).

	A	B	C	D
1	**Compound Interest Calculation**			
2	***Monthly compounding***			
3				
4	Investment amount:	$1,000.00		
5	Annual interest rate:	3.00%		
6	Investment term (months):	12		
7				
8	Month	Interest Earned	Balance	
9	Beginning Balance		$1,000.00	
10	1	$2.50	$1,002.50	
11	2	$2.51	$1,005.01	
12	3	$2.51	$1,007.52	
13	4	$2.52	$1,010.04	
14	5	$2.53	$1,012.56	
15	6	$2.53	$1,015.09	
16	7	$2.54	$1,017.63	
17	8	$2.54	$1,020.18	
18	9	$2.55	$1,022.73	
19	10	$2.56	$1,025.28	
20	11	$2.56	$1,027.85	
21	12	$2.57	$1,030.42	
22				

Figure 11-8: Using a series of formulas to calculate compound interest.

Column B contains formulas to calculate the interest for one month. For example, the formula in B10 is

```
=C9*($B$5*(1/12))
```

The formulas in column C simply add the monthly interest amount to the balance. For example, the formula in C10 is

```
=C9+B10
```

At the end of the 12-month term, the CD balance is $1,030.42. In other words, monthly compounding results in an additional $0.42 (compared with simple interest).

You can use the FV (future value) function to calculate the final investment amount without using a series of formulas. Figure 11-9 shows a worksheet set up to calculate compound interest. Cell B6 is an input cell that holds the number of compounding periods per year. For monthly compounding, the value in B6 would be 12. For quarterly compounding, the value would be 4. For daily compounding, the value would be 365. Cell B7 holds the term of the investment expressed in years.

	A	B	C
1	**Compound Interest Calculation**		
2	***Single formula general solution***		
3			
4	Investment amount:	$5,000.00	
5	Annual interest rate:	4.25%	
6	Compounding periods/year	4	
7	Term (years)	3	
8			
9	Periodic interest rate:	1.0625%	
10	Investment value at end of term:	$5,676.11	
11	Total interest earned:	$676.11	
12			
13	Annual yield:	4.51%	
14			
15			

Figure 11-9: Using a single formula to calculate compound interest.

Cell B9 contains the following formula that calculates the periodic interest rate. This value is the interest rate used for each compounding period:

```
=B5*(1/B6)
```

The formula in cell B10 uses the FV function to calculate the value of the investment at the end of the term. The formula follows:

```
=FV(B9,B6*B7,,-B4)
```

The first argument for the FV function is the periodic interest rate, which is calculated in cell B9. The second argument represents the total number of compounding periods. The third argument (pmt) is omitted, and the fourth argument is the original investment amount (expressed as a negative value).

The total interest is calculated with a simple formula in cell B11:

```
=B10-B4
```

Another formula, in cell B13, calculates the annual yield on the investment:

```
=(B11/B4)/B7
```

For example, suppose that you deposit $5,000 into a three-year CD with a 4.25% annual interest rate compounded quarterly. In this case, the investment has four compounding periods per year, so you enter **4** into cell B6. The term is three years, so you enter **3** into cell B7. The formula in B10 returns *$5,676.11*.

Perhaps you want to see how this rate stacks up against another account that offers daily compounding. Figure 11-10 shows a calculation with daily compounding using a $5,000 investment (compare this with Figure 11-9). As you can see, the difference is small ($679.88 versus $676.11). Over a period of three years, the account with daily compounding earns a total of $3.77 more interest. In terms of annual yield, quarterly compounding earns 4.51%, and daily compounding earns 4.53%.

	A	B	C
1	**Compound Interest Calculation**		
2	***Single formula general solution***		
3			
4	Investment amount:	$5,000.00	
5	Annual interest rate:	4.25%	
6	Compounding periods/year	365	
7	Term (years)	3	
8			
9	Periodic interest rate:	0.0116%	
10	Investment value at end of term:	$5,679.88	
11	Total interest earned:	$679.88	
12			
13	Annual yield:	4.53%	
14			
15			
16			

Figure 11-10: Calculating interest by using daily compounding.

Calculating interest with continuous compounding

The term *continuous compounding* refers to interest that is accumulated continuously. In other words, the investment has an infinite number of compounding periods per year. The following formula calculates the future value of a $5,000 investment at 4.25% compounded continuously for three years:

```
=5000*EXP(4.25&*3)
```

The formula returns *$5,679.92,* which is an additional $0.04 compared with daily compounding.

Note

You can calculate compound interest without using the FV function. The general formula to calculate compound interest is this:

```
Principal*(1+Periodic Rate)^Number of Periods
```

For example, consider a five-year, $5,000 investment that earns an annual interest rate of 4%, compounded monthly. The formula to calculate the future value of this investment follows:

```
=5000*(1+4&/12)^(12*5)
```

The Rule of 72

Need to make an investment decision but don't have a computer handy? You can use the Rule of 72 to determine the number of years required to double your money at a particular interest rate using annual compounding. Just divide 72 by the interest rate. For example, consider a $10,000 investment at 4% interest. How many years will it take to turn that 10 grand into 20 grand? Take 72, divide it by 4, and you get 18 years. What if you can get a 5% interest rate? If so, you can double your money in a little over 14 years.

How accurate is the Rule of 72? The table that follows shows Rule of 72 estimated years versus the actual years for various interest rates. As you can see, this simple rule is remarkably accurate. However, for interest rates that exceed 30%, the accuracy drops off considerably.

Interest Rate	Rule of 72	Actual
1%	72.00	69.66
2%	36.00	35.00
3%	24.00	23.45
4%	18.00	17.67
5%	14.40	14.21
6%	12.00	11.90
7%	10.29	10.24
8%	9.00	9.01
9%	8.00	8.04
10%	7.20	7.27
15%	4.80	4.96
20%	3.60	3.80
25%	2.88	3.11
30%	2.40	2.64

The Rule of 72 also works in reverse. For example, if you want to double your money in six years, divide 6 into 72; you discover that you need to find an investment that pays an annual interest rate of about 12%.

Present value of a series of payments

The example in this section computes the present value of a series of future receipts, sometimes called an *annuity.*

A man gets lucky and wins the $1,000,000 jackpot in the state lottery. Lottery officials offer a choice:

- Receive the $1 million as 20 annual payments of $50,000
- In lieu of the $1 million, receive an immediate lump sum of $500,000

Ignoring tax implications, which is the better offer? In other words, what's the present value of 20 years of annual $50,000 payments? And is the present value greater than the single lump sum payment of $500,000 (which has a present value of $500,000)?

The answer depends on making a prediction: if Mr. Lucky invests the money, what interest rate can be expected?

Assuming an expected 6% return on investment, calculate the present value of 20 annual $50,000 payments using this formula:

```
=PV(6&,20,50000,0,1)
```

The result is –$573,496.

Note

The present value is negative because it represents the amount Mr. Lucky would have to pay today to get those 20 years of payments at the stated interest rate. For this example, we can ignore the negative sign and treat it as positive value to be compared with the lump sum of $500,000.

What's the decision? The lump sum amount would need to exceed $573,496 to make it a better deal for the lottery winner. The lump sum payout probably isn't negotiable, so (based on an interest rate assumption of 6%) the 20 annual payments is a better deal for the lottery winner.

The PV calculation is sensitive to the interest rate assumption, which is often unknown. For example, if the lottery winner assumed an interest rate of 8% in the calculation, the present value of the 20 payments would be $490,907. Under this scenario, the lump sum would be a better choice.

In the extreme case, an interest rate of 0%, the PV calculates to $1,000,000. The lottery organization would have to pay the winner a lump sum of more than $1 million to make it more valuable than the payments spread over 20 years—not likely.

Future value of a series of deposits

Now consider another type of investment, one in which you make a regular series of deposits into an account. This type of investment is an *annuity.*

The worksheet functions discussed in the "Loan Calculations" section earlier in this chapter also apply to annuities, but you need to use the perspective of a lender, not a borrower. A simple example of this type of investment is a holiday club savings program offered by some banking institutions. A fixed amount is deducted from each of your paychecks and deposited into an interest-earning account. At the end of the year, you withdraw the money (with accumulated interest) to use for holiday expenses.

Suppose that you deposit $200 at the beginning of each month (for 12 months) into an account that pays 2.5% annual interest compounded monthly. The following formula calculates the future value of your series of deposits:

```
=FV(2.5&/12,12,-200,,1)
```

This formula returns *$2,432.75*, which represents the total of your deposits ($2,400.00) plus the interest ($32.75). The last argument for the FV function is 1, which means that you make payments at the beginning of the month. Figure 11-11 shows a worksheet set up to calculate annuities. Table 11-4 describes the contents of this sheet.

	A	B	C
1	**Annuity Calculator**		
2			
3	**Deposits...**		
4	Initial investment:	$0.00	
5	Periodic deposit amount:	$200.00	
6	No. periodic deposits per year :	12	
7	Deposits made at beginning of period?	TRUE	
8			
9	**Investment Period...**		
10	Length of investment (years):	1	
11			
12	**Interest Rate...**		
13	Annual interest rate:	2.50%	
14			
15	**Calculations**		
16	Initial investment:	$0.00	
17	Additional deposits:	$2,400.00	
18	Total amount invested:	$2,400.00	
19	Periodic interest rate:	0.21%	
20	Value of investment at end of term:	$2,432.75	
21	Interest earned on investment:	$32.75	
22			

Figure 11-11: This worksheet contains formulas to calculate annuities.

On the Web

The workbook shown in Figure 11-11 is available at this book's website. The file is named annuity calculator.xlsx.

Table 11-4: The Annuity Calculator Worksheet

Cell	Formula	Description
B4	None (input cell)	Initial investment (can be 0)
B5	None (input cell)	The amount deposited on a regular basis
B6	None (input cell)	The number of deposits made in 12 months
B7	None (input cell)	*TRUE* if you make deposits at the beginning of period; otherwise, *FALSE*
B10	None (input cell)	The length of the investment, in years (can be fractional)
B13	None (input cell)	The annual interest rate
B16	`=B4`	The initial investment amount
B17	`=B5*B6*B10`	The total of all regular deposits
B18	`=B16+B17`	The initial investment added to the sum of the deposits
B19	`=B13*(1/B6)`	The periodic interest rate
B20	`=FV(B19,B6*B10,-B5,-B4,IF(B7,1,0))`	The future value of the investment
B21	`=B20-B18`	The interest earned from the investment

12

Discounting and Depreciation Formulas

In This Chapter

- Calculating the net present value of future cash flows
- Using cross-checking to verify results
- Calculating the internal rate of return
- Calculating the net present value of irregular cash flows
- Finding the internal rate of return on irregular cash flows
- Using the depreciation functions

The NPV (Net Present Value) and IRR (Internal Rate of Return) functions are perhaps the most commonly used financial analysis functions. This chapter provides many examples that use these functions for various types of financial analyses.

Using the NPV Function

The NPV function returns the sum of a series of cash flows, discounted to the present day using a single discount rate. The cash flow amounts can vary, but they must be at regular intervals (for example, monthly). The syntax for Excel's NPV function is shown here; arguments in bold are required:

```
NPV(rate,value1,value2, ...)
```

Cash inflows are represented as positive values, and cash outflows are negative values. The NPV function is subject to the same restrictions that apply to financial functions, such as PV, PMT, FV, NPER, and RATE (see Chapter 11, "Borrowing and Investing Formulas").

If the discounted negative flows exceed the discounted positive flows, the function returns a negative amount. Conversely, if the discounted positive flows exceed the discounted negative flows, the NPV function returns a positive amount.

The rate argument is the discount rate—the rate at which future cash flows are discounted. It represents the rate of return that the investor requires. If NPV returns zero, it indicates that the future cash flows provide a rate of return exactly equal to the specified discount rate.

If the NPV is positive, it indicates that the future cash flows provide a better rate of return than the specified discount rate. The positive amount returned by NPV is the amount that the investor could add to the initial cash flow (called *Point 0*) to get the exact rate of return specified.

As you may have guessed, a negative NPV signifies that the investor does not get the required discount rate, often called a *hurdle rate*. To achieve the desired rate, the investor must reduce the initial cash outflow (or increase the initial cash inflow) by the amount returned by the negative NPV.

Note

The discount rate used must be a single effective rate for the period used for the cash flows. Therefore, if flows are set to monthly, you must use the monthly effective rate.

Definition of NPV

Excel's NPV function assumes that the first cash flow is received at the *end* of the first period.

Warning

This assumption differs from the definition used by most financial calculators, and it is at odds with the definition used by institutions such as the Appraisal Institute of America (AIA). For example, the AIA defines NPV as the difference between the present value of positive cash flows and the present value of negative cash flows. If you use Excel's NPV function without making an adjustment, the result does not adhere to this definition.

The point of an NPV calculation is to determine whether an investment will provide an appropriate return. The typical sequence of cash flows is an initial cash outflow followed by a series of cash inflows. For example, you buy a hot dog cart and some hot dogs (initial outflow) and spend the summer months selling them on a street corner (series of inflows). If you include the initial cash flow as an argument, NPV assumes the initial investment isn't made right now but instead at the end of the first month (or some other time period).

Figure 12-1 shows three calculations using the same cash flows: a $20,000 initial outflow, a series of monthly inflows, and an 8% discount rate.

	A	B	C	D	E
1	Cash Flow Calculations				
2					
3	Month	Cash Flows	Cash Flows	Cash Flows	
4	Initial Investment	(20,000.00)	(20,000.00)	(20,000.00)	
5	June	4,000.00	4,000.00	4,000.00	
6	July	5,000.00	5,000.00	5,000.00	
7	August	10,000.00	10,000.00	10,000.00	
8	September	2,000.00	2,000.00	2,000.00	
9		($2,408.54)	($2,601.22)	($2,601.22)	
10		-- Caution --			
11					

Figure 12-1: Three methods of computing NPV.

The formulas in row 9 are as follows:

```
B9:   =NPV(8%,B4:B8)
C9:   =NPV(8%,C5:C8)+C4
D9:   =NPV(8%,D4:D8)*(1+8%)
```

The formula in B9 produces a result that differs from the other two. It assumes the $20,000 investment is made one month from now. There are applications where this is useful, but they rarely (if ever) involve an initial investment. The other two formulas answer the question of whether a $20,000 investment right now will earn 8%, assuming the future cash flows. The formulas in C9 and D9 produce the same result and can be used interchangeably.

NPV function examples

This section contains a number of examples that demonstrate the NPV function.

On the Web

All the examples in this section are available in the workbook net present value.xlsx at this book's website.

Initial investment

Many NPV calculations start with an initial cash outlay followed by a series of inflows. In this example, the Time 0 cash flow is the purchase of a snowplow. Over the next ten years, the plow will be used to clear driveways and earn revenue. Experience shows that such a snowplow lasts 10 years. After that time, it will be broken down and worthless. Figure 12-2 shows a worksheet set up to calculate the NPV of the future cash flows associated with buying the plow.

	A	B	C
1	NPV Example		
2			
3	Discount Rate:	10%	
4			
5	Time	Cash Flow	
6	0	($200,000.00)	
7	1	20,000.00	
8	2	22,500.00	
9	3	25,000.00	
10	4	27,500.00	
11	5	30,000.00	
12	6	32,500.00	
13	7	35,000.00	
14	8	37,500.00	
15	9	40,000.00	
16	10	42,500.00	
17			
18	NPV =	($19,880.30)	
19			

Figure 12-2: An initial investment returns positive future cash flows.

The NPV calculation in cell B18 uses the following formula, which returns *–$19,880.30*:

```
=NPV($B$3,B7:B16)+B6
```

The NPV is negative, so this analysis indicates that buying the snowplow is not a good investment. Here are several factors that influence the result:

- First, a "good investment" is defined in the formula as one that returns 10%. If you can settle for a lesser return, lower the discount rate.
- The future cash flows are generally (but not always) estimates. In this case, the potential plow owner assumes increasing revenue over the 10-year life of the equipment. Unless he has a 10-year contract to plow snow that sets forth the exact amounts to be received, the future cash flows are educated guesses at how much money he can make.
- Finally, the initial investment plays a significant role in the calculation. If you can get the snowplow dealer to lower his price, the 10-year investment may prove worthwhile.

No initial investment

You can look at the snowplow example in a different way. In the previous example, you knew the cost of the snowplow and included that as the initial investment. The calculation determines whether the initial investment would produce a 10% return. You can also use NPV to tell what initial investment is required to produce the required return. That is, how much should you pay for the snowplow? Figure 12-3 shows the calculation of the NPV of a series of cash flows with no initial investment.

	A	B	C
1	Calculating a Required Initial Investment		
2			
3	Discount Rate:	10%	
4			
5	Time	Cash Flow	
6	0	$0.00	
7	1	20,000.00	
8	2	22,500.00	
9	3	25,000.00	
10	4	27,500.00	
11	5	30,000.00	
12	6	32,500.00	
13	7	35,000.00	
14	8	37,500.00	
15	9	40,000.00	
16	10	42,500.00	
17			
18	NPV=	$180,119.70	
19			

Figure 12-3: The NPV function can be used to determine the initial investment required.

The NPV calculation in cell B18 uses the following formula:

```
=NPV($B$3,B7:B16)+B6
```

If the potential snowplow owner can buy the snowplow for $180,119.70, it results in a 10% rate of return—assuming that the cash flow projections are accurate, of course.

Note

The formula adds the value in B6 to the end to be consistent with the formula from the previous example. Obviously, because the initial cash flow is zero, adding B6 is superfluous.

Initial cash inflow

Figure 12-4 shows an example in which the initial cash flow (the Time 0 cash flow) is an inflow. Like the previous example, this calculation returns the amount of an initial investment that is necessary to achieve the desired rate of return. In this example, however, the initial investment entitles you to receive the first inflow immediately.

	A	B	C	D
1	Calculating Value of a Cash Flow with Initial Flow			
2				
3	Rate:	10%		
4				
5	Time	Cash Flow		
6	0	$30,000.00		
7	1	30,000.00		
8	2	32,500.00		
9	3	32,500.00		
10	4	35,000.00		
11	5	35,000.00		
12	6	40,000.00		
13	7	40,000.00		
14				
15	NPV=	$197,292.96		
16				

Figure 12-4: Some NPV calculations include an initial cash inflow.

The NPV calculation is in cell B15, which contains the following formula:

```
=NPV(B3,B7:B13)+B6
```

This example might seem unusual, but it is common in real estate situations in which rent is paid in advance. This calculation indicates that you can pay $197,292.96 for a rental property that pays back the future cash flows in rent. The first year's rent, however, is due immediately. Therefore, the first year's rent is shown at Time 0.

Terminal values

The previous example is missing one key element: namely, the disposition of the property after seven years. You can keep renting it forever, in which case you need to increase the number of cash flows in the calculation. Or you can sell it, as shown in Figure 12-5.

	A	B	C	D	E
1	Cash Flows with Terminal Values				
2					
3	Rate:	10%			
4					
5	Time	Income Flow	Capital Flow	Cash Flow	
6	0	$30,000.00		$30,000.00	
7	1	30,000.00		30,000.00	
8	2	32,500.00		32,500.00	
9	3	32,500.00		32,500.00	
10	4	35,000.00		35,000.00	
11	5	35,000.00		35,000.00	
12	6	40,000.00		40,000.00	
13	7	40,000.00	450,000.00	490,000.00	
14					
15			NPV=	$428,214.11	
16					
17					

Figure 12-5: The initial investment may still have value at the end of the cash flows.

The NPV calculation in cell D15 follows:

```
=NPV(B3,D7:D13)+D6
```

In this example, the investor can pay $428,214.11 for the rental property, collect rent for seven years, sell the property for $450,000, and make 10% on his investment.

Initial and terminal values

This example uses the same cash flows as the previous example except that you know how much the owner of the investment property wants. It represents a typical investment example in which the aim is to determine if, and by how much, an asking price exceeds a desired rate of return, as you can see in Figure 12-6.

The following formula indicates that at a $360,000 asking price, the discounted positive cash at the desired rate of return is $68,214.11:

```
-NPV(B3,D9:D15)+D8
```

	A	B	C	D	E
1	Cash Flows with an Initial and Terminal Value				
2					
3	Rate:	10%			
4					
5	Time	Income Flow	Capital Flow	Cash Flow	
6	0	$30,000.00	($360,000.00)	($330,000.00)	
7	1	30,000.00		30,000.00	
8	2	32,500.00		32,500.00	
9	3	32,500.00		32,500.00	
10	4	35,000.00		35,000.00	
11	5	35,000.00		35,000.00	
12	6	40,000.00		40,000.00	
13	7	40,000.00	450,000.00	490,000.00	
14					
15			NPV=	$68,214.11	
16					

Figure 12-6: The NPV function can include an initial value and a terminal value.

The resulting positive NPV means that the investor can pay the asking price and make more than his desired rate of return. In fact, he can pay $68,214.11 more than the asking price and still meet his objective.

Future outflows

Although the typical investment decision may consist of an initial cash outflow resulting in periodic inflows, that's certainly not always the case. The flexibility of NPV is that you can have varying amounts, both positive and negative, at all the points in the cash flow schedule.

In this example, a company wants to roll out a new product. It needs to purchase equipment for $475,000 and needs to spend another $225,000 to overhaul the equipment after five years. Also, the new product won't be profitable at first but will be eventually.

Figure 12-7 shows a worksheet set up to account for all these varying cash flows. The formula in cell E18 is this:

```
=NPV(B3,E7:E16)+E6
```

The positive NPV indicates that the company should invest in the equipment and start producing the new product. If it does, and the estimates of gross margin and expenses are accurate, the company will earn better than 10% on its investment.

	A	B	C	D	E	F
1	Multiple Outflows					
2						
3	Rate:	10%				
4						
5	Time	Capital Flow	Gross Margin	Fixed Expenses	Cash Flow	
6	0	($475,000.00)	$0.00	($25,000.00)	($500,000.00)	
7	1	-	$0.00	(25,000.00)	(25,000.00)	
8	2	-	20,000.00	(25,000.00)	(5,000.00)	
9	3	-	40,000.00	(25,000.00)	15,000.00	
10	4	-	100,000.00	(25,000.00)	75,000.00	
11	5	(225,000.00)	175,000.00	(25,000.00)	(75,000.00)	
12	6	-	200,000.00	(25,000.00)	175,000.00	
13	7	-	250,000.00	(25,000.00)	225,000.00	
14	8	-	275,000.00	(25,000.00)	250,000.00	
15	9	-	275,000.00	(25,000.00)	250,000.00	
16	10	-	275,000.00	(25,000.00)	250,000.00	
17						
18			NPV=		$22,347.71	
19						

Figure 12-7: The NPV function can accept multiple positive and negative cash flows.

Using the IRR Function

Excel's IRR function returns the discount rate that makes the NPV of an investment zero. In other words, the IRR function is a special-case NPV.

The syntax of the IRR function follows:

```
IRR(range,guess)
```

Warning

The range argument must contain values. Empty cells are not treated as zero. If the range contains empty cells or text, the cells are ignored.

In most cases, the IRR can be calculated only by iteration. The guess argument, if supplied, acts as a "seed" for the iteration process. It has been found that a guess of –90% will almost always produce an answer. Other guesses, such as 0, usually (but not always) produce an answer.

An essential requirement of the IRR function is that there must be both negative and positive income flows. To get a return, there must be an outlay, and there must be a payback. There is no essential requirement for the outlay to come first. For a loan analysis using IRR, the loan amount is positive (and comes first), and the repayments that follow are negative.

The IRR is a powerful tool, and its uses extend beyond simply calculating the return from an investment. This function can be used in any situation in which you need to calculate a time- and data-weighted average return.

The examples in this section are in a workbook named internal rate of return.xlsx, which is available at this book's website.

Rate of return

This example sets up a basic IRR calculation (see Figure 12-8). An important consideration when calculating IRR is the payment frequency. If the cash flows are monthly, the IRR is monthly. In general, you want to convert the IRR to an annual rate. The example uses data validation in cell C3 to allow the user to select the type of flow (annual, monthly, daily, and so on) that displays in cell D3. That choice determines the appropriate interest conversion calculation; it also affects the labels in row 5, which contain formulas that reference the text in cell D3.

	A	B	C	D	E	F
1	Calculation of IRR					
2						
3	Cash Flow Frequency:		12	Monthly		
4						
5	Monthly Number	Monthly Income Flow	Capital Flow	Net Monthly Flow		
6	0	$0.00	($2,000,000.00)	($2,000,000.00)		
7	1	$50,000.00		$50,000.00		
8	2	$50,000.00		$50,000.00		
9	3	$50,000.00		$50,000.00		
10	4	$50,000.00		$50,000.00		
11	5	$50,000.00		$50,000.00		
12	6	$50,000.00		$50,000.00		
13	7	$50,000.00		$50,000.00		
14	8	$50,000.00		$50,000.00		
15	9	$50,000.00		$50,000.00		
16	10	$50,000.00		$50,000.00		
17	11	$50,000.00		$50,000.00		
18	12	$50,000.00	$2,500,000.00	$2,550,000.00		
19						
20		IRR of Net Monthly Flow		4.14958%	Monthly	
21		IRR p.a.		62.88844%	per annum	
22		Check NPV		($0.00)		

Figure 12-8: The IRR returns the rate based on the cash flow frequency and should be converted into an annual rate.

Cell D20 contains this formula:

```
=IRR(D6:D18,-90%)
```

Cell D21 contains this formula:

```
=FV(D20,C3,0,-1)-1
```

The following formula, in cell D22, is a validity check:

```
=NPV(D20,D7:D18)+D6
```

The IRR is the rate at which the discounting of the cash flow produces an NPV of zero. The formula in cell D22 uses the IRR in an NPV function applied to the same cash flow. The NPV discounting at the IRR (per month) is $0.00, so the calculation checks.

Geometric growth rates

You may have a need to calculate an average growth rate or average rate of return. Because of compounding, a simple arithmetic average does not yield the correct answer. Even worse, if the flows are different, an arithmetic average does not take these variations into account.

A solution uses the IRR function to calculate a *geometric* average rate of return. This is simply a calculation that determines the single percentage rate per period that exactly replaces the varying ones.

This example (see Figure 12-9) shows the IRR function being used to calculate a geometric average return based on index data (in column B). The calculations of the growth rate for each year are in column C. For example, the formula in cell C5 follows:

```
=(B5/B4)-1
```

	A	B	C	D	E	F	G	H
1	IRR to Calculate Geometric Average Growth							
2								
3	Year	Index	Growth P.A.	2012-2013	2013-2014	2014-2015	2015-2016	
4	2012	100.00		-100.00	-100.00	-100.00	-100.00	
5	2013	105.21	5.21%	105.21	0	0	0	
6	2014	110.32	4.86%		110.32	0	0	
7	2015	116.56	5.66%			116.56	0	
8	2016	119.94	2.90%				119.94	
9								
10	Average Growth Since 2012:			5.210%	5.033%	5.241%	4.650%	
11								

Figure 12-9: Using the IRR function to calculate geometric average growth.

The remaining columns show the geometric average growth rate between different periods. The formulas in row 10 use the IRR function to calculate the internal rate of return. For example, the formula in cell F10, which returns 5.241%, is this:

```
=IRR(F4:F8,-90%)
```

In other words, the growth rates of 5.21%, 4.86%, and 5.66% are equivalent to a geometric average growth rate of 5.241%.

The IRR calculation takes into account the direction of flow and places a greater value on the larger flows.

Checking results

Figure 12-10 shows a worksheet that demonstrates the relationship between IRR, NPV, and PV by verifying the results of some calculations. This verification is based on the definition of IRR: the rate at which the sum of positive and negative discounted flows is 0.

	A	B	C	D	E
1	Checking IRR & NPV Using Sum of PV Approach				
2					
3	Discount Rate for NPV			10%	
4					
5	Period	Flow	PV IRR Check	PV NPV Check	
6	0	($100,000.00)	($100,000.00)	($100,000.00)	
7	1	14,000.00	13,570.24	12,727.27	
8	2	14,000.00	13,153.68	11,570.25	
9	3	14,000.00	12,749.90	10,518.41	
10	4	14,000.00	12,358.52	9,562.19	
11	5	14,000.00	11,979.15	8,692.90	
12	6	15,000.00	12,440.82	8,467.11	
13	7	15,000.00	12,058.92	7,697.37	
14	8	15,000.00	11,688.75	6,997.61	
15					
16	NPV	($23,766.89)	$0.00	($23,766.89)	
17	IRR	3.167%			
18					

Figure 12-10: Checking IRR and NPV using the sum of PV approach.

The NPV is calculated in cell B16:

```
=NPV(D3,B7:B14)+B6
```

The internal rate of return is calculated in cell B17:

```
=IRR(B6:B14,-90%)
```

In column C, formulas calculate the present value. They use the IRR (calculated in cell B17) as the discount rate and use the period number (in column A) for the nper argument. For example, the formula in cell C6 follows:

```
=PV($B$17,A6,0,-B6)
```

The sum of the values in column C is 0, which verifies that the IRR calculation is accurate.

The formulas in column D use the discount rate (in cell D3) to calculate the present values. For example, the formula in cell D6 is this:

```
=PV($D$3,A6,0,-B6)
```

The sum of the values in column D is equal to the NPV.

For serious applications of NPV and IRR functions, it is an excellent idea to use this type of cross-checking.

Irregular Cash Flows

All the functions discussed so far—NPV, IRR, and MIRR—deal with cash flows that are *regular*. That is, they occur monthly, quarterly, yearly, or at some other periodic interval. Excel provides two functions for dealing with cash flows that don't occur regularly: XNPV and XIRR.

Net present value

The syntax for XNPV follows:

```
XNPV(rate,values,dates)
```

The difference between XNPV and NPV is that XNPV requires a series of dates to which the values relate. In the example shown in Figure 12-11, the NPV of a series of irregular cash flows is found using XNPV.

	A	B	C	D
1	The XNPV Function			
2				
3	Interest Rate:	8.00%		
4				
5	Date	Flow	Revised Flow	
6	Jul-27-2015	$250.00	($3,026.49)	
7	Aug-16-2015	250.00	250.00	
8	Sep-15-2015	250.00	250.00	
9	Oct-25-2015	500.00	500.00	
10	Nov-04-2015	500.00	500.00	
11	Dec-04-2015	600.00	600.00	
12	Dec-24-2015	400.00	400.00	
13	Dec-29-2015	200.00	200.00	
14	Jan-18-2016	200.00	200.00	
15	Jan-28-2016	200.00	200.00	
16				
17	XNPV:	$3,276.49	$0.00	

Figure 12-11: The XNPV function works with irregular cash flows.

On the Web

This book's website contains the workbook irregular cash flows.xlsx, which contains all the examples in this section.

The formula in cell B17 is

```
=XNPV(B3,B6:B15,A6:A15)
```

Similar to NPV, the result of XNPV can be checked by duplicating the cash flows and netting the result with the first cash flow. The XNPV of the revised cash flows will be zero.

Note

Unlike the NPV function, XNPV assumes that the cash flows are at the beginning of each period instead of at the end. With NPV, we had to exclude the initial cash flow from the arguments and add it to the end of the formula. With XNPV, there is no need to do that.

Internal rate of return

The syntax for the XIRR function follows:

```
XIRR(value,dates,guess)
```

Just like XNPV, XIRR differs from its regular cousin by requiring dates. Figure 12-12 shows an example of computing the internal rate of return on a series of irregular cash flows.

	A	B	C
1	The XIRR Function		
2			
3	Date	Flow	
4	Jul-27-2015	($3,000.00)	
5	Aug-16-2015	$250.00	
6	Sep-15-2015	$250.00	
7	Oct-25-2015	$500.00	
8	Nov-04-2015	$500.00	
9	Dec-04-2015	$600.00	
10	Dec-24-2015	$400.00	
11	Dec-29-2015	$200.00	
12	Jan-18-2016	$200.00	
13	Jan-28-2016	$200.00	
14			
15	XIRR:	11.0966%	
16	Check XNPV:	($0.00)	
17			

Figure 12-12: The XIRR function works with irregular cash flows.

The formula in B15 is:

```
=XIRR(B4:B13,A4:A13)
```

Warning

The XIRR function has the same problem with multiple rates of return as IRR. It expects that the cash flow changes signs only once: that is, goes from negative to positive or from positive to negative. If the sign changes more than once, it is essential that you plug the XIRR result back into an XNPV function to verify that it returns zero. Figure 12-12 shows such a verification, although the sign only changes once in that example.

Depreciation Calculations

Depreciation is an accounting concept whereby the value of an asset is expensed over time. Some expenditures affect only the current period and are expensed fully in that period. Other expenditures, however, affect multiple periods. These expenditures are *capitalized* (made into an asset) and *depreciated* (written off a little each period). A forklift, for example, may be useful for five years. Expensing the full cost of the forklift in the year it was purchased would not put the correct cost into the correct years. Instead, the forklift is capitalized, and one-fifth of its cost is expensed in each year of its useful life.

On the Web

The examples in this section are available at this book's website. The workbook is named depreciation.xlsx.

Table 12-1 summarizes Excel's depreciation functions and the arguments used by each. For complete details, consult Excel's Help system.

Table 12-1: Excel Depreciation Functions

Function	Depreciation Method	Arguments*
SLN	Straight-line. The asset depreciates by the same amount each year of its life.	cost, salvage, life
DB	Declining balance. Computes depreciation at a fixed rate.	cost, salvage, life, period, [month]
DDB	Double-declining balance. Computes depreciation at an accelerated rate. Depreciation is highest in the first period and decreases in successive periods.	cost, salvage, life, period, month, [factor]
SYD	Sum of the year's digits. Allocates a larger depreciation in the earlier years of an asset's life.	cost, salvage, life, period
VDB	Variable-declining balance. Computes the depreciation of an asset for any period (including partial periods) using the double-declining balance method or some other method you specify.	cost, salvage, life, start period, end period, [factor], [no switch]

** Arguments in brackets are optional.*

The arguments for the depreciation functions are described as follows:

- **cost:** Original cost of the asset.
- **salvage:** Salvage cost of the asset after it has fully depreciated.
- **life:** Number of periods over which the asset will depreciate.
- **period:** Period in the life for which the calculation is being made. The VBD function uses two arguments: **start period** and **end period**.
- **month:** Number of months in the first year; if omitted, Excel uses 12.
- **factor:** Rate at which the balance declines; if omitted, it is assumed to be 2 (that is, double-declining).
- **no switch:** *TRUE* or *FALSE*. Specifies whether to switch to straight-line depreciation when depreciation is greater than the declining balance calculation.

Figure 12-13 shows depreciation calculations using the SLN, DB, DDB, and SYD functions. The asset's original cost, $10,000, is assumed to have a useful life of ten years, with a salvage value of $1,000. The range labeled Depreciation Amount shows the annual depreciation of the asset. The range labeled Value of Asset shows the asset's depreciated value over its life.

	A	B	C	D	E	F
1	Asset:	Office Furniture				
2	Original Cost:	$10,000				
3	Life (years):	10				
4	Salvage Value:	$1,000				
5						
6	***Depreciation Amount***					
7	Year	SLN	DB	DDB	SYD	
8	1	$900.00	$2,060.00	$2,000.00	$1,636.36	
9	2	$900.00	$1,635.64	$1,600.00	$1,472.73	
10	3	$900.00	$1,298.70	$1,280.00	$1,309.09	
11	4	$900.00	$1,031.17	$1,024.00	$1,145.45	
12	5	$900.00	$818.75	$819.20	$981.82	
13	6	$900.00	$650.08	$655.36	$818.18	
14	7	$900.00	$516.17	$524.29	$654.55	
15	8	$900.00	$409.84	$419.43	$490.91	
16	9	$900.00	$325.41	$335.54	$327.27	
17	10	$900.00	$258.38	$268.44	$163.64	
18						
19						
20	***Value of Asset***					
21	Year	SLN	DB	DDB	SYD	
22	0	$10,000.00	$10,000.00	$10,000.00	$10,000.00	
23	1	$9,100.00	$7,940.00	$8,000.00	$8,363.64	
24	2	$8,200.00	$6,304.36	$6,400.00	$6,890.91	
25	3	$7,300.00	$5,005.66	$5,120.00	$5,581.82	
26	4	$6,400.00	$3,974.50	$4,096.00	$4,436.36	
27	5	$5,500.00	$3,155.75	$3,276.80	$3,454.55	
28	6	$4,600.00	$2,505.67	$2,621.44	$2,636.36	
29	7	$3,700.00	$1,989.50	$2,097.15	$1,981.82	
30	8	$2,800.00	$1,579.66	$1,677.72	$1,490.91	
31	9	$1,900.00	$1,254.25	$1,342.18	$1,163.64	
32	10	$1,000.00	$995.88	$1,073.74	$1,000.00	

Figure 12-13: A comparison of four depreciation functions.

Figure 12-14 shows a chart that graphs the asset's value. As you can see, the SLN function produces a straight line; the other functions produce curved lines because the depreciation is greater in the earlier years of the asset's life.

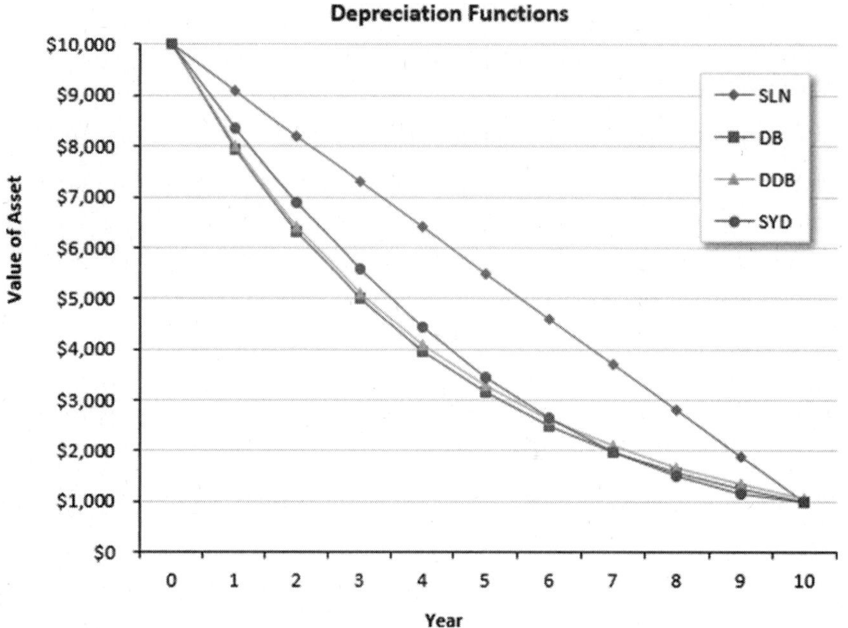

Figure 12-14: This chart shows an asset's value over time, using four depreciation functions.

The VDB (variable declining balance) function is useful if you need to calculate depreciation for multiple periods, such as when you need to figure accumulated depreciation on an asset that has been sold. Figure 12-15 shows a worksheet set up to calculate the gain or loss on the sale of some office furniture. The formula in cell B12 is this:

```
=VDB(B2,B4,B3,0,DATEDIF(B5,B6,"y"),B7,B8)
```

The formula computes the depreciation taken on the asset from the date it was purchased until the date it was sold. The DATEDIF function is used to determine how many years the asset has been in service.

	A	B	C	D
1	Asset:	Office Furniture		
2	Original Cost:	$10,000.00		
3	Life (years):	10		
4	Salvage Value:	$1,000.00		
5	Purchase Date:	3/15/2013		
6	Disposal Date:	3/15/2016		
7	Factor:	2		
8	No-Switch:	TRUE		
9				
10	Proceeds:		$5,875.00	
11	Cost:	10,000.00		
12	Accumulated Depreciation:	4,880.00		
13	Net Asset Value:		5,120.00	
14	Gain on sale of asset:		$755.00	
15				

Figure 12-15: Using the VDB function to calculate accumulated depreciation.

13

Financial Schedules

In This Chapter

- Setting up a basic amortization schedule
- Setting up a dynamic amortization schedule
- Evaluating loan options with a data table
- Creating two-way data tables
- Creating financial statements
- Understanding credit card repayment calculations
- Calculating and evaluating financial ratios
- Creating indices

This chapter, which makes use of much of the information contained in the two previous chapters, contains helpful examples of a variety of financial calculations.

Creating Financial Schedules

Financial schedules present financial information in many different forms. Some present a summary of information, such as a profit and loss statement. Others present a detailed list, such as an amortization schedule, which schedules the payments for a loan.

Financial schedules can be static or dynamic. Static schedules generally use a few Excel functions but mainly exist in Excel to take advantage of its grid system, which lends itself well for formatting schedules. Dynamic schedules, on the other hand, usually contain an area for user input. A user can change certain input parameters and affect the results.

The sections that follow demonstrate summary and detail schedules, as well as static and dynamic schedules.

Creating Amortization Schedules

In its simplest form, an *amortization schedule* tracks the payments (including interest and principal components) and the loan balance for a particular loan. This section presents several examples of amortization schedules.

A simple amortization schedule

This example uses a simple loan to demonstrate the basic concepts involved in creating a schedule. Refer to the worksheet in Figure 13-1. Notice that rows 19 through 370 are hidden, so only the first four payments and last four payments are visible.

	A	B	C	D	E	F
1	**Simple Amortization Schedule**					
2		**Input Area**				
3	Purchase Price		$ 225,000.00			
4	Down Payment		45,000.00			
5	Amount Financed		180,000.00			
6						
7	Annual Interest Rate		5.90%			
8	Term (years)		30			
9	Monthly Payment		$1,067.65			
10	Loan Date		1/15/2016			
11						
12	**Pmt. No**	**Date**	**Payment**	**Interest**	**Principal**	**Balance**
13		Totals:	384,352.46	204,352.46	180,000.00	
14		1/15/2016				$180,000.00
15	1	2/15/2016	1,067.65	885.00	182.65	179,817.35
16	2	3/15/2016	1,067.65	884.10	183.54	179,633.81
17	3	4/15/2016	1,067.65	883.20	184.45	179,449.36
18	4	5/15/2016	1,067.65	882.29	185.35	179,264.01
371	357	10/15/2045	1,067.65	20.74	1,046.90	3,171.70
372	358	11/15/2045	1,067.65	15.59	1,052.05	2,119.65
373	359	12/15/2045	1,067.65	10.42	1,057.22	1,062.42
374	360	1/15/2046	1,067.65	5.22	1,062.42	(0.00)
375						

Figure 13-1: A simple amortization schedule.

On the Web

All the examples in this section are available at this book's website in the workbook loan amortization.xlsx.

User input section

The area above the schedule contains cells for user input and for intermediate calculations. The user input cells are shaded, making it easy to distinguish between cells that can be changed and cells that are calculated by formulas.

The user can enter the purchase price and the down payment. The amount financed is calculated for use in the amortization calculation. Here's the formula in cell B5:

```
=Purchase_Price-Down_Payment
```

Tip

Names are used to make the formulas more readable. More information on named cells and ranges is in Chapter 3, "Working with Names."

The other calculation necessary to complete the schedule is the monthly payment. Here's the formula in B9:

```
=-PMT(Rate/12,Term*12,Amount_Financed)
```

The PMT function is used to determine the monthly payment amount. The rate (B7) is divided by 12, and the term (B8) is multiplied by 12, so that the arguments are on a monthly basis. This ensures that the result of PMT is also on a monthly basis.

Because this is a simple amortization schedule, the loan term is fixed at 30 years. Using a different term requires adding or deleting rows of formulas and changing the summary formulas.

Summary information

The first line of the schedule (row 13) contains summary formulas. Placing the summary information above the schedule eliminates the need to scroll to the end of the worksheet.

In this example, only the totals are shown. However, you can include subtotals by year, quarter, or any other interval you like. The formula in C13 sums 360 cells and is copied across the next two columns:

```
=SUM(C15:C374)
```

The schedule

The schedule starts in row 14, which shows the loan date and the amount financed (the beginning balance). The first payment is made exactly one month after the loan is initiated. The first payment row (row 15) and all subsequent rows contain the same formulas, which we describe later.

The Payment column simply references the Monthly_Payment cell in the user input section.

The Interest column computes a monthly interest based on the previous loan balance. The formula in D15 is this:

```
=F14*(Rate/12)
```

The previous balance, in cell F14, is multiplied by the annual interest rate, which is divided by 12. The annual interest rate is in cell B7, named Rate.

Whatever portion of the payment doesn't go toward interest goes toward reducing the principal balance. The formula in E15 is this:

```
=C15-D15
```

Finally, the balance is updated to reflect the principal portion of the payment. The formula in E15 is this:

```
=F14-E15
```

Loan amortization schedules are self-checking. If everything is set up correctly, the final balance at the end of the term is 0 (or close to 0, given rounding errors). Another check is to add all the monthly Principal components. The sum of these values should equal the original loan amount.

Limitations

This type of schedule is suitable for loans that will likely never change. It can be set up one time and referred to throughout the life of the loan. Further, you can copy it to create a new loan with just a few adjustments. However, this schedule lacks flexibility:

- The payment is computed and applied every month but cannot account for overpayments. Borrowers often pay an additional amount that is applied to the principal, thereby reducing the pay-off period.
- Many loans have variable interest rates, and this schedule provides no way to adjust the interest rate per period.
- The schedule has a fixed term of 30 years. A loan with a shorter or longer term would require that formulas be deleted or added to compensate.

In the next section, we address some of the flexibility issues and create a more dynamic amortization schedule.

A dynamic amortization schedule

The example in this section builds on the previous example. Figure 13-2 shows part of a loan amortization schedule that allows the user to define input parameters beyond the loan amount and rate.

The first difference you'll notice is that this schedule has two additional columns: APR and Addt'l Pmt. These columns are shaded, which indicates that the values can be changed.

	A	B	C	D	E	F	G	H	I
1	**Dynamic Amortization Schedule**								
2		**Input Area**							
3	Purchase Price:		$ 225,000.00						
4	Down Payment:		45,000.00						
5	Amount Financed:		180,000.00						
6	Starting Rate:		5.90%						
7	Term (years):		15.0						
8	Computed Payment:		$1,509.23						
9	Loan Date:		1/15/2016						
10									
11									
12	Pmt. No	Date	APR	Payment	Addt'l Pmt	Interest	Principal	Balance	
13		Totals:		$263,171.46	$500.00	$83,671.46	$180,000.00		
14		1/15/2016						$180,000.00	
15	1	2/15/2016	5.90%	1,509.23		885.00	624.23	179,375.77	
16	2	3/15/2016	5.90%	1,509.23		881.93	627.30	178,748.46	
17	3	4/15/2016	5.90%	1,509.23		878.85	630.39	178,118.07	
18	4	5/15/2016	5.90%	1,509.23		875.75	633.49	177,484.59	
19	5	8/30/2013	5.90%	1,509.23		872.63	636.60	176,847.98	
20	6	7/15/2016	5.90%	1,509.23		869.50	639.73	176,208.25	
21	7	8/15/2016	5.75%	1,495.14		844.33	650.81	175,557.44	
22	8	9/15/2016	5.75%	1,495.14		841.21	653.93	174,903.51	
23	9	10/15/2016	5.75%	1,495.14		838.08	657.06	174,246.45	
24	10	11/15/2016	5.75%	1,495.14	500.00	834.93	1,160.21	173,086.24	
25	11	12/15/2016	5.75%	1,495.14		829.37	665.77	172,420.47	
26	12	1/15/2017	5.75%	1,495.14		826.18	668.96	171,751.52	
27	13	2/15/2017	5.40%	1,459.20		772.88	686.32	171,065.20	
28	14	3/15/2017	5.40%	1,459.20		769.79	689.40	170,375.80	
191	177	10/15/2030	5.40%	1,459.20		25.97	1,433.22	4,338.49	
192	178	11/15/2030	5.40%	1,459.20		19.52	1,439.67	2,898.81	
193	179	12/15/2030	5.40%	1,459.20		13.04	1,446.15	1,452.66	
194									

Figure 13-2: A dynamic amortization schedule.

User input section

This schedule has a few changes in the Input Area at the top. The interest rate is labeled Starting Rate, and the payment is labeled Computed Payment, indicating that they are subject to change. Also, the user can now specify the term of the loan.

Summary information

Because the user can now change the term and make additional payments, the maturity date isn't always fixed. The formulas are set up for a maximum of 360 payments, but not all these rows need to be summed. For the summary information, you want to sum only the rows up until the loan is paid off. The formula in D13 follows:

```
=SUMIF($H15:$H374,">=-1",D15:D374)
```

After the Balance in column H is zero, the amortization is complete. This SUMIF function sums only those payments up until that point. This formula is copied across the next three columns. Note that the condition is "greater than or equal to –1." This handles the situation in which the final balance isn't exactly zero (but close to it).

Changing the APR

If the interest rate changes, the user can enter the new rate in the APR column. That new rate is in effect until a different rate is entered.

The formula in cell C15 retrieves the Starting_Rate value from the input area. The formula in cell C16, and copied down, is this:

```
=C15
```

If a new rate is entered, it overwrites the formula, and that new rate is propagated down the column. The effect is that the new rate is in effect for all subsequent payments—at least until it changes again.

In Figure 13-2, the rate was changed to 5.75% beginning with the seventh payment. The lower rate also affected the payments. The rate changed again beginning with the thirteenth payment, and again the payment amount was adjusted.

Note

We used conditional formatting for the cells in the APR column to make the rate changes stand out.

When the APR is changed, the payment amount is adjusted. The loan is essentially reamortized for the remaining term, using the new interest rate. Here's the formula in cell D16:

```
=IF(C16<>C15,-PMT(C16/12,(Term*12)-A15,H15),D15)
```

This formula checks the value in the APR column. If it's different from the APR in the previous row, the PMT function calculates the new payment. If the APR hasn't changed, the previous payment is returned.

Handling additional payments

If additional payments are made, they are entered in column E. In Figure 13-2, an additional payment of $500 was applied to the tenth payment. Extra payments are applied to the principal.

The formula in cell G15 (and copied down) calculates the principal portion of the payment (and additional payment, if made):

```
=(D15-F15)+E15
```

Finishing touches

Because the loan term is specified by the user, we used conditional formatting to hide the rows that extend beyond the specified term.

All the cells in the schedule, starting in row 15, have conditional formatting applied to them. If column G of the row above is zero or less, both the background color and the font color are white, rendering them invisible.

To apply conditional formatting, select the range A15:H374 and choose the Home ➜ Styles ➜ Conditional Formatting command. Add a formula rule with this formula:

```
=$H15<0
```

Cross-Ref

For more information on conditional formatting, see Chapter 19, "Conditional Formatting."

Credit card calculations

Another type of loan amortization schedule is for credit card loans. Credit cards are different because the minimum payment varies, based on the balance. You could use the method in which the payments are entered directly into the schedule. When the payments are different every time, however, the schedule loses its value as a predictor or planner. Here, we describe a schedule that can predict the payments of a credit card loan.

Credit card calculations represent several nonstandard problems. Excel's financial functions (PV, FV, RATE, and NPER) require that the regular payments are at a single level. In addition, the PMT function returns a single level of payments. With IRR and NPV analysis, the user inserts the varying payments into a cash flow.

Credit card companies calculate payments based on the following relatively standard set of criteria:

- **A minimum payment is required.** For example, a credit card account might require a minimum monthly payment of $25.
- **The payment must be at least equal to a base percentage of the debt.** Usually, the payment is a percentage of the balance but not less than a specified amount.
- **The payment is rounded**, usually to the nearest $0.05.
- **Interest is invariably quoted at a given rate per month.**

Figure 13-3 shows a worksheet set up to calculate credit card payments.

The formula for the minimum payment is rather complicated—just like the terms of a credit card. This example uses a minimum payment amount of $25 or 3% of the balance, whichever is larger. This small minimum payment results in a long payback period. If this borrower ever hopes to pay off that balance in a reasonable amount of time, he needs to use that additional payment column.

	A	B	C	D	E	F	G
1	**Credit Card Amortization**						
2		**Input Area**					
3	Starting Balance			$ 3,200.00			
4	Starting Date			2/3/2013			
5	Monthly Interest Rate			1.500%			
6	Minimum Payment Percent			3.000%			
7	Minimum Payment Dollars			$ 25.00			
8	Payment Rounding			$ 0.05			
9							
10	**Date**	**Minimum Payment**	**Additional Payment**	**Interest**	**Principal**	**Balance**	
11	Totals	$5,896.92	$0.00	$2,696.92	$3,200.00		
12	2/3/2013					$ 3,200.00	
13	3/3/2013	96.00		48.00	48.00	3,152.00	
14	4/3/2013	94.55		47.28	47.27	3,104.73	
15	5/3/2013	93.15		46.57	46.58	3,058.15	
16	6/3/2013	91.75		45.87	45.88	3,012.27	
17	7/3/2013	90.35		45.18	45.17	2,967.10	
18	8/3/2013	89.00		44.51	44.49	2,922.61	
19	9/3/2013	87.70		43.84	43.86	2,878.75	
20	10/3/2013	86.35		43.18	43.17	2,835.58	
21	11/3/2013	85.05		42.53	42.52	2,793.06	
22	12/3/2013	83.80		41.90	41.90	2,751.16	
23	1/3/2014	82.55		41.27	41.28	2,709.88	
24	2/3/2014	81.30		40.65	40.65	2,669.23	
25	3/3/2014	80.10		40.04	40.06	2,629.17	
26	4/3/2014	78.90		39.44	39.46	2,589.71	
27	5/3/2014	77.70		38.85	38.85	2,550.86	
28	6/3/2014	76.55		38.26	38.29	2,512.57	
29	7/3/2014	75.40		37.69	37.71	2,474.86	
30	8/3/2014	74.25		37.12	37.13	2,437.73	
31	9/3/2014	73.15		36.57	36.58	2,401.15	
32	10/3/2014	72.05		36.02	36.03	2,365.12	
33	11/3/2014	70.95		35.48	35.47	2,329.65	
34	12/3/2014	69.90		34.94	34.96	2,294.69	

Figure 13-3: Calculating a credit card payment schedule.

The minimum payment formula, such as the one in B13, follows:

```
=MIN(F12+D13,MROUND(MAX(MinDol,ROUND(MinPct*F12,2)),PayRnd))
```

From the inside out: the larger of the minimum dollar amounts and the minimum percent are calculated. The result is rounded to the nearest five cents. This rounded amount is then compared with the outstanding balance (plus interest), and the lesser of the two is used.

Of course, things get much more complicated when additional charges are made. In such a case, the formulas need to account for "grace periods" for purchases (but not cash withdrawals). A further complication is that interest is calculated on the daily outstanding balance at the daily effective equivalent of the quoted rate.

Summarizing Loan Options Using a Data Table

If you're faced with making a decision about borrowing money, you have to choose between many variables, not the least of which is the interest rate. Fortunately, Excel's data table feature can help by summarizing the results of calculations using different inputs.

On the Web

The workbook loan data tables.xlsx contains the examples in this section and can be found at this book's website.

The data table feature is one of Excel's most under-used tools. A data table is a dynamic range that summarizes formula cells for varying input cells. You can create a data table fairly easily, but it has some limitations. In particular, a data table can deal with only one or two input cells at a time. This limitation becomes clear as you view the examples.

Creating a one-way data table

A *one-way data table* shows the results of any number of calculations for different values of a single input cell. Figure 13-4 shows the general layout for a one-way data table.

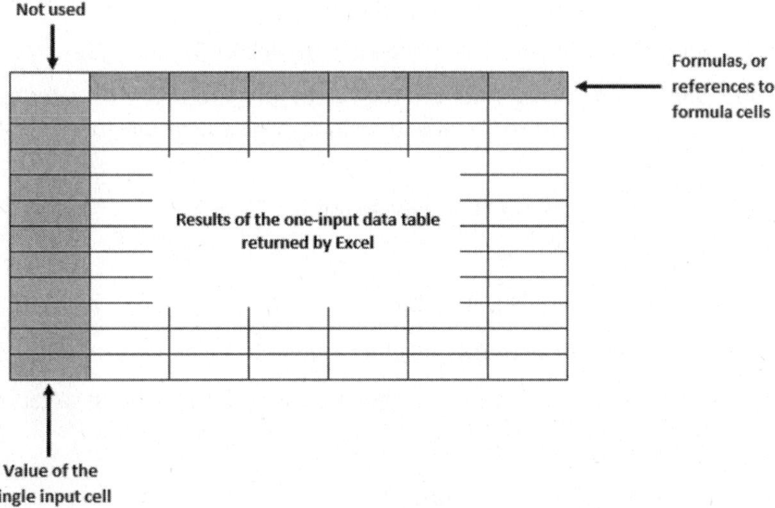

Figure 13-4: The layout for a one-way data table.

Figure 13-5 shows a one-way data table (in D2:G9) that displays three calculations (payment amount, total payments, and total interest) for a loan, using eight interest rates ranging from 6.75% to 8.50%. In this example, the input cell is cell B2. Note that the range E1:G1 is not part of the data table. These cells contain descriptive labels.

	A	B	C	D	E	F	G	H
1	Loan Amount:	$10,000.00			*Payment Amt*	*Total Payments*	*Total Interest*	
2	Annual Interest Rate:	6.75%		6.75%	$307.63	$11,074.65	$1,074.65	
3	Pmt. Period (mos):	1		7.00%	$308.77	$11,115.75	$1,115.75	
4	No. of Periods:	36		7.25%	$309.92	$11,156.95	$1,156.95	
5				7.50%	$311.06	$11,198.24	$1,198.24	
6	Payment Amount:	$307.63		7.75%	$312.21	$11,239.62	$1,239.62	
7	Total Payments:	$11,074.65		8.00%	$313.36	$11,281.09	$1,281.09	
8	Total Interest:	$1,074.65		8.25%	$314.52	$11,322.66	$1,322.66	
9				8.50%	$315.68	$11,364.31	$1,364.31	
10								

Figure 13-5: Using a one-way data table to display three loan calculations for various interest rates.

To create this one-way data table, follow these steps:

1. **In the first row of the data table, enter the formulas that returns the results.**

   The interest rate varies in the data table, but it doesn't matter which interest rate you use for the calculations as long as the calculations are correct. In this example, the formulas in E2:G2 contain references to other formulas in column B:

   ```
   E2: =B6
   F2: =B7
   G2: =B8
   ```

2. **In the first column of the data table, enter various values for a single input cell.**

   In this example, the input value is an interest rate, and the values for various interest rates appear in D2:D9. Note that the first row of the data table (row 2) displays the results for the first input value (in cell D2).

3. **Select the range that contains the entries from the previous steps.**

   In this example, select D2:G9.

4. **Choose Data➜ Forecast➜ What-If Analysis➜ Data Table.**

   Excel displays the Data Table dialog box, as shown in Figure 13-6.

5. **For the Column Input Cell field, specify the formula cell that corresponds to the input variable.**

   In this example, the Column Input Cell is B2.

6. **Leave the Row Input Cell field empty. Then click OK.**

   Excel inserts an array formula that uses the TABLE function with a single argument.

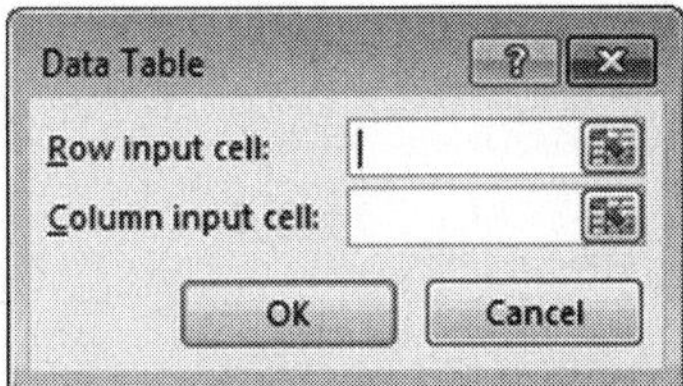

Figure 13-6: The Data Table dialog box

Note that the array formula is not entered into the entire range that you selected in step 3. The first column and the first row of your selection are not changed.

Creating a two-way data table

A *two-way data table* shows the results of a single calculation for different values of two input cells. Figure 13-7 shows the general layout of a two-way data table.

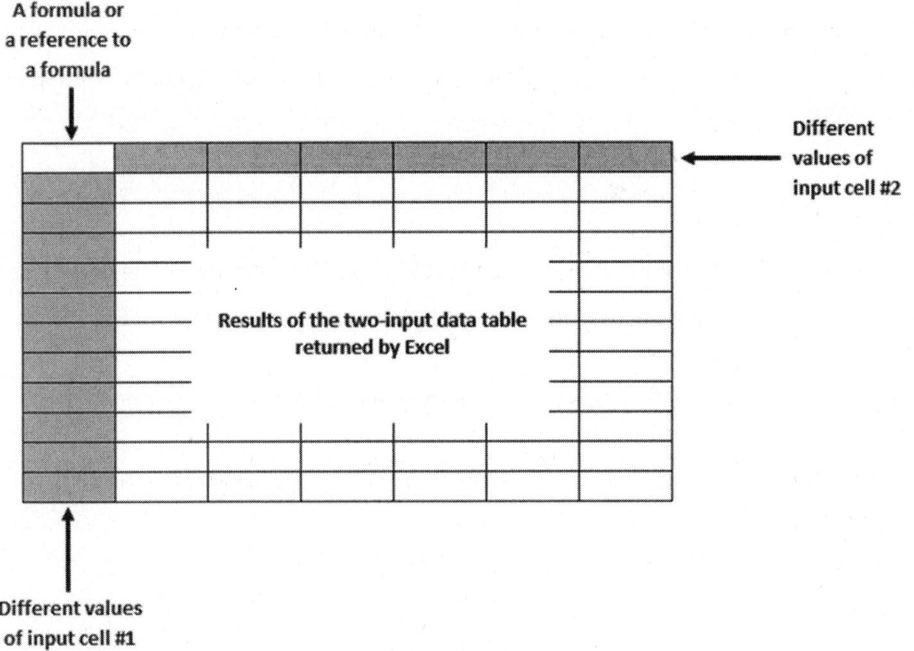

Figure 13-7: The structure for a two-way data table.

Figure 13-8 shows a two-way data table (in B7:J16) that displays a calculation (payment amount) for a loan, using eight interest rates and nine loan amounts.

	A	B	C	D	E	F	G	H	I	J	K
1	Loan Amount:	$10,000									
2	Annual Interest Rate:	7.25%									
3	Pmt. Period (mos):	1									
4	No. of Periods:	36									
5	Payment:	$309.92									
6						*Interest Rate*					
7		$310	6.75%	7.00%	7.25%	7.50%	7.75%	8.00%	8.25%	8.50%	
8	*Loan Amount*	$8,000	$246.10	$247.02	$247.93	$248.85	$249.77	$250.69	$251.61	$252.54	
9		$8,500	$261.48	$262.46	$263.43	$264.40	$265.38	$266.36	$267.34	$268.32	
10		$9,000	$276.87	$277.89	$278.92	$279.96	$280.99	$282.03	$283.07	$284.11	
11		$9,500	$292.25	$293.33	$294.42	$295.51	$296.60	$297.70	$298.79	$299.89	
12		$10,000	$307.63	$308.77	$309.92	$311.06	$312.21	$313.36	$314.52	$315.68	
13		$10,500	$323.01	$324.21	$325.41	$326.62	$327.82	$329.03	$330.24	$331.46	
14		$11,000	$338.39	$339.65	$340.91	$342.17	$343.43	$344.70	$345.97	$347.24	
15		$11,500	$353.77	$355.09	$356.40	$357.72	$359.04	$360.37	$361.70	$363.03	
16		$12,000	$369.16	$370.53	$371.90	$373.27	$374.65	$376.04	$377.42	$378.81	
17											

Figure 13-8: Using a two-way data table to display payment amounts for various loan amounts and interest rates.

To create this two-way data table, follow these steps:

1. **Enter a formula that returns the results that you want to use in the data table.**

   In this example, the formula in cell B7 is a simple reference to cell B5, which contains the payment calculation:

   ```
   =B5
   ```

2. **Enter various values for the first input in successive columns of the first row of the data table.**

   In this example, the first input value is interest rate, and the values for various interest rates appear in C7:J7.

3. **Enter various values for the second input cell in successive rows of the first column of the data table.**

   In this example, the second input value is the loan amount, and the values for various loan amounts are in B8:B16.

4. **Select the range that contains the entries from the preceding steps.**

   For this example, select B7:J16.

5. **Choose Data ➜ Forecast ➜ What-If Analysis ➜ Data Table.**

   Excel displays the Data Table dialog box.

6. **For the Row Input Cell field, specify the cell reference that corresponds to the first input cell.**

   In this example, the Row Input Cell is B2.

7. For the Column Input Cell field, specify the cell reference that corresponds to the second input cell.

   In this example, the Column Input Cell is B1.

8. Click OK.

   Excel inserts an array formula that uses the TABLE function with two arguments.

After you create the two-way data table, you can change the formula in the upper-left cell of the data table. In this example, you can change the formula in cell B7 to

```
=PMT(B2*(B3/12),B4,-B1)*B4-B1
```

This causes the TABLE function to display total interest rather than payment amounts.

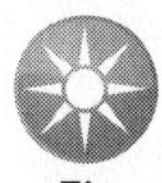
Tip

If you find that using data tables slows down the calculation of your workbook, choose Formulas ➜ Calculation ➜ Calculation Options ➜ Automatic Except for Data Tables. Then you can recalculate by pressing F9.

Financial Statements and Ratios

Many companies use Excel to evaluate their financial health and report financial results. Financial statements and financial ratios are two types of analyses a company can use to accomplish those goals. Excel is well suited for financial statements because its grid layout allows for easy adjustment of columns. Ratios are simple financial calculations—something Excel was designed for.

Basic financial statements

Financial statements summarize the financial transactions of a business. The two primary financial statements are the balance sheet and the income statement:

- The *balance sheet* reports the state of a company at a particular moment in time. It shows the following:
  - **Assets:** What the company owns
  - **Liabilities:** What the company owes
  - **Equity:** What the company is worth
- The *income statement* summarizes the transactions of a company over a certain period of time, such as a month, quarter, or year.
- A typical income statement reports the sales, costs, and net income (or loss) of the company.

Converting trial balances

Most accounting software produces financial statements for you. However, many of those applications do not give you the flexibility and formatting options that you have in Excel. One way to produce your own financial statements is to export the trial balance from your accounting software package and use Excel to summarize the transactions for you. Figure 13-9 shows part of a *trial balance,* which lists all the accounts and their balances.

	A	B	C	D
1	Account Name	Account No.	Balance	Class
2	Cash-Petty Cash	1010	449.87	Cash
3	Checking Account	1110	2,412.23	Cash
4	Investment Account	1115	327,283.53	Marketable Securities
5	Accounts Receivable	1210	16,586.25	Accounts Receivable
6	Prepaid Expenses	1420	2,587.50	Prepaid and Other
7	Prepaid Insurance	1425	1,000.00	Prepaid and Other
8	Inventory Asset	1310	46,005.75	Inventory
9	Property and Equipment	1510	65,000.00	Property and Equipment
10	Accum. Depr.Property and Equipment	1511	(6,750.00)	Accumulated Depreciation
11	Office/Store Furniture and Fixtures	1520	12,000.00	Property and Equipment
12	Accum. Depr. Furniture and Fixtures	1521	(9,525.00)	Accumulated Depreciation
13	Accounts Payable	2010	(15,502.62)	Accounts Payable
14	Pending Item Receipts	2015	(846.59)	Accrued Expenses
15	Sales Tax Payable	2110	(11,426.42)	Accrued Expenses
16	Federal Tax Liability	2210	(1,517.30)	Accrued Expenses
17	Federal Tax Liability (FUTA)	2215	(145.00)	Accrued Expenses
18	State Tax Liability	2220	(740.00)	Accrued Expenses
19	401 (k) Liability	2230	(2,000.00)	Accrued Expenses
20	Union Dues Liability	2240	(85.00)	Accrued Expenses
21	Medical/Dental Liability	2250	(990.00)	Accrued Expenses
22	Other Payables	2310	(500.00)	Accrued Expenses
23	Interest Payable	2315	(2,000.00)	Accrued Expenses
24	Visa Credit Card	2610	(300.00)	Accrued Expenses
25	Note Payable to Bank	2710	(20,000.00)	Long Term Debt
26	Common Stock	3015	(1,000.00)	Common Stock
27	APIC	3016	(36,000.00)	Additional Paid in Capital
28	Owners' Withdrawals	3020	12,000.00	Dividends
29	Retained Earnings	3025	(76,484.48)	Beginning Retained Earnings
30	Sales	4010	(1,198,873.98)	Revenue
31	Cash Discount Given	4020	3,414.90	Revenue
32	Write off	4210	8.83	Revenue

Figure 13-9: A trial balance lists all accounts and balances.

Figure 13-10 shows a balance sheet that summarizes the balance sheet accounts from the trial balance.

The Class column of the trial balance is used to classify that account on the balance sheet or income statement. The formula in cell B4 on the balance sheet follows:

```
=SUMIF(Class,A4,Balance)
```

	A		B
1	**Balance Sheet**		
2			
3	**Assets**		
4	Cash	$	2,862.10
5	Marketable Securities		327,283.53
6	Accounts Receivable		16,586.25
7	Inventory		46,005.75
8	Prepaid and Other		3,587.50
9	Total Current Assets	$	396,325.13
10			
11	Property and Equipment	$	77,000.00
12	Accumulated Depreciation		16,275.00
13	Net PP&E	$	60,725.00
14			
15	Total Assets	$	457,050.13
16			
17	**Liabilities**		
18	Accounts Payable	$	15,502.62
19	Accrued Expenses		20,550.31
20	Total Current Liabilities	$	36,052.93
21			
22	Long Term Debt	$	20,000.00
23			
24	**Equity**		
25	Common Stock	$	1,000.00
26	Additional Paid in Capital		36,000.00
27	Retained Earnings		363,997.20
28			
29	Total Liabilities and Equity	$	457,050.13
30			

Figure 13-10: A balance sheet summarizes certain accounts.

On the Web

The file financial statements.xlsx contains all the examples in this chapter and can be found at this book's website.

For all the accounts on the trial balance whose class equals Cash, their total is summed here. The formula is repeated for every financial statement classification on both the balance sheet and the income statement. For classifications that typically have a credit balance—such as liabilities, equity, and revenue—the formula starts with a negative sign. Here's the formula for Accounts Payable, cell B18:

```
=-SUMIF(Class,A18,Balance)
```

The account that ties the balance sheet and income statement together is Retained Earnings. Figure 13-11 shows an income statement that includes a statement of retained earnings at the bottom.

	A		B	C
1	**Income Statement**			
2	**with Statement of Retained Earnings**			
3				
4	Revenue	$	1,195,450.25	
5	Cost of Goods Sold		870,175.83	
6	Gross Margin	$	325,274.42	
7				
8	Overhead		29,879.65	
9	Net Ordinary Income (Loss)	$	295,394.77	
10				
11	Interest Expense		1,269.08	
12	Interest Income		5,387.03	
13	Net Income (Loss)	$	299,512.72	
14				
15	Beginning Retained Earnings	$	76,484.48	
16	Net Income (Loss)		299,512.72	
17	Dividends		(12,000.00)	
18	Ending Retained Earnings	$	363,997.20	
19				
20				

Figure 13-11: The income statement can include a statement of retained earnings.

The Retained Earnings classification on the balance sheet refers to the Ending Retained Earnings classification on the income statement. Ending Retained Earnings is computed by taking Beginning Retained Earnings, adding net income (or subtracting net loss), and subtracting dividends.

Finally, the balance sheet must be in balance: hence, the name. Total assets must equal total liabilities and equity. This error-checking formula is used in cell B31 on the balance sheet:

```
=IF(ABS(B29-B15)>0.01,"Out of Balance","")
```

If the difference between assets and liabilities and equity is more than a penny, an error message is displayed below the schedule; otherwise, the cell appears blank. The ABS function is used to check for assets being more or less than liabilities and equity. Because the balance sheet is in balance, the formula returns an empty string.

Common size financial statements

Comparing financial statements from different companies can be difficult. One such difficulty is comparing companies of different sizes. A small retailer might show $1 million in revenue, but a multinational retailer might show $1 billion. The sheer scale of the numbers makes it difficult to compare the health and results of operations of these very different companies.

Common size financial statements summarize accounts relative to a single number. For balance sheets, all entries are shown relative to total assets. For the income statement, all entries are shown relative to total sales. Figure 13-12 shows a common size income statement.

	A	B	C	D
1	**Income Statement**			
3				
4	Revenue	$ 1,195,450.25	100.00%	
5	Cost of Goods Sold	870,175.83	72.79%	
6	Gross Margin	$ 325,274.42	27.21%	
7				
8	Overhead	29,879.65	2.50%	
9	Net Ordinary Income (Loss)	$ 295,394.77	24.71%	
10				
11	Interest Expense	1,269.08	0.11%	
12	Interest Income	5,387.03	0.45%	
13	Net Income (Loss)	$ 299,512.72	25.05%	
14				
15	Beginning Retained Earnings	$ 76,484.48		
16	Net Income (Loss)	299,512.72		
17	Distributions	-		
18	Ending Retained Earnings	$ 375,997.20		
19				
20				
21				

Figure 13-12: Entries on a common size income statement are shown relative to revenue.

The formula in cell C4 follows:

```
=B4/$B$4
```

The denominator is absolute with respect to both rows and columns so that when this formula is copied to other areas of the income statement, it shows the percentage of revenue. To display only the percentage figures, you can hide column B.

Ratio analysis

Financial ratios are calculations that are derived from the financial statements and other financial data to measure various aspects of a company. They can be compared with other companies or to industry standards. This section demonstrates how to calculate several financial ratios. See Figure 13-13.

	A	B	C
1			
2	**Liquidity**		
3	Current Assets	396,325.13	
4	Current Liabilities	36,052.93	
5	Net Working Capital	360,272.20	
6	Current Ratio	10.99:1	
7	Quick Ratio	9.16:1	
8			
9	**Asset Use**		
10	Accounts Receivable Turnover	70.59	
11	Average Collection Period	5.17	
12	Inventory Turnover	20.41	
13	Average Age of Inventory	17.88	
14	Operating Cycle	23.05	
15			
16	**Solvency**		
17	Debt Ratio	8.15:1	
18	Debt-to-Equity	0.14:1	
19	Times Interest Earned	237.01	
20			
21	**Profitability**		
22	Gross Profit Margin	27.21%	
23	Net Profit Margin	25.05%	
24	Return on Assets	63.77%	
25	Return on Equity	116.43%	
26			

Figure 13-13: Various financial ratio calculations.

Liquidity ratios

Liquidity ratios measure a company's ability to pay its bills in the short term. Poor liquidity ratios may indicate that the company has a high cost of financing or is on the verge of bankruptcy.

Net working capital is computed by subtracting current liabilities from current assets:

```
=Total_Current_Assets-Total_Current_Liabilities
```

Current assets are turned into cash within one accounting period (usually one year). *Current liabilities* are debts that will be paid within one period. A positive number here indicates that the company has enough assets to pay for its short-term liabilities.

The current ratio is a similar measure that divides current assets by current liabilities:

```
=Total_Current_Assets/Total_Current_Liabilities
```

When this ratio is greater than 1:1, it's the same as when net working capital is positive.

The final liquidity ratio is the quick ratio. Although the current ratio includes assets, such as inventory and accounts receivable that will be converted into cash in a short time, the quick ratio includes only cash and assets that can be converted into cash immediately.

```
=(Cash+Marketable_Securities)/Total_Current_Liabilities
```

A quick ratio greater than 1:1 indicates that the company can pay all its short-term liabilities right now.

Tip

The following custom number format can be used to format the result of the current ratio and the quick ratio:

```
0.00":1"_)
```

Asset use ratios

Asset use ratios measure how efficiently a company is using its assets: that is, how quickly the company is turning its assets back into cash. The accounts receivable turnover ratio divides sales by average accounts receivable:

```
=Revenue/((Account_Receivable+LastYear_Accounts_Receivable)/2)
```

Accounts receivable turnover is then used to compute the average collection period:

```
=365/Accounts_receivable_turnover
```

The average collection period is generally compared against the company's credit terms. If the company allows 30 days for its customers to pay and the average collection period is greater than 30 days, it can indicate a problem with the company's credit policies or collection efforts.

The efficiency with which the company uses its inventory can be similarly computed. Inventory turnover divides cost of sales by average inventory:

```
=Cost_of_Goods_Sold/((Inventory+LastYear_Inventory)/2)
```

The average age of inventory tells how many days' inventory is in stock before it is sold:

```
=365/Inventory_turnover
```

By adding the average collection period to the average age of inventory, the total days to convert inventory into cash can be computed. This is the operating cycle and is computed as follows:

```
=Average_collection_period+Average_age_of_inventory
```

Solvency ratios

Whereas *liquidity ratios* compute a company's ability to pay short-term debt, *solvency ratios* compute its ability to pay long-term debt. The debt ratio compares total assets with total liabilities:

```
=Total_Assets/(Total_Current_Liabilities+Long_Term_Debt)
```

The debt-to-equity ratio divides total liabilities by total equity. It's used to determine whether a company is primarily equity financed or debt financed:

```
=(Total_Current_Liabilities+Long_Term_Debt)/
(Common_Stock+Additional_Paid_in_Capital+Retained_Earnings)
```

The times interest earned ratio computes how many times a company's profit would cover its interest expense:

```
=(Net_Income__Loss+Interest_Expense)/Interest_Expense
```

Profitability ratios

As you might guess, *profitability ratios* measure how much profit a company makes. Gross profit margin and net profit margin can be seen on the earlier common size financial statements because they are both ratios computed relative to sales. The formulas for gross profit margin and net profit margin follow:

```
=Gross_Margin/Revenue
=Net_Income__Loss/Revenue
```

The return on assets computes how well a company uses its assets to produce profits:

```
=Net_Income__Loss/((Total_Assets+LastYear_Total_Assets)/2)
```

The return on equity computes how well the owners' investments are performing:

```
=Net_Income__Loss/((Total_Equity+LastYear_Total_Equity)/2)
```

Creating Indices

The final topic in this chapter demonstrates how to create an index from schedules of changing values. An index is commonly used to compare how data changes over time. An index allows easy cross-comparison between different periods and between different data sets.

For example, consumer price changes are recorded in an index in which the initial "shopping basket" is set to an index of 100. All subsequent changes are made relative to that base. Therefore, any two points show the cumulative effect of increases.

Tip

Using indices makes it easier to compare data that uses vastly different scales—such as comparing a consumer price index with a wage index.

Perhaps the best approach is to use a two-step illustration:

1. Convert the second and subsequent data in the series to percentage increases from the previous item.
2. Set up a column in which the first entry is 100, and successive entries increase by the percentage increases previously determined.

Although a two-step approach is not required, a major advantage is that the calculation of the percentage changes is often useful data in its own right.

The example, shown in Figure 13-14, involves rentals per square foot of different types of space between 2010 and 2016. The raw data is contained in the first table. This data is converted to percentage changes in the second table, and this information is used to create the indices in the third table.

Creating an Index from Growth Data

Rentals Per Square Foot

	2010	2011	2012	2013	2014	2015	2016
Retail	89.4	92.3	97.8	101.9	105.7	108.4	116.4
Office	60.3	58.6	60.2	72.1	84.3	89.9	92.3
Industrial	12.0	11.2	12.5	17.9	18.2	19.7	20.2
Other	33.5	32.1	35.8	51.7	35.7	36.4	37.7
All Property	39.2	37.8	40.2	58.9	60.4	69.2	74.5

Growth Data

	2010	2011	2012	2013	2014	2015	2016	Average
Retail		3.13%	5.63%	3.98%	3.62%	2.49%	6.90%	4.28%
Office		-2.82%	2.61%	16.56%	14.46%	6.24%	2.57%	6.38%
Industrial		-7.71%	11.08%	29.94%	1.76%	7.61%	2.13%	6.87%
Other		-4.33%	10.31%	30.75%	-44.94%	1.90%	3.61%	-3.61%
All Property		-3.76%	5.88%	31.83%	2.42%	12.71%	7.22%	8.84%

Index Data

	2010	2011	2012	2013	2014	2015	2016	Average
Retail	100.0	103.1	108.9	113.3	117.4	120.3	128.6	4.28%
Office	100.0	97.2	99.7	116.2	133.0	141.3	145.0	6.38%
Industrial	100.0	92.3	102.5	133.2	135.6	145.9	149.0	6.87%
Other	100.0	95.7	105.5	138.0	76.0	77.4	80.2	-3.61%
All Property	100.0	96.2	101.9	134.3	137.6	155.1	166.3	8.84%

Figure 13-14: Creating an index from growth data.

This example is available at this book's website in the workbook indices.xlsx.

The formulas for calculating the growth rates (in the second table) are simple. For example, the formula in cell C14 follows:

```
=(C5-B5)/B5
```

This formula returns 3.13%, which represents the change in retail space (from $89.4 to $92.3). This formula is copied to the other cells in the table (range C14:H18). This information is useful, but it is difficult to track overall performance between periods of more than a year. That's why indices are required.

Calculating the indices in the third table is also straightforward. The 2010 index is set at 100 (column B) and is the base for the indices. The formula in cell C23 follows:

```
=B23*(1+C14)
```

This formula is copied to the other cells in the table (range C23:H27).

These indices make it possible to compare performance of, say, offices between any two years and to track the relative performance over any two years of any two types of property. So it is clear, for example, that industrial property rental grew faster than retail property rentals between 2013 and 2016.

The average figures (column I) are calculated by using the RATE function. This results in an annual growth rate over the entire period.

Here's the formula in cell I23 that calculates the average growth rate over the term:

```
=RATE(6,0,B23,-H23,0)
```

The nper argument is 6 in the formula because that is the number of years since the base date.

Array Formulas

14

Introducing Arrays

In This Chapter

- Defining arrays and array formulas
- One-dimensional versus two-dimensional arrays
- How to work with array constants
- Techniques for working with array formulas
- Examples of multicell array formulas
- Examples of array formulas that occupy a single cell

One of Excel's most interesting (and most powerful) features is its ability to work with arrays in a formula. When you understand this concept, you can create elegant formulas that appear to perform magic. This chapter introduces the concept of arrays and is required reading for anyone who wants to become a master of Excel formulas. Chapter 15, "Performing Magic with Array Formulas," continues with lots of useful examples.

Introducing Array Formulas

If you do any computer programming, you've probably been exposed to the concept of an *array*, which is a collection of items operated on collectively or individually. In Excel, an array can be one dimensional or two dimensional. These dimensions correspond to rows and columns. For example, a *one-dimensional array* can be stored in a range that consists of one row (a horizontal array) or one column (a vertical array). A *two-dimensional array* can be stored in a rectangular range of cells. Excel doesn't support three-dimensional arrays (although its VBA programming language does).

As you'll see, though, arrays need not be stored in cells. You can also work with arrays that exist only in Excel's memory. You can then use an *array formula* to manipulate this information and return a result. Excel supports two types of array formulas:

➤ **Multicell array formulas:** This type of array formula works with arrays stored in ranges or in memory, and it produces an array as a result. Because a cell can hold only one value, a multicell array formula is entered into a range of cells.

➤ **Single-cell array formulas:** This type of array formula works with arrays stored in ranges or in memory, and it produces a result displayed in a single cell.

This section presents two array formula examples: an array formula that occupies multiple cells and another array formula that occupies only one cell.

On the Web

All the examples in this chapter are available at this book's website. The filename is `array examples.xlsx`.

A multicell array formula

Figure 14-1 shows a simple worksheet set up to calculate product sales. Normally, you would calculate the value in column D (total sales per product) with a formula such as the one that follows and then copy this formula down the column:

```
=B2*C2
```

	A	B	C	D
1	Product	Units Sold	Unit Price	Total
2	AR-998	3	$50	$150
3	BZ-011	10	$100	$1,000
4	MR-919	5	$20	$100
5	TR-811	9	$10	$90
6	TS-333	3	$60	$180
7	ZL-001	1	$200	$200

Figure 14-1: Column D contains formulas to calculate the total sales for each product.

After you copy the formula, the worksheet contains six formulas in column D.

Another alternative uses a *single* formula (an array formula) to calculate all six values in D2:D7. This single formula occupies six cells and returns an array of six values.

To create a single array formula to perform the calculations, follow these steps:

1. Select a range to hold the results.

   In this example, the range is D2:D7.

2. Enter the following formula, either by typing it or by pointing to the ranges:

   ```
   =B2:B7*C2:C7
   ```

3. Normally, you press Enter to enter a formula. Because this is an array formula, however, you press Ctrl+Shift+Enter.

The formula is entered into all six selected cells. If you examine the Formula bar, you see the following:

```
{=B2:B7*C2:C7}
```

Excel places curly brackets around the formula to indicate that it's an array formula.

This formula performs its calculations and returns a six-item array. The array formula actually works with two other arrays, both of which happen to be stored in ranges. The values for the first array are stored in B2:B7, and the values for the second array are stored in C2:C7.

Because displaying more than one value in a single cell is not possible, six cells are required to display the resulting array. That explains why you selected six cells before you entered the array formula.

This array formula, of course, returns the same values as these six normal formulas entered into individual cells in D2:D7:

```
=B2*C2
=B3*C3
=B4*C4
=B5*C5
=B6*C6
=B7*C7
```

Using a single array formula rather than individual formulas does offer a few advantages:

- It's a good way of ensuring that all formulas in a range are identical.
- Using a multicell array formula makes it less likely that you will overwrite a formula accidentally. You cannot change or delete one cell in a multicell array formula.
- Using a multicell array formula almost certainly prevents novices from tampering with your formulas.

As you see later, multicell array formulas can be more useful than this trivial introductory example.

A single-cell array formula

Now take a look at a single-cell array formula in Figure 14-2. The following array formula is in cell C9:

```
{=SUM(B2:B7*C2:C7)}
```

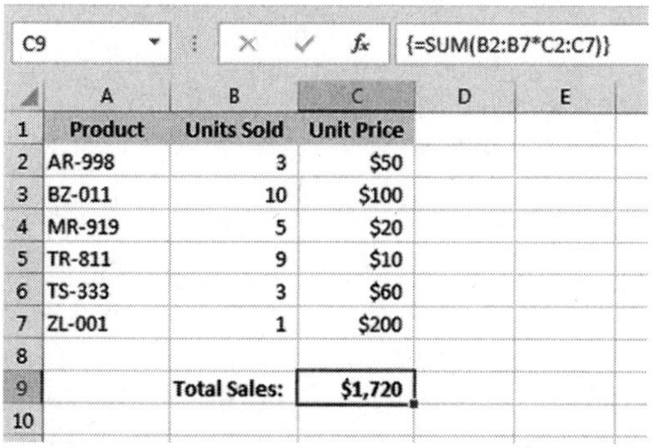

C9 | {=SUM(B2:B7*C2:C7)}

	A	B	C	D	E
1	Product	Units Sold	Unit Price		
2	AR-998	3	$50		
3	BZ-011	10	$100		
4	MR-919	5	$20		
5	TR-811	9	$10		
6	TS-333	3	$60		
7	ZL-001	1	$200		
8					
9		Total Sales:	$1,720		
10					

Figure 14-2: An array formula to calculate the total sales.

You can enter this formula into any cell. Remember: when you enter this formula, make sure you press Ctrl+Shift+Enter (and don't type the curly brackets).

This formula works with two arrays, both of which are stored in cells. The first array is stored in B2:B7, and the second array is stored in C2:C7. The formula multiplies the corresponding values in these two arrays and creates a new array (which exists only in memory). The new array consists of six values, which can be represented like this. (The reason for using semicolons is explained a bit later.)

```
{150;1000;100;90;180;200}
```

The SUM function then operates on this new array and returns the sum of its values.

Note

In this case, you can use Excel's SUMPRODUCT function to obtain the same result without using an array formula:

```
=SUMPRODUCT(B2:B7,C2:C7)
```

However, array formulas allow many other types of calculations that are otherwise not possible.

Creating an array constant

The examples in the previous section used arrays stored in worksheet ranges. The examples in this section demonstrate an important concept: An array does not have to be stored in a range of cells. This type of array, which is stored in memory, is referred to as an *array constant.*

You create an array constant by listing its items and surrounding them with curly brackets. Here's an example of a five-item horizontal array constant:

```
{1,0,1,0,1}
```

The following formula uses the SUM function, with the preceding array constant as its argument. The formula returns the sum of the values in the array (which is 3). Notice that this formula uses an array, but it is not an array formula. Therefore, you do not use Ctrl+Shift+Enter to enter the formula.

```
=SUM({1,0,1,0,1})
```

Note

When you specify an array directly (as shown previously), you must provide the curly brackets around the array elements. When you enter an array formula, on the other hand, you do not supply the curly brackets.

At this point, you probably don't see any advantage to using an array constant. The formula that follows, for example, returns the same result as the previous formula:

```
=SUM(1,0,1,0,1)
```

Keep reading, and the advantages will become apparent.

Following is a formula that uses two array constants:

```
=SUM({1,2,3,4}*{5,6,7,8})
```

This formula creates a new array (in memory) that consists of the product of the corresponding elements in the two arrays. The new array is as follows:

```
{5,12,21,32}
```

This new array is then used as an argument for the SUM function, which returns the result (70). The formula is equivalent to the following formula, which doesn't use arrays:

```
=SUM(1*5,2*6,3*7,4*8)
```

A formula can work with both an array constant and an array stored in a range. The following formula, for example, returns the sum of the values in A1:D1, each multiplied by the corresponding element in the array constant:

```
{=SUM(A1:D1*{1,2,3,4})}
```

Because one of our arrays in this formula is a range, the formula is entered with Ctrl+Shift+Enter to let Excel know we want to convert any ranges to array. The formula is equivalent to this:

```
=SUM(A1*1,B1*2,C1*3,D1*4)
```

Array constant elements

An array constant can contain numbers, text, logical values (*TRUE* or *FALSE*), and even error values such as *#N/A*. Numbers can be in integer, decimal, or scientific format. You must enclose text in double quotation marks (for example, "Tuesday"). You can use different types of values in the same array constant, as in this example:

```
{1,2,3,TRUE,FALSE,TRUE,"Moe","Larry","Curly"}
```

An array constant cannot contain formulas, functions, or other arrays. Numeric values cannot contain dollar signs, commas, parentheses, or percent signs. For example, the following is an invalid array constant:

```
{SQRT(32),$56.32,12.5%}
```

Understanding the Dimensions of an Array

As stated previously, an array can be either one dimensional or two dimensional. A one-dimensional array's orientation can be either vertical or horizontal.

One-dimensional horizontal arrays

The elements in a one-dimensional horizontal array are separated by commas. The following example is a one-dimensional horizontal array constant:

```
{1,2,3,4,5}
```

Displaying this array in a range requires five consecutive cells in a single row. To enter this array into a range, select a range of cells that consists of one row and five columns. Then enter **={1,2,3,4,5}** and press Ctrl+Shift+Enter.

Note

If you enter this array into a horizontal range that consists of more than five cells, the extra cells contain #N/A (which denotes unavailable values). If you enter this array into a *vertical* range of cells, only the first item (1) appears in each cell.

The following example is another horizontal array; it has seven elements and is made up of text strings:

```
{"Sun","Mon","Tue","Wed","Thu","Fri","Sat"}
```

To enter this array, select seven cells in one row and then type the following (followed by pressing Ctrl+Shift+Enter):

```
={"Sun","Mon","Tue","Wed","Thu","Fri","Sat"}
```

One-dimensional vertical arrays

The elements in a one-dimensional vertical array are separated by semicolons. The following is a six-element vertical array constant:

```
{10;20;30;40;50;60}
```

Displaying this array in a range requires six cells in a single column. To enter this array into a range, select a range of cells that consists of six rows and one column. Then enter the following formula and press Ctrl+Shift+Enter:

```
={10;20;30;40;50;60}
```

The following is another example of a vertical array; this one has four elements:

```
{"Widgets";"Sprockets";"Do-Dads";"Thing-A-Majigs"}
```

To enter this array into a range, select four cells in a column, enter the following formula, and then press Ctrl+Shift+Enter:

```
={"Widgets";"Sprockets";"Do-Dads";"Thing-A-Majigs"}
```

Two-dimensional arrays

A *two-dimensional array* uses commas to separate its horizontal elements and semicolons to separate its vertical elements.

Note

Other language versions of Excel may use characters other than commas and semicolons.

The following example shows a 3 × 4 array constant:

```
{1,2,3,4;5,6,7,8;9,10,11,12}
```

Displaying this array in a range requires 12 cells. To enter this array into a range, select a range of cells that consists of three rows and four columns. Then type the following formula and press Ctrl+Shift+Enter:

```
={1,2,3,4;5,6,7,8;9,10,11,12}
```

Figure 14-3 shows how this array appears when entered into a range (in this case, B3:E5).

B3 | {=\{1,2,3,4;5,6,7,8;9,10,11,12\}}

	A	B	C	D	E	F
1						
2						
3		1	2	3	4	
4		5	6	7	8	
5		9	10	11	12	
6						

Figure 14-3: A 3 × 4 array entered into a range of cells.

If you enter an array into a range that has more cells than array elements, Excel displays #N/A in the extra cells. Figure 14-4 shows a 3 × 4 array entered into a 10 × 5 cell range.

B3 | {=\{1,2,3,4;5,6,7,8;9,10,11,12\}}

	A	B	C	D	E	F	G
1							
2							
3		1	2	3	4	#N/A	
4		5	6	7	8	#N/A	
5		9	10	11	12	#N/A	
6		#N/A	#N/A	#N/A	#N/A	#N/A	
7		#N/A	#N/A	#N/A	#N/A	#N/A	
8		#N/A	#N/A	#N/A	#N/A	#N/A	
9		#N/A	#N/A	#N/A	#N/A	#N/A	
10		#N/A	#N/A	#N/A	#N/A	#N/A	
11		#N/A	#N/A	#N/A	#N/A	#N/A	
12		#N/A	#N/A	#N/A	#N/A	#N/A	
13							
14							

Figure 14-4: A 3 × 4 array entered into a 10 × 5 cell range.

Each row of a two-dimensional array must contain the same number of items. The array that follows, for example, is not valid because the third row contains only three items:

```
{1,2,3,4;5,6,7,8;9,10,11}
```

Excel does not allow you to enter a formula that contains an invalid array.

You can use #N/A as a placeholder for a missing element in an array. For example, the following array is missing the element in the third row of the first column:

```
={1,2,3,4;5,6,7,8;#N/A,10,11,12}
```

Naming Array Constants

You can create an array constant, give it a name, and then use this named array in a formula. Technically, a named array is a named formula.

Cross-Ref

Chapter 3, "Working with Names," covers names and named formulas in detail.

To create a named constant array, use the New Name dialog box (choose Formulas ➜ Defined Names ➜ Define Name). In Figure 14-5, the name of the array is *DayNames,* and it refers to the following array constant:

```
{"Sun","Mon","Tue","Wed","Thu","Fri","Sat"}
```

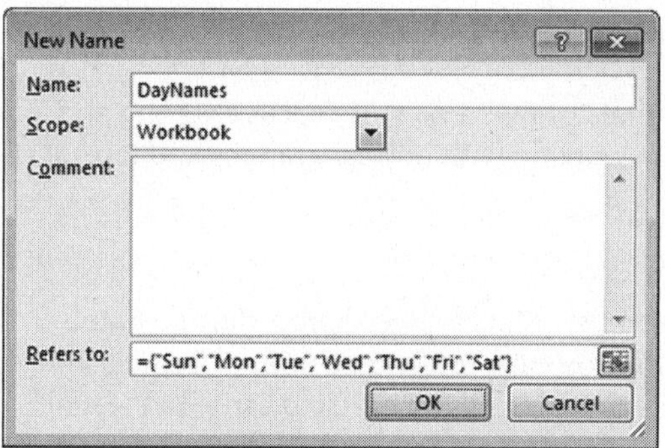

Figure 14-5: Creating a named array constant.

Notice that in the New Name dialog box, the array is defined by using a leading equal sign (=). Without this equal sign, the array is interpreted as a text string rather than an array. Also, you must type the curly brackets when defining a named array constant; Excel does not enter them for you.

After creating this named array, you can use it in a formula. Figure 14-6 shows a worksheet that contains a single array formula entered into the range B2:H2. The formula follows:

```
{=DayNames}
```

B2 | {=DayNames}

	A	B	C	D	E	F	G	H
1								
2		Sun	Mon	Tue	Wed	Thu	Fri	Sat
3								
4								

Figure 14-6: Using a named array constant in an array formula.

To enter this formula, select seven cells in a row, type **=DayNames**, and press Ctrl+Shift+Enter.

Because commas separate the array elements, the array has a horizontal orientation. Use semicolons to create a vertical array. Or you can use Excel's TRANSPOSE function to insert a horizontal array into a vertical range of cells. (See the "Transposing an array" section later in this chapter.) The following array formula, which is entered into a seven-cell vertical range, uses the TRANSPOSE function:

```
{=TRANSPOSE(DayNames)}
```

You also can access individual elements from the array by using Excel's INDEX function. The following formula, for example, returns *Wed*, the fourth item in the *DayNames* array:

```
=INDEX(DayNames,4)
```

Working with Array Formulas

This section deals with the mechanics of selecting cells that contain arrays, as well as entering and editing array formulas. These procedures differ a bit from working with ordinary ranges and formulas.

Entering an array formula

When you enter an array formula into a cell or range, you must follow a special procedure so Excel knows that you want an array formula rather than a normal formula. You enter a normal formula into a cell by pressing Enter. You enter an array formula into one or more cells by pressing Ctrl+Shift+Enter.

You can easily identify an array formula because the formula is enclosed in curly brackets in the Formula bar. The following formula, for example, is an array formula:

```
{=SUM(LEN(A1:A5))}
```

Don't enter the curly brackets when you create an array formula; Excel inserts them for you after you press Ctrl+Shift+Enter. If the result of an array formula consists of more than one value, you must select all the cells in the results range *before* you enter the formula. If you fail to do this, only the first element of the result is returned.

Selecting an array formula range

You can select the cells that contain a multicell array formula manually by using the normal cell selection procedures. Alternatively, you can use either of the following methods:

- Activate any cell in the array formula range. Choose Home ➜ Editing ➜ Find & Select ➜ Go to Special, and then select the Current Array option. When you click OK to close the dialog box, Excel selects the array.
- Activate any cell in the array formula range and press Ctrl+/ to select the entire array.

Editing an array formula

If an array formula occupies multiple cells, you must edit the entire range as though it were a single cell. The key point to remember is that you can't change just one element of an array formula. If you attempt to do so, Excel displays the warning message shown in Figure 14-7. Click OK and press Esc to exit edit mode; then select the entire range and try again.

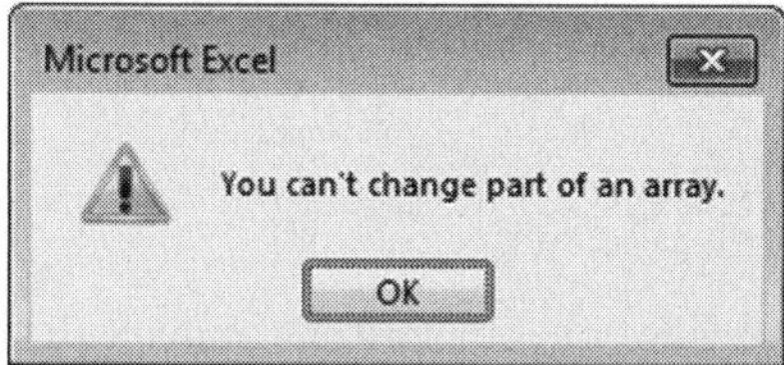

Figure 14-7: Excel's warning message reminds you that you can't edit just one cell of a multicell array formula.

The following rules apply to multicell array formulas. If you try to do any of these things, Excel lets you know about it:

- You can't change the contents of individual cells that make up an array formula.
- You can't move cells that make up part of an array formula (although you can move an entire array formula).
- You can't delete cells that form part of an array formula (although you can delete an entire array).
- You can't insert new cells into an array range. This rule includes inserting rows or columns that add new cells to an array range.
- You can't use multicell array formulas inside of a table that was created by choosing Insert ➜ Tables ➜ Table. Similarly, you can't convert a range to a table if the range contains a multicell array formula.

To edit an array formula, select all the cells in the array range and activate the Formula bar as usual (click it or press F2). Excel removes the brackets from the formula while you edit it. Edit the formula and then press Ctrl+Shift+Enter to enter the changes. Excel adds the curly brackets, and all the cells in the array now reflect your editing changes.

Warning

If you accidentally press Ctrl+Enter (instead of Ctrl+Shift+Enter) after editing an array formula, the formula is entered into each selected cell, but it will no longer be an array formula. And it will probably return an incorrect result. Just reselect the cells, press F2, and then press Ctrl+Shift+Enter.

Although you can't change any individual cell that makes up a multicell array formula, you can apply formatting to the entire array or to only parts of it.

Expanding or contracting a multicell array formula

Often, you may need to expand a multicell array formula (to include more cells) or contract it (to include fewer cells). Doing so requires a few steps:

1. Select the entire range that contains the array formula.

   You can use Ctrl+/ to automatically select the cells in an array that includes the active cell.

2. Press F2 to enter edit mode.
3. Press Ctrl+Enter.

   This step enters an identical (nonarray) formula into each selected cell.

4. Change your range selection to include additional or fewer cells, making sure the active cell is part of the original array.
5. Press F2 to reenter edit mode.
6. Press Ctrl+Shift+Enter.
7. If you contracted the range, clear the contents of any cells that still contain the nonarray formula.

Array formulas: The downside

If you've read straight through to this point in the chapter, you probably understand some of the advantages of using array formulas. The main advantage, of course, is that an array formula enables you to perform otherwise impossible calculations. As you gain more experience with arrays, you undoubtedly will discover some disadvantages.

Array formulas are one of the least understood features of Excel. Consequently, if you plan to share a workbook with someone who may need to make modifications, you should probably avoid using array formulas. Encountering an array formula when you don't know what it is can be confusing.

You might also discover that you can easily forget to enter an array formula by pressing Ctrl+Shift+Enter. If you edit an existing array, you still must use these keys to complete the edits. Except for logical errors, this is probably the most common problem that users have with array formulas. If you press Enter by mistake after editing an array formula, just press F2 to get back into edit mode and then press Ctrl+Shift+Enter.

Another potential problem with array formulas is that they can sometimes slow your worksheet's recalculations, especially if you use large arrays. On a faster system, this may not be a problem. But, conversely, using an array formula is almost always faster than using a custom VBA function. (Part VI of this book, "Developing Custom Worksheet Functions," covers custom VBA functions.)

Using Multicell Array Formulas

This section contains examples that demonstrate additional features of multicell array formulas. A multicell array formula is a single formula that's entered into a range of cells. These features include creating arrays from values, performing operations, using functions, transposing arrays, and generating consecutive integers.

Creating an array from values in a range

The following array formula creates an array from a range of cells. Figure 14-8 shows a workbook with some data entered into A1:C4. The range D8:F11 contains a single array formula:

```
{=A1:C4}
```

D8 | {=A1:C4}

	A	B	C	D	E	F	G
1	1	dog	3				
2	4	5	cat				
3	7	FALSE	9				
4	monkey	8	12				
5							
6							
7							
8				1	dog	3	
9				4	5	cat	
10				7	FALSE	9	
11				monkey	8	12	
12							
13							
14							

Figure 14-8: Creating an array from a range.

The array in D8:F11 is linked to the range A1:C4. Change any value in A1:C4, and the corresponding cell in D8:F11 reflects that change.

Creating an array constant from values in a range

In the previous example, the array formula in D8:F11 essentially created a link to the cells in A1:C4. It's possible to sever this link and create an array constant made up of the values in A1:C4.

To do so, select the cells that contain the array formula (the range D8:F11, in this example). Press F2 to edit the array formula and then press F9 to convert the cell references to values. Press Ctrl+Shift+Enter to reenter the array formula (which now uses an array constant). The array constant is as follows:

```
{1,"dog",3;4,5,"cat";7,FALSE,9;"monkey",8,12}
```

Figure 14-9 shows how this looks after pressing F9 to convert the cell references.

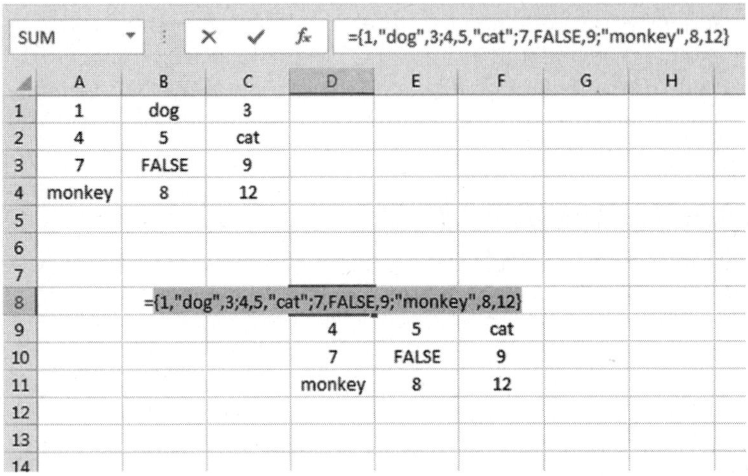

	A	B	C	D	E	F	G	H
1	1	dog	3					
2	4	5	cat					
3	7	FALSE	9					
4	monkey	8	12					
5								
6								
7								
8		={1,"dog",3;4,5,"cat";7,FALSE,9;"monkey",8,12}						
9				4	5	cat		
10				7	FALSE	9		
11				monkey	8	12		
12								
13								
14								

Formula bar: SUM ={1,"dog",3;4,5,"cat";7,FALSE,9;"monkey",8,12}

Figure 14-9: After you press F9, the cell references are converted to an array constant.

Performing operations on an array

So far, most of the examples in this chapter simply entered arrays into ranges. The following array formula creates a rectangular array and multiplies each array element by 2:

```
{={1,2,3,4;5,6,7,8;9,10,11,12}*2}
```

Figure 14-10 shows the result when you enter this formula into a range:

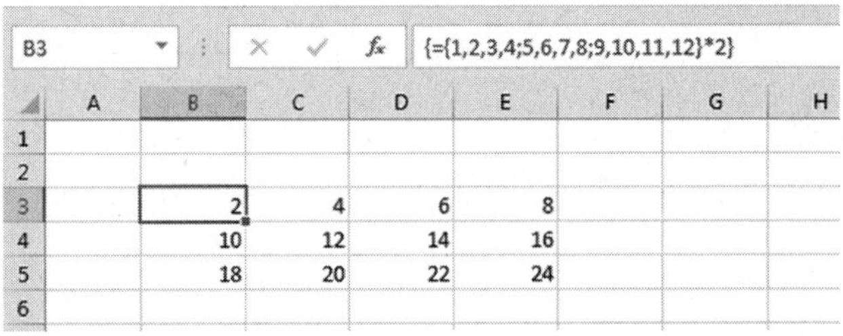

Formula bar: B3 {={1,2,3,4;5,6,7,8;9,10,11,12}*2}

	A	B	C	D	E	F	G	H
1								
2								
3		2	4	6	8			
4		10	12	14	16			
5		18	20	22	24			
6								

Figure 14-10: Performing a mathematical operation on an array.

The following array formula multiplies each array element by itself:

```
{={1,2,3,4;5,6,7,8;9,10,11,12}*{1,2,3,4;5,6,7,8;9,10,11,12}}
```

The following array formula is a simpler way of obtaining the same result:

```
{={1,2,3,4;5,6,7,8;9,10,11,12}^2}
```

Figure 14-11 shows the result when you enter this formula into a range (B8:E10).

B8 {={1,2,3,4;5,6,7,8;9,10,11,12}^2}

	A	B	C	D	E	F	G	H
7								
8		1	4	9	16			
9		25	36	49	64			
10		81	100	121	144			
11								
12								

Figure 14-11: Multiplying each array element by itself.

If the array is stored in a range (such as A1:D3), the array formula returns the square of each value in the range, as follows:

```
{=A1:D3^2}
```

Tip

In some of these examples are brackets that you must enter to define an array constant as well as brackets that Excel enters when you define an array by pressing Ctrl+Shift+Enter. An easy way to tell whether you must enter the brackets is to note the position of the opening curly bracket. If it's before the equal sign, Excel enters the brackets. If it's after the equal sign, you enter them.

Using functions with an array

As you might expect, you also can use functions with an array. The following array formula, which you can enter into a ten-cell vertical range, calculates the square root of each array element in the array constant:

```
{=SQRT({1;2;3;4;5;6;7;8;9;10})}
```

If the array is stored in a range, a multicell array formula such as the one that follows returns the square root of each value in the range:

```
{=SQRT(A1:A10)}
```

Transposing an array

When you transpose an array, you essentially convert rows to columns and columns to rows. In other words, you can convert a horizontal array to a vertical array and vice versa. Use Excel's TRANSPOSE function to transpose an array.

Consider the following one-dimensional horizontal array constant:

```
{1,2,3,4,5}
```

You can enter this array into a vertical range of cells by using the TRANSPOSE function. To do so, select a range of five cells that occupy five rows and one column. Then enter the following formula and press Ctrl+Shift+Enter:

```
=TRANSPOSE({1,2,3,4,5})
```

The horizontal array is transposed, and the array elements appear in the vertical range.

Transposing a two-dimensional array works in a similar manner. Figure 14-12 shows a two-dimensional array entered into a range normally and entered into a range using the TRANSPOSE function. The formula in A1:D3 follows:

```
{={1,2,3,4;5,6,7,8;9,10,11,12}}
```

A6 {={1,5,9;2,6,10;3,7,11;4,8,12}}

	A	B	C	D	E	F	G
1	1	2	3	4			
2	5	6	7	8			
3	9	10	11	12			
4							
5							
6	1	5	9				
7	2	6	10				
8	3	7	11				
9	4	8	12				
10							
11							
12							

Figure 14-12: Using the TRANSPOSE function to transpose a rectangular array.

Here's the formula in A6:C9:

```
{=TRANSPOSE({1,2,3,4;5,6,7,8;9,10,11,12})}
```

You can, of course, use the TRANSPOSE function to transpose an array stored in a range. The following formula, for example, uses an array stored in A1:C4 (four rows, three columns). You can enter this array formula into a range that consists of three rows and four columns:

```
{=TRANSPOSE(A1:C4)}
```

Generating an array of consecutive integers

As you will see in Chapter 15, it's often useful to generate an array of consecutive integers for use in an array formula. Excel's ROW function, which returns a row number, is ideal for this. Consider the array formula shown here, entered into a vertical range of 12 cells:

```
{=ROW(1:12)}
```

This formula generates a 12-element array that contains integers from 1 to 12. To demonstrate, select a range that consists of 12 rows and 1 column, and then enter the array formula into the range. The range is filled with 12 consecutive integers (see Figure 14-13).

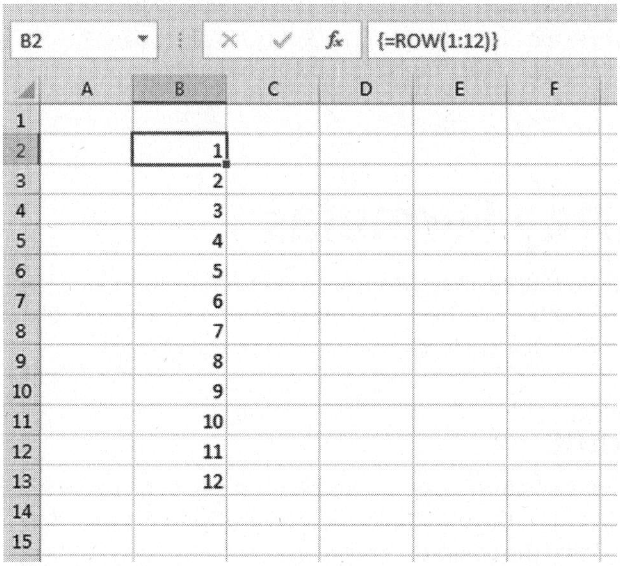

B2 {=ROW(1:12)}

	A	B	C	D	E	F
1						
2		1				
3		2				
4		3				
5		4				
6		5				
7		6				
8		7				
9		8				
10		9				
11		10				
12		11				
13		12				
14						
15						

Figure 14-13: Using an array formula to generate consecutive integers.

If you want to generate an array of consecutive integers, a formula like the one shown previously is good—but not perfect. To see the problem, insert a new row above the range that contains the array formula. Excel adjusts the row references so the array formula now reads like this:

```
{=ROW(2:13)}
```

The formula that originally generated integers from 1 to 12 now generates integers from 2 to 13.

For a better solution, use this formula:

```
{=ROW(INDIRECT("1:12"))}
```

This formula uses the INDIRECT function, which takes a text string as its argument. Excel does not adjust the references contained in the argument for the INDIRECT function. Therefore, this array formula *always* returns integers from 1 to 12.

Cross-Ref

Chapter 15 contains several examples that use the technique for generating consecutive integers.

Worksheet functions that return an array

Several of Excel's worksheet functions use arrays; you must enter a formula that uses one of these functions into multiple cells as an array formula. These functions are as follows: FORECAST, FREQUENCY, GROWTH, LINEST, LOGEST, MINVERSE, MMULT, and TREND. Consult the Help system for more information.

Using Single-Cell Array Formulas

All the examples in the previous section used a multicell array formula—a single array formula entered into a range of cells. The real power of using arrays becomes apparent when you use single-cell array formulas. This section contains examples of array formulas that occupy a single cell.

Counting characters in a range

Suppose you have a range of cells that contains text entries (see Figure 14-14). If you need to get a count of the total number of characters in that range, the traditional method involves creating a formula like the one that follows and copying it down the column:

```
=LEN(A1)
```

Then you use a SUM formula to calculate the sum of the values that the intermediate formulas return.

The following array formula does the job without using intermediate formulas:

```
{=SUM(LEN(A1:A14))}
```

The array formula uses the LEN function to create a new array (in memory) that consists of the number of characters in each cell of the range. In this case, the new array follows:

```
{10,9,8,5,6,5,5,10,11,14,6,8,8,7}
```

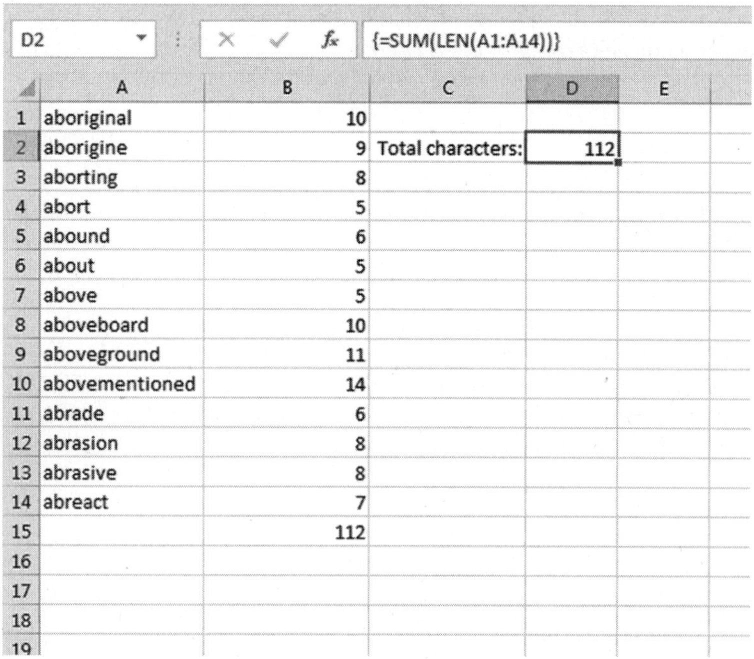

D2	{=SUM(LEN(A1:A14))}			
	A	B	C	D
1	aboriginal	10		
2	aborigine	9	Total characters:	112
3	aborting	8		
4	abort	5		
5	abound	6		
6	about	5		
7	above	5		
8	aboveboard	10		
9	aboveground	11		
10	abovementioned	14		
11	abrade	6		
12	abrasion	8		
13	abrasive	8		
14	abreact	7		
15		112		

Figure 14-14: The goal is to count the number of characters in a range of text.

The array formula is then reduced to the following:

```
=SUM({10,9,8,5,6,5,5,10,11,14,6,8,8,7})
```

Summing the three smallest values in a range

If you have values in a range named *Data*, you can determine the smallest value by using the SMALL function:

```
=SMALL(Data,1)
```

You can determine the second smallest and third smallest values by using these formulas:

```
=SMALL(Data,2)
=SMALL(Data,3)
```

To add the three smallest values, you can use a formula like this:

```
=SUM(SMALL(Data,1), SMALL(Data,2), SMALL(Data,3)
```

This formula works fine, but using an array formula is more efficient. The following array formula returns the sum of the three smallest values in a range named *Data*:

```
{=SUM(SMALL(Data,{1,2,3}))}
```

The formula uses an array constant as the second argument for the SMALL function. This generates a new array, which consists of the three smallest values in the range. This array is then passed to the SUM function, which returns the sum of the values in the new array.

Figure 14-15 shows an example that sums the three smallest values in the range A1:A10. The SMALL function is evaluated three times, each with a different second argument. The first time, the SMALL function has a second argument of 1, and it returns *–5*. The second time, the second argument for the SMALL function is 2 and it returns *0* (the second-smallest value in the range). The third time, the SMALL function has a second argument of 3 and returns the third-smallest value of *2*.

D2 {=SUM(SMALL(A1:A10,{1,2,3}))}

	A	B	C	D	E	F	G
1	12						
2	-5		Sum of three smallest:	-3			
3	3						
4	2						
5	0						
6	6						
7	13						
8	7						
9	4						
10	8						
11							
12							
13							
14							

Figure 14-15: An array formula returns the sum of the three smallest values in A1:A10.

Therefore, the array that's passed to the SUM function is

```
{-5,0,2}
```

The formula returns the sum of the array (*–3*).

Counting text cells in a range

Suppose that you need to count the number of text cells in a range. The COUNTIF function seems like it might be useful for this task, but it's not. COUNTIF is useful only if you need to count values in a range that meet some criterion (for example, values greater than 12).

To count the number of text cells in a range, you need an array formula. The following array formula uses the IF function to examine each cell in a range. It then creates a new array (of the same size and dimensions as the original range) that consists of 1s and 0s, depending on whether the cell contains text. This new array is then passed to the SUM function, which returns the sum of the items in the array. The result is a count of the number of text cells in the range.

```
{=SUM(IF(ISTEXT(A1:D5),1,0))}
```

Cross-Ref

This general array formula type (that is, an IF function nested in a SUM function) is useful for counting. See Chapter 7, "Counting and Summing Techniques," for additional examples.

Figure 14-16 shows an example of the preceding formula in cell C7. The array created by the IF function is as follows:

```
{0,1,1,1;1,0,0,0;1,0,0,0;1,0,0,0;1,0,0,0}
```

C7 | {=SUM(IF(ISTEXT(A1:D5),1,0))}

	A	B	C	D	E	F	G	H
1		Jan	Feb	Mar				
2	Region 1	7	4	9				
3	Region 2	8	2	8				
4	Region 3	12	1	9				
5	Region 4	14	6	10				
6								
7	No. of text cells:		7					
8								

Figure 14-16: An array formula returns the number of text cells in the range.

Notice that this array contains four rows of three elements (the same dimensions as the range).

A variation on this formula follows:

```
{=SUM(ISTEXT(A1:D5)*1)}
```

This formula eliminates the need for the IF function and takes advantage of the fact that

```
TRUE * 1 = 1
```

and

```
FALSE * 1 = 0
```

TRUE and *FALSE* in array formulas

When your arrays return Boolean values (*TRUE* or *FALSE*), you must coerce these Boolean values into numbers. Excel's SUM function ignores Booleans, but you can still perform mathematical operations on them. In Excel, *TRUE* is equivalent to a value of 1, and *FALSE* is equivalent to a value of 0. Converting *TRUE* and *FALSE* to these values ensures the SUM function treats them appropriately.

You can use three mathematical operations to convert *TRUE* and *FALSE* to numbers without changing their values, called *identity operations.*

- Multiply by 1: (x * 1 = x)
- Add zero: (x + 0 = x)
- Double negative: (—x = x)

Applying any of these operations to a Boolean value causes Excel to convert it to a number. The following formulas return the same answer:

```
{=SUM(ISTEXT(A1:D5)*1)}
{=SUM(ISTEXT(A1:D5)+0)}
{=SUM(--ISTEXT(A1:D5))}
```

There is no "best" way to convert Boolean values to numbers. Pick a method that you like and use that. However, be aware of all three methods so that you can identify them in other people's spreadsheets.

Eliminating intermediate formulas

One of the main benefits of using an array formula is that you can eliminate intermediate formulas in your worksheet. This makes your worksheet more compact and eliminates the need to display irrelevant calculations. Figure 14-17 shows a worksheet that contains pretest and posttest scores for students. Column D contains formulas that calculate the changes between the pretest and the posttest scores. Cell D17 contains the following formula, which calculates the average of the values in column D:

```
=AVERAGE(D2:D15)
```

With an array formula, you can eliminate column D. The following array formula calculates the average of the changes but does not require the formulas in column D:

```
{=AVERAGE(C2:C15-B2:B15)}
```

D17 =AVERAGE(D2:D15)

	A	B	C	D	E	F
1	Student	Pre-Test	Post-Test	Change		
2	Andy	56	67	11		
3	Beth	59	74	15		
4	Cindy	98	92	-6		
5	Duane	78	79	1		
6	Eddy	81	100	19		
7	Francis	92	94	2		
8	Georgia	100	100	0		
9	Hilda	92	99	7		
10	Isabel	54	69	15		
11	Jack	91	92	1		
12	Kent	80	88	8		
13	Linda	45	68	23		
14	Michelle	71	92	21		
15	Nancy	94	83	-11		
16						
17		Average Change:		7.57		
18						

Figure 14-17: Without an array formula, calculating the average change requires intermediate formulas in column D.

How does it work? The formula uses two arrays, the values of which are stored in two ranges (B2:B15 and C2:C15). The formula creates a *new* array that consists of the differences between each corresponding element in the other arrays. This new array is stored in Excel's memory, not in a range. The AVERAGE function then uses this new array as its argument and returns the result.

The new array consists of the following elements:

```
{11,15,-6,1,19,2,0,7,15,1,8,23,21,-11}
```

The formula, therefore, is reduced to the following:

```
=AVERAGE({11,15,-6,1,19,2,0,7,15,1,8,23,21,-11})
```

Excel evaluates the function and displays the result: 7.57.

You can use additional array formulas to calculate other measures for the data in this example. For instance, the following array formula returns the largest change (that is, the greatest improvement). This formula returns *23,* which represents Linda's test scores:

```
{=MAX(C2:C15-B2:B15)}
```

The following array formula returns the smallest change (that is, the least improvement). This formula returns *–11,* which represents Nancy's test scores:

```
{=MIN(C2:C15-B2:B15)}
```

Using an array in lieu of a range reference

If your formula uses a function that requires a range reference, you may be able to replace that range reference with an array constant. This is useful when the values in the referenced range do not change.

Note

A notable exception to using an array constant in place of a range reference in a function is with the database functions that use a reference to a criteria range (for example, DSUM). Unfortunately, using an array constant instead of a reference to a criteria range does not work.

Figure 14-18 shows a worksheet that uses a lookup table to display a word that corresponds to an integer. For example, looking up a value of 9 returns *Nine* from the lookup table in D1:E10. Here's the formula in cell C1:

```
=VLOOKUP(B1,D1:E10,2,FALSE)
```

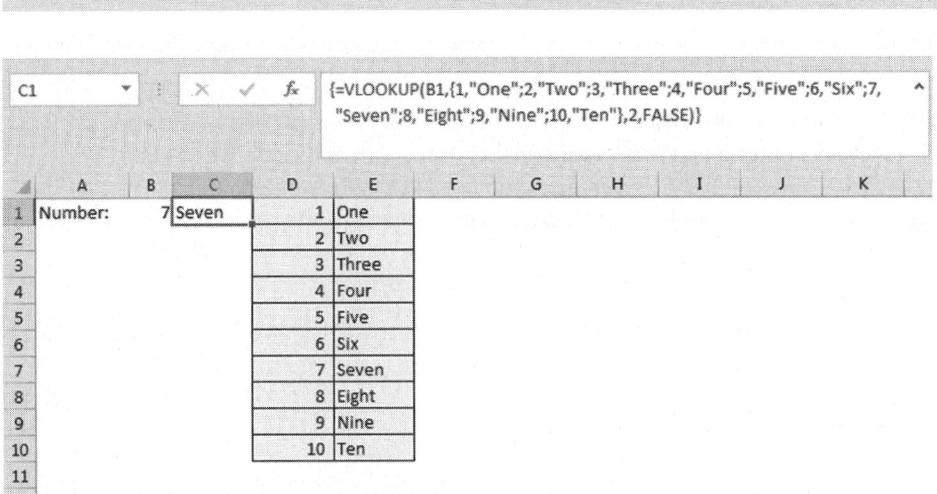

Figure 14-18: You can replace the lookup table in D1:E10 with an array constant.

You can use a two-dimensional array in place of the lookup range. The following formula returns the same result as the previous formula, but it does not require the lookup range in D1:E10:

```
=VLOOKUP(B1,{1,"One";2,"Two";3,"Three";4,"Four";5,"Five";
6,"Six";7,"Seven";8,"Eight";9,"Nine";10,"Ten"},2,FALSE)
```

This chapter introduced arrays. Chapter 15 explores the topic further and provides many additional examples.

Performing Magic with Array Formulas

In This Chapter

- More examples of single-cell array formulas
- More examples of multicell array formulas

The previous chapter introduced arrays and array formulas and presented some basic examples to whet your appetite. This chapter continues the saga and provides many useful examples that further demonstrate the power of this feature.

We selected the examples in this chapter to provide a good assortment of the various uses for array formulas. Most can be used as is. You do, of course, need to adjust the range names or references that you use. Also, you can modify many of the examples easily to work in a slightly different manner.

Working with Single-Cell Array Formulas

As we describe in the preceding chapter, you enter single-cell array formulas into a single cell (not into a range of cells). These array formulas work with arrays contained in a range or that exist in memory. This section provides some additional examples of such array formulas.

On the Web

The examples in this section are available at this book's website. The file is named single-cell array formulas.xlsx.

About the examples in this chapter

This chapter contains many examples of array formulas. Keep in mind that you press Ctrl+Shift+Enter to enter an array formula. Excel places curly brackets around the formula to remind you that it's an array formula. The array formula examples shown here are surrounded by curly brackets, but you should not enter the brackets because Excel does that for you when the formula is entered.

Summing a range that contains errors

You may have discovered that the SUM function doesn't work if you attempt to sum a range that contains one or more error values (such as #DIV/0! or #N/A). Figure 15-1 shows an example. The formula in cell D11 returns an error value because the range that it sums (D4:D10) contains errors.

D13 {=SUM(IFERROR(D4:D10,""))}

	A	B	C	D	E
1	**Summing a range that contains error values**				
2					
3	Item	Cost	Number	Total	
4	A-933	10	4	40	
5	A-833	6	4	24	
6	C-902	#N/A	3	#N/A	
7	F-902	#N/A	10	#N/A	
8	J-111	3	12	36	
9	R-234	20	6	120	
10	S-984	5	4	20	
11			TOTAL:	#N/A	
12					
13				240	<-- SUM, excluding errors
14					
15					

Figure 15-1: An array formula can sum a range of values, even if the range contains errors.

The following array formula, in cell D13, overcomes this problem and returns the sum of the values, even if the range contains error values:

```
{=SUM(IFERROR(D4:D10,""))}
```

This formula works by creating a new array that contains the original values but without the errors. The IFERROR function effectively filters out error values by replacing them with an empty string. The SUM function then works on this "filtered" array. This technique also works with other functions, such as AVERAGE, MIN, and MAX.

Note

The IFERROR function was introduced in Excel 2007. Following is a modified version of the formula that's compatible with older versions of Excel:

```
{=SUM(IF(ISERROR(D4:D10),"",D4:D10))}
```

The AGGREGATE function, which works only in Excel 2010 and later, provides another way to sum a range that contains one or more error values. Here's an example:

```
=AGGREGATE(9,2,D4:D10)
```

The first argument, 9, is the code for SUM. The second argument, 2, is the code for "ignore error values."

Counting the number of error values in a range

The following array formula is similar to the previous example, but it returns a count of the number of error values in a range named *Data*:

```
{=SUM(IF(ISERROR(Data),1,0))}
```

This formula creates an array that consists of 1s (if the corresponding cell contains an error) and 0s (if the corresponding cell does not contain an error value).

You can simplify the formula a bit by removing the third argument for the IF function. If this argument isn't specified, the IF function returns FALSE if the condition is not satisfied (that is, the cell does not contain an error value). In this context, Excel treats FALSE as a 0 value. The array formula shown here performs exactly like the previous formula, but it doesn't use the third argument for the IF function:

```
{=SUM(IF(ISERROR(Data),1))}
```

Actually, you can simplify the formula even more:

```
{=SUM(ISERROR(Data)*1)}
```

This version of the formula relies on the fact that

```
TRUE * 1 = 1
```

and

```
FALSE * 1 = 0
```

Summing the *n* largest values in a range

The following array formula returns the sum of the ten largest values in a range named *Data*:

```
{=SUM(LARGE(Data,ROW(INDIRECT("1:10"))))}
```

The LARGE function is evaluated ten times, each time with a different second argument (1, 2, 3, and so on up to 10). The results of these calculations are stored in a new array, and that array is used as the argument for the SUM function.

To sum a different number of values, replace the 10 in the argument for the INDIRECT function with another value.

If the number of cells to sum is contained in cell C17, use the following array formula, which uses the concatenation operator (&) to create the range address for the INDIRECT function:

```
{=SUM(LARGE(Data,ROW(INDIRECT("1:"&C17))))}
```

To sum the *n smallest* values in a range, use the SMALL function instead of the LARGE function.

Computing an average that excludes zeros

Figure 15-2 shows a simple worksheet that calculates average sales. The formula in cell C13 follows:

```
=AVERAGE(B4:B11)
```

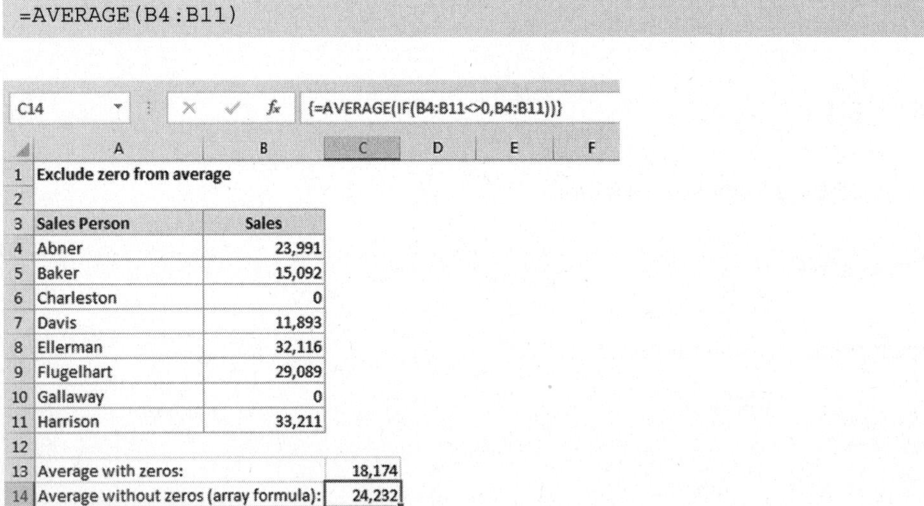

C14 {=AVERAGE(IF(B4:B11<>0,B4:B11))}

	A	B	C
1	Exclude zero from average		
2			
3	Sales Person	Sales	
4	Abner	23,991	
5	Baker	15,092	
6	Charleston	0	
7	Davis	11,893	
8	Ellerman	32,116	
9	Flugelhart	29,089	
10	Gallaway	0	
11	Harrison	33,211	
12			
13	Average with zeros:		18,174
14	Average without zeros (array formula):		24,232

Figure 15-2: The calculated average includes cells that contain a 0.

Two of the sales staff had the week off, however, so including their 0 sales in the calculated average doesn't accurately describe the average sales per representative.

Note

The AVERAGE function ignores blank cells, but it does not ignore cells that contain 0.

The following array formula (in cell C14) returns the average of the range but excludes the cells containing 0:

```
{=AVERAGE(IF(B4:B11<>0,B4:B11))}
```

This formula creates a new array that consists only of the nonzero values in the range and *FALSE* in place of zero values. Many aggregate functions, including AVERAGE, ignore Boolean values just like they ignore blanks and text. The AVERAGE function then uses this new array as its argument.

You also can get the same result with a regular (nonarray) formula:

```
=SUM(B4:B11)/COUNTIF(B4:B11,"<>0")
```

This formula uses the COUNTIF function to count the number of nonzero values in the range. This value is divided into the sum of the values. This formula does not work if the range contains blank cells.

Note

The only reason to use an array formula to calculate an average that excludes zero values is for compatibility with versions prior to Excel 2007. A simple approach is to use the AVERAGEIF function in a nonarray formula:

```
=AVERAGEIF(B4:B11,"<>0",B4:B11)
```

Determining whether a particular value appears in a range

To determine whether a particular value appears in a range of cells, you can press Ctrl+F and do a search of the worksheet—or, you can make this determination by using an array formula.

Figure 15-3 shows a worksheet with a list of names in A5:E24 (named *NameList*). An array formula in cell D3 checks the name entered into cell C3 (named *TheName*). If the name exists in the list of names, the formula then displays the text *Found*. Otherwise, it displays *Not Found*.

D3 {=IF(OR(TheName=NameList),"Found","Not Found")}

	A	B	C	D	E	F	G	H
1	**Is a value contained in a range?**							
2								
3		Enter a Name:	Donald	**Found**				
4								
5	Al	Daniel	Harold	Lyle	Richard			
6	Allen	Dave	Ian	Maggie	Rick			
7	Andrew	David	Jack	Margaret	Robert			
8	Anthony	Dennis	James	Marilyn	Rod			
9	Arthur	Don	Jan	Mark	Roger			
10	Barbara	Donald	Jeff	Marvin	Ronald			
11	Bernard	Doug	Jeffrey	Mary	Russ			
12	Beth	Douglas	Jerry	Matt	Sandra			
13	Bill	Ed	Jim	Mel	Scott			
14	Bob	Edward	Joe	Merle	Simon			
15	Brian	Eric	John	Michael	Stacy			
16	Bruce	Fran	Joseph	Michelle	Stephen			
17	Cark	Frank	Kathy	Mike	Steven			
18	Carl	Fred	Kathy	Norman	Stuart			
19	Charles	Gary	Keith	Patrick	Susan			
20	Chris	George	Kenneth	Paul	Terry			
21	Chuck	Glenn	Kevin	Peter	Thomas			
22	Clark	Gordon	Larry	Phillip	Timothy			
23	Curt	Greg	Leonard	Ray	Vincent			
24	Dan	Gregory	Louise	Rebecca	Wendy			
25								
26								

Figure 15-3: Using an array formula to determine whether a range contains a particular value.

The array formula in cell D3 is

```
{=IF(OR(TheName=NameList),"Found","Not Found")}
```

This formula compares *TheName* to each cell in the *NameList* range. It builds a new array that consists of logical *TRUE* or *FALSE* values. The OR function returns *TRUE* if any one of the values in the new array is *TRUE*. The IF function uses this result to determine which message to display.

A simpler form of this formula follows. This formula displays *TRUE* if the name is found and returns *FALSE* otherwise:

```
{=OR(TheName=NameList)}
```

Yet another approach uses the COUNTIF function in a nonarray formula:

```
=IF(COUNTIF(NameList,TheName)>0,"Found","Not Found")
```

Counting the number of differences in two ranges

The following array formula compares the corresponding values in two ranges (named *MyData* and *YourData*) and returns the number of differences in the two ranges. If the contents of the two ranges are identical, the formula returns 0.

```
{=SUM(IF(MyData=YourData,0,1))}
```

Figure 15-4 shows an example.

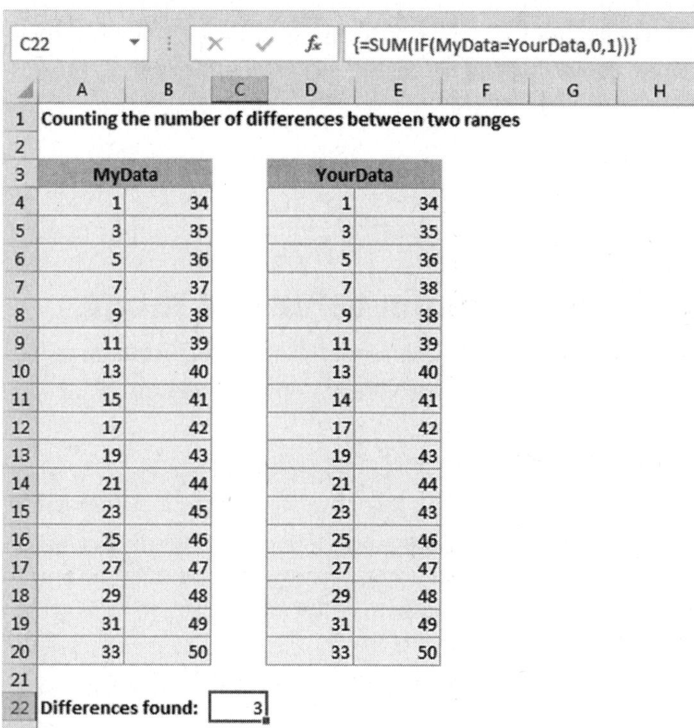

C22 {=SUM(IF(MyData=YourData,0,1))}

	A	B	C	D	E
1	Counting the number of differences between two ranges				
2					
3	MyData			YourData	
4	1	34		1	34
5	3	35		3	35
6	5	36		5	36
7	7	37		7	38
8	9	38		9	38
9	11	39		11	39
10	13	40		13	40
11	15	41		14	41
12	17	42		17	42
13	19	43		19	43
14	21	44		21	44
15	23	45		23	43
16	25	46		25	46
17	27	47		27	47
18	29	48		29	48
19	31	49		31	49
20	33	50		33	50
21					
22	Differences found:		3		

Figure 15-4: Using an array formula to count the number of differences in two ranges.

Note

The two ranges must be the same size and of the same dimensions.

This formula works by creating a new array of the same size as the ranges being compared. The IF function fills this new array with 0s and 1s (0 if a difference is found, and 1 if the corresponding cells are the same). The SUM function then returns the sum of the values in the array.

The following array formula, which is simpler, is another way of calculating the same result:

```
{=SUM(1*(MyData<>YourData))}
```

This version of the formula relies on the fact that

```
TRUE * 1 = 1
```

and

```
FALSE * 1 = 0
```

Once you know that comparisons return *TRUE* or *FALSE* and that Excel converts those to 1 and 0, respectively, you can manipulate the data in different ways to get the result you want. In yet another version of this formula, 1 is subtracted from each *TRUE* and *FALSE*, turning *TRUE* values into 0 and *FALSE* values into –1. Then the ABS function switches the sign:

```
{=ABS(SUM((MyData=YourData)-1))}
```

Returning the location of the maximum value in a range

The following array formula returns the row number of the maximum value in a single-column range named *Data*:

```
{=MIN(IF(Data=MAX(Data),ROW(Data), ""))}
```

The IF function creates a new array that corresponds to the *Data* range. If the corresponding cell contains the maximum value in *Data*, the array contains the row number; otherwise, it contains an empty string. The MIN function uses this new array as its second argument, and it returns the smallest value, which corresponds to the row number of the maximum value in *Data*.

If the *Data* range contains more than one cell that has the maximum value, the row of the first maximum cell is returned.

The following array formula is similar to the previous one, but it returns the actual cell address of the maximum value in the *Data* range. It uses the ADDRESS function, which takes two arguments: a row number and a column number.

```
{=ADDRESS(MIN(IF(Data=MAX(Data),ROW(Data), "")),COLUMN(Data))}
```

The previous formulas work only with a single-column range. The following variation works with any sized range and returns the address of the largest value in the range named *Data*:

```
{=ADDRESS(MIN(IF(Data=MAX(data),ROW(Data), "")),MIN(IF(Data=MAX(Data),COLUMN(D
  ata), "")))}
```

Finding the row of a value's *n*th occurrence in a range

The following array formula returns the row number within a single-column range named *Data* that contains the *n*th occurrence of the value in a cell named *Value*:

```
{=SMALL(IF(Data=Value,ROW(Data), ""),n)}
```

The IF function creates a new array that consists of the row number of values from the *Data* range that are equal to *Value*. Values from the *Data* range that aren't equal to *Value* are replaced with an empty string. The SMALL function works on this new array and returns the *n*th smallest row number.

The formula returns *#NUM!* if the value is not found or if *n* exceeds the number of occurrences of the value in the range.

Returning the longest text in a range

The following array formula displays the text string in a range (named *Data*) that has the most characters. If multiple cells contain the longest text string, the first cell is returned:

```
{=INDEX(Data,MATCH(MAX(LEN(Data)),LEN(Data),FALSE),1)}
```

This formula works with two arrays, both of which contain the length of each item in the *Data* range. The MAX function determines the largest value, which corresponds to the longest text item. The MATCH function calculates the offset of the cell that contains the maximum length. The INDEX function returns the contents of the cell containing the most characters. This function works only if the *Data* range consists of a single column.

Figure 15-5 shows an example.

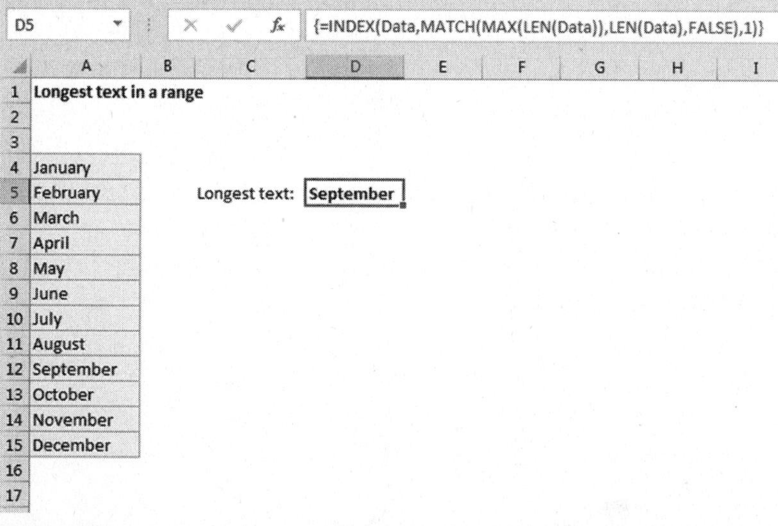

Figure 15-5: Using an array formula to return the longest text in a range.

Determining whether a range contains valid values

You may have a list of items that you need to check against another list. For example, you may import a list of part numbers into a range named *MyList*, and you want to ensure that all the part numbers are valid. You can do so by comparing the items in the imported list to the items in a master list of part numbers (named *Master*). Figure 15-6 shows an example.

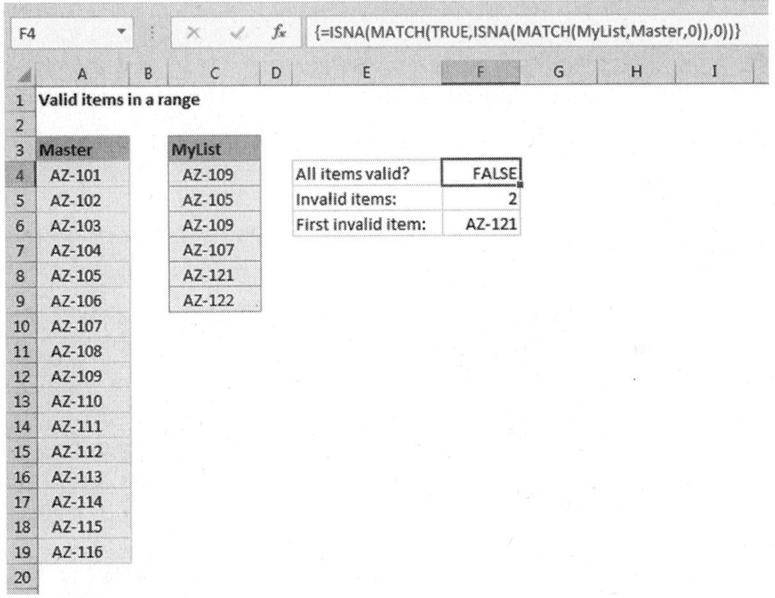

Figure 15-6: Using an array formula to count and identify items that aren't in a list.

The following array formula returns *TRUE* if every item in the range named *MyList* is found in the range named *Master*. Both ranges must consist of a single column, but they don't need to contain the same number of rows:

```
{=ISNA(MATCH(TRUE,ISNA(MATCH(MyList,Master,0)),0))}
```

The array formula that follows returns the number of invalid items. In other words, it returns the number of items in *MyList* that do not appear in *Master*:

```
{=SUM(1*ISNA(MATCH(MyList,Master,0)))}
```

To return the first invalid item in *MyList*, use the following array formula:

```
{=INDEX(MyList,MATCH(TRUE,ISNA(MATCH(MyList,Master,0)),0))}
```

Summing the digits of an integer

We can't think of any practical application for the example in this section, but it's a good demonstration of the potential power of an array formula. The following array formula calculates the sum of the digits in a positive integer, which is stored in cell A1. For example, if cell A1 contains the value 409, the formula returns *13* (the sum of 4, 0, and 9).

```
{=SUM(MID(A1,ROW(INDIRECT("1:"&LEN(A1))),1)*1)}
```

To understand how this formula works, start with the ROW function, as shown here:

```
{=ROW(INDIRECT("1:"&LEN(A1)))}
```

This function returns an array of consecutive integers beginning with 1 and ending with the number of digits in the value in cell A1. For example, if cell A1 contains the value 409, the LEN function returns *3*, and the array generated by the ROW functions is

```
{1,2,3}
```

Cross-Ref

For more information about using the INDIRECT function to return this array, see Chapter 14, "Introducing Arrays."

This array is then used as the second argument for the MID function. The MID part of the formula, simplified a bit and expressed as values, is the following:

```
{=MID(409,{1,2,3},1)*1}
```

This function generates an array with three elements:

```
{4,0,9}
```

By simplifying again and adding the SUM function, the formula looks like this:

```
{=SUM({4,0,9})}
```

This formula produces the result of *13*.

Note

The values in the array created by the MID function are multiplied by 1 because the MID function returns a string. Multiplying by 1 forces a numeric value result. Alternatively, you can use the VALUE function to force a numeric string to become a numeric value.

Notice that the formula doesn't work with a negative value because the negative sign is not a numeric value. Also, the formula fails if the cell contains nonnumeric values (such as 123A6). The following formula solves this problem by checking for errors in the array and replacing them with zero:

```
{=SUM(IFERROR(MID(A1,ROW(INDIRECT("1:"&LEN(A1))),1)*1,0))}
```

Note

This formula uses the IFERROR function, which was introduced in Excel 2007.

Figure 15-7 shows a worksheet that uses both versions of this formula.

C9 {=SUM(IFERROR(MID(A9,ROW(INDIRECT("1:"& LEN(A9))),1)*1,0))}

	A	B	C
1	**Sum of the digits of a value**		
2			
3	**Number**	**Sum of Digits**	**Improved Version**
4	132	6	1
5	9	9	9
6	111111	6	6
7	980991	36	36
8	-980991	#VALUE!	36
9	409	13	13
10	123A6	#VALUE!	12
11	12	3	3
12	98,763,023	38	38
13	111,111,111	9	9
14			

Figure 15-7: Two versions of an array formula that calculates the sum of the digits in an integer.

Summing rounded values

Figure 15-8 shows a simple worksheet that demonstrates a common spreadsheet problem: rounding errors. As you can see, the grand total in cell E7 appears to display an incorrect amount. (That is, it's off by a penny.) The values in column E use a number format that displays two decimal places. The actual values, however, consist of additional decimal places that do not display due to rounding (as a result of the number format). The net effect of these rounding errors is a seemingly incorrect total. The total, which is actually $168.320997, displays as $168.32.

E9 {=SUM(ROUND(E4:E6,2))}

	A	B	C	D	E	F	G	H	I
1	Summing rounded values								
2									
3	Description	Quantity	Unit Price	Discount	Total				
4	Widgets	6	$11.69	5.23%	$66.47				
5	Sprockets	8	$9.74	5.23%	$73.84				
6	Snapholytes	3	$9.85	5.23%	$28.00				
7	GRAND TOTAL				$168.32		<-- appears to be incorrect		
8									
9				Sum of rounded values	$168.31				
10									
11									
12									

Figure 15-8: Using an array formula to correct rounding errors.

The following array formula creates a new array that consists of values in column E, rounded to two decimal places:

```
{=SUM(ROUND(E4:E6,2))}
```

This formula returns *$168.31*.

You also can eliminate these types of rounding errors by using the ROUND function in the formula that calculates each row total in column E (which does not require an array formula).

Summing every *n*th value in a range

Suppose that you have a range of values and you want to compute the sum of every third value in the list—the first, the fourth, the seventh, and so on. One solution is to hard-code the cell addresses in a formula. But a better solution is to use an array formula.

Note

In Figure 15-9, the values are stored in a range named Data, and the value of n is in cell D4 (named *n*).

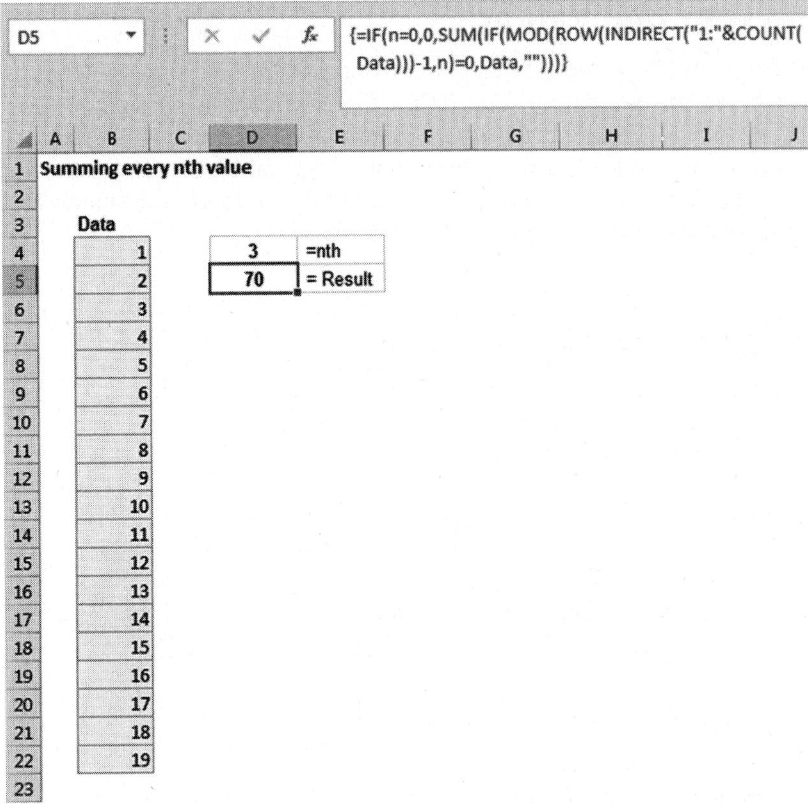

Figure 15-9: An array formula returns the sum of every nth value in the range.

The following array formula returns the sum of every *n*th value in the range:

```
{=SUM(IF(MOD(ROW(INDIRECT("1:"&COUNT(Data)))-1,n)=0,Data,""))}
```

This formula returns *70,* which is the sum of every third value in the range.

This formula generates an array of consecutive integers, and the MOD function uses this array as its first argument. The second argument for the MOD function is the value of *n*. The MOD function creates another array that consists of the remainders when each row number minus 1 is divided by *n*. When the array item is 0 (that is, the row is evenly divisible by *n*), the corresponding item in the *Data* range is included in the sum.

You find that this formula fails when *n* is 0 (that is, when it sums no items). The modified array formula that follows uses an IF function to handle this case:

```
{=IF(n=0,0,SUM(IF(MOD(ROW(INDIRECT("1:"&COUNT(data)))-1,n)=0,data,"")))}
```

This formula works only when the *Data* range consists of a single column of values. It does not work for a multicolumn range or for a single row of values.

To make the formula work with a horizontal range, you need to transpose the array of integers generated by the ROW function. Excel's TRANPOSE function is just the ticket. The modified array formula that follows works only with a horizontal *Data* range:

```
{=IF(n=0,0,SUM(IF(MOD(TRANSPOSE(ROW(INDIRECT("1:"&COUNT(Data))))-1,n)=0,Data,"")))}
```

Removing nonnumeric characters from a string

The following array formula extracts a number from a string that contains text. For example, consider the string *ABC145Z*. The formula returns the numeric part, *145*.

```
{=MID(A1,MATCH(0,(ISERROR(MID(A1,ROW(INDIRECT("1:"&LEN(A1))),1)*1)*1),0),
LEN(A1)-SUM((ISERROR(MID(A1,ROW(INDIRECT("1:"&LEN(A1))),1)*1)*1)))}
```

This formula works only with a single embedded number. For example, it gives an incorrect result with a string like *X45Z99* because the string contains two embedded numbers.

Using Excel's Formula Evaluator

If you would like to better understand how some of these complex array formulas work, consider using a handy tool: the Formula Evaluator. Select the cell that contains the formula and then choose Formulas ➜ Formula Auditing ➜ Evaluate Formula. You'll see the Evaluate Formula dialog box as shown in the figure.

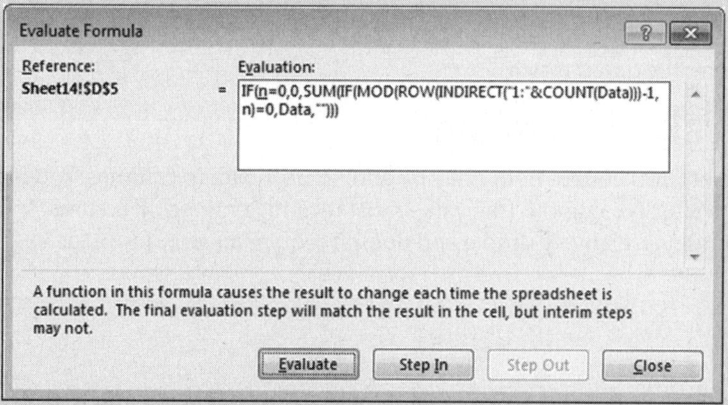

Click the Evaluate button repeatedly to see the intermediate results as the formula is being calculated. It's like watching a formula calculate in slow motion.

Determining the closest value in a range

The formula in this section performs an operation that none of Excel's lookup functions can do. The array formula that follows returns the value in a range named *Data* that is closest to another value (named *Target*):

```
{=INDEX(Data,MATCH(SMALL(ABS(Target-Data),1),ABS(Target-Data),0))}
```

If two values in the *Data* range are equidistant from the *Target* value, the formula returns the first one in the list. Figure 15-10 shows an example of this formula. In this case, the *Target* value is 45. The array formula in cell D4 returns *48*—the value closest to 45.

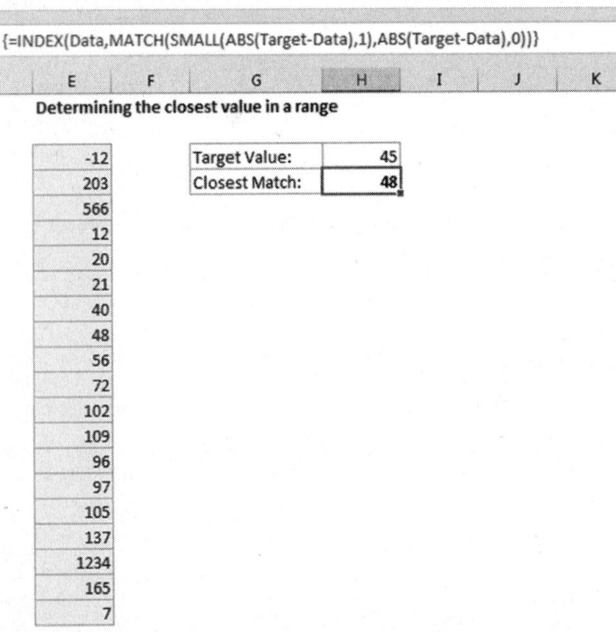

Figure 15-10: An array formula returns the closest match.

Returning the last value in a column

Suppose that you have a worksheet you update frequently by adding new data to columns. You may need a way to reference the last value in column A (the value most recently entered). If column A contains no empty cells, the solution is relatively simple and doesn't require an array formula:

```
=OFFSET(A1,COUNTA(A:A)-1,0)
```

This formula uses the COUNTA function to count the number of nonempty cells in column A. This value (minus 1) is used as the second argument for the OFFSET function. For example, if the last value is in row 100, COUNTA returns *100*. The OFFSET function returns the value in the cell 99 rows down from cell A1 in the same column.

If column A has one or more empty cells interspersed, which is frequently the case, the preceding formula doesn't work because the COUNTA function doesn't count the empty cells.

The following array formula returns the contents of the last nonempty cell in column A:

```
{=INDEX(A:A,MAX(ROW(A:A)*(NOT(ISBLANK(A:A)))))}
```

You can, of course, modify the formula to work with a column other than column A. To use a different column, change the column references from A to whatever column you need.

This formula does not work if the column contains error values.

Warning

You can't use this formula, as written, in the same column in which it's working. Attempting to do so generates a circular reference. You can, however, modify it. For example, to use the function in cell A1, change the references so that they begin with row 2 rather than the entire column. For example, use A2:A1000 to return the last nonempty cell in the range A2:A1000.

Tip

The formula that follows is an alternate (nonarray) formula that returns the last value in a column. This formula returns the last nonempty cell in column A:

```
=LOOKUP(2,1/(NOT(ISBLANK(A:A))),A:A )
```

The lookup_vector argument returns an array of 1 divided by either *TRUE* or *FALSE*, depending on whether the value in column A is blank. That evaluates down to an array of 1 for *TRUE* and a #DIV/0 error for *FALSE*. Finally, the LOOKUP function attempts to find a 2 in lookup_vector, ignoring errors along the way. When it gets to the end, not having found a 2, it returns the last value. It differs from the array formula in one way: it ignores error values. So it actually returns the last nonempty nonerror cell in a column.

Returning the last value in a row

The following array formula is similar to the previous formula, but it returns the last nonempty cell in a row (in this case, row 1):

```
{=INDEX(1:1,MAX(COLUMN(1:1)*(NOT(ISBLANK(1:1)))))}
```

To use this formula for a different row, change the 1:1 reference to correspond to the row.

Figure 15-11 shows an example for the last value in a column and the last value in a row.

E4 | {=INDEX(A1:A501,MAX(ROW(A:A)*(NOT(ISBLANK(A:A)))))}

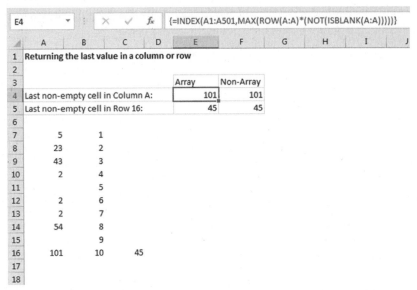

	A	B	C	D	E	F
1	**Returning the last value in a column or row**					
2						
3					Array	Non-Array
4	Last non-empty cell in Column A:				101	101
5	Last non-empty cell in Row 16:				45	45
6						
7	5	1				
8	23	2				
9	43	3				
10	2	4				
11		5				
12	2	6				
13	2	7				
14	54	8				
15		9				
16	101	10	45			
17						
18						

Figure 15-11: Using array formulas to return the last nonempty cell in a column or row.

An alternative, non-array formula that returns the last nonempty non-error cell in a row is

```
=LOOKUP(2,1/(NOT(ISBLANK(1:1))),1:1 )
```

Working with Multicell Array Formulas

The preceding chapter introduces array formulas that you can enter into multicell ranges. In this section, we present a few more multicell array formulas. Most of these formulas return some or all of the values in a range but are rearranged in some way.

When you enter a multicell array formula, you must select the entire range first. Then type the formula and press Ctrl+Shift+Enter.

On the Web

The examples in this section are available at this book's website. The file is named multi-cell array formulas.xlsx.

Returning only positive values from a range

The following array formula works with a single-column vertical range (named *Data*). The array formula is entered into a range that's the same size as *Data* and returns only the positive values in the *Data* range. (Zeroes and negative numbers are ignored.)

```
{=INDEX(Data,SMALL(IF(Data>0,ROW(INDIRECT("1:"&ROWS(Data)))),
ROW(INDIRECT("1:"&ROWS(Data)))))}
```

As you can see in Figure 15-12, this formula works, but not perfectly. The *Data* range is A4:A23, and the array formula is entered into C4:C23. However, the array formula displays *#NUM!* error values for cells that don't contain a value.

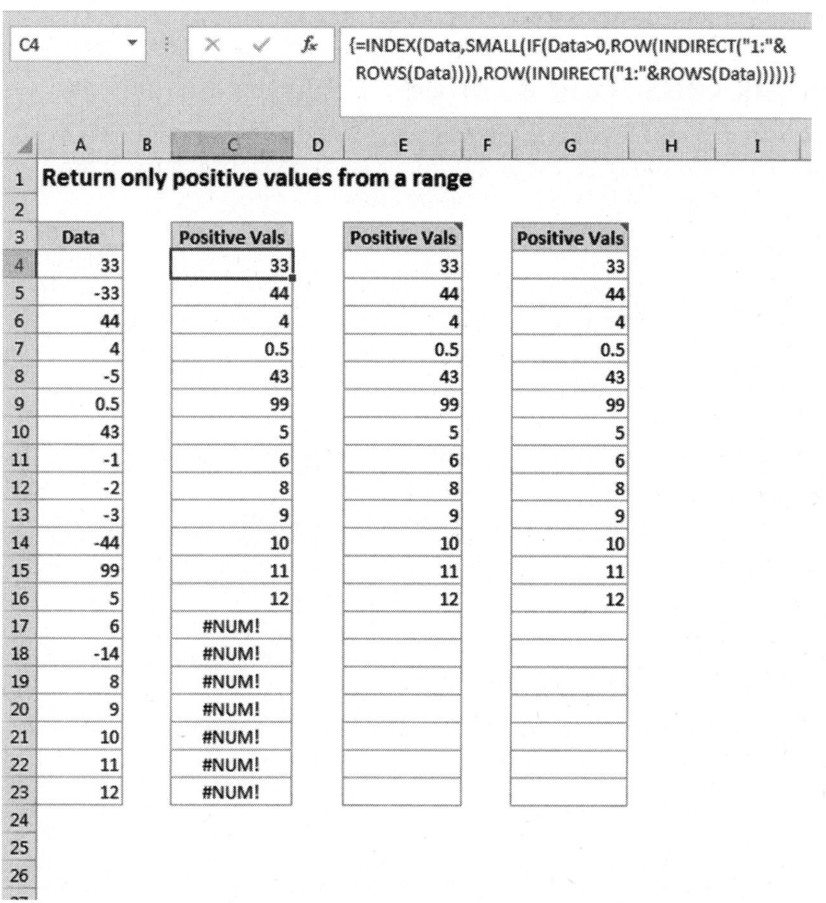

C4 {=INDEX(Data,SMALL(IF(Data>0,ROW(INDIRECT("1:"&ROWS(Data)))),ROW(INDIRECT("1:"&ROWS(Data)))))}

Return only positive values from a range

	A	B	C	D	E	F	G
3	Data		Positive Vals		Positive Vals		Positive Vals
4	33		33		33		33
5	-33		44		44		44
6	44		4		4		4
7	4		0.5		0.5		0.5
8	-5		43		43		43
9	0.5		99		99		99
10	43		5		5		5
11	-1		6		6		6
12	-2		8		8		8
13	-3		9		9		9
14	-44		10		10		10
15	99		11		11		11
16	5		12		12		12
17	6		#NUM!				
18	-14		#NUM!				
19	8		#NUM!				
20	9		#NUM!				
21	10		#NUM!				
22	11		#NUM!				
23	12		#NUM!				

Figure 15-12: Using an array formula to return only the positive values in a range.

This modified array formula, entered into range E4:E23, uses the IFERROR function to avoid the error value display:

```
{=IFERROR(INDEX(Data,SMALL(IF(Data>0,ROW(INDIRECT("1:"&ROWS(Data)))),
ROW(INDIRECT("1:"&ROWS(Data))))),"")}
```

The IFERROR function was introduced in Excel 2007. For compatibility with older versions, use this formula entered in G4:G23:

```
{=IF(ISERR(SMALL(IF(Data>0,ROW(INDIRECT("1:"&ROWS(Data)))),
ROW(INDIRECT("1:"&ROWS(Data))))),"",INDEX(Data,SMALL(IF
(Data>0,ROW(INDIRECT("1:"&ROWS(Data)))),ROW(INDIRECT
("1:"&ROWS(Data)))))))}
```

Returning nonblank cells from a range

The following formula is a variation on the formula in the preceding section. This array formula works with a single-column vertical range named *Data*. The array formula is entered into a range of the same size as *Data* and returns only the nonblank cell in the *Data* range:

```
{=IFERROR(INDEX(Data,SMALL(IF(Data<>"",ROW(INDIRECT("1:"&ROWS(Data)))),
ROW(INDIRECT("1:"&ROWS(Data))))),"")}
```

For compatibility with versions prior to Excel 2007, use this formula:

```
{=IF(ISERR(SMALL(IF(Data<>"",ROW(INDIRECT("1:"&ROWS(Data)))),
ROW(INDIRECT("1:"&ROWS(Data))))),"",INDEX(Data,SMALL(IF(Data
<>"",ROW(INDIRECT("1:"&ROWS(Data)))),ROW(INDIRECT("1:"&ROWS
(Data))))))}
```

Reversing the order of cells in a range

In Figure 15-13, cells C4:C13 contain a multicell array formula that reverses the order of the values in the range A4:A13 (which is named *Data*).

The array formula is

```
{=IF(INDEX(Data,ROWS(Data)-ROW(INDIRECT
("1:"&ROWS(Data)))+1)="","",INDEX(Data,ROWS(Data)-
ROW(INDIRECT("1:"&ROWS(Data)))+1))}
```

To reverse the order, a consecutive integer is subtracted from the total number of rows in the data. On its first iteration through the array, the first consecutive integer (1) is subtracted from the total rows (10) and 1 is added back to return 10. This is used in INDEX to retrieve the 10th cell in the range. The formula returns zero for blank cells, so an IF statement corrects that situation.

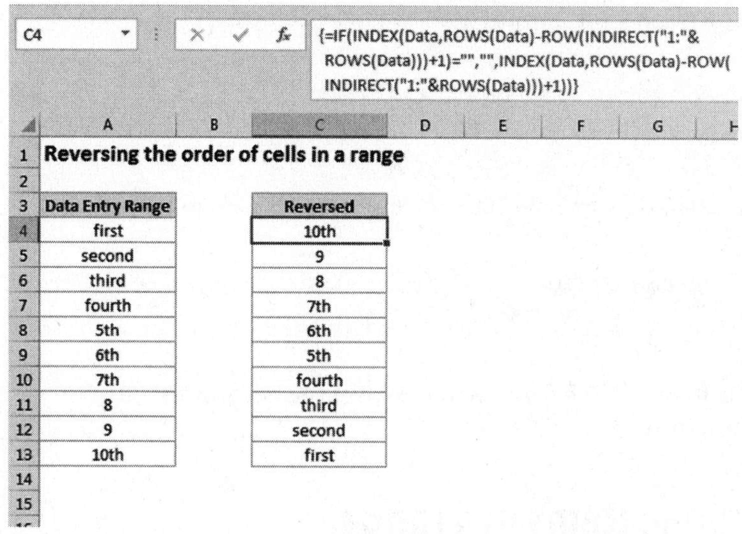

Figure 15-13: A multicell array formula displays the entries in A4:A13 in reverse order.

Sorting a range of values dynamically

Figure 15-14 shows a data entry range in column A (named *Data*). As the user enters values into that range, the values are displayed sorted from largest to smallest in column C. The array formula in column C is rather simple:

```
{=LARGE(Data,ROW(INDIRECT("1:"&ROWS(Data))))}
```

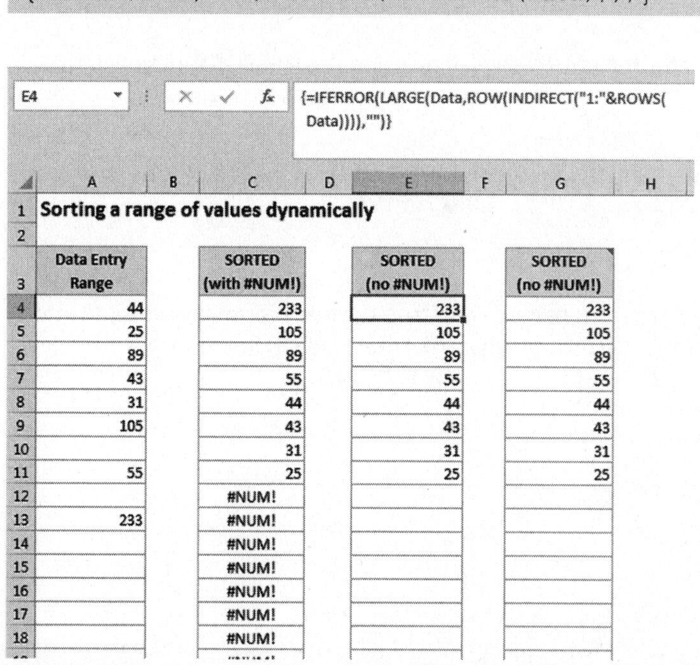

Figure 15-14: A multicell array formula displays the values in column A, sorted.

If you prefer to avoid the *#NUM!* error display, the formula gets a bit more complex:

```
{=IF(ISERR(LARGE(Data,ROW(INDIRECT("1:"&ROWS(Data))))),
"",LARGE(Data,ROW(INDIRECT("1:"&ROWS(Data)))))}
```

If you require compatibility with versions prior to Excel 2007, the formula gets even more complex:

```
{=IF(ISERR(LARGE(Data,ROW(INDIRECT("1:"&ROWS(Data))))),"",LARGE(Data,ROW(INDIRECT(
  "1:"&ROWS(Data)))))}
```

Note that this formula works only with values. The file at this book's website has a similar array formula example that works only with text.

Returning a list of unique items in a range

If you have a single-column range named *Data,* the following array formula returns a list of the unique items in the range (the list with no duplicated items):

```
{=INDEX(Data,SMALL(IF(MATCH(Data,Data,0)=ROW(INDIRECT
("1:"&ROWS(Data))),MATCH(Data,Data,0),""),ROW(INDIRECT
("1:"&ROWS(Data)))))}
```

This formula doesn't work if the *Data* range contains blank cells. The unfilled cells of the array formula display *#NUM!*.

The following modified version eliminates the *#NUM!* display by using the IFERROR function, introduced in Excel 2007:

```
{=IFERROR(INDEX(Data,SMALL(IF(MATCH(Data,Data,0)=ROW(INDIRECT
("1:"&ROWS(data))),MATCH(Data,Data,0),""),ROW(INDIRECT
("1:"&ROWS(Data))))),"")}
```

Figure 15-15 shows an example. Range A4:A22 is named *Data,* and the array formula is entered into range C4:C22. Range E4:E23 contains the array formula that uses the IFERROR function.

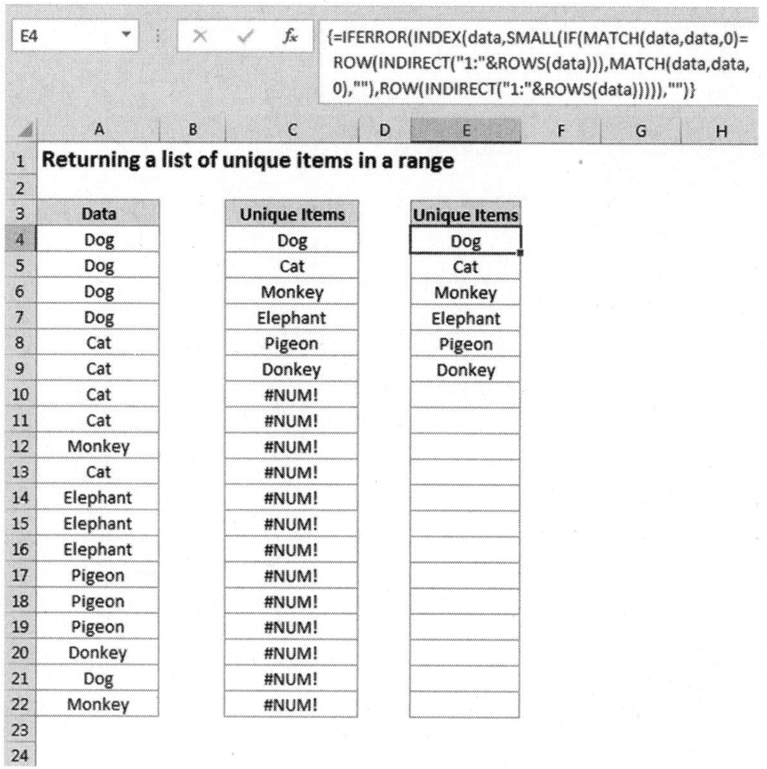
E4 {=IFERROR(INDEX(data,SMALL(IF(MATCH(data,data,0)=ROW(INDIRECT("1:"&ROWS(data))),MATCH(data,data,0),""),ROW(INDIRECT("1:"&ROWS(data))))),"")}

Returning a list of unique items in a range

Data	Unique Items	Unique Items
Dog	Dog	Dog
Dog	Cat	Cat
Dog	Monkey	Monkey
Dog	Elephant	Elephant
Cat	Pigeon	Pigeon
Cat	Donkey	Donkey
Cat	#NUM!	
Cat	#NUM!	
Monkey	#NUM!	
Cat	#NUM!	
Elephant	#NUM!	
Elephant	#NUM!	
Elephant	#NUM!	
Pigeon	#NUM!	
Pigeon	#NUM!	
Pigeon	#NUM!	
Donkey	#NUM!	
Dog	#NUM!	
Monkey	#NUM!	

Figure 15-15: Using an array formula to return unique items from a list.

Displaying a calendar in a range

Figure 15-16 shows the results of one of our favorite multicell array formulas: a "live" calendar displayed in a range of cells. If you change the date at the top, the calendar recalculates to display the dates for the month and year.

On the Web

This workbook is available at this book's website. The file is named array formula calendar.xlsx. In addition, the workbook contains an example that uses this technique to display a calendar for a complete year.

After you create this calendar, you can easily copy it to other worksheets or workbooks.

To create this calendar in the range B2:H9, follow these steps:

1. Select B2:H2 and merge the cells by choosing Home ➜ Alignment ➜ Merge & Center.
2. Type a date into the merged range.

   The day of the month isn't important.

October, 2015

Sun	Mon	Tue	Wed	Thu	Fri	Sat
				1	2	3
4	5	6	7	8	9	10
11	12	13	14	15	16	17
18	19	20	21	22	23	24
25	26	27	28	29	30	31

Week starts on Sunday

October, 2015

Mon	Tue	Wed	Thu	Fri	Sat	Sun
			1	2	3	4
5	6	7	8	9	10	11
12	13	14	15	16	17	18
19	20	21	22	23	24	25
26	27	28	29	30	31	

Week starts on Monday

October, 2015

Sun	Mon	Tue	Wed	Thu	Fri	Sat
27	28	29	30	1	2	3
4	5	6	7	8	9	10
11	12	13	14	15	16	17
18	19	20	21	22	23	24
25	26	27	28	29	30	31
1	2	3	4	5	6	7

Simpler formula that shows other months
(Uses conditional formatting)

Figure 15-16: Displaying a calendar by using a single array formula.

3. Enter the abbreviated day names in the range B3:H3.
4. Select B4:H9 and enter this array formula.

   Remember, to enter an array formula, use Ctrl+Shift+Enter (not just Enter).

```
{=IF(MONTH(DATE(YEAR(B2),MONTH(B2),1))<>MONTH(DATE(YEAR(B2),
MONTH(B2),1)-(WEEKDAY(DATE(YEAR(B2),MONTH(B2),1))-1)+
{0;1;2;3;4;5}*7+{1,2,3,4,5,6,7}-1),"",
DATE(YEAR(B2),MONTH(B2),1)-
(WEEKDAY(DATE(YEAR(B2),MONTH(B2),1))-1)+
{0;1;2;3;4;5}*7+{1,2,3,4,5,6,7}-1)}
```

5. Format the range B4:H9 to use this custom number format: d.

   This step formats the dates to show only the day. Use the Custom category in the Number tab in the Format Cells dialog box to specify this custom number format.

6. Adjust the column widths and format the cells as you like.

Change the month and year in cell B2, and the calendar updates automatically. After creating this calendar, you can copy the range to any other worksheet or workbook.

The array formula actually returns date values, but the cells are formatted to display only the day portion of the date. Also, notice that the array formula uses array constants.

Cross-Ref

See Chapter 14 for more information about array constants.

The array formula can be simplified quite a bit by removing the IF function, which checks to make sure that the date is in the specified month:

```
=DATE(YEAR(B2),MONTH(B2),1)-(WEEKDAY(DATE(YEAR(B2),MONTH(B2),1))
-1)+{0;1;2;3;4;5}*7+{1,2,3,4,5,6,7}-1
```

This version of the formula displays the days from the preceding month and the next month.

Figure 15-17 shows 12 instances of the array formula calendar for an entire year.

2016

January

Sun	Mon	Tue	Wed	Thu	Fri	Sat
					1	2
3	4	5	6	7	8	9
10	11	12	13	14	15	16
17	18	19	20	21	22	23
24	25	26	27	28	29	30
31						

February

Sun	Mon	Tue	Wed	Thu	Fri	Sat
	1	2	3	4	5	6
7	8	9	10	11	12	13
14	15	16	17	18	19	20
21	22	23	24	25	26	27
28	29					

March

Sun	Mon	Tue	Wed	Thu	Fri	Sat
		1	2	3	4	5
6	7	8	9	10	11	12
13	14	15	16	17	18	19
20	21	22	23	24	25	26
27	28	29	30	31		

April

Sun	Mon	Tue	Wed	Thu	Fri	Sat
					1	2
3	4	5	6	7	8	9
10	11	12	13	14	15	16
17	18	19	20	21	22	23
24	25	26	27	28	29	30

May

Sun	Mon	Tue	Wed	Thu	Fri	Sat
1	2	3	4	5	6	7
8	9	10	11	12	13	14
15	16	17	18	19	20	21
22	23	24	25	26	27	28
29	30	31				

June

Sun	Mon	Tue	Wed	Thu	Fri	Sat
			1	2	3	4
5	6	7	8	9	10	11
12	13	14	15	16	17	18
19	20	21	22	23	24	25
26	27	28	29	30		

July

Sun	Mon	Tue	Wed	Thu	Fri	Sat
					1	2
3	4	5	6	7	8	9
10	11	12	13	14	15	16
17	18	19	20	21	22	23
24	25	26	27	28	29	30
31						

August

Sun	Mon	Tue	Wed	Thu	Fri	Sat
	1	2	3	4	5	6
7	8	9	10	11	12	13
14	15	16	17	18	19	20
21	22	23	24	25	26	27
28	29	30	31			

September

Sun	Mon	Tue	Wed	Thu	Fri	Sat
				1	2	3
4	5	6	7	8	9	10
11	12	13	14	15	16	17
18	19	20	21	22	23	24
25	26	27	28	29	30	

October

Sun	Mon	Tue	Wed	Thu	Fri	Sat
						1
2	3	4	5	6	7	8
9	10	11	12	13	14	15
16	17	18	19	20	21	22
23	24	25	26	27	28	29
30	31					

November

Sun	Mon	Tue	Wed	Thu	Fri	Sat
		1	2	3	4	5
6	7	8	9	10	11	12
13	14	15	16	17	18	19
20	21	22	23	24	25	26
27	28	29	30			

December

Sun	Mon	Tue	Wed	Thu	Fri	Sat
				1	2	3
4	5	6	7	8	9	10
11	12	13	14	15	16	17
18	19	20	21	22	23	24
25	26	27	28	29	30	31

Figure 15-17: An annual calendar made from array formulas.

PART V

Miscellaneous Formula Techniques

16

Importing and Cleaning Data

In This Chapter

- Ways to import data into Excel
- Many techniques to manipulate and clean data
- Using the new Fill Flash feature
- A checklist for data cleaning
- Exporting data to other formats

One common use for Excel is as a tool to "clean up" data. Cleaning up data involves getting raw data into a worksheet and then manipulating it so it conforms to various requirements. In the process, the data will be made consistent so that it can be properly analyzed.

This chapter describes various ways to get data into a worksheet and provides some tips to help you clean it up.

A Few Words About Data

Data is everywhere. For example, if you run a website, you're collecting data continually, and you may not even know it. Every visit to your site generates information stored in a file on your server. This file contains lots of useful information—if you take the time to examine it.

That's just one example of data collection. Virtually every automated system collects data and stores it. Most of the time, the system that collects the data is also equipped to verify and analyze it. Not always, though. And, of course, data is also collected manually. An example is a telephone survey.

Excel is a good tool for analyzing data, and it's often used to summarize the information and display it in the form of tables and charts. But often, the data that's collected isn't perfect. For one reason or another, it needs to be cleaned up before it can be analyzed.

Importing Data

Before you can do anything with data, you must get it into a worksheet. Excel can import most common text file formats and can retrieve data from websites.

Importing from a file

This section describes file types that Excel can open directly, using the File ➜ Open command. Figure 16-1 shows the list of file filter options you can specify from this dialog box.

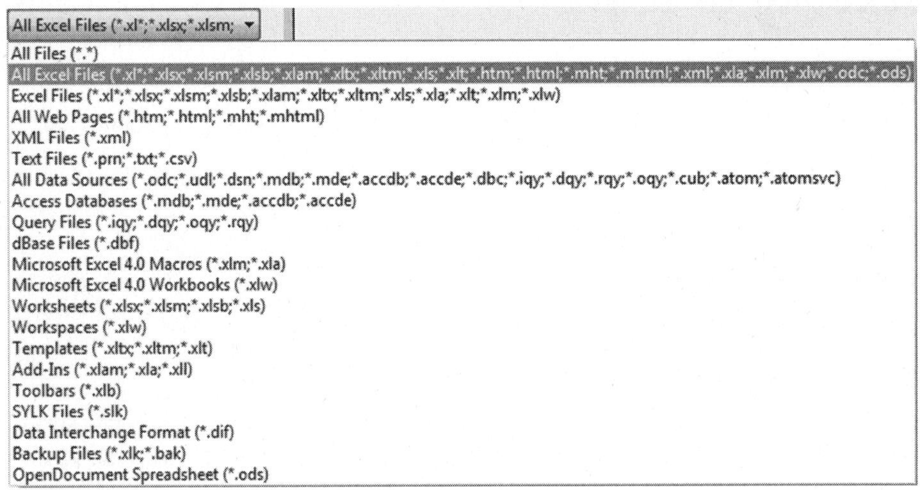

Figure 16-1: Filtering by file extension in the Open dialog box.

Spreadsheet file formats

In addition to the current file formats (XLSX, XLSM, XLSB, XLTX, XLTM, and XLAM), Excel 2016 can open workbook files from all previous versions of Excel:

- **XLS:** Binary files created by Excel 4, Excel 95, Excel 97, Excel 2000, Excel 2002, and Excel 2003
- **XLM:** Binary files that contain Excel 4 macros (no data)
- **XLT:** Binary files for an Excel template
- **XLA:** Binary files for an Excel add-in

Excel can also open one file format created by other spreadsheet products:

- **ODS:** OpenDocument spreadsheet. These files are produced by a variety of open-source software, including Google Drive, OpenOffice, LibreOffice, StarOffice, and several others.

Note that Excel does not support Lotus 1-2-3 files, Quattro Pro files, or Microsoft Works files.

Database file formats

Excel 2016 can open the following database file formats:

- **Access files:** These files have various extensions, including MDB and ACCDB.
- **dBase files:** These are produced by dBase III and dBase IV. Excel does not support dBase II files.

In addition, Excel supports various types of database connections that enable you to access data selectively. For example, you can perform a query on a large database to retrieve only the records you need (rather than the entire database).

Text file formats

A text file contains raw characters with no formatting. Excel can open most types of text files:

- **CSV:** Comma-separated values. Columns are delimited with a comma, and rows are delimited with a carriage return.
- **TXT:** Columns are delimited with a tab, and rows are delimited with a carriage return.
- **PRN:** Columns are delimited with multiple space characters, and rows are delimited with a carriage return. Excel imports this type of file into a single column.
- **DIF:** The file format originally used by the VisiCalc spreadsheet. Rarely used.
- **SYLK:** The file format originally used by Multiplan. Rarely used.

Most of these text file types have variants. For example, text files produced by a Mac computer have different end-of-row characters. Excel can usually handle the variants without a problem.

When you attempt to open a text file in Excel, the Text Import Wizard might kick in to help you specify how you want the data to be retrieved.

Tip

To bypass the Text Import Wizard, press Shift while you click the Open button in the Open dialog box.

When Excel can't open a file

If Excel doesn't support a particular file form, don't be too quick to give up. Other folks have likely had the same problem. Try searching the web for the file extension, plus the word *excel*. Maybe a file converter is available, or someone has figured out how to use an intermediary program to open the file and export it into a format that Excel recognizes.

Importing HTML files

Excel can open most HTML files, which can be stored on your local drive or on a web server. Choose File ➜ Open and locate the HTML file. If the file is on a web server, copy the URL and paste it into the File Name field in the Open dialog box.

The way the HTML code renders in Excel varies considerably. Sometimes the HTML file may look exactly as it does in a browser. Other times, it may bear little resemblance, especially if the HTML file uses cascading style sheets (CSS) for layout.

In some cases, you can access data on the Web by using a Web Query (Data ➜ Get External Data ➜ From Web).

Importing XML files

XML (eXtensible Markup Language) is a text file format suitable for structured data. Data is enclosed in tags, which also serve to describe the data.

Excel can open XML files, and simple files will display with little or no effort. Complex XML files will require some work, however. A discussion of this topic is beyond the scope of this book. You'll find information about getting data from XML files in Excel's Help system and online.

Importing a text file into a specified range

If you need to insert a text file into a specific range in a worksheet, you might think that your only choice is to import the text into a new workbook and then to copy the data and paste it to the range where you want it to appear. However, you can do it in a more direct way.

Figure 16-2 shows a small CSV file. The following instructions describe how to import this file, named monthly.csv, beginning at cell C3.

monthly.csv - Notepad

File Edit Format View Help

```
January,55,85,40,66,53
February,36,39,44,59,54
March,61,77,81,82,48
April,32,38,90,89,84
May,84,73,32,81,47
June,32,66,82,83,73
July,68,40,85,70,57
August,83,37,39,74,78
September,63,46,63,66,46
October,84,51,56,32,68
November,72,52,82,48,45
December,49,58,65,85,42
```

Figure 16-2: This CSV file will be imported into a range.

1. Choose Data ➜ Get External Data ➜ From Text to display the Import Text File dialog box.
2. Navigate to the folder that contains the text file.
3. Select the file from the list and then click the Import button to display the Text Import Wizard.
4. Use the Text Import Wizard to specify how the data will be imported. For a CSV file, specify Delimited with a Comma Delimiter.
5. Click the Finish button. Excel displays the Import Data dialog box, shown in Figure 16-3.

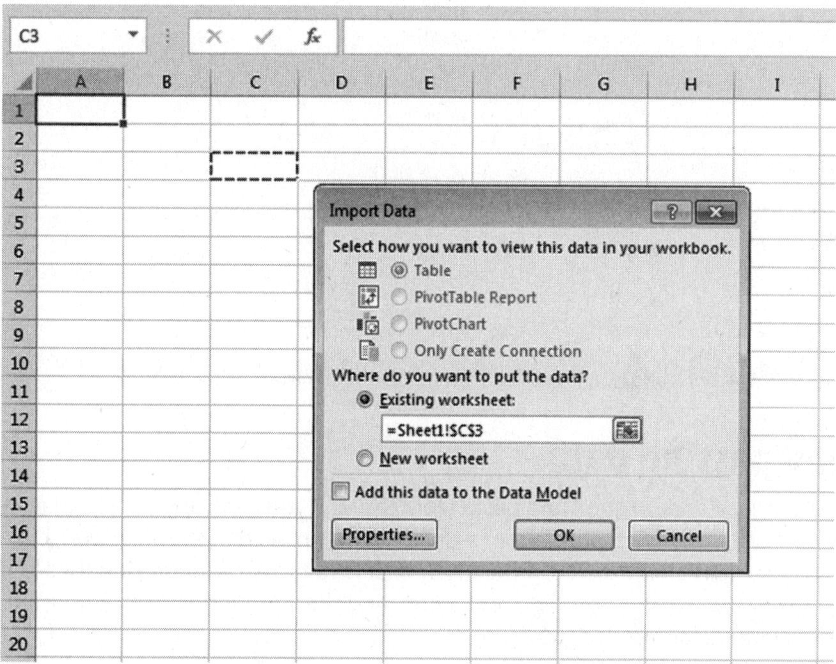

Figure 16-3: Using the Import Data dialog box to import a CSV file at a particular location.

6. In the Import Data dialog box, click the Properties button to display the External Data Range Properties dialog box.
7. In the External Data Range Properties dialog box, deselect the Save Query Definition check box and click OK to return to the Import Data dialog box.
8. In the Import Data dialog box, specify the location for the imported data. (It can be a cell in an existing worksheet or a new worksheet.)
9. Click OK, and Excel imports the data (see Figure 16-4).

Note

You can ignore Step 7 if the data you're importing will be changing. By saving the query definition, you can quickly update the imported data by right-clicking any cell in the range and choosing Refresh Data.

	A	B	C	D	E	F	G	H	I	J
1										
2										
3			January	55	85	40	66	53		
4			February	36	39	44	59	54		
5			March	61	77	81	82	48		
6			April	32	38	90	89	84		
7			May	84	73	32	81	47		
8			June	32	66	82	83	73		
9			July	68	40	85	70	57		
10			August	83	37	39	74	78		
11			September	63	46	63	66	46		
12			October	84	51	56	32	68		
13			November	72	52	82	48	45		
14			December	49	58	65	85	42		
15										
16										
17										
18										

Figure 16-4: This range contains data imported directly from a CSV file.

Copying and pasting data

If all else fails, you can try standard copy and paste techniques. If you can copy data from an application (for example, a word processing program or a document displayed in a PDF viewer), chances are good that you can paste it into an Excel workbook. For best results, try pasting using the Home ➜ Clipboard ➜ Paste ➜ Paste Special command and employing the various paste options listed. Usually, pasted data requires some cleanup.

Data Cleanup Techniques

This section discusses a variety of techniques that you can use to clean up data in a worksheet.

Cross-Ref

Chapter 5, "Manipulating Text," contains additional examples of text-related formulas that may be helpful when cleaning data.

Removing duplicate rows

If data is compiled from multiple sources, it may contain duplicate rows. Most of the time, you want to eliminate the duplicates. In the past, removing duplicate data was essentially a manual task, although it could be automated by using a fairly nonintuitive advanced filter technique. Now removing duplicate rows is easy, thanks to Excel's Remove Duplicates command (introduced in Excel 2007).

Start by moving the cell cursor to any cell within your data range. Choose Data ➜ Data Tools ➜ Remove Duplicates, and Excel displays the Remove Duplicates dialog box shown in Figure 16-5.

If your data is in a table, you can also use Table Tools ➜ Design ➜ Data Tools ➜ Remove Duplicates. These two commands work the same.

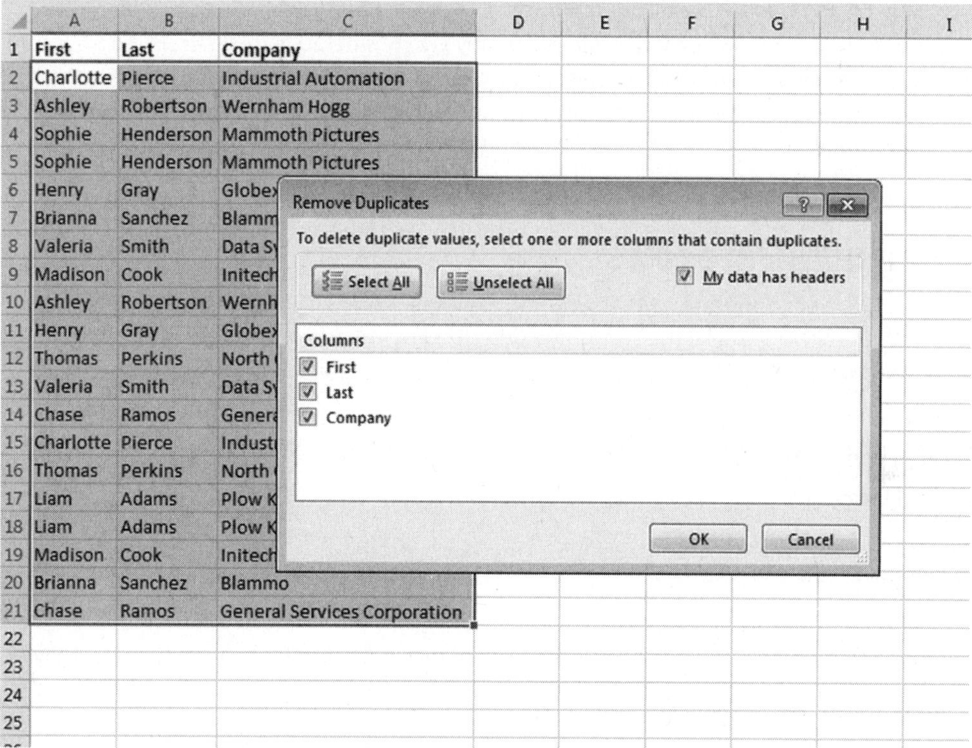

Figure 16-5: Use the Remove Duplicates dialog box to delete duplicate rows.

The Remove Duplicates dialog box lists all the columns in your data range or table. Place a check mark next to the columns that you want to be included in the duplicate search. Most of the time, you'll want to select all the columns, which is the default. Click OK, and Excel weeds out the duplicate rows and displays a message that tells you how many duplicates it removed. It would be nice if Excel gave you the option to just highlight the duplicates so you could look them over, but it doesn't. If Excel deletes too many rows, you can undo the procedure by clicking Undo on the Quick Access Toolbar (or by pressing Ctrl+Z).

When you select all columns in the Remove Duplicates dialog box, Excel deletes a row only if the content of every column is duplicated. In some situations, you may not care about matching some columns, so you would deselect those columns in the Remove Duplicates dialog box. For example, if each row has a unique ID code, Excel would never find duplicate rows, so you'd want to uncheck that column in the Remove Duplicates dialog box.

When duplicate rows are found, the first row is kept, and subsequent duplicate rows are deleted.

Warning

Duplicate values are determined by the value *displayed* in the cell—not necessarily the value *stored* in the cell. For example, assume that two cells contain the same date. One of the dates is formatted to display as 5/15/2013, and the other is formatted to display as May 15, 2013. When removing duplicates, Excel considers these dates to be different. Similarly, values that are formatted differently are considered to be different. So $1,209.32 is not the same as 1209.32. Therefore, you might want to apply formatting to entire columns to ensure that duplicate rows are not overlooked just because of a formatting difference.

Identifying duplicate rows

If you would like to identify duplicate rows so you can examine them without automatically deleting them, here's another method. Unlike the technique described in the previous section, this method looks at actual values, not formatted values.

Create a formula to the right of your data that concatenates each of the cells to the left. The following formulas assume that the data is in columns A:C.

Enter this formula in cell D2:

```
=CONCATENATE(A2,B2,C2)
```

Add another formula in cell E2. This formula displays the number of times that a value in column D occurs:

```
=COUNTIF(D:D,D2)
```

Copy these formulas down the column for each row of your data.

Column E displays the number of occurrences of that row. Unduplicated rows display 1. Duplicated rows display a number that corresponds to the number of times that row appears.

Figure 16-6 shows a simple example. If you don't care about a particular column, just omit it from the formula in column D. For example, if you want to find duplicates regardless of the Company column, just omit C2 from the CONCATENATE formula.

D2 =CONCATENATE(A2,B2,C2)

	A	B	C	D	E	F
1	First	Last	Company	Concatentate	Countif	
2	Charlotte	Pierce	Industrial Automation	CharlottePierceIndustrial Automation	2	
3	Ashley	Robertson	Wernham Hogg	AshleyRobertsonWernham Hogg	1	
4	Sophie	Henderson	Mammoth Pictures	SophieHendersonMammoth Pictures	2	
5	Sophie	Henderson	Mammoth Pictures	SophieHendersonMammoth Pictures	2	
6	Henry	Gray	Globex Corporation	HenryGrayGlobex Corporation	1	
7	Brianna	Sanchez	Blammo	BriannaSanchezBlammo	2	
8	Valeria	Smith	Data Systems	ValeriaSmithData Systems	3	
9	Valeria	Smith	Data Systems	ValeriaSmithData Systems	3	
10	Charlotte	Pierce	Industrial Automation	CharlottePierceIndustrial Automation	2	
11	Thomas	Perkins	North Central Positronics	ThomasPerkinsNorth Central Positronics	1	
12	Liam	Adams	Plow King	LiamAdamsPlow King	2	
13	Liam	Adams	Plow King	LiamAdamsPlow King	2	
14	Madison	Cook	Initech	MadisonCookInitech	1	
15	Brianna	Sanchez	Blammo	BriannaSanchezBlammo	2	
16	Chase	Ramos	General Services Corporation	ChaseRamosGeneral Services Corporation	1	
17	Valeria	Smith	Data Systems	ValeriaSmithData Systems	3	
18						
19						

Figure 16.6: Using formulas to identify duplicate rows.

Splitting text

When importing data, you might find that multiple values are imported into a single column. Figure 16-7 shows an example of this type of import problem.

	A	B
1	January,55,85,40,66,53	
2	February,36,39,44,59,54	
3	March,61,77,81,82,48	
4	April,32,38,90,89,84	
5	May,84,73,32,81,47	
6	June,32,66,82,83,73	
7	July,68,40,85,70,57	
8	August,83,37,39,74,78	
9	September,63,46,63,66,46	
10	October,84,51,56,32,68	
11	November,72,52,82,48,45	
12	December,49,58,65,85,42	
13		
14		
15		
16		
17		

Figure 16-7: The imported data was put in one column rather than multiple columns.

If all the text is the same length (knows as a fixed-width text file), you might be able to write a series of formulas that extract the information to separate columns. The LEFT, RIGHT, and MID functions are useful for this task. (See Chapter 5.)

You should also be aware that Excel offers two nonformula methods to assist in splitting data so it occupies multiple columns: Text to Columns and Flash Fill.

Using Text to Columns

The Text to Columns command is a handy tool that can parse strings into their component parts.

First, make sure that the column that contains the data to be split up has enough empty columns to the right to accommodate the extracted data. Then select the data to be parsed and choose Data ➜ Data Tools ➜ Text to Columns.

Excel displays the Convert Text to Columns Wizard, which consists of a series of dialog boxes that walk you through the steps to convert a single column of data into multiple columns. Figure 16-8 shows the initial step, in which you choose the type of data:

- **Delimited:** The data to be split is separated by delimiters such as commas, spaces, slashes, or other characters.
- **Fixed Width:** Each component occupies the same number of characters.

Make your choice and click Next to move on to step 2, which depends on the choice you made in step 1.

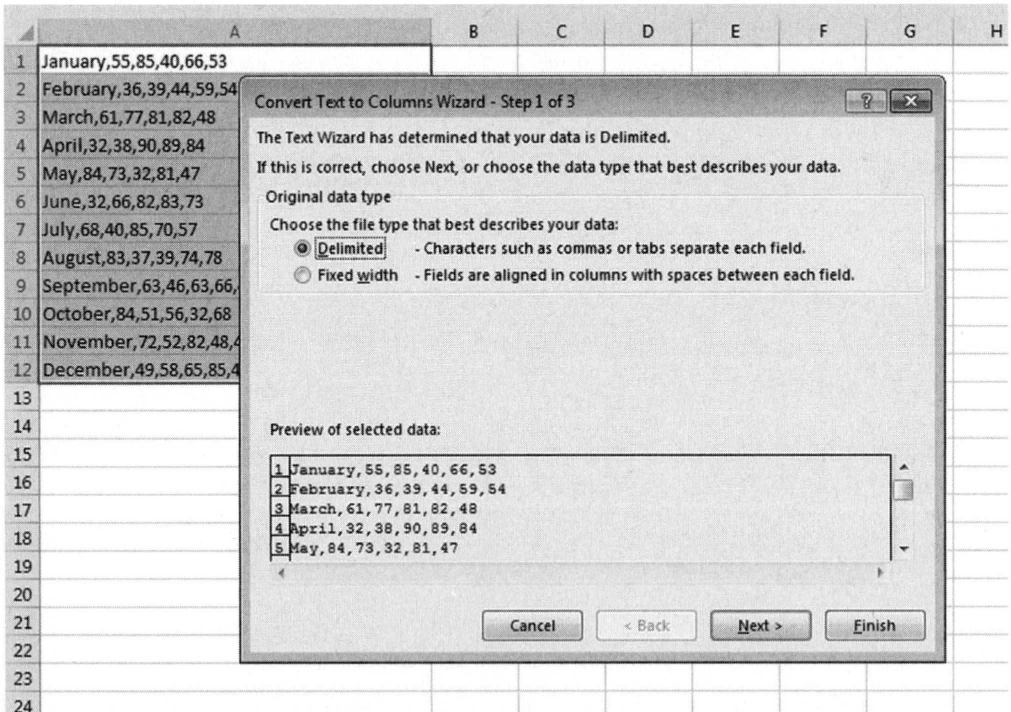

Figure 16-8: The first dialog box in the Convert Text to Columns Wizard.

If you're working with delimited data, specify the delimiting character or characters (a comma in this example). You'll see a preview of the result. If you're working with fixed width data, you can modify the column breaks directly in the preview window. Click and drag the vertical lines to move the column break to another location. Single-click to add a new vertical line. Double-click an existing vertical line to remove it.

When you're satisfied with the column breaks, click Next to move to step 3. In this step, you can click a column in the preview window and specify formatting for the column, or you can indicate that the column should be skipped. Click Finish, and Excel will split the data as specified. The original data will be replaced.

Using Flash Fill

The Text to Columns Wizard works well for many types of data, but sometimes you'll encounter data that can't be parsed by that wizard. For example, the Text to Columns Wizard is useless if you have variable width data that doesn't have delimiters. In such a case, using the Flash Fill feature might save the day.

Flash Fill uses pattern recognition to extract data (and concatenate data). Just enter a few examples in a column that's adjacent to the data and then choose Data ➜ Data Tools ➜ Flash Fill (or press Ctrl+E). Excel analyzes the examples and attempts to fill in the remaining cells. If Excel didn't recognize the pattern you had in mind, press Ctrl+Z, add another example or two, and try again.

Figure 16-9 shows a worksheet with some text in a single column. The goal is to extract the number from each cell and put it into a separate cell. The Text to Columns Wizard can't do it because the space delimiters aren't consistent. You could write an array formula, but it would be complicated. Another option is to write a custom worksheet function using VBA. This might be a good job for Flash Fill.

	A	B
1	The boy weighed 20 pounds	
2	Bob is 6 feet tall	
3	She drove for 9.5 hours straight	
4	Pi is 3.14159	
5	He drank 5 cups of coffee	
6	The sales tax was $3.12 for that item	
7	15 people showed up for jury duty	
8	He was in 7th heaven	
9	The square root of 16 is four	
10	Where is the 90210 zip code?	
11		
12		
13		

Figure 16-9: The goal is to extract the numbers in column A.

To try using Flash Fill, select cell B1 and type the first number (20). Move to B2 and type the second number (6). Can Flash Fill identify the remaining numbers and fill them in? Choose Data ➜ Data Tools ➜ Flash Fill (or press Ctrl+E), and Excel fills in the remaining cells in a flash. Figure 16-10 shows the result.

	A	B	C
1	The boy weighed 20 pounds	20	
2	Bob is 6 feet tall	6	
3	She drove for 9.5 hours straight	5	
4	Pi is 3.14159	14159	
5	He drank 5 cups of coffee	5	
6	The sales tax was $3.12 for that item	12	
7	15 people showed up for jury duty	15	
8	He was in 7th heaven	7	
9	The square root of 16 is four	16	
10	Where is the 90210 zip code?	90210	
11			
12			
13			
14			

Figure 16-10: Using manually entered examples in B1 and B2, Excel makes some incorrect guesses.

It looks good. Excel somehow managed to extract the numbers from the text. Examine the results more closely, though, and you see that it failed for numbers that include decimal points. Accuracy increases if you provide more examples—such as an example of a decimal number. Delete the suggested values, enter **3.12** into cell B6, and press Ctrl+E. This time, Excel gets them all correct (see Figure 16-11).

	A	B	C	D
1	The boy weighed 20 pounds	20		
2	Bob is 6 feet tall	6		
3	She drove for 9.5 hours straight	9.5		
4	Pi is 3.14159	3.14159		
5	He drank 5 cups of coffee	5		
6	The sales tax was $3.12 for that item	3.12		
7	15 people showed up for jury duty	15		
8	He was in 7th heaven	7		
9	The square root of 16 is four	16		
10	Where is the 90210 zip code?	90210		
11				
12				
13				
14				

Figure 16.11: After entering an example of a decimal number, Excel gets them all correct.

This simple example demonstrates two important points:

- You must examine your data carefully after using Flash Fill. Just because the first few rows are correct, you can't assume that Flash Fill worked correctly for all rows.
- Flash Fill increases accuracy when you provide more examples.

Figure 16-12 shows another example: names in column A. The goal is to use Flash Fill to extract the first, last, and middle name (if it has one). In column B, Flash Fill works great if you give it only two examples (Mark and Tim). Plus, it successfully extracts all the last names, using Russell and Colman as examples. Flash Fill has trouble extracting the middle names if some of the names have them and some don't. In that case you can use the following formula to get the middle name or initial:

```
=TRIM(SUBSTITUTE(SUBSTITUTE(A1,B1,""),C1,""))
```

The inner SUBSTITUTE replaces the first name with an empty string, the outer SUBSTITUTE replaces the last name with an empty string, and the TRIM function removes any extra spaces.

Cross-Ref

See Chapter 5 for a formula-based solution for splitting names.

D1 | =TRIM(SUBSTITUTE(SUBSTITUTE(A1,B1,""),C1,""))

	A	B	C	D	E	F	G
1	Mark Russel	Mark	Russel				
2	Tim Colman	Tim	Colman				
3	Sam Daniel Bains	Sam	Bains	Daniel			
4	Fred James Foster	Fred	Foster	James			
5	James J. Wehr	James	Wehr	J.			
6	Mitch Nichols	Mitch	Nichols				
7	Neal McCaslin	Neal	McCaslin				
8	Ned Poulakis	Ned	Poulakis				
9	Paul T. Wingfield	Paul	Wingfield	T.			
10	Peter Gans	Peter	Gans				
11	Ron E. Hoffman	Ron	Hoffman	E.			
12	Julia Hayes	Julia	Hayes				
13	Richard P Light	Richard	Light	P			
14	Ray Walker	Ray	Walker				
15	Robert F. Mahoney	Robert	Mahoney	F.			
16	Robert Fist	Robert	Fist				
17							
18							

Figure 16-12: Using Flash Fill to split names.

In addition to clicking the Flash Fill button on the Data tab of the Ribbon or using the Ctrl+E shortcut, Excel may recognize that you're attempting to extract data and suggest an extraction as you type. Figure 16-13 shows Excel's Flash Fill suggestion after typing **Mark** in cell B1 and the first two letters of **Tim** in B2.

	A	B	C
1	Mark Russel	Mark	
2	Tim Colman	Tim	
3	Sam Daniel Bains	Sam	
4	Fred James Foster	Fred	
5	James J. Wehr	James	
6	Mitch Nichols	Mitch	
7	Neal McCaslin	Neal	
8	Ned Poulakis	Ned	
9	Paul T. Wingfield	Paul	
10	Peter Gans	Peter	
11	Ron E. Hoffman	Ron	
12	Julia Hayes	Julia	
13	Richard P Light	Richard	
14	Ray Walker	Ray	
15	Robert F. Mahoney	Robert	
16	Robert Fist	Robert	
17			
18			
19			

Figure 16-13: Excel suggests a Flash Fill as you type.

At this point, pressing the down arrow will complete the Flash Fill. Note that if you type the entire name, **Tim**, the suggestion goes away. You can simply move to the next cell and begin typing that name to get the suggestions to show again.

Here's another example of using Flash Fill. Say you have a list of URLs and need to extract the domain (the part of the URL that ends in .com, .net, and so on).

Figure 16-14 shows a list of URLs. Flash Fill required just two examples of the domain entered into column B. As we typed **31engine** in cell B2, Flash Fill suggested the remaining rows and we pressed the down arrow to fill them.

	A	B	C	D
1	http://1470.net/api/ping	1470.net		
2	http://31engine.com/weblogUpdates/1.cgi	31engine.com		
3	http://a2b.cc/setloc/bp.a2b	a2b.cc		
4	http://api.blogblogs.com.br/api/ping	api.blogblogs.com.br		
5	http://api.moreover.com/RPC2	api.moreover.com		
6	http://api.my.yahoo.com/RPC2	api.my.yahoo.com		
7	http://bblog.com/ping.php	bblog.com		
8	http://bitacoles.net/notificacio.php	bitacoles.net		
9	http://blog-search.net/up.php	blog-search.net		
10	http://blog.goo.ne.jp/XMLRPC	blog.goo.ne.jp		
11	http://blogbot.dk/io/xml-rpc.php	blogbot.dk		
12	http://blogdigger.com/RPC2	blogdigger.com		
13	http://bloglines.com/ping	bloglines.com		
14	http://blogpeople.net/servlet/weblogUpdates	blogpeople.net		
15	http://blogsdominicanos.com/ping/	blogsdominicanos.com		
16	http://blogsearch.google.com/ping/RPC2	blogsearch.google.com		
17	http://blogshares.com/rpc.php	blogshares.com		
18				
19				
20				
21				

Figure 16-14: Using Flash Fill to extract domains from URLs.

Unlike formulas, Flash Fill is not dynamic. That is, if your data changes, the flash-filled column does not update.

Flash Fill seems to work reliably if the data is consistent, but it's still a good idea to examine the results carefully. And think twice before trusting Flash Fill with important data. There's no way to document how the data was extracted. You just have to trust Excel.

Note

You can also use the Flash Fill feature to create new data from multiple columns. Just provide a few examples of how you want the data combined, and Excel will figure out the pattern and fill in the column.

Changing the case of text

Often, you'll want to make text in a column consistent in terms of case. Excel provides no direct way to change the case of text, but it's easy to do with formulas. See the sidebar "Transforming data with formulas."

The three relevant functions are

- **UPPER:** Converts the text to ALL UPPERCASE.
- **LOWER:** Converts the text to all lowercase.
- **PROPER:** Converts the text to Proper Case. (The first letter in each word is capitalized, as in a proper name.)

These functions are quite straightforward. They operate only on alphabetic characters. They ignore all other characters and return them unchanged.

If you use the PROPER function, you'll probably need to do some additional cleanup to handle exceptions. Here are some examples of transformations that you'd probably consider incorrect:

- The letter following an apostrophe is always capitalized (for example, Don'T). This is done, apparently, to handle names like O'Reilly.
- The PROPER function doesn't handle names with an embedded capital letter, such as McDonald.
- "Minor" words—such as *and* and *the*—are always capitalized. For example, some would prefer that the third word in *United States Of America* not be capitalized.

You can correct some of these problems by using Find and Replace.

Transforming data with formulas

Many of the data cleanup examples in this chapter describe how to use formulas and functions to transform data in some way. For example, you can use the UPPER function to transform text into uppercase. When the data is transformed, you'll have two columns: the original data and the

continued

continued

transformed data. Almost always, you'll want to replace the original data with the transformed data. Here's how:

1. Insert a new temporary column for formulas to transform the original data.
2. Create your formulas in the temporary column and make sure that the formulas do what they were intended to do.
3. Select the formula cells.
4. Choose Home ➜ Clipboard ➜ Copy (or press Ctrl+C).
5. Select the original data cells.
6. Choose Home ➜ Clipboard ➜ Paste ➜ Values (V).

This procedure replaces the original data with the transformed data. Then you can delete the temporary column that holds the formulas.

Removing extra spaces

It's usually a good idea to ensure that data doesn't have extra spaces. It's impossible to spot a space character at the end of a text string. Extra spaces can cause lots of problems, especially when you need to compare text strings. The text *July* is not the same as the text *July* with a space appended to the end. The first is four characters long, and the second is five characters long.

Create a formula that uses the TRIM function to remove all leading and trailing spaces, and replace multiple spaces with a single space. This example uses the TRIM function. The formula returns *Fourth Quarter Earnings* (with no excess spaces):

```
=TRIM("    Fourth     Quarter     Earnings     ")
```

Data that is imported from a web page often contains a different type of space: a nonbreaking space, indicated by   in HTML code. In Excel, this character can be generated by this formula:

```
=CHAR(160)
```

You can use a formula like this to replace those spaces with normal spaces:

```
=SUBSTITUTE(A2,CHAR(160)," ")
```

Or use this formula to replace the nonbreaking space character with normal spaces and remove excess spaces:

```
=TRIM(SUBSTITUTE(A2,CHAR(160)," "))
```

Removing strange characters

Often, data imported into an Excel worksheet contains strange (often unprintable) characters. You can use the CLEAN function to remove all nonprinting characters from a string. If the data is in cell A2, this formula will do the job:

```
=CLEAN(A2)
```

The CLEAN function can miss some nonprinting Unicode characters. This function is programmed to remove the first 32 nonprinting characters in the 7-bit ASCII code. Consult the Excel Help system for information on how to remove the nonprinting Unicode characters. (Search Help for the CLEAN function.)

Converting values

You may need to convert values from one system to another. For example, you may import a file that has values in fluid ounces, but those values need to be expressed in milliliters. Excel's handy CONVERT function can perform that and many other conversions.

If cell A2 contains a value in ounces, the following formula converts it to milliliters.

```
=CONVERT(A2,"oz","ml")
```

This function is extremely versatile and can handle most common measurement units.

See Chapter 10, "Miscellaneous Calculations," for more information about the CONVERT function.

Excel can also convert between number bases. You may import a file that contains hexadecimal values, and you need to convert them to decimal. Use the HEX2DEC function to perform this conversion. For example, the following formula returns *1,279,* which is the decimal equivalent of its hex argument:

```
=HEX2DEC("4FF")
```

Excel can also convert from binary to decimal (BIN2DEC) and from octal to decimal (OCT2DEC).

Functions that convert from decimal to another number base are DEC2HEX, DEC2BIN, and DEC2OCT.

The BASE function, introduced in Excel 2013, converts a decimal number to any number base. Note that there is not a function that works in the opposite direction. Excel does not provide a function that converts any number base to decimal. You're limited to binary, octal, and hexadecimal.

Classifying values

Often, you may have values that need to be classified into a group. For example, if you have ages of people, you might want to classify them into groups such as 17 or younger, 18 to 24, 25 to 34, and so on.

The easiest way to perform this classification is with a lookup table. Figure 16-15 shows ages in column A and classifications in column B. Column B uses the lookup table in D2:E9. The formula in cell B2 is

```
=VLOOKUP(A2,$D$2:$E$9,2)
```

This formula was copied to the cells below.

B2 =VLOOKUP(A2,$D$2:$E$9,2)

	A	B	C	D	E	F
1	Age	Classification				
2	24	18-24		0	<18	
3	42	35-44		18	18-24	
4	44	35-44		25	25-34	
5	17	<18		35	35-44	
6	72	65-74		45	45-54	
7	51	45-54		55	55-64	
8	40	35-44		65	65-74	
9	51	45-54		75	75+	
10	34	25-34				
11	51	45-54				
12	81	75+				
13	18	18-24				
14	46	45-54				
15	60	55-64				
16	32	25-34				
17						
18						
19						

Figure 16-15: Using a lookup table to classify ages into age ranges.

You can also use a lookup table for nonnumeric data. Figure 16-16 shows a lookup table that is used to assign a region to a state.

B2 =VLOOKUP(A2,$D$2:$E$51,2,FALSE)

	A	B	C	D	E	F	G
1	State	Region					
2	Florida	Region IV		Alabama	Region III		
3	Ohio	Region IV		Alaska	Region IV		
4	Louisiana	Region II		Arizona	Region V		
5	Connecticut	Region I		Arkansas	Region III		
6	New Hampshire	Region I		California	Region II		
7	Kansas	Region I		Colorado	Region III		
8	Utah	Region V		Connecticut	Region I		
9				Delaware	Region II		
10				Florida	Region IV		
11				Georgia	Region IV		
12				Hawaii	Region V		
13				Idaho	Region II		
14				Illinois	Region II		
15				Indiana	Region I		
16				Iowa	Region V		
17				Kansas	Region I		
18				Kentucky	Region IV		
19				Louisiana	Region II		
20				Maine	Region IV		
21				Maryland	Region III		

Figure 16-16: Using a lookup table to assign a region for a state.

The two-column lookup table is in the range D2:E51. The formula in cell B2, which was copied to the cells below, is

```
=VLOOKUP(A2,$D$2:$E$51,2,FALSE)
```

Tip

A side benefit is that the VLOOKUP function will return #N/A if an exact match is not found—a good way to spot misspelled states. Using FALSE as the last argument in the function indicates that an exact match is required.

Joining columns

To combine data in two more columns, you can usually use the concatenation operator (&) in a formula. For example, the following formula combines the contents of cells A1, B1, and C1:

```
=A1&B1&C1
```

Often, you'll need to insert spaces between the cells, such as if the columns contain a title, first name, and last name. Concatenating using the preceding formula would produce something like *Mr. ThomasJones*. To add spaces (to produce *Mr. Thomas Jones*), modify the formula like this:

```
=A1&" "&B1&" "&C1
```

You can also use the Flash Fill feature to join columns without using formulas. Just provide an example or two in an adjacent column, and press Ctrl+E.

Rearranging columns

If you need to rearrange the columns in a worksheet, you can insert a blank column and then drag another column into the new blank column. But then the moved column leaves a gap, which you need to delete.

Here's an easier way:

1. Click the column header of the column you want to move.
2. Choose Home ➜ Clipboard ➜ Cut.
3. Click the column header to the right of where you want the column to go.
4. Right-click and choose Insert Cut Cells from the shortcut menu that appears.

Repeat these steps until the columns are in the order you desire.

You can also move or copy columns by dragging them with your mouse. Select the entire column by clicking on the column header, and then click on the column border and drag. (The cursor turns into four arrows when you're on the border.) Hold down the Ctrl key while you drag, and you create a copy of the column in the new location while the original column remains where it was. Hold down the Shift key while you drag to move the column and insert it where you drop, shifting all other columns to the right.

Randomizing the rows

If you need to arrange rows in random order, here's a quick way to do it. In the column to the right of the data, insert this formula into the first cell and copy it down:

```
=RAND()
```

Then sort the data using this column. The rows will be in random order, and you can delete the column.

Matching text in a list

You may have some data that you need to check against another list. For example, you may want to identify rows in which data in a particular column appears in a different list. Figure 16-17 shows a simple example. The data is in columns A:C. The goal is to identify the rows in which the Member Num appears in the Resigned Members list, in column F. These rows can then be deleted.

Here's a formula entered into cell D2, and copied down, that will do the job:

```
=IF(COUNTIF($F$2:$F$5,A2)>0,"Resigned","" )
```

This formula displays the word *Resigned* if the Member Num in column A is found in the Resigned Members list. If the member number is not found, it returns an empty string. If the list is sorted by column D, the rows for all resigned members will appear together and can be quickly deleted.

This technique can be adapted to other types of list matching tasks.

D2 =IF(COUNTIF($F$2:$F$5,A2)>0,"Resigned","")

	A	B	C	D	E	F	G
1	Member Num	First Name	Last Name	Status		Resigned	
2	851	Chloe	Mitchell			393	
3	444	Isabelle	Harper	Resigned		444	
4	275	Gracie	Pierce			471	
5	393	Bryan	Dunn	Resigned		189	
6	471	Zoey	Sanchez	Resigned			
7	237	Mason	Warren				
8	657	Joshua	Peterson				
9	189	Riley	Rodriguez	Resigned			
10	284	Elijah	Bell				
11	723	Ian	Owens				
12	554	Charles	Murphy				
13	264	Claire	Cooper				
14	992	Hayden	Ross				
15	524	Angelina	Coleman				
16	103	Katherine	Hicks				
17	483	Bryan	Carpenter				
18	359	Lauren	Hamilton				
19	777	Justin	Gibson				
20	902	Alexa	Butler				
21	839	Ariana	Morgan				
22							
23							
24							

Figure 16.17: The goal is to identify member numbers that are in the resigned members list.

Change vertical data to horizontal data

Figure 16-18 shows a common type of data layout that you might see when importing a file. Each record consists of three consecutive cells in a single column: Department, Name, and Location. The goal is to convert this data so that each record appears as a single row with three columns.

	A	B	C	D
1				
2	Customer Service			
3	Taylor Gonzalez			
4	Lahore			
5				
6	Quality Asurance			
7	Evelyn Burns			
8	Hyderabad			
9				
10	Logistics			
11	Isabella Reynolds			
12	Chongqing			
13				
14	Insurance			
15	Madison Gibson			
16	Johannesburg			
17				
18	Services			
19	Kaylee Wright			
20	Buenos Aires			
21				
22	IT			
23	Leah Hughes			
24	Santiago			
25				
26	Business Development			
27	Christopher Carroll			
28	Mexico City			

Figure 16-18: Vertical data that needs to be converted to three columns.

There are several ways to convert this type of data, but here's a method that's fairly easy. Start by creating column headers for Department, Name, and Location in row 1. In row 2, enter these four formulas as shown in Figure 16-19:

```
B2: =A2
C2: =A3
D2: =A4
E2: =MOD(ROW(),4)
```

E2 =MOD(ROW(),4)

	A	B	C	D	E	F
1		Department	Name	Location	Mod	
2	Customer Service	Customer Service	Taylor Gonzalez	Lahore	2	
3	Taylor Gonzalez					
4	Lahore					
5						
6	Quality Asurance					
7	Evelyn Burns					
8	Hyderabad					
9						
10	Logistics					
11	Isabella Reynolds					
12	Chongqing					
13						
14	Insurance					
15	Madison Gibson					
16	Johannesburg					
17						
18	Services					
19	Kaylee Wright					
20	Buenos Aires					
21						
22	IT					
23	Leah Hughes					
24	Santiago					

Figure 16-19: Use formulas to convert column data to row data.

Copy the four formulas down as far as you have data. Each record is three pieces of data and a blank line. The MOD function returns the remainder when the row number is divided by four. All the rows with a 2 in the Mod column will be the ones you want to keep.

Copy columns B:E and choose Home ➜ Paste ➜ Values to convert the formulas to their values and delete column A. Select all the data and choose Sort from the Data tab on the Ribbon and sort on the Mod column (see Figure 16-20).

Delete any rows that do not contain 2 in the Mod column, and you're left with data in which each record is on its own row, as shown in Figure 16-21. You can now delete the Mod column.

You can easily adapt this technique to work with vertical data that contains a different number of rows. Simply add as many formulas across as you need and change the second argument of the MOD function to the number of rows that represent one record.

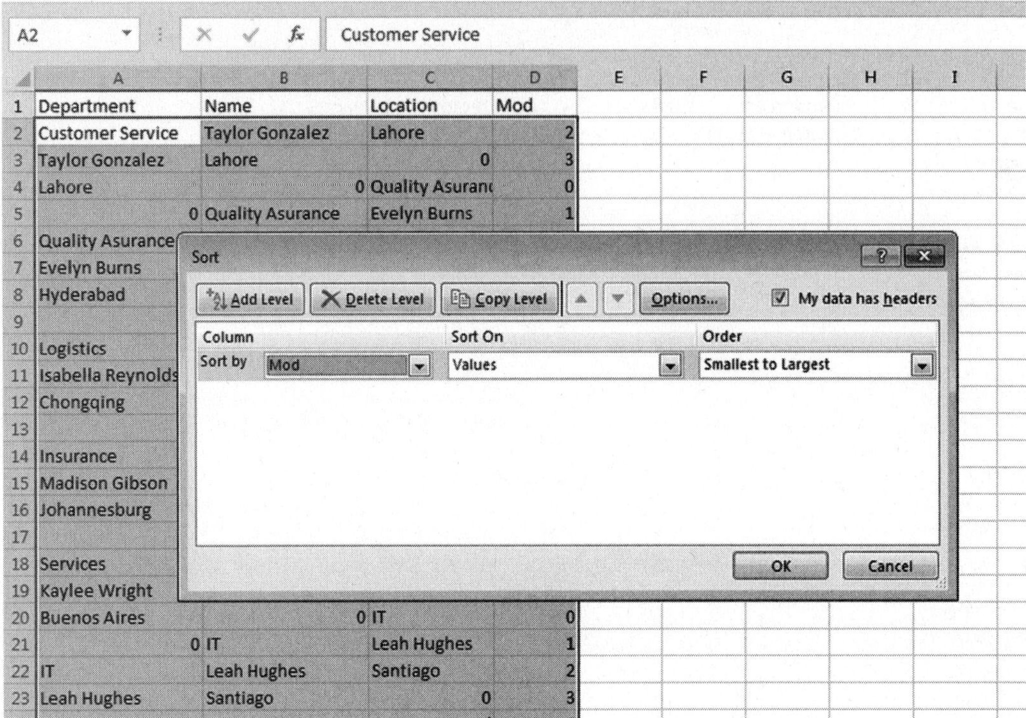

Figure 16.20: Sort the data on the Mod column to group the data.

	A	B	C	D	E
1	Department	Name	Location	Mod	
2	Customer Service	Taylor Gonzalez	Lahore	2	
3	Quality Asurance	Evelyn Burns	Hyderabad	2	
4	Logistics	Isabella Reynolds	Chongqing	2	
5	Insurance	Madison Gibson	Johannesburg	2	
6	Services	Kaylee Wright	Buenos Aires	2	
7	IT	Leah Hughes	Santiago	2	
8	Business Development	Christopher Carroll	Mexico City	2	
9	Business Development	Mackenzie Perez	Pune	2	
10	Licenses	Dominic Ramirez	Kolkata	2	
11	Marketing	Anna Garcia	Bangalore	2	
12	Customer Service	Isabelle Howard	Shanghai	2	
13					
14					
15					

Figure 16.21: Each record of data is on its own row.

Filling gaps in an imported report

When you import data, you can sometimes end up with a worksheet that looks something like the one shown in Figure 16-22. This type of report formatting is common. As you can see, an entry in column A applies to several rows of data. If you sort this type of list, the missing data messes things up, and you can no longer tell who sold what when.

	A	B	C	D	E
1	Sales Rep	Month	Units Sold	Amount	
2	Jane	Jan	182	$35,263.00	
3		Feb	3,350	25,666.00	
4		Mar	114	15,553.00	
5	George	Jan	135	2,719.00	
6		Feb	401	26,631.00	
7		Mar	357	17,853.00	
8	Beth	Jan	509	10,860.00	
9		Feb	414	12,392.00	
10		Mar	53	25,952.00	
11	Dan	Jan	32	32,167.00	
12		Feb	283	33,395.00	
13		Mar	401	19,516.00	
14					
15					
16					

Figure 16-22: This report contains gaps in the Sales Rep column.

If the report is small, you can enter the missing cell values manually or by using a series of Home ➜ Editing ➜ Fill ➜ Down commands (or its Ctrl+D shortcut). If you have a large list that's in this format, here's a better way:

1. Select the range that has the gaps (A2:A13, in this example).
2. Choose Home ➜ Editing ➜ Find & Select ➜ Go to Special to display the Go to Special dialog box.
3. In the Go to Special dialog box, select the Blanks option and click OK. This action selects the blank cells in the original selection.
4. In the formula bar, type an equal sign (=) followed by the address of the first cell with an entry in the column (**=A2**, in this example), and then press Ctrl+Enter. Figure 16-23 shows the blank cells filled in.
5. Reselect the original range and press Ctrl+C to copy the selection.
6. Choose Home ➜ Clipboard ➜ Paste ➜ Paste Values to convert the formulas to values.

After you complete these steps, the gaps are filled in with the correct information.

A3 =A2

	A	B	C	D	E
1	Sales Rep	Month	Units Sold	Amount	
2	Jane	Jan	182	$35,263.00	
3	Jane	Feb	3,350	25,666.00	
4	Jane	Mar	114	15,553.00	
5	George	Jan	135	2,719.00	
6	George	Feb	401	26,631.00	
7	George	Mar	357	17,853.00	
8	Beth	Jan	509	10,860.00	
9	Beth	Feb	414	12,392.00	
10	Beth	Mar	53	25,952.00	
11	Dan	Jan	32	32,167.00	
12	Dan	Feb	283	33,395.00	
13	Dan	Mar	401	19,516.00	
14					
15					
16					

Figure 16-23: The gaps are gone, and this list can now be sorted.

Spelling checking

If you use a word processing program, you probably take advantage of its spelling checker feature. Spelling mistakes can be embarrassing when they appear in a text document, but they can cause serious problems when they occur within your data. For example, if you tabulate data by month using a pivot table, a misspelled month name will make it appear that a year has 13 months.

To access the Excel spell checker, choose Review ➜ Proofing ➜ Spelling or press F7. To check the spelling in just a particular range, select the range before you activate the spell checker.

If the spell checker finds any words that it does not recognize as correct, it displays the Spelling dialog box. Figure 16-24 shows the Spelling dialog box where you can ignore the misspelling, change it to a suggested spelling, or add the word to the dictionary.

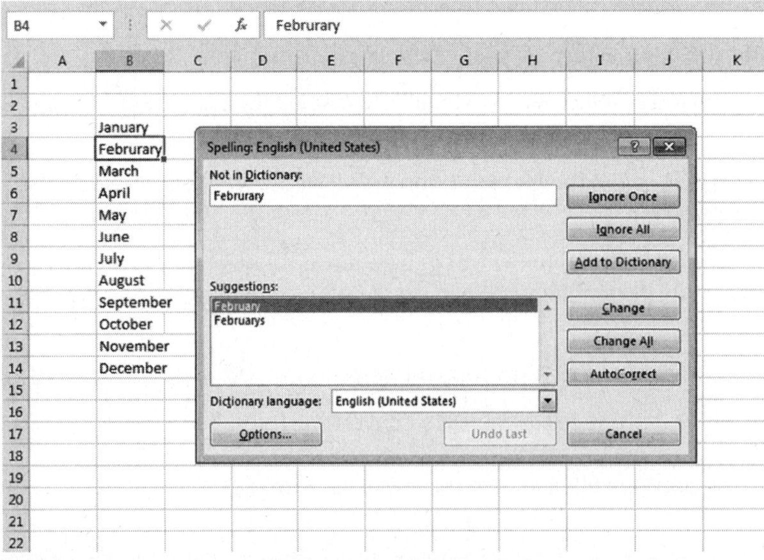

Figure 16.24: Misspelled words can be ignored or changed.

Replacing or removing text in cells

You may need to systematically replace (or remove) certain characters in a column of data. For example, you may need to replace all backslash characters with forward slash characters. In many cases, you can use Excel's Find and Replace dialog box to accomplish this task. To remove text using the Find and Replace dialog box, just leave the Replace With field empty.

In other situations, you may need a formula-based solution. Consider the data shown in Figure 16-25. The goal is to replace the second hyphen character with a colon. Using Find and Replace wouldn't work because there's no way to specify that only the second hyphen should be replaced.

B2 =SUBSTITUTE(A2,"-",":",2)

	A	B	C	D	E	F
1						
2	201-FIN-6438	201-FIN:6438				
3	201-SUB-5230	201-SUB:5230				
4	201-SUB-4936	201-SUB:4936				
5	203-PRT-2562	203-PRT:2562				
6	202-SUB-5616	202-SUB:5616				
7	202-PRT-1605	202-PRT:1605				
8	202-SUB-5917	202-SUB:5917				
9	203-SUB-6350	203-SUB:6350				
10	202-PRT-1984	202-PRT:1984				
11	201-PRT-7841	201-PRT:7841				
12	201-PRT-1380	201-PRT:1380				
13	203-FIN-5656	203-FIN:5656				
14	203-FIN-5721	203-FIN:5721				
15	201-SUB-3964	201-SUB:3964				
16	201-FIN-4618	201-FIN:4618				
17						
18						

Figure 16.25: To replace only the second hyphen in these cells, Find and Replace is not an option.

In this case, the solution is a fairly simple formula that replaces the second occurrence of a hyphen with a colon:

```
=SUBSTITUTE(A2,"-",":",2)
```

To remove the second occurrence of a hyphen, just omit the third argument for the SUBSTITUTE function:

```
=SUBSTITUTE(A2,"-",,2)
```

This is another example in which Flash Fill can also do the job.

Note

If you've worked with programming languages, you may be familiar with the concept of regular expressions. A *regular expression* is a way to match strings of text using concise (and often confusing) codes. Excel does not support regular expressions, but if you search the Web, you'll find ways to incorporate regular expressions in VBA, plus a few add-ins that provide this feature in the workbook environment.

Adding text to cells

If you need to add text to a cell, the only solution is to use a new column of formulas. Here are some examples.

This formula adds: "ID: " to the beginning of a cell:

```
="ID: "&A2
```

This formula adds ".mp3" to the end of a cell:

```
=A2&".mp3"
```

This formula inserts a hyphen after the third character in a cell:

```
=LEFT(A2,3)&"-"&RIGHT(A2,LEN(A2)-3)
```

You can also use Flash Fill to add text to cells.

Fixing trailing minus signs

Imported data sometimes displays negative values with a trailing minus sign. For example, a negative value may appear as **3,498**- rather than the more common **-3,498**. Excel does not convert these values. In fact, it considers them to be nonnumeric text.

The solution is so simple it may even surprise you:

1. Select the data that has the trailing minus signs. The selection can also include positive values.
2. Choose Data ➜ Data Tools ➜ Text to Columns.
3. When the Text to Columns dialog box appears, click Finish.

This procedure works because of a default setting in the Advanced Text Import Settings dialog box (which you don't even see, normally). To display this dialog box, shown in Figure 16-26, go to step 3 in the Text to Columns Wizard dialog box and click Advanced.

Or you can use Flash Fill to fix the trailing minus signs. If the range contains positive values, you may need to provide several examples.

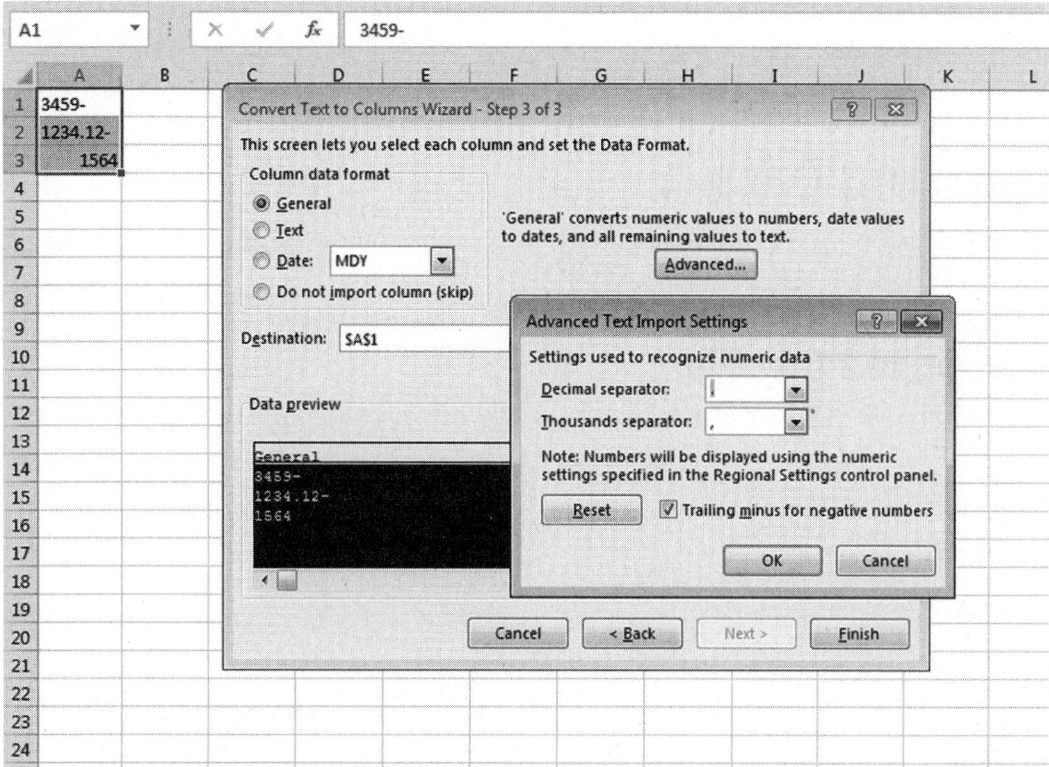

Figure 16-26: The Trailing Minus for Negative Numbers option makes it easy to fix trailing minus signs in a range of data.

A Data Cleaning Checklist

This section contains a list of items that could cause problems with data. Not all these are relevant to every set of data:

- Does each column have a unique and descriptive header?
- Is each column of data formatted consistently?
- Did you check for duplicate or missing rows?
- For text data, are the words consistent in terms of case?
- Does the data include any unprintable characters?
- Did you check for spelling errors?
- Does the data contain extra spaces?

- Are the columns arranged in the proper (or logical) order?
- Are any cells blank that shouldn't be?
- Did you correct any trailing minus signs?
- Are the columns wide enough to display all data?

Exporting Data

This chapter began with a section on importing data, so it's only appropriate to end it with a discussion of exporting data to a file that's not a standard Excel file.

Exporting to a text file

When you choose File ➜ Save As, the Save As dialog box offers you a variety of text file formats. The three types are

- **CSV:** Comma-separated value files
- **TXT:** Tab-delimited files
- **PRN:** Formatted text

I discuss these files types in the sections that follow.

CSV files

When you export a worksheet to a CSV file, the data is saved as displayed. In other words, if a cell contains 12.8312344 but is formatted to display with two decimal places, the value will be saved as 12.83.

Cells are delimited with a comma character, and rows are delimited with a carriage return and line feed.

Note

If you export a file using the Macintosh variant, rows are delimited with a carriage return only (no line feed character).

Note that if a cell contains a comma, the cell value is saved within quotation marks. If a cell contains a quotation mark character, that character appears twice.

TXT files

Exporting a workbook to a TXT file is almost identical to the CSV file format described earlier. The only difference is that cells are separated by a tab character instead of a comma.

If your worksheet contains any Unicode characters, you should export the file using the Unicode variant. Otherwise, Unicode characters will be saved as question mark characters.

PRN files

A PRN file is much like a printed image of the worksheet. The cells are separated by multiple space characters. Also, a line is limited to 240 characters. If a line exceeds that limit, the remainder appears on the next line. PRN files are rarely used.

Exporting to other file formats

Excel also lets you save your work in several other formats:

- **Data Interchange Format:** These files have a DIF extension. Not used very often.
- **Symbolic Link:** These files have an SYLK extension. Not used very often.
- **Portable Document Format:** These files have a PDF extension. This is a common "read-only" file format.
- **XML Paper Specification Document:** These files have an XPS extension; they're Microsoft's alternative to PDF files. Not used very often.
- **Web Page:** These files have an HTM extension. Often, saving a file as a web page generates a directory of ancillary files required to render the page accurately.
- **OpenDocument Spreadsheet:** These files have an ODS extension. They are compatible with various open source spreadsheet programs.

Charting Techniques

In This Chapter

- Understanding how a chart's SERIES formula works
- Plotting functions with one and two variables
- Creating awesome designs with formulas
- Working with linear and nonlinear trendlines
- Using new forecasting functions
- Useful charting examples that demonstrate key concepts

When most people think of Excel, they think of analyzing rows and columns of numbers. As you probably know already, though, Excel is no slouch when it comes to presenting data visually in the form of a chart. In fact, it's a safe bet that Excel is the most commonly used software for creating charts.

After you create a chart, you have almost complete control over nearly every aspect of each chart. This chapter, which assumes that you're familiar with Excel's charting features, demonstrates some useful charting techniques—most of which involve formulas.

Understanding the SERIES Formula

You create charts from numbers that appear in a worksheet. You can enter these numbers directly, or you can derive them as the result of formulas. Normally, the data used by a chart resides in a single worksheet, within one file, but that's not a strict requirement. A single chart can use data from any number of worksheets or even from different workbooks.

A *chart* consists of one or more data series, and each data series appears as a line, column, bar, and so on. Each series in a chart has a SERIES formula. When you select a data series in a chart, Excel highlights the worksheet data with an outline, and its SERIES formula appears in the Formula bar (see Figure 17-1).

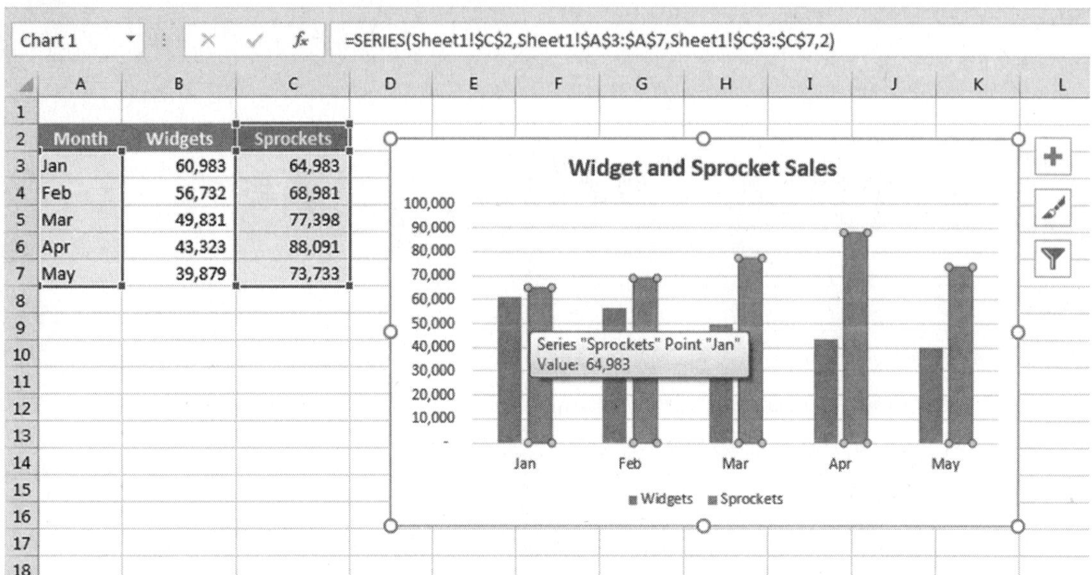

Figure 17-1: The Formula bar displays the SERIES formula for the selected data series in a chart.

Note

A SERIES formula is not a "real" formula. In other words, you can't use it in a cell, and you can't use worksheet functions within the SERIES formula. You can, however, edit the arguments in the SERIES formula to change the data that's used by the chart. You can also drag the outlines in the worksheet to change the chart's data.

A SERIES formula has the following syntax:

```
=SERIES(series_name, category_labels, values, order, sizes)
```

The arguments that you can use in the SERIES formula include

- **series_name:** (Optional) A reference to the cell that contains the series name used in the legend. If the chart has only one series, the series_name argument is used as the title. The series_name argument can also consist of text, in quotation marks. If omitted, Excel creates a default series name (for example, Series1).
- **category_labels:** (Optional) A reference to the range that contains the labels for the category axis. If omitted, Excel uses consecutive integers beginning with 1. For XY charts, this argument specifies the *x* values. A noncontiguous range reference is also valid. (The range's addresses are separated by a comma and enclosed in parentheses.) The argument may also consist of an array of comma-separated values (or text in quotation marks) enclosed in curly brackets.
- **values:** (Required) A reference to the range that contains the values for the series. For XY charts, this argument specifies the *y* values. A noncontiguous range reference is also valid. (The range's addresses are separated by a comma and enclosed in parentheses.) The argument may also consist of an array of comma-separated values enclosed in curly brackets.

- **order:** (Required) An integer that specifies the plotting order of the series. This argument is relevant only if the chart has more than one series. Using a reference to a cell is not allowed.
- **sizes:** (Only for bubble charts) A reference to the range that contains the values for the size of the bubbles in a bubble chart. A noncontiguous range reference is also valid. (The range's addresses are separated by a comma and enclosed in parentheses.) The argument may also consist of an array of values enclosed in curly brackets.

Range references in a SERIES formula are always absolute, and (with one exception) they always include the sheet name. Here's an example of a SERIES formula that doesn't use category labels:

```
=SERIES(Sheet1!$B$1,,Sheet1!$B$2:$B$7,1)
```

A range reference can consist of a noncontiguous range. If so, each range is separated by a comma, and the argument is enclosed in parentheses. In the following SERIES formula, the values range consists of B2:B3 and B5:B7:

```
=SERIES(,,(Sheet1!$B$2:$B$3,Sheet1!$B$5:$B$7),1)
```

Although a SERIES formula can refer to data in other worksheets, all the data for a series must reside on a single sheet. The following SERIES formula, for example, is not valid because the data series references two different worksheets:

```
=SERIES(,,(Sheet1!$B$2,Sheet2!$B$2),1)
```

Using names in a SERIES formula

You can substitute range names for the range references in a SERIES formula. When you do so, Excel changes the reference in the SERIES formula to include the workbook name. For example, the SERIES formula shown here uses a range named *MyData* (located in a workbook named `budget.xlsx`). Excel added the workbook name and exclamation point.

```
=SERIES(Sheet1!$B$1,,budget.xlsx!MyData,1)
```

Using names in a SERIES formula provides a significant advantage: if you change the range reference for the name, the chart automatically displays the new data. In the preceding SERIES formula, for example, assume that the range named *MyData* refers to A1:A20. The chart displays the 20 values in that range. You can then use the Name Manager to redefine *MyData* as a different range—say, A1:A30. The chart then displays the 30 data points defined by *MyData*. (No chart editing is necessary.)

Note

A SERIES formula does not use structured table referencing. If you edit the SERIES formula to include a table reference such as Table1[Widgets], Excel converts the table reference to a standard range address. However, if the chart is based on data in a table, the references in the SERIES formula adjust automatically if you add or remove data from the table.

As noted previously, a SERIES formula cannot use worksheet functions. You *can,* however, create named formulas (which use functions) and use these named formulas in your SERIES formula. As you see later in this chapter, this technique enables you to perform some useful charting tricks.

Unlinking a chart series from its data range

Normally, an Excel chart uses data stored in a range. If you change the data in the range, the chart updates automatically. In some cases, you may want to "unlink" the chart from its data ranges and produce a *static chart*—a chart that never changes. For example, if you plot data generated by various what-if scenarios, you may want to save a chart that represents some baseline so you can compare it with other scenarios.

There are two ways to create a static chart:

- **Paste it as a picture.** Activate the chart and then choose Home ➜ Clipboard ➜ Copy ➜ Copy as Picture. (Accept the default settings from the Copy Picture dialog box.) Then activate any cell and choose Home ➜ Clipboard ➜ Paste (or press Ctrl+V). The result is a picture of the copied chart. You can then delete the original chart if you like. When a chart is converted to a picture, you can use all of Excel's image editing tools. Figure 17-2 shows an example.
- **Convert the range references to arrays.** Click a chart series and then click the Formula bar to activate the SERIES formula. Press F9 to convert the ranges to arrays. Repeat this for each series in the chart. This technique (as opposed to creating a picture) enables you to continue to edit and format the chart. Here's an example of a SERIES formula after the range references were converted to arrays:

```
=SERIES(,{"Jan","Feb","Mar"},{1869,2085,2451},1)
```

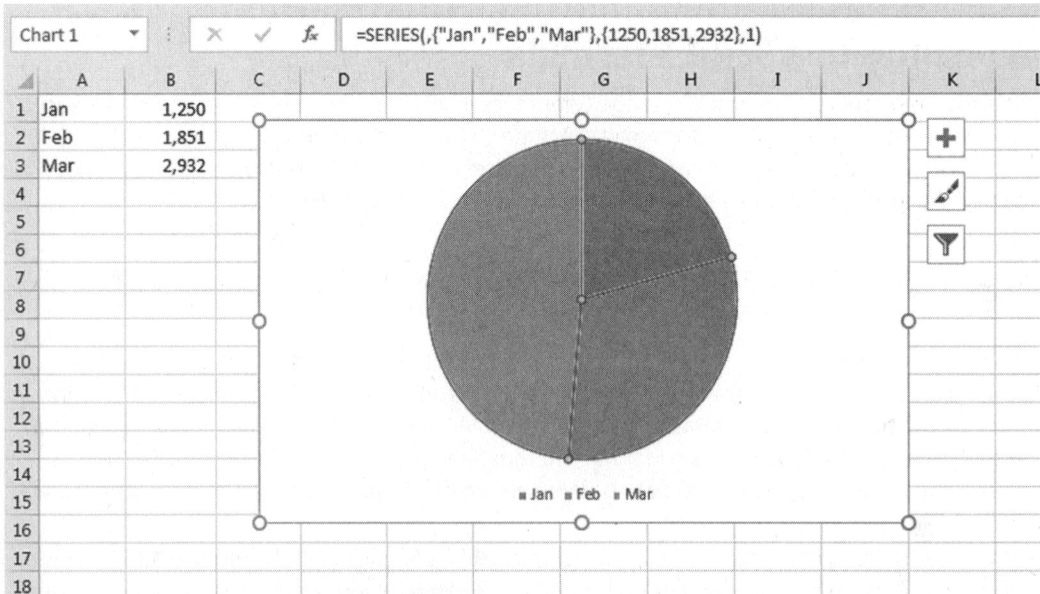

Figure 17-2: A chart after being converted to a picture (and then edited).

Creating Links to Cells

You can add cell links to various elements of a chart. Adding cell links can make your charts more dynamic. You can set dynamic links for chart titles, data labels, and axis labels. In addition, you can insert a text box that links to a cell.

Adding a chart title link

The chart title is normally not linked to a cell. In other words, it contains static text that changes only when you edit the title manually. You can, however, create a link so that a title refers to a worksheet cell.

Here's how to create a linked title:

1. Select the title in the chart.
2. Activate the Formula bar and type an equal sign (=).
3. Click the cell that contains the title text.
4. Press Enter.

The result is a formula that contains the sheet reference and the cell reference as an absolute reference (for example, `=Sheet3!$A$1`). Figure 17-3 shows a chart in which the chart title is linked to cell A1 on Sheet3.

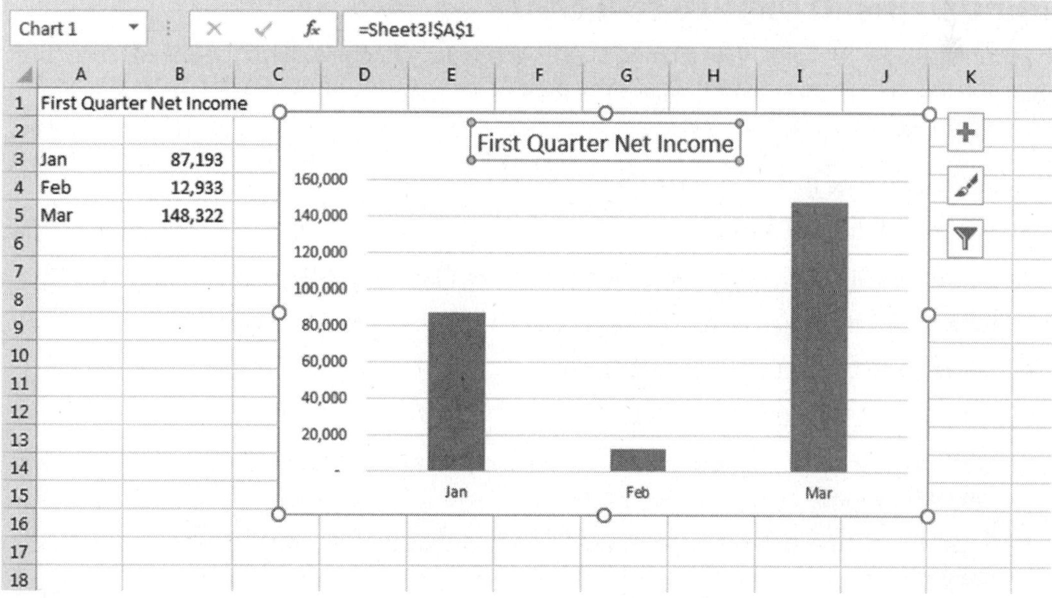

Figure 17-3: The chart title is linked to cell A1.

Adding axis title links

The axis titles are optional and are used to describe the data for an axis. The process for adding a link to an axis title is identical to that described in the previous section for a chart title.

Adding text links

You can also add a linked text box to a chart. The process is a bit tricky, however. Follow these steps exactly:

1. Select the chart and then choose Insert ➜ Text ➜ Text Box.
2. Drag the mouse inside the chart to create the text box.
3. Press Esc to exit text entry mode and select the text box object.
4. Click in the Formula bar and then type an equal sign (=).
5. Use your mouse and click the cell that you want linked.
6. Press Enter.

You can apply any type of formatting you like to the text box.

Tip

After you add a text box to a chart, you can change it to any other shape that supports text. Select the text box and choose Drawing Tools ➜ Format ➜ Insert Shapes ➜ Edit Shape ➜ Change Shape. Then choose a new shape from the gallery.

Adding a linked picture to a chart

A chart can display a "live" picture of a range of cells. When you change a cell in the linked range, the change appears in the linked picture. Again, the process isn't exactly intuitive. Start by creating a chart. Then do this:

1. Select the range that you want to insert into the chart.
2. Press Ctrl+C to copy the range.
3. Activate a cell (not the chart) and choose Home ➜ Clipboard ➜ Paste ➜ Linked Picture (I).

   Excel inserts the linked picture of the range on the worksheet's draw layer.
4. Select the linked picture and press Ctrl+X.
5. Activate the chart and press Ctrl+V.

   The linked picture is cut from the worksheet and pasted into the chart. However, the link no longer functions.
6. Select the picture in the chart, activate the Formula bar, type an equal sign, and select the range *again*.
7. Press Enter, and the picture is now linked to the range.

Chart Examples

This section contains a variety of chart examples that you may find useful or informative. At the very least, they may inspire you to create charts that are relevant to your work.

Single data point charts

Effective charts don't always have to be complicated. This section presents some charts that display a single data point.

A workbook with these examples is available at this book's website. The filename is single data point charts.xlsx.

Figure 17-4 shows five charts, each of which uses one data point. These are minimalistic charts. The only chart elements are the single data point series, the data label for that data point, and the chart title (displayed on the left). The single column fills the entire width of the plot area.

One of the charts is grouped with a shape object that contains text.

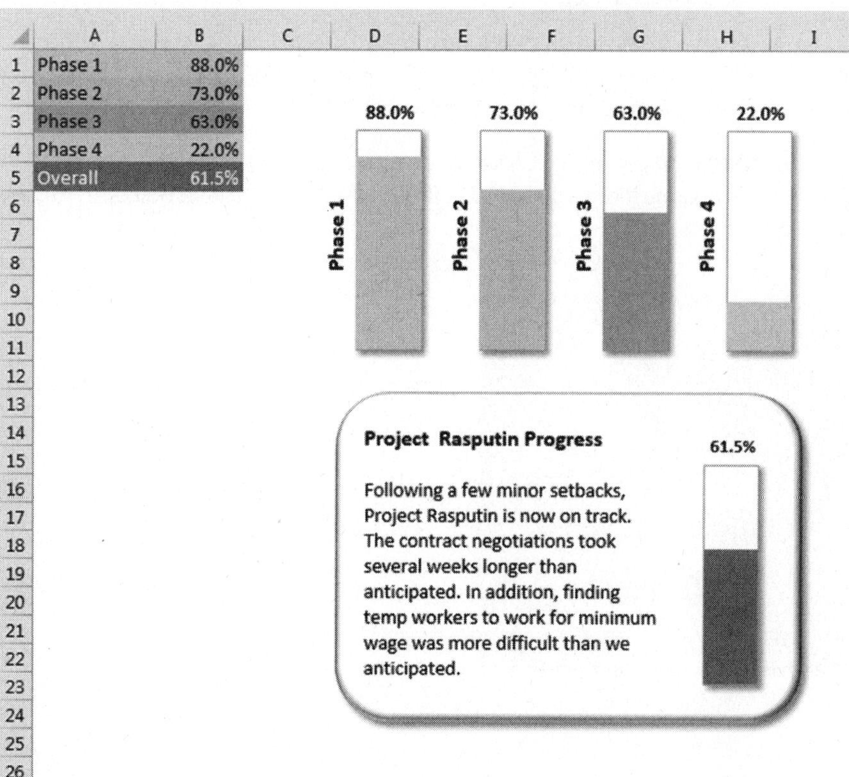

Figure 17-4: Five single data point charts.

Figure 17-5 shows another single data point chart. The chart, which shows the value in cell B21, is actually a line chart with markers. A shape object was copied and pasted to replace the normal line marker. The chart contains a second series, which was added for the secondary axis.

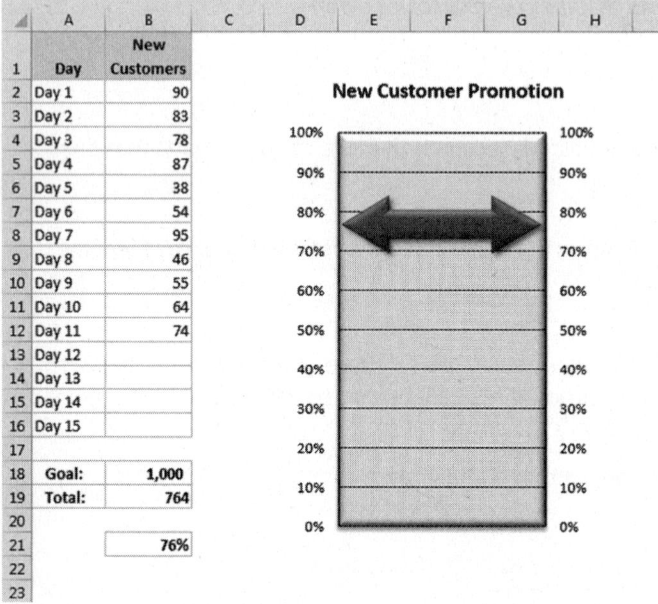

Figure 17-5: This single data point chart is a line chart, with a shape used as the marker.

Figure 17-6 shows another chart based on a single cell. It's a pie chart set up to resemble a gauge. Although this chart displays only one value (entered in cell B1), it actually uses three data points (in A4:A6).

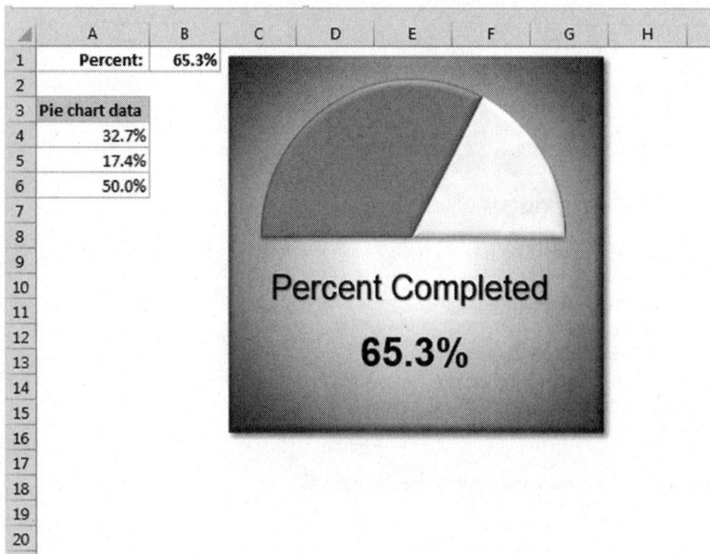

Figure 17-6: This chart resembles a speedometer gauge and displays a value between 0 and 100 percent.

One slice of the pie—the slice at the bottom—always consists of 50 percent. The pie has been rotated so that the 50 percent slice is at the bottom. Then that slice was hidden by specifying No Fill and No Border for the data point.

The other two slices are apportioned based on the value in cell B1. The formula in cell A4 is

```
=MIN(B1,100%)/2
```

This formula uses the MIN function to display the smaller of two values: either the value in cell B1 or 100 percent. It then divides this value by 2 because only the top half of the pie is relevant. Using the MIN function prevents the chart from displaying more than 100 percent.

The formula in cell A5 simply calculates the remaining part of the pie—the part to the right of the gauge's "needle":

```
=50%-A4
```

The chart's title (Percent Completed) was moved below the half-pie. A linked text box displays the percent completed value in cell B1.

Displaying conditional colors in a column chart

This section describes how to create a column chart in which the color of each column depends on the value that it's displaying. Figure 17-7 shows such a chart. (It's more impressive when you see it in color.) The data used to create the chart is in range A2:F14.

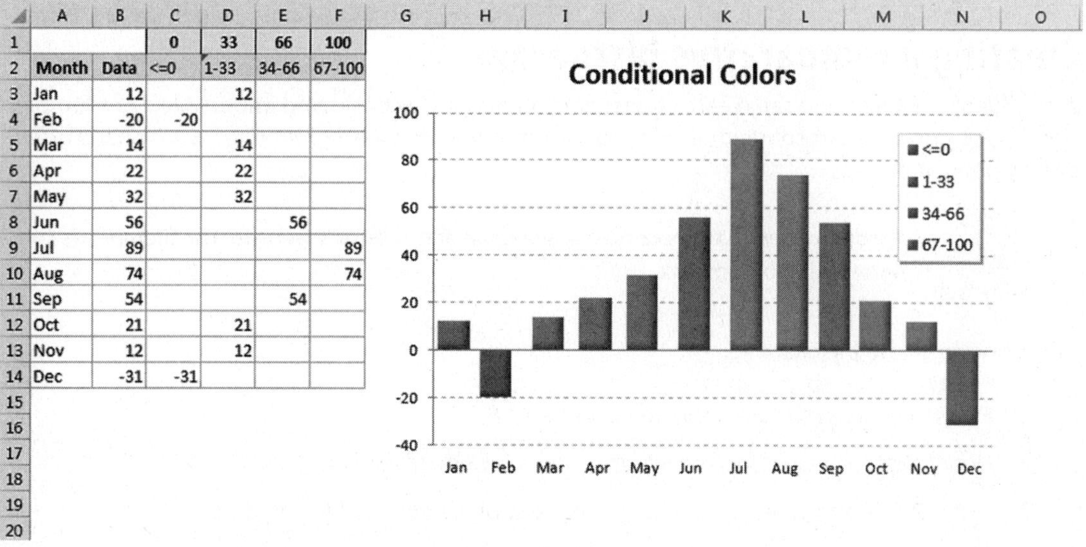

	A	B	C	D	E	F
1			0	33	66	100
2	Month	Data	<=0	1-33	34-66	67-100
3	Jan	12		12		
4	Feb	-20	-20			
5	Mar	14		14		
6	Apr	22		22		
7	May	32		32		
8	Jun	56			56	
9	Jul	89				89
10	Aug	74				74
11	Sep	54			54	
12	Oct	21		21		
13	Nov	12		12		
14	Dec	-31	-31			
15						
16						
17						
18						
19						
20						

Figure 17-7: The color of the column varies with the value.

On the Web

A workbook with this example is available at this book's website. The filename is conditional colors.xlsx.

This chart actually displays four data series, but some data is missing for each series. The data for the chart is entered into column B. Formulas in columns C:F determine which series the number belongs to by referencing the cut-off values in row 1. For example, the formula in cell C3 is

```
=IF(B3<=$C$1,B3,"")
```

If the value in column B is less than the value in cell C1, the value goes in this column. The formulas are set up such that a value in column B goes into only one column in the row.

The formula in cell D3 is a bit more complex because it must determine whether cell C3 is greater than the value in cell C1 and less than or equal to the value in cell D1:

```
=IF(AND($B3>C$1,$B3<=D$1),$B3,"")
```

The four data series are overlaid on top of each other in the chart. The trick involves setting the Series Overlap value to a large number. This setting determines the spacing between the series. Use the Series Options section of the Format Data Series task pane to adjust this setting. That section has another setting, Gap Width. In this case, the Gap Width essentially controls the width of the columns.

Note

Series Overlap and Gap Width apply to the entire chart. If you change the setting for one series, the other series change to the same value.

Creating a comparative histogram

With a bit of creativity, you can create charts that you may have considered impossible. For example, Figure 17-8 shows a chart sometimes referred to as a *comparative histogram chart.* Such charts often display population data.

On the Web

A workbook with this example is available at this book's website. The filename is comparative histogram.xlsx.

Here's how to create the chart:

1. Enter the data in A1:C8, as shown in Figure 17-8.

   Notice that the values for females are entered as negative values.

2. Select A1:C8 and create a bar chart. Use the subtype labeled Clustered Bar.
3. Select the horizontal axis and display the Format Axis task pane.

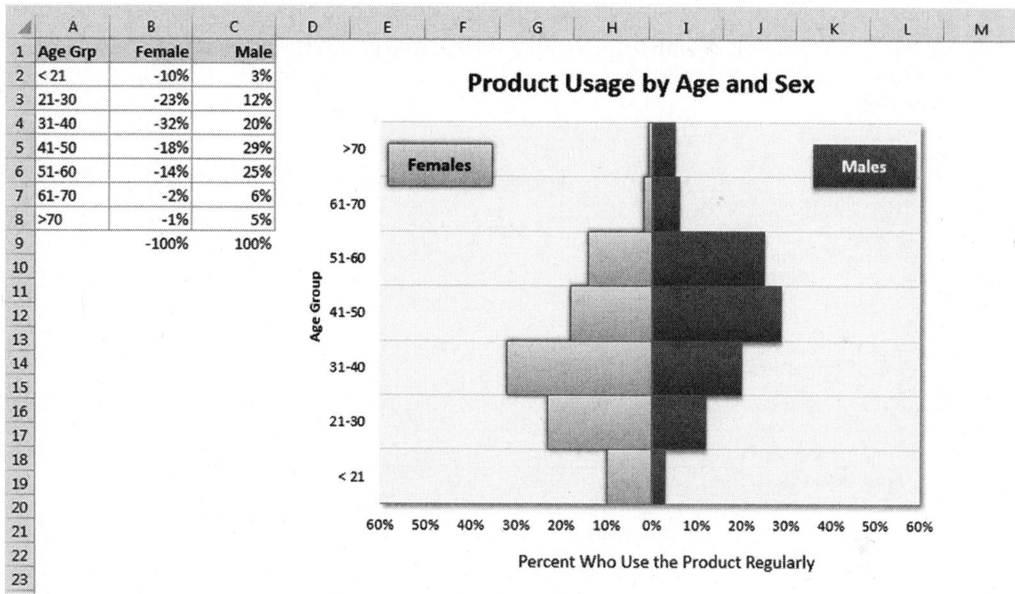

Age Grp	Female	Male
< 21	-10%	3%
21-30	-23%	12%
31-40	-32%	20%
41-50	-18%	29%
51-60	-14%	25%
61-70	-2%	6%
>70	-1%	5%
	-100%	100%

Figure 17-8: A comparative histogram.

4. Expand the Number section and specify the following custom number format:

   0%;0%;0%

   This custom format eliminates the negative signs in the percentages.
5. Select the vertical axis and display the Format Axis task pane.

   In the Tick Marks section, set all tick marks to None, and in the Labels section, set the Label Position option to Low.
6. This setting keeps the vertical axis in the center of the chart but displays the axis labels at the left side.
7. Select either of the data series and display the Format Data Series task pane.
8. In the Series Options section, set the Series Overlap to 100% and the Gap Width to 0%.
9. Delete the legend and add two text boxes to the chart (Females and Males) to substitute for the legend.
10. Apply other formatting and labels as desired.

Creating a Gantt chart

A *Gantt chart* is a horizontal bar chart often used in project management applications. Although Excel doesn't support Gantt charts per se, creating a simple Gantt chart is fairly easy. The key is getting your data set up properly.

Figure 17-9 shows a Gantt chart that depicts the schedule for a project that is in the range A2:C13. The horizontal axis represents the total time span of the project, and each bar represents a project task. The viewer can quickly see the duration for each task and identify overlapping tasks.

On the Web

A workbook with this example is available at this book's website. The filename is gantt chart.xlsx.

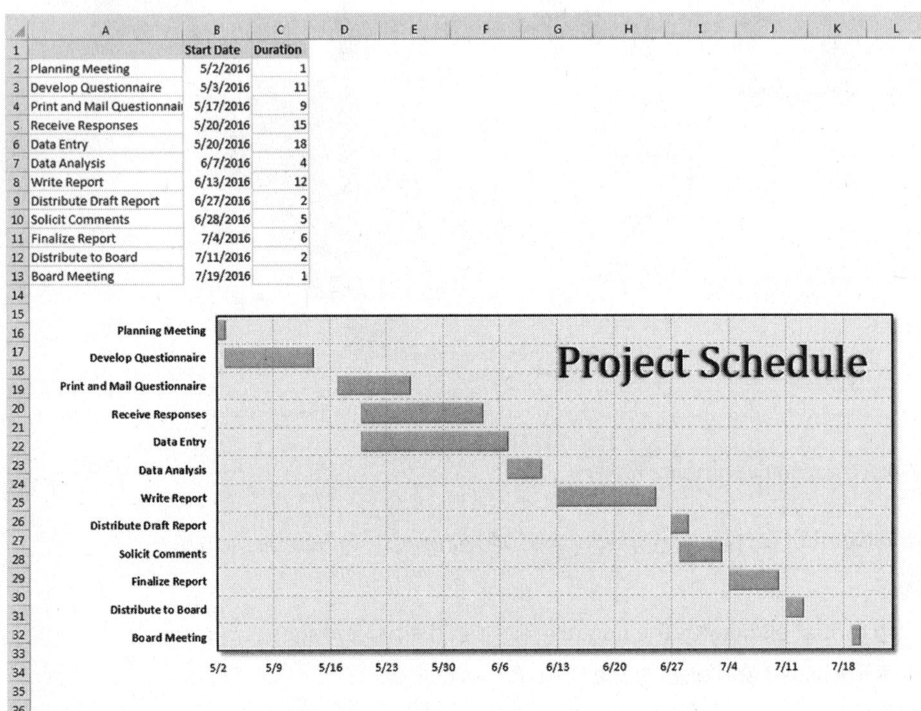

	Start Date	Duration
Planning Meeting	5/2/2016	1
Develop Questionnaire	5/3/2016	11
Print and Mail Questionnai	5/17/2016	9
Receive Responses	5/20/2016	15
Data Entry	5/20/2016	18
Data Analysis	6/7/2016	4
Write Report	6/13/2016	12
Distribute Draft Report	6/27/2016	2
Solicit Comments	6/28/2016	5
Finalize Report	7/4/2016	6
Distribute to Board	7/11/2016	2
Board Meeting	7/19/2016	1

Figure 17-9: You can create a simple Gantt chart from a bar chart.

Column A contains the task name, column B contains the corresponding start date, and column C contains the duration of the task, in days. Note that cell A1 does *not* have a descriptive label. Leaving that cell empty ensures that Excel does not use columns A and B as the category axis.

Follow these steps to create this chart:

1. Select the range A1:C13 and create a Stacked Bar Chart.
2. Delete the legend.
3. Select the category (vertical) axis and display the Format Axis task pane.
4. In the Axis Options section, specify Categories in Reverse Order to display the tasks in order, starting at the top. Choose Horizontal Axis Crosses at Maximum Category to display the dates at the bottom.
5. Select the Start Date data series and display the Format Data Series task pane.
6. In the Series Options section, set the Series Overlap to 100%. In the Fill section, specify No Fill. In the Border section, specify No Line.

   These steps effectively hide the data series.

7. Select the value (horizontal) axis and display the Format Axis task pane.
8. In the Axis Options, adjust the Minimum and Maximum settings to accommodate the dates that you want to display on the axis.

   You can enter a date value, and Excel converts it to a date serial number. In the example, the Minimum is 5/2/2016, and the Maximum is 7/24/2016.
9. Apply other formatting as desired.

Handling missing data

Sometimes data that you're charting may be missing one or more data points. As shown in the accompanying figure, Excel offers three ways to handle the missing data:

- **Gaps:** Missing data is simply ignored, and the data series will have a gap.

  This is the default.
- **Zero:** Missing data is treated as zero.
- **Connect with Line:** Missing data is interpolated—calculated by using data on either side of the missing point(s).

  This option is available only for line charts, area charts, and XY charts.

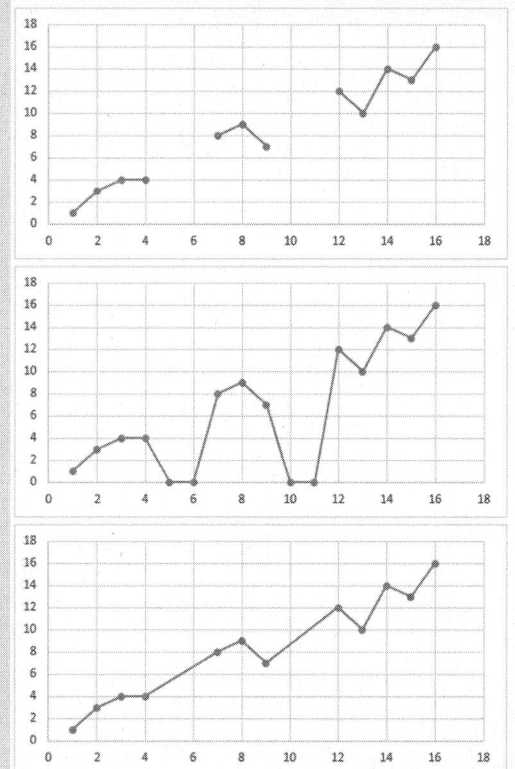

continued

continued

To specify how to deal with missing data for a chart, choose Chart Tools ➜ Design ➜ Data ➜ Select Data. In the Select Data Source dialog box, click the Hidden and Empty Cells button. Excel displays its Hidden and Empty Cell Settings dialog box. Make your choice in the dialog box. The option that you select applies to the entire chart, and you can't set a different option for different series in the same chart.

Normally, a chart doesn't display data that's in a hidden row or columns. You can use the Hidden and Empty Cell Settings dialog box to force a chart to use hidden data.

Creating a box plot

A *box plot* (sometimes known as a *quartile plot*) is often used to summarize data. Figure 17-10 shows a box plot created for four groups of data. The raw data appears in columns A through D. The range G2:J7, used in the chart, contains formulas that summarize the data. Table 17.1 lists the formulas in column G (which were copied to the three columns to the right).

On the Web

A workbook with this example is available at this book's website. The filename is box plot.xlsx.

	A	B	C	D
1	Group 1	Group 2	Group 3	Group 4
2	1,664	2,646	2,768	657
3	1,084	2,465	2,265	5,034
4	1,780	912	3,379	4,756
5	144	2,319	3,345	3,370
6	921	553	2,132	1,575
7	2,402	2,349	3,120	1,474
8	2,253	2,575	1,731	4,503
9	2,458	2,144	2,242	3,395
10	1,031	850	3,016	1,363
11	2,101	2,552	2,640	2,670
12	1,312	1,472	3,596	597
13	2,422	2,530	869	3,822
14	1,376	1,317	1,994	3,340
15	667	2,347	2,929	2,757
16	652	2,051	1,487	651
17	1,380	1,645	1,884	4,196
18	1,961	1,962	4,543	2,041
19	1,794	2,243	4,415	272
20	2,022	385	1,685	3,644
21	2,059	432	1,442	3,040
22	544	2,265	1,364	3,656
23	2,254	302	2,279	3,525
24	2,115	2,433	2,575	3,023
25	1,943	1,501	2,694	1,306
26	1,091	1,408	1,677	1,559

	F	G	H	I	J
1		Group 1	Group 2	Group 3	Group 4
2	25th Percentile	1,084	1,317	1,731	1,474
3	Minimum	144	302	869	272
4	Mean	1,577	1,746	2,483	2,649
5	50th Percentile	1,780	2,051	2,279	3,023
6	Maximum	2,458	2,646	4,543	5,034
7	75th Percentile	2,101	2,349	3,016	3,644

Figure 17-10: This box plot summarizes the data in columns A through D.

Table 17-1: Formulas Used to Create a Box Plot

Cell	Calculation	Formula
G2	25th Percentile	`=QUARTILE(A2:A26,1)`
G3	Minimum	`=MIN(A2:A26)`
G4	Mean	`=AVERAGE(A2:A26)`
G5	50th Percentile	`=QUARTILE(A2:A26,2)`
G6	Maximum	`=MAX(A2:A26)`
G7	75th Percentile	`=QUARTILE(A2:A26,3)`

Follow these steps to create the box plot:

1. Select the range F1:J7 and create a line chart with markers.
2. Choose Chart Tools ➜ Design ➜ Data ➜ Switch Row/Column to change the orientation of the chart.
3. Choose Chart Tools ➜ Design ➜ Chart Layouts ➜ Add Chart Element ➜ Up/Down Bars to add up/down bars that connect the first data series (25th Percentile) with the last data series (75th Percentile).
4. Remove the markers from the 25th Percentile series and the 75th Percentile series.
5. Choose Chart Tools ➜ Design ➜ Chart Layouts ➜ Add Chart Element ➜ Lines ➜ High-Low Lines to add a vertical line between each point to connect the Minimum and Maximum data series.
6. Remove the lines from each of the six data series.
7. Change the series marker to a horizontal line for the following series: Minimum, Maximum, and 50th Percentile.
8. Make other formatting changes as required.

The chart shown here does not have a legend. It's been replaced with a graphic that explains how to read the chart. The legend for this chart displays the series in the order in which they are plotted—which is not the optimal order and can be very confusing. Unfortunately, you can't change the plot order because the order is important. (The up/down bars use the first and last series.) Creating a descriptive graphic seems like a good alternative to a confusing legend.

Tip

After performing all these steps, you may want to create a template to simplify the creation of additional box plots. Right-click the chart and choose Save as Template.

Plotting every *n*th data point

Normally, Excel doesn't plot data that resides in a hidden row or column. You can sometimes use this to your advantage because it's an easy way to control what data appears in the chart.

Suppose you have a lot of data in a column and you want to plot only every 10th data point. One way to accomplish this is to use filtering in conjunction with a formula. Figure 17-11 shows a two-column table with filtering in effect. The chart plots only the data in the visible (filtered) rows and ignores the values in the hidden rows.

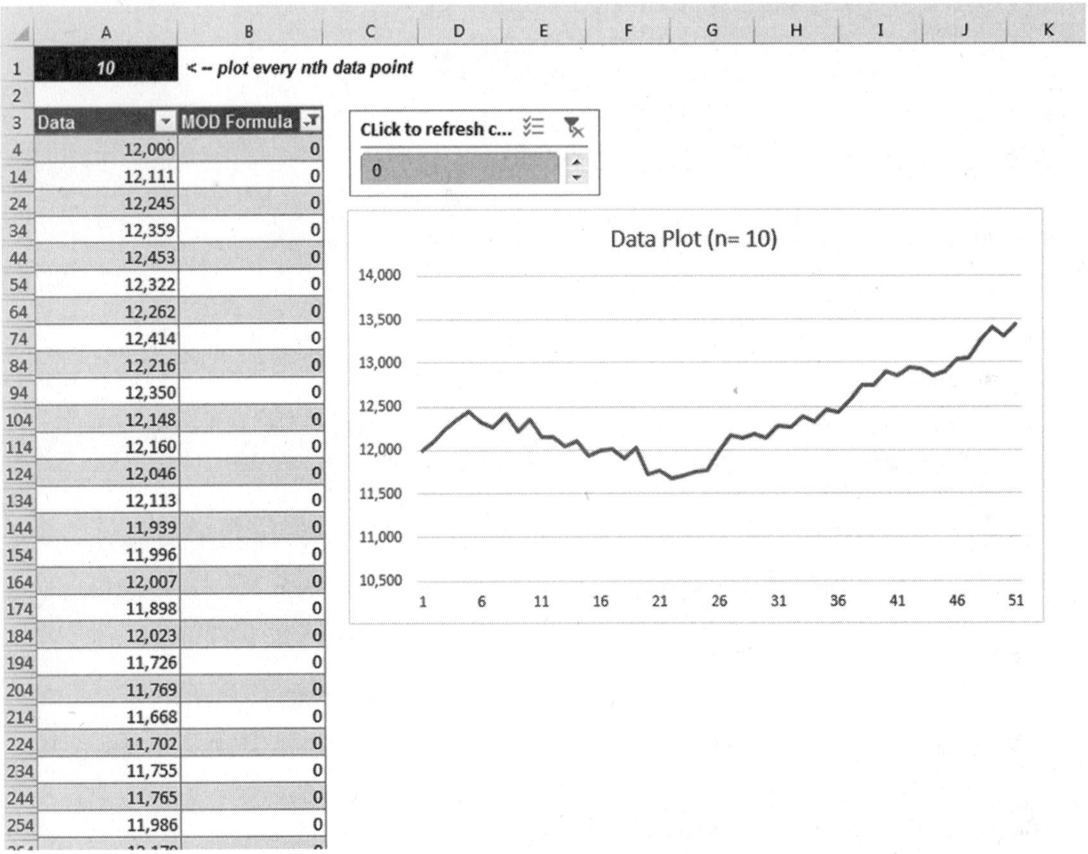

	A	B
1	10	<-- plot every nth data point
2		
3	Data	MOD Formula
4	12,000	0
14	12,111	0
24	12,245	0
34	12,359	0
44	12,453	0
54	12,322	0
64	12,262	0
74	12,414	0
84	12,216	0
94	12,350	0
104	12,148	0
114	12,160	0
124	12,046	0
134	12,113	0
144	11,939	0
154	11,996	0
164	12,007	0
174	11,898	0
184	12,023	0
194	11,726	0
204	11,769	0
214	11,668	0
224	11,702	0
234	11,755	0
244	11,765	0
254	11,986	0

CLick to refresh c...

0

Data Plot (n= 10)

Figure 17-11: This chart plots every *n*th data point (specified in A1) by ignoring data in the rows hidden by filtering.

On the Web

The example in this section, named plot every nth data point.xlsx, is available at this book's website.

Cell A1 contains the value 10. The value in this cell determines which rows to hide. Column B contains identical formulas that use the value in cell A1. For example, the formula in cell B4 is as follows:

```
=MOD(ROW()-ROW($A$4),$A$1)
```

This formula subtracts the current row number from the first data row number in the table and uses the MOD function to calculate the remainder when that value is divided by the value in A1. As a result, every *n*th cell (beginning with row 4) contains 0. Use the filter drop-down list in cell B3 to specify a filter that shows only the rows that contain a 0 in column B.

Note

If you change the value in cell A1, you must respecify the filter criteria for column B because the rows will not hide automatically. Just click the filter icon in the column heading and then click OK. The example uses a table Slicer, so clicking the 0 value applies the filter. Add a Slicer to a table by choosing Table Tools ➜ Design ➜ Tools ➜ Insert Slicer.

Although this example uses a table (created using Insert ➜ Tables ➜ Table), the technique also works with a normal range of data as long as it has column headers. Choose Data ➜ Sort & Filter ➜ Filter to enable filtering.

Identifying maximum and minimum values in a chart

Figure 17-12 shows a line chart that has its maximum and minimum values identified with a circle and a square, respectively. These identifiers are the result of using two additional series in the chart. You can achieve this effect manually, by adding two shapes, but using the additional series makes it fully automated.

On the Web

This example is available at this book's website. The filename is identify max and min data points.xlsx.

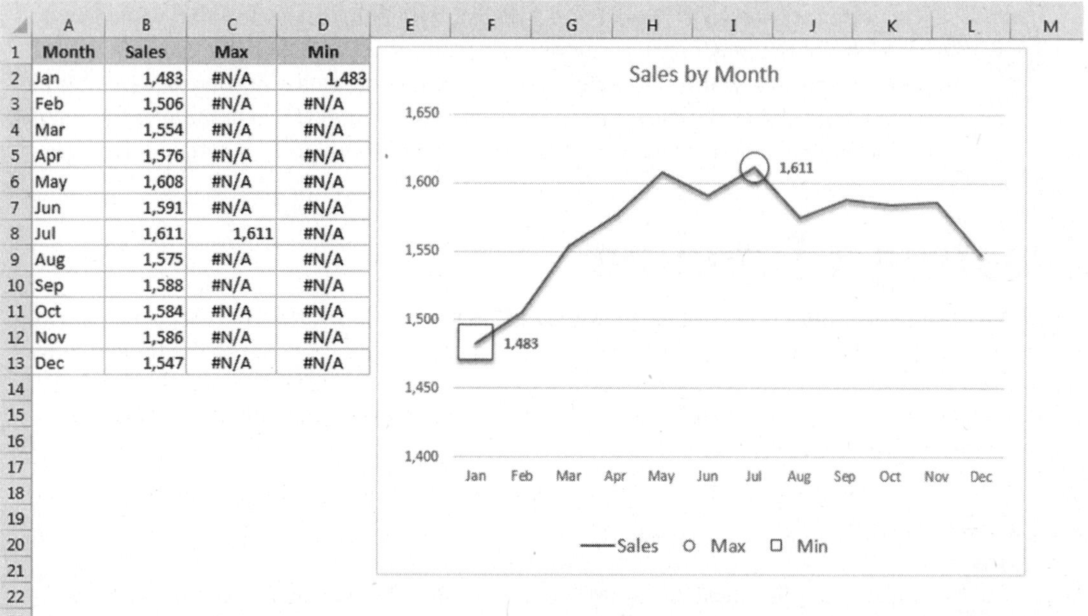

	A	B	C	D
1	Month	Sales	Max	Min
2	Jan	1,483	#N/A	1,483
3	Feb	1,506	#N/A	#N/A
4	Mar	1,554	#N/A	#N/A
5	Apr	1,576	#N/A	#N/A
6	May	1,608	#N/A	#N/A
7	Jun	1,591	#N/A	#N/A
8	Jul	1,611	1,611	#N/A
9	Aug	1,575	#N/A	#N/A
10	Sep	1,588	#N/A	#N/A
11	Oct	1,584	#N/A	#N/A
12	Nov	1,586	#N/A	#N/A
13	Dec	1,547	#N/A	#N/A

Figure 17-12: This chart uses two XY series to highlight the maximum and minimum data points in the line series.

Start by creating a line chart using the data in range A1:B13:

1. Enter the following formula in cell C2:

```
=IF(B2=MAX($B$2:$B$13),B2,NA())
```

2. Enter this formula in cell D2:

```
=IF(B2=MIN($B$2:$B$13),B2,NA())
```

3. Copy range C2:D2 down, ending in row 13. These formulas display the maximum and minimum values in column B, and all other cells display *#NA*.
4. Select C1:D13 and press Ctrl+C.
5. Select the chart and choose Home ➜ Clipboard ➜ Paste ➜ Paste Special. In the Paste Special dialog box, choose New series, Values (Y) in Columns, and Series Names in First Row. This adds two new series, named Max and Min.
6. Select the Max series and access the Format Data Series task pane. Specify a circle marker, with no fill, and increase the size of the marker.
7. Repeat step 6 for the Min series, but use a large square for the marker.
8. Add data labels to the Max and Min series. (The *#NA* values will not appear.)
9. Apply other cosmetic formatting as desired.

Note

The formulas entered in steps 1 and 2 display *#NA* if the corresponding value in column B is not the maximum or minimum. In a line chart, an #NA value causes a gap to appear in the line, which is exactly what is needed. As a result, only one data point is plotted (or more, if there is a tie for the maximum or minimum). If two or more values are tied for the minimum or maximum, all the values will be identified with a square or circle.

Creating a Timeline

Figure 17-13 shows a scatter chart, set up to display a timeline of events. The chart uses the data in columns A and B, and the series uses vertical error bars to connect each marker to the timeline (the horizontal value axis). The text consists of data labels from column C. The vertical value axis for the chart is hidden, but it is set to display Values In Reverse Order so that the earliest events display higher in the vertical dimension.

This type of chart is limited to relatively small amounts of text. Otherwise, the data labels wrap, and the text may be obscured.

On the Web

This example is available at this book's website. The filename is scatter chart timeline.xlsx.

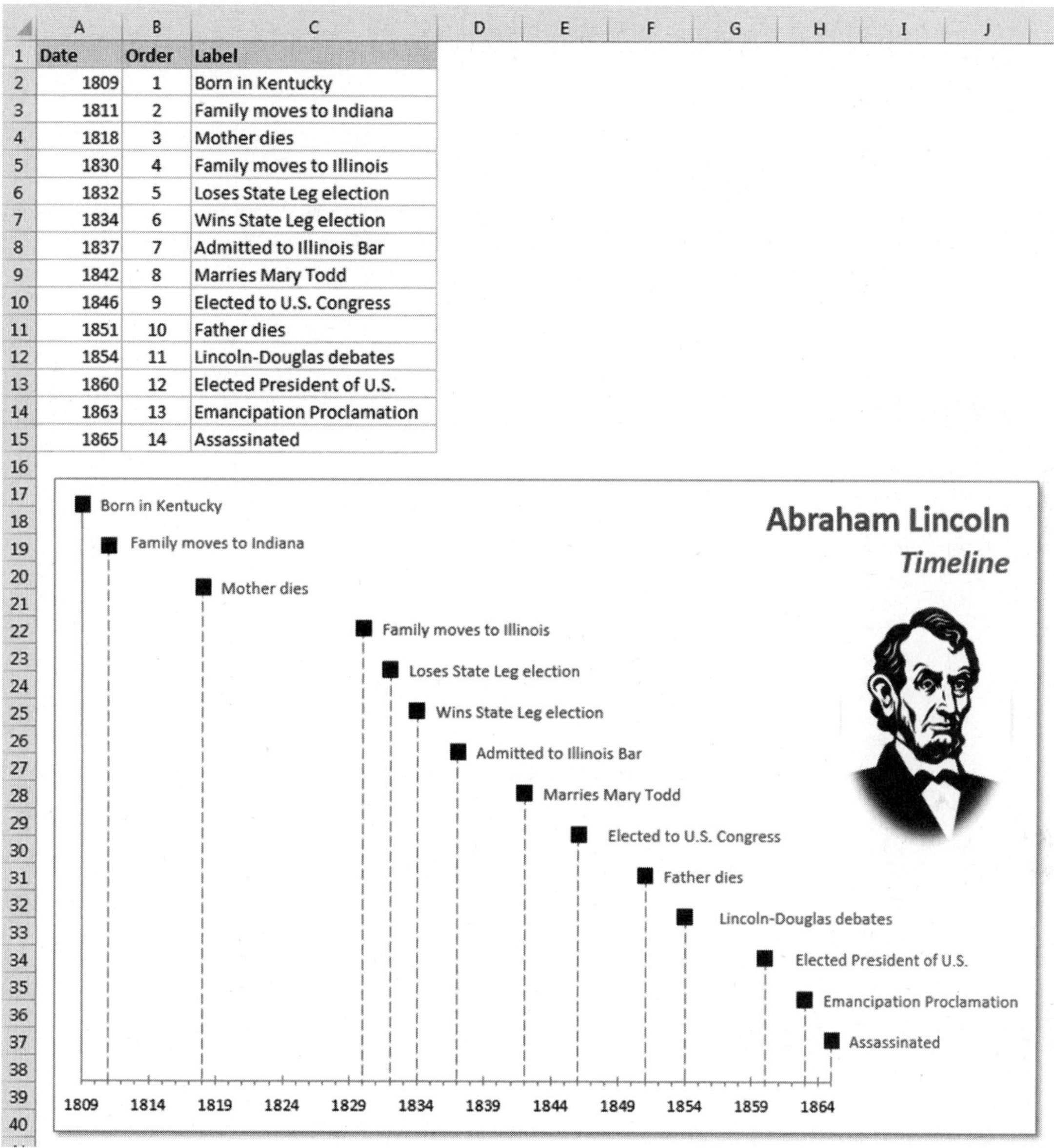

Date	Order	Label
1809	1	Born in Kentucky
1811	2	Family moves to Indiana
1818	3	Mother dies
1830	4	Family moves to Illinois
1832	5	Loses State Leg election
1834	6	Wins State Leg election
1837	7	Admitted to Illinois Bar
1842	8	Marries Mary Todd
1846	9	Elected to U.S. Congress
1851	10	Father dies
1854	11	Lincoln-Douglas debates
1860	12	Elected President of U.S.
1863	13	Emancipation Proclamation
1865	14	Assassinated

Figure 17-13: A scatter chart disguised as a timeline.

Plotting mathematical functions

The examples in this section demonstrate how to plot mathematical functions that use one variable (a 2D line chart) and two variables (a 3D surface chart). Some of the examples make use of Excel's Data Table feature, which enables you to evaluate a formula with varying input values.

Note

A Data Table is not the same as a table, created by choosing Insert ➜ Tables ➜ Table.

Plotting functions with one variable

An XY chart (also known as a *scatter chart*) is useful for plotting various mathematical and trigonometric functions. For example, Figure 17-14 shows a plot of the SIN function. The chart plots *y* for values of *x* (expressed in radians) from –5 to +5 in increments of 0.5. Each pair of *x* and *y* values appears as a data point in the chart, and the points connect with a line.

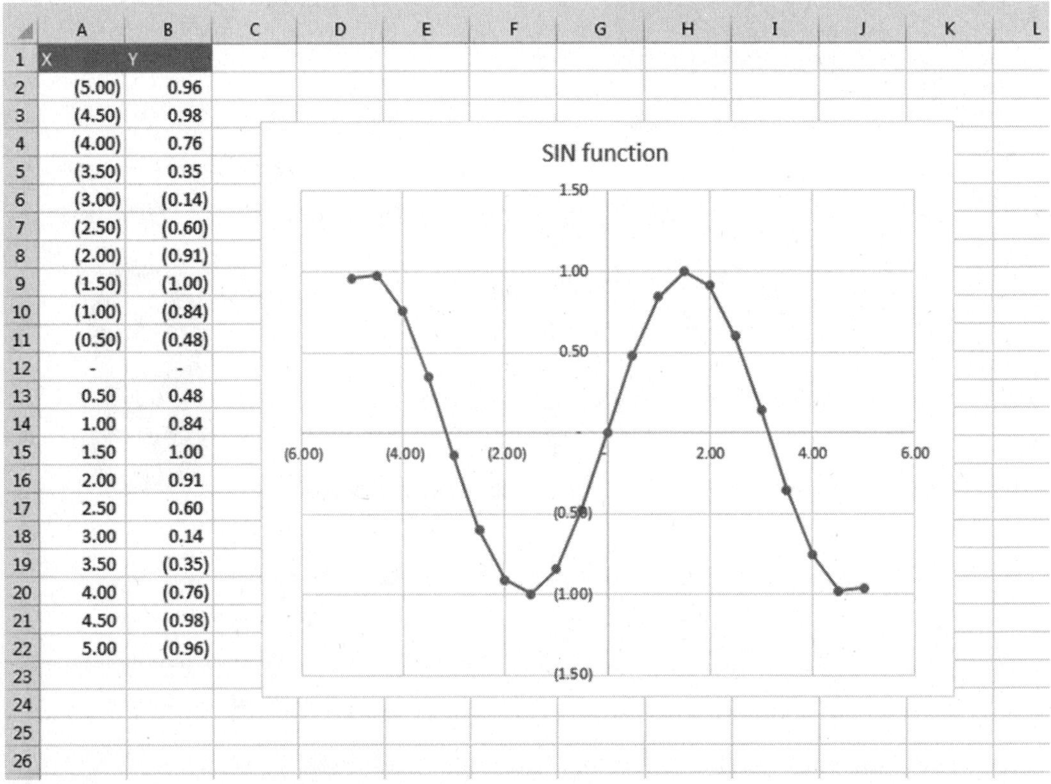

	A	B
1	X	Y
2	(5.00)	0.96
3	(4.50)	0.98
4	(4.00)	0.76
5	(3.50)	0.35
6	(3.00)	(0.14)
7	(2.50)	(0.60)
8	(2.00)	(0.91)
9	(1.50)	(1.00)
10	(1.00)	(0.84)
11	(0.50)	(0.48)
12	-	-
13	0.50	0.48
14	1.00	0.84
15	1.50	1.00
16	2.00	0.91
17	2.50	0.60
18	3.00	0.14
19	3.50	(0.35)
20	4.00	(0.76)
21	4.50	(0.98)
22	5.00	(0.96)

Figure 17-14: This chart plots the SIN(*x*).

Tip

Excel's trigonometric functions use angles expressed in radians. To convert degrees to radians, use the RADIANS function.

The function is expressed like this:

```
y = SIN(x)
```

The corresponding formula in cell B2 (which is copied to the cells below) is

```
=SIN(A2)
```

Figure 17-15 shows a general-purpose, single-variable plotting application. The data for the chart is calculated by a data table in columns I:J. Follow these steps to use this application:

1. Enter a formula in cell B7. The formula should contain at least one *x* variable.

   In the figure, the formula in cell B7 is

   ```
   =SIN(x^3)*COS(x^2)
   ```

2. Type the minimum value for *x* in cell B8.
3. Type the maximum value for *x* cell B9.

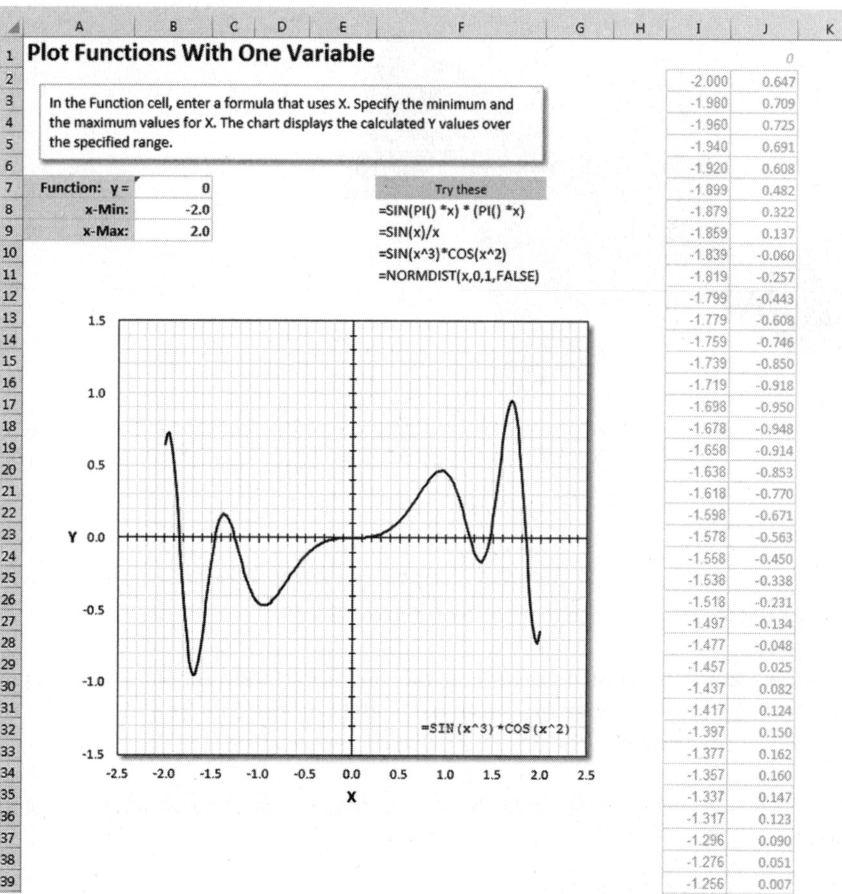

Figure 17-15: A general-purpose, single-variable plotting workbook.

The formula in cell B7 displays the value of *y* for the minimum value of *x*. The data table, however, evaluates the formula for 200 equally spaced values of *x*, and these values appear in the chart.

On the Web

This workbook, named function plot 2D.xlsx, is available at this book's website.

Plotting functions with two variables

The preceding section describes how to plot functions that use a single variable (*x*). You also can plot functions that use two variables. For example, the following function calculates a value of *z* for various values of two variables (*x* and *y*):

```
z = SIN(x)*COS(y)
```

Figure 17-16 shows a surface chart that plots the value of *z* for 25 *x* values ranging from –1 to 1 (in 0.1 increments) and for 25 *y* values ranging from –2 to 2 (in 0.2 increments).

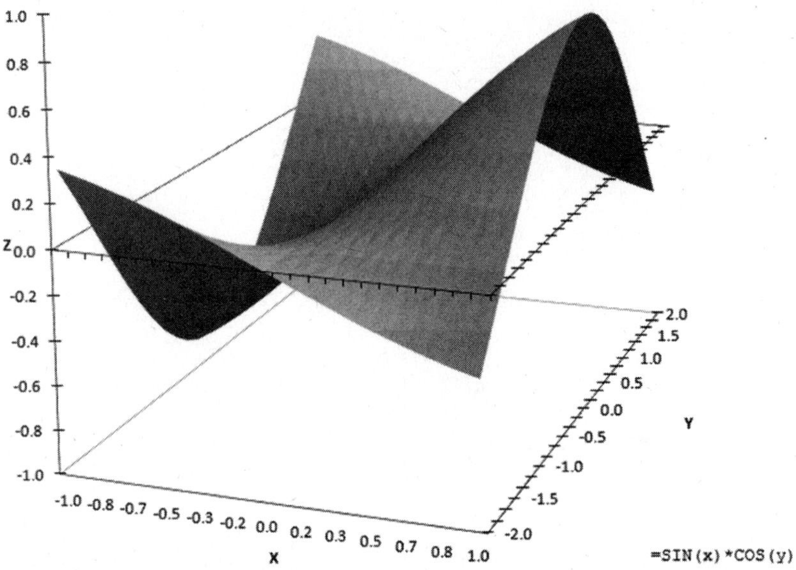

Figure 17-16: Using a surface chart to plot a function with two variables.

Figure 17-17 shows a general-purpose, two-variable plotting application, similar to the single-variable workbook described in the previous section. The data for the chart is a 25 × 25 data table in range M7:AL32 (not shown in the figure). To use this application

1. Enter a formula in cell B3. The formula should contain at least one *x* variable and at least one *y* variable.

   In the figure, the formula in cell B3 is

   ```
   =SIN(SQRT(x^2 + y^2))
   ```

2. Enter the minimum *x* value in cell B4 and the maximum *x* value in cell B5.
3. Enter the minimum *y* value in cell B6 and the maximum *y* value in cell B7.

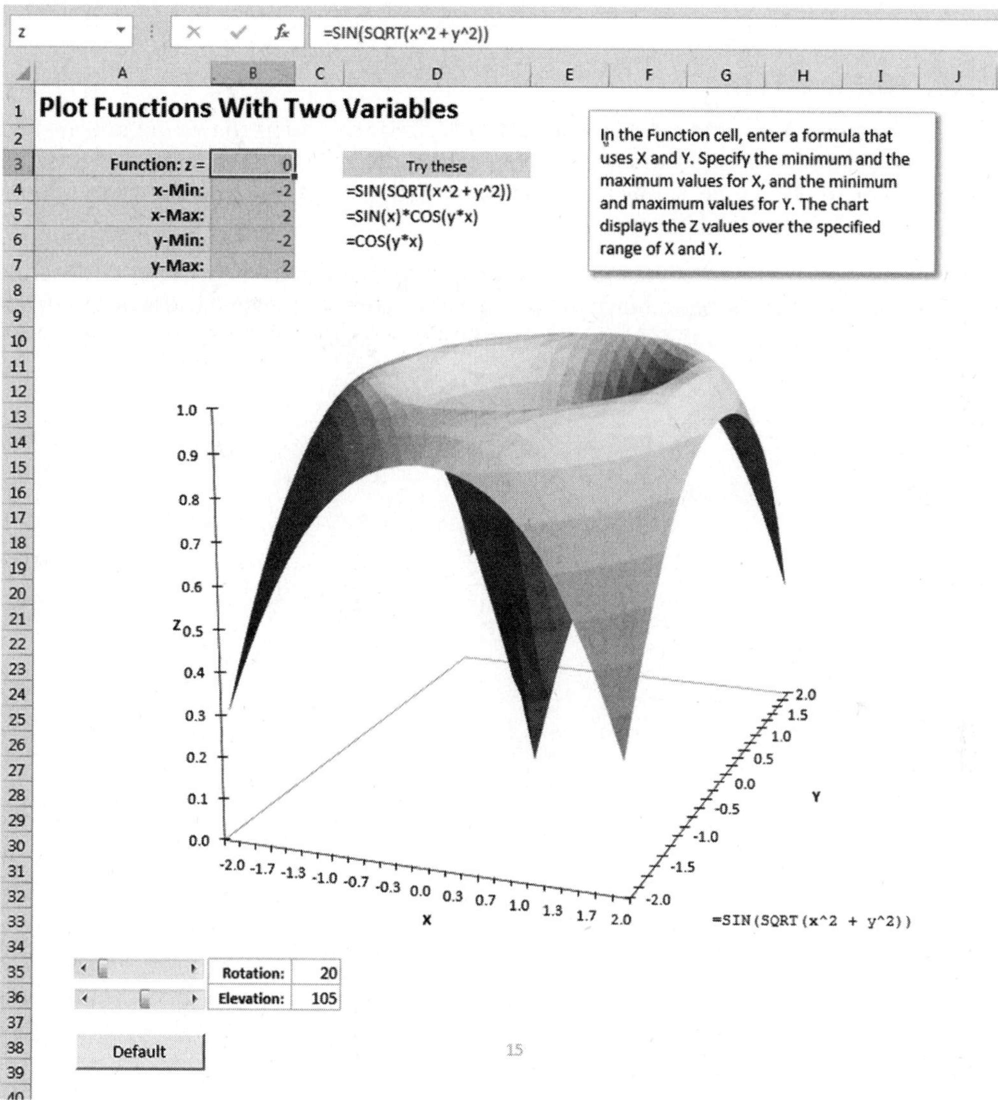

Figure 17-17: A general-purpose, two-variable plotting workbook.

The formula in cell B3 displays the value of *z* for the minimum values of *x* and *y*. The data table evaluates the formula for 25 equally spaced values of *x* and 25 equally spaced values of *y*. These values are plotted in the surface chart.

On the Web

This workbook, which is available at this book's website, contains simple macros that enable you to easily change the rotation and elevation of the chart by using scrollbars. The file is named function plot 3D.xlsm.

Plotting a circle

You can create an XY chart that draws a perfect circle. To do so, you need two ranges: one for the *x* values and another for the *y* values. The number of data points in the series determines the smoothness of the circle. Or you can simply select the Smoothed Line option in the Format Data Series dialog box (Line Style tab) for the data series.

Figure 17-18 shows a chart that uses 13 points to create a circle. If you work in degrees, generate a series of values such as the ones shown in column A. The series starts with 0 and increases in 30-degree increments. If you work in radians (column B), the first series starts with 0 and increments by π/6.

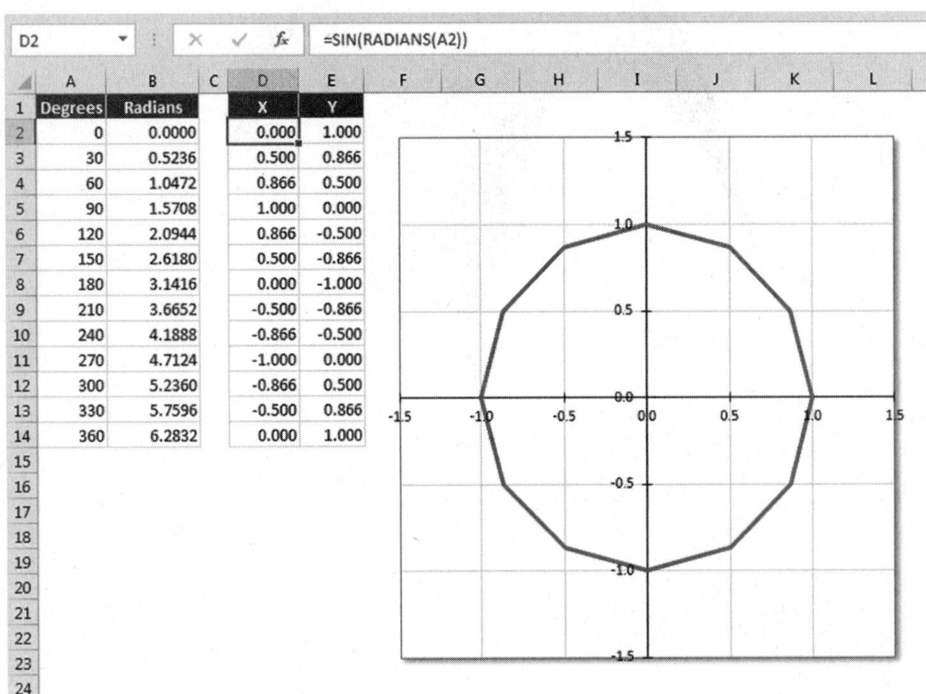

D2 =SIN(RADIANS(A2))

Degrees	Radians	X	Y
0	0.0000	0.000	1.000
30	0.5236	0.500	0.866
60	1.0472	0.866	0.500
90	1.5708	1.000	0.000
120	2.0944	0.866	-0.500
150	2.6180	0.500	-0.866
180	3.1416	0.000	-1.000
210	3.6652	-0.500	-0.866
240	4.1888	-0.866	-0.500
270	4.7124	-1.000	0.000
300	5.2360	-0.866	0.500
330	5.7596	-0.500	0.866
360	6.2832	0.000	1.000

Figure 17-18: Creating a circle using an XY chart.

The ranges used in the chart appear in columns D and E. If you work in degrees, the formula in cell D2 is

```
=SIN(RADIANS(A2))
```

The formula in cell E2 is

```
=COS(RADIANS(A2))
```

If you work in radians, use this formula in cell D2:

```
=SIN(B2)
```

And use this formula in cell E2:

```
=COS(B2)
```

The formulas in cells D2 and E2 are copied down to subsequent rows.

To plot a circle with more data points, you need to adjust the increment value and the number of data points in column A (or column B if working in radians). The final value should be the same as those shown in row 14. In degrees, the increment is 360 divided by the number of data points minus 1. In radians, the increment is π divided by (the number of data points minus 1, divided by 2).

Figure 17-19 shows a general circle plotting application that uses 37 data points. In range H27:H29, you can specify the *x* origin, the *y* origin, and the radius for the circle (these are named cells). A second series plots the origin as a single data point. In the figure, the circle's origin is at 2,3, and it has a radius of 7.25.

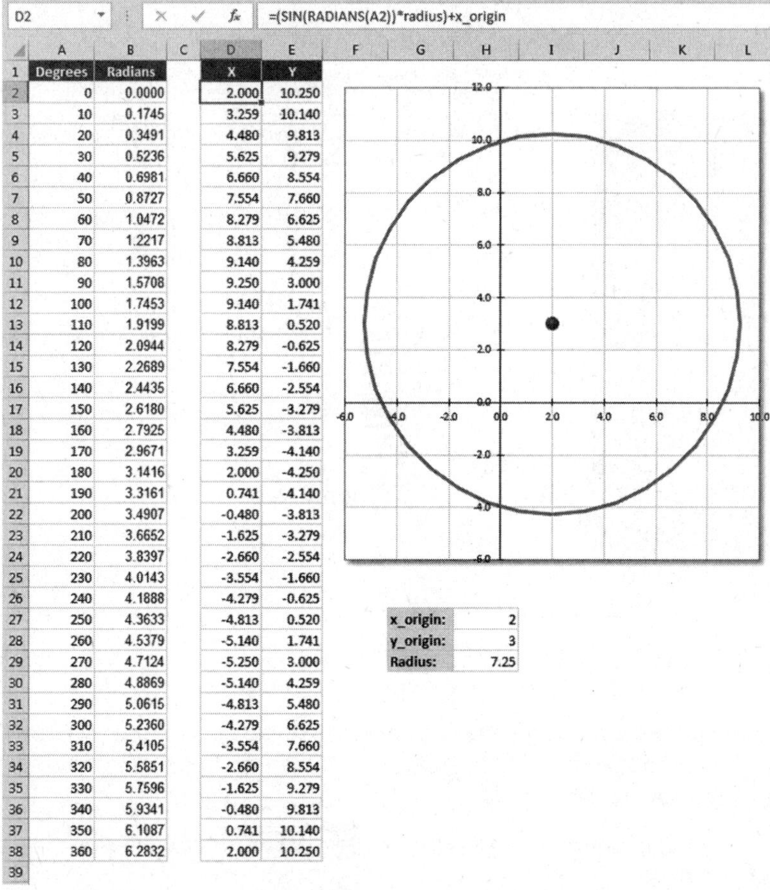

D2 =(SIN(RADIANS(A2))*radius)+x_origin

Degrees	Radians	X	Y
0	0.0000	2.000	10.250
10	0.1745	3.259	10.140
20	0.3491	4.480	9.813
30	0.5236	5.625	9.279
40	0.6981	6.660	8.554
50	0.8727	7.554	7.660
60	1.0472	8.279	6.625
70	1.2217	8.813	5.480
80	1.3963	9.140	4.259
90	1.5708	9.250	3.000
100	1.7453	9.140	1.741
110	1.9199	8.813	0.520
120	2.0944	8.279	-0.625
130	2.2689	7.554	-1.660
140	2.4435	6.660	-2.554
150	2.6180	5.625	-3.279
160	2.7925	4.480	-3.813
170	2.9671	3.259	-4.140
180	3.1416	2.000	-4.250
190	3.3161	0.741	-4.140
200	3.4907	-0.480	-3.813
210	3.6652	-1.625	-3.279
220	3.8397	-2.660	-2.554
230	4.0143	-3.554	-1.660
240	4.1888	-4.279	-0.625
250	4.3633	-4.813	0.520
260	4.5379	-5.140	1.741
270	4.7124	-5.250	3.000
280	4.8869	-5.140	4.259
290	5.0615	-4.813	5.480
300	5.2360	-4.279	6.625
310	5.4105	-3.554	7.660
320	5.5851	-2.660	8.554
330	5.7596	-1.625	9.279
340	5.9341	-0.480	9.813
350	6.1087	0.741	10.140
360	6.2832	2.000	10.250

x_origin:	2
y_origin:	3
Radius:	7.25

Figure 17-19: A general circle plotting application.

The formula in cell D2 is

```
=(SIN(RADIANS(A2))*radius)+x_origin
```

The formula in cell E2 is

```
=(COS(RADIANS(A2))*radius)+y_origin
```

On the Web

This example, named plot circles.xlsx, is available at this book's website.

Creating a clock chart

Figure 17-20 shows an XY chart formatted to look like a clock. It not only looks like a clock but also functions like a clock. There is really no reason why anyone would need to display a clock such as this on a worksheet, but creating the workbook was challenging, and you may find it instructive.

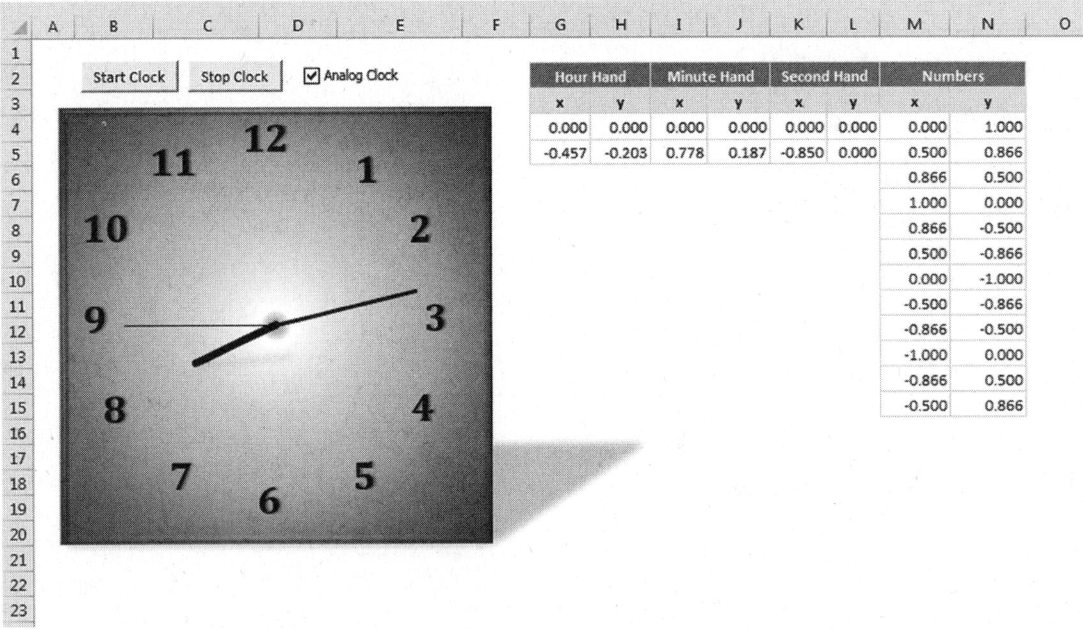

Hour Hand		Minute Hand		Second Hand		Numbers	
x	y	x	y	x	y	x	y
0.000	0.000	0.000	0.000	0.000	0.000	0.000	1.000
-0.457	-0.203	0.778	0.187	-0.850	0.000	0.500	0.866
						0.866	0.500
						1.000	0.000
						0.866	-0.500
						0.500	-0.866
						0.000	-1.000
						-0.500	-0.866
						-0.866	-0.500
						-1.000	0.000
						-0.866	0.500
						-0.500	0.866

Figure 17-20: This fully functional clock is actually an XY chart in disguise.

The chart uses four data series: one for the hour hand, one for the minute hand, one for the second hand, and one for the numbers. The last data series draws a circle with 12 points (but no line). The numbers consist of manually entered data labels.

The formulas listed in Table 17-2 use basic trigonometry to calculate the data series for the clock hands. (The range G4:L4 contains zero values, not formulas.)

Table 17-2: Formulas Used to Generate a Clock Chart

Cell	Description	Formula
G5	Origin of hour hand	`=0.5*SIN((HOUR(NOW())+(MINUTE(NOW())/60))*(2*PI()/12))`
H5	End of hour hand	`=0.5*COS((HOUR(NOW())+(MINUTE(NOW())/60))*(2*PI()/12))`
I5	Origin of minute hand	`=0.8*SIN((MINUTE(NOW())+(SECOND(NOW())/60))*(2*PI()/60))`
J5	End of minute hand	`=0.8*COS((MINUTE(NOW())+(SECOND(NOW())/60))*(2*PI()/60))`
K5	Origin of second hand	`=0.85*SIN(SECOND(NOW())*(2*PI()/60))`
L5	End of second hand	`=0.85*COS(SECOND(NOW())*(2*PI()/60))`

This workbook uses a simple VBA procedure that schedules an event every second, which causes the formula to recalculate.

In addition to the clock chart, the workbook contains a text box that displays the time using the NOW function, as shown in Figure 17-21. Normally hidden behind the analog clock, you can display this text box by deselecting the Analog Clock check box. A simple VBA procedure attached to the check box hides and unhides the chart, depending on the status of the check box.

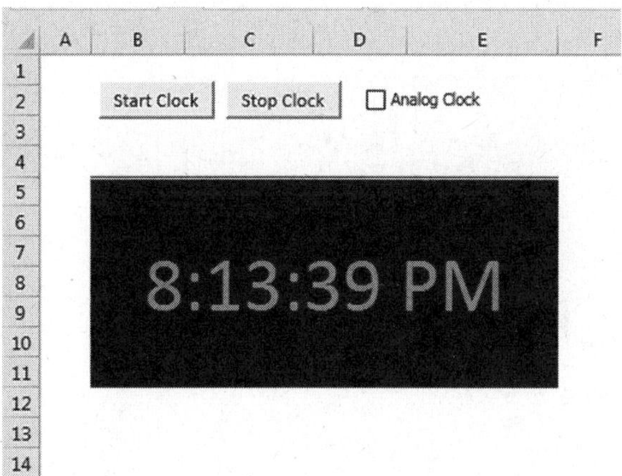

Figure 17-21: Displaying a digital clock in a worksheet is much easier but not as much fun to create.

On the Web

The workbook with the animated clock example appears at this book's website. The filename is clock chart.xlsx.

When you examine the workbook, keep the following points in mind:

- The ChartObject, named *ClockChart,* covers up a range named *DigitalClock,* which is used to display the time digitally.
- The two buttons on the worksheet are from the Forms group (Developer ➜ Controls ➜ Insert), and each has a VBA procedure assigned to it (`StartClock` and `StopClock`).
- Selecting the check box control executes a procedure named `cbClockType_Click`, which simply toggles the `Visible` property of the chart. When the chart is hidden, the digital clock is revealed.

- The `UpdateClock` procedure uses the `OnTime` method of the `Application` object. This method enables you to execute a procedure at a specific time. Before the `UpdateClock` procedure ends, it sets up a new `OnTime` event that occurs in one second. In other words, the `UpdateClock` procedure is called every second.
- The `UpdateClock` procedure inserts the following formula into the cell named *DigitalClock:*

```
=NOW()
```

- Inserting this formula causes the workbook to calculate, updating the clock.

Creating awesome designs

Figure 17-22 shows an example of an XY chart that displays hypocycloid curves using random values. This type of curve is the same as that generated by Hasbro's popular Spirograph toy, which you may remember from childhood.

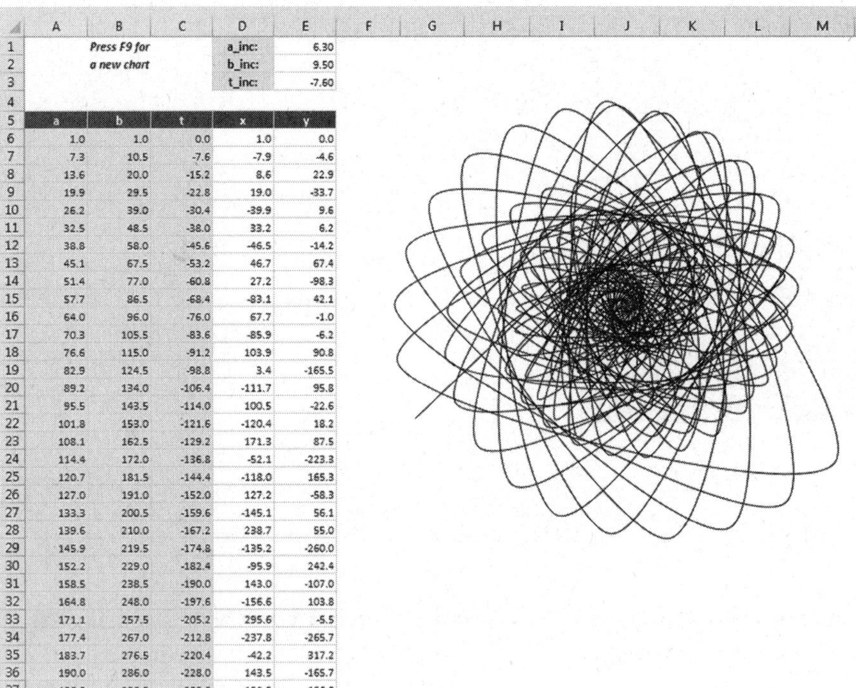

	A	B	C	D	E
1		*Press F9 for*		a_inc:	6.30
2		*a new chart*		b_inc:	9.50
3				t_inc:	-7.60
4					
5	a	b	t	x	y
6	1.0	1.0	0.0	1.0	0.0
7	7.3	10.5	-7.6	-7.9	-4.6
8	13.6	20.0	-15.2	8.6	22.9
9	19.9	29.5	-22.8	19.0	-33.7
10	26.2	39.0	-30.4	-39.9	9.6
11	32.5	48.5	-38.0	33.2	6.2
12	38.8	58.0	-45.6	-46.5	-14.2
13	45.1	67.5	-53.2	46.7	67.4
14	51.4	77.0	-60.8	27.2	-98.3
15	57.7	86.5	-68.4	-83.1	42.1
16	64.0	96.0	-76.0	67.7	-1.0
17	70.3	105.5	-83.6	-85.9	-6.2
18	76.6	115.0	-91.2	103.9	90.8
19	82.9	124.5	-98.8	3.4	-165.5
20	89.2	134.0	-106.4	-111.7	95.8
21	95.5	143.5	-114.0	100.5	-22.6
22	101.8	153.0	-121.6	-120.4	18.2
23	108.1	162.5	-129.2	171.3	87.5
24	114.4	172.0	-136.8	-52.1	-223.3
25	120.7	181.5	-144.4	-118.0	165.3
26	127.0	191.0	-152.0	127.2	-58.3
27	133.3	200.5	-159.6	-145.1	56.1
28	139.6	210.0	-167.2	238.7	55.0
29	145.9	219.5	-174.8	-135.2	-260.0
30	152.2	229.0	-182.4	-95.9	242.4
31	158.5	238.5	-190.0	143.0	-107.0
32	164.8	248.0	-197.6	-156.6	103.8
33	171.1	257.5	-205.2	295.6	-5.5
34	177.4	267.0	-212.8	-237.8	-265.7
35	183.7	276.5	-220.4	-42.2	317.2
36	190.0	286.0	-228.0	143.5	-165.7

Figure 17-22: A hypocycloid curve.

On the Web

This book's website contains two hypocycloid workbooks: the simple example shown in Figure 17-22 (named hypocycloid chart.xlsx) and a much more complex example (named hypocycloid animated.xlsm) that adds animation and a few other accoutrements. The animated version uses VBA macros.

The chart uses data in columns D and E (the *x* and *y* ranges). These columns contain formulas that rely on data in columns A through C. The formulas in columns A through C rely on the values stored in E1:E3. The data column for the *x* values (column D) consists of the following formula:

```
=(A6-B6)*COS(C6)+B6*COS((A6/B6-1)*C6)
```

The formula for the *y* values (column E) is as follows:

```
=(A6-B6)*SIN(C6)-B6*SIN((A6/B6-1)*C6)
```

Pressing F9 recalculates the worksheet, which generates new random increment values for E1:E3 and creates a new display in the chart. The variety (and beauty) of charts generated using these formulas may amaze you.

Working with Trendlines

With some charts, you may want to plot a trendline that describes the data. A *trendline* points out general trends in your data. In some cases, you can forecast data with trendlines. A single series can have more than one trendline.

To add a trendline in Excel 2016, select the chart series, click the Chart Elements icon (to the right of the chart), and select Trendline. The default trendline is Linear, but you can expand the selection choice and choose a different type. For additional options (and more control over the trendline), choose More Options to display the Format Trendline task pane (see Figure 17-23).

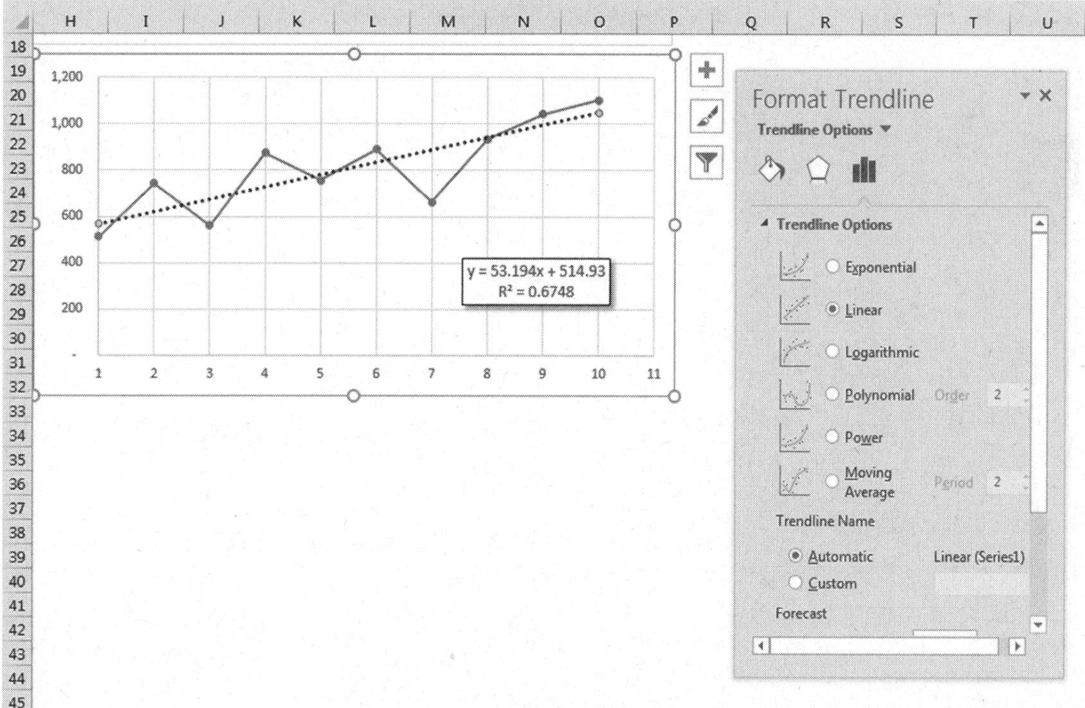

Figure 17-23: Use the Format Trendline task pane to fine-tune trendlines.

The type of trendline that you choose depends on your data. Linear trends are the most common type, but you can describe some data more effectively with another type.

On the Trendline Options tab, you can specify a name to appear in the legend and the number of periods that you want to forecast (if any). Additional options there enable you to set the intercept value, specify that the equation used for the trendline should appear on the chart, and choose whether the R-squared value appears on the chart.

When Excel inserts a trendline, it may look like a new data series, but it's not. It's a new chart element with a name, such as Series 1 Trendline 1. And, of course, a trendline does not have a corresponding SERIES formula.

Linear trendlines

Figure 17-24 shows two charts. The first chart depicts a data series without a trendline. As you can see, the data seems to be "linear" over time. The next chart is the same chart but with a linear trendline that shows the trend in the data.

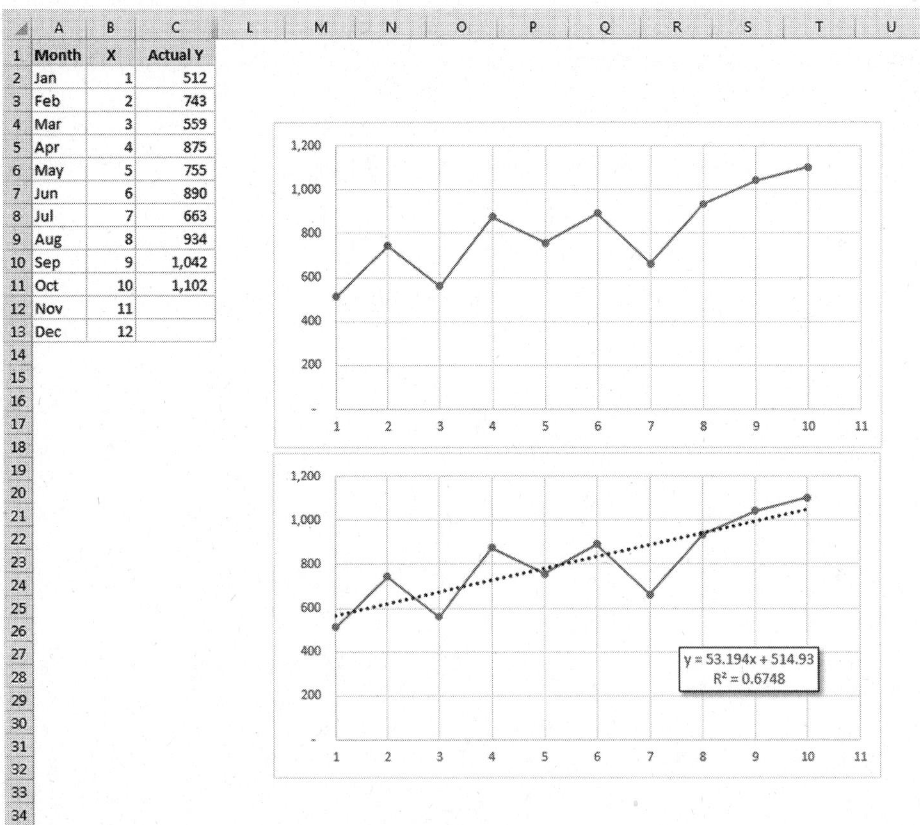

Month	X	Actual Y
Jan	1	512
Feb	2	743
Mar	3	559
Apr	4	875
May	5	755
Jun	6	890
Jul	7	663
Aug	8	934
Sep	9	1,042
Oct	10	1,102
Nov	11	
Dec	12	

Figure 17-24: Adding a linear trendline to an existing chart.

On the Web

The workbook used in this example is available at this book's website. The file is named linear trendline.xlsx.

The second chart also uses the options to display the equation and the R-squared value. In this example, the equation is as follows:

```
y = 53.194x + 514.93
```

The R-squared value is 0.6748.

What do these numbers mean? You can describe a straight line with an equation of the form:

```
y = mx +b
```

For each value of *x* (the horizontal axis), you can calculate the predicted value of *y* (the value on the trendline) by using this equation. The variable *m* represents the slope of the line, and *b* represents the *y*-intercept. For example, when *x* is 3 (for March), the predicted value of *y* is 674.47, calculated with this formula:

```
=(53.19*3)+514.9
```

The R-squared value, sometimes referred to as the *coefficient of determination,* ranges in value from 0 to 1. This value indicates how closely the estimated values for the trendline correspond to the actual data. A trendline is most reliable when its R-squared value is closer to 1.

Calculating the slope and y-intercept

This section describes how to use the LINEST function to calculate the slope (*m*) and *y*-intercept (*b*) of the best-fit linear trendline.

Figure 17-25 shows ten data points (*x* values in column B, actual *y* values in column C).

G2 {=LINEST(C2:C11,B2:B11)}

	A	B	C	G	H	J	K
1	Month	X	Actual Y	m	b		
2	Jan	1	512	53.19394	514.9333		
3	Feb	2	743				
4	Mar	3	559				
5	Apr	4	875				
6	May	5	755				
7	Jun	6	890				
8	Jul	7	663				
9	Aug	8	934				
10	Sep	9	1,042				
11	Oct	10	1,102				
12	Nov	11					
13	Dec	12					
14							
15							

Figure 17-25: Using the LINEST function to calculate slope and *y*-intercept.

The formula that follows is a multicell array formula that displays its result (the slope and *y*-intercept) in two cells:

```
{=LINEST(C2:C11,B2:B11)}
```

To enter this formula, start by selecting two cells (in this example, G2:H2). Then type the formula (without the curly brackets) and press Ctrl+Shift+Enter. Cell G2 displays the slope; cell H2 displays the *y*-intercept. Note that these are the same values displayed in the chart for the linear trendline.

Calculating predicted values

After you know the values for the slope and *y*-intercept, you can calculate the predicted *y* value for each *x*. Figure 17-26 shows the result. Cell E2 contains the following formula, which is copied down the column:

```
=(B2*$G$2)+$H$2
```

E2 | {=TREND(C2:C11,B2:B11)}

	A	B	C	D	E	F	G	H	I
1	Month	X	Actual Y		Predicted Y			m	b
2	Jan	1	512		568.13			53.19394	514.9333
3	Feb	2	743		621.32				
4	Mar	3	559		674.52				
5	Apr	4	875		727.71				
6	May	5	755		780.90				
7	Jun	6	890		834.10				
8	Jul	7	663		887.29				
9	Aug	8	934		940.48				
10	Sep	9	1,042		993.68				
11	Oct	10	1,102		1,046.87				
12	Nov	11							
13	Dec	12							
14									
15									

Figure 17-26: Column E contains formulas that calculate the predicted values for *y*.

The calculated values in column E represent the values used to plot the linear trendline.

You can also calculate predicted values of *y* without first computing the slope and *y*-intercept. You do so with an array formula that uses the TREND function. Select D2:D11, type the following formula (without the curly brackets), and press Ctrl+Shift+Enter:

```
{=TREND(C2:C11,B2:B11)}
```

Linear forecasting

When your chart contains a trendline, you can instruct Excel to extend the trendline to forecast additional values. You do this on the Trendline Options section of the Format Trendline task pane. (Read earlier in this section to see how to open this task pane.) Just specify the number of periods to forecast. Figure 17-27 shows a chart with a trendline that's extended to forecast two subsequent periods.

F12 =FORECAST(B12,$C$2:$C$11,$B$2:$B$11)

	A	B	C	D	E	F	G	H
1	Month	X	Actual Y	Predicted Y	Predicted Y	Forecasted	m	b
2	Jan	1	512	568.13	568.13		53.19394	514.9333
3	Feb	2	743	621.32	621.32			
4	Mar	3	559	674.52	674.52			
5	Apr	4	875	727.71	727.71			
6	May	5	755	780.90	780.90			
7	Jun	6	890	834.10	834.10			
8	Jul	7	663	887.29	887.29			
9	Aug	8	934	940.48	940.48			
10	Sep	9	1,042	993.68	993.68			
11	Oct	10	1,102	1,046.87	1,046.87			
12	Nov	11			1,100.07	1,100.07		
13	Dec	12			1,153.26	1,153.26		
14								

Figure 17-27: Using a trendline to forecast values for two additional periods of time.

If you know the values of the slope and *y*-intercept (see the "Calculating the slope and *y*-intercept" section, earlier in the chapter), you can calculate forecasts for other values of *x*. For example, to calculate the value of *y* when *x* = 11 (November), use the following formula:

```
=(53.194*11)+514.93
```

You can also forecast values by using the FORECAST function. The following formula, for example, forecasts the value for November (that is, *x* = 11) using known *x* and known *y* values:

```
=FORECAST(11,C2:C11,B2:B11)
```

Forecasting future values with forecasting functions

The preceding example uses the FORECAST function to predict future months' values. Excel 2016 introduces five new forecasting functions to give you more algorithm options. The new functions use advanced machine learning algorithms, which are beyond the scope of this book. But we include a brief summary and the syntax of the new functions here:

```
FORECAST.LINEAR(x, known_y's, known_x's)
```

FORECAST.LINEAR is the direct replacement for the deprecated FORECAST function. It uses linear regression to predict a *y* value for the given *x* value:

```
FORECAST.ETS(target_date, values, timeline, seasonality, data_completion,
  aggregation)
```

FORECAST.ETS uses the AAA version of an algorithm called Exponential Smoothing, or ETS. The first three arguments—target_date, values, and timeline—are similar to the arguments for FORECAST.LINEAR. Target_date can be any number, not just a date, but it must be larger than the largest date in timeline. That is, it only predicts future values.

The timeline argument is a series of dates that have a *consistent step*. That is, each element of the series must be one day apart, one month apart, one year apart, or any other value as long as it's consistent. There are a few exceptions to this rule depending on the values you provide for the optional arguments.

The remaining arguments are optional.

- **Seasonality:** Adjusts the forecast for changes in values based on seasons. A seasonality of 0 indicates no seasonality, 1 tells the algorithm to detect seasonality based on the provided values, and any other positive number indicates the interval to use for seasonality. For example, a seasonality of 3 instructs the algorithm to use three periods as a season.
- **Data completion:** Accounts for up to 30% missing data in timeline. You can indicate that missing values are zeros or tell the algorithm to use an average of the missing data's neighbors.
- **Aggregation:** Allows you to have duplicate values in the timeline. If you have duplicate data, aggregation will combine it into one data point using an aggregate you specify here:

```
FORECAST.ETS.SEASONALITY(target_date, values, timeline, seasonality, data_
  completion)
```

FORECAST.ETS.SEASONALITY uses many of the same arguments as FORECAST.ETS. If you specify 1 as the seasonality argument of FORECAST.ETS, the algorithm determines the seasonality. This function returns what the algorithm calculates for seasonality. In Figure 17-28, cell G12 shows that two periods is the seasonality computed from the data.

```
FORECAST.ETS.CONFINT(target_date, values, timeline, confidence_level,
  seasonality, data_completion, aggregation)
```

FORECAST.ETS.CONFINT returns the confidence interval for the forecasted data using ETS. It has the same arguments as FORECAST.ETS except for confidence_level. Confidence_level is a number between 0 and 1. (The default is 95%.) Cell H12 in Figure 17-28 uses a confidence_level of .9 (90%)

and calculates that there is 90% confidence that the actual future values will be +/-131 of the predicted values in column F:

```
FORECAST.ETS.STAT(target_date, values, timeline, statistic_type,
   seasonality, data_completion, aggregation)
```

FORECAST.ETS.STAT returns one of several statistical measures from the data provided. Again, the arguments are mostly the same as FORECAST.ETS. The exception is statistic_type, where you indicate which statistic you want the formula to return. The list of statistics can be found in Excel's help. Figure 17-28 uses the Step size detected statistic in cell I12 to report that it determined that the values in column B incremented by 1.

F12 =FORECAST.ETS(B12,$C$2:$C$11,$B$2:$B$11,1)

	A	B	C	D	E	F	G	H	I	J
1	Month	X	Actual Y	FORECAST	LINEAR	ETS	SEASONALITY	CONFINT	STAT	
2	Jan	1	512							
3	Feb	2	743							
4	Mar	3	559							
5	Apr	4	875							
6	May	5	755							
7	Jun	6	890							
8	Jul	7	663							
9	Aug	8	934							
10	Sep	9	1,042							
11	Oct	10	1,102							
12	Nov	11		1,100	1,100	995	2	131	1	
13	Dec	12		1,153	1,153	1,202				
14										
15										

Figure 17-28: Using Excel 2016's new forecasting functions.

Calculating R-Squared

The accuracy of forecasted values depends on how well the linear trendline fits your actual data. The value of R-squared represents the degree of fit. R-squared values closer to 1 indicate a better fit—and more accurate predictions. In other words, you can interpret R-squared as the proportion of the variance in *y* attributable to the variance in *x*.

As described previously, you can instruct Excel to display the R-squared value in the chart. Or you can calculate it directly in your worksheet using the RSQ function. The following formula calculates R-squared for *x* values in B2:B11 and *y* values for C2:C11:

```
=RSQ(B2:B11,C2:C11)
```

Caution

The value of R-squared calculated by the RSQ function is valid only for a linear trendline.

Working with nonlinear trendlines

Besides linear trendlines, an Excel chart can display trendlines of the following types:

- **Logarithmic:** Used when the rate of change in the data increases or decreases quickly and then flattens out.
- **Power:** Used when the data consists of measurements that increase at a specific rate. The data cannot contain zero or negative values.
- **Exponential:** Used when data values rise or fall at increasingly higher rates. The data cannot contain zero or negative values.
- **Polynomial:** Used when data fluctuates. You can specify the order of the polynomial (from 2 to 6) depending on the number of fluctuations in the data.

Note

The Trendline Options tab of the Format Trendline task pane offers the option of Moving Average, which really isn't a trendline. This option, however, can be useful for smoothing out "noisy" data. The Moving Average option enables you to specify the number of data points to include in each average. For example, if you select 5, Excel averages every group of five data points and displays the points on a trendline.

Figure 17-29 shows charts that depict each of the trendline options.

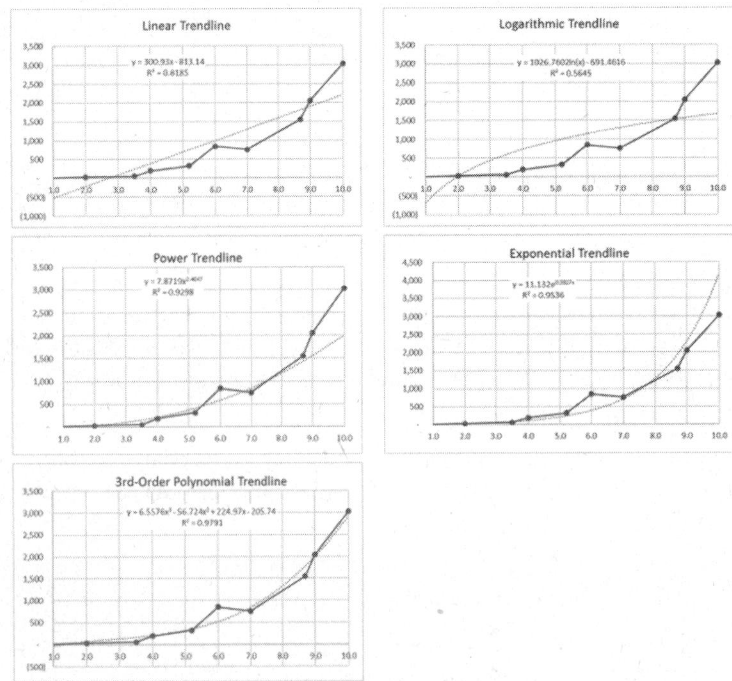

Figure 17-29: Charts with various trendline options.

Earlier in this chapter, you learned how to calculate the slope and *y*-intercept for the linear equation that describes a linear trendline. Nonlinear trendlines also have equations, and they are a bit more complex.

On the Web

This book's website contains a workbook with nonlinear trendline examples. The file is named nonlinear trendlines.xlsx.

Summary of trendline equations

This section contains a concise summary of trendline equation. These equations assume that your sheet has two named ranges: x and y.

Linear trendline

```
Equation: y = m * x + b
m: =SLOPE(y,x)
b: =INTERCEPT(y,x)
```

Logarithmic trendline

```
Equation: y = (c * LN(x)) + b
c: =INDEX(LINEST(y,LN(x)),1)
b: =INDEX(LINEST(y,LN(x)),1,2)
```

Power trendline

```
Equation: y=c*x^b
c: =EXP(INDEX(LINEST(LN(y),LN(x),,),1,2))
b: =INDEX(LINEST(LN(y),LN(x),,),1)
```

Exponential trendline

```
Equation: y = c *e ^(b * x)
c: =EXP(INDEX(LINEST(LN(y),x),1,2))
b: =INDEX(LINEST(LN(y),x),1)
```

Second order polynomial trendline

```
Equation: y = (c2 * x^2) + (c1 * x ^1) + b
c2: =INDEX(LINEST(y,x^{1,2}),1)
c1: =INDEX(LINEST(y,x^{1,2}),1,2)
b = INDEX(LINEST(y,x^{1,2}),1,3)
```

Third order polynomial trendline

```
Equation: y = (c3 * x^3) + (c2 * x^2) + (c1 * x^1) + b
c3: =INDEX(LINEST(y,x^{1,2,3}),1)
c2: =INDEX(LINEST(y,x^{1,2,3}),1,2)
c1: =INDEX(LINEST(y,x^{1,2,3}),1,3)
b: =INDEX(LINEST(y,x^{1,2,3}),1,4)
```

Creating Interactive Charts

An *interactive chart* allows the user to easily change various parameters that affect what's displayed in the chart. Often, VBA macros are used to make charts interactive. The examples in this section use no macros and demonstrate what can be done using only the tools built into Excel.

Selecting a series from a drop-down list

Figure 17-30 shows a chart that displays data as specified by a drop-down list in cell F2. Cell F2 uses data validation, which allows the user to select a month from a list. The chart uses the data in F1:I2, but the values depend on the selected month. The formulas in range G2:I2 retrieve the values from columns B:D that correspond to the selected month.

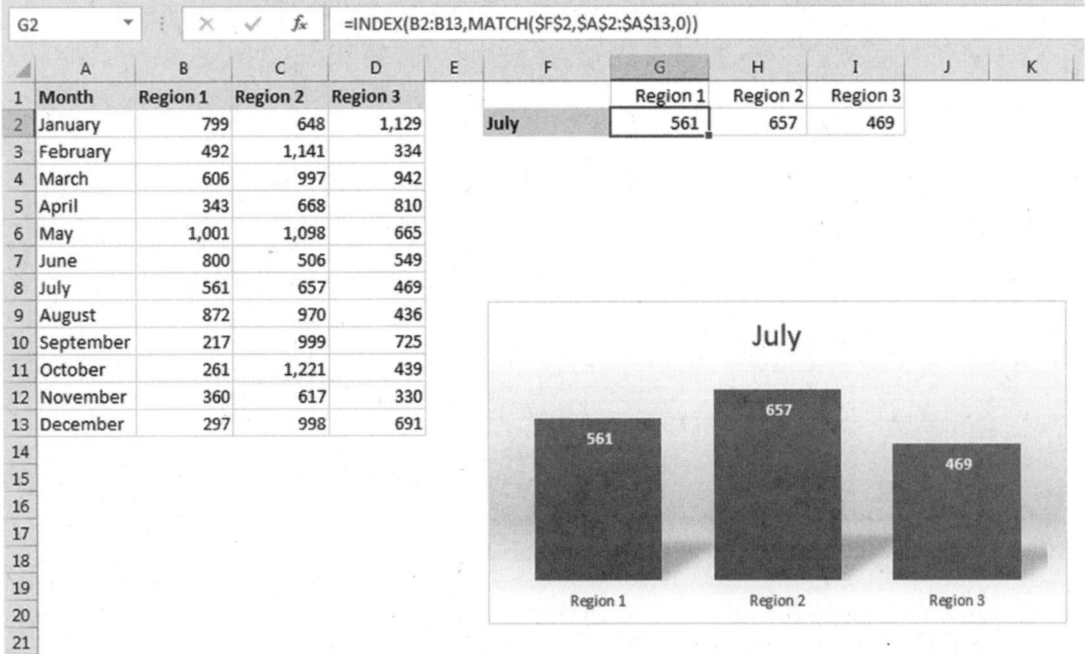

G2 =INDEX(B2:B13,MATCH($F$2,$A$2:$A$13,0))

	A	B	C	D	E	F	G	H	I
1	Month	Region 1	Region 2	Region 3			Region 1	Region 2	Region 3
2	January	799	648	1,129		July	561	657	469
3	February	492	1,141	334					
4	March	606	997	942					
5	April	343	668	810					
6	May	1,001	1,098	665					
7	June	800	506	549					
8	July	561	657	469					
9	August	872	970	436					
10	September	217	999	725					
11	October	261	1,221	439					
12	November	360	617	330					
13	December	297	998	691					

Figure 17-30: Selecting data to plot using a drop-down list.

The formula in cell G2, which was copied to the two cells to the right, is

```
=INDEX(B2:B13,MATCH($F$2,$A$2:$A$13,0))
```

On the Web

This example is available at this book's website. The filename is series from drop-down.xlsx.

Plotting the last *n* data points

You can use a technique that makes your chart show only the most recent data points in a column. For example, you can create a chart that always displays the most recent six months of data. Figure 17-31 shows a worksheet set up so the user can specify the number of data points.

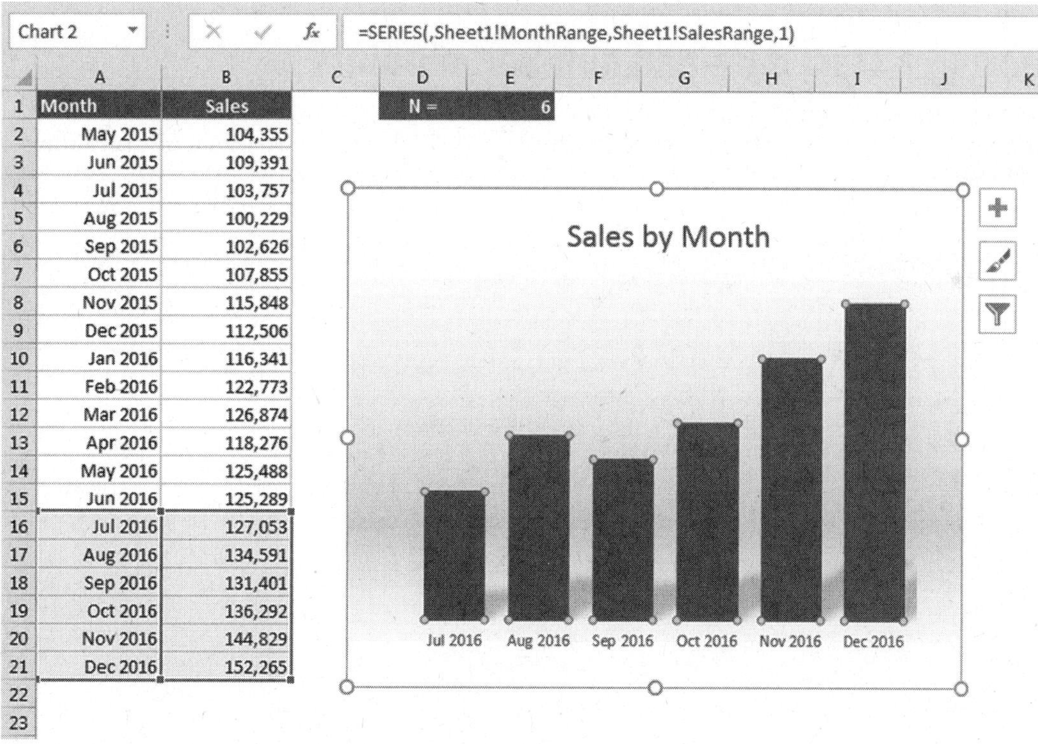

Figure 17-31: This chart displays the most recent data points.

The workbook uses three names. *N* is the name for cell E3, which holds the number of data points to plot.

MonthRange is a dynamic named formula, defined as

```
=OFFSET(Sheet1!$A$1,COUNTA(Sheet1!$A:$A)-Sheet1!N,0,Sheet1!N,1)
```

SalesRange is a dynamic named formula, defined as

```
=OFFSET(Sheet1!$B$1,COUNTA(Sheet1!$B:$B)-Sheet1!N,0,Sheet1!N,1)
```

The chart's SERIES formula uses the two named formulas:

```
=SERIES(,Sheet1!MonthRange,Sheet1!SalesRange,1)
```

The example in this section, named plot last n data points.xlsx, is available at this book's website.

Choosing a start date and number of points

This example uses dynamic formulas to allow the user to display a chart with a specified number of data points, beginning with a selected starting date. Figure 17-32 shows a worksheet with 365 rows of daily sales data.

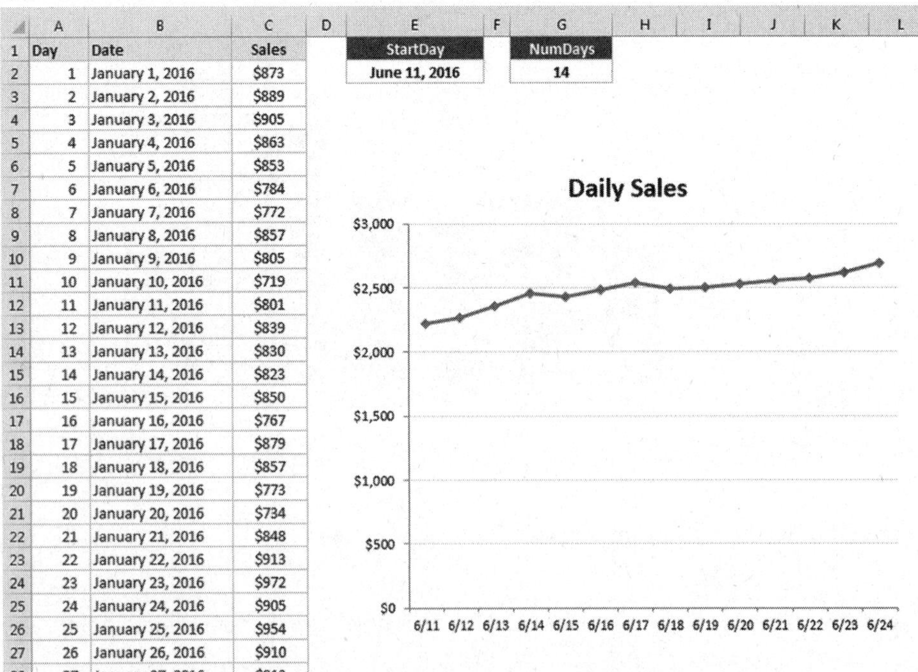

	A	B	C
1	Day	Date	Sales
2	1	January 1, 2016	$873
3	2	January 2, 2016	$889
4	3	January 3, 2016	$905
5	4	January 4, 2016	$863
6	5	January 5, 2016	$853
7	6	January 6, 2016	$784
8	7	January 7, 2016	$772
9	8	January 8, 2016	$857
10	9	January 9, 2016	$805
11	10	January 10, 2016	$719
12	11	January 11, 2016	$801
13	12	January 12, 2016	$839
14	13	January 13, 2016	$830
15	14	January 14, 2016	$823
16	15	January 15, 2016	$850
17	16	January 16, 2016	$767
18	17	January 17, 2016	$879
19	18	January 18, 2016	$857
20	19	January 19, 2016	$773
21	20	January 20, 2016	$734
22	21	January 21, 2016	$848
23	22	January 22, 2016	$913
24	23	January 23, 2016	$972
25	24	January 24, 2016	$905
26	25	January 25, 2016	$954
27	26	January 26, 2016	$910

	E	G
1	StartDay	NumDays
2	June 11, 2016	14

Figure 17-32: This chart displays data based on values specified by the user.

The start date is indicated in cell E2 (named *StartDay*), and the number of data points is specified in cell G2 (named *NumDays*). Both cells use data validation to display a drop-down list of options.

What makes this work is two named formulas. The formula named *Date* is

```
=OFFSET(Sheet1!$B$2,MATCH(StartDay,Sheet1!$B:$B,1)-2,0,NumDays,1)
```

The formula named *Sales* is

```
=OFFSET(Sheet1!$B$2,MATCH(StartDay,Sheet1!$B:$B,1)-2,1,NumDays,1)
```

These are both dynamic names that return a range that depends on the value of *StartDay* and *NumDays*. The two names are used in the chart's SERIES formula. (The filename qualifier was removed for simplicity.)

```
=SERIES(,Date,Sales,1)
```

On the Web

The example in this section, named first point and number of points.xlsx, is available at this book's website.

Displaying population data

The example in this section uses the population pyramid technique described earlier in this chapter. (See "Creating a comparative histogram.") Here, the user can choose two years to view population by age groups side by side.

Figure 17-33 shows the age distribution for 1950 and 2013.

The years are entered in cells C2 and G2. The years can be entered manually or specified by using a scrollbar linked to a cell. Formulas below the chart retrieve data from a table that has population statistics (and projections) from 1950 through 2100.

For each year, the chart also displays the total population and the percentage of people age 65 or older. That information is displayed by using text boxes linked to cells.

On the Web

This workbook, named US population chart.xlsx, is available at this book's website.

Displaying weather data

The example shown in Figure 17-34 is a useful application that allows the user to choose two U.S. cities (from a list of 284 cities) and view a chart that compares the cities by month in any of the following categories: average precipitation, average temperature, percent sunshine, and average wind speed.

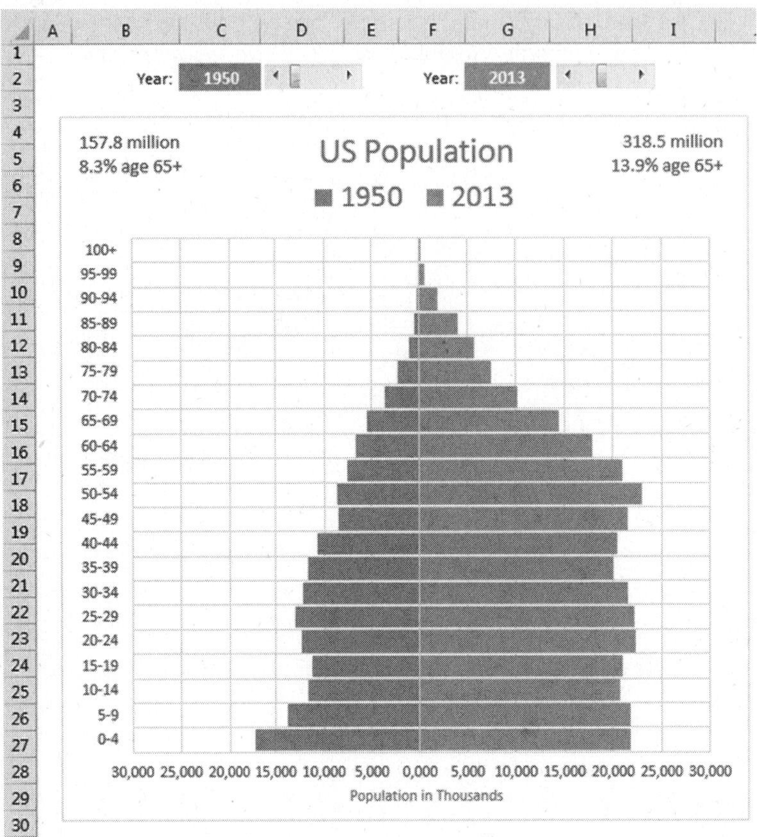

Figure 17-33: Population by age group, for two years.

The cities are chosen from a drop-down list using Excel's data validation feature, and the data option is selected using four OptionButton controls, which are linked to a cell. All the pieces are connected using a few formulas.

On the Web

This workbook, named climate data.xlsx, is available at this book's website.

The key to this application is that the chart uses data in a specific range. The data in this range is retrieved from the appropriate data table by using formulas that use the VLOOKUP function.

The formula in cell A23, which looks up data based on the contents of City1, is

```
=VLOOKUP(City1,INDIRECT(DataTable),COLUMN(),FALSE)
```

The formula in cell A24 is the same except that it looks up data based on the contents of City2:

```
=VLOOKUP(City2,INDIRECT(DataTable),COLUMN(),FALSE)
```

These formulas were entered and then copied across to the next 12 columns (see Figure 17-34).

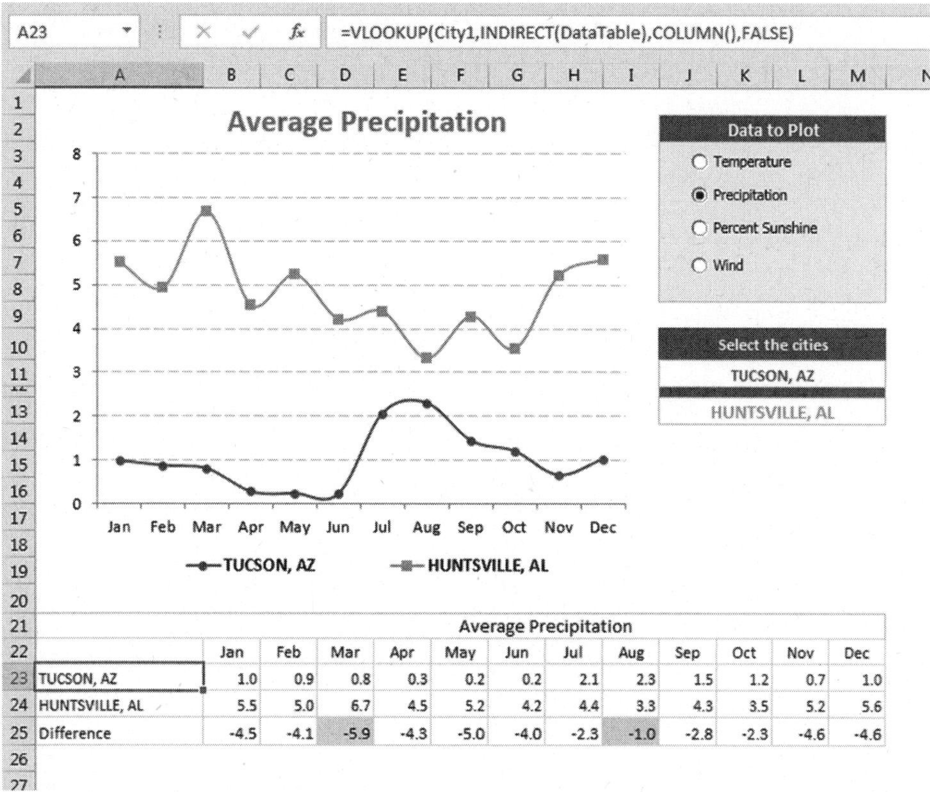

	Average Precipitation											
	Jan	Feb	Mar	Apr	May	Jun	Jul	Aug	Sep	Oct	Nov	Dec
TUCSON, AZ	1.0	0.9	0.8	0.3	0.2	0.2	2.1	2.3	1.5	1.2	0.7	1.0
HUNTSVILLE, AL	5.5	5.0	6.7	4.5	5.2	4.2	4.4	3.3	4.3	3.5	5.2	5.6
Difference	-4.5	-4.1	-5.9	-4.3	-5.0	-4.0	-2.3	-1.0	-2.8	-2.3	-4.6	-4.6

Figure 17-34: This application uses a variety of techniques (but no VBA code) to plot monthly climate data for two selected U.S. cities.

Note

You may be wondering about the use of the COLUMN function for the third argument of the VLOOKUP function. This function returns the column number of the cell that contains the formula. This is a convenient way to avoid hard-coding the column to be retrieved and allows the same formula to be used in each column.

Row 25 contains formulas that calculate the difference between the two cities for each month. Conditional formatting was used to apply a different color background for the largest difference and the smallest difference.

The label above the month names is generated by a formula that refers to the DataTable cell and constructs a descriptive title. The formula is

```
="Average " & LEFT(DataTable,LEN(DataTable)-4)
```

After you've completed the previous tasks, the final step—creating the actual chart—is a breeze. The line chart has two data series and uses the data in A22:M24. The chart title is linked to cell B21. The data in A23:M24 changes, of course, whenever an OptionButton control is selected or a new city is selected from either of the Data Validation lists.

18

Pivot Tables

In This Chapter

- An introduction to pivot tables
- How to create a pivot table from a worksheet database or table
- How to group items in a pivot table
- How to create a calculated field or a calculated item in a pivot table
- The Data Model feature
- How to create pivot charts

Excel's pivot table feature is perhaps the most technologically sophisticated component in Excel. This chapter may seem a bit out of place in a book devoted to formulas. After all, a pivot table does its job *without* using formulas. That's exactly the point. If you haven't yet discovered the power of pivot tables, this chapter demonstrates how using a pivot table can serve as an excellent alternative to creating many complex formulas.

About Pivot Tables

A *pivot table* is essentially a dynamic summary report generated from a database. The database can reside in a worksheet or in an external file. A pivot table can help transform endless rows and columns of numbers into a meaningful presentation of the data.

For example, a pivot table can create frequency distributions and cross-tabulations of several different data dimensions. In addition, you can display subtotals and any level of detail that you want. Perhaps the most innovative aspect of a pivot table lies in its interactivity. After you create a pivot table, you can rearrange the information in almost any way imaginable and insert special formulas that perform calculations. You can even create post-hoc groupings of summary items: for example, combining Northern Region totals with Western Region totals. And the icing on the cake is that with but a few mouse clicks, you can apply formatting to a pivot table to convert it to boardroom-quality attractiveness.

Pivot tables were introduced in Excel 97, and this feature improves with every version of Excel. You can create pivot tables from multiple data tables. Unfortunately, many users avoid pivot tables because they think that they are too complicated. Our goal in this chapter is to dispel that myth.

One minor drawback to using a pivot table is that unlike a formula-based summary report, a pivot table does not update automatically when you change the source data. This does not pose a serious problem, however, because a single click of the Refresh button forces a pivot table to update itself with the latest data.

A Pivot Table Example

The best way to understand the concept of a pivot table is to see one. Start with Figure 18-1, which shows a portion of the data used in creating the pivot table in this chapter.

	A	B	C	D	E	F	G
1	Date	Weekday	Amount	AcctType	OpenedBy	Branch	Customer
2	Nov-01	Friday	5,000	IRA	New Accts	Central	Existing
3	Nov-01	Friday	14,571	CD	Teller	Central	New
4	Nov-01	Friday	500	Checking	New Accts	Central	Existing
5	Nov-01	Friday	15,000	CD	New Accts	Central	Existing
6	Nov-01	Friday	4,623	Savings	New Accts	North County	Existing
7	Nov-01	Friday	8,721	Savings	New Accts	Westside	New
8	Nov-01	Friday	15,276	Savings	New Accts	North County	Existing
9	Nov-01	Friday	5,000	Savings	New Accts	Westside	Existing
10	Nov-01	Friday	15,759	CD	Teller	Westside	Existing
11	Nov-01	Friday	12,000	CD	New Accts	Westside	Existing
12	Nov-01	Friday	7,177	Savings	Teller	North County	Existing
13	Nov-01	Friday	6,837	Savings	New Accts	Westside	Existing
14	Nov-01	Friday	3,171	Checking	New Accts	Westside	Existing
15	Nov-01	Friday	50,000	Savings	New Accts	Central	Existing
16	Nov-01	Friday	4,690	Checking	New Accts	North County	New
17	Nov-01	Friday	12,438	Checking	New Accts	Central	Existing
18	Nov-01	Friday	5,000	Checking	New Accts	North County	Existing
19	Nov-01	Friday	7,000	Savings	New Accts	North County	New
20	Nov-01	Friday	11,957	Checking	New Accts	Central	Existing
21	Nov-01	Friday	13,636	CD	New Accts	North County	Existing
22	Nov-01	Friday	16,000	CD	New Accts	Central	New
23	Nov-01	Friday	5,879	Checking	New Accts	Central	Existing

Figure 18-1: This table is used to create a pivot table.

This table consists of a month's worth of new account information for a three-branch bank. The table contains 712 rows, and each row represents a new account opened at the bank. The table has the following columns:

- The date when the account was opened
- The day of the week the account was opened
- The opening amount
- The account type: CD, checking, savings, or IRA (Individual Retirement Account)
- The person who opened the account: a teller or a new-account representative
- The branch at which it was opened: Central, Westside, or North County
- The type of customer: an existing customer or a new customer

On the Web

This workbook, named bank accounts.xlsx, is available at this book's website.

The bank accounts database contains quite a bit of information, but in its current form, the data doesn't reveal much. To make the data more useful, you need to summarize it. Summarizing a database is essentially the process of answering questions about the data. Following are a few questions that may be of interest to the bank's management:

- What is the daily total new deposit amount for each branch?
- Which day of the week accounts for the most deposits?
- How many accounts were opened at each branch, broken down by account type?
- What's the dollar distribution of the different account types?
- What types of accounts do tellers open most often?
- How does the Central branch compare with the other two branches?
- In which branch do tellers open the most checking accounts for new customers?

You can, of course, spend time sorting the data and creating formulas to answer these questions. Often, however, a pivot table is a much better choice. Creating a pivot table takes only a few seconds, doesn't require a single formula, and produces a nice-looking report. In addition, pivot tables are much less prone to error than creating formulas.

By the way, we provide answers to these questions later in the chapter by presenting several additional pivot tables created from the data.

Figure 18-2 shows a pivot table created from the bank data. Keep in mind that no formulas are involved. This pivot table shows the amount of new deposits, broken down by branch and account type. This particular summary represents one of dozens of summaries that you can produce from this data.

	A	B	C	D	E	F
1						
2						
3	Sum of Amount	AcctType				
4	Branch	CD	Checking	IRA	Savings	Grand Total
5	Central	1,359,385	802,403	68,380	885,757	3,115,925
6	North County	1,137,911	392,516	134,374	467,414	2,132,215
7	Westside	648,549	292,995	10,000	336,088	1,287,632
8	Grand Total	3,145,845	1,487,914	212,754	1,689,259	6,535,772
9						
10						

Figure 18-2: A simple pivot table.

Figure 18-3 shows another pivot table generated from the bank account data. This pivot table uses the drop-down filter for the Customer field (in row 2). In the figure, the pivot table displays the data only for Existing customers. The user can also select New or All from the drop-down control.

	A	B	C	D	E	F
1						
2	Customer	Existing				
3						
4	Sum of Amount	Branch				
5		⊟Central	⊟Group1		Grand Total	
6	Row Labels	Central	North County	Westside		
7	CD	973,112	845,522	356,079	2,174,713	
8	Checking	505,822	208,375	144,391	858,588	
9	IRA	68,380	125,374	10,000	203,754	
10	Savings	548,198	286,891	291,728	1,126,817	
11	Grand Total	2,095,512	1,466,162	802,198	4,363,872	
12						
13						
14						

Figure 18-3: A pivot table that uses a report filter.

Notice the change in the orientation of the table. For this pivot table, branches appear as column labels, and account types appear as row labels. This change, which took about five seconds to make, is another example of the flexibility of a pivot table.

Data Appropriate for a Pivot Table

A pivot table requires that your data be in the form of a rectangular table. You can store the data in either a worksheet range (which can either be a normal range or a table created by choosing Insert ➜ Tables ➜ Table) or an external database file. Although Excel can generate a pivot table from any table, not all tables are appropriate.

Generally speaking, fields in the database table consist of two types of information:

- **Data:** Contains a value or data that you want to summarize. For the bank account example, the Amount field is a data field.
- **Category:** Describes the data. For the bank account data, the Date, Weekday, AcctType, OpenedBy, Branch, and Customer fields are category fields because they describe the data in the Amount field.

A single table can have any number of data fields and category fields. When you create a pivot table, you usually want to summarize one or more of the data fields. Conversely, the values in the category fields appear in the pivot table as row labels, column labels, or filters.

Exceptions exist, however, and you may find Excel's pivot table feature useful even for a table that doesn't contain numerical data fields. In such a case, the pivot table provides counts rather than sums.

Figure 18-4 shows an example of an Excel range that is *not* appropriate for a pivot table. Although the range contains descriptive information about each value, it does *not* consist of normalized data. In fact, this range actually resembles a pivot table summary, but it is much less flexible.

This workbook, named normalized data.xlsx, is available at this book's website.

	A	B	C	D	E	F	G	H	I	J	K
1	State	Jan	Feb	Mar	*Qtr-1*	Apr	May	Jun	*Qtr-2*	*Total*	
2	California	1,118	1,960	1,252	*4,330*	1,271	1,557	1,679	*4,507*	8,837	
3	Washington	1,247	1,238	1,028	*3,513*	1,345	1,784	1,574	*4,703*	8,216	
4	Oregon	1,460	1,954	1,726	*5,140*	1,461	1,764	1,144	*4,369*	9,509	
5	Arizona	1,345	1,375	1,075	*3,795*	1,736	1,555	1,372	*4,663*	8,458	
6	**West Total**	**5,170**	**6,527**	**5,081**	**16,778**	**5,813**	**6,660**	**5,769**	**18,242**	**35,020**	
7	New York	1,429	1,316	1,993	*4,738*	1,832	1,740	1,191	*4,763*	9,501	
8	New Jersey	1,735	1,406	1,224	*4,365*	1,706	1,320	1,290	*4,316*	8,681	
9	Massachusetts	1,099	1,233	1,110	*3,442*	1,637	1,512	1,006	*4,155*	7,597	
10	Florida	1,705	1,792	1,225	*4,722*	1,946	1,327	1,357	*4,630*	9,352	
11	**East Total**	**5,968**	**5,747**	**5,552**	**17,267**	**7,121**	**5,899**	**4,844**	**17,864**	**35,131**	
12	Kentucky	1,109	1,078	1,155	*3,342*	1,993	1,082	1,551	*4,626*	7,968	
13	Oklahoma	1,309	1,045	1,641	*3,995*	1,924	1,499	1,941	*5,364*	9,359	
14	Missouri	1,511	1,744	1,414	*4,669*	1,243	1,493	1,820	*4,556*	9,225	
15	Illinois	1,539	1,493	1,211	*4,243*	1,165	1,013	1,445	*3,623*	7,866	
16	Kansas	1,973	1,560	1,243	*4,776*	1,495	1,125	1,387	*4,007*	8,783	
17	**Central Total**	**7,441**	**6,920**	**6,664**	**21,025**	**7,820**	**6,212**	**8,144**	**22,176**	**43,201**	
18	**Grand Total**	**18,579**	**19,194**	**17,297**	**55,070**	**20,754**	**18,771**	**18,757**	**58,282**	**113,352**	
19											
20											

Figure 18-4: This range is not appropriate for a pivot table.

Figure 18-5 shows the same data but rearranged in such a way that makes it normalized. *Normalized* data contains one data point per row, with an additional column that classifies the data point.

The normalized range contains 78 rows of data—one for each of the six monthly sales values for the 13 states. Notice that each row contains category information for the sales value. This table is an ideal candidate for a pivot table and contains all the information necessary to summarize the information by region or quarter.

Figure 18-6 shows a pivot table created from the normalized data. As you can see, it's virtually identical to the nonnormalized data shown in Figure 18-4.

	A	B	C	D	E	F
1	**State**	**Region**	**Month**	**Qtr**	**Sales**	
2	California	West	Jan	Qtr-1	1,118	
3	California	West	Feb	Qtr-1	1,960	
4	California	West	Mar	Qtr-1	1,252	
5	California	West	Apr	Qtr-2	1,271	
6	California	West	May	Qtr-2	1,557	
7	California	West	Jun	Qtr-2	1,679	
8	Washington	West	Jan	Qtr-1	1,247	
9	Washington	West	Feb	Qtr-1	1,238	
10	Washington	West	Mar	Qtr-1	1,028	
11	Washington	West	Apr	Qtr-2	1,345	
12	Washington	West	May	Qtr-2	1,784	
13	Washington	West	Jun	Qtr-2	1,574	
14	Oregon	West	Jan	Qtr-1	1,460	
15	Oregon	West	Feb	Qtr-1	1,954	
16	Oregon	West	Mar	Qtr-1	1,726	
17	Oregon	West	Apr	Qtr-2	1,461	
18	Oregon	West	May	Qtr-2	1,764	
19	Oregon	West	Jun	Qtr-2	1,144	
20	Arizona	West	Jan	Qtr-1	1,345	
21	Arizona	West	Feb	Qtr-1	1,375	
22	Arizona	West	Mar	Qtr-1	1,075	
23	Arizona	West	Apr	Qtr-2	1,736	

Figure 18-5: This range contains normalized data and is appropriate for a pivot table.

	A	B	C	D	E	F	G	H	I	J
1										
2										
3	**Sum of Sales**	**Column Labels**								
4		**⊟Qtr-1**			**Qtr-1 Total**	**⊟Qtr-2**			**Qtr-2 Total**	**Grand Total**
5	**Row Labels**	**Jan**	**Feb**	**Mar**		**Apr**	**May**	**Jun**		
6	**⊟Central**	**7,441**	**6,920**	**6,664**	**21,025**	**7,820**	**6,212**	**8,144**	**22,176**	**43,201**
7	Illinois	1,539	1,493	1,211	4,243	1,165	1,013	1,445	3,623	7,866
8	Kansas	1,973	1,560	1,243	4,776	1,495	1,125	1,387	4,007	8,783
9	Kentucky	1,109	1,078	1,155	3,342	1,993	1,082	1,551	4,626	7,968
10	Missouri	1,511	1,744	1,414	4,669	1,243	1,493	1,820	4,556	9,225
11	Oklahoma	1,309	1,045	1,641	3,995	1,924	1,499	1,941	5,364	9,359
12	**⊟East**	**5,968**	**5,747**	**5,552**	**17,267**	**7,121**	**5,899**	**4,844**	**17,864**	**35,131**
13	Florida	1,705	1,792	1,225	4,722	1,946	1,327	1,357	4,630	9,352
14	Massachusetts	1,099	1,233	1,110	3,442	1,637	1,512	1,006	4,155	7,597
15	New Jersey	1,735	1,406	1,224	4,365	1,706	1,320	1,290	4,316	8,681
16	New York	1,429	1,316	1,993	4,738	1,832	1,740	1,191	4,763	9,501
17	**⊟West**	**5,170**	**6,527**	**5,081**	**16,778**	**5,813**	**6,660**	**5,769**	**18,242**	**35,020**
18	Arizona	1,345	1,375	1,075	3,795	1,736	1,555	1,372	4,663	8,458
19	California	1,118	1,960	1,252	4,330	1,271	1,557	1,679	4,507	8,837
20	Oregon	1,460	1,954	1,726	5,140	1,461	1,764	1,144	4,369	9,509
21	Washington	1,247	1,238	1,028	3,513	1,345	1,784	1,574	4,703	8,216
22	**Grand Total**	**18,579**	**19,194**	**17,297**	**55,070**	**20,754**	**18,771**	**18,757**	**58,282**	**113,352**
23										
24										

Figure 18-6: A pivot table created from normalized data.

A reverse pivot table

Excel's pivot table feature creates a summary table from a list. But what if you want to perform the opposite operation? Often, you may have a two-way summary table, and it would be convenient if the data were in the form of a normalized list.

In this figure, range A1:E13 contains a summary table with 48 data points. Notice that this summary table is similar to a pivot table. Column G:I shows part of a 48-row table that was derived from the summary table. In other words, every value in the original summary table gets converted to a row, which also contains the region name and month. This type of table is useful because it can be sorted and manipulated in other ways. And you can create a pivot table from this transformed table.

	North	South	East	West
Jan	132	233	314	441
Feb	143	251	314	447
Mar	172	252	345	450
Apr	184	290	365	452
May	212	299	401	453
Jun	239	317	413	457
Jul	249	350	427	460
Aug	263	354	448	468
Sep	291	373	367	472
Oct	294	401	392	479
Nov	302	437	495	484
Dec	305	466	504	490

Select a cell in the summary table above, then click the button to create a table with one row per data point.
Replace the column headings to describe the fields.
This macro can be used with any 2-way table

Convert

Col1	Col2	Col3
Jan	North	132
Jan	South	233
Jan	East	314
Jan	West	441
Feb	North	143
Feb	South	251
Feb	East	314
Feb	West	447
Mar	North	172
Mar	South	252
Mar	East	345
Mar	West	450
Apr	North	184
Apr	South	290
Apr	East	365
Apr	West	452
May	North	212
May	South	299
May	East	401
May	West	453
Jun	North	239
Jun	South	317
Jun	East	413
Jun	West	457
Jul	North	249

This book's website contains a workbook, reverse pivot.xlsm, which has a macro that will convert any two-way summary table into a three-column normalized table.

Creating a Pivot Table Automatically

How easy is it to create a pivot table? This task requires practically no effort if you choose a recommended pivot table.

If your data is in a worksheet, select any cell within the data range and choose Insert ➜ Tables ➜ Recommended PivotTables, Excel quickly scans your data, and the Recommended PivotTables dialog box presents thumbnails that depict some pivot tables that you can choose from (see Figure 18-7).

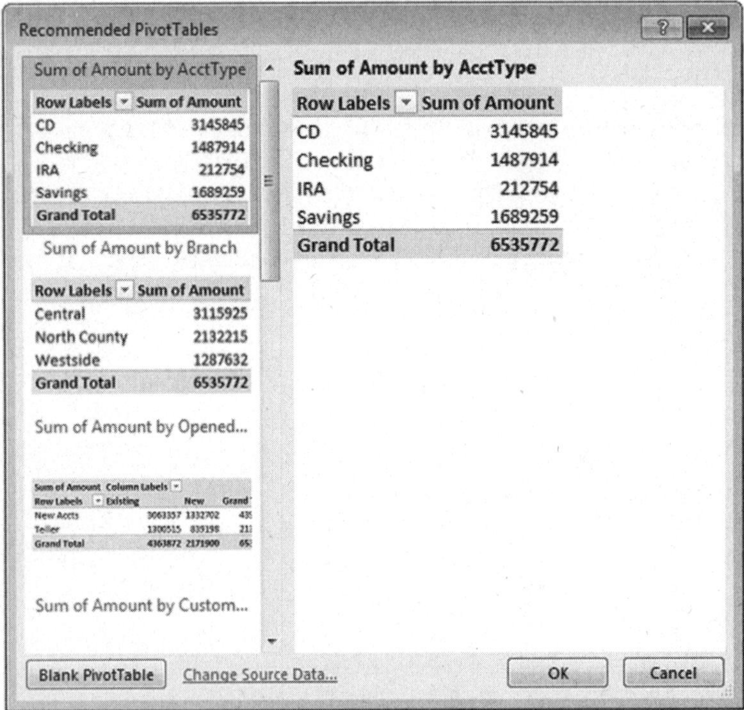

Figure 18-7: Selecting a recommended pivot table.

The pivot table thumbnails use your actual data, and there's a good chance that one of them will be exactly what you're looking for, or at least close. Select a thumbnail, click OK, and Excel creates the pivot table on a new worksheet.

When any cell in a pivot table is selected, Excel displays the PivotTable Fields task pane. You can use this task pane to make changes to the layout of the pivot table.

Note

If your data is in an external database, start by selecting a blank cell. When you choose Insert ➜ Tables ➜ Recommended PivotTables, Excel displays the Choose Data Source dialog box. Select Use an External Data Source and then click Choose Connection to specify the data source. You will then see the thumbnails of the list of recommended pivot tables.

If none of the recommended pivot tables is suitable, you have two choices:

- Create a pivot table that's close to what you want and then use the PivotTable Fields task pane to modify it.
- Click the Blank PivotTable button (at the bottom of the Recommended PivotTables dialog box) and create a pivot table manually. See the next section.

Creating a Pivot Table Manually

Using a recommended pivot table is easy, but you might prefer to create a pivot table manually. And if you use a version prior to Excel 2013, manually creating a pivot table is your only option.

In this section, we describe the basic steps required to create a pivot table using the bank account data from earlier in this chapter. Creating a pivot table is an interactive process. It's not at all uncommon to experiment with various layouts until you find one that you're satisfied with.

Specifying the data

If your data is in a worksheet range or table, select any cell in that range and then choose Insert ➜ Tables ➜ PivotTable, which displays the dialog box shown in Figure 18-8.

Figure 18-8: In the Create PivotTable dialog box, you tell Excel where the data is and then specify a location for the pivot table.

Excel attempts to guess the range, based on the location of the active cell. If you're creating a pivot table from an external data source, you need to select that option and then click the Choose Connection button to specify the data source.

Note

The Create PivotTable dialog box includes this check box: Add This Data to the Data Model. Use this option only if your pivot table will use data from more than one table or from an external data connection that uses multiple tables. We provide an example of using the Data Model later in this chapter.

Tip

If you're creating a pivot table from data in a worksheet, it's a good idea to first create a table for the range (by choosing Insert ➜ Tables ➜ Table). Then, if you expand the table by adding new rows of data, Excel refreshes the pivot table without your needing to manually indicate the new data range.

Specifying the location for the pivot table

Use the bottom section of the Create PivotTable dialog box to indicate the location for your pivot table. The default location is on a new worksheet, but you can specify any range on any worksheet, including the worksheet that contains the data.

Click OK, and Excel creates an empty pivot table and displays its PivotTable Fields task pane, as shown in Figure 18-9.

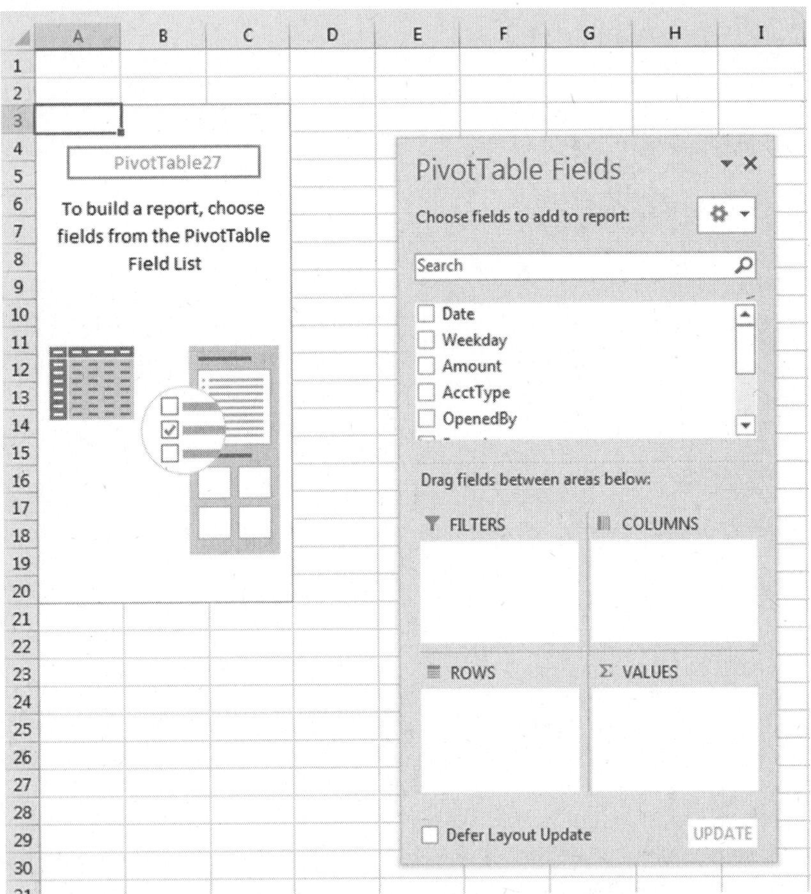

Figure 18-9: Use the PivotTable Fields task pane to build the pivot table.

Tip

The PivotTable Fields task pane is normally docked on the right side of Excel's window. By dragging its title bar, you can move it anywhere you like. Also, if you click a cell outside the pivot table, the PivotTable task pane is temporarily hidden. To dock the task pane back on the right side, simply double-click the title bar.

Pivot table terminology

Understanding the terminology associated with pivot tables is the first step in mastering this feature. Refer to the accompanying figure to get your bearings.

OpenedBy	Teller			
Sum of Amount		**Customer**		
Branch	**AcctType**	**Existing**	**New**	**Grand Total**
Central	CD	215,468	137,443	352,911
	Checking	210,543	173,830	384,373
	IRA	9,095		9,095
	Savings	195,277	127,237	322,514
Central Total		**630,383**	**438,510**	**1,068,893**
North County	CD	151,858	58,837	210,695
	Checking	95,105	90,566	185,671
	IRA	89,820	2,000	91,820
	Savings	83,117	73,396	156,513
North County Total		**419,900**	**224,799**	**644,699**
Westside	CD	104,803	92,135	196,938
	Checking	82,269	72,988	155,257
	Savings	63,160	10,766	73,926
Westside Total		**250,232**	**175,889**	**426,121**
Grand Total		**1,300,515**	**839,198**	**2,139,713**

- **Column Labels:** A field that has a column orientation in the pivot table. Each item in the field occupies a column. In the figure, Customer represents a column field that contains two items: Existing and New. You can have nested column fields.
- **Grand Total:** A row or column that displays totals for all cells in a row or column in a pivot table. You can specify that grand totals be calculated for rows, columns, or both (or neither). The pivot table in the figure shows grand totals for both rows and columns.
- **Group:** A collection of items treated as a single item. You can group items manually or automatically (group dates into months, for example). The pivot table in the figure does not have defined groups.
- **Item:** An element in a field that appears as a row or column header in a pivot table. In the figure, Existing and New are items for the Customer field. The Branch field has three items: Central, North County, and Westside. AcctType has four items: CD, Checking, IRA, and Savings.
- **Refresh:** Recalculates the pivot table after making changes to the source data.
- **Row Labels:** A field that has a row orientation in the pivot table. Each item in the field occupies a row. You can have nested row fields. In the figure, both Branch and AcctType represent row fields.
- **Source Data:** The data used to create a pivot table. It can reside in a worksheet or an external database.

continued

continued

- **Subtotals:** A row or column that displays subtotals for detail cells in a row or column in a pivot table. The pivot table in the figure displays subtotals for each branch below the data. You can also display subtotals below the data or hide subtotals.
- **Report Filter:** A field that limits what data is shown in the pivot table. You can display one item, multiple items, or all items in a table filter. In the figure, OpenedBy represents a table filter that displays the Teller item.
- **Values Area:** The cells in a pivot table that contain the summary data. Excel offers several ways to summarize the data (sum, average, count, and so on).

Laying out the pivot table

Next, set up the actual layout of the pivot table. You can do so by using any of these techniques:

- Drag the field names (at the top of the PivotTable Fields task pane) to one of the four areas at the bottom of the PivotTable Field task pane.
- Place a check mark next to the item. Excel places the field into one of the four areas at the bottom. You can drag it to a different area if necessary.
- Right-click a field name at the top of the PivotTable Fields task pane and choose its location from the shortcut menu (for example, add to Row Labels).

The following steps create the pivot table presented earlier in this chapter. (See the earlier "A Pivot Table Example" section.) For this example, we drag the items from the top of the PivotTable Field task pane to the areas in the bottom of the PivotTable Field task pane.

1. Drag the Amount field into the Values area. At this point, the pivot table displays the total of all the values in the Amount column of the data source.
2. Excel guesses at the way you want to aggregate the Values data. Sometimes it guesses wrong. For example, it may guess that you want to count the data when you want to sum it. To change the aggregation, right-click on the data, choose Summarize Values By, and choose the proper aggregate (see Figure 18-10). For more aggregation options, see the "Pivot table calculations" sidebar later in this chapter.
3. Drag the AcctType field into the Rows area. Now the pivot table shows the total amount for each of the account types.
4. Drag the Branch field into the Columns area. The pivot table shows the amount for each account type, cross-tabulated by branch (see Figure 18-11). The pivot table updates itself automatically with every change you make in the PivotTable Fields task pane.

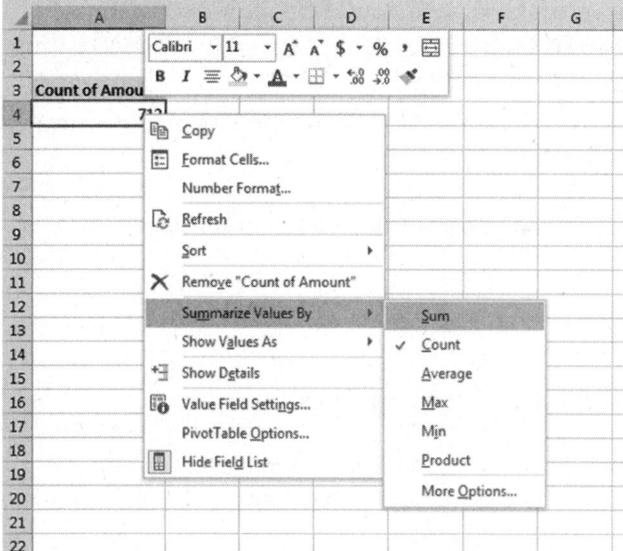

Figure 18-10: Right-click anywhere in the data to summarize using a different aggregate.

Sum of Amount	Column Labels			
Row Labels	Central	North County	Westside	Grand Total
CD	1359385	1137911	648549	3145845
Checking	802403	392516	292995	1487914
IRA	68380	134374	10000	212754
Savings	885757	467414	336088	1689259
Grand Total	3115925	2132215	1287632	6535772

Figure 18-11: After a few simple steps, the pivot table shows a summary of the data.

Formatting the pivot table

Notice that the pivot table uses General number formatting. To change the number format for all data, right-click any value and choose Number Format from the shortcut menu. Then use the Format Cells dialog box to change the number format for the displayed data.

Tip

You might be tempted to use the cell formatting controls on the Home tab of the Ribbon. When you use those controls, it only formats the cells you have selected. However, when you use the Number Format option on the right-click menu, all the data is formatted.

You can apply any of several built-in styles to a pivot table. Select any cell in the pivot table and choose PivotTable Tools ➜ Design ➜ PivotTable Styles to select a style. Fine-tune the display by using the controls in the PivotTable Tools ➜ Design ➜ PivotTable Style Options group.

You also can use the controls in the PivotTable ➜ Design ➜ Layout group to control various elements in the pivot table. You can adjust any of the following elements:

- **Subtotals:** Hide subtotals or choose where to display them (above or below the data).
- **Grand Totals:** Choose which types, if any, to display.
- **Report Layout:** Choose from three different layout styles (compact, outline, or tabular). You can also choose to hide repeating labels.
- **Blank Row:** Add a blank row between items to improve readability.

The PivotTable Tools ➜ Analyze ➜ Show group contains additional options that affect the appearance of your pivot table. For example, you use the Field Headers button to toggle the display of the field headings.

Still more pivot table options are available in the PivotTable Options dialog box, shown in Figure 18-12. To display this dialog box, choose PivotTable Tools ➜ Analyze ➜ PivotTable ➜ Options. Or right-click any cell in the pivot table and choose PivotTable Options from the shortcut menu.

The best way to become familiar with all these layout and formatting options is to experiment.

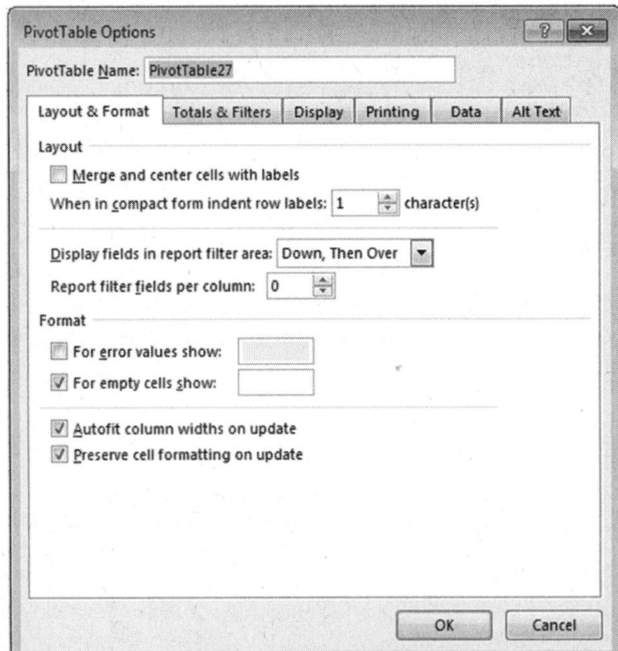

Figure 18-12: The PivotTable Options dialog box.

Pivot table calculations

Pivot table data is most frequently summarized using a sum. However, you can display your data using a number of different summary techniques, specified in the Value Field Settings dialog box. The quickest way to display this dialog box is to right-click any value in the pivot table and choose Value Field Settings from the shortcut menu. This dialog box has two tabs: Summarize Values By and Show Values As.

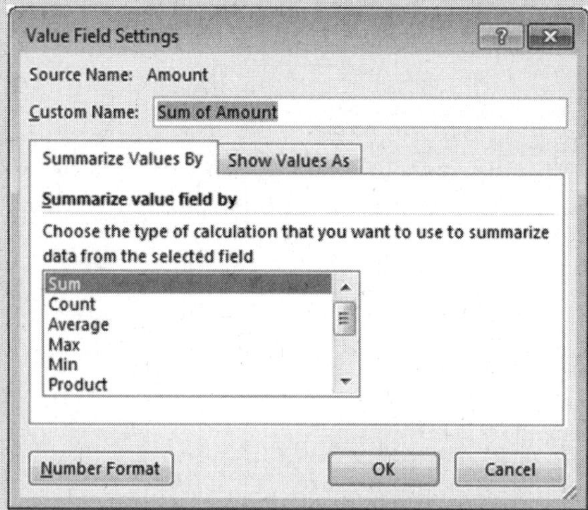

Use the Summarize Values By tab to select a different summary function. Your choices are Sum, Count, Average, Max, Min, Product, Count Numbers, StdDev, StdDevp, Var, and Varp.

To display your values in a different form, use the drop-down control on the Show Values As tab. You have many options to choose from, including as a percentage of the total or subtotal.

This dialog box also provides a way to apply a number format to the values. Just click the button and choose your number format.

Modifying the pivot table

After you create a pivot table, changing it is easy. For example, you can add further summary information by using the PivotTable Field task pane. Figure 18-13 shows the pivot table after we dragged a second field (OpenedBy) to the Rows section in the PivotTable task pane.

Following are some tips on other pivot table modifications that you can make:

- To remove a field from the pivot table, select it in the bottom part of the PivotTable Field task pane and drag it away.
- If an area has more than one field, you can change the order in which the fields are listed by dragging the field names. Doing so determines how nesting occurs and affects the appearance of the pivot table.

- To temporarily remove a field from the pivot table, remove the check mark from the field name in the top part of the PivotTable Field task pane. The pivot table is redisplayed without that field. Place the check mark back on the field name, and it appears in its previous section.
- If you add a field to the Filters section, the field items appear in a drop-down list, which allows you to filter the displayed data by one or more items. Figure 18-14 shows an example. We dragged the Date field to the Filters area. The pivot table is now showing the data only for a single day (which we selected from the drop-down list).

	A	B	C	D	E
1					
2					
3	Sum of Amount	Column Labels			
4	Row Labels	Central	North County	Westside	Grand Total
5	⊟CD	1,359,385	1,137,911	648,549	3,145,845
6	New Accts	1,006,474	927,216	451,611	2,385,301
7	Teller	352,911	210,695	196,938	760,544
8	⊟Checking	802,403	392,516	292,995	1,487,914
9	New Accts	418,030	206,845	137,738	762,613
10	Teller	384,373	185,671	155,257	725,301
11	⊟IRA	68,380	134,374	10,000	212,754
12	New Accts	59,285	42,554	10,000	111,839
13	Teller	9,095	91,820		100,915
14	⊟Savings	885,757	467,414	336,088	1,689,259
15	New Accts	563,243	310,901	262,162	1,136,306
16	Teller	322,514	156,513	73,926	552,953
17	Grand Total	3,115,925	2,132,215	1,287,632	6,535,772
18					

Figure 18-13: Two fields are used for row labels.

	A	B	C	D	E	F
1	Date	Nov-05				
2						
3	Sum of Amount	Column Labels				
4	Row Labels	Central	North County	Westside	Grand Total	
5	⊟CD	58,961	19,307	84,705	162,973	
6	New Accts	30,666	19,307	71,705	121,678	
7	Teller	28,295		13,000	41,295	
8	⊟Checking	23,124	12,375	400	35,899	
9	New Accts	11,459	8,100	200	19,759	
10	Teller	11,665	4,275	200	16,140	
11	⊟IRA		7,000		7,000	
12	New Accts		7,000		7,000	
13	⊟Savings	19,395	11,612	12,310	43,317	
14	New Accts		10,612	12,310	22,922	
15	Teller	19,395	1,000		20,395	
16	Grand Total	101,480	50,294	97,415	249,189	
17						
18						

Figure 18-14: The pivot table is filtered by date.

Copying a pivot table's content

A pivot table is flexible, but it does have some limitations. For example, you can't insert new rows or columns, change any of the calculated values, or enter formulas within the pivot table. If you want to manipulate a pivot table in ways not normally permitted, make a copy of it so it's no longer linked to its source data.

To copy a pivot table, select the entire table and choose Home ➜ Clipboard ➜ Copy (or press Ctrl+C). Then select a new worksheet and choose Home Clipboard ➜ Paste ➜ Paste Values. The contents of the pivot table are copied to the new location so that you can do whatever you like to them. You also may want to copy the formats from the pivot table. Select the entire pivot table and then choose Home ➜ Clipboard ➜ Format Painter. Then click the upper-left corner of the copied range.

Note that the copied information is not a pivot table, and it is no longer linked to the source data. If the source data changes, your copied pivot table does not reflect these changes.

More Pivot Table Examples

To demonstrate the flexibility of pivot tables, we created some additional pivot tables. The examples use the bank account data and answer the questions posed earlier in this chapter. (See the "A Pivot Table Example" section.)

Question 1

What is the daily total new deposit amount for each branch?

Figure 18-15 shows the pivot table that answers this question:

- The Branch field is in the Columns section.
- The Date field is in the Rows section.
- The Amount field is in the Value section and is summarized by Sum.

Note that you can sort the pivot table by any column. For example, you can sort the Grand Total column in descending order to find out which day of the month had the largest amount of new funds. To sort, just right-click any cell in the column and choose Sort from the shortcut menu.

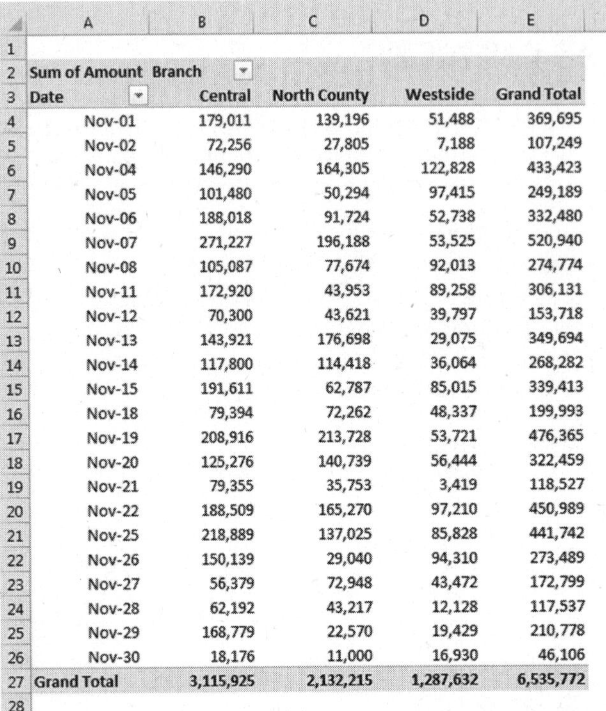

Sum of Amount	Branch			
Date	Central	North County	Westside	Grand Total
Nov-01	179,011	139,196	51,488	369,695
Nov-02	72,256	27,805	7,188	107,249
Nov-04	146,290	164,305	122,828	433,423
Nov-05	101,480	50,294	97,415	249,189
Nov-06	188,018	91,724	52,738	332,480
Nov-07	271,227	196,188	53,525	520,940
Nov-08	105,087	77,674	92,013	274,774
Nov-11	172,920	43,953	89,258	306,131
Nov-12	70,300	43,621	39,797	153,718
Nov-13	143,921	176,698	29,075	349,694
Nov-14	117,800	114,418	36,064	268,282
Nov-15	191,611	62,787	85,015	339,413
Nov-18	79,394	72,262	48,337	199,993
Nov-19	208,916	213,728	53,721	476,365
Nov-20	125,276	140,739	56,444	322,459
Nov-21	79,355	35,753	3,419	118,527
Nov-22	188,509	165,270	97,210	450,989
Nov-25	218,889	137,025	85,828	441,742
Nov-26	150,139	29,040	94,310	273,489
Nov-27	56,379	72,948	43,472	172,799
Nov-28	62,192	43,217	12,128	117,537
Nov-29	168,779	22,570	19,429	210,778
Nov-30	18,176	11,000	16,930	46,106
Grand Total	3,115,925	2,132,215	1,287,632	6,535,772

Figure 18-15: This pivot table shows daily totals for each branch.

Question 2

Which day of the week accounts for the most deposits?

Figure 18-16 shows the pivot table that answers this question:

- The Weekday field is in the Rows section.
- The Amount field is in the Values section and is summarized by Sum.

Conditional formatting data bars have been added to make it easier to visualize how the days compare.

Weekday	Sum of Amount
Monday	1,381,289
Tuesday	1,152,761
Wednesday	1,177,432
Thursday	1,025,286
Friday	1,645,649
Saturday	153,355
Grand Total	6,535,772

Figure 18-16: This pivot table shows totals by day of the week.

Question 3

How many accounts were opened at each branch, broken down by account type?

Figure 18-17 shows a pivot table that answers this question:

- The AcctType field is in the Columns section.
- The Branch field is in the Rows section.
- The Amount field is in the Value section and is summarized by Count.

	A	B	C	D	E	F
1						
2	Count of Amount	AcctType				
3	Branch	CD	Checking	IRA	Savings	Grand Total
4	Central	97	158	8	99	362
5	North County	60	61	15	61	197
6	Westside	54	59	5	35	153
7	Grand Total	211	278	28	195	712
8						

Figure 18-17: This pivot table uses the Count function to summarize the data.

So far, all the pivot table examples have used the Sum summary function. In this case, though, the summary function has been changed to Count. To change the summary function to Count, right-click any cell in the Values area and choose Summarize Data By ➜ Count from the shortcut menu.

Question 4

What's the dollar distribution of the different account types?

Figure 18-18 shows a pivot table that answers this question. For example, 253 (or 35.53%) of the new accounts were for an amount of $5,000 or less.

	A	B	C
1			
2	Amount	Count	Pct
3	1-5000	253	35.53%
4	5001-10000	193	27.11%
5	10001-15000	222	31.18%
6	15001-20000	19	2.67%
7	20001-25000	3	0.42%
8	25001-30000	1	0.14%
9	30001-35000	3	0.42%
10	40001-45000	3	0.42%
11	45001-50000	5	0.70%
12	60001-65000	2	0.28%
13	70001-75000	5	0.70%
14	85001-90000	3	0.42%
15	Grand Total	712	100.00%
16			

Figure 18-18: This pivot table counts the number of accounts that fall into each value range.

This pivot table is unusual because it uses three instances of a single field: Amount.

- The Amount field is in the Rows section (grouped, to show dollar ranges).
- The Amount field is also in the Values section and is summarized by Count.
- A third instance of the Amount field is the Values section, summarized by Percent of Total.

When we initially added the Amount field to the Rows section, the pivot table showed a row for each unique dollar amount. To group the values, we right-clicked one of the amounts and chose Group from the shortcut menu. Then we used Excel's Grouping dialog box to set up bins of $5,000 increments. Note that the Grouping dialog box does not appear if you select more than one Row label.

The second instance of the Amount field (in the Values section) is summarized by Count. We right-clicked a value and chose Summarize Data By ➜ Count.

We added another instance of Amount to the Values section, and we set it up to display the percentage. We right-clicked a value in column C and chose Show Values As ➜ % of Column Total. This option is also available on the Show Values As tab of the Value Field Settings dialog box.

Question 5

What types of accounts do tellers open most often?

The pivot table in Figure 18-19 shows that the most common account opened by tellers is a checking account:

- The AcctType field is in the Rows section.
- The OpenedBy field is in the Filters section.
- The Amount field is in the Values section (summarized by Count).
- A second instance of the Amount field is in the Values section (shown as Percent of GrandTotal).

	A	B	C	D
1				
2	OpenedBy	Teller		
3				
4	Row Labels	Accounts	Pct	
5	Checking	99	39.92%	
6	CD	71	28.63%	
7	Savings	68	27.42%	
8	IRA	10	4.03%	
9	Grand Total	248	100.00%	
10				

Figure 18-19: This pivot table uses a report filter to show only the teller data.

This pivot table uses the OpenedBy field as a filter and is showing the data only for tellers. We sorted the data so that the largest value is at the top, and we used conditional formatting to display data bars for the percentages.

When we added the first instance of Amount to the Value section, Excel labeled it Count of Amount. For the second instance, it labeled it as Count of Amount2. To change these to Accounts and Pct as shown in the figure, select the cell with the title (cells B3 and B4, respectively) and simply type the desired name.

Question 6

How does the Central branch compare with the other two branches?

Figure 18-20 shows a pivot table that sheds some light on this rather vague question. It shows how the Central branch compares with the other two branches combined:

- The AcctType field is in the Rows section.
- The Branch field is in the Columns section.
- The Amount field is in the Values section.

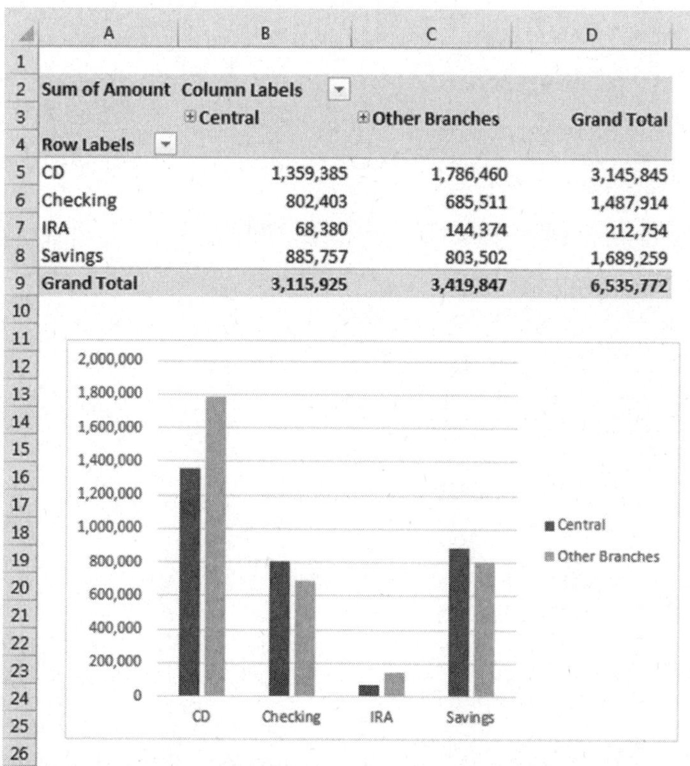

Sum of Amount	Column Labels		
	Central	Other Branches	Grand Total
Row Labels			
CD	1,359,385	1,786,460	3,145,845
Checking	802,403	685,511	1,487,914
IRA	68,380	144,374	212,754
Savings	885,757	803,502	1,689,259
Grand Total	3,115,925	3,419,847	6,535,772

Figure 18-20: This pivot table (and pivot chart) compares the Central branch with the other two branches combined.

We selected the North County and Westside labels, right-clicked, and chose Group to combine those two branches into a new category. Grouping also creates a new field in the PivotTable Fields task pane. In this case, the new field is named Branch2. We changed the label in the pivot table to Other Branches.

Note

The new field, Branch2, is also available for use in other pivot tables created from the data.

After grouping the North County and Westside branches, the pivot table allows easy comparison between the Central branch and the other branches combined.

We also created a pivot chart for good measure. We discuss pivot charts later in this chapter.

Question 7

In which branch do tellers open the most checking accounts for new customers?

Figure 18-21 shows a pivot table that answers this question. At the Central branch, tellers opened 23 checking accounts for new customers:

- The Customer field is in the Filters section.
- The OpenedBy field is in the Filters section.
- The AcctType field is in the Filters section.
- The Branch field is in the Rows section.
- The Amount field is in the Values section, summarized by Count.

	A	B	C
1			
2	Customer	New	
3	OpenedBy	Teller	
4	AcctType	Checking	
5			
6	**Branch**	**Accounts**	
7	Central	23	
8	North County	10	
9	Westside	10	
10	**Grand Total**	**43**	
11			
12			
13			

Figure 18-21: This pivot table uses three report filters.

This pivot table uses three filters. The Customer field is filtered to show only New, the OpenedBy field is filtered to show only Teller, and the AcctType field is filtered to show only Checking.

Grouping Pivot Table Items

One of the more useful features of a pivot table is the ability to combine items into groups. You can group items that appear as Row Labels or Column Labels. Excel offers two ways to group items:

- **Manually:** After creating the pivot table, select the items to be grouped and then choose PivotTable Tools ➜ Options ➜ Group ➜ Group Selection. Or you can right-click and choose Group from the shortcut menu.
- **Automatically:** If the items are numeric (or dates), use the Grouping dialog box to specify how you would like to group the items. Select any item in the Row Labels or Column Labels and then choose PivotTable Tools ➜ Options ➜ Group ➜ Group Selection. Or you can right-click and choose Group from the shortcut menu. In either case, Excel displays its Grouping dialog box.

Note

If you create a pivot table using the Data Model, grouping is not an option.

A manual grouping example

Figure 18-22 shows a pivot table created from an employee list in columns A:C, which has the following fields: Employee, Location, and Sex. The pivot table, in columns E:H, shows the number of employees in each of six states, cross-tabulated by sex.

	A	B	C
1	Employee	Location	Sex
2	Al Grubbs	California	Male
3	Sarah Parks	New York	Female
4	Cheryl Cory	California	Female
5	Gregory Steiger	California	Male
6	Sheila Wigfall	California	Female
7	Pedro H. Nicholson	Arizona	Male
8	Howard Keach	California	Male
9	Heather Lichtenstein	Washington	Female
10	Janet Woodson	Arizona	Female
11	Hosea Pierson	New York	Male

Count	Female	Male	Total
Arizona	5	15	20
California	44	64	108
Massachusetts	43	47	90
New York	51	40	91
Pennsylvania	17	29	46
Washington	16	29	45
Total	176	224	400

Figure 18-22: A pivot table before creating groups of states.

The goal is to create two groups of states: Western Region (Arizona, California, and Washington) and Eastern Region (Massachusetts, New York, and Pennsylvania). One solution is to add a new column (Region) to the data table and enter the Region for each row. In this case, it's easier to create groups directly in the pivot table.

To create the first group, we held the Ctrl key while selecting Arizona, California, and Washington. Then we right-clicked and chose Group from the shortcut menu. We repeated the operation with the remaining states to create the second group. Then we replaced the default group names (Group 1 and Group 2) with more meaningful names (Eastern Region and Western Region). Figure 18-23 shows the result of the grouping.

Count	Female	Male	Total
⊟Western Region	65	108	173
Arizona	5	15	20
California	44	64	108
Washington	16	29	45
⊟Eastern Region	111	116	227
Massachusetts	43	47	90
New York	51	40	91
Pennsylvania	17	29	46
Total	176	224	400

Figure 18-23: A pivot table with two groups and subtotals for the groups.

You can create any number of groups and even create groups of groups.

On the Web

The workbook used in this example is available at this book's website. The file is named employee list.xlsx.

Multiple groups from the same data source

If you create multiple pivot tables from the same data source, you may have noticed that grouping a field in one pivot table affects the other pivot tables. Specifically, all the other pivot tables automatically use the same grouping. Sometimes, this is exactly what you want. Other times, it's not at all what you want. For example, you might like to see two pivot table reports: one that summarizes data by month and year, and another that summarizes the data by quarter and years.

Grouping affects other pivot tables because all the pivot tables are using the same pivot table "cache." Unfortunately, there is no direct way to force a pivot table to use a new cache. But there *is* a way to trick Excel into using a new cache. The trick involves giving multiple range names to the source data.

For example, name your source range *Table1* and then give the same range a second name: *Table2*. The easiest way to name a range is to use the Name box, to the left of the Formula bar. Select the range, type a name in the Name box, and press Enter. Then, with the range still selected, type a different name and press Enter. Excel will display only the first name, but you can verify that both names exist by choosing Formulas ➜ Define Names ➜ Name Manager.

When you create the first pivot table, specify *Table1* as the Table/Range. When you create the second pivot table, specify *Table2* as the Table/Range. Each pivot table will use a separate cache, and you can create groups in one pivot table, independent of the other pivot table.

You can use this trick with existing pivot tables. Make sure that you give the data source a different name. Then select the pivot table and choose PivotTable Tools ➜ Analyze ➜ Data ➜ Change Data Source. In the Change PivotTable Data Source dialog box, type the new name that you gave to the range. This will cause Excel to create a new pivot cache for the pivot table.

Viewing grouped data

Excel provides a number of options for displaying a pivot table, and you may want to experiment with these options when you use groups. These commands are on the PivotTable Tools ➜ Design ➜ Layout tab of the Ribbon. There are no rules for these options. The key is to try a few and see which makes your pivot table look the best. In addition, try various PivotTable Styles, with options for banded rows or banded columns. Often, the style that you choose can greatly enhance readability.

Figure 18-24 shows pivot tables using various options for displaying subtotals, grand totals, and styles.

Count	Female	Male	Total
⊟Western Region	65	108	173
Arizona	5	15	20
California	44	64	108
Washington	16	29	45
⊟Eastern Region	111	116	227
Massachusetts	43	47	90
New York	51	40	91
Pennsylvania	17	29	46
Total	176	224	400

Count	Female	Male	Total
⊟Western Region			
Arizona	5	15	20
California	44	64	108
Washington	16	29	45
Western Region Total	65	108	173
⊟Eastern Region			
Massachusetts	43	47	90
New York	51	40	91
Pennsylvania	17	29	46
Eastern Region Total	111	116	227
Total	176	224	400

Count	Female	Male
⊟Western Region		
Arizona	5	15
California	44	64
Washington	16	29
⊟Eastern Region		
Massachusetts	43	47
New York	51	40
Pennsylvania	17	29

Count	Female	Male
⊟Western Region	65	108
Arizona	5	15
California	44	64
Washington	16	29
⊟Eastern Region	111	116
Massachusetts	43	47
New York	51	40
Pennsylvania	17	29
Total	176	224

Figure 18-24: Pivot tables with options for subtotals and grand totals.

Automatic grouping examples

When a field contains numbers, dates, or times, Excel can create groups automatically by assigning each item to a bin. The two examples in this section demonstrate automatic grouping.

Grouping by date

Figure 18-25 shows a portion of a simple table with two fields: Date and Sales. This table has 730 rows of data and covers the dates between January 1, 2015 and December 31, 2016. The goal is to summarize the sales information by month.

	A	B	C
1	Date	Sales	
2	1/1/2015	3,830	
3	1/2/2015	3,763	
4	1/3/2015	4,362	
5	1/4/2015	3,669	
6	1/5/2015	3,942	
7	1/6/2015	4,488	
8	1/7/2015	4,416	
9	1/8/2015	3,371	
10	1/9/2015	3,628	
11	1/10/2015	4,548	
12	1/11/2015	5,493	
13	1/12/2015	5,706	
14	1/13/2015	6,579	
15	1/14/2015	6,333	
16	1/15/2015	6,101	
17	1/16/2015	5,289	
18	1/17/2015	5,349	
19	1/18/2015	5,814	
20	1/19/2015	6,501	
21	1/20/2015	6,513	
22	1/21/2015	5,970	
23	1/22/2015	5,791	
24	1/23/2015	5,478	

Figure 18-25: You can use a pivot table to summarize the sales data by month.

On the Web

A workbook demonstrating how to group pivot table items by date is available at this book's website. The file is named grouping sales by date.xlsx.

Figure 18-26 shows part of a pivot table created from the data. The Date field is in the Row Labels section, and the Sales field is in the Values section. Not surprisingly, the pivot table looks exactly like the input data because the dates have not been grouped.

Row Labels	Sum of Sales
1/1/2015	3,830
1/2/2015	3,763
1/3/2015	4,362
1/4/2015	3,669
1/5/2015	3,942
1/6/2015	4,488
1/7/2015	4,416
1/8/2015	3,371
1/9/2015	3,628
1/10/2015	4,548
1/11/2015	5,493
1/12/2015	5,706
1/13/2015	6,579
1/14/2015	6,333
1/15/2015	6,101
1/16/2015	5,289
1/17/2015	5,349
1/18/2015	5,814
1/19/2015	6,501
1/20/2015	6,513
1/21/2015	5,970
1/22/2015	5,791
1/23/2015	5,478
1/24/2015	6,564

Figure 18-26: The pivot table, before grouping by month.

To group the items by month, select any date and choose PivotTable Tools ➜ Analyze ➜ Group ➜ Group Field (or, right-click and choose Group from the shortcut menu). You see the Grouping dialog box in Figure 18-27.

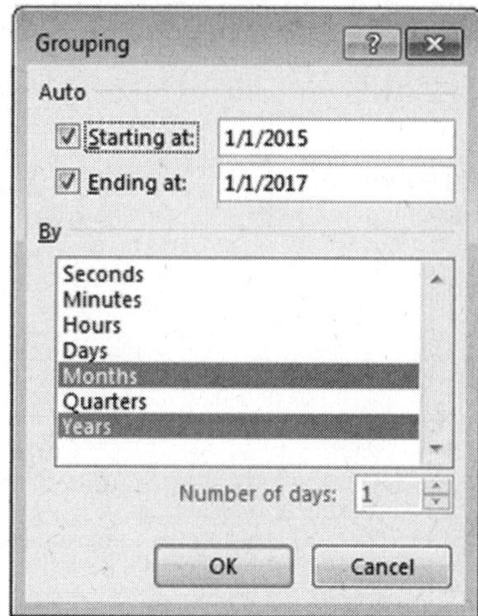

Figure 18-27: Use the Grouping dialog box to group pivot table items by dates.

In the By list box, select Months and Years and verify that the starting and ending dates are correct. Click OK. The Date items in the pivot table are grouped by years and by months, as shown in Figure 18-28.

Row Labels	Sum of Sales
2015	
Jan	167,624
Feb	137,825
Mar	214,896
Apr	100,872
May	158,005
Jun	117,649
Jul	295,248
Aug	518,966
Sep	612,673
Oct	699,854
Nov	863,085
Dec	970,441
2016	
Jan	974,625
Feb	969,696
Mar	1,081,596
Apr	983,306
May	1,044,322
Jun	930,076
Jul	961,557
Aug	938,433
Sep	975,503
Oct	948,120
Nov	950,493
Dec	906,389
Grand Total	16,521,254

Figure 18-28: The pivot table, after grouping by years and months.

Note

If you select only Months from the By list box of the Grouping dialog box, months in different years combine. For example, the January item would display sales for both 2015 and 2016.

Figure 18-29 shows another view of the data, grouped by quarter and by year.

Row Labels	Sum of Sales
2015	
Qtr1	520,345
Qtr2	376,526
Qtr3	1,426,887
Qtr4	2,533,380
2016	
Qtr1	3,025,917
Qtr2	2,957,704
Qtr3	2,875,493
Qtr4	2,805,002
Grand Total	16,521,254

Figure 18-29: This pivot table shows sales by quarter and by year.

Grouping by time

Figure 18-30 shows a pivot table that groups instrument reading data into hours. Each row of the source data is a reading from an instrument, taken at one-minute intervals throughout an entire day. The source table has 1,440 rows, each representing one minute. The pivot table summarizes the data by hour.

D	E	F	G	H
	Average	Minimum	Maximum	
12 AM	110.50	104.37	116.21	
1 AM	118.57	112.72	127.14	
2 AM	124.39	115.75	130.36	
3 AM	122.74	112.85	132.90	
4 AM	129.29	123.99	133.52	
5 AM	132.91	125.88	141.04	
6 AM	139.67	132.69	146.06	
7 AM	128.18	117.53	139.65	
8 AM	119.24	112.10	129.38	
9 AM	134.36	129.11	142.79	
10 AM	136.16	130.91	142.89	
11 AM	122.79	108.63	138.10	
12 PM	111.76	106.43	116.71	
1 PM	104.91	98.48	111.86	
2 PM	119.71	110.37	130.55	
3 PM	131.83	121.92	139.65	
4 PM	131.05	123.36	137.94	
5 PM	138.90	133.05	145.06	
6 PM	134.71	129.29	139.89	
7 PM	123.09	113.97	135.23	
8 PM	118.13	112.64	125.65	
9 PM	112.64	108.09	117.72	
10 PM	103.19	96.13	110.49	
11 PM	106.01	100.03	111.76	
Grand Total	123.11	96.13	146.06	

Figure 18-30: This pivot table is grouped by hours.

On the Web

This workbook, named time based grouping.xlsx, is available at this book's website.

Following are the settings we used for this pivot table:

- The Values area has three instances of the Reading field. We used the Data Field Setting dialog box (the Summarize Values By tab) to summarize the first instance by Average, the second instance by Min, and the third instance by Max.
- The Time field is in the Row Labels section, and we used the Grouping dialog box to group by Hours.

Creating a Frequency Distribution

Excel provides a number of ways to create a frequency distribution, but none of those methods is easier than using a pivot table. Figure 18-31 shows part of a table of 221 students and the test score for each. The goal is to determine how many students are in each ten-point range (1–10, 11–20, and so on).

On the Web

This workbook, named test scores.xlsx, is available at this book's website.

	A	B
1	Student	Score
2	Rhea Madsen	69
3	Jennifer Mendez	81
4	Brett Broyles	100
5	Shirley Smith	28
6	John Brown	93
7	Michael G. Welch	50
8	Donald Tse	100
9	Madeline Stevens	82
10	Howard Porter	86
11	Helen Craven	81
12	Lillie Schultz	75
13	Emily Li	80
14	Michael Long	71
15	Chris Herrman	88
16	Marshall Sherman	48
17	William Grindle	82
18	Pauline Haun	85
19	Lydia J. Evans	82
20	James Weaver	80
21	Barbara Billings	77
22	William Hernandez	35
23	Robert Griffin	90

Figure 18-31: Creating a frequency distribution for these test scores is simple.

The pivot table is simple:

- The Score field is in the Rows section (grouped).
- Another instance of the Score field is in the Values section (summarized by Count).

The Grouping dialog box that generated the bins specified that the groups start at 1 and end at 100, in increments of 10.

Note

By default, Excel does not display items with a count of zero. In this example, no test scores are below 21, so the 1–10 and 11–20 items are hidden. To display items that have no data, choose PivotTable Tools ➜ Analyze ➜ Active Field ➜ Field Settings. In the Field Settings dialog box, click the Layout & Print tab. Then select the Show Items with No Data check box.

Figure 18-32 shows the frequency distribution of the test scores, along with a pivot chart, created by choosing PivotTable Tools ➜ Analyze ➜ Tools ➜ PivotChart.

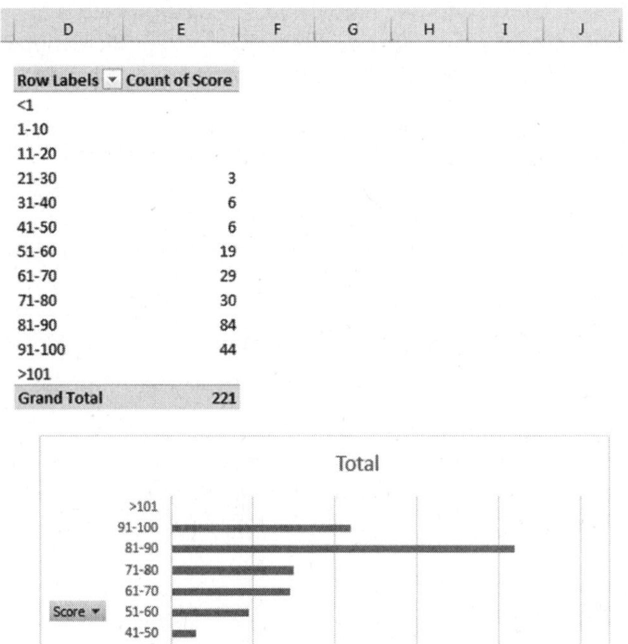

Row Labels	Count of Score
<1	
1-10	
11-20	
21-30	3
31-40	6
41-50	6
51-60	19
61-70	29
71-80	30
81-90	84
91-100	44
>101	
Grand Total	221

Figure 18-32: The pivot table and pivot chart show the frequency distribution for the test scores.

Note

This example uses Excel's Grouping dialog box to create the groups automatically. If you don't want to group in equal-sized bins, you can create your own groups. For example, you may want to assign letter grades based on the test score. Select the rows for the first group and then choose Group from the shortcut menu. Repeat these steps for each additional group. Then replace the default group names with more meaningful names.

Creating a Calculated Field or Calculated Item

Perhaps the most confusing aspect of pivot tables is calculated fields versus calculated items. Many pivot table users simply avoid dealing with calculated fields and items. However, these features can be useful, and they really aren't that complicated after you understand how they work.

First, some basic definitions:

- **Calculated field:** A calculated field is a new field created from other fields in the pivot table. If your pivot table source is a worksheet table, an alternative to using a calculated field is to add a new column to the table and then create a formula to perform the desired calculation. A calculated field must reside in the Values area of the pivot table. You can't use a calculated field in the Columns area, Rows area, or Filter area.
- **Calculated item:** A calculated item uses the contents of other items within a field of the pivot table. If your pivot table source is a worksheet table, an alternative to using a calculated item is to insert one or more rows and write formulas that use values in other rows. A calculated item must reside in the Columns area, Rows area, or Filter area of a pivot table. You can't use a calculated item in the Values area.

The formulas used to create calculated fields and calculated items aren't standard Excel formulas. In other words, you don't enter the formulas into cells. Rather, you enter these formulas in a dialog box, and they're stored along with the pivot table data.

The examples in this section use the worksheet table shown in Figure 18-33. The table consists of 5 fields and 48 rows. Each row describes monthly sales information for a particular sales representative. For example, Amy is a sales rep for the North region, and she sold 239 units in January for total sales of $23,040.

	A	B	C	D	E
1	SalesRep	Region	Month	Sales	Units Sold
2	Amy	North	Jan	$23,040	239
3	Amy	North	Feb	$24,131	79
4	Amy	North	Mar	$24,646	71
5	Amy	North	Apr	$22,047	71
6	Amy	North	May	$24,971	157
7	Amy	North	Jun	$24,218	92
8	Amy	North	Jul	$25,735	175
9	Amy	North	Aug	$23,638	87
10	Amy	North	Sep	$25,749	557
11	Amy	North	Oct	$24,437	95
12	Amy	North	Nov	$25,355	706
13	Amy	North	Dec	$25,899	180
14	Bob	North	Jan	$20,024	103
15	Bob	North	Feb	$23,822	267
16	Bob	North	Mar	$24,854	96
17	Bob	North	Apr	$22,838	74
18	Bob	North	May	$25,320	231
19	Bob	North	Jun	$24,733	164
20	Bob	North	Jul	$21,184	68
21	Bob	North	Aug	$23,174	114
22	Bob	North	Sep	$25,999	84
23	Bob	North	Oct	$22,639	260
24	Bob	North	Nov	$23,949	109
25	Bob	North	Dec	$23,179	465
26	Chuck	South	Jan	$19,886	95
27	Chuck	South	Feb	$23,494	148
28	Chuck	South	Mar	$21,824	83
29	Chuck	South	Apr	$22,058	96
30	Chuck	South	May	$20,280	453
31	Chuck	South	Jun	$23,965	760

Figure 18-33: This data demonstrates calculated fields and calculated items.

A workbook that demonstrates calculated fields and items is available at this book's website. The file is named calculated fields and items.xlsx.

Figure 18-34 shows a pivot table created from the data. This pivot table shows Sales (Values area), cross-tabulated by Month (Rows area) and by SalesRep (Columns area).

G	H	I	J	K
Sum of Sales	**Column Labels**			
Row Labels	**Amy**	**Bob**	**Chuck**	**Doug**
Group1				
Jan	23,040	20,024	19,886	26,264
Feb	24,131	23,822	23,494	29,953
Mar	24,646	24,854	21,824	25,041
Apr	22,047	22,838	22,058	29,338
May	24,971	25,320	20,280	25,150
Jun	24,218	24,733	23,965	27,371
Jul	25,735	21,184	23,032	25,044
Aug	23,638	23,174	21,273	29,506
Sep	25,749	25,999	21,584	29,061
Oct	24,437	22,639	19,625	27,113
Nov	25,355	23,949	19,832	25,953
Dec	25,899	23,179	20,583	28,670
Grand Total	**293,866**	**281,715**	**257,436**	**328,464**

Figure 18-34: This pivot table was created from the sales data.

The examples that follow create the following:

- A calculated field, to compute average sales per unit
- Four calculated items, to compute the quarterly sales commission

Creating a calculated field

Because a pivot table is a special type of range, you can't insert new rows or columns within the pivot table, which means that you can't insert formulas to perform calculations with the data in a pivot table. However, you can create calculated fields for a pivot table. A *calculated field* consists of a calculation that can involve other fields.

A calculated field is basically a way to display new information in a pivot table: an alternative to creating a new column field in your source data. In many cases, you may find it easier to insert a new column in the source range with a formula that performs the desired calculation. A calculated field is most useful when the data comes from a source that you can't easily manipulate, such as an external database.

Calculated fields can be used in the Values area of a pivot table. They cannot be used in the Columns, Rows, or Filter areas of a pivot table.

In the sales example, for example, suppose that you want to calculate the average sales amount per unit. You can compute this value by dividing the Sales field by the Units Sold field. The result shows a new field (a calculated field) for the pivot table.

Use the following procedure to create a calculated field that consists of the Sales field divided by the Units Sold field:

1. Select any cell within the pivot table.
2. Choose PivotTable Tools ➜ Analyze ➜ Calculations ➜ Fields, Items & Sets ➜ Calculated Field.

   Excel displays the Insert Calculated Field dialog box.
3. Type a descriptive name in the Name field and specify the formula in the Formula field (see Figure 18-35).

   The formula can use worksheet functions and other fields from the data source. For this example, the calculated field name is Average Unit Price, and the formula is

   ```
   =Sales/'Units Sold'
   ```
4. Click the Add button to add this new field.
5. Click OK to close the Insert Calculated Field dialog box.

Note

You can create the formula manually by typing it or by double-clicking items in the Fields list box. Double-clicking an item transfers it to the Formula field. Because the Units Sold field contains a space, Excel adds single quotes around the field name.

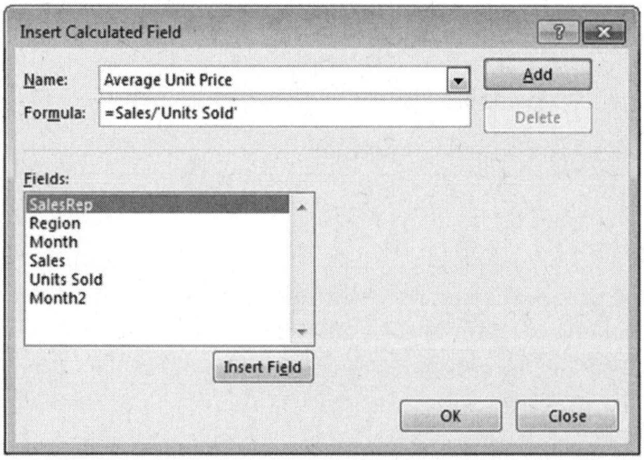

Figure 18-35: The Insert Calculated Field dialog box.

After you create the calculated field, Excel adds it to the Values area of the pivot table (and it appears in the PivotTable Field task pane). You can treat it just like any other field, with one exception: you can't move it to the Rows, Columns, or Filter areas. It must remain in the Values area.

Figure 18-36 shows the pivot table after adding the calculated field. The new field displayed Sum of Avg Unit Price, but we changed this label to Avg Price.

	Column Labels							
	Amy		Bob		Chuck		Doug	
Row Labels	**Tot Sales**	**Avg Price**	**Tot Sales**	**Avg Price**	**Tot Sales**	**Avg Price**	**Tot Sales**	**Avg Price**
Group1								
Jan	23,040	$96	20,024	$194	19,886	$209	26,264	$285
Feb	24,131	$305	23,822	$89	23,494	$159	29,953	$35
Mar	24,646	$347	24,854	$259	21,824	$263	25,041	$291
Apr	22,047	$311	22,838	$309	22,058	$230	29,338	$132
May	24,971	$159	25,320	$110	20,280	$45	25,150	$104
Jun	24,218	$263	24,733	$151	23,965	$32	27,371	$288
Jul	25,735	$147	21,184	$312	23,032	$149	25,044	$305
Aug	23,638	$272	23,174	$203	21,273	$28	29,506	$286
Sep	25,749	$46	25,999	$310	21,584	$189	29,061	$199
Oct	24,437	$257	22,639	$87	19,625	$236	27,113	$226
Nov	25,355	$36	23,949	$220	19,832	$283	25,953	$320
Dec	25,899	$144	23,179	$50	20,583	$116	28,670	$145
Grand Total	**293,866**	**$117**	**281,715**	**$138**	**257,436**	**$86**	**328,464**	**$142**

Figure 18-36: This pivot table uses a calculated field.

Tip

The formulas that you develop can also use worksheet functions, but the functions can't refer to cells or named ranges.

Inserting a calculated item

The preceding section describes how to create a calculated field. Excel also enables you to create a *calculated item* for a pivot table field. Keep in mind that a calculated field can be an alternative to adding a new field (column) to your data source. A calculated item, on the other hand, is an alternative to adding new rows to the data source—rows that contain formulas that refer to other rows.

In this example, you create four calculated items. Each item represents the commission earned on the quarter's sales, according to the following schedule:

- **Quarter 1:** 10% of January, February, and March sales
- **Quarter 2:** 11% of April, May, and June sales
- **Quarter 3:** 12% of July, August, and September sales
- **Quarter 4:** 12.5% of October, November, and December sales

Note

Modifying the source data to obtain this information would require inserting 16 new rows, each with formulas. So, for this example, creating four calculated items may be an easier task.

To create a calculated item to compute the commission for January, February, and March, follow these steps:

1. Move the cell pointer to the Rows area of the pivot table and choose PivotTable Tools ➜ Analyze ➜ Calculations ➜ Fields, Items, & Sets ➜ Calculated Item. Excel displays the Insert Calculated Item dialog box.
2. Type a name for the new item in the Name field and specify the formula in the Formula field (see Figure 18-37).

   The formula can use items in other fields, but it can't use worksheet functions. For this example, the new item is named Qtr1 Commission, and the formula appears as follows:

   ```
   =10%*(Jan+Feb+Mar)
   ```

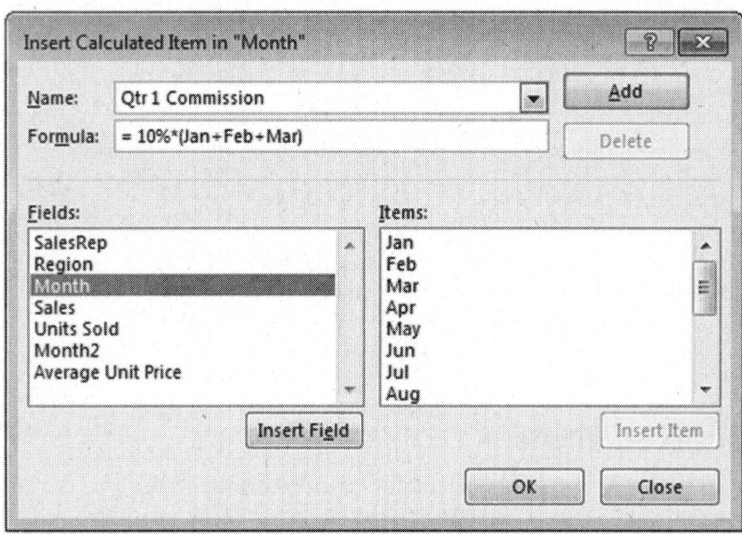

Figure 18-37: The Insert Calculated Item dialog box.

3. Click the Add button.
4. Repeat steps 2 and 3 to create three additional calculated items:
   - `Qtr2 Commission: =11%*(Apr+May+Jun)`
   - `Qtr3 Commission: =12%*(Jul+Aug+Sep)`
   - `Qtr4 Commission: =12.5%*(Oct+Nov+Dec)`
5. Click OK to close the dialog box.

Note

A calculated item, unlike a calculated field, does not appear in the PivotTable Field task pane. Only fields appear in the field list.

Warning

If you use a calculated item in your pivot table, you may need to turn off the Grand Total display for columns to avoid double counting. In this example, the Grand Total includes the calculated item, so the commission amounts are included with the sales amounts. To turn off Grand Totals, choose PivotTable Tools ➜ Design ➜ Layout ➜ Grand Totals.

After you create the calculated items, they appear in the pivot table. Figure 18-38 shows the pivot table after adding the four calculated items. Notice that the calculated items are added to the end of the Month items. You can rearrange the items by selecting the cell and dragging its border. Another option is to create two groups: one for the sales numbers and one for the commission calculations. Figure 18-39 shows the pivot table after creating the two groups and adding subtotals.

G	H	I	J	K
Tot Sales	Column Labels			
Row Labels	Amy	Bob	Chuck	Doug
Jan	23,040	20,024	19,886	26,264
Feb	24,131	23,822	23,494	29,953
Mar	24,646	24,854	21,824	25,041
Apr	22,047	22,838	22,058	29,338
May	24,971	25,320	20,280	25,150
Jun	24,218	24,733	23,965	27,371
Jul	25,735	21,184	23,032	25,044
Aug	23,638	23,174	21,273	29,506
Sep	25,749	25,999	21,584	29,061
Oct	24,437	22,639	19,625	27,113
Nov	25,355	23,949	19,832	25,953
Dec	25,899	23,179	20,583	28,670
Qtr1 Commission	7,182	6,870	6,520	8,126
Qtr2 Commission	7,836	8,018	7,293	9,004
Qtr3 Commission	9,015	8,443	7,907	10,033
Qtr4 Commission	9,461	8,721	7,505	10,217

Figure 18-38: This pivot table uses calculated items for quarterly totals.

G	H	I	J	K
Tot Sales	Column Labels			
Row Labels	Amy	Bob	Chuck	Doug
⊟Monthly Sales				
Jan	23,040	20,024	19,886	26,264
Feb	24,131	23,822	23,494	29,953
Mar	24,646	24,854	21,824	25,041
Apr	22,047	22,838	22,058	29,338
May	24,971	25,320	20,280	25,150
Jun	24,218	24,733	23,965	27,371
Jul	25,735	21,184	23,032	25,044
Aug	23,638	23,174	21,273	29,506
Sep	25,749	25,999	21,584	29,061
Oct	24,437	22,639	19,625	27,113
Nov	25,355	23,949	19,832	25,953
Dec	25,899	23,179	20,583	28,670
⊟Commissions				
Qtr1 Commission	7,182	6,870	6,520	8,126
Qtr2 Commission	7,836	8,018	7,293	9,004
Qtr3 Commission	9,015	8,443	7,907	10,033
Qtr4 Commission	9,461	8,721	7,505	10,217

Figure 18-39: The pivot table, after creating two groups and adding subtotals.

Filtering Pivot Tables with Slicers

A slicer makes it easy to filter data in a pivot table. Figure 18-40 shows a pivot table with three slicers. Each slicer represents a particular field. In this case, the pivot table is displaying data for new customers, opened by tellers at the Central branch.

The same type of filtering can be accomplished by using the field labels in the pivot table, but slicers are intended for those who might not understand how to filter data in a pivot table. You can also use slicers to create an attractive and easy-to-use interactive "dashboard."

	A	B	C
1	OpenedBy	Teller	
2			
3	Count of Amount	Column Labels	
4	Row Labels	New	Grand Total
5	Central	52	52
6	CD	14	14
7	Checking	23	23
8	Savings	15	15
9	Grand Total	52	52

OpenedBy
New Accts
Teller

Branch
Central
North County
Westside

Customer
Existing
New

Figure 18-40: Using slicers to filter the data displayed in a pivot table.

To add one or more slicers to a worksheet, start by selecting any cell in a pivot table and then choose PivotTable Tools ➜ Filter ➜ Insert Slicer. The Insert Slicers dialog box appears with a list of all fields in the pivot table. Place a check mark next to the slicers you want and then click OK.

Note

Slicers aren't limited to pivot tables. Slicers can also be used with a table (choose Insert ➜ Tables ➜ Table).

To use a slicer to filter data in a pivot table, just click a button. To display multiple values, press Ctrl while you click the buttons in a Slicer. Press Shift and click to select a series of consecutive buttons.

Figure 18-41 shows a pivot table and a pivot chart. Two slicers are used to filter the data (by state and by month). In this case, the pivot table (and pivot chart) shows only the data for Kansas, Missouri, and New York for the months of January through March. Slicers provide a quick and easy way to create an interactive chart.

This workbook, named pivot table slicers.xlsx, is available at this book's website.

G H I J K L M N O P Q

Sum of Sales	Column Labels			
Row Labels	Kansas	Missouri	New York	Grand Total
Jan	1973	1511	1429	4913
Feb	1560	1744	1316	4620
Mar	1243	1414	1993	4650
Grand Total	4776	4669	4738	14183

2500
2000
1500
1000
500
0
Jan
Feb
Mar
Kansas
Missouri
New York

State
Kansas
Kentucky
Massachusetts
Missouri
New Jersey
New York
Oklahoma
Oregon
Washington

Month
Jan
Feb
Mar
Apr
May
Jun

Figure 18-41: Using a slicer to filter a pivot table by state.

Filtering Pivot Tables with a Timeline

A timeline is conceptually similar to a slicer, but this control is designed to simplify time-based filtering in a pivot table.

A timeline is relevant only if your pivot table has a field formatted as a date. This feature does not work with times. To add a timeline, select a cell in a pivot table and choose Insert ➜ Filter ➜ Timeline. Excel displays a dialog box that lists all date-based fields. If your pivot table doesn't have a field formatted as a date, Excel displays an error.

Figure 18-42 shows a pivot table created from the data in columns A:E. This pivot table uses a timeline, set to allow date filtering by quarters. Click a button that corresponds to the quarter you want to view, and the pivot table is updated immediately. To select a range of quarters, press Shift while you click the first and last buttons in the range. Other filtering options (selectable from the drop-down in the upper-right corner) are Year, Month, and Day. In the figure, the pivot table displays data from the last two quarters of 2011 and the first quarter of 2012.

A workbook that uses a timeline is available at this book's website. The filename is pivot table timeline.xlsx.

You can, of course, use both slicers and a timeline for a pivot table. A timeline has the same type of formatting options as slicers, so you can create an attractive interactive dashboard that simplifies pivot table filtering.

N34

	A	B	C	D	E
1	Ordered	Customer	Product	Units	TOTAL
2	1/2/2009	Existing	Doodads	2	198.00
3	1/2/2009	Existing	Sprockets	1	178.00
4	1/2/2009	Existing	Sprockets	1	178.00
5	1/2/2009	New	Snapholytes	1	188.00
6	1/2/2009	New	Doodads	1	212.95
7	1/2/2009	New	Doodads	1	197.95
8	1/3/2009	New	Sprockets	1	213.00
9	1/3/2009	New	Sprockets	1	213.00
10	1/4/2009	New	Doodads	2	206.95
11	1/4/2009	New	Doodads	1	186.95
12	1/4/2009	Existing	Doodads	2	198.00
13	1/4/2009	New	Sprockets	1	213.00
14	1/5/2009	New	Doodads	1	212.95
15	1/5/2009	New	Doodads	1	212.95
16	1/6/2009	Existing	Doodads	1	178.00
17	1/6/2009	Existing	Sprockets	2	183.00
18	1/6/2009	New	Doodads	2	232.95
19	1/7/2009	Existing	Doodads	1	178.00
20	1/7/2009	Existing	Doodads	1	178.00
21	1/7/2009	Existing	Sprockets	2	198.00
22	1/7/2009	New	Snapholytes	1	188.00
23	1/7/2009	New	Snapholytes	1	188.00
24	1/7/2009	New	Doodads	1	212.95
25	1/7/2009	New	Doodads	2	232.95
26	1/7/2009	New	Sprockets	2	233.00

	Customer		
Products	Existing	New	Grand Total
Doodads	2,688	6,945	9,632
Sprockets	56,516	92,689	149,205
Snapholytes	0	26,565	26,565
Grand Total	59,204	126,199	185,403

Ordered
Q3 2011 - Q1 2012
QUARTERS
2010 2011 2012
Q3 Q4 Q1 Q2 Q3 Q4 Q1 Q2 Q3 Q4

Product
Doodads
Snapholytes
Sprockets
Widgets

Figure 18-42: Using a timeline to filter a pivot table by date.

Referencing Cells Within a Pivot Table

In some cases, you may want to create a formula that references one or more cells within a pivot table. Figure 18-43 shows a simple pivot table that displays income and expense information for three years. In this pivot table, the Month field is hidden, so the pivot table shows the year totals.

This workbook, named pivot table referencing.xlsx, is available at this book's website.

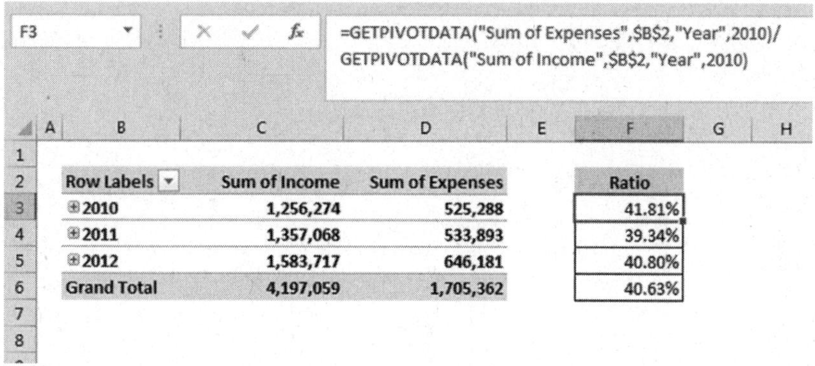

Figure 18-43: The formulas in column F reference cells in the pivot table.

Column F contains formulas, and this column is not part of the pivot table. These formulas calculate the expense-to-income ratio for each year. We created these formulas by pointing to the cells. You may expect to see this formula in cell F3:

```
=D3/C3
```

In fact, the formula in cell F3 is

```
=GETPIVOTDATA("Sum of Expenses",$B$2,"Year",2010)/GETPIVOTDATA("Sum of
  Income",$B$2,"Year",2010)
```

When you use the pointing technique to create a formula that references a cell in a pivot table, Excel replaces those simple cell references with a much more complicated GETPIVOTDATA function. If you type the cell references manually (rather than pointing to them), Excel does not use the GETPIVOTDATA function.

The reason? Using the GETPIVOTDATA function helps ensure that the formula will continue to reference the intended cells if the pivot table layout is changed. Figure 18-44 shows the pivot table after expanding the years to show the month detail. As you can see, the formulas in column F still show the correct result even though the referenced cells are in a different location. Had we used simple cell references, the formula would have returned incorrect results after expanding the years.

Warning

Using the GETPIVOTDATA function has one caveat: the data that it retrieves must be visible in the pivot table. If you modify the pivot table so that the value used by GETPIVOTDATA is no longer visible, the formula returns an error.

Tip

You may want to prevent Excel from using the GETPIVOTDATA function when you point to pivot table cells when creating a formula. If so, choose PivotTable Tools ➜ Analyze ➜ PivotTable ➜ Options ➜ Generate GetPivot Data. (This command is a toggle.)

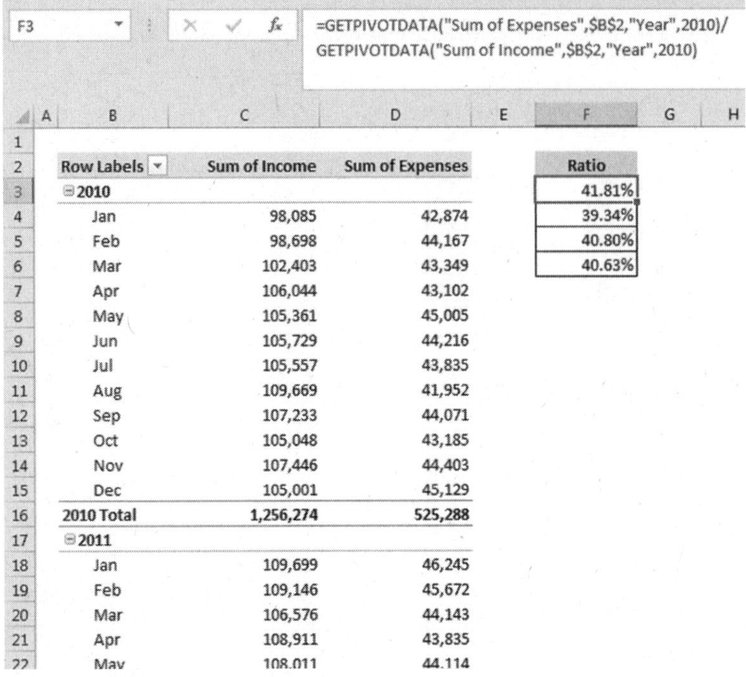

Row Labels	Sum of Income	Sum of Expenses
2010		
Jan	98,085	42,874
Feb	98,698	44,167
Mar	102,403	43,349
Apr	106,044	43,102
May	105,361	45,005
Jun	105,729	44,216
Jul	105,557	43,835
Aug	109,669	41,952
Sep	107,233	44,071
Oct	105,048	43,185
Nov	107,446	44,403
Dec	105,001	45,129
2010 Total	1,256,274	525,288
2011		
Jan	109,699	46,245
Feb	109,146	45,672
Mar	106,576	44,143
Apr	108,911	43,835
May	108,011	44,114

Figure 18-44: After expanding the pivot table, formulas that used the GETPIVOTDATA function continue to display the correct result.

Another Pivot Table Example

The pivot table example in this section demonstrates some useful ways to work with pivot tables. Figure 18-45 shows a table with 3,144 data rows, one for each county in the United States. The fields are

- **County:** The name of the county
- **State Name:** The state of the county
- **Region:** The region (Roman number ranging from I to XII)
- **Census 2000:** The population of the county, according to the 2000 Census
- **Census 1990:** The population of the county, according to the 1990 Census
- **Land Area:** The area, in square miles (excluding water-covered area)
- **Water Area:** The area, in square miles, covered by water

On the Web

This workbook, named county data.xlsx, is available at this book's website.

	A	B	C	D	E	F	G
1	County	State Name	Region	Census 2000	Census 1990	Land Area	WaterArea
2	Los Angeles	California	Region IX	9,519,338	8,863,164	4,060.87	691.45
3	Cook	Illinois	Region V	5,376,741	5,105,067	945.68	689.36
4	Harris	Texas	Region VI	3,400,578	2,818,199	1,728.83	48.87
5	San Diego	California	Region IX	2,813,833	2,498,016	4,199.89	325.62
6	Orange	California	Region IX	2,846,289	2,410,556	789.40	158.57
7	Kings	New York	Region II	2,465,326	2,300,664	70.61	26.29
8	Maricopa	Arizona	Region IX	3,072,149	2,122,101	9,203.14	21.13
9	Wayne	Michigan	Region V	2,061,162	2,111,687	614.15	58.05
10	Queens	New York	Region II	2,229,379	1,951,598	109.24	69.04
11	Dade	Florida	Region IV	2,253,362	1,937,094	1,946.21	77.85
12	Dallas	Texas	Region VI	2,218,899	1,852,810	879.60	28.96
13	Philadelphia	Pennsylvania	Region III	1,517,550	1,585,577	135.09	7.55
14	King	Washington	Region X	1,737,034	1,507,319	2,126.04	180.48
15	Santa Clara	California	Region IX	1,682,585	1,497,577	1,290.69	13.32
16	New York	New York	Region II	1,537,195	1,487,536	22.96	10.81
17	San Bernardino	California	Region IX	1,709,434	1,418,380	20,052.50	52.82
18	Cuyahoga	Ohio	Region V	1,393,978	1,412,140	458.49	787.07
19	Middlesex	Massachusetts	Region I	1,465,396	1,398,468	823.46	24.08
20	Allegheny	Pennsylvania	Region III	1,281,666	1,336,449	730.17	14.54
21	Suffolk	New York	Region II	1,419,369	1,321,864	912.20	1,460.87
22	Nassau	New York	Region II	1,334,544	1,287,348	286.69	166.39
23	Alameda	California	Region IX	1,443,741	1,279,182	737.57	83.57

Figure 18-45: This table contains data for each county in the United States.

	A	B	C	D	E	F	G
1	**Population Growth by State (1990 - 2000)**						
2							
3			Census 1990 Population	Census 2000 Population	Pop Change	Pct Pop Change	Pop/Sq Mile
4	**Region I**		**13,206,943**	**13,922,517**	**715,574**	**5.4%**	**222**
5		Connecticut	3,287,116	3,405,565	118,449	3.6%	703
6		Maine	1,227,928	1,274,923	46,995	3.8%	41
7		Massachusetts	6,016,425	6,349,097	332,672	5.5%	810
8		New Hampshire	1,109,252	1,235,786	126,534	11.4%	138
9		Rhode Island	1,003,464	1,048,319	44,855	4.5%	1,003
10		Vermont	562,758	608,827	46,069	8.2%	66
11							
12	**Region II**		**25,720,643**	**27,390,807**	**1,670,164**	**6.5%**	**501**
13		New Jersey	7,730,188	8,414,350	684,162	8.9%	1,134
14		New York	17,990,455	18,976,457	986,002	5.5%	402
15							
16	**Region III**		**25,917,014**	**27,828,549**	**1,911,535**	**7.4%**	**231**
17		Delaware	666,168	783,600	117,432	17.6%	401
18		District of Columbia	606,900	572,059	(34,841)	-5.7%	9,316
19		Maryland	4,781,468	5,296,486	515,018	10.8%	542
20		Pennsylvania	11,881,643	12,281,054	399,411	3.4%	274
21		Virginia	6,187,358	7,087,006	899,648	14.5%	179
22		West Virginia	1,793,477	1,808,344	14,867	0.8%	75
23							
24	**Region IV**		**46,643,644**	**55,506,328**	**8,862,684**	**19.0%**	**150**
25		Alabama	4,040,587	4,447,100	406,513	10.1%	88
26		Florida	[illegible]	[illegible]	[illegible]	[illegible]	[illegible]

Figure 18-46: This pivot table was created from the county data.

I created three calculated fields to display additional information:

- **Change (displayed as Pop Change):** The difference between Census 2000 and Census 1990
- **Pct Change (displayed as Pct Pop Change):** The population change expressed as a percentage of the 1990 population
- **Density (displayed as Pop/Sq Mile):** The population per square mile of land

You might want to document your calculated fields and calculated items. Choose PivotTable Tools ➜ Analyze ➜ Calculations ➜ Fields, Items, & Sets ➜ List Formulas, and Excel inserts a new worksheet with information about your calculated fields and items. Figure 18-47 shows an example.

	A	B	C	D
1	*Calculated Field*			
2	Solve Order	Field	Formula	
3	1	Change	='Census 2000'-'Census 1990'	
4	2	Pct Change	=('Census 2000'-'Census 1990')/'Census 1990'	
5	3	Density	='Census 2000'/'Land Area'	
6				
7	*Calculated Item*			
8	Solve Order	Item	Formula	
9				

Figure 18-47: This worksheet lists calculated fields and items for the pivot table.

This pivot table is sorted on two columns. The main sort is by Region, and states within each region are sorted alphabetically. To sort, just select a cell that contains a data point to be included in the sort. Right-click and choose Sort from the shortcut menu.

Sorting by Region required some additional effort because Roman numerals are not in alphabetical order. Therefore, we had to create a custom list. To create a custom sort list, access the Excel Options dialog box, click the Advanced tab, and scroll down and click Edit Custom Lists. In the Custom Lists dialog box, select New List, type your list entries, and click Add. Figure 18-48 shows the custom list that we created for the region names.

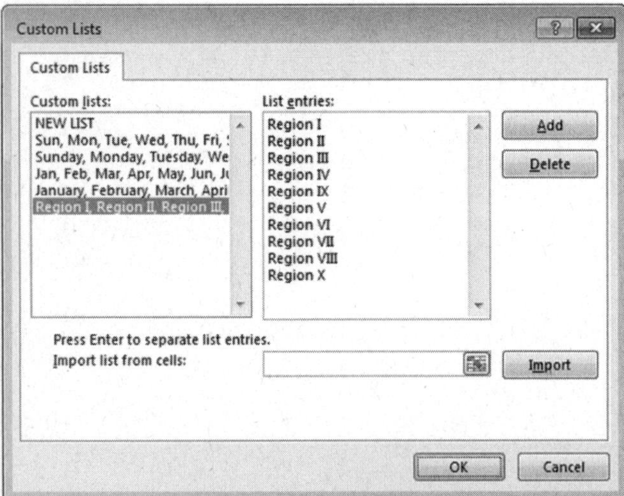

Figure 18-48: This custom list ensures that the Region names are sorted correctly.

Using the Data Model

This chapter, so far, has focused exclusively on pivot tables that are created from a single table of data. With the Data Model, you can use multiple tables of data in a single pivot table. You will need to create one or more "table relationships" so that the data can be tied together.

Figure 18-49 shows parts of three tables that are in a single workbook. (Each sheet is in its own worksheet and is shown in a separate window.) The tables are named Orders, Customers, and Regions. The Orders table contains information about product orders. The Customers table contains information about the company's customers. The Regions table contains a region identifier for each state.

Notice that the Orders and Customers tables have a CustomerID column in common, and Customers and Regions tables have a State column in common. The common columns will be used to form relationship among the tables.

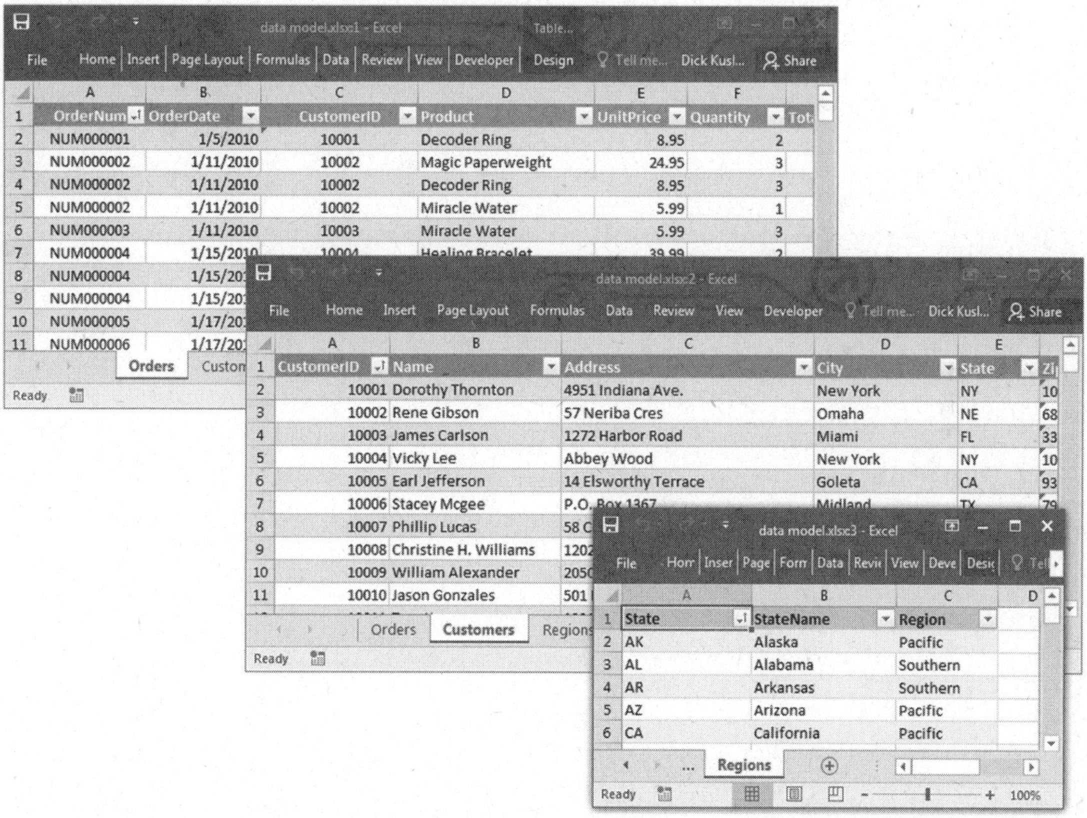

OrderNum	OrderDate	CustomerID	Product	UnitPrice	Quantity
NUM000001	1/5/2010	10001	Decoder Ring	8.95	2
NUM000002	1/11/2010	10002	Magic Paperweight	24.95	3
NUM000002	1/11/2010	10002	Decoder Ring	8.95	3
NUM000002	1/11/2010	10002	Miracle Water	5.99	1
NUM000003	1/11/2010	10003	Miracle Water	5.99	3

CustomerID	Name	Address	City	State
10001	Dorothy Thornton	4951 Indiana Ave.	New York	NY
10002	Rene Gibson	57 Neriba Cres	Omaha	NE
10003	James Carlson	1272 Harbor Road	Miami	FL
10004	Vicky Lee	Abbey Wood	New York	NY
10005	Earl Jefferson	14 Elsworthy Terrace	Goleta	CA
10006	Stacey Mcgee			
10007	Phillip Lucas			
10008	Christine H. Williams			
10009	William Alexander			
10010	Jason Gonzales			

State	StateName	Region
AK	Alaska	Pacific
AL	Alabama	Southern
AR	Arkansas	Southern
AZ	Arizona	Pacific
CA	California	Pacific

Figure 18-49: These three tables will be used for a pivot table, using the Data Model.

On the Web

The example in this section is available at this book's website. The workbook is named data model.xlsx.

Note

Compared with a pivot table created from a single table, pivot data created using the Data Model has some restrictions. Most notably, you cannot create groups. In addition, you cannot create calculated fields or calculated items.

The goal is to summarize sales by state, region, and year. Notice that the sales (and date) information is in the Orders table, the state information is in the Customers table, and the region names are in the Regions table. Therefore, all three tables will be used for this pivot table.

Start by creating a pivot table (in a new worksheet) from the Orders table. Select any cell within the table and choose Insert ➜ Tables ➜ Pivot Tables. In the Create PivotTable dialog box, make sure you select the Add This Data to the Data Model check box.

Notice that the PivotTable Fields task pane is a bit different when you're working with the Data Model. The task pane contains two tabs: Active and All. The Active tab lists only the Orders table. The All tab lists all of the tables in the workbook. To make things easier, switch to the All tab, right-click the Customers table, and choose Show in Active Tab. Then do the same for the Regions table.

Figure 18-50 shows the active tab of the PivotTable Fields task pane, with all three tables expanded to show their column headers.

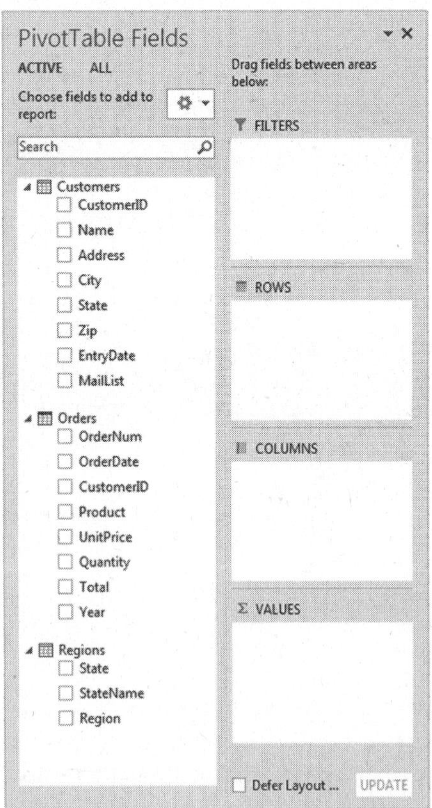

Figure 18-50: The PivotTable Fields task pane, with three active tables.

The next step is to set up the relationships among the tables. Choose PivotTable Tools ➜ Analyze ➜ Calculations ➜ Relationships. Excel displays its Manage Relationships dialog box. Click the New button, and the Create Relationship dialog box appears.

For the Table, specify Orders; for the Foreign Column, specify CustomerID. For the Related Table, specify Customers; for the Related Column (Primary), specify CustomerID (see Figure 18-51).

Figure 18-51: Creating a relationship between two tables.

Click OK to return to the Manage Relationships dialog box. Click New again and set up a relationship between the Customers table and the Regions table. Both will use the State column. The Manage Relationships dialog box will now show two relationships.

Note

If you don't set up the table relationships in advance, Excel prompts you to do so when you add a field to the pivot table that's from a different table than you started with.

Now it's simply a matter of dragging the field names to the appropriate section of the PivotTable Fields task pane:

1. Drag the Total field to the Values area.
2. Drag the Year field to the Columns area.
3. Drag the Region field to the Rows area.
4. Drag the StateName field to the Rows area.

Figure 18-52 shows part of the pivot table. We added two slicers to enable filtering the table by customers who are on the mailing list, and by product.

Tip

When you create a pivot chart using the Data Model, you can convert the pivot table to formulas. Select any cell in the pivot table and choose PivotTable Tools ➜ Analyze ➜ OLAP Tools ➜ Convert to Formulas. The pivot table is replaced by cells that use formulas. These formulas use CUBEMEMBER and CUBEVALUE functions. Although the range is no longer a pivot table, the formulas update when the data changes.

	A	B	C	D	E
1					
2					
3	**Sum of Total**	**Column Labels**			
4	**Row Labels**	**2010**	**2011**	**2012**	**Grand Total**
5	**Central**	**362.05**	**970.19**	**1,310.62**	**2,642.86**
6	IA			155.64	155.64
7	IL	12.99	277.06	235.48	525.53
8	IN	12.99	53.70	61.78	128.47
9	KY	49.90			49.90
10	MI	88.63	235.48	383.12	707.23
11	MN	17.90	25.98		43.88
12	MO			260.43	260.43
13	OH	170.69	319.12	138.53	628.34
14	WI	8.95	58.85	75.64	143.44
15	**Northern**	**831.58**	**823.27**	**1,434.41**	**3,089.26**
16	CT	42.85	199.52	112.55	354.92
17	DC			106.77	106.77
18	DE			12.99	12.99
19	MA	66.69	8.95	75.64	151.28
20	MD	39.84	12.99	162.37	215.20
21	ME	17.90	8.95	8.95	35.80
22	NH			87.84	87.84
23	NJ	51.96	190.49	300.98	543.43
24	NY	435.71	326.49	415.83	1,178.03
25	PA	176.63	25.98	150.49	353.10
26	VT		49.90		49.90
27	**Pacific**	**902.63**	**1,209.31**	**1,206.23**	**3,318.17**
28	AK	80.79	56.87	52.83	190.49

MailList
- FALSE
- TRUE

Product
- All-Purpose Magic Word
- Decoder Ring
- Healing Bracelet
- Magic Paperweight
- Miracle Water
- Mystery Stone
- Super Crystal

Figure 18-52: The pivot table, after adding two slicers.

Creating Pivot Charts

A *pivot chart* is a graphical representation of a data summary displayed in a pivot table. If you're familiar with creating charts in Excel, you'll have no problem creating and customizing pivot charts. All Excel charting features are available in a pivot chart.

Excel provides several ways to create a pivot chart:

- Select any cell in an existing pivot table and then choose PivotTable Tools ➜ Analyze ➜ Tools ➜ PivotChart.
- Select any cell in an existing pivot table and then choose Insert ➜ Charts ➜ PivotChart.
- Choose Insert ➜ Charts ➜ PivotChart ➜ PivotChart. Excel prompts you for the data source and creates a pivot chart.
- Choose Insert ➜ Charts ➜ Pivot Chart ➜ PivotChart & PivotTable. Excel prompts you for the data source and creates a pivot table and a pivot chart.

A pivot chart example

Figure 18-53 shows part of a table that tracks daily sales by region. The Date field contains dates for the entire year (excluding weekends), the Region field contains the region name (Eastern, Southern, or Western), and the Sales field contains the sales amount.

On the Web

This workbook, named sales by region pivot chart.xlsx, is available at this book's website.

	A	B	C	D
1	Date	Region	Sales	
2	1/2/2013	Eastern	10,909	
3	1/3/2013	Eastern	11,126	
4	1/4/2013	Eastern	11,224	
5	1/5/2013	Eastern	11,299	
6	1/6/2013	Eastern	11,265	
7	1/9/2013	Eastern	11,328	
8	1/10/2013	Eastern	11,494	
9	1/11/2013	Eastern	11,328	
10	1/12/2013	Eastern	11,598	
11	1/13/2013	Eastern	11,868	
12	1/16/2013	Eastern	11,702	
13	1/17/2013	Eastern	11,846	
14	1/18/2013	Eastern	11,898	
15	1/19/2013	Eastern	11,871	
16	1/20/2013	Eastern	12,053	
17	1/23/2013	Eastern	12,073	
18	1/24/2013	Eastern	12,153	
19	1/25/2013	Eastern	12,226	
20	1/26/2013	Eastern	12,413	
21	1/27/2013	Eastern	12,663	
22	1/30/2013	Eastern	12,571	
23	1/31/2013	Eastern	12,508	
24	2/1/2013	Eastern	12,390	
25	2/2/2013	Eastern	12,649	
26	2/3/2013	Eastern	12,697	
27	2/6/2013	Eastern	12,878	
28	2/7/2013	Eastern	13,082	

Figure 18-53: This data will be used to create a pivot chart.

Figure 18-54 shows the pivot table created from the table. The Date field is in the Rows area, and the daily dates have been grouped into months. The Region field is in the Columns area. The Sales field is in the Values area.

The pivot table is certainly easier to interpret than the raw data, but the trends are easier to spot in a chart.

To create a pivot chart, select any cell in the pivot table and choose PivotTable Tools ➜ Analyze ➜ Tools ➜ PivotChart. Excel displays its Insert Chart dialog box, from which you can choose a chart type. For this example, select a Line with Markers chart and then click OK. Excel creates the pivot chart shown in Figure 18-55.

	A	B	C	D
1				
2				
3	**Sum of Sales**	**Column Label**		
4	**Row Labels**	**Eastern**	**Southern**	**Western**
5	Jan	259,416	171,897	99,833
6	Feb	255,487	135,497	100,333
7	Mar	296,958	147,425	107,884
8	Apr	248,956	131,401	110,628
9	May	293,192	132,165	144,889
10	Jun	281,641	122,156	133,153
11	Jul	263,899	110,844	147,484
12	Aug	283,917	107,935	176,325
13	Sep	252,049	101,233	181,518
14	Oct	273,592	104,542	212,932
15	Nov	292,585	98,041	232,032
16	Dec	288,378	95,986	239,514
17	**Grand Total**	**3,290,070**	**1,459,122**	**1,886,525**
18				

Figure 18-54: This pivot table summarizes sales by region and by month.

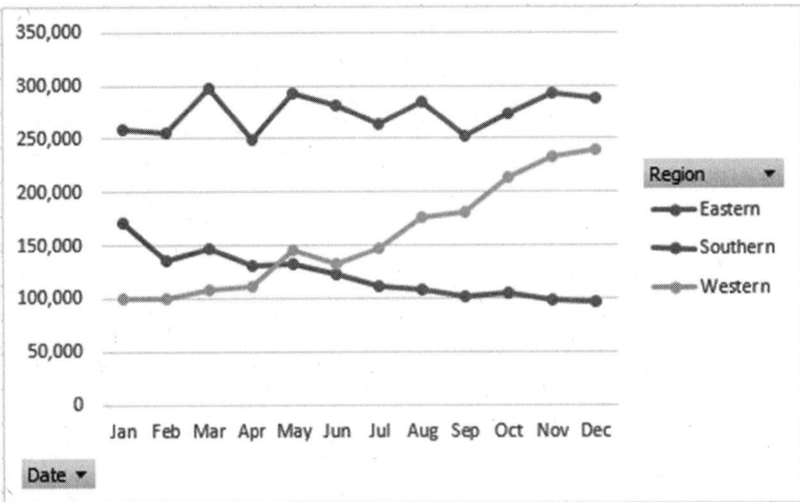

Figure 18-55: The pivot chart uses the data displayed in the pivot table.

The chart makes it easy to see an upward sales trend for the Western division, a downward trend for the Southern division, and relatively flat sales for the Eastern division.

A pivot chart includes field buttons that let you filter the chart's data. To remove the field buttons, right-click a button and choose the Hide command from the shortcut menu.

When you select a pivot chart, the Ribbon displays a contextual tab: PivotChart Tools. The commands are virtually identical to those for a standard Excel chart, so you can manipulate the pivot chart any way you like.

If you modify the underlying pivot table, the chart adjusts automatically to display the new summary data. Figure 18-56 shows the pivot chart after we changed the Date group to quarters.

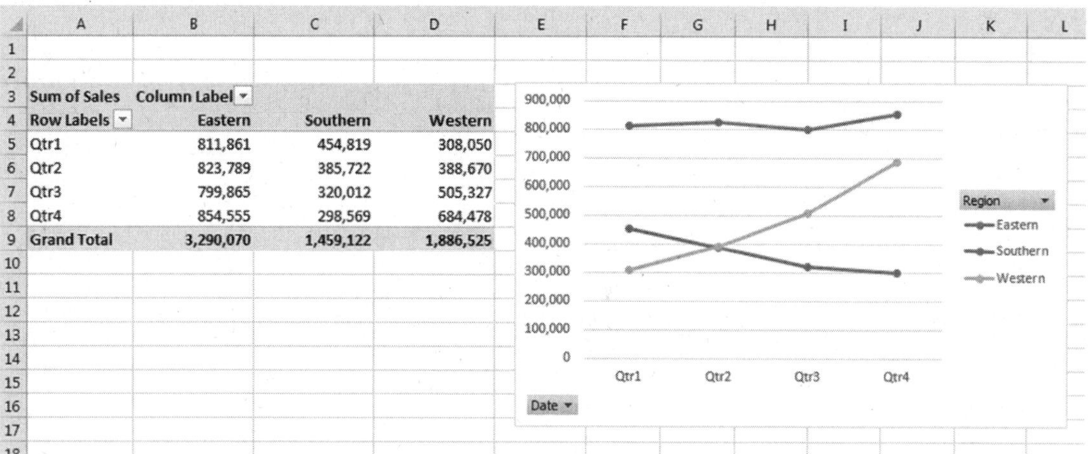

Figure 18-56: If you modify the pivot table, the pivot chart is also changed.

More about pivot charts

Keep in mind these points when using pivot charts:

- A pivot table and a pivot chart are joined in a two-way link. If you make structural or filtering changes to one, the other is also changed.
- When you activate a pivot chart, the PivotTable Fields task pane changes to the PivotChart Fields task pane. In this task pane, Legend (Series) replaces the Columns area, and Axis (Category) replaces the Rows area.
- The field buttons in a pivot chart contain the same controls as the pivot chart's field headers. These controls allow you to filter the data that's displayed in the pivot table (and pivot chart). If you make changes to the chart using these buttons, those changes are also reflected in the pivot table.
- If you have a pivot chart and you delete the underlying pivot table, the pivot chart remains. The chart's SERIES formulas contain the original data, stored in arrays.
- By default, pivot charts are embedded in the sheet that contains the pivot table. To move the pivot chart to a different worksheet (or to a Chart sheet), choose PivotChart Tools ➜ Analyze ➜ Actions ➜ Move Chart.
- You can create multiple pivot charts from a pivot table, and you can manipulate and format the charts separately. However, all the charts display the same data.
- Slicers and timelines also work with pivot charts. See the examples earlier in this chapter.
- Don't forget about themes. You can choose Page Layout ➜ Themes ➜ Themes to change the workbook theme, and your pivot table and pivot chart will both reflect the new theme.

19

Conditional Formatting

In This Chapter

- An overview of Excel's conditional formatting feature
- How to use the graphical conditional formats
- Examples of using conditional formatting formulas
- Tips for using conditional formatting

This chapter explores the topic of conditional formatting, one of Excel's most versatile features. You can apply conditional formatting to a cell so that the cell looks different, depending on its contents.

Conditional formatting is a useful tool for visualizing numeric data. In some cases, conditional formatting may be a viable alternative to creating a chart.

About Conditional Formatting

Conditional formatting enables you to apply cell formatting selectively and automatically, based on the contents of the cells. For example, you can apply conditional formatting in such a way that all negative values in a range have a light-yellow background color. When you enter or change a value in the range, Excel examines the value and checks the conditional formatting rules for the cell. If the value is negative, the background is shaded. If not, no formatting is applied.

Conditional formatting is an easy way to quickly identify erroneous cell entries or cells of a particular type. You can use a format (such as bright-red cell shading) to make particular cells easy to identify.

Figure 19-1 shows a worksheet with nine ranges, each with a different type of conditional formatting rule applied. Here's a brief explanation of each:

- **Greater than ten:** Values greater than 10 are highlighted with a different background color. This rule is just one of many numeric value related rules that you can apply.
- **Above average:** Values that are higher than the average value are highlighted.
- **Duplicate values:** Values that appear in the range more than one time are highlighted.
- **Words that contain X:** If the cell contains X (upper- or lowercase), the cell is highlighted.
- **Data bars:** Each cell displays a horizontal bar, the length of which is proportional to its value.

- **Color scale:** The background color varies, depending on the value of the cells. You can choose from several different color scales or create your own.
- **Icon set:** One of several icon sets. It displays a small graphic in the cell. The graphic varies, depending on the cell value.
- **Icon set:** Another icon set, with all but one icon in the set hidden.
- **Custom rule:** The rule for this checkerboard pattern is based on a formula:

```
=MOD(ROW(),2)=MOD(COLUMN(),2)
```

On the Web

This workbook, named conditional formatting examples.xlsx, is available at this book's website.

	A	B	C	D	E	F	G	H	I	J	K	L
1			Greater than ten				Above average				Duplicate values	
2		10	3	6		27	42	78		47	68	34
3		7	8	11		80	42	38		64	22	17
4		2	11	3		26	36	17		65	25	69
5		6	10	1		60	32	34		5	13	3
6		4	7	10		13	88	9		95	59	60
7		5	12	9		86	95	20		66	20	24
8		9	7	2		50	53	34		92	98	48
9		9	9	10		29	54	69		85	24	3
10		3	11	4		96	42	42		13	62	57
11		8	2	4		5	21	35		24	54	22
12												
13			Words that contain X				Data bars				Color scale	
14		apple	kite	urn		3	2	-3		1	11	21
15		baby	light	violin		0	10	-2		2	12	22
16		cry	max	wax		6	8	7		3	13	23
17		dog	night	X-ray		-2	-2	1		4	14	24
18		elf	oxen	young		0	4	0		5	15	25
19		fox	purple	zebra		-1	10	10		6	16	26
20		garage	quaint	angle		6	-1	1		7	17	27
21		hex	right	boy		8	1	7		8	18	28
22		icon	sled	chump		4	8	3		9	19	29
23		jewel	turtle	dusty		0	10	2		10	20	30
24												
25			Icon set				Icon set				Custom rule	
26		78	80	63		2	1	5				
27		77	78	41		5	4	4				
28		10	36	76		4	2	0				
29		83	80	63		3	4	3				
30		95	77	57		0	4	4				
31		24	95	32		5	2	1				
32		31	19	52		5	5	0				
33		71	66	51		3	5	2				
34		21	35	36		3	2	5				
35		67	26	2		5	2	5				
36		25	46	9		4	4	4				
37												

Figure 19-1: This worksheet demonstrates a few conditional formatting rules.

Specifying Conditional Formatting

To apply a conditional formatting rule to a cell or range, select the cells and then use one of the commands from the Home ➜ Styles ➜ Conditional Formatting drop-down list to specify a rule. The choices include these:

- **Highlight Cell Rules:** Examples include highlighting cells that are greater than a particular value, are between two values, contain a specific text string, contain a date, or are duplicated.
- **Top Bottom Rules:** Examples include highlighting the top 10 items, the items in the bottom 20 percent, and items that are above average.
- **Data Bars:** Applies graphics bars directly in the cells proportional to the cell's value.
- **Color Scales:** Applies background color proportional to the cell's value.
- **Icon Sets:** Displays icons directly in the cells. The icons depend on the cell's value.
- **New Rule:** Enables you to specify other conditional formatting rules, including rules based on a logical formula.
- **Clear Rules:** Deletes all the conditional formatting rules from the selected cells, the entire sheet, a table, or a pivot table.
- **Manage Rules:** Displays the Conditional Formatting Rules Manager dialog box in which you create new conditional formatting rules, edit rules, or delete rules.

Formatting types you can apply

When you select a conditional formatting rule, Excel displays a dialog box specific to that rule. These dialog boxes have one thing in common: a drop-down list with common formatting suggestions.

Figure 19-2 shows the dialog box that appears when you choose Home ➜ Styles ➜ Conditional Formatting ➜ Highlight Cells Rules ➜ Between. This particular rule applies the formatting if the value in the cell falls between two specified values. In this case, you enter the two values (or specify cell references) and then use choices from the drop-down list to set the type of formatting to display if the condition is met.

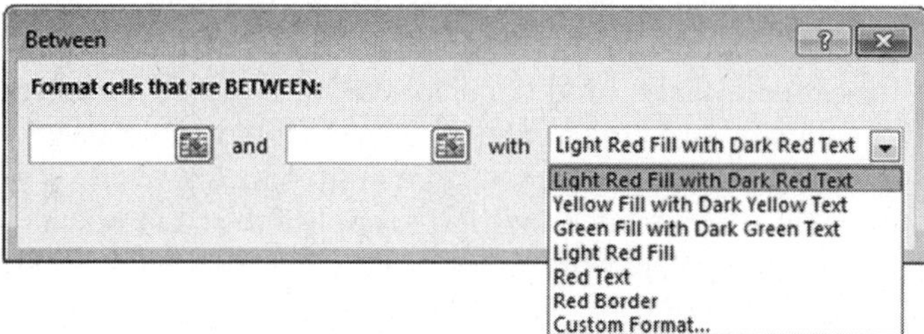

Figure 19-2: One of several different conditional formatting dialog boxes.

The formatting suggestions in the drop-down list are just a few of thousands of different formatting combinations. If none of Excel's suggestions is what you want, choose the Custom Format option from the drop-down list to display the Format Cells dialog box. You can specify the format in any or all of the four tabs: Number, Font, Border, and Fill.

Note

The Format Cells dialog box used for conditional formatting is a modified version of the standard Format Cells dialog box. It doesn't have the Alignment and Protection tabs, and some of the Font formatting options are disabled. The dialog box also includes a Clear button that clears any formatting already selected.

Making your own rules

For maximum control, Excel provides the New Formatting Rule dialog box, shown in Figure 19-3. Access this dialog box by choosing Home ➜ Styles ➜ Conditional Formatting ➜ New Rule.

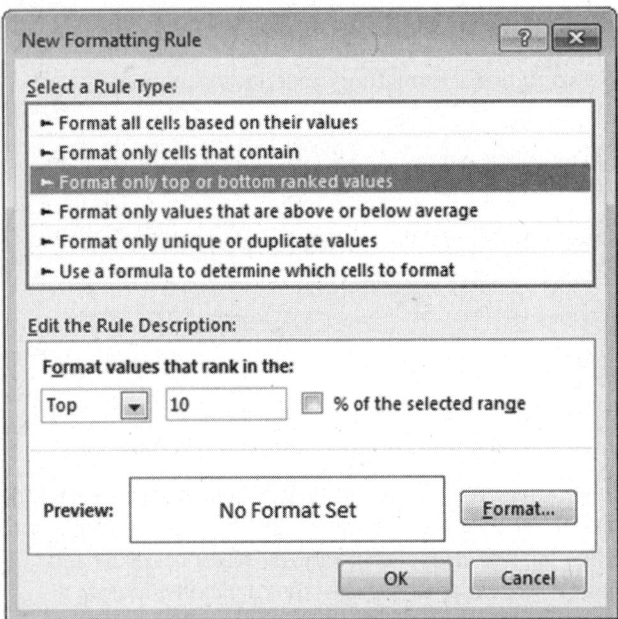

Figure 19-3: Use the New Formatting Rule dialog box to create your own conditional formatting rules.

Use the New Formatting Rule dialog box to re-create all the conditional format rules available via the Ribbon, as well as custom rules. First, select a general rule type from the list at the top of the dialog box. The bottom part of the dialog box varies, depending on your selection at the top. After you specify the rule, click the Format button to specify the type of formatting to apply if the condition is met. An exception is the first rule type (Format All Cells Based on Their Values), which doesn't have a Format button. (It uses graphics rather than cell formatting.)

Here is a summary of the rule types:

- **Format All Cells Based on Their Values:** Use this rule type to create rules that display data bars, color scales, or icon sets.

- **Format Only Cells That Contain:** Use this rule type to create rules that format cells based on mathematical comparisons (greater than, less than, greater than or equal to, less than or equal to, equal to, not equal to, between, not between). You can also create rules based on text, dates, blank cells, nonblank cells, and cells that contain errors.
- **Format Only Top or Bottom Ranked Values:** Use this rule type to create rules that involve identifying cells in the top *n*, top *n* percent, bottom *n*, and bottom *n* percent.
- **Format Only Values That Are Above or Below Average:** Use this rule type to create rules that identify cells that are above average, below average, or within a specified standard deviation from the average.
- **Format Only Unique or Duplicate Values:** Use this rule type to create rules that format unique or duplicate values in a range.
- **Use a Formula to Determine Which Cells to Format:** Use this rule type to create rules based on a logical formula. See "Creating Formula-Based Rules," later in this chapter.

Conditional Formats That Use Graphics

This section describes the three conditional formatting options that display graphics: data bars, color scales, and icon sets. These types of conditional formatting can be useful for visualizing the values in a range.

Using data bars

The data bars conditional format displays horizontal bars directly in the cell. The length of the bar is based on the value of the cell, relative to the other values in the range.

A simple data bar

Figure 19-4 shows an example of data bars. It's a list of tracks on Bob Dylan albums, with the length of each track in column D. I applied data bar conditional formatting to the values in column D. You can tell at a glance which tracks are longer.

On the Web

The examples in the section are available on this book's website. The workbook is named data bars examples.xlsx.

Tip

When you adjust the column width, the bar lengths adjust accordingly. The differences among the bar lengths are more prominent when the column is wider.

	A	B	C	D
1	Artist	Album	Title	Length
2	Bob Dylan	Planet Waves	Never Say Goodbye	0:02:53
3	Bob Dylan	Bob Dylan	Fixin' To Die Blues	0:02:21
4	Bob Dylan	Tell Tale Signs (Disc 1)	Huck's Tune (from "Lucky You" Soundtrack)	0:04:04
5	Bob Dylan	World Gone Wrong	Blood in My Eyes	0:05:04
6	Bob Dylan	Good As I Been to You	Blackjack Davey	0:05:50
7	Bob Dylan	Good As I Been to You	Froggie Went a Courtin'	0:06:23
8	Bob Dylan	Self Portrait	The Mighty Quinn (Quinn the Eskimo)	0:02:48
9	Bob Dylan	Good As I Been to You	Canadee-I-O	0:04:23
10	Bob Dylan	Bringing it All Back Home	Outlaw Blues	0:03:06
11	Bob Dylan	World Gone Wrong	Love Henry	0:04:24
12	Bob Dylan	Down in the Groove	Had A Dream About You, Baby	0:02:50
13	Bob Dylan	Tell Tale Signs (Disc 1)	Dignity (Piano Demo, Oh Mercy)	0:02:12
14	Bob Dylan	Tell Tale Signs (Disc 1)	Someday Baby (Alternate Version, Modern Times)	0:05:57
15	Bob Dylan	Bob Dylan	Freight Train Blues	0:02:19
16	Bob Dylan	Tell Tale Signs (Disc 1)	High Water (for Charley Patton) (Live, 2003)	0:06:46
17	Bob Dylan	The Freewheelin' Bob Dylan	Don't Think Twice, It's All Right	0:03:40
18	Bob Dylan	Tempest	Tempest	0:13:54
19	Bob Dylan	Another Side of Bob Dylan	I Shall Be Free No. 10	0:04:47
20	Bob Dylan	Highway 61 Revisited	Just Like Tom Thumb's Blues	0:05:32
21	Bob Dylan	30th Anniversary Concert	When I Paint My Masterpiece	0:04:23
22	Bob Dylan	Bob Dylan	Highway 51 blues	0:02:53
23	Bob Dylan	The Freewheelin' Bob Dylan	Down The Highway	0:03:27
24	Bob Dylan	MTV Unplugged	Shooting Star	0:04:06

Figure 19-4: The length of the data bars is proportional to the track length in the cell in column D.

Excel provides quick access to 12 data bar styles via Home ➜ Styles ➜ Conditional Formatting ➜ Data Bars. For additional choices, click the More Rules option, which displays the New Formatting Rule dialog box. Use this dialog box to do the following:

- Show the bar only (hide the numbers).
- Specify minimum and maximum values for the scaling.
- Change the appearance of the bars.
- Specify how negative values and the axis are handled.
- Specify the direction of the bars.

Note

Oddly, if you add data bars using one of the 12 data bar styles, the colors used for data bars are *not* theme colors. If you apply a new document theme, the data bar colors do not change. However, if you add the data bars by using the New Formatting Rule dialog box, the colors that you choose *are* theme colors.

Using data bars in lieu of a chart

Using the data bars conditional formatting can sometimes serve as a quick alternative to creating a chart. Figure 19-5 shows a three-column range (in B3:D14) with data bars conditional formatting to the data in column D. (Column D contains references to the values in the second column.) The conditional formatting in the third column uses the Show Bars Only option, so the values are not displayed.

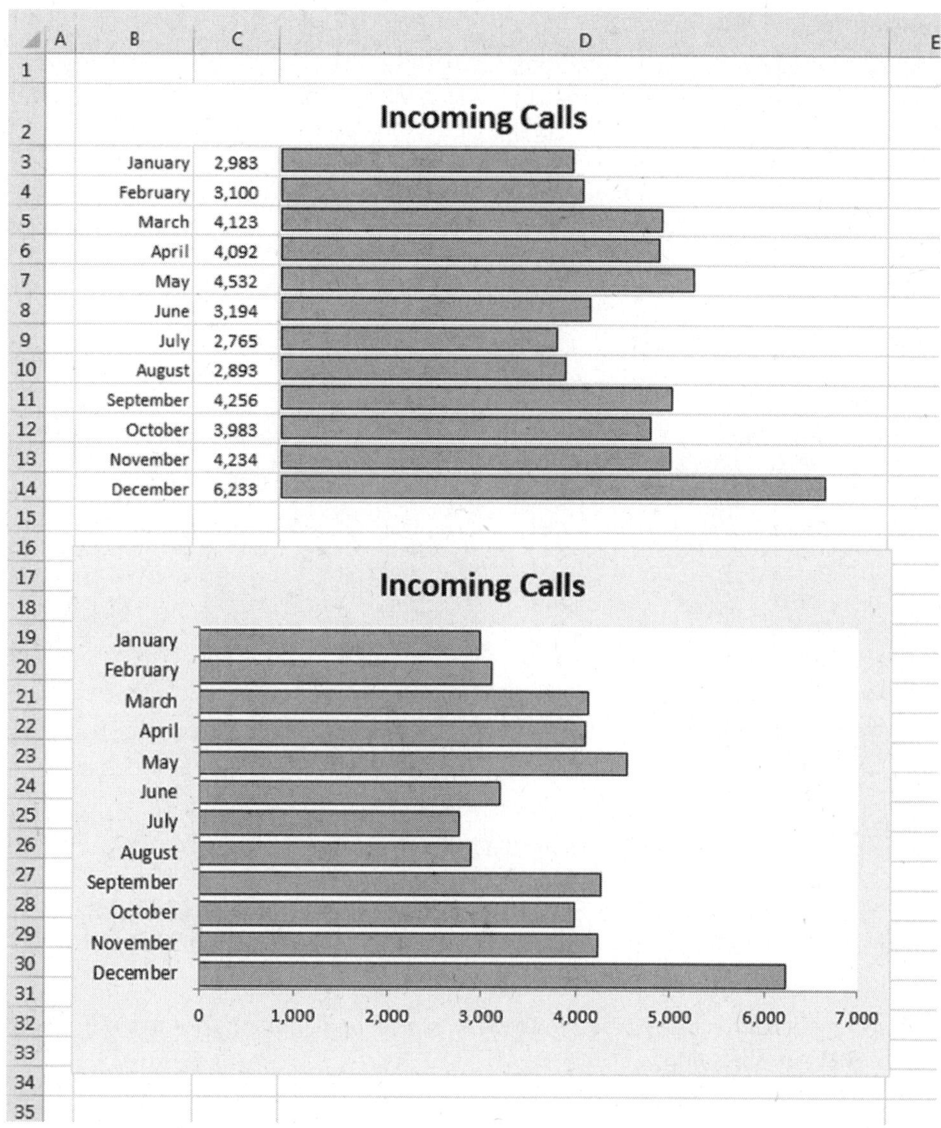

Figure 19-5: Comparing data bars conditional formatting (top) with a bar chart.

Figure 19-5 also shows an actual bar chart created from the same data. The bar chart takes about the same amount of time to create and is a lot more flexible. But for a quick-and-dirty chart, data bars may be a good option—especially when you need to create several such charts.

Using color scales

The color scale conditional formatting option varies the background color of a cell based on the cell's value, relative to other cells in the range.

A color scale example

Figure 19-6 shows examples of color scale conditional formatting. The example on the left depicts monthly sales for three regions. Conditional formatting was applied to the range B4:D15. The conditional formatting uses a 3-color scale, with red (in this book, the darkest gray) for the lowest value, yellow for the midpoint, and green for the highest value. Values in between are displayed using a color within the gradient. It's clear that the Central region consistently has lower sales volumes, but the conditional formatting doesn't help identify monthly difference for a particular region.

	A	B	C	D	E	F	G	H	I
1	**A single conditional formatting rule**					**A separate rule for each region**			
2									
3	**Month**	**Western**	**Central**	**Eastern**		**Month**	**Western**	**Central**	**Eastern**
4	January	214,030	103,832	225,732		January	214,030	103,832	225,732
5	February	214,492	103,604	229,058		February	214,492	103,604	229,058
6	March	213,478	106,119	216,188		March	213,478	106,119	216,188
7	April	220,744	100,971	229,798		April	220,744	100,971	229,798
8	May	222,948	105,423	221,455		May	222,948	105,423	221,455
9	June	222,874	98,692	222,927		June	222,874	98,692	222,927
10	July	219,854	91,818	206,120		July	219,854	91,818	206,120
11	August	211,832	91,796	217,313		August	211,832	91,796	217,313
12	September	208,991	88,106	227,096		September	208,991	88,106	227,096
13	October	199,728	88,522	239,841		October	199,728	88,522	239,841
14	November	190,624	92,035	248,976		November	190,624	92,035	248,976
15	December	194,289	88,800	253,194		December	194,289	88,800	253,194
16									

Figure 19-6: Two examples of color scale conditional formatting.

The example on the right shows the same data, but conditional formatting was applied to each region separately. This approach facilitates comparisons within a region and can help identify high or low sales months.

Neither one of these approach is necessarily better. The way you set up conditional formatting depends entirely on what you are trying to visualize.

On the Web

This workbook, named color scale example.xlsx, is available at this book's website.

Excel provides four 2-color scale presets and four 3-color scales presets, which you can apply to the selected range by choosing Home ➜ Styles ➜ Conditional Formatting ➜ Color Scales.

To customize the colors and other options, choose Home ➜ Styles ➜ Conditional Formatting ➜ Color Scales ➜ More Rules. This command displays the Edit Formatting Rule dialog box, shown in Figure 19-7. Adjust the settings and watch the Preview box to see the effects of your changes.

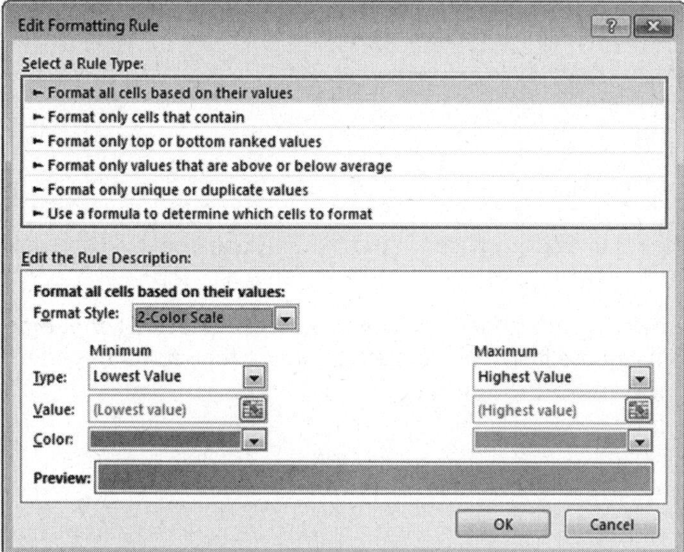

Figure 19-7: Use the Edit Formatting Rule dialog box to customize a color scale.

An extreme color scale example

It's important to understand that color scale conditional formatting uses a gradient. For example, if you format a range using a 2-color scale, you will get a lot more than two colors. You'll also get colors within the gradient between the two specified colors.

Figure 19-8 shows an extreme example that uses color scale conditional formatting on a range of more than 6,000 cells. The worksheet contains average daily temperatures for an 18-year period. Each row contains 365 (or 366) temperatures for the year. The columns are narrow, so the entire year can be visualized.

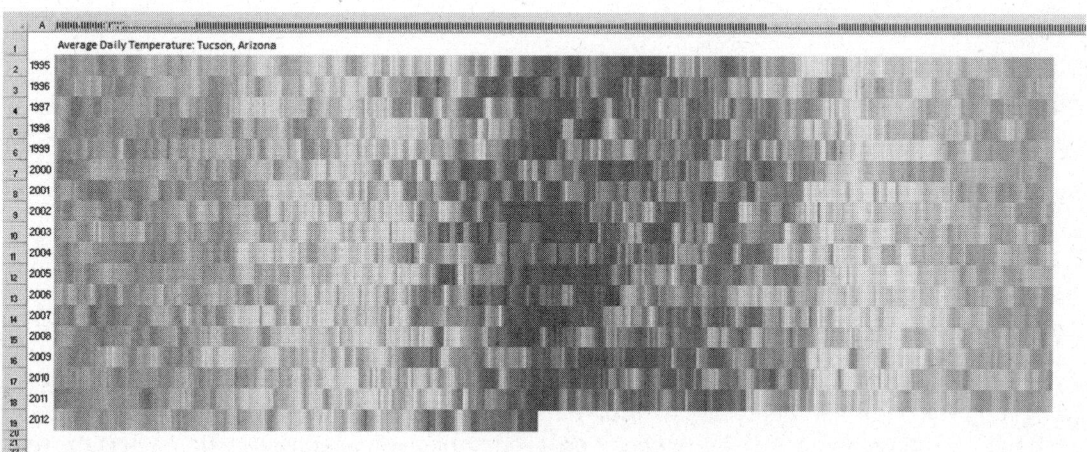

Figure 19-8: This worksheet uses color scale conditional formatting to display daily temperatures.

This workbook, named extreme color scale.xlsx, is available at this book's website. The workbook contains a second example of extreme color scale.

Using icon sets

Yet another conditional formatting option is to display an icon in the cell. The icon displayed depends on the value of the cell.

To assign an icon set to a range, select the cells and choose Home ➜ Styles ➜ Conditional Formatting ➜ Icon Sets. Excel provides 20 icon sets to choose from. The number of icons in the sets ranges from three to five. You cannot create a custom icon set.

An icon set example

Figure 19-9 shows an example that uses an icon set. The symbols graphically depict the status of each project, based on the value in column C.

The icon set examples in this section are available at this book's website. The workbook is named icon set examples.xlsx.

Project Status Report

Project	Pct Completed	
Project 1	✔	95%
Project 2	✔	100%
Project 3	!	50%
Project 4	✖	0%
Project 5	!	20%
Project 6	!	80%
Project 7	✔	100%
Project 8	✖	0%
Project 9	✖	0%
Project 10	!	50%

Figure 19-9: Using an icon set to indicate the status of projects.

By default, the symbols are assigned using percentiles. For a 3-symbol set, the items are grouped into three percentiles. For a 4-symbol set, they're grouped into four percentiles. And for a 5-symbol set, the items are grouped into five percentiles.

If you would like more control over how the icons are assigned, choose Home ➜ Styles ➜ Conditional Formatting ➜ Icon Sets ➜ More Rules to display the New Formatting Rule dialog box. To modify an existing rule, choose Home ➜ Styles ➜ Conditional Formatting ➜ Manage Rules. Then select the rule to modify and click the Edit Rule button to display the Edit Formatting Rule dialog box.

Figure 19-10 shows how to modify the icon set rules such that only projects that are 100% completed get the check mark icons. Projects that are 0% completed get the X icon. All other projects get no icon.

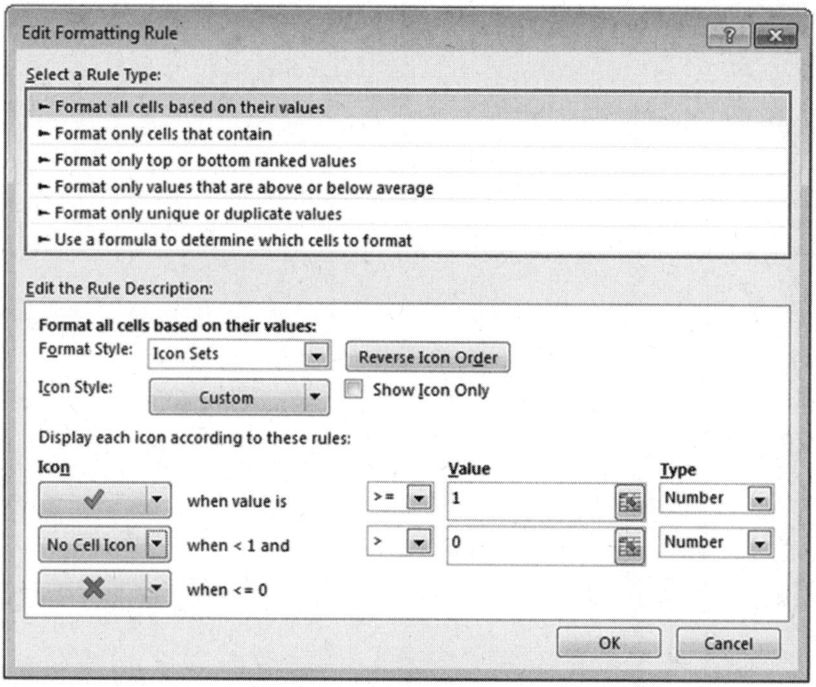

Edit Formatting Rule

Select a Rule Type:

- Format all cells based on their values
- Format only cells that contain
- Format only top or bottom ranked values
- Format only values that are above or below average
- Format only unique or duplicate values
- Use a formula to determine which cells to format

Edit the Rule Description:

Format all cells based on their values:

Format Style: Icon Sets | Reverse Icon Order

Icon Style: Custom | Show Icon Only

Display each icon according to these rules:

Icon			Value	Type
✔	when value is	>=	1	Number
No Cell Icon	when < 1 and	>	0	Number
✖	when <= 0			

OK | Cancel

Figure 19-10: Changing the icon assignment rule.

Figure 19-11 shows the project status list after making this change.

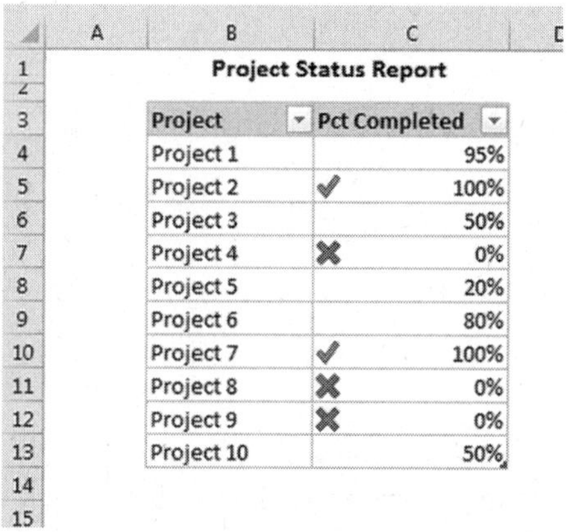

Project Status Report

Project	Pct Completed
Project 1	95%
Project 2	✔ 100%
Project 3	50%
Project 4	✖ 0%
Project 5	20%
Project 6	80%
Project 7	✔ 100%
Project 8	✖ 0%
Project 9	✖ 0%
Project 10	50%

Figure 19-11: Using a modified rule and eliminating an icon makes the table more readable.

Another icon set example

Figure 19-12 shows a table that contains two test scores for each student. The Change column contains a formula that calculates the difference between the two tests. The Trend column uses an icon set to display the trend graphically.

Student	Test 1	Test 2	Change	Trend
Amy	59	65	6	↑
Bob	82	78	-4	→
Calvind	98	92	-6	↓
Doug	56	69	13	↑
Ephraim	98	89	-9	↓
Frank	67	75	8	↑
Gretta	78	87	9	↑
Harold	87	92	5	↑
Inez	56	85	29	↑
June	87	72	-15	↓
Kenny	87	88	1	→
Lance	92	92	0	→
Marvin	82	73	-9	↓
Noel	98	100	2	→
Opie	84	73	-11	↓
Paul	94	93	-1	→
Quinton	68	92	24	↑
Rasmus	91	90	-1	→
Sam	85	86	1	→
Ted	72	92	20	↑
Ursie	80	75	-5	↓
Valerie	77	65	-12	↓
Wally	64	45	-19	↓
Xerxes	59	63	4	→
Yolanda	89	99	10	↑
Zippy	85	82	-3	→

Figure 19-12: The arrows depict the trend from Test 1 to Test 2.

This example uses the icon set named 3 Arrows, and we customized the rule using the Edit Formatting Rule dialog box:

- **Up arrow:** When value is ≥ 5
- **Level arrow:** When value < 5 and > –5
- **Down arrow:** When value is ≤ –5

In other words, a difference of no more than five points in either direction is considered an even trend. An improvement of at least five points is considered a positive trend, and a decline of five points or more is considered a negative trend.

Note

The Trend column contains the same formula as the Change column. We used the Show Icon Only option in the Trend column, which also centers the icon in the column.

In some cases, using icon sets can cause your worksheet to look cluttered. Displaying an icon for every cell in a range might result in visual overload.

Figure 19-13 shows the test results table after hiding the level arrow by choosing No Cell Icon in the Edit Formatting Rule dialog box.

Student	Test 1	Test 2	Change	Trend
Amy	59	65	6	↑
Bob	82	78	-4	
Calvind	98	92	-6	↓
Doug	56	69	13	↑
Ephraim	98	89	-9	↓
Frank	67	75	8	↑
Gretta	78	87	9	↑
Harold	87	92	5	↑
Inez	56	85	29	↑
June	87	72	-15	↓
Kenny	87	88	1	
Lance	92	92	0	
Marvin	82	73	-9	↓
Noel	98	100	2	
Opie	84	73	-11	↓
Paul	94	93	-1	
Quinton	68	92	24	↑
Rasmus	91	90	-1	
Sam	85	86	1	
Ted	72	92	20	↑
Ursie	80	75	-5	↓
Valerie	77	65	-12	↓
Wally	64	45	-19	↓
Xerxes	59	63	4	
Yolanda	89	99	10	↑
Zippy	85	82	-3	

Figure 19-13: Hiding one of the icons makes the table less cluttered.

Creating Formula-Based Rules

Excel's conditional formatting feature is versatile, but sometimes it's just not quite versatile enough. Fortunately, you can extend its versatility by writing conditional formatting formulas.

The examples later in this section describe how to create conditional formatting formulas for the following:

- To identify text entries
- To identify dates that fall on a weekend
- To format cells that are in odd-numbered rows or columns (for dynamic alternate row or columns shading)
- To format groups of rows (for example, shade every group of two rows)
- To display a sum only when all precedent cells contain values

Some of these formulas may be useful to you. If not, they may inspire you to create other conditional formatting formulas.

On the Web

This book's website contains all the examples in this section. The file is named conditional formatting formulas.xlsx.

To specify conditional formatting based on a formula, select the cells and then choose Home ➜ Styles ➜ Conditional Formatting ➜ New Rule. This command displays the New Formatting Rule dialog box. Click the rule type Use a Formula to Determine Which Cells to Format and you can specify the formula.

You can type the formula directly into the box, or you can enter a reference to a cell that contains a logical formula. As with normal Excel formulas, the formula you enter here must begin with an equal sign (=).

Note

The formula must be a logical formula that returns either *TRUE* or *FALSE*. If the formula evaluates to *TRUE*, the condition is satisfied, and the conditional formatting is applied. If the formula evaluates to *FALSE*, the conditional formatting is not applied.

Understanding relative and absolute references

If the formula that you enter into the Conditional Formatting dialog box contains a cell reference, that reference is considered a *relative reference* based on the upper-left cell in the selected range.

For example, suppose that you want to set up a conditional formatting condition that applies shading to cells in range A1:B10 only if the cell contains text. None of Excel's conditional formatting options can do this task, so you need to create a formula that will return *TRUE* if the cell contains text and *FALSE* otherwise. Follow these steps:

1. Select the range A1:B10 and ensure that cell A1 is the active cell.

2. Choose Home ➜ Styles ➜ Conditional Formatting ➜ New Rule to display the New Formatting Rule dialog box. See Figure 19-14.

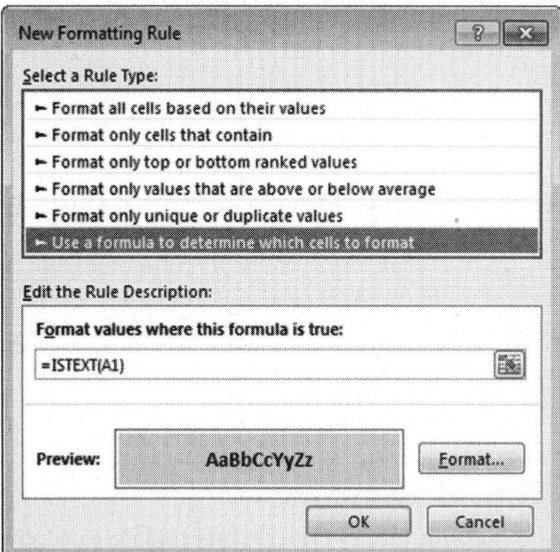

Figure 19-14: Creating a conditional formatting rule based on a formula.

3. Click the Use a Formula to Determine Which Cells to Format rule type.
4. Enter the following formula in the formula box:

```
=ISTEXT(A1)
```

Note

Notice that the formula entered in step 4 contains a relative reference to the upper-left cell in the selected range.

5. Click the Format button to display the Format Cells dialog box.
6. From the Fill tab, specify the cell shading that will be applied if the formula returns *TRUE*.
7. Click OK to return to the New Formatting Rule dialog box.
8. Click OK to close the New Formatting Rule dialog box.

Generally, when entering a conditional formatting formula for a range of cells, you'll use a reference to the active cell, which is typically the upper-left cell in the selected range. One exception is when you need to refer to a specific cell. For example, suppose that you select range A1:B10, and you want to apply formatting to all cells in the range that exceed the value in cell C1. Enter this conditional formatting formula:

```
=A1>$C$1
```

In this case, the reference to cell C1 is an *absolute reference;* it will not be adjusted for the cells in the selected range. In other words, the conditional formatting formula for cell A2 looks like this:

```
=A2>$C$1
```

The relative cell reference is adjusted, but the absolute cell reference is not.

Conditional formatting formula examples

Each of these examples uses a formula entered directly into the New Formatting Rule dialog box, after selecting the Use a Formula to Determine Which Cells to Format rule type. You decide the type of formatting that you apply conditionally.

Identifying weekend days

Excel provides a number of conditional formatting rules that deal with dates, but it doesn't let you identify dates that fall on a weekend. Use this formula to identify weekend dates:

```
=WEEKDAY(A1,2)>=6
```

This formula assumes that a range is selected and that cell A1 is the active cell. The WEEKDAY function's second argument, 2 in this example, indicates that Monday returns 1 and Sunday returns 7. The default for this argument is that Sunday starts with 1, but by specifying this argument you can test that weekday is at least 6 (Saturday).

Highlighting a row based on a value

Figure 19-15 shows a worksheet that contains a conditional format in the range A3:G28. If a name entered in cell B1 is found in the first column, the entire row for that name is highlighted.

	A	B	C	D	E	F	G	H
1	**Name:**	Noel						
2								
3	Alice	7	118	61	55	85	26	
4	Bob	198	134	180	3	132	63	
5	Carl	2	46	59	63	59	26	
6	Denise	190	121	12	26	68	97	
7	Elvin	174	42	176	68	124	14	
8	Francis	129	114	83	103	129	129	
9	George	9	128	24	44	139	108	
10	Harald	168	183	200	167	134	83	
11	Ivan	165	141	95	91	100	144	
12	June	116	171	109	84	148	15	
13	Kathy	131	43	197	82	103	163	
14	Larry	139	30	171	122	34	196	
15	Mary	31	171	185	162	171	17	
16	Noel	78	126	190	78	123	2	
17	Oliver	157	98	100	75	137	10	
18	Patrick	120	144	106	39	39	119	
19	Quincey	156	200	58	74	37	76	
20	Raul	58	147	160	182	11	79	
21	Shiela	79	183	5	161	104	23	
22	Todd	91	54	100	174	198	78	
23	Ursula	53	140	188	58	54	36	
24	Vince	121	13	2	139	148	101	
25	Walter	132	65	123	129	174	90	
26	Xenu	162	127	86	51	164	35	
27	Yolanda	60	116	107	117	189	200	
28	Zed	103	142	103	165	89	37	
29								

Figure 19-15: Highlighting a row, based on a matching name.

The conditional formatting formula follows:

```
=$A3=$B$1
```

Notice that a mixed reference is used for cell A3. Because the column part of the reference is absolute, the comparison is always done using the contents of column A.

Displaying alternate-row shading

The conditional formatting formula that follows was applied to the range A1:D18, as shown in Figure 19-16, to apply shading to alternate rows:

```
=MOD(ROW(),2)=0
```

Q33

	A	B	C	D	E
1	319	629	185	152	
2	50	741	148	133	
3	968	607	749	970	
4	72	523	133	46	
5	681	34	825	247	
6	887	263	699	949	
7	449	388	919	670	
8	398	941	41	889	
9	561	277	134	135	
10	314	687	504	35	
11	22	572	690	224	
12	983	248	100	977	
13	72	993	778	283	
14	713	625	341	859	
15	599	65	616	255	
16	872	689	522	735	
17	282	691	241	700	
18	734	960	977	448	
19					

Figure 19-16: Using conditional formatting to apply formatting to alternate rows.

Alternate row shading can make your spreadsheets easier to read. If you add or delete rows within the conditional formatting area, the shading is updated automatically.

This formula uses the ROW function (which returns the row number) and the MOD function (which returns the remainder of its first argument divided by its second argument). For cells in even-numbered rows, the MOD function returns *0*, and cells in that row are formatted.

For alternate shading of columns, use the COLUMN function instead of the ROW function.

Creating checkerboard shading

The following formula is a variation on the example in the preceding section. It applies formatting to alternate rows and columns, creating a checkerboard effect:

```
=MOD(ROW(),2)=MOD(COLUMN(),2)
```

Instead of comparing the results of MOD to 0 or 1 as in the last example, this example compares the modulo of the ROW to the modulo of the COLUMN. For odd-numbered rows, only cells in odd-numbered columns are formatted. And for even-numbered rows, only cells in even-numbered columns are formatted.

Shading groups of rows

Here's another row shading variation. The following formula shades alternate groups of rows. It produces four rows of shaded rows, followed by four rows of unshaded rows, followed by four more shaded rows, and so on:

```
=MOD(INT((ROW()-1)/4)+1,2)=1
```

Figure 19-17 shows an example.

	A	B	C	D	E
1	200	306	416	5	
2	439	297	496	271	
3	143	376	244	74	
4	186	184	173	380	
5	303	290	304	247	
6	193	336	323	79	
7	74	222	230	334	
8	460	414	4	242	
9	460	499	464	145	
10	488	93	297	362	
11	196	292	251	330	
12	288	416	294	282	
13	174	22	216	263	
14	217	389	73	245	
15	320	351	157	402	
16	424	79	230	380	
17	25	18	374	131	
18	155	354	234	71	
19	106	391	125	40	
20	50	499	395	445	
21	163	327	127	267	
22	373	32	282	487	
23					

Figure 19-17: Conditional formatting produces these groups of alternate shaded rows.

For different sized groups, change the 4 to some other value. For example, use this formula to shade alternate groups of two rows:

```
=MOD(INT((ROW()-1)/2)+1,2)=1
```

Displaying a total only when all values are entered

Figure 19-18 shows a range with a formula that uses the SUM function in cell C6. Conditional formatting is used to display the sum only when all of the four cells above are nonblank. The conditional formatting formula for cell C6 (and cell B6, which contains a label) is this:

```
=COUNT($C$2:$C$5)=COUNTA($B$2:$B$5)
```

This formula returns *TRUE* only if C2:C5 contains an entry for every label in B2:B5. The conditional formatting applied is a dark background color. The text color is white, so it's legible only when the conditional formatting rule is satisfied.

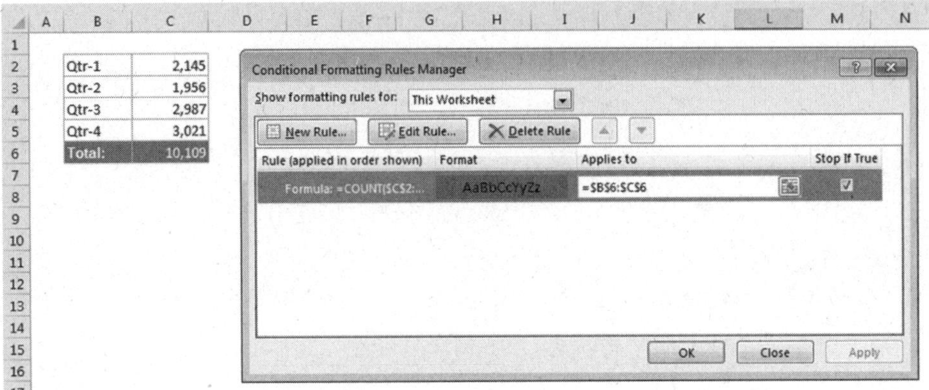

Figure 19-18: The sum is displayed only when all four values have been entered.

Figure 19-19 shows the worksheet when one of the values is missing.

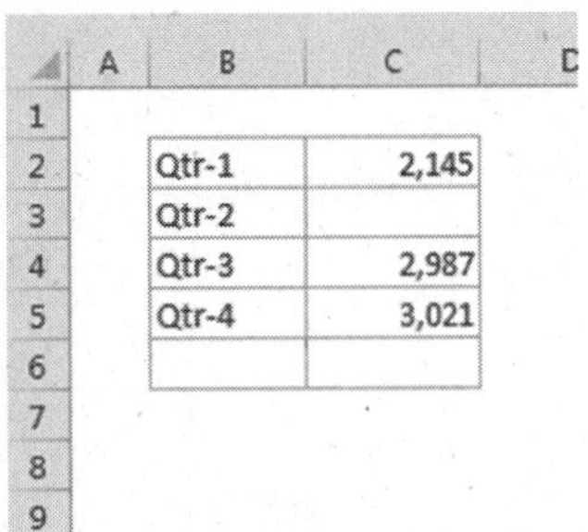

Figure 19-19: A missing value causes the sum to be hidden.

Using custom functions in conditional formatting formulas

Excel's conditional formatting feature is versatile, and the ability to create your own formulas to define the conditions will cover most needs. But if custom formulas still aren't versatile enough, you can create custom VBA functions and use those in a conditional formatting formula.

This section provides three examples of VBA functions that you can use in conditional formatting formulas.

Cross-Ref

Part VI, "Developing Custom Worksheet Functions," provides an overview of VBA, with specific information about creating custom worksheet functions.

On the Web

This book's website contains all the examples in this section. The file is named conditional formatting with VBA functions.xlsm.

Identifying formula cells

You can use the ISFORMULA function in a conditional formatting formula to highlight all the cells in a range that contain a formula. If your workbook must be compatible with versions of Excel prior to 2013 (the version in which ISFORMULA was introduced), you can create a simple VBA function. The following custom VBA function uses the VBA HasFormula property. The function, which you can enter into a VBA module, returns *TRUE* if the cell (specified as its argument) contains a formula; otherwise, it returns *FALSE*:

```
Function CELLHASFORMULA(cell) As Boolean
    CELLHASFORMULA = cell.HasFormula
End Function
```

After you enter this function into a VBA module, you can use the function in your worksheet formulas. For example, the following formula returns *TRUE* if cell A1 contains a formula:

```
=CELLHASFORMULA(A1)
```

You also can use this function in a conditional formatting formula. The worksheet in Figure 19-20, for example, uses conditional formatting to identify cells that contain a formula. In this case, formula cells display a background color.

	A	B	C	D	E
1		Last Year	This Year	Difference	
2	Jan	143	155	12	
3	Feb	155	188	33	
4	Mar	133	122	-11	
5	Q1	431	465	34	
6	Apr	160	178	18	
7	May	187	203	16	
8	Jun	199	221	22	
9	Q2	546	602	56	
10	Jul	201	273	72	
11	Aug	177	212	35	
12	Sep	191	198	7	
13	Q3	569	683	114	
14	Oct	244	255	11	
15	Nov	199	188	-11	
16	Dec	211	233	22	
17	Q4	654	676	22	
18	Total	2200	2426	226	
19					

Figure 19-20: Using a custom VBA function to apply conditional formatting to cells that contain a formula.

Identifying date cells

Excel lacks a function to determine whether a cell contains a date. The following VBA function, which uses the VBA IsDate function, overcomes this limitation. The custom CELLHASDATE function returns *TRUE* if the cell contains a date:

```
Function CELLHASDATE(cell) As Boolean
    CELLHASDATE = IsDate(cell)
End Function
```

The following conditional formatting formula applies formatting to cell A1 if it contains a date and the month is June:

```
=AND(CELLHASDATE(A1),MONTH(A1)=6)
```

The following conditional formatting formula applies formatting to cell A1 if it contains a date and the date falls on a weekend:

```
=AND(CELLHASDATE(A1), WEEKDAY(A1,2)>=6)
```

Identifying invalid data

You might have a situation in which the data entered must adhere to some specific rules, and you'd like to apply special formatting if the data entered is not valid. For example, consider part numbers that consist of seven characters: four uppercase alphabetic characters, followed by a hyphen, and then a two-digit number—for example, ADSS-09 or DYUU-43.

You can write a conditional formatting formula to determine whether part numbers adhere to this structure, but the formula is complex. The following formula, for example, returns *TRUE* only if the value in A1 meets the part number rules specified:

```
=AND(LEN(A1)=7,AND(LEFT(A1)>="A",LEFT(A1)<="Z"),
AND(MID(A1,2,1)>="A",MID(A1,2,1)<="Z"),AND(MID(A1,3,1)>="A",
MID(A1,3,1)<="Z"),AND(MID(A1,4,1)>="A",MID(A1,4,1)<="Z"),
MID(A1,5,1)="-",AND(VALUE(MID(A1,6,2))>=0,
VALUE(MID(A1,6,2))<=99))
```

For a simpler approach, write a custom VBA worksheet function. The VBA Like operator makes this sort of comparison relatively easy. The following VBA function procedure returns *TRUE* if its argument does not correspond to the part number rules outlined previously:

```
Function INVALIDPART(Part) As Boolean
    If Part Like "[A-Z][A-Z][A-Z][A-Z]-##" Then
        INVALIDPART = False
    Else
        INVALIDPART = True
    End If
End Function
```

After defining this function in a VBA module, you can enter the following conditional formatting formula to apply special formatting if cell A1 contains an invalid part number:

```
=INVALIDPART(A1)
```

Figure 19-21 shows a range that uses the custom INVALIDPART function in a conditional formatting formula. Cells that contain invalid part numbers have a colored background.

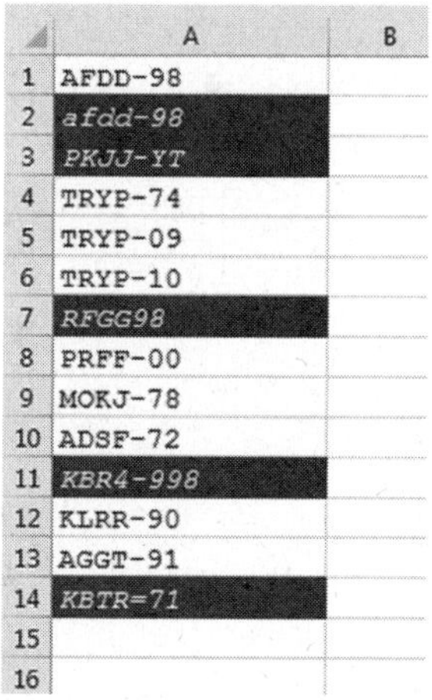

	A	B
1	AFDD-98	
2	afdd-98	
3	PKJJ-YT	
4	TRYP-74	
5	TRYP-09	
6	TRYP-10	
7	RFGG98	
8	PRFF-00	
9	MOKJ-78	
10	ADSF-72	
11	KBR4-998	
12	KLRR-90	
13	AGGT-91	
14	KBTR=71	
15		
16		

Figure 19-21: Using conditional formatting to highlight cells with invalid entries.

In many cases, you can simply take advantage of Excel's data validation feature, which is described next.

Working with Conditional Formats

This section describes some additional information about conditional formatting that you may find useful.

Managing rules

The Conditional Formatting Rules Manager dialog box is useful for checking, editing, deleting, and adding conditional formats. First select any cell in the range that contains conditional formatting. Then choose Home ➜ Styles ➜ Conditional Formatting ➜ Manage Rules.

You can specify as many rules as you like by clicking the New Rule button. As you can see in Figure 19-22, cells can even use data bars, color scales, and icon sets at the same time—although we can't think of a good reason to do so.

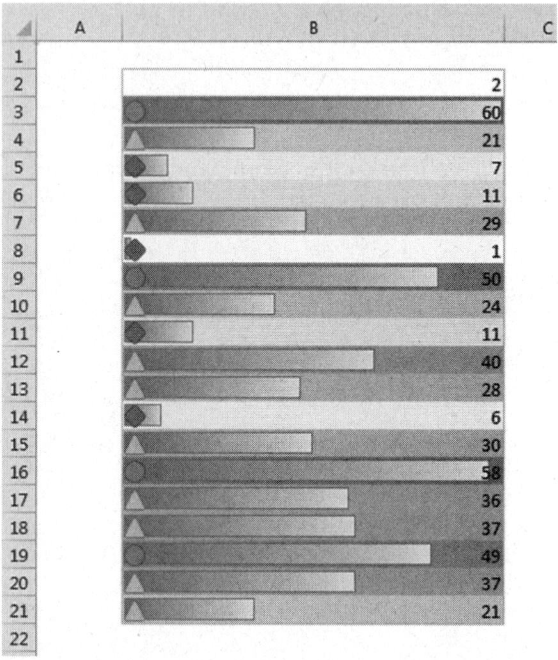

Figure 19-22: This range uses data bars, color scales, and icon sets.

Copying cells that contain conditional formatting

Conditional formatting information is stored with a cell, much like standard formatting information is stored with a cell. As a result, when you copy a cell that contains conditional formatting, you also copy the conditional formatting.

Tip

To copy only the formatting (including conditional formatting), copy the cells and then use the Paste Special dialog box and select the Formats option. Or use Home ➜ Clipboard ➜ Paste ➜ Formatting (R).

If you insert rows or columns within a range that contains conditional formatting, the new cells have the same conditional formatting.

Deleting conditional formatting

When you press Delete to delete the contents of a cell, you do not delete the conditional formatting for the cell (if any). To remove all conditional formats (as well as all other cell formatting), select the cell. Then choose Home ➜ Editing ➜ Clear ➜ Clear Formats. Or choose Home ➜ Editing ➜ Clear ➜ Clear All to delete the cell contents and the conditional formatting.

To remove only conditional formatting (and leave the other formatting intact), use Home ➜ Styles ➜ Conditional Formatting ➜ Clear Rules. Or to remove only one of many conditional formats, use Home ➜ Styles ➜ Conditional Formatting ➜ Manage Rules, select the rule to delete, and click the Delete Rule button.

Locating cells that contain conditional formatting

You can't always tell, just by looking at a cell, whether it contains conditional formatting. You can, however, use the Go To dialog box to select such cells.

1. Choose Home ➜ Editing ➜ Find & Select ➜ Go to Special.
2. In the Go to Special dialog box, select the Conditional Formats option.
3. Click OK. Excel selects the cells for you.

Note

The Excel Find and Replace dialog box includes a feature that allows you to search your worksheet to locate cells that contain specific formatting. This feature does *not* locate cells that contain formatting resulting from conditional formatting.

20

Using Data Validation

In This Chapter

- An overview of Excel's data validation feature
- Practical examples of using data validation formulas

This chapter explores a useful Excel feature: data validation. Data validation enables you to add rules for what's acceptable in specific cells and allows you to add dynamic elements to your worksheet without using macro programming.

About Data Validation

The Excel data validation feature allows you to set up rules that dictate what can be entered into a cell. For example, you may want to limit data entry in a particular cell to whole numbers between 1 and 12. You can specify an input message to help the user know what kind of data to enter in the cell. If the user makes an invalid entry, you can display a custom message. Figure 20.1 shows an example of both the input message and the message generated from an invalid entry.

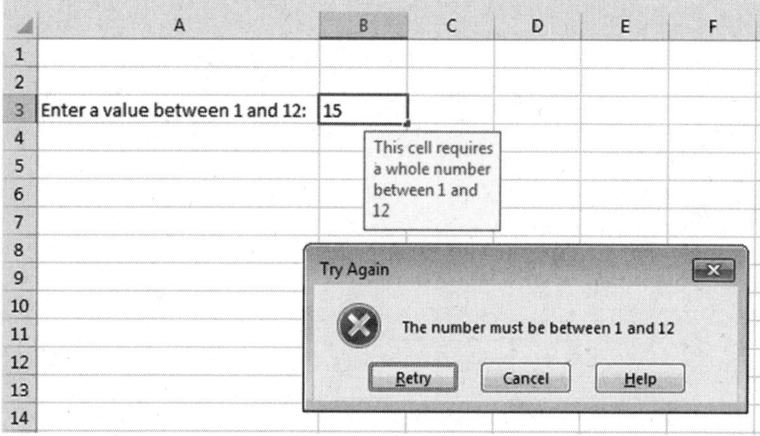

Figure 20-1: Displaying an input message and a message when the user makes an invalid entry.

Excel makes it easy to specify the validation criteria, and you can also use a formula for more complex criteria.

Caution

The Excel data validation feature suffers from a potentially serious problem: if the user copies a cell that does not use data validation and pastes it to a cell that *does* use data validation, the data validation rules are deleted. In other words, the cell then accepts any type of data. This has always been a problem, but Microsoft still hasn't fixed it in Excel 2016.

Specifying Validation Criteria

To specify the type of data allowable in a cell or range, follow these steps while you refer to Figure 20.2, which shows all three tabs of the Data Validation dialog box:

1. Select the cell or range.
2. Choose Data ➜ Data Tools ➜ Data Validation. Excel displays its Data Validation dialog box.
3. Click the Settings tab.

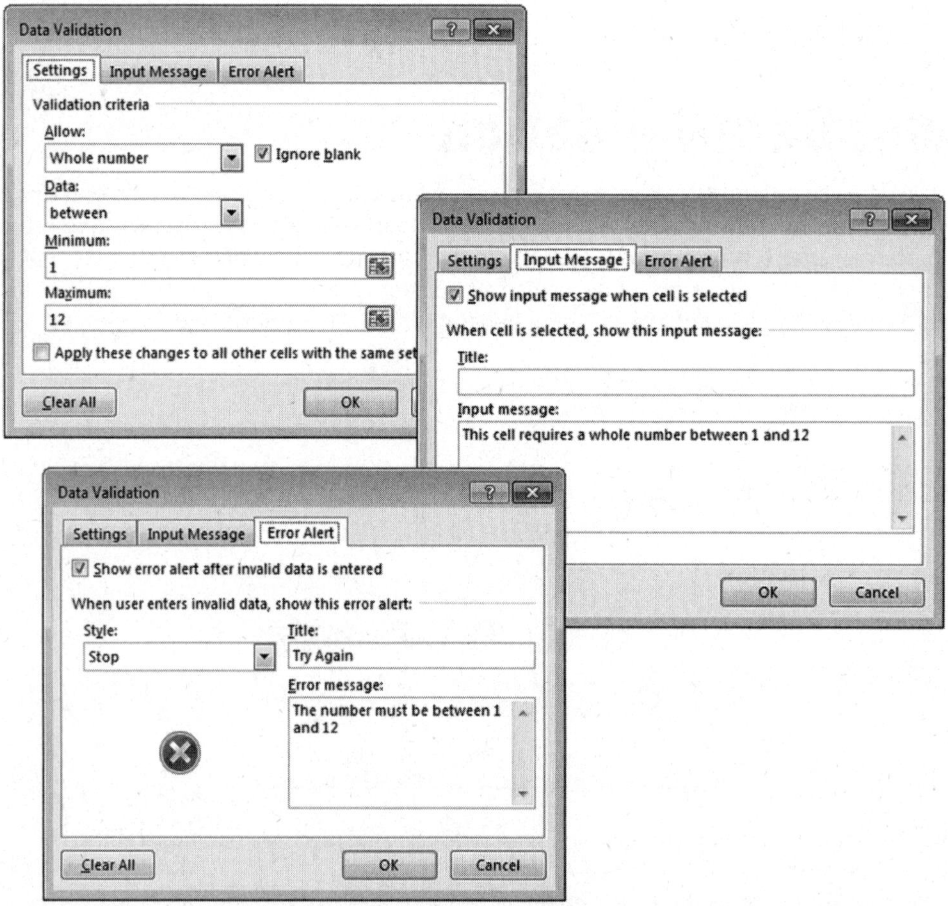

Figure 20-2: The three tabs of the Data Validation dialog box.

4. Choose an option from the Allow drop-down list. The contents of the Data Validation dialog box will change, displaying controls based on your choice. To specify a formula, select Custom.
5. Specify the conditions by using the displayed controls. Your selection in step 4 determines what other controls you can access.
6. (Optional) Click the Input Message tab and specify which message to display when a user selects the cell. You can use this optional step to tell the user what type of data is expected. If this step is omitted, no message will appear when the user selects the cell.
7. (Optional) Click the Error Alert tab and specify which error message to display when a user makes an invalid entry. The selection for Style determines what choices users have when they make invalid entries. To prevent an invalid entry, choose Stop. If this step is omitted, a standard message will appear if the user makes an invalid entry.

Caution

Even with data validation in effect, a user can enter invalid data. If the Style setting on the Error Alert tab of the Data Validation dialog box is set to anything except Stop, invalid data *can* be entered. You can identify invalid entries by having Excel circle them (explained later).

8. Click OK. The cell or range contains the validation criteria you specified.

Tip

You can use the optional Input Message with a criteria of Any Value. This allows you to display a message to the user even for cells whose value you don't want to restrict.

Types of Validation Criteria You Can Apply

From the Settings tab of the Data Validation dialog box, you can specify a variety of data validation criteria. The following options are available from the Allow drop-down list. Keep in mind that the other controls on the Settings tab vary, depending on your choice from the Allow drop-down list.

- **Any Value:** Selecting this option removes any existing data validation. Note, however, that the input message, if any, still displays if the check box is selected on the Input Message tab.
- **Whole Number:** The user must enter a whole number. You specify a valid range of whole numbers by using the Data drop-down list. For example, you can specify that the entry must be a whole number greater than or equal to 100.
- **Decimal:** The user must enter a number. You specify a valid range of numbers by refining the criteria from choices in the Data drop-down list. For example, you can specify that the entry must be greater than or equal to 0 and less than or equal to 1.
- **List:** The user must choose from a list of entries you provide. This option is useful, and we discuss it in detail later in this chapter. (See "Creating a Drop-Down List.")

- **Date:** The user must enter a date. You specify a valid date range from choices in the Data drop-down list. For example, you can specify that the entered data must be greater than or equal to January 1, 2016, and less than or equal to December 31, 2016.
- **Time:** The user must enter a time. You specify a valid time range from choices in the Data drop-down list. For example, you can specify that the entered data must be later than 12:00 p.m.
- **Text Length:** The length of the data (number of characters) is limited. You specify a valid length by using the Data drop-down list. For example, you can specify that the length of the entered data be 1 (a single alphanumeric character).
- **Custom:** To use this option, you must supply a logical formula that determines the validity of the user's entry. (A logical formula returns either *TRUE* or *FALSE*.) You can enter the formula directly into the Formula control (which appears when you select the Custom option), or you can specify a cell reference that contains a formula. This chapter contains examples of useful formulas.

Tip

All the data validation criteria can accept typed values or references to cells. For instance, you can type 1 and 12 to limit whole numbers, or you can point to cells that contain the values 1 and 12.

The Settings tab of the Data Validation dialog box contains two other check boxes:

- **Ignore Blank:** If selected, blank entries are allowed.
- **Apply These Changes to All Other Cells with the Same Setting:** If selected, the changes you make apply to all other cells that contain the original data validation criteria.

Tip

The Data ➜ Data Tools ➜ Data Validation drop-down list contains an item labeled Circle Invalid Data. When you select this item, circles appear around cells that contain incorrect entries. If you correct an invalid entry, the circle disappears. To get rid of the circles, choose Data ➜ Data Tools ➜ Data Validation ➜ Clear Validation Circles. In Figure 20.3, invalid entries are defined as values that are less than 1 or greater than 100.

	A	B	C	D	E	F	G	H	I	J
1	4	-8	32	53	37	-5	46	52	110	
2	7	104	109	42	28	4	37	46	84	
3	0	12	49	66	48	42	46	86	104	
4	-8	95	29	1	61	74	21	23	51	
5	31	68	-1	47	32	72	100	53	42	
6	102	70	82	20	69	17	100	86	108	
7	50	95	103	40	51	99	51	99	76	
8	19	68	78	54	46	-2	-6	86	108	
9	82	87	18	101	35	67	36	1	6	
10	5	77	63	19	18	107	6	12	33	
11	20	34	86	50	12	88	20	102	40	
12	91	68	89	33	76	10	85	107	59	
13	97	35	20	44	84	33	52	49	106	
14	103	95	11	34	-5	69	22	86	10	
15	35	83	54	1	43	21	53	15	83	
16	63	41	52	1	7	25	42	1	91	
17	52	46	79	48	10	83	2	22	23	
18										
19										

Figure 20-3: Excel can draw circles around invalid entries (in this case, cells that contain values less than 1 or greater than 100).

Creating a Drop-Down List

Perhaps one of the most common uses of data validation is to create a drop-down list in a cell. Figure 20.4 shows an example that uses the month names in A1:A12 as the list source.

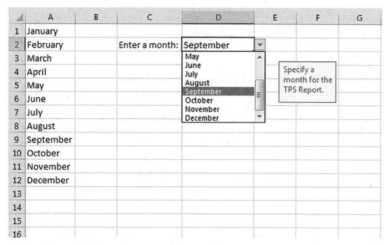

	A	B	C	D	E	F	G
1	January						
2	February		Enter a month:	September			
3	March						
4	April						
5	May						
6	June						
7	July						
8	August						
9	September						
10	October						
11	November						
12	December						
13							
14							
15							
16							

Figure 20-4: This drop-down list (with an Input Message) was created using data validation.

To create a drop-down list in a cell, do the following:

1. Enter the list items into a single-row or single-column range. These items will appear in the drop-down list.
2. Select the cell that will contain the drop-down list and then access the Data Validation dialog box. (Choose Data ➜ Data Tools ➜ Data Validation.)
3. From the Settings tab, select the List option (from the Allow drop-down list) and specify the range that contains the list, using the Source control. The range can be in a different worksheet but must be in the same workbook.
4. Make sure that the In-Cell Dropdown check box is selected.
5. Set any other Data Validation options as desired.
6. Click OK. The cell displays an input message (if specified) and a drop-down arrow when it's activated. Click the arrow and choose an item from the list that appears.

Tip

If you have a short list, you can enter the items directly into the Source control of the Settings tab of the Data Validation dialog box. (This control appears when you choose the List option in the Allow drop-down list.) Just separate each item with list separators specified in your regional settings (a comma if you use the U.S. regional settings).

Using Formulas for Data Validation Rules

For simple data validation, the data validation feature is quite straightforward and easy to use. The real power of this feature, though, becomes apparent when you use data validation formulas.

Note

The formula that you specify must be a logical formula that returns either *TRUE* or *FALSE*. If the formula evaluates to *TRUE*, the data is considered valid and remains in the cell. If the formula evaluates to *FALSE*, a message box appears that displays the message you specify on the Error Alert tab of the Data Validation dialog box. Specify a formula in the Data Validation dialog box by selecting the Custom option from the Allow drop-down list of the Settings tab. Enter the formula directly into the Formula control or enter a reference to a cell that contains a formula. The Formula control appears on the Setting tab of the Data Validation dialog box when the Custom option is selected.

We present several examples of formulas used for data validation in the upcoming section "Data Validation Formula Examples."

Understanding Cell References

If the formula that you enter into the Data Validation dialog box contains a cell reference, that reference is considered a *relative reference,* based on the upper-left cell in the selected range.

The following example clarifies this concept. Suppose that you want to allow only an odd number to be entered into the range B2:B10. None of the Excel data validation rules can limit entry to odd numbers, so a formula is required.

Follow these steps:

1. Select the range (B2:B10 for this example) and ensure that cell B2 is the active cell.
2. Choose Data ➜ Data Tools ➜ Data Validation. The Data Validation dialog box appears.
3. Click the Settings tab and select Custom from the Allow drop-down list.
4. Enter the following formula in the Formula field, as shown in Figure 20.5:

```
=ISODD(B2)
```

This formula uses the ISODD function, which returns *TRUE* if its numeric argument is an odd number. Notice that the formula refers to the active cell, which is cell B2.

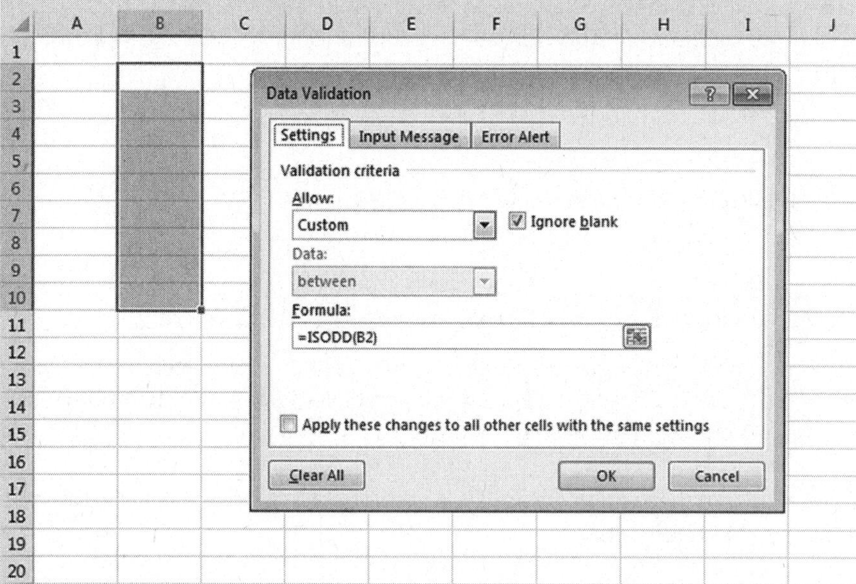

Figure 20-5: Entering a data validation formula.

5. On the Error Alert tab, choose Stop for the Style and then type **An odd number is required here** as the error message.
6. Click OK to close the Data Validation dialog box.

Notice that the formula entered contains a reference to the upper-left cell in the selected range. This data validation formula was applied to a range of cells, so you might expect that each cell would contain the same data validation formula. Because you entered a relative cell reference as the argument for the ISODD function, Excel adjusts the formula for the other cells in the B2:B10 range. To demonstrate that the reference is relative, select cell B5 and examine its formula displayed in the Data Validation dialog box. You'll see that the formula for this cell is

```
=ISODD(B5)
```

Generally, when entering a data validation formula for a range of cells, you use a reference to the active cell, which is normally the upper-left cell in the selected range. An exception is when you need to refer to a specific cell. For example, suppose that you select range A1:B10 and you want your data validation to allow only values that are greater than the value in cell C1. You would use this formula:

```
=A1>$C$1
```

In this case, the reference to cell C1 is an *absolute reference;* it will not be adjusted for the cells in the selected range, which is just what you want. The data validation formula for cell A2 looks like this:

```
=A2>$C$1
```

The relative cell reference is adjusted, but the absolute cell reference is not.

Data Validation Formula Examples

The following sections contain a few data validation examples that use a formula entered directly into the Formula control on the Settings tab of the Data Validation dialog box. These examples help you understand how to create your own data validation formulas.

On the Web

All the examples in this section are available at this book's website. The file is named data validation examples.xlsx.

Accepting text only

Excel has a data validation option to limit the length of text entered into a cell, but it doesn't have an option to force text (rather than a number) into a cell. To force a cell or range to accept only text (no values), use the following data validation formula:

```
=ISTEXT(A1)
```

This formula assumes that the active cell in the selected range is cell A1.

Accepting a larger value than the previous cell

The following data validation formula enables the user to enter a value only if it's greater than the value in the cell directly above it:

```
=A2>A1
```

This formula assumes that A2 is the active cell in the selected range. Note that you can't use this formula for a cell in row 1.

Accepting nonduplicate entries only

The following data validation formula does not permit the user to make a duplicate entry in the range A1:C20:

```
=COUNTIF($A$1:$C$20,A1)=1
```

This is a logical formula that returns *TRUE* if the value in the cell occurs only one time in the A1:C20 range. Otherwise, it returns *FALSE*, and the Duplicate Entry dialog box is displayed.

This formula assumes that A1 is the active cell in the selected range. Note that the first argument for COUNTIF is an absolute reference. The second argument is a relative reference, and it adjusts for each cell in the validation range. Figure 20.6 shows this validation criterion in effect, using a custom error alert message. The user is attempting to enter a value into cell B5 that already exists in the A1:C20 range.

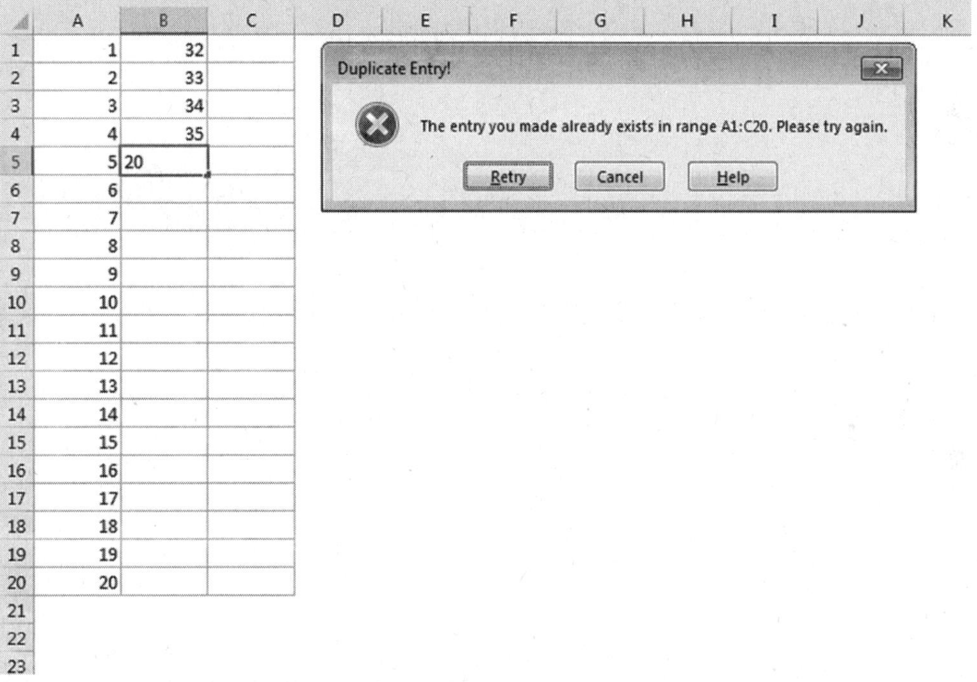

Figure 20-6: Using data validation to prevent duplicate entries in a range.

Accepting text that begins with a specific character

The following data validation formula demonstrates how to check for a specific character. In this case, the formula ensures that the user's entry is a text string that begins with the letter *A* (uppercase or lowercase):

```
=LEFT(A1)="a"
```

This is a logical formula that returns *TRUE* if the first character in the cell is the letter *A*. Otherwise, it returns *FALSE*. This formula assumes that the active cell in the selected range is cell A1.

If case sensitivity is important and you want to limit entries to only those that start with a lowercase *a*, you can use the EXACT worksheet function as shown here:

```
=EXACT(LEFT(A1,1),"a")
```

The following formula is a variation of the non–case sensitive validation formula. It uses wildcard characters in the second argument of the COUNTIF function. In this case, the formula ensures that the entry begins with the letter *A* and contains exactly five characters:

```
=COUNTIF(A1,"A????")=1
```

Accepting dates by the day of the week

The following data validation formula ensures that the cell entry is a date and that the date is a Monday:

```
=WEEKDAY(A1)=2
```

This formula assumes that the active cell in the selected range is cell A1. It uses the WEEKDAY function, which returns *1* for Sunday, *2* for Monday, and so on.

Accepting only values that don't exceed a total

Figure 20.7 shows a simple budget worksheet, with the budget item amounts in the range B1:B6. The planned budget is in cell E5, and the user is attempting to enter a value in cell B4 that would cause the total (cell E6) to exceed the budget. The following data validation formula ensures that the sum of the budget items does not exceed the budget:

```
=SUM($B$1:$B$6)<=$E$5
```

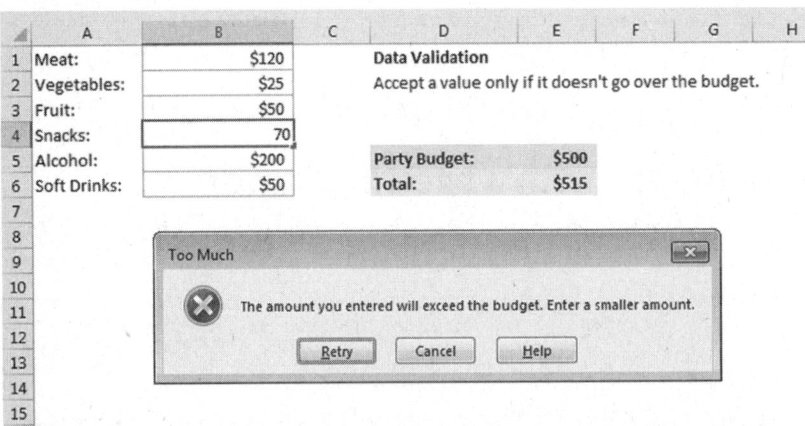

Figure 20-7: Using data validation to ensure that the sum of a range does not exceed a certain value.

Creating a dependent list

As we described previously, you can use data validation to create a drop-down list in a cell (see "Creating a Drop-Down List"). This section explains how to use a drop-down list to control the entries that appear in a second drop-down list. In other words, the second drop-down list is dependent upon the value selected in the first drop-down list.

Figure 20.8 shows a simple example of a dependent list created by using data validation. Cell E2 contains data validation that displays a three-item list from the range A1:C1 (Vegetables, Fruits, and Meats). When the user chooses an item from the list, the second list (in cell F2) displays the appropriate items. Cell E2 contains data validation with its Allow criterion set to List and its Source criterion shown below:

```
=$A$1:$C$1
```

This worksheet uses three named ranges:

- **Vegetables**: A2:A15
- **Fruits**: B2:B9
- **Meats**: C2:C5

For this technique to work, your range names must match the values in A1:C1. For example, if you type **Veggies** in cell A1 and name the range Vegetables, the list in F2 won't contain items. Cell F2 contains data validation that uses this formula:

```
=INDIRECT($E$2)
```

The INDIRECT function converts its argument into a range if it can. If cell E2 contains the text Fruits, for instance, INDIRECT looks for a range named Fruits and supplies that range to the data validation list.

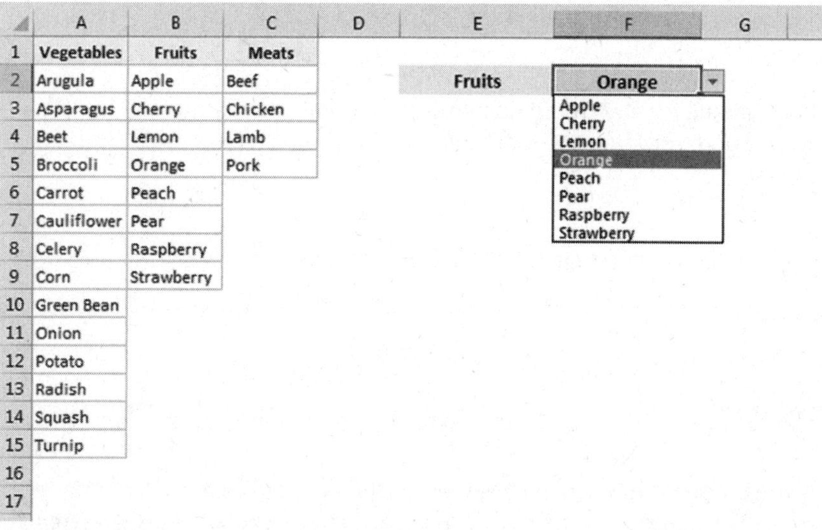

	A	B	C	D	E	F	G
1	Vegetables	Fruits	Meats				
2	Arugula	Apple	Beef		Fruits	Orange	
3	Asparagus	Cherry	Chicken				
4	Beet	Lemon	Lamb				
5	Broccoli	Orange	Pork				
6	Carrot	Peach					
7	Cauliflower	Pear					
8	Celery	Raspberry					
9	Corn	Strawberry					
10	Green Bean						
11	Onion						
12	Potato						
13	Radish						
14	Squash						
15	Turnip						
16							
17							

Figure 20-8: The items displayed in the list in cell F2 depend on the list item selected in cell E2.

Caution

Dependent data validation lists have a flaw. If you select a fruit from the list (see Figure 20.8) and then change cell E2 to Meats, the value you selected in F2 will become invalid. The only way you'll know this is if you pull down the list in F2 or circle invalid data.

Using Structured Table Referencing

With Excel Tables (Insert ➜ Table) you can use structured table referencing in your formulas. Figure 20.9 shows a simple table consisting of one column of names. You can create a formula like this one that matches a name to the list:

```
=MATCH("Joe",Table1[Name],FALSE)
```

C2 =MATCH("Joe",Table1[Name],FALSE)

	A	B	C	D	E	F	G	H
1	Name							
2	Mike		2					
3	Joe							
4	Bonnie							
5	Harry							
6	Linda							
7	Debra							
8								
9								
10								
11								
12								

Figure 20-9: Structured references grow or shrink with the table.

The second argument, Table1[Name], is a structured reference that returns the Name column of the table named Table1. As you add or remove rows to that table, the structured reference adjusts and your formulas continue to work.

Cross-Ref

See Chapter 9, "Working with Tables and Lists," for more information on structured table references.

Unfortunately, you can't use structured table references in your data validation criteria. To overcome this, you can create a named range that uses a structured table reference and use that name in your data validation.

To create a named range, choose Formulas ➜ Defined Names ➜ Define Name for the Ribbon. Enter the name, such as dvTable1Name, and point to the table's column in the Refers To box. The reference changes to =Table1[Name], as shown in Figure 20.10.

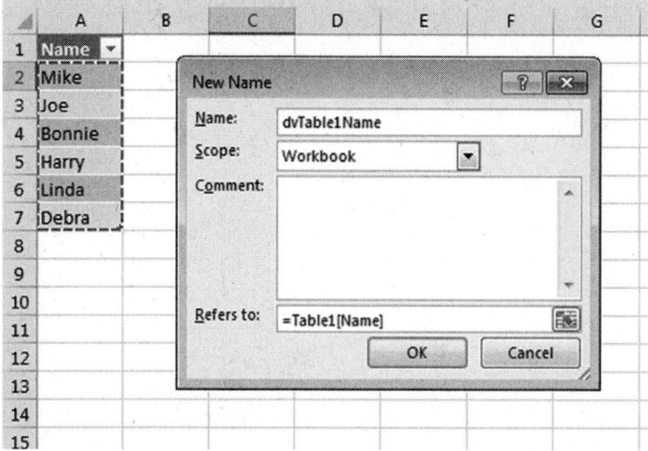

Figure 20-10: Named ranges can refer to tables using structured references.

Now you can use dvTable1Name in your data validation to get a list that grows or shrinks with the table. Figure 20.11 shows a cell with such validation.

This example used a naming convention of dv plus the table name plus the column name. You don't have to use a convention like this; you can use any valid named range.

	A	B	C	D	E
1	Name				
2	Mike		2		
3	Joe				
4	Bonnie				
5	Harry		Enter a name:	Bonnie	
6	Linda			Mike	
7	Debra			Joe	
8				Bonnie	
9				Harry	
10				Linda	
11				Debra	
12					

Figure 20-11: A defined name can be used in data validation to avoid the structured reference limitation.

21

Creating Megaformulas

In This Chapter

- What a megaformula is and why you would want to use such a thing
- How to create a megaformula
- Examples of megaformulas
- How to use named formulas to create a megaformula
- Pros and cons of using megaformulas

This chapter describes a useful technique that combines several formulas into a single formula—what we call a *megaformula*. This technique can eliminate intermediate formulas and may even speed up recalculation. The downside, as you'll see, is that the resulting formula is virtually incomprehensible and may be impossible to edit.

What Is a Megaformula?

Often, a worksheet may require intermediate formulas to produce a desired result. In other words, a formula may depend on other formulas, which in turn depend on other formulas. After you get all these formulas working correctly, you often can eliminate the intermediate formulas and create a single (and more complex) formula. For lack of a better term, we call such a formula a megaformula.

What are the advantages of employing megaformulas? They use fewer cells (less clutter), and recalculation may be faster. And you can impress people in the know with your formula-building abilities. The disadvantages? The formula probably will be impossible to decipher or modify, even by the person who created it.

Note

We use the techniques described in this chapter to create many of the complex formulas presented elsewhere in this book.

Using megaformulas is actually a rather controversial issue. Some claim that the clarity that results from having multiple formulas far outweighs any advantages in having a single incomprehensible formula. You can decide for yourself.

Creating a Megaformula: A Simple Example

Creating a megaformula basically involves copying formula text and pasting it into another formula. We start with a relatively simple example. Examine the spreadsheet shown in Figure 21-1. This sheet uses formulas to calculate mortgage loan information.

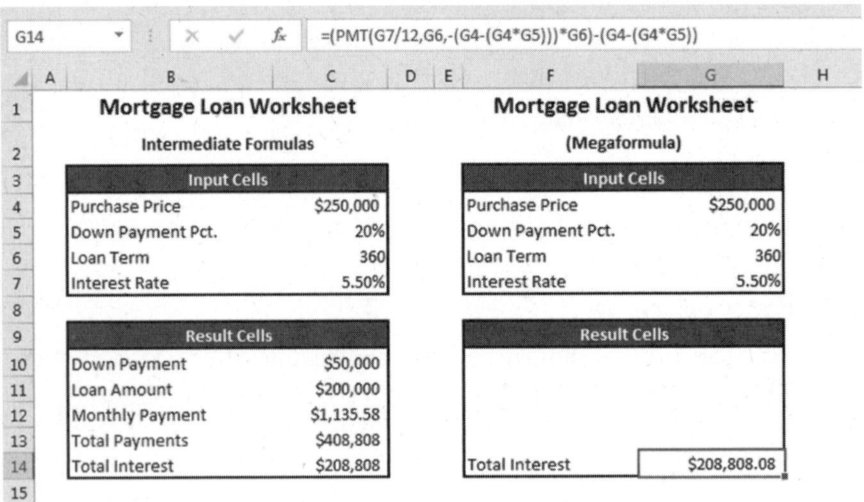

Figure 21-1: This spreadsheet uses multiple formulas to calculate mortgage loan information.

On the Web

This workbook, named total interest.xlsx, is available at this book's website.

The Result Cells section of the worksheet uses information entered into the Input Cells section and contains the formulas shown in Table 21-1.

Table 21-1: Formulas Used to Calculate Total Interest

Cell	Formula	What It Does
C10	`=C4*C5`	Calculates the down payment amount
C11	`=C4-C10`	Calculates the loan amount
C12	`=PMT(C7/12,C6,-C11)`	Calculates the monthly payment
C13	`=C12*C6`	Calculates the total payments
C14	`=C13-C11`	Calculates the total interest

Suppose you're really interested in the total interest paid (cell C14). You could, of course, simply hide the rows that contain the extraneous information. However, it's also possible to create a single formula that does the work of several intermediary formulas.

Note

This example is for illustration only. The CUMIPMT function provides a more direct way to calculate total interest on a loan.

The formula that calculates total interest depends on the formulas in cells C11 and C13 (which are the direct precedent cells). In addition, the formula in cell C13 depends on the formula in cell C12. And cell C12, in turn, depends on cell C11. Therefore, calculating the total interest in this example uses five formulas. The steps that follow describe how to create a single formula to calculate total interest so that you can eliminate the four intermediate formulas.

C14 contains the following formula:

```
=C13-C11
```

The steps that follow describe how to convert this formula into a megaformula:

1. Substitute the formula contained in cell C13 for the reference to cell C13.

   Before doing this, add parentheses around the formula in C13. (Without the parentheses, the calculations occur in the wrong order.) Now the formula in C14 is

   ```
   =(C12*C6)-C11
   ```

2. Substitute the formula contained in cell C12 for the reference to cell C12. Now the formula in C14 is

   ```
   =(PMT(C7/12,C6,-C11)*C6)-C11
   ```

3. Substitute the formula contained in cell C11 for the two references to cell C11. Before copying the formula, you need to insert parentheses around it. Now the formula in C14 is

   ```
   =(PMT(C7/12,C6,-(C4-C10))*C6)-(C4-C10)
   ```

4. Substitute the formula contained in cell C10 for the two references to cell C10. Before copying the formula, insert parentheses around it. Now the formula in C14 is

   ```
   =(PMT(C7/12,C6,-(C4-(C4*C5)))*C6)-(C4-(C4*C5))
   ```

At this point, the formula contains references only to input cells. The formulas in range C10:C13 are not referenced, so you can delete them. The single megaformula now does the work previously performed by the intermediary formulas.

Unless you're a world-class Excel formula wizard, it's quite unlikely that you could arrive at that formula without first creating intermediate formulas.

Creating a megaformula essentially involves substituting formula text for cell references in a formula. You perform substitutions until the megaformula contains no references to formula cells. At each step along the way, you can check your work by ensuring that the formula continues to display the same result. In the previous example, a few of the steps required parentheses around the copied formula to ensure the correct order of calculation.

Copying text from a formula

Creating megaformulas involves copying formula text and then replacing a cell reference with the copied text. To copy the contents of a formula, activate the cell and press F2. Select the formula text (without the equal sign) by pressing Shift+Home, followed by Shift+right arrow. Press Ctrl+C to copy the selected text to the Clipboard, and then press Esc to cancel cell editing. Activate the cell that contains the megaformula and press F2. Use the arrow keys, and hold down Shift to select the cell reference that you want to replace. Finally, press Ctrl+V to replace the selected text with the Clipboard contents.

In some cases, you need to insert parentheses around the copied formula text to make the formula calculate correctly. If the formula returns a different result after you paste the formula text, press Ctrl+Z to undo the paste. Insert parentheses around the formula you want to copy and paste it into the megaformula. It should then calculate correctly.

Megaformula Examples

This section contains three additional examples of megaformulas. These examples provide a thorough introduction to applying the megaformula technique for streamlining a variety of tasks, including cleaning up a list of names by removing middle names and initials, returning the position of the last space character in a string, determining whether a credit card number is valid, and generating a list of random names.

Using a megaformula to remove middle names

Consider a worksheet with a column of names, like the one shown in Figure 21-2. Suppose you have a worksheet with thousands of such names, and you need to remove all the middle names and middle initials from the names. Editing the cells manually would take hours, and you're not up to writing a VBA macro, so that leaves using a formula-based solution. Notice that not all the names have a middle name or a middle initial, which makes the task a bit trickier. Although this is not a difficult task, it normally involves several intermediate formulas.

	A
1	Robert E. Lee
2	Jim Jones
3	R. L Burnside
4	Michael J. Hammer
5	Timothy Franklin
6	T. Henry Jackson
7	Frank J Thomas
8	Mary Richards Helton
9	Tom A. Smith
10	

Figure 21-2: The goal is to remove the middle name or middle initial from each name.

Cross-Ref

The Flash Fill feature, introduced in Excel 2013, can handle this task without using formulas. See Chapter 16, "Importing and Cleaning Data," for more information about Flash Fill.

Figure 21-3 shows the results of the more conventional solution, which requires six intermediate formulas, as shown in Table 21-2. The names are in column A; column H displays the end result. Columns B:G hold the intermediate formulas.

	A	B	C	D	E	F	G	H
1	Robert E. Lee	Robert E. Lee	7	10	10	Robert	Lee	Robert Lee
2	Jim Jones	Jim Jones	4	#VALUE!	4	Jim	Jones	Jim Jones
3	R. L Burnside	R. L Burnside	3	5	5	R.	Burnside	R. Burnside
4	Michael J. Hammer	Michael J. Hammer	8	11	11	Michael	Hammer	Michael Hammer
5	Timothy Franklin	Timothy Franklin	8	#VALUE!	8	Timothy	Franklin	Timothy Franklin
6	T. Henry Jackson	T. Henry Jackson	3	9	9	T.	Jackson	T. Jackson
7	Frank J Thomas	Frank J Thomas	6	8	8	Frank	Thomas	Frank Thomas
8	Mary Richards Helton	Mary Richards Helton	5	14	14	Mary	Helton	Mary Helton
9	Tom A. Smith	Tom A. Smith	4	7	7	Tom	Smith	Tom Smith
10								
11								

Figure 21-3: Removing the middle names and initials requires six intermediate formulas.

On the Web

You can access the workbook for removing middle names and initials at this book's website. The filename is no middle name.xlsx.

Table 21-2: Intermediate Formulas in the First Row of Sheet1 in Figure 21-3

Cell	Intermediate Formula	What It Does
B1	`=TRIM(A1)`	Removes excess spaces
C1	`=FIND(" ",B1)`	Locates the first space
D1	`=FIND(" ",B1,C1+1)`	Locates the second space, if any
E1	`=IFERROR(D1,C1)`	Uses the first space if no second space exists
F1	`=LEFT(B1,C1-1)`	Extracts the first name
G1	`=RIGHT(B1,LEN(B1)-E1)`	Extracts the last name
H1	`=F1&" "&G1`	Concatenates the two names

Note that cell E1 uses the IFERROR function, which was introduced in Excel 2007. For compatibility with earlier versions, use this formula:

```
=IF(ISERROR(D1),C1,D1)
```

Note

Notice that the result isn't perfect. For example, it will not work if the cell contains only one name (for example, Enya). This method also fails if a name has two middle names (such as John Jacob Robert Smith). That occurs because the formula simply searches for the second space character in the name. In this example, the megaformula returns *John Robert Smith.* Later in this chapter, we present an array formula method to identify the last space character in a string.

With a bit of work, you can eliminate all the intermediate formulas and replace them with a single megaformula. You do so by creating all the intermediate formulas and then editing the final result formula (in this case, the formula in column H) by replacing each cell reference with a copy of the formula in the cell referred to. Fortunately, you can use the Clipboard to copy and paste. (See the sidebar "Copying text from a formula," earlier in this chapter.) Keep repeating this process until cell H1 contains nothing but references to cell A1. You end up with the following megaformula in one cell:

```
=LEFT(TRIM(A1),FIND(" ",TRIM(A1))-1)&" "&RIGHT
(TRIM(A1),LEN(TRIM(A1))-IFERROR(FIND(" ",TRIM(A1),
FIND(" ",TRIM(A1))+1),FIND(" ",TRIM(A1))))
```

When you're satisfied that the megaformula works, you can delete the columns that hold the intermediate formulas because they are no longer used.

The step-by-step procedure

If you're still not clear about this process, take a look at the step-by-step procedure:

1. Examine the formula in H1. This formula contains two cell references (F1 and G1):

```
=F1&" "&G1
```

2. Activate cell G1 and copy the contents of the formula (without the equal sign) to the Clipboard.
3. Activate cell H1 and replace the reference to cell G1 with the Clipboard contents.

   Now cell H1 contains the following formula:

```
=F1&" "&RIGHT(B1,LEN(B1)-E1)
```

4. Activate cell F1 and copy the contents of the formula (without the equal sign) to the Clipboard.
5. Activate cell H1 and replace the reference to cell F1 with the Clipboard contents.

   Now the formula in cell H1 is as follows:

```
=LEFT(B1,C1-1)&" "&RIGHT(B1,LEN(B1)-E1)
```

6. Cell H1 contains references to three cells (B1, C1, and E1).

   The formulas in those cells will replace each of the three references.
7. Replace the reference to cell E1 with the formula in cell E1. The result is

```
=LEFT(B1,C1-1)&" "&RIGHT(B1,LEN(B1)-IFERROR(D1,C1))
```

8. Replace the reference to cell D1 with the formula in cell D1.

   The formula now looks like this:

```
=LEFT(B1,C1-1)&" "&RIGHT(B1,LEN(B1)-IFERROR(FIND(" ",B1,C1+1),C1))
```

9. The formula has three references to cell C1. Replace all three of those references to cell C1 with the formula contained in cell C1.

   The formula in cell H1 is as follows:

```
=LEFT(B1,FIND(" ",B1)-1)&" "&RIGHT(B1,LEN(B1)-IFERROR
(FIND(" ",B1,FIND(" ",B1)+1),FIND(" ",B1)))
```

10. Finally, replace the seven references to cell B1 with the formula in cell B1. The result is

```
=LEFT(TRIM(A1),FIND(" ",TRIM(A1))-1)&" "&RIGHT
(TRIM(A1),LEN(TRIM(A1))-IFERROR(FIND(" ",TRIM(A1),
FIND(" ",TRIM(A1))+1),FIND(" ",TRIM(A1))))
```

Notice that the formula in cell H1 now contains references only to cell A1. The megaformula is complete, and it performs exactly the same tasks as all the intermediate formulas (which you can now delete).

After you create a megaformula, you can create a name for it to simplify using the formula. Here's an example:

1. Copy the megaformula text to the Clipboard.

   In this example, the megaformula refers to cell A1.
2. Activate cell B1, which is the cell to the right of the cell referenced in the megaformula.
3. Choose Formulas ➜ Defined Names ➜ Define Name to display the New Name dialog box.
4. In the Name field, type **NoMiddleName**.
5. Activate the Refers To field and press Ctrl+V to paste the megaformula text.
6. Click OK to close the New Name dialog box.

After performing these steps and creating the named formula, you can enter the following formula, and it will return the result using the cell directly to the left:

```
=NoMiddleName
```

If you enter this formula in cell K8, it displays the name in cell J8, with no middle name.

Cross-Ref

See Chapter 3, "Working with Names," for more information about creating and using named formulas.

This megaformula uses the IFERROR function, so it will not work with versions prior to Excel 2007. A comparable formula that's compatible with previous versions follows:

```
=LEFT(TRIM(A1),FIND(" ",TRIM(A1),1)-1)&" "&RIGHT
(TRIM(A1),LEN(TRIM(A1))-IF(ISERROR(FIND(" ",TRIM(A1),
FIND(" ",TRIM(A1),1)+1)),FIND(" ",TRIM(A1),1),FIND(" ",TRIM
(A1),FIND(" ",TRIM(A1),1)+1)))
```

Comparing speed and efficiency

Because a megaformula is so complex, you may think that using one slows down recalculation. Actually, that's not the case. As a test, we created three workbooks (each with 175,000 names): one that used six intermediate formulas, one that used a megaformula, and one that used a named megaformula. We compared the results in terms of calculation time and file size; see Table 21-3.

Table 21-3: Comparing Intermediate Formulas and Megaformulas

Method	Recalculation Time (Seconds)	File Size
Intermediate formulas	3.1	13.5MB
Megaformula	2.3	3.07MB
Named megaformula	2.3	2.67MB

Of course, the actual results will vary depending on your system's processor speed.

As you can see, using a megaformula (or a named megaformula) in this case resulted in slightly faster recalculations as well as a *much* smaller workbook.

On the Web

The three test workbooks that we used are available at this book's website. The filenames are time test intermediate.xlsx, time test megaformula.xlsx, and time test named megaformula.xlsx. To perform your own time tests, change the name in cell A1 and start your stopwatch when you press Enter. Keep your eye on the status bar, which indicates when the calculation is finished.

Using a megaformula to return a string's last space character position

As previously noted, the "remove middle name" example presented earlier contains a flaw: to identify the last name, the formula searches for the second space character. A better solution is to search for the *last* space character. Unfortunately, Excel doesn't provide a simple way to locate the position of the first occurrence of a character from the *end* of a string. The example in this section solves that problem and describes a way to determine the position of the first occurrence of a specific character going backward from the end of a text string.

Cross-Ref

This technique involves arrays, so you might want to review the material in Part IV, "Array Formulas," to familiarize yourself with this topic.

This example describes how to create a megaformula that returns the character position of the last *space character* in a string. You can, of course, modify the formula to work with any other character.

Creating the intermediate formulas

The general plan is to create an array of characters in the string, but in reverse order. After that array is created, you can use the MATCH function to locate the first space character in the array.

Refer to Figure 21-4, which shows the results of the intermediate formulas. Cell A1 contains an arbitrary name, which happens to use 12 characters. The range B1:B12 contains the following array formula:

```
{=ROW(INDIRECT("1:"&LEN(A1)))}
```

	A	B	C	D	E	F
1	Ann R. Smith	1	12	h	6	7
2		2	11	t		
3		3	10	i		
4		4	9	m		
5		5	8	S		
6		6	7			
7		7	6	.		
8		8	5	R		
9		9	4			
10		10	3	n		
11		11	2	n		
12		12	1	A		
13						
14						
15						

Figure 21-4: These intermediate formulas will eventually be converted to a single megaformula.

On the Web

This example, named position of last space.xlsx, is available at this book's website.

You enter this multicell array formula into the entire B1:B12 range by selecting the range, typing the formula, and pressing Ctrl+Shift+Enter. Don't type the curly brackets. Excel adds the curly brackets to indicate an array formula. This formula returns an array of 12 consecutive integers.

The range C1:C12 contains the following array formula:

```
{=LEN(A1)+1-B1:B12}
```

This formula reverses the integers generated in column B.

The range D1:D12 contains the following array formula:

```
{=MID(A1,C1:C12,1)}
```

This formula uses the MID function to extract the individual characters in cell A1. The MID function uses the array in C1:C12 as its second argument. The result is an array of the name's characters in reverse order.

The formula in cell E1 is as follows:

```
=MATCH(" ",D1:D12,0)
```

This formula, which is *not* an array formula, uses the MATCH function to return the position of the first space character in the range D1:D12. In the example shown in Figure 21-4, the formula returns 6, which means that the first space character is six characters from the end of the text in cell A1.

The formula in cell F1 follows:

```
=LEN(A1)+1-E1
```

This formula returns the character position of the last space in the string.

You may wonder how all these formulas can possibly be combined into a single formula. Keep reading for the answer.

Creating the megaformula

At this point, cell F1 contains the result that you're looking for—the number that indicates the position of the last space character. The challenge is consolidating all those intermediate formulas into a single formula. The goal is to produce a formula that contains only references to cell A1. These steps will get you to that goal:

1. The formula in cell F1 contains a reference to cell E1. Replace that reference with the text of the formula in cell E1.

   As a result, the formula in cell F1 becomes this:

   ```
   =LEN(A1)+1-MATCH(" ",D1:D12,0)
   ```

2. The formula contains a reference to D1:D12. This range contains a single array formula.

   Replacing the reference to D1:D12 with the array formula results in the following array formula in cell F1:

   ```
   {=LEN(A1)+1-MATCH(" ",MID(A1,C1:C12,1),0)}
   ```

Note

Because an array formula replaced the reference in cell F1, you must now enter the formula in F1 as an array formula (enter by pressing Ctrl+Shift+Enter).

3. The formula in cell F1 contains a reference to C1:C12, which also contains an array formula. Replace the reference to C1:C12 with the array formula in C1:C12 to get this array formula in cell F1:

   ```
   {=LEN(A1)+1-MATCH(" ",MID(A1,LEN(A1)+1-B1:B12,1),0)}
   ```

4. Replace the reference to B1:B12 with the array formula in B1:B12. The result is

```
{=LEN(A1)+1-MATCH(" ",MID(A1,LEN(A1)+1-ROW(INDIRECT
("1:"&LEN(A1))),1),0)}
```

Now the array formula in cell F1 refers only to cell A1, which is exactly what you want. The megaformula does the job, and you can delete all the intermediate formulas.

Note

Although you use a 12-digit value and arrays stored in 12-row ranges to create the formula, the final formula does not use any of these range references. Consequently, the megaformula works with text of any length.

Putting the megaformula to work

Figure 21-5 shows a worksheet with names in column A. Column B contains the megaformula developed in the previous section. Column C contains a formula that extracts the characters beginning after the last space, which represents the last name of the name in column A.

	A	B	C	D
1	Paula M. Smith	9	Smith	
2	Michael Alan Jones	13	Jones	
3	Mike Helton	5	Helton	
4	Tom Alvin Jacobs	10	Jacobs	
5	John Jacob Robert Smith	18	Smith	
6	Mr. Hank R. Franklin	12	Franklin	
7	James Jackson Jr.	14	Jr.	
8	Jill M. Horneg	8	Horneg	
9	Rodger K. Moore	10	Moore	
10	Andy R. Maxwell	8	Maxwell	
11	Michelle Theresa Hunt	17	Hunt	
12				
13				

Figure 21-5: Column B contains a megaformula that returns the character position of the last space of the name in column A.

Cell C1, for example, contains this formula:

```
=RIGHT(A1,LEN(A1)-B1)
```

If you like, you can eliminate the formulas in column B and create a specialized formula that returns the last name. To do so, substitute the formula in cell B1 for the reference to cell B1 in the formula. The result is the following array formula:

```
{=RIGHT(A1,LEN(A1)-(LEN(A1)+1-MATCH(" ",MID(A1,LEN(A1)+
1-ROW(INDIRECT("1:"&LEN(A1))),1),0)))}
```

Note

You must insert parentheses around the formula text copied from cell B1. Without the parentheses, the formula does not evaluate correctly.

Using a megaformula to determine the validity of a credit card number

Many people are not aware that you can determine the validity of a credit card number by using a relatively complex algorithm to analyze the digits of the number. In addition, you can determine the type of credit card by examining the initial digits and the length of the number. Table 21-4 shows information about four major credit cards.

Table 21-4: Information About Four Major Credit Cards

Credit Card	Prefix Digits	Total Digits
MasterCard	51–55	16
Visa	4	13 or 16
American Express	34 or 37	15
Discover	6011	16

Note

***Validity*, as used here, means whether the credit card number *itself* is a valid number as determined by the following steps. This technique, of course, cannot determine whether the number represents an actual credit card account.**

You can test the validity of a credit card account number by processing its checksum. All account numbers used in major credit cards use a Mod 10 check-digit algorithm. The general process is as follows:

1. Add leading zeros to the account number to make the total number of digits equal 16.
2. Beginning with the first digit, double the value of alternate digits of the account number. If the result is a two-digit number, add the two digits together.
3. Add the eight values generated in step 2 to the sum of the skipped digits of the original number.
4. If the sum obtained in step 3 is evenly divisible by 10, the number is a valid credit card number.

The example in this section describes a megaformula that determines whether a credit card number is a valid number.

The basic formulas

Figure 21-6 shows a worksheet set up to analyze a credit card number and determine its validity. This workbook uses quite a few formulas to make the determination.

G1 =IF(MOD(E21,10)=0,"VALID","INVALID")

	A	B	C	D	E	F	G	H
1				Credit Card Number:		4384842201065	INVALID	
2						0004384842201065		
3								
4	Digit Number	Digit	Digit Multiplier	Equals	Sum of the digits			
5	1	0	2	0	0			
6	2	0	1	0	0			
7	3	0	2	0	0			
8	4	4	1	4	4			
9	5	3	2	6	6			
10	6	8	1	8	8			
11	7	4	2	8	8			
12	8	8	1	8	8			
13	9	4	2	8	8			
14	10	2	1	2	2			
15	11	2	2	4	4			
16	12	0	1	0	0			
17	13	1	2	2	2			
18	14	0	1	0	0			
19	15	6	2	12	3			
20	16	5	1	5	5			
21					58			
22								
23								

Figure 21-6: The formulas in this worksheet determine the validity of a credit card number.

On the Web

You can access the credit card number validation workbook at this book's website. The file is named credit card validation.xlsx.

In this worksheet, the credit card number is entered in cell F1, with no spaces or hyphens. The formula in cell F2 follows. This formula appends leading zeros, if necessary, to make the card number exactly 16 digits long. The other formulas use the string in cell F2.

```
=REPT("0",16-LEN(F1))&F1
```

Warning

When entering a credit card number that contains more than 15 digits, you must be careful that Excel does not round the number to 15 digits. You can precede the number with an apostrophe or preformat the cell as Text (using Home ➜ Number ➜ Number Format ➜ Text).

Column A contains a series of integers from 1 to 16, each representing the digit positions of the credit card.

Column B contains formulas that extract each digit from cell F2. For example, the formula in cell B5 is as follows:

```
=MID($F$2,A5,1)
```

Column C contains the multipliers for each digit: alternating 2s and 1s.

Column D contains formulas that multiply the digit in column B by the multiplier in column C. For example, the formula in cell D5 is

```
=B5*C5
```

Column E contains formulas that sum the digits displayed in column D. A single digit value in column D is returned directly. For two-digit values, the sum of the digits is displayed in column E. For example, if column D displays 12, the formula in column E returns 3: that is, 1 + 2. The formula that accomplishes this is as follows:

```
=INT((D5/10)+MOD((D5),10))
```

Cell E21 contains a simple SUM formula to add the values in column E:

```
=SUM(E5:E20)
```

The formula in cell G1, which follows, calculates the remainder when cell E21 is divided by 10. If the remainder is 0, the card number is valid, and the formula displays *VALID*. Otherwise, the formula displays *INVALID*.

```
=IF(MOD(E21,10)=0,"VALID","INVALID")
```

Convert to array formulas

The megaformula that performs all these calculations will be an array formula because the intermediary formulas occupy multiple rows.

First, you need to convert all the formulas to array formulas. Note that columns A and C consist of values, not formulas. To use the values in a megaformula, they must be generated by formulas—more specifically, array formulas.

Enter the following array formula into the range A5:A20. This array formula returns a series of 16 consecutive integers:

```
{=ROW(INDIRECT("1:16"))}
```

1. For column B, select B5:B20 and enter the following array formula, which extracts the digits from the credit card number:

```
{=MID($F$2,A5:A20,1)}
```

2. Column C requires an array formula that generates alternating values of 2 and 1.

   Such a formula, entered into the range C5:C20, is shown here:

```
{=(MOD(ROW(INDIRECT("1:16")),2)+1)}
```

3. For column D, select D5:D20 and enter the following array formula:

```
{=B5:B20*C5:C20}
```

4. Select E5:E20 and enter this array formula:

```
{=INT((D5:D20/10)+MOD((D5:D20),10))}
```

Now the worksheet contains five columns of 16 rows but only five actual formulas (which are multi-cell array formulas).

Build the megaformula

To create the megaformula for this task, start with cell G1, which is the cell that has the final result. The original formula in G1 is

```
=IF(MOD(E21,10)=0,"VALID","INVALID")
```

1. Replace the reference to cell E21 with the formula in E21.

   Doing so results in the following formula in cell G1:

```
=IF(MOD(SUM(E5:E20),10)=0,"VALID","INVALID")
```

2. Replace the reference to E5:E20 with the array formula contained in that range. Now the formula becomes an array formula, so you must enter it by pressing Ctrl+Shift+Enter.

   After the replacement, the formula in G1 is as follows:

```
{=IF(MOD(SUM(INT((D5:D20/10)+MOD((D5:D20),10))),10)=0,
"VALID","INVALID")}
```

3. Replace the two references to range D5:D20 with the array formula contained in D5:20.

   Doing so results in the following array formula in cell G1:

```
{=IF(MOD(SUM(INT((B5:B20*C5:C20/10)+MOD((B5:B20*C5:C20),
10))),10)=0,"VALID","INVALID")}
```

4. Replace the references to cell C5:C20 with the array formula in C5:C20.

   Note that you must have a set of parentheses around the copied formula text. The result is as follows:

```
{=IF(MOD(SUM(INT((B5:B20*(MOD(ROW(INDIRECT("1:16")),
2)+1)/10)+MOD((B5:B20*(MOD(ROW(INDIRECT("1:16")),2)+1)),
10))),10)=0,"VALID","INVALID")}
```

5. Replacing the references to B5:B20 with the array formula contained in B5:B20 yields the following:

```
{=IF(MOD(SUM(INT((MID($F$2,A5:A20,1)*(MOD(ROW(INDIRECT
("1:16")),2)+1)/10)+MOD((MID($F$2,A5:A20,1)*(MOD(ROW
(INDIRECT("1:16")),2)+1)),10))),10)
=0,"VALID","INVALID")}
```

6. Substitute the array formula in range A5:A20 for the references to that range.

   The resulting array formula is as follows:

```
{=IF(MOD(SUM(INT((MID($F$2,ROW(INDIRECT("1:16")),1)*(MOD(ROW
(INDIRECT("1:16")),2)+1)/10)+MOD((MID($F$2,ROW(INDIRECT
("1:16")),1)*(MOD(ROW(INDIRECT("1:16")),2)+1)),10))),10)=0,
"VALID","INVALID")}
```

7. Substitute the formula in cell F2 for the two references to cell F2.

   After making the substitutions, the formula is as follows:

```
{=IF(MOD(SUM(INT((MID(REPT("0",16-LEN(F1))&F1,
ROW(INDIRECT("1:16")),1)*(MOD(ROW(INDIRECT("1:16")),2)+1)/
10)+MOD((MID(REPT("0",16-LEN(F1))&F1,ROW(INDIRECT("1:16")),
1)*(MOD(ROW(INDIRECT("1:16")),2)+1)),10))),10)=0,"VALID",
"INVALID")}
```

You can delete the now superfluous intermediate formulas. The final megaformula, a mere 229 characters in length, does the work of 51 intermediary formulas!

Figure 21-7 shows this formula at work.

	A	B	C
1	Credit Card Number	Valid/Invalid	
2	4012888888881881	VALID	
3	5610591081018250	VALID	
4	4387841401865332	INVALID	
5	3043878414018656	INVALID	
6	6011111111111117	VALID	
7			
8			
9			

Figure 21-7: Using a megaformula to determine the validity of credit card numbers.

Using Intermediate Named Formulas

One way you can make your mega formulas easier to read is to name them. This technique was described in an earlier section about removing middle names. A variation of this technique is to use several named formulas rather than one named megaformula.

The credit card validation formula could be made to look like this:

```
=IF(MOD(SUM(SumOfDigits),10)=0,"VALID","INVALID")
```

There's still a lot you can't see in that formula, but it does give you a feel for what the formula is doing, as opposed to a named megaformula, which might look like this:

```
=IsCreditCardValid
```

This technique involves creating a series of named formulas. Some of the names will refer to previously created names. Start by creating a name called Padded for this formula:

```
=REPT("0",16-LEN(INDIRECT("RC[-1]",FALSE)))&INDIRECT("RC[-1]",FALSE)
```

This simply uses the formula from cell F2 in the previous example, except that it uses INDIRECT and R1C1 notation to refer to the cell just to the left of where this name is used. You could use this named formula as is. Simply type **=Padded** into a cell with a credit card number in the cell to the left, and it will return the number padded with zeros.

The remaining formulas either refer to Padded, another named formula, or a formula with no cell references. Table 21-5 shows the remaining named formulas.

Table 21-5: Named Formulas to Validate Credit Card Numbers

Name	Refers To	References
OneToSixteen	`=ROW(INDIRECT("1:16"))`	No cell references. Returns an array of numbers 1 to 16.
Digit	`=MID(Padded,OneToSixteen,1)`	Refers to Padded and OneToSixteen. Returns an array of all the digits.
Multiplier	`=MOD(ROW(INDIRECT("1:16")),2)+1`	No cell references. Returns an array of 1s and 2s.
SumOfDigits	`=INT((Digit*Multiplier/10)+MOD((Digit*Multiplier),10))`	Refers to Digit and Multiplier. Returns an array of processed digits.

None of these named formulas refers to a fixed cell, so you can use them in any cell on any worksheet (as long as there's a cell to the left). If something goes wrong, you can inspect each intermediate named formula to help you troubleshoot the problem.

Generating random names

The final example is a useful application that generates random names. It uses three name lists compiled by the U.S. Census Bureau: 4,275 female first names; 1,219 male first names; and 18,839 last names. The names are sorted by frequency of occurrence. The megaformula selects random names such that more frequently occurring names have a higher probability of being selected. Therefore, if you create a list of random names, they will appear to be somewhat realistic. (Common names will appear more often than uncommon names.)

Figure 21-8 shows the workbook. Cells B7 and B8 contain values that determine the probability that the random name is a male as well as the probability that the random name contains a middle initial. The randomly generated names begin in cell A11.

On the Web

This workbook, named name generator.xlsx, is available at this book's website.

The megaformula is as follows. (The workbook uses several names.)

```
=IF(RAND()<=PctMale,INDEX(MaleNames,MATCH(RAND(),
MaleProbability,-1)),INDEX(FemaleNames,MATCH(RAND(),
FemaleProbability,-1)))&IF(RAND()<=PctMiddle," "&
INDEX(MiddleInitials,MATCH(RAND(),MiddleProbability,-1))&
".","")&" "&INDEX(LastNames,MATCH(RAND(),LastProbability,-1))
```

We don't list the intermediate formulas here, but you can examine them by opening the file at this book's website.

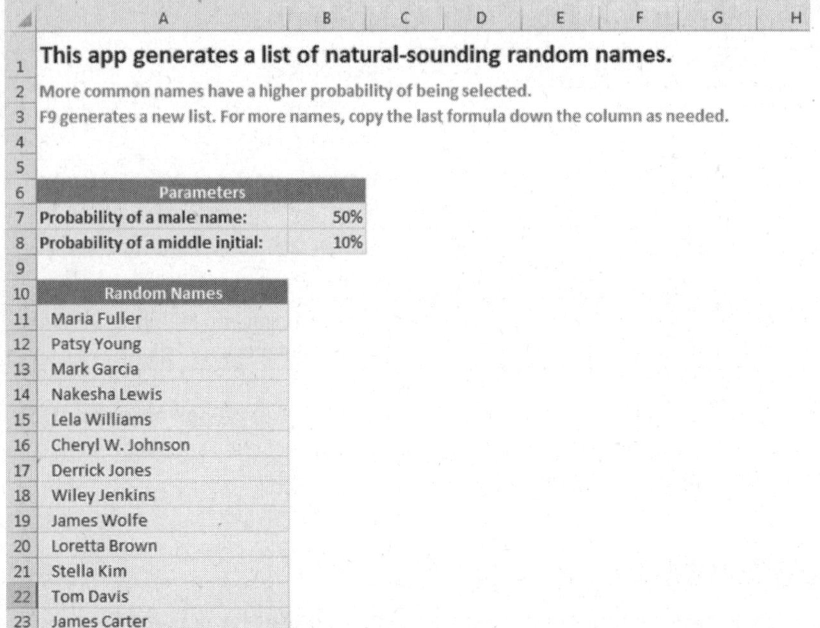

Figure 21-8: This workbook uses a megaformula to generate realistic random names.

The Pros and Cons of Megaformulas

If you followed the examples in this chapter, you probably realize that the main advantage of creating a megaformula is to eliminate intermediate formulas. Doing so can streamline your worksheet and reduce the size of your workbook files, and it may even result in slightly faster recalculations.

The downside? Creating a megaformula does, of course, require some additional time and effort. And, as you've undoubtedly noticed, a megaformula is virtually impossible for anyone (even the author) to figure out. If you decide to use megaformulas, take extra care to ensure that the intermediate formulas are performing correctly before you start building a megaformula. Even better, keep a single copy of the intermediate formulas somewhere in case you discover an error or need to make a change.

22

Tools and Methods for Debugging Formulas

In This Chapter

- What is formula debugging?
- How to identify and correct common formula errors
- A description of Excel's auditing tools

Errors happen. And when you create Excel formulas, errors happen frequently. This chapter describes common formula errors and discusses tools and methods that you can use to help create formulas that work as they are intended to.

Formula Debugging?

Debugging refers to identifying and correcting errors in a computer program. Strictly speaking, an Excel formula is not a computer program. Formulas, however, are subject to the same types of problems that occur in a computer program. If you create a formula that does not work as it should, you need to identify and correct the problem.

The ultimate goal in developing a spreadsheet solution is to generate accurate results. For simple worksheets, this is not difficult, and you can usually tell whether the formulas are producing correct results. But as your worksheets grow in size or complexity, ensuring accuracy becomes more difficult.

Making a change in a worksheet—even a relatively minor one—may produce a ripple effect that introduces errors in other cells. For example, accidentally entering a value into a cell that previously held a formula is all too easy to do. This simple error can have a major impact on other formulas, and you may not discover the problem until long after you made the change—or you may *never* discover the problem.

Research on spreadsheet errors

Using a spreadsheet can be hazardous to your company's bottom line. It's tempting to simply assume that your spreadsheet produces accurate results. If you use the results of a spreadsheet to make a major decision, it's especially important to make sure that the formulas return accurate and meaningful results.

Researchers have conducted quite a few studies that deal with spreadsheet errors. Generally, these studies have found that between 20 and 40 percent of all spreadsheets contain some type of error. If this type of research interests you, check out the European Spreadsheet Risk Interest Group. The URL follows:

```
http://eusprig.org/
```

Formula Problems and Solutions

Formula errors tend to fall into one of the following general categories:

- **Syntax errors:** You have a problem with the syntax of a formula. For example, a formula may have mismatched parentheses, or a function may not have the correct number of arguments.
- **Logical errors:** A formula does not return an error, but it contains a logical flaw that causes it to return an incorrect result.
- **Incorrect reference errors:** The logic of the formula is correct, but the formula uses an incorrect cell reference. As a simple example, the range reference in a SUM formula may not include all the data that you want to sum.
- **Semantic errors:** An example of a semantic error is a function name that is spelled incorrectly. Excel attempts to interpret the misspelled function as a name and displays the *#NAME?* error.
- **Circular references:** A circular reference occurs when a formula refers to its own cell, either directly or indirectly. Circular references are useful in a few cases, but most of the time, a circular reference indicates a problem.
- **Array formula entry error:** When entering (or editing) an array formula, you must press Ctrl+Shift+Enter to enter the formula. If you fail to do so, Excel does not recognize the formula as an array formula. The formula may return an error or (even worse) an incorrect result.
- **Incomplete calculation errors:** The formulas simply aren't calculated fully. To ensure that your formulas are fully calculated, press Ctrl+Alt+Shift+F9.

Syntax errors are usually the easiest to identify and correct. In most cases, you will know when your formula contains a syntax error. For example, Excel won't permit you to enter a formula with mismatched parentheses. Other syntax errors also usually result in an error display in the cell.

The remainder of this section describes some common formula problems and offers advice on identifying and correcting them.

Mismatched parentheses

In a formula, every left parenthesis must have a corresponding right parenthesis. If your formula has mismatched parentheses, Excel usually doesn't permit you to enter it. An exception to this rule involves a simple formula that uses a function. For example, if you enter the following formula (which is missing a closing parenthesis), Excel accepts the formula and provides the missing parenthesis:

```
=SUM(A1:A500
```

And even though a formula may have an equal number of left and right parentheses, the parentheses might not match properly. For example, consider the following formula, which converts a text string such that the first character is uppercase, and the remaining characters are lowercase. This formula has five pairs of parentheses, and they match properly:

```
=UPPER(LEFT(A1))&RIGHT(LOWER(A1),LEN(A1)-1)
```

The following formula also has five pairs of parentheses, but they are mismatched. The result displays a syntactically correct formula that simply returns the wrong result:

```
=UPPER(LEFT(A1)&RIGHT(LOWER(A1),LEN(A1)-1))
```

Often, parentheses that are in the wrong location will result in a syntax error, which is usually a message that tells you that you entered too many or too few arguments for a function.

Tip

Excel can help you with mismatched parentheses. When you edit a formula, use the arrow keys to move the cursor to a parenthesis and pause. Excel displays it (and its matching parenthesis) in bold for about one second. In addition, nested parentheses appear in a different color.

Using Formula AutoCorrect

When you enter a formula that has a syntax error, Excel attempts to determine the problem and offers a suggested correction. The accompanying figure shows an example of a proposed correction.

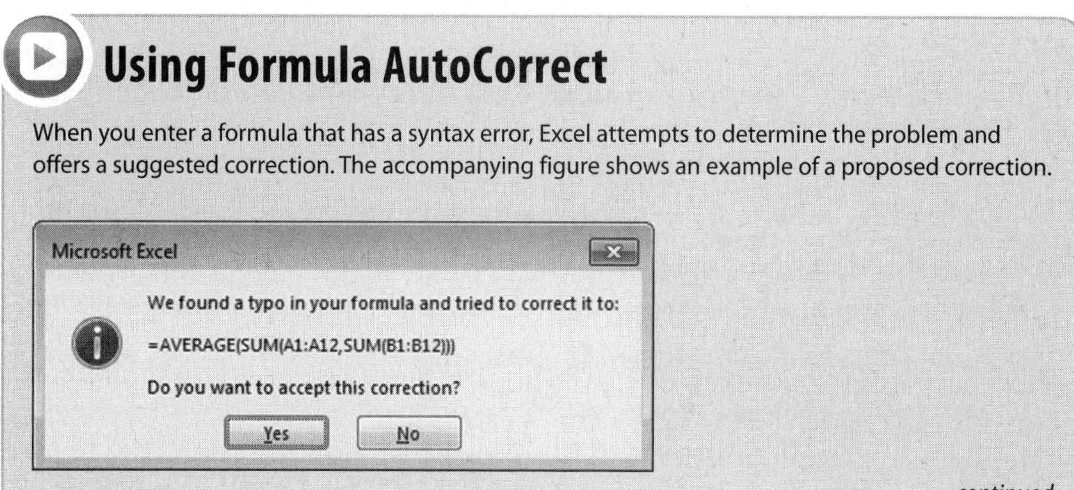

continued

continued

Be careful when accepting corrections for your formulas from Excel because it does not always guess correctly. For example, we entered the following formula (which has mismatched parentheses):

```
=AVERAGE(SUM(A1:A12,SUM(B1:B12))
```

Excel then proposed the following correction to the formula:

```
=AVERAGE(SUM(A1:A12,SUM(B1:B12)))
```

You may be tempted to accept the suggestion without even thinking. In this case, the proposed formula is syntactically correct—but not what we intended. The correct formula is as follows:

```
=AVERAGE(SUM(A1:A12),SUM(B1:B12))
```

Cells are filled with hash marks

A cell displays a series of hash marks (#) for one of two reasons:

- The column is not wide enough to accommodate the formatted numeric value. To correct it, you can make the column wider or use a different number format.
- The cell contains a formula that returns an invalid date or time. For example, Excel does not support dates prior to 1900 or the use of negative time values. Attempting to display either of these will result in a cell filled with hash marks. Widening the column won't fix it.

Blank cells are not blank

Some Excel users have discovered that by pressing the spacebar, the contents of a cell seem to erase. Actually, pressing the spacebar inserts an invisible space character, which is not the same as erasing the cell.

For example, the following formula returns the number of nonempty cells in range A1:A10. If you "erase" any of these cells by using the spacebar, these cells are included in the count, and the formula returns an incorrect result:

```
=COUNTA(A1:A10)
```

If your formula doesn't ignore blank cells the way that it should, check to make sure that the blank cells are really blank cells. Here's how to search for cells that contain only a blank character:

1. Press Ctrl+F to display the Find and Replace dialog box.
2. In the Find What box, type a space character.
3. Make sure the Match Entire Cell Contents check box is selected.
4. Click Find All.

If any cells that contain only a space character are found, you'll be able to spot them in the list displayed at the bottom of the Find and Replace dialog box.

Extra space characters

If you have formulas that rely on comparing text, be careful that your text doesn't contain additional space characters. Adding an extra space character is particularly common when data has been imported from another source.

Excel automatically removes trailing spaces from values that you enter, but trailing spaces in text entries are not deleted. It's impossible to tell just by looking at a cell whether text contains one or more trailing space characters.

The TRIM function removes leading spaces, trailing spaces, and multiple spaces within a text string.

Figure 22-1 shows some text in column A. The formula in B1, which was copied down the column, is

```
=TRIM(A1)=A1
```

This formula returns *FALSE* if the text in column A contains leading spaces, trailing spaces, or multiple spaces. In this case, the word *Dog* in cell A2 contains a trailing space.

	A	B	C
1	Horse	TRUE	
2	Cat	TRUE	
3	Dog	FALSE	
4	Cow	TRUE	
5	Chicken	TRUE	
6			
7			
8			
9			

Figure 22-1: Using a formula to identify cells that contain extra space characters.

Formulas returning an error

A formula may return any of the following error values:

- *#DIV/0!*
- *#N/A*
- *#NAME?*
- *#NULL!*
- *#NUM!*
- *#REF!*
- *#VALUE!*

The following sections summarize possible problems that may cause these errors.

Tip

Excel allows you to choose the way error values are printed. To access this feature, display the Page Setup dialog box and click the Sheet tab. In the Cell Errors As drop-down, you can choose to print error values as displayed (the default) or as blank cells, dashes, or *#N/A*. To display the Page Setup dialog box, click the dialog box launcher in the Page Layout ➜ Page Setup group.

Tracing error values

Often, an error in one cell is the result of an error in a precedent cell (a cell that is used by the formula). To help track down the source of an error value in a cell, select the cell and choose Formulas ➜ Formula Auditing ➜ Error Checking ➜ Trace Error. Excel draws arrows to indicate the error source.

	A	B	C	D	E	F	G	H
1		Units	Price	Total				
2	North	82	1.2	98.4				
3	South	396	1.8	712.8				
4	East	473	1.[illegible]9	#VALUE!				
5	West	437	1.1	480.7				
6	Total Sales	1388		#VALUE!				
7						Sales	#VALUE!	
8						Cost	1450	
9						Profit	#VALUE!	
10								
11								

After you identify the error, use Formulas ➜ Formula Auditing ➜ Error Checking ➜ Remove Arrows to get rid of the arrow display.

#DIV/0! errors

Division by zero is not a valid operation. If you create a formula that attempts to divide by zero, Excel displays its familiar *#DIV/0!* error value.

Because Excel considers a blank cell to be zero, you also get this error if your formula divides by a missing value. This problem is common when you create formulas for data that you haven't entered yet or that simply doesn't exist, as shown in Figure 22-2. The formula in cell D2, which was copied to the cells below it, is as follows:

```
=(C2-B2)/B2
```

	A	B	C	D	E
1	Product	Last Year	This Year	Change	
2	Widget 4	175	162	-7.43%	
3	Widget 4s	156	147	-5.77%	
4	Widget 5	198	202	2.02%	
5	Widget 5c	144	166	15.28%	
6	Widget 6		149	#DIV/0!	
7					
8					
9					
10					
11					

Figure 22-2: *#DIV/0!* errors occur when the data in column B is missing.

This formula calculates the percentage growth of a list of products from last year to this year. Because the newest product didn't exist last year, there is no data for it, and the formula returns a *#DIV/0!* error.

To avoid the error display, you can use an IF function to check for a blank cell in column B:

```
=IF(B2=0,"", (C2-B2)/B2)
```

This formula displays an empty string if cell B2 is blank or contains 0; otherwise, it displays the calculated value.

Another approach is to use the IFERROR function to check for *any* error condition. The following formula, for example, displays an empty string if the formula results in any type of error:

```
=IFERROR((C2-B2)/B2,"")
```

IFERROR was introduced in Excel 2007. For compatibility with previous versions, use this formula:

```
=IF(ISERROR((C2-B2)/B2),"", (C2-B2)/B2)
```

#N/A errors

The *#N/A* error occurs if any cell referenced by a formula displays *#N/A*.

Note

Some users like to enter =NA() or #N/A explicitly for missing data (that is, Not Available). This method makes it perfectly clear that the data is not available and hasn't been deleted accidentally.

The *#N/A* error also occurs when a lookup function (HLOOKUP, LOOKUP, MATCH, or VLOOKUP) can't find a match.

If you would like to display an empty string instead of *#N/A*, use the IFNA function in a formula like this:

```
=IFNA(VLOOKUP(A1,C1:F50,4,FALSE),"")
```

Tip

The IFNA function was introduced in Excel 2013. For compatibility with previous versions, use a formula like this:

```
=IF(ISNA(VLOOKUP(A1,C1:F50,4,FALSE)),"",VLOOKUP(A1,C1:F50,4,FALSE))
```

A third common cause of *#N/A* errors occurs when the components of an array formula don't contain the same number of elements. In this example, an array formula is used to find the largest value where column A is North and column B is June.

```
{=MAX((A1:A100="North")*(B1:B99="June")*(C1:C100))}
```

The first and third arrays look at 100 rows, whereas the second array only includes 99 rows. Because of this difference, this formula will return *#N/A*.

Cross-Ref

Array formulas are discussed in Chapter 14, "Introducing Arrays."

#NAME? errors

The *#NAME?* error occurs under these conditions:

- The formula contains an undefined range or cell name.
- The formula contains text that Excel *interprets* as an undefined name. A misspelled function name, for example, generates a *#NAME?* error.
- The formula contains text that isn't enclosed in quotation marks.
- The formula contains a range reference that omits the colon between the cell addresses.
- The formula uses a worksheet function that's defined in an add-in, and the add-in is not installed.

Note

Excel has a bit of a problem with range names. If you delete a name for a cell or range and the name is used in a formula, the formula continues to use the name even though it's no longer defined. As a result, the formula displays #NAME?. You may expect Excel to automatically convert the names to their corresponding cell references, but this does not happen. In fact, Excel does not even provide a way to convert the names used in a formula to the equivalent cell references!

#NULL! errors

The *#NULL!* error occurs when a formula attempts to use the intersection of two ranges that don't actually intersect. Excel's intersection operator is a space. The following formula, for example, returns *#NULL!* because the two ranges have no cells in common:

```
=SUM(B5:B14 A16:F16)
```

The following formula does not return *#NULL!* but instead displays the contents of cell B9—which represents the intersection of the two ranges:

```
=SUM(B5:B14 A9:F9)
```

You also see a *#NULL!* error if you accidentally omit an operator in a formula. For example, this formula is missing the second operator:

```
= A1+A2 A3
```

#NUM! errors

A formula returns a *#NUM!* error if any of the following occurs:

- You pass a nonnumeric argument to a function when a numeric argument is expected: for example, $1,000 instead of 1000.
- You pass an invalid argument to a function. For example, this formula returns *#NUM!*:

  ```
  =SQRT(-1)
  ```
- A function that uses iteration can't calculate a result. Examples of functions that use iteration are IRR and RATE.
- A formula returns a value that is too large or too small. Excel supports values between –1E–307 and 1E+307.

#REF! errors

The *#REF!* error occurs when a formula uses an invalid cell reference. This error can occur in the following situations:

- You delete a cell or the row or column of a cell that is referenced by the formula. For example, the following formula displays a *#REF!* error if row 1, column A, or column B is deleted:

  ```
  =A1/B1
  ```
- You delete the worksheet of a cell that is referenced by the formula. For example, the following formula displays a *#REF!* error if Sheet2 is deleted:

  ```
  =Sheet2!A1
  ```

- You copy a formula to a location that invalidates the relative cell references. For example, if you copy the following formula from cell A2 to cell A1, the formula returns *#REF!* because it attempts to refer to a nonexistent cell:

```
=A1-1
```

- You cut a cell (by choosing Home ➜ Clipboard ➜ Cut) and then paste it to a cell that's referenced by a formula. The formula displays *#REF!*.

#VALUE! errors

The *#VALUE!* error is common and can occur under the following conditions:

- An argument for a function is of an incorrect data type or the formula attempts to perform an operation using incorrect data. For example, a formula that adds a value to a text string returns the *#VALUE!* error.
- A function's argument is a range when it should be a single value.
- A custom worksheet function (created using VBA) is not calculated. With some versions of Excel, inserting or moving a sheet may cause this error. You can press Ctrl+Alt+F9 to force a recalculation.
- A custom worksheet function attempts to perform an operation that is not valid. For example, custom functions cannot modify the Excel environment or make changes to other cells.
- You forget to press Ctrl+Shift+Enter when entering an array formula.

Pay attention to the colors

When you edit a cell that contains a formula, Excel color-codes the cell and range references in the formula. Excel also outlines the cells and ranges used in the formula by using corresponding colors. Therefore, you can see at a glance the cells that are used in the formula.

You also can manipulate the colored outline to change the cell or range reference. To change the references that are used in the formula, drag the outline's border or fill handle (at the lower-right corner of the outline). Using this technique is often easier than editing the formula.

Absolute/relative reference problems

As we describe in Chapter 2, "Basic Facts About Formulas," a cell reference can be relative (for example, A1), absolute (for example, $A$1), or mixed (for example, $A1 or A$1). The type of cell reference that you use in a formula is relevant only if the formula will be copied to other cells.

A common problem is to use a relative reference when you should use an absolute reference. As shown in Figure 22-3, cell C1 contains a tax rate, which is used in the formulas in column C. The formula in cell C4 is as follows:

```
=B4*(1+$C$1)
```

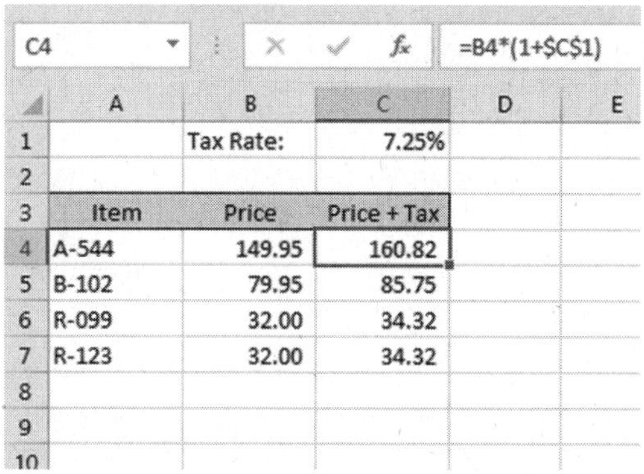

C4 =B4*(1+$C$1)

	A	B	C	D	E
1		Tax Rate:	7.25%		
2					
3	Item	Price	Price + Tax		
4	A-544	149.95	160.82		
5	B-102	79.95	85.75		
6	R-099	32.00	34.32		
7	R-123	32.00	34.32		
8					
9					
10					

Figure 22-3: Formulas in the range C4:C7 use an absolute reference to cell C1.

Notice that the reference to cell C1 is an absolute reference. When the formula is copied to other cells in column C, the formula continues to refer to cell C1. If the reference to cell C1 were a relative reference, the copied formulas would return an incorrect result or #VALUE!.

Operator precedence problems

Excel has some straightforward rules about the order in which mathematical operations are performed in a formula. In Table 22-1, operations with a lower precedence number are performed before operations with a higher precedence number. This table, for example, shows that multiplication has a higher precedence than addition. Therefore, multiplication is performed first.

Table 22-1: Operator Precedence in Excel Formulas

Symbol	Operator	Precedence
–	Negation	1
%	Percent	2
^	Exponentiation	3
* and /	Multiplication and division	4
+ and –	Addition and subtraction	5
&	Text concatenation	6
=, <, >, and <>	Comparison	7

When in doubt (or when you simply need to clarify your intentions), use parentheses to ensure that operations are performed in the correct order. For example, the following formula multiplies A1 by A2 and then adds 1 to the result. The multiplication is performed first because it has a higher order of precedence.

```
=1+A1*A2
```

The following is a clearer version of this formula. The parentheses aren't necessary—but in this case, the order of operations is perfectly obvious.

```
=1+(A1*A2)
```

Notice that the negation operator symbol is the same as the subtraction operator symbol. This, as you may expect, can cause some confusion. Consider these two formulas:

```
=-3^2
=0-3^2
```

The first formula, as expected, returns 9. The second formula, however, returns –9. Squaring a number always produces a positive result, so how is it that Excel can return the *–9* result?

In the first formula, the minus sign is a negation operator and has the highest precedence. However, in the second formula, the minus sign is a subtraction operator, which has a lower precedence than the exponentiation operator. Therefore, the value 3 is squared, and the result is subtracted from zero, producing a negative result.

Note

Excel is a bit unusual in interpreting the negation operator. Other spreadsheet products (for example, Lotus 1-2-3 and Quattro Pro) return –9 for both formulas. Excel's VBA language also returns –9 for these expressions.

Formulas are not calculated

If you use custom worksheet functions written in VBA, you may find that formulas that use these functions fail to get recalculated and may display incorrect results. For example, assume that you wrote a VBA function that returns the number format of a referenced cell. If you change the number format, the function continues to display the previous number format. That's because changing a number format doesn't trigger a recalculation.

To force a single formula to be recalculated, select the cell, press F2, and then press Enter. To force a recalculation of all formulas, press Ctrl+Alt+F9.

See Part VI, "Developing Custom Worksheet Functions," for more information about creating custom worksheet functions with VBA.

Actual versus displayed values

You may encounter a situation in which values in a range don't appear to add up properly. For example, Figure 22-4 shows a worksheet with the following formula entered into each cell in the range B3:B5:

```
=1/3
```

Cell B6 contains the following formula:

```
=SUM(B3:B5)
```

All the cells are formatted to display with three decimal places. As you can see, the formula in cell B6 appears to display an incorrect result. (You may expect it to display 0.999.) The formula, of course, *does* return the correct result. The formula uses the *actual* values in the range B3:B5, not the displayed values.

	A	B	C	D
1				
2				
3		0.333		
4		0.333		
5		0.333		
6		1.000		
7				
8				
9				
10				

Figure 22-4: A simple demonstration of numbers that appear to add up incorrectly.

You can instruct Excel to use the displayed values by selecting the Set Precision as Displayed check box on the Advanced tab of the Excel Options dialog box. (Choose File ➜ Options to display this dialog box.) This setting applies to the active workbook.

Warning

Use the Set Precision as Displayed option with caution, and make sure that you understand how it works. This setting also affects normal values (nonformulas) that have been entered into cells. For example, if a cell contains the value 4.68 and is displayed with no decimal places (that is, 5), selecting the Set Precision as Displayed check box converts 4.68 to 5.00. This change is permanent, and you can't restore the original value if you later clear the Set Precision as Displayed check box. A better approach is to use Excel's ROUND function to round the values to the desired number of decimal places. (See Chapter 10, "Miscellaneous Calculations.")

Floating-point number errors

Computers, by their very nature, don't have infinite precision. Excel stores numbers in binary format by using 8 bytes, which can handle numbers with 15-digit accuracy. Some numbers can't be expressed precisely by using 8 bytes, so the number is stored as an approximation.

To demonstrate how this limited precision may cause problems, enter the following formula into cell A1:

```
=(5.1-5.2)+1
```

The result should be 0.9. However, if you format the cell to display 15 decimal places, you'll discover that Excel calculates the formula with a result of *0.899999999999999*. This small error occurs because the operation in parentheses is performed first, and this intermediate result stores in binary format by using an approximation. The formula then adds 1 to this value, and the approximation error is propagated to the final result.

In many cases, this type of error does not present a problem. However, if you need to test the result of that formula by using a logical operator, it *may* present a problem. For example, the following formula (which assumes that the previous formula is in cell A1) returns *FALSE*:

```
=A1=.9
```

One solution to this type of error is to use Excel's ROUND function. The following formula, for example, returns *TRUE* because the comparison is made by using the value in A1 rounded to one decimal place:

```
=ROUND(A1,1)=0.9
```

Here's another example of a "precision" problem. Try entering the following formula:

```
=(1.333-1.233)-(1.334-1.234)
```

This formula should return *0*, but it actually returns *–2.22045E–16* (a number very close to zero).

If that formula were in cell A1, the following formula would return the string *Not Zero*.

```
=IF(A1=0,"Zero","Not Zero")
```

One way to handle these very-close-to-zero rounding errors is to use a formula like this:

```
=IF(ABS(A1)<1E-6,"Zero","Not Zero")
```

This formula uses the less-than operator to compare the absolute value of the number with a very small number. This formula would return *Zero*.

Phantom link errors

You may open a workbook and see a message like the one shown in Figure 22-5. This message sometimes appears even when a workbook contains no linked formulas.

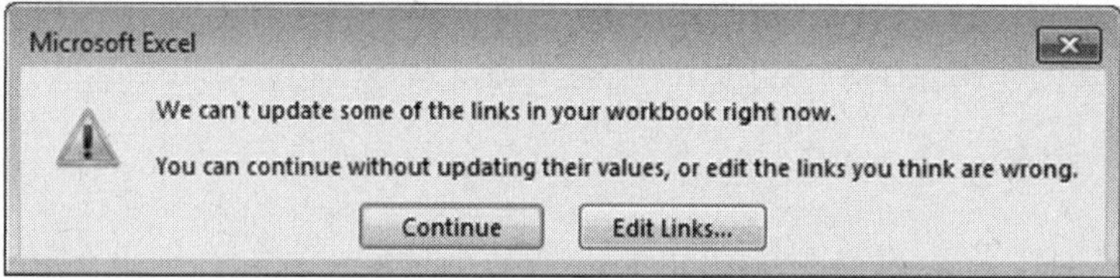

Figure 22-5: Excel's way of asking whether you want to update links in a workbook.

First, try choosing File ➜ Info ➜ Edit Links to Files to display the Edit Links dialog box. Then select each link and click Break Link. If that doesn't solve the problem, this phantom link may be caused by an erroneous name. Choose Formulas ➜ Defined Names ➜ Name Manager, and scroll through the list of names in the Name Manager dialog box. If you see a name that refers to *#REF!*, delete the name. The Name Manager dialog box has a Filter button that lets you filter the names. For example, you can filter the lists to display only the names with errors.

These phantom links may be created when you copy a worksheet that contains names. See Chapter 3, "Working with Names," for more information about names.

Logical value errors

As you know, you can enter *TRUE* or *FALSE* into a cell to represent logical True or logical False. Although these values seem straightforward enough, Excel is inconsistent about how it treats *TRUE* and *FALSE*.

Figure 22-6 shows a worksheet with three logical values in A1:A3 as well as four formulas that sum these logical values in A5:A8. As you see, these formulas return different answers.

	A	B	C
1	TRUE		
2	TRUE		
3	FALSE		
4			
5	2	=A1+A2+A3	
6	0	=SUM(A1:A3)	
7	2	{=SUM(--A1:A3)}	
8	-2	=VBASUM(A1:A3)	
9			
10			
11			
12			
13			

Figure 22-6: This worksheet demonstrates an inconsistency when summing logical values.

The formula in cell A5 uses the addition operator. The sum of these three cells is 2. The conclusion: Excel treats *TRUE* as 1 and *FALSE* as 0.

But wait! The formula in cell A6 uses Excel's SUM function. In this case, the sum of these three cells is 0. In other words, the SUM function ignores logical values. However, it's possible to force these logical values to be treated as values by the SUM function by using an array formula. The array formula in A7 uses double negation to coerce the *TRUE* and *FALSE* values to numbers.

To add to the confusion, the SUM function *does* return the correct answer if the logical values are passed as literal arguments. The following formula returns *2:*

```
=SUM(TRUE,TRUE,FALSE)
```

Although the VBA macro language is tightly integrated with Excel, sometimes it appears that the two applications don't understand each other. We created a simple VBA function that adds the values in a range. The function (which follows) returns *–2!*

```
Function VBASUM(rng)
    Dim cell As Range
    VBASUM = 0
    For Each cell In rng
        VBASUM = VBASUM + cell.Value
    Next cell
End Function
```

VBA considers *TRUE* to be –1 and *FALSE* to be 0.

The conclusion is that you need to be aware of Excel's inconsistencies and be careful when summing a range that contains logical values.

Circular reference errors

A *circular reference* is a formula that contains a reference to the cell that contains the formula. The reference may be direct or indirect. For help tracking down a circular reference, see the following section.

Excel's Auditing Tools

Excel includes a number of tools that can help you track down formula errors. The following sections describe the auditing tools built into Excel.

Identifying cells of a particular type

The Go to Special dialog box is a handy tool that enables you to locate cells of a particular type. Choose Home ➜ Editing ➜ Find & Select ➜ Go to Special; see Figure 22-7.

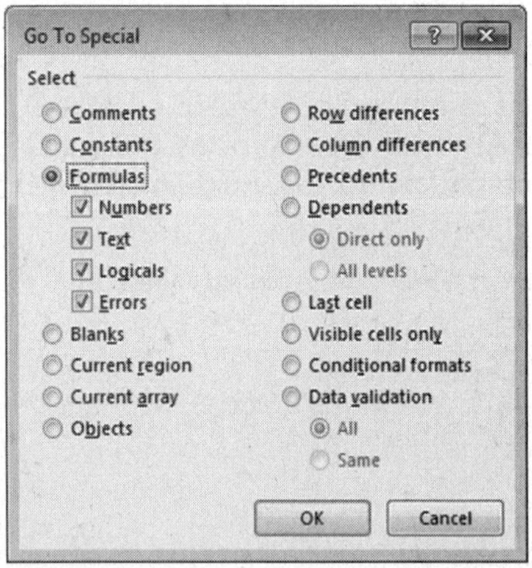

Figure 22-7: The Go to Special dialog box.

Note

If you select a multicell range before displaying the Go to Special dialog box, the command operates only within the selected cells. If a single cell is selected, the command operates on the entire worksheet.

You can use the Go to Special dialog box to select cells of a certain type, which can often help you identify errors. For example, if you choose the Formulas option, Excel selects all the cells that contain a formula. If you find a cell that's not selected amid a group of selected formula cells, chances are good that the cell previously contained a formula that has been replaced by a value.

Viewing formulas

You can often understand an unfamiliar workbook by displaying the formulas rather than the results of the formulas. To toggle the display of formulas, choose Formulas ➜ Formula Auditing ➜ Show Formulas. You may want to create a second window for the workbook before issuing this command. This way, you can see the formulas in one window and the results of the formula in the other window. Choose View ➜ Window ➜ New Window to open a new window.

Tip

You can also use Ctrl+` (the accent grave key, usually located above the Tab key) to toggle between Formula view and Normal view.

Figure 22-8 shows an example of a worksheet displayed in two windows. The window on the top shows Normal view (formula results), and the window on the bottom displays the formulas. The View ➜ Window ➜ View Side by Side command, which allows synchronized scrolling, is also useful for viewing two windows.

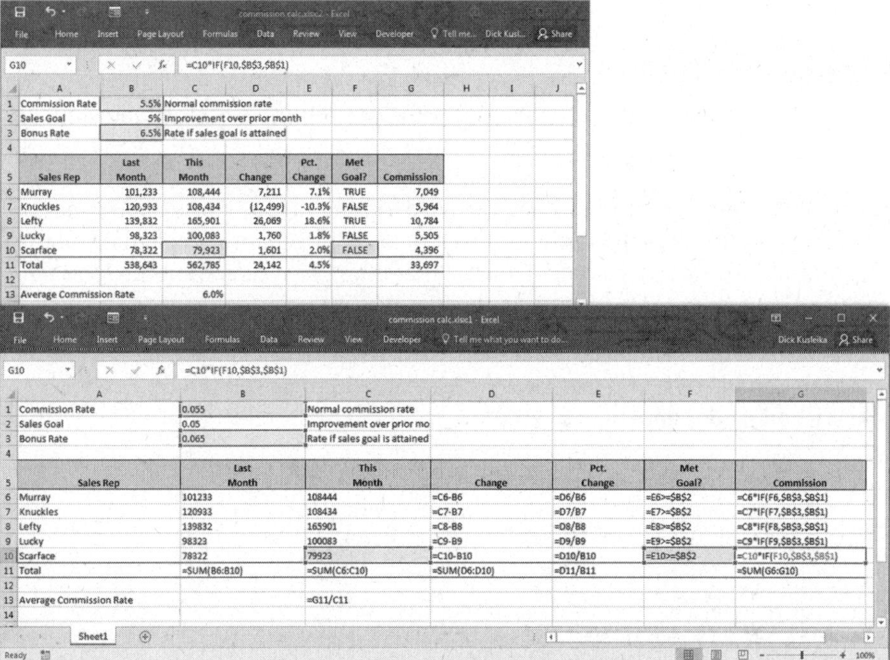

Figure 22-8: Displaying formulas (bottom window) and their results (top window).

When Formula view is in effect, Excel highlights the cells that are used by the formula in the active cell. In Figure 22-8, for example, the active cell is G10. The four cells used by this formula are highlighted in both windows.

Using the Inquire add-in

Some versions of Excel 2016 include a useful auditing add-in called Inquire. To install Inquire, choose File ➜ Options to display the Excel Options dialog box. Click the Add-Ins tab. At the bottom of the dialog box, choose COM Add-Ins from the Manage drop-down list, and click Go.

In the COM Add-Ins dialog box, place a checkmark next to Inquire Add-In and click OK. The add-in will be loaded automatically when Excel starts. If Inquire is not listed, your version of Excel does not include the add-in.

Inquire is accessible from the Inquire tab on the Ribbon. You can use this add-in to accomplish the following:

- Compare versions of a workbook
- Analyze a workbook for potential problems and inconsistencies
- Display interactive diagnostics
- Visualize links between workbook and worksheets
- Clear excess cell formatting
- Manage passwords

Tracing cell relationships

To understand how to trace cell relationships, you need to familiarize yourself with the following two concepts:

- **Cell precedents:** Applicable only to cells that contain a formula; a formula cell's precedents are all the cells that contribute to the formula's result. A *direct precedent* is a cell that you use directly in the formula. An *indirect precedent* is a cell that is not used directly in the formula but is instead used by a cell that you refer to in the formula.
- **Cell dependents:** These are formula cells that depend on a particular cell. A cell's dependents consist of all formula cells that use the cell. Again, the formula cell can be a direct dependent or an indirect dependent.

For example, consider this simple formula entered into cell A4:

```
=SUM(A1:A3)
```

Cell A4 has three precedent cells (A1, A2, and A3), which are all direct precedents. Cells A1, A2, and A3 each have at least one dependent cell (cell A4), and A4 is a direct dependent of all of them.

Identifying cell precedents for a formula cell often sheds light on why the formula is not working correctly. Conversely, knowing which formula cells depend on a particular cell is also helpful. For example, if you're about to delete a formula, you may want to check whether it has dependents.

Identifying precedents

You can identify cells used by a formula in the active cell in a number of ways:

- **Press F2.** The cells that are used directly by the formula are outlined in color, and the color corresponds to the cell reference in the formula. This technique is limited to identifying cells on the same sheet as the formula.
- **Display the Go to Special dialog box.** (Choose Home ➜ Editing ➜ Find & Select ➜ Go To Special.) Select the Precedents option and then select either Direct Only (for direct precedents only) or All Levels (for direct and indirect precedents). Click OK, and Excel selects the precedent cells for the formula. This technique is limited to identifying cells on the same sheet as the formula.
- **Press Ctrl+[** to select all direct precedent cells on the active sheet.
- **Press Ctrl+Shift+[** to select all precedent cells (direct and indirect) on the active sheet.
- **Choose Formulas ➜ Formula Auditing ➜ Trace Precedents.** Excel draws arrows to indicate the cell's precedents. Click this button multiple times to see additional levels of precedents. Choose Formulas ➜ Formula Auditing ➜ Remove Arrows to hide the arrows. Figure 22-9 shows a worksheet with precedent arrows drawn to indicate the precedents for the formula in cell C13.

	A	B	C	D	E	F	G	H
1	Commission Rate	5.5%	Normal commission rate					
2	Sales Goal	5%	Improvement over prior month					
3	Bonus Rate	6.5%	Rate if sales goal is attained					
4								
5	Sales Rep	Last Month	This Month	Change	Pct. Change	Met Goal?	Commission	
6	Murray	101,233	108,444	7,211	7.1%	TRUE	7,049	
7	Knuckles	120,933	108,434	(12,499)	-10.3%	FALSE	5,964	
8	Lefty	139,832	165,901	26,069	18.6%	TRUE	10,784	
9	Lucky	98,323	100,083	1,760	1.8%	FALSE	5,505	
10	Scarface	78,322	79,923	1,601	2.0%	FALSE	4,396	
11	Total	538,643	562,785	24,142	4.5%		33,697	
12								
13	Average Commission Rate		6.0%					
14								
15								
16								

Figure 22-9: This worksheet displays lines that indicate cell precedents for the formula in cell C13.

Identifying dependents

You can identify formula cells that use a particular cell in a number of ways:

- **Display the Go to Special dialog box.** Select the Dependents option and then select either Direct Only (for direct dependents only) or All Levels (for direct and indirect dependents). Click OK. Excel selects the cells that depend on the active cell. This technique is limited to identifying cells on the active sheet only.
- **Press Ctrl+]** to select all direct dependent cells on the active sheet.
- **Press Ctrl+Shift+]** to select all dependent cells (direct and indirect) on the active sheet.
- **Choose Formulas ➜ Formula Auditing ➜ Trace Dependents.** Excel draws arrows to indicate the cell's dependents. Click this button multiple times to see additional levels of dependents. Choose Formulas ➜ Formula Auditing ➜ Remove Arrows to hide the arrows.

Tracing error values

If a formula displays an error value, Excel can help you identify the cell that is causing that error value. An error in one cell is often the result of an error in a precedent cell. Activate a cell that contains an error value and choose Formulas ➜ Formula Auditing ➜ Error Checking ➜ Trace Error. Excel draws arrows to indicate the error source.

Fixing circular reference errors

If you accidentally create a circular reference formula, Excel displays a warning message, displays Circular Reference (with the cell address) in the status bar, and draws arrows on the worksheet to help you identify the problem.

If you can't figure out the source of the problem, use Formulas ➜ Formula Auditing ➜ Error Checking ➜ Circular References. This command displays a list of all cells that are involved in the circular references. Start by selecting the first cell listed and then work your way down the list until you figure out the problem.

Using background error checking

Some people may find it helpful to take advantage of Excel's automatic error-checking feature. This feature is enabled or disabled via the Enable Background Error Checking check box, on the Formulas tab of the Excel Options dialog box shown in Figure 22-10. In addition, you can specify which types of errors to check for by using the check boxes in the Error Checking Rules section.

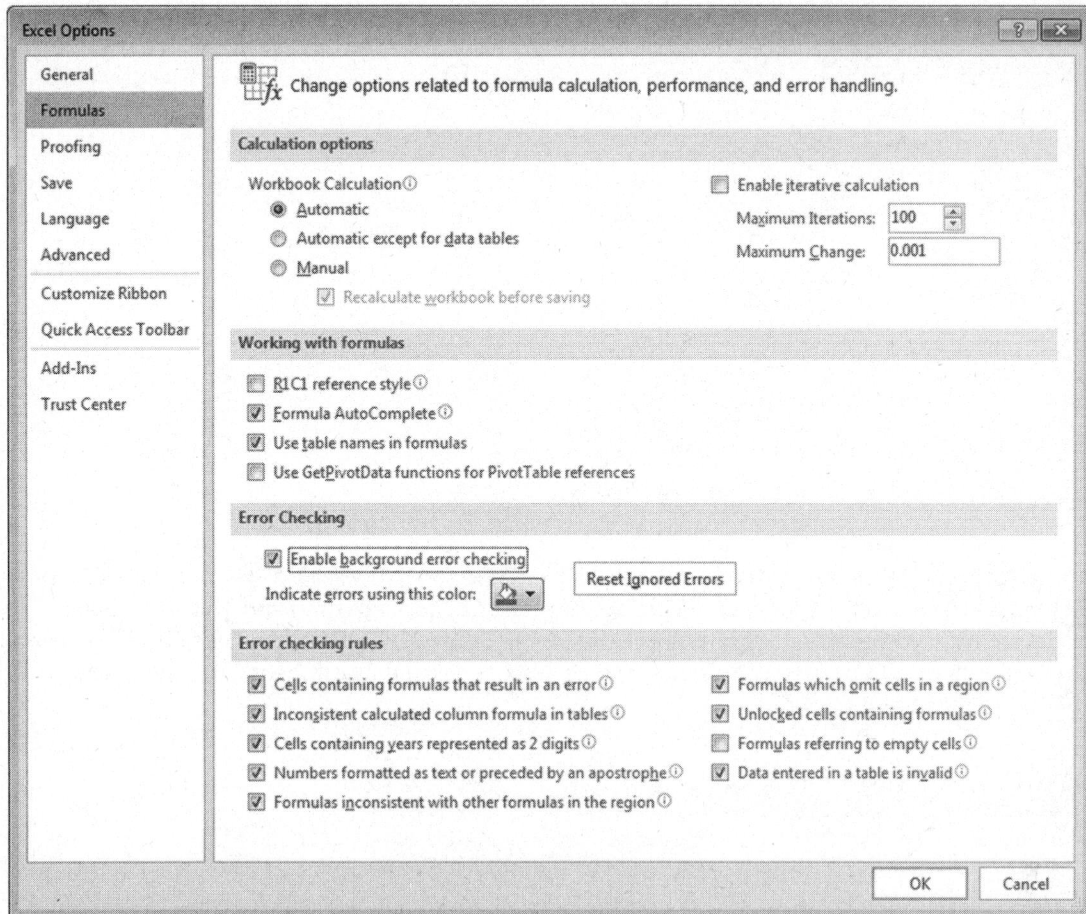

Figure 22-10: Excel can check your formulas for potential errors.

When error checking is turned on, Excel continually evaluates your worksheet, including its formulas. If a potential error is identified, Excel places a small triangle in the upper-left corner of the cell. When the cell is activated, an icon appears. Clicking this icon provides options. Figure 22-11 shows the options that appear when you click the icon in a cell that contains a *#DIV/0!* error. The options vary, depending on the type of error.

In many cases, you will choose to ignore an error by selecting the Ignore Error option. Selecting this option eliminates the cell from subsequent error checks. However, all previously ignored errors can be reset so that they appear again. (Use the Reset Ignored Errors button in the Formulas tab of the Excel Options dialog box.)

	A	B	C	D	E	F
1	Product	Last Year	This Year	Change		
2	Widget 4	175	162	-7.43%		
3	Widget 4s	156	147	-5.77%		
4	Widget 5	198	202	2.02%		
5	Widget 5c	144	166	15.28%		
6	Widget 6			#DIV/0!		

Divide by Zero Error
Help on this error
Show Calculation Steps...
Ignore Error
Edit in Formula Bar
Error Checking Options...

Figure 22-11: Clicking an error's icon gives you a list of options.

You can choose Formulas ➜ Formula Auditing ➜ Error Checking to display a dialog box that describes each potential error cell in sequence, much like using a spell-checking command. This command is available even if you disable background error checking. Figure 22-12 shows the Error Checking dialog box. Note that this dialog box is *modeless,* so you can still access your worksheet when the Error Checking dialog box is displayed.

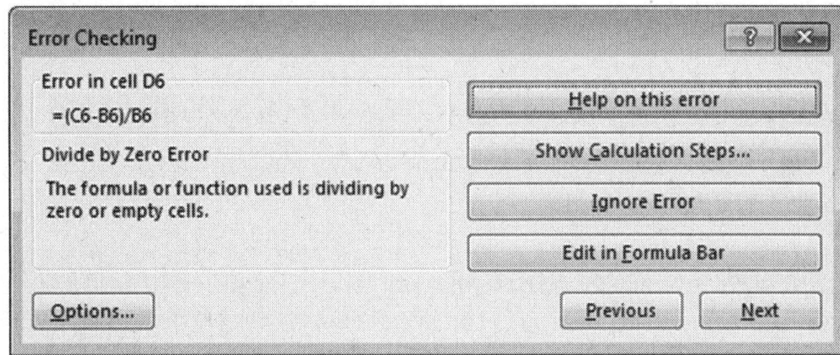

Figure 22-12: Using the Error Checking dialog box to cycle through potential errors that Excel identifies.

Warning

It's important to understand that the error-checking feature is not perfect. In fact, it's not even close to perfect. In other words, you can't assume that you have an error-free worksheet simply because Excel does not identify potential errors! Also, be aware that this error checking feature won't catch a common type of error: overwriting a formula cell with a value.

Using Excel's Formula Evaluator

Excel's Formula Evaluator enables you to see the various parts of a nested formula evaluated in the order that the formula is calculated.

To use the Formula Evaluator, select the cell that contains the formula and then choose Formula ➜ Formula Auditing ➜ Evaluate Formula to display the Evaluate Formula dialog box, as shown in Figure 22-13.

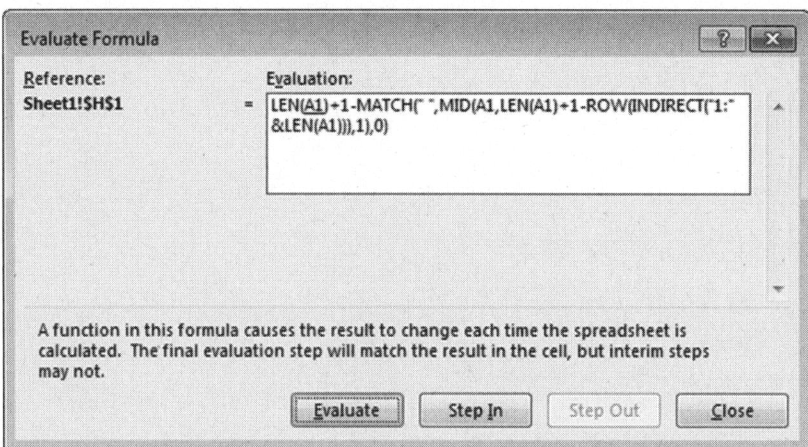

Figure 22-13: Excel's Formula Evaluator shows a formula being calculated one step at a time.

Click the Evaluate button to show the result of calculating the expressions within the formula. Each click of the button evaluates the underlined portion of the formula. This feature may seem a bit complicated at first, but if you spend some time working with it, you'll understand how it works and see the value.

Excel provides another way to evaluate a part of a formula:

1. Select the cell that contains the formula.
2. Press F2 to get into cell edit mode.
3. Use your mouse to highlight the portion of the formula that you want to evaluate or press Shift and use the arrow keys.
4. Press F9.

The highlighted portion of the formula displays the calculated result. You can evaluate other parts of the formula or press Esc to cancel and return your formula to its previous state.

Warning

Be careful when using this technique because if you press Enter (rather than Esc), the formula is modified to use the calculated values.

PART VI

Developing Custom Worksheet Functions

23

Introducing VBA

In This Chapter

- An introduction to VBA
- How to use the Visual Basic Editor
- How to work in the code windows of the Visual Basic Editor

VBA (Visual Basic for Applications) is Excel's programming language, and it is used to create macros and custom worksheet functions that you can employ in formulas. In its broadest sense, a macro is a sequence of instructions that automates some aspect of Excel so that you can work more efficiently and with fewer errors.

Excel programming terminology can be a bit confusing. For example, VBA is a programming language, but it also serves as a macro language. What do you call something written in VBA and executed in Excel? Is it a macro or is it a program? Excel's Help system often refers to VBA procedures as macros, so this is the terminology used in this book.

Over the next few chapters, we will introduce you to the world of VBA through the prism of creating worksheet functions. But before you can create custom functions by using VBA, you need to have some basic background knowledge of VBA as well as some familiarity with the Visual Basic Editor (VBE).

Fundamental Macro Concepts

Most Excel users think of macros as a way of recording actions so that Excel can duplicate those actions on demand. Recording a macro is like programming a phone number into your cell phone. You first manually dial and save a number. Then when you want, you can redial those numbers with the touch of a button. Just as on a cell phone, you can record your actions in Excel while you perform them.

While you record, Excel gets busy in the background, translating your keystrokes and mouse clicks to written VBA code.

Activating the Developer tab

If you plan to work with VBA macros, you need to make sure that the Developer tab is visible. To display this tab, do the following:

1. Choose File ➜ Options.
2. In the Excel Options dialog box, select Customize Ribbon.
3. In the list box on the right, place a check mark next to Developer.
4. Click OK to return to Excel.

Recording a macro

Now that you have the Developer tab showing in the Excel Ribbon, you can start working with VBA. You have the option of either manually creating a macro or recording a macro. It's often useful to start programming a procedure by recording a macro and letting Excel write the initial code for you.

Activate the Macro Recorder by selecting Record Macro from the Developer tab. This activates the Record Macro dialog box, as shown in Figure 23-1.

Figure 23-1: The Record Macro dialog box.

Here are the four parts of the Record Macro dialog box:

- **Macro Name:** This should be self-explanatory. Excel gives a default name to your macro, such as Macro1, but you should give your macro a name that's more descriptive of what it actually does. For example, you might name a macro that formats a generic table as FormatTable.
- **Shortcut Key:** Every macro needs an event, or something to happen, for it to run.

  This event can be a button press, a workbook opening, or in this case, a keystroke combination. When you assign a shortcut key to your macro, entering that combination of keys triggers your macro to run. This is an optional field.

- **Store Macro In:** This Workbook is the default option. Storing your macro in This Workbook simply means that the macro is stored along with the active Excel file. The next time you open that particular workbook, the macro is available to run. Similarly, if you send the workbook to another user, that user can run the macro as well (provided the macro security is properly set by your user—more on that later in this chapter).
- **Description:** This is an optional field, but it can come in handy if you have numerous macros in a spreadsheet or if you need to give a user a more detailed description about what the macro does.

With the Record Macro dialog box open, follow these steps to create a simple macro that enters your name into a worksheet cell:

1. Enter a new single-word name for the macro to replace the default Macro1 name. A good name for this example is MyName.
2. Assign this macro to the shortcut key Ctrl+Shift+N by entering uppercase **N** in the edit box labeled Shortcut Key.
3. Click OK to close the Record Macro dialog box and begin recording your actions.
4. Select any cell on your Excel spreadsheet, type your name into the selected cell, and then press Enter.
5. Choose Developer ➜ Code ➜ Stop Recording (or click the Stop Recording button in the status bar).

Examining the macro

The macro was recorded in a new module named Module1. To view the code in this module, you must activate the VB Editor. You can activate the VB Editor in either of two ways:

- Press Alt+F11.
- Choose Developer ➜ Code ➜ Visual Basic.

In the VB Editor, the Project window displays a list of all open workbooks and add-ins. This list is displayed as a tree diagram, which you can expand or collapse. The code that you recorded previously is stored in Module1 in the current workbook. When you double-click Module1, the code in the module appears in the code window.

The macro should look something like this:

```
Sub MyName()
'
' MyName Macro
'
' Keyboard Shortcut: Ctrl+Shift+N
'
    ActiveCell.FormulaR1C1 = "Michael Alexander"
End Sub
```

The macro recorded is a Sub procedure that is named MyName. The statements tell Excel what to do when the macro is executed.

Notice that Excel inserted some comments at the top of the procedure. These comments are some of the information that appeared in the Record Macro dialog box. These comment lines (which begin with an apostrophe) aren't really necessary, and deleting them has no effect on how the macro runs. If you ignore the comments, you'll see that this procedure has only one VBA statement:

```
ActiveCell.FormulaR1C1 = "Michael Alexander"
```

This single statement causes the name you typed while recording to be inserted into the active cell.

Testing the macro

Before you recorded this macro, you set an option that assigned the macro to the Ctrl+Shift+N shortcut key combination. To test the macro, return to Excel by using either of the following methods:

- Press Alt+F11.
- Click the View Microsoft Excel button on the VB Editor toolbar.

When Excel is active, activate a worksheet. (It can be in the workbook that contains the VBA module or in any other workbook.) Select a cell and press Ctrl+Shift+N. The macro immediately enters your name into the cell.

Editing the macro

After you record a macro, you can make changes to it. For example, assume that you want your name to be bold. You can rerecord the macro, but this modification is simple, so editing the code is more efficient. Press Alt+F11 to activate the VB Editor window. Then activate Module1 and insert the following statement before the End Sub statement:

```
ActiveCell.Font.Bold = True
```

The edited macro appears as follows:

```
Sub MyName()
'
' MyName Macro
'
' Keyboard Shortcut: Ctrl+Shift+N
'
    ActiveCell.FormulaR1C1 = "Michael Alexander"

    ActiveCell.Font.Bold = True

End Sub
```

Understanding macro-enabled extensions

Beginning with Excel 2007, Excel workbooks were given the standard file extension .xlsx. Files with the .xlsx extension cannot contain macros. If your workbook contains macros and you then save that workbook as an .xlsx file, your macros are removed automatically. Excel warns you that macro content will be disabled in that case.

If you want to retain the macros, you must save your file as an Excel Macro-Enabled Workbook. This gives your file an .xlsm extension. The idea is that all workbooks with an .xlsx file extension are automatically known to be safe, whereas you can recognize .xlsm files as a potential threat.

Macro security in Excel

With the release of Office 2010, Microsoft introduced significant changes to its Office security model. One of the most significant changes is the concept of trusted documents. Without getting into the technical minutia, a trusted document is essentially a workbook you have deemed safe by enabling macros.

If you open a workbook that contains macros in Excel, you see a yellow bar message under the Ribbon stating that macros have been disabled.

If you click Enable content, it automatically becomes a trusted document. This means you no longer are prompted to enable the content as long as you open that file on your computer. The basic idea is that if you told Excel that you "trust" a particular workbook by enabling macros, it is highly likely you will enable macros each time you open it. Thus, Excel remembers that you've enabled macros before and inhibits any further messages about macros for that workbook.

This is great news for you and your clients. After enabling your macros just one time, your clients won't be annoyed at the constant messages about macros, and you won't have to worry that your macro-enabled dashboard will fall flat because macros have been disabled.

Trusted locations

If the thought of any macro message coming up (even one time) unnerves you, you can set up a trusted location for your files. A trusted location is a directory that is deemed a safe zone in which only trusted workbooks are placed. A trusted location allows you and your clients to run a macro-enabled workbook with no security restrictions as long as the workbook is in that location.

To set up a trusted location, follow these steps:

1. Select the Macro Security button on the Developer tab. This activates the Trust Center dialog box.
2. Click the Trusted Locations button. This opens the Trusted Locations window (see Figure 23-2), which shows you all the directories that are considered trusted.
3. Click the Add New Location button.
4. Click Browse to find and specify the directory that will be considered a trusted location.

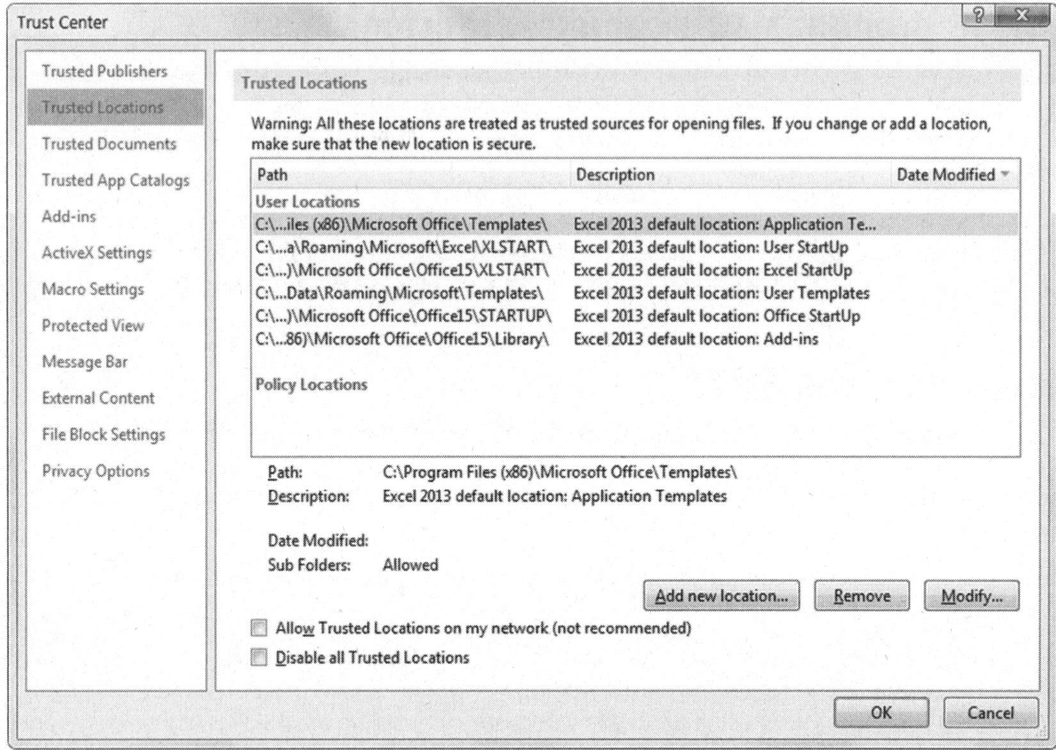

Figure 23-2: The Trusted Locations window allows you to add directories that are considered trusted.

After you specify a trusted location, any Excel file that is opened from this location will have macros automatically enabled.

Storing macros in your Personal Macro Workbook

Most user-created macros are designed for a specific workbook, but you may want to use some macros in all your work. You can store these general-purpose macros in the Personal Macro Workbook so that they're always available to you. The Personal Macro Workbook is loaded whenever you start Excel. This file, named personal.xlsb, doesn't exist until you record a macro using Personal Macro Workbook as the destination.

To record the macro in your Personal Macro Workbook, select the Personal Macro Workbook option in the Record Macro dialog box before you start recording. This option is in the Store Macro In drop-down list (refer to Figure 23-1).

If you store macros in the Personal Macro Workbook, you don't have to remember to open the Personal Macro Workbook when you load a workbook that uses macros. When you want to exit, Excel asks whether you want to save changes to the Personal Macro Workbook.

Assigning a macro to a button and other form controls

When you create macros, you may want to have a clear and easy way to run each macro. A basic button can provide a simple but effective user interface.

As luck would have it, Excel offers a set of form controls designed specifically for creating user interfaces directly on spreadsheets. There are several types of form controls, from buttons (the most commonly used control) to scrollbars.

The idea behind using a form control is simple. You place a form control on a spreadsheet and then assign a macro to it—that is, a macro you've already recorded. When a macro is assigned to the control, that macro is executed, or played, when the control is clicked.

Here's how:

1. Click the Insert button under the Developer tab. (See Figure 23-3.)
2. Select the Form Control button from the drop-down list that appears.
3. Click the location where you want to place your button.

   When you drop the button control onto your spreadsheet, the Assign Macro dialog box, as shown in Figure 23-4, activates and asks you to assign a macro to this button.
4. Select the macro you want to assign to the button and then click OK.

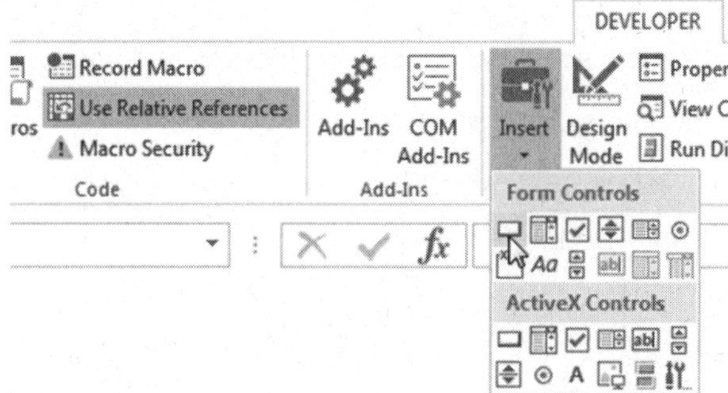

Figure 23-3: You can find the form controls in the Developer tab.

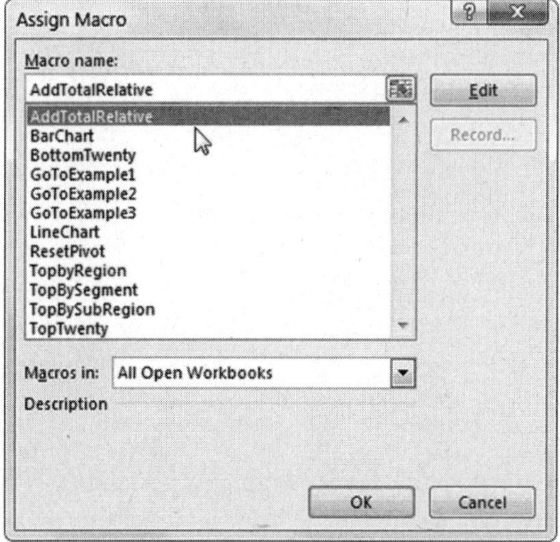

Figure 23-4: Assign a macro to the newly added button.

At this point, you have a button that runs your macro when you click it. Keep in mind that all the controls in the Form Controls group (shown in Figure 23-3) work in the same way as the command button in that you assign a macro to run when the control is selected.

Note

Notice the form controls and ActiveX controls in Figure 23-3. Although they look similar, they're quite different. Form controls are designed specifically for use on a spreadsheet, and ActiveX controls are typically used on Excel user forms. As a general rule, you should always use form controls when working on a spreadsheet. Why? Form controls need less overhead, so they perform better, and configuring form controls is far easier than configuring their ActiveX counterparts.

Placing a macro on the Quick Access toolbar

You can also assign a macro to a button in Excel's Quick Access toolbar. The Quick Access toolbar sits either above or below the Ribbon. You can add a custom button that runs your macro by following these steps:

1. Right-click your Quick Access toolbar and select Customize Quick Access Toolbar. This opens the dialog box illustrated in Figure 23-5.
2. Click the Quick Access Toolbar button on the left of the Excel Options dialog box.
3. Select Macros from the Choose Commands From drop-down list on the left.
4. Select the macro you want to add and click the Add button.
5. Change the icon by clicking the Modify button.

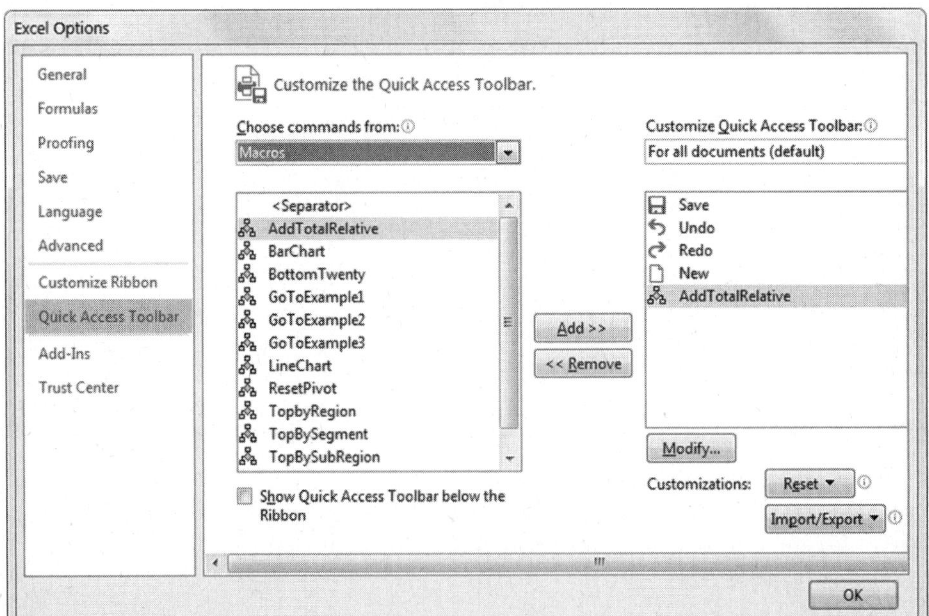

Figure 23-5: Adding a macro to the Quick Access toolbar.

Working in the Visual Basic Editor

The VBE is actually a separate application that runs when you open Excel. To see this hidden VBE environment, you need to activate it. The quickest way to activate the VBE is to press Alt+F11 when Excel is active. To return to Excel, press Alt+F11 again.

You can also activate the VBE by using the Visual Basic command found on Excel's Developer tab.

Understanding VBE components

Figure 23-6 shows the VBE program with some of the key parts identified. Chances are your VBE program window doesn't look exactly like what you see in the figure. The VBE contains several windows and is highly customizable. You can hide windows, rearrange windows, dock windows, and so on.

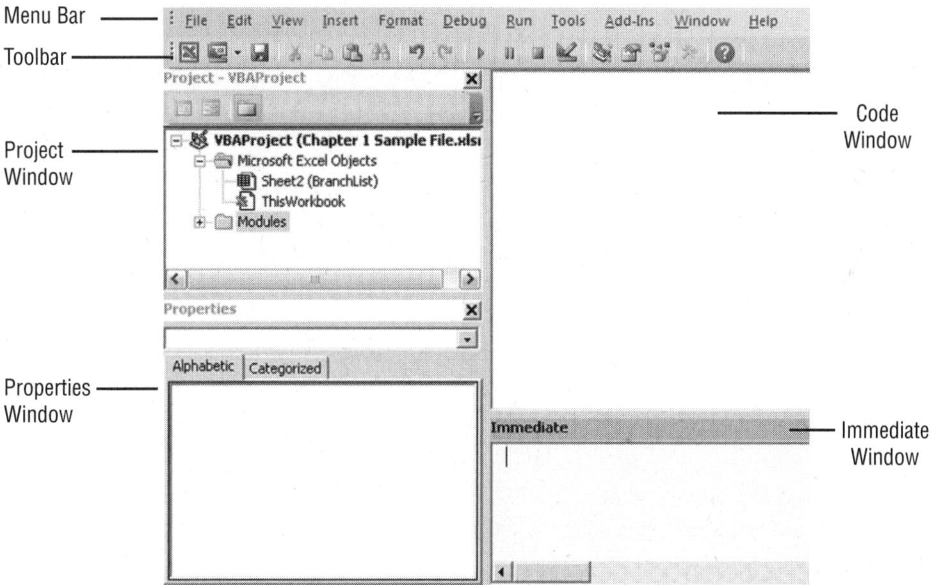

Figure 23-6: The VBE with significant elements identified.

Menu bar

The VBE menu bar works just like every other menu bar you've encountered. It contains commands that you use to do things with the various components in the VBE. Many of the menu commands have shortcut keys associated with them.

The VBE also features shortcut menus. You can right-click virtually anything in the VBE and get a shortcut menu of common commands.

Toolbar

The Standard toolbar, which is directly under the menu bar by default, is one of four VBE toolbars available. You can customize the toolbars, move them around, display other toolbars, and so on. If you're so inclined, use the View ➜ Toolbars command to work with VBE toolbars. Most people just leave them as they are.

Project window

The Project window displays a tree diagram that shows every workbook currently open in Excel (including add-ins and hidden workbooks). Double-click items to expand or contract them. You'll explore this window in more detail in the "Working with the Project window" section later in this chapter.

If the Project window is not visible, press Ctrl+R or use the View ➜ Project Explorer command. To hide the Project window, click the Close button in its title bar. Alternatively, right-click anywhere in the Project window and select Hide from the shortcut menu.

Code window

A code window contains VBA code. Every object in a project has an associated code window. To view an object's code window, double-click the object in the Project window. For example, to view the code window for the Sheet1 object, double-click Sheet1 in the Project window. Unless you've added some VBA code, the code window will be empty.

You find out more about code windows later in this chapter's "Working with a code window" section.

Immediate window

The Immediate window may or may not be visible. If it isn't visible, press Ctrl+G or use the View ➜ Immediate Window command. To close the Immediate window, click the Close button in its title bar (or right-click anywhere in the Immediate window and select Hide from the shortcut menu).

The Immediate window is most useful for executing VBA statements directly and for debugging your code. If you're just starting out with VBA, this window won't be all that useful, so feel free to hide it and free up some screen space for other things.

Working with the Project window

When you're working in the VBE, each Excel workbook and add-in that's open is a project. You can think of a project as a collection of objects arranged as an outline. You can expand a project by clicking the plus sign (+) at the left of the project's name in the Project window. Contract a project by clicking the minus sign (–) to the left of a project's name. Or you can double-click the items to expand and contract them.

Figure 23-7 shows a Project window with two projects listed: a workbook named Book1 and a workbook named Book2.

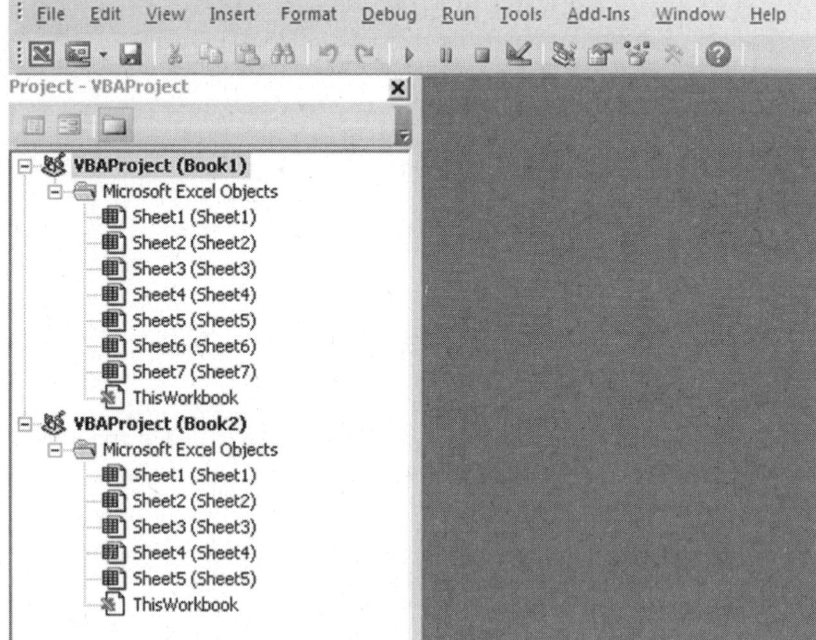

Figure 23-7: This Project window lists two projects. They are expanded to show their objects.

Every project expands to show at least one node called Microsoft Excel Objects. This node expands to show an item for each sheet in the workbook (each sheet is considered an object) and another object called ThisWorkbook (which represents the Workbook object). If the project has VBA modules, the project listing also shows a Modules node.

Adding a new VBA module

When you record a macro, Excel automatically inserts a VBA module to hold the recorded code. The workbook that holds the module for the recorded macro depends on where you chose to store the recorded macro, just before you started recording.

In general, a VBA module can hold three types of code:

- **Declarations:** One or more information statements that you provide to VBA. For example, you can declare the data type for variables you plan to use or set some other module-wide options.
- **Sub procedures:** A set of programming instructions that performs some action. All recorded macros are Sub procedures.
- **Function procedures:** A set of programming instructions that returns a single value (similar in concept to a worksheet function, such as Sum).

A single VBA module can store any number of Sub procedures, Function procedures, and declarations. The way you organize a VBA module is completely up to you. Some people prefer to keep all their VBA code for an application in a single VBA module; others like to split up the code into several modules. It's a personal choice, just like arranging furniture.

Follow these steps to manually add a new VBA module to a project:

1. Select the project's name in the Project window.
2. Choose Insert ➜ Module.

Or you can do the following:

1. Right-click the project's name.
2. Choose Insert ➜ Module from the shortcut menu.

The new module is added to a Modules folder in the Project window (see Figure 23-8). Any modules you create in a given workbook are placed in this Modules folder.

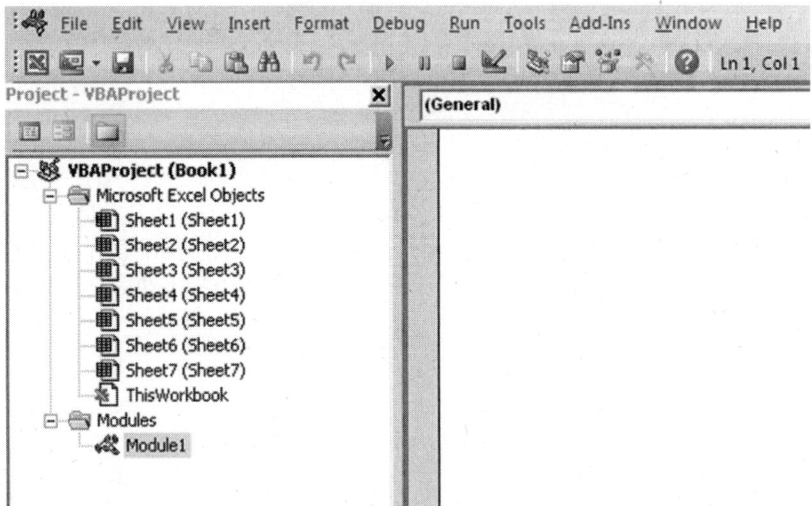

Figure 23-8: Code modules are visible in the Project window in a folder called Modules.

Removing a VBA module

You may want to remove a code module that is no longer needed. To do so, follow these steps:

1. Select the module's name in the Project window.
2. Choose File ➜ Remove *xxx*, where *xxx* is the module name.

Or do the following:

1. Right-click the module's name.
2. Choose Remove *xxx* from the shortcut menu.

Working with a code window

As you become proficient with VBA, you spend lots of time working in code windows. Macros that you record are stored in a module that is visible in the code window, and you can type VBA code directly into a VBA module.

Minimizing and maximizing windows

Code windows are much like workbook windows in Excel. You can minimize them, maximize them, resize them, hide them, rearrange them, and so on. It's often much easier to maximize the code window that you're working on. Doing so lets you see more code and keeps you from getting distracted.

To maximize a code window, click the Maximize button in its title bar (right next to the X). Or just double-click its title bar to maximize it. To restore a code window to its original size, click the Restore button. When a window is maximized, its title bar isn't really visible, so you'll find the Restore button to the right of the Help box.

Sometimes you may want to have two or more code windows visible. For example, you may want to compare the code in two modules or copy code from one module to another. You can arrange the windows manually or use the Window ➜ Tile Horizontally or Window ➜ Tile Vertically commands to arrange them automatically.

You can quickly switch among code windows by pressing Ctrl+Tab. If you repeat that key combination, you keep cycling through all the open code windows. Pressing Ctrl+Shift+Tab cycles through the windows in reverse order.

Minimizing a code window gets it out of the way. You can also click the window's Close button in a code window's title bar to close the window completely. (Closing a window just hides it; you won't lose anything.) To open it again, just double-click the appropriate object in the Project window. Working with these code windows sounds more difficult than it really is.

Getting VBA code into a module

Before you can do anything meaningful, you must have some VBA code in the VBA module. You can get VBA code into a VBA module in three ways:

- Use the Excel macro recorder to record your actions and convert them to VBA code.
- Enter the code directly.
- Copy code from another module (or any online resource) and paste it into the code window.

You have discovered the excellent method for creating code by using the Excel Macro recorder. However, not all tasks can be translated to VBA by recording a macro. You often have to enter your code directly into the module. Entering code directly basically means either typing the code yourself or copying and pasting code you have found somewhere else.

Entering and editing text in a VBA module works as you might expect. You can select, copy, cut, paste, and do other things to the text.

A single line of VBA code can be as long as you like. However, you may want to use the line continuation character to break up lengthy lines of code. To continue a single line of code (also known as a statement) from one line to the next, end the first line with a space followed by an underscore (_). Then continue the statement on the next line. Here's an example of a single statement split into three lines:

```
Selection.Sort Key1:=Range("A1"), _
    Order1:=xlAscending, Header:=xlGuess, _
    Orientation:=xlTopToBottom
```

This statement would perform the same way if it were entered in a single line (with no line-continuation characters). Notice that the second and third lines of this statement are indented. Indenting is optional, but it helps clarify the fact that these lines are not separate statements.

The VBE has multiple levels of undo and redo. If you deleted a statement that you shouldn't have, use the Undo button on the toolbar (or press Ctrl+Z) until the statement appears again. After undoing, you can use the Redo button to perform the changes you've undone.

Ready to enter some real, live code? Try the following steps:

1. Create a new workbook in Excel.
2. Press Alt+F11 to activate the VBE.
3. Click the new workbook's name in the Project window.
4. Choose Insert ➜ Module to insert a VBA module into the project.
5. Type the following code into the module:

```
Sub GuessName()
    Dim Msg as String
    Dim Ans As Long
    Msg = "Is your name " & Application.UserName & "?"
    Ans = MsgBox(Msg, vbYesNo)
    If Ans = vbNo Then MsgBox "Oh, never mind."
    If Ans = vbYes Then MsgBox "I must be clairvoyant!"
End Sub
```

6. Make sure the cursor is located anywhere within the text you typed and press F5 to execute the procedure. F5 is a shortcut for the Run ➜ Run Sub/UserForm command.

When you enter the code listed in step 5, you might notice that the VBE makes some adjustments to the text you enter. For example, after you type the Sub statement, the VBE automatically inserts the End Sub statement. And if you omit the space before or after an equal sign, the VBE inserts the space for you. Also, the VBE changes the color and capitalization of some text. This is all perfectly normal. It's just the VBE's way of keeping things neat and readable.

If you followed the previous steps, you just created a VBA Sub procedure, also known as a macro. When you press F5 with the cursor in the procedure, Excel executes the code and follows the instructions. In other words, Excel evaluates each statement and does what you told it to do. You can execute this macro any number of times, although it tends to lose its appeal after a few dozen executions.

This simple macro uses the following concepts:

- Defining a Sub procedure (the first line)
- Declaring variables (the Dim statements)
- Assigning values to variables (Msg and Ans)
- Concatenating (joining) strings (using the & operator)
- Using a built-in VBA function (MsgBox)
- Using built-in VBA constants (vbYesNo, vbNo, and vbYes)
- Using an If-Then construct (twice)
- Ending a Sub procedure (the last line)

As mentioned previously, you can copy and paste code into a VBA module. For example, a Sub or Function procedure that you write for one project might also be useful in another project. Instead of wasting time reentering the code, you can activate the module and use the normal copy-and-paste procedures (Ctrl+C to copy and Ctrl+V to paste). After pasting it into a VBA module, you can modify the code as necessary.

Saving your project

As with any application, you should save your work frequently while working in the VB Editor. To do so, use File ➜ Save *xxxx* (where *xxxx* is the name of the active workbook), press Ctrl+S, or click the Save button on the standard toolbar.

Note

When you save your project, you actually save your Excel workbook. By the same token, if you save your workbook in Excel, you also save the changes made in the workbook's VB project.

The VB Editor does not have a Save As command. If you save a workbook for the first time from the Editor, you are presented with Excel's standard Save As dialog box. If you want to save your project with a different name, you need to activate Excel and use Excel's Save As command.

Customizing the VBA environment

If you're serious about becoming an Excel programmer, you'll spend a lot of time with VBA modules on your screen. To help make things as comfortable as possible, the VBE provides quite a few customization options.

When the VBE is active, choose Tools ➜ Options. You'll see a dialog box with four tabs: Editor, Editor Format, General, and Docking. Take a moment to explore some of the options found on each tab.

The Editor tab

Figure 23-9 shows the options accessed by clicking the Editor tab of the Options dialog box. Use the options in the Editor tab to control the way certain things work in the VBE.

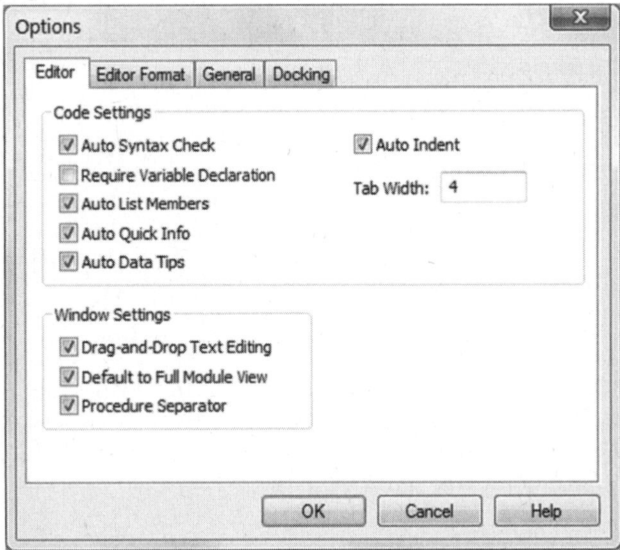

Figure 23-9: The Editor tab in the Options dialog box.

The Auto Syntax Check option

The Auto Syntax Check setting determines whether the VBE pops up a dialog box if it discovers a syntax error while you're entering your VBA code. The dialog box tells roughly what the problem is. If you don't choose this setting, VBE flags syntax errors by displaying them in a different color from the rest of the code, and you don't have to deal with any dialog boxes popping up on your screen.

The Require Variable Declaration option

If the Require Variable Declaration option is set, VBE inserts the following statement at the beginning of each new VBA module you insert:

```
Option Explicit
```

Changing this setting affects only new modules, not existing modules. If this statement appears in your module, you must explicitly define each variable you use. Using a Dim statement is one way to declare variables.

The Auto List Members option

If the Auto List Members option is set, VBE provides some help when you're entering your VBA code. It displays a list that logically completes the statement you're typing. This is one of the best features of the VBE.

The Auto Quick Info option

If the Auto Quick Info option is selected, VBE displays information about functions and their arguments as you type. This is similar to the way Excel lists the arguments for a function as you start typing a new formula.

The Auto Data Tips option

If the Auto Data Tips option is set, VBE displays the value of the variable over which your cursor is placed when you're debugging code. This is turned on by default and is often quite useful. There is no reason to turn this option off.

The Auto Indent setting

The Auto Indent setting determines whether VBE automatically indents each new line of code the same as the previous line. Most Excel developers are keen on using indentations in their code, so this option is typically kept on.

Tip

By the way, you should use the Tab key to indent your code, not the spacebar. Also, you can use Shift+Tab to "unindent" a line of code. If you want to indent more than just one line, select all lines you want to indent and then press the Tab key.

The VBE's Edit toolbar (which is hidden by default) contains two useful buttons: Indent and Outdent. These buttons let you quickly indent or "unindent" a block of code. Select the code and click one of these buttons to change the block's indenting.

The Drag-and-Drop Text Editing option

The Drag-and-Drop Text Editing option, when enabled, lets you copy and move text by dragging and dropping with your mouse.

The Default to Full Module View option

The Default to Full Module View option sets the default state for new modules. (It doesn't affect existing modules.) If set, procedures in the code window appear as a single scrollable list. If this option is turned off, you can see only one procedure at a time.

The Procedure Separator option

When the Procedure Separator option is turned on, separator bars appear at the end of each procedure in a code window. Separator bars provide a nice visual line between procedures, making it easy to see where one piece of code ends and where another starts.

The Editor Format tab

Figure 23-10 shows the Editor Format tab of the Options dialog box. With this tab, you can customize the way the VBE looks.

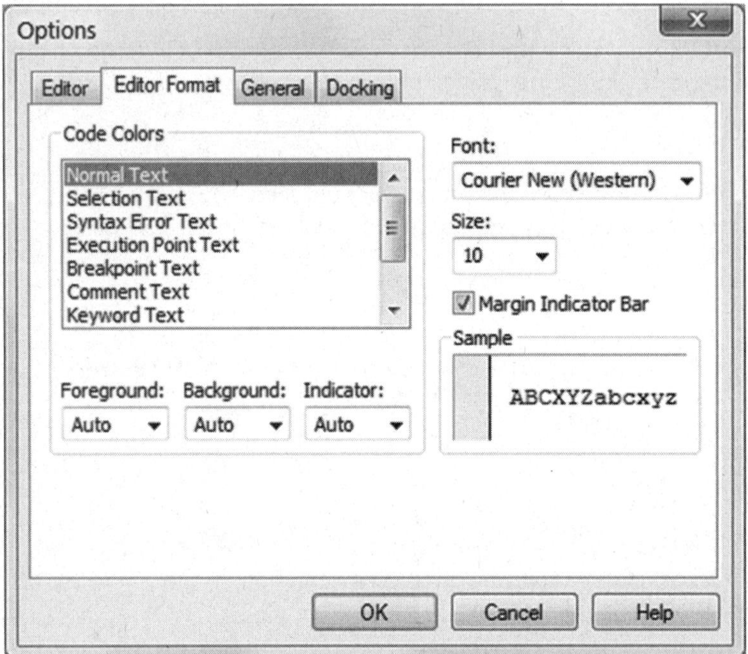

Figure 23-10: Change the VBE's looks with the Editor Format tab.

The Code Colors option

The Code Colors option lets you set the text color and background color displayed for various elements of VBA code. This is largely a matter of personal preference. Most Excel developers stick with the default colors. But if you like to change things up, you can play around with these settings.

The Font option

The Font option lets you select the font that's used in your VBA modules. For best results, stick with a fixed-width font such as Courier New. In a fixed-width font, all characters are the same width. This makes your code more readable because the characters are nicely aligned vertically and you can easily distinguish multiple spaces (which is sometimes useful).

The Size setting

The Size setting specifies the point size of the font in the VBA modules. This setting is a matter of personal preference determined by your video display resolution and how good your eyesight is.

The Margin Indicator Bar option

This option controls the display of the vertical margin indicator bar in your modules. You should keep this turned on; otherwise, you can't see the helpful graphical indicators when you're debugging your code.

The General tab

Figure 23-11 shows the options available under the General tab in the Options dialog box. In almost every case, the default settings are just fine.

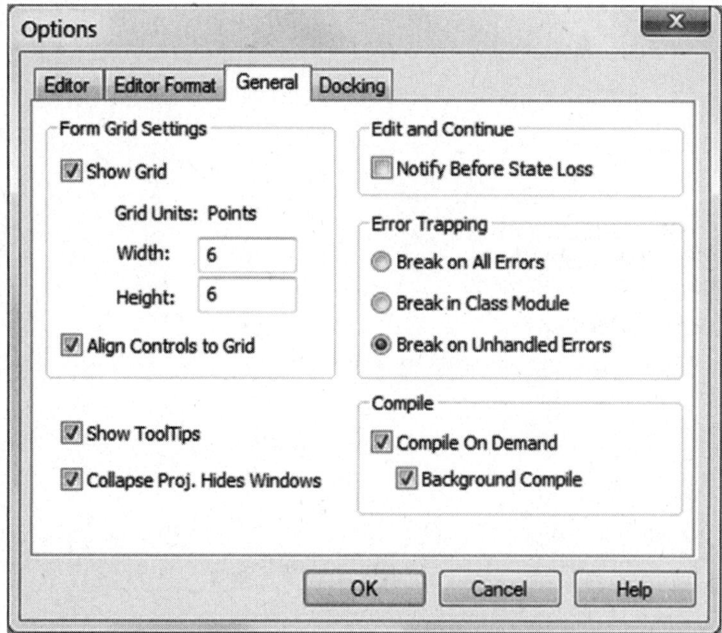

Figure 23-11: The General tab of the Options dialog box.

The most important setting on the General tab is Error Trapping. If you are just starting your Excel macro writing career, it's best to leave the Error Trapping set to Break on Unhandled Errors. This ensures Excel can identify errors as you type your code.

The Docking tab

Figure 23-12 shows the Docking tab. These options determine how the various windows in the VBE behave. When a window is docked, it is fixed in place along one of the edges of the VBE program window. This makes it much easier to identify and locate a particular window. If you turn off all docking, you have a big, confusing mess of windows. Generally, the default settings work fine.

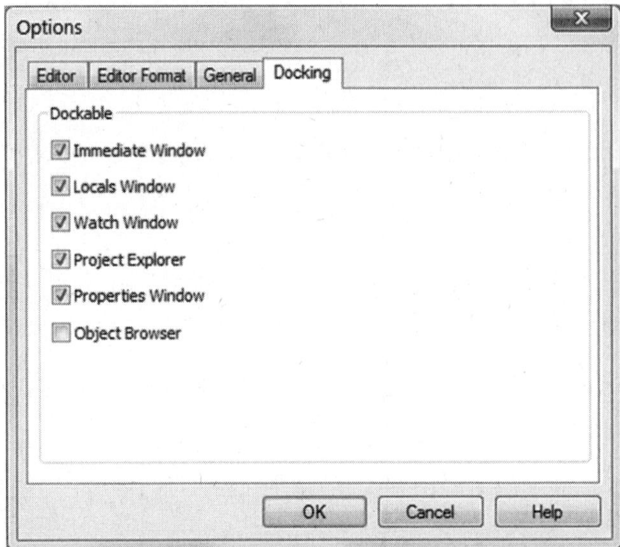

Figure 23-12: The Docking tab of the Options dialog box.

24

VBA Programming Concepts

In This Chapter

- Understanding VBA's language elements, including variables, data types, and constants
- Using the built-in VBA functions
- Controlling the execution of your Function procedures
- Using ranges in your code

To truly go beyond recording macros and into writing your own custom functions, it's important to understand the underlying Visual Basic for Applications (VBA) typically used in Excel macros.

This chapter starts you on that journey by giving you a primer on some of the objects, variables, events, and error handlers you will encounter in the examples found in this book.

On the Web

Many of the code examples in this chapter are available at this book's website. The file is named function examples.xlsm.

A Brief Overview of the Excel Object Model

VBA is an object-oriented programming language. The basic concept of object-oriented programming is that a software application (Excel in this case) consists of various individual objects, each of which has its own set of features and uses. An Excel application contains cells, worksheets, charts, pivot tables, drawing shapes—the list of Excel's objects is seemingly endless. Each object has its own set of features, which are called *properties*, and its own set of uses, called *methods*.

You can think of this concept just as you would the objects you encounter every day, such as your computer, your car, and the refrigerator in your kitchen. Each of those objects has identifying qualities, such as height, weight, and color. Each has its own distinct uses, such as your computer for working with Excel, your car to transport you over long distances, and your refrigerator to keep your perishable foods cold.

VBA objects also have their identifiable properties and methods of use. A worksheet cell is an object, and among its describable features (its properties) are its address, its height, and its formatted fill color. A workbook is also a VBA object, and among its usable features (its methods) are its abilities to be opened, closed, and have a chart or pivot table added to it.

In Excel you deal with workbooks, worksheets, and ranges on a daily basis. You likely think of each of these "objects" as part of Excel, not really separating them in your mind. However, Excel thinks about these internally as part of a hierarchical model called the Excel Object Model. The Excel Object Model is a clearly defined set of objects that are structured according to the relationships between them.

Understanding objects

In the real world, you can describe everything you see as an object. When you look at your house, it is an object. Your house has rooms; those rooms are also separate objects. Those rooms may have closets. Those closets are likewise objects. As you think about your house, the rooms, and the closets, you may see a hierarchical relationship between them. Excel works in the same way.

In Excel, the Application object is the all-encompassing object—similar to your house. Inside the Application object, Excel has a workbook. Inside a workbook is a worksheet. Inside that is a range. All these are objects that live in a hierarchical structure.

To point to a specific object in VBA, you can traverse the object model. For example, to get to cell A1 on Sheet 1, you can enter this code:

```
Activeworkbook.Sheets("Sheet1").Range("A1").Select
```

In most cases, the object model hierarchy is understood, so you don't have to type every level. Entering this code also gets you to cell A1 because Excel infers that you mean the active workbook and the active sheet:

```
Range("A1").Select
```

Indeed, if you have your cursor already in cell A1, you can simply use the ActiveCell object, negating the need to actually spell out the range:

```
Activecell.Select
```

Understanding collections

Many of Excel's objects belong to collections. For example, your house sits within a collection of houses that are called a neighborhood. Each neighborhood sits in a collection of neighborhoods called a city. Excel considers collections to be objects themselves.

In each workbook object, you have a collection of worksheets. The Worksheets collection is an object that you can call upon through VBA. Each worksheet in your workbook lives in the Worksheets collection.

If you want to refer to a worksheet in the Worksheets collection, you can refer to it by its position in the collection, as an index number starting with 1, or by its name, as quoted text. If you run these two lines of code in a workbook that has only one worksheet called MySheet, they both do the same thing:

```
Worksheets(1).Select
Worksheets("MySheet").Select
```

If you have two worksheets in the active workbook that have the names MySheet and YourSheet, in that order, you can refer to the second worksheet by typing either of these statements:

```
Worksheets(2).Select
Worksheets("YourSheet").Select
```

If you want to refer to a worksheet called MySheet in a particular workbook called MyData.xlsx that is not active, you must qualify the worksheet reference and the workbook reference, as follows:

```
Workbooks("MyData.xlsx").Worksheets("MySheet").Select
```

Understanding properties

Properties are essentially the characteristics of an object. Your house has a color, a square footage, an age, and so on. Some properties can be changed, such as the color of your house. Other properties can't be changed, such as the age of your house.

Likewise, an object in Excel like the Worksheet object has a sheet name property that can be changed and a Rows.Count row property that cannot.

You refer to the property of an object by referring to the object and then the property. For instance, you can change the name of your worksheet by changing its Name property.

In this example, you are renaming Sheet1 to MySheet:

```
Sheets("Sheet1").Name = "MySheet"
```

Some properties are read only, which means that you can't assign a value to them directly; an example is the Text property of a cell. The Text property gives you the formatted appearance of value in a cell, but you cannot overwrite or change it.

Understanding methods

Methods are the actions that can be performed against an object. It helps to think of methods as verbs. You can paint your house, so in VBA, that translates to something like this:

```
house.paint
```

A simple example of an Excel method is the Select method of the Range object:

```
Range("A1").Select
```

Another is the Copy method of the Range object:

```
Range("A1").Copy
```

Some methods have parameters that can dictate how they are applied. For instance, the Paste method can be used more effectively by explicitly defining the Destination parameter:

```
ActiveSheet.Paste Destination:=Range("B1")
```

A brief look at variables

Another concept you will see throughout the macros in this book is variables. It's important to dedicate a few words to this concept because it will play a big part in most of the macros you will encounter here.

You can think of variables as memory containers that you can use in your procedures. There are different types of variables, each tasked with holding a specific type of data.

Following are some of the common types of variables you will see in this book:

- **String:** Holds textual data
- **Integer:** Holds numeric data ranging from –32,768 to 32,767
- **Long:** Holds numeric data ranging from –2,147,483,648 to 2,147,483,647
- **Double:** Holds floating point numeric data
- **Variant:** Holds any kind of data
- **Boolean:** Holds binary data that returns *TRUE* or *FALSE*
- **Object:** Holds an actual object from the Excel Object Model

The term used for creating a variable in a macro is *declaring a variable*. You do so by entering Dim (abbreviation for dimension), then the name of your variable, and then the type. For instance:

```
Dim MyText as String

Dim MyNumber as Integer
Dim MyWorksheet as Worksheet
```

Once you create your variable, you can fill it with data. Here are a few simple examples of how you would create a variable and then assign values to them:

```
Dim MyText as String
Mytext = Range("A1").Value

Dim MyNumber as Integer
MyNumber = Range("B1").Value * 25

Dim MyObject as Worksheet
Set MyWorksheet = Sheets("Sheet1")
```

The values you assign to your variables often come from data stored in your cells. However, the values may also be information that you yourself create. It all depends on the task at hand. This notion will become clearer as you go through the macros in this book.

What's so great about variables?

Although it is possible to create code that does not use variables, you will encounter many examples of VBA code where variables are employed. There are two main reasons for this.

First, Excel doesn't inherently know what your data is used for. It doesn't see numerals, symbols, or letters. It just sees data. When you declare variables with specific data types, you help Excel know how it should handle certain pieces of data so that your macros will produce the results you'd expect.

Second, variables help by making your code more efficient and easier to understand. For example, suppose you have a number in cell A1 that you are repeatedly referring to in your macro. You can retrieve that number by pointing to cell A1 each time you need it:

```
Sub Macro1()
Range("B1").Value = Range("A1").Value * 5
Range("C1").Value = Range("A1").Value * 10
Range("D1").Value = Range("A1").Value * 15
End Sub
```

However, this forces Excel to waste cycles storing the same number into memory every time you point to cell A1. Also, if you need to change your workbook so that the target number is not in cell A1, but in, let's say, cell A2, you must edit your code by changing all the references from A1 to A2.

A better way is to store the number in cell A1 just once. For example, you can store the value in cell A1 in an Integer variable called myValue.

```
Sub WithVariable()
Dim myValue As Integer
myValue = Range("A1").Value
Range("B1").Value = myValue * 5
Range("C1").Value = myValue * 10
Range("D1").Value = myValue * 15
End Sub
```

This not only improves the efficiency of your code (ensuring Excel reads the number in Cell A1 just once) but ensures that you only have to edit one line should the design of your workbook change.

Using assignment statements

An *assignment statement* is a VBA instruction that evaluates an expression and assigns the result to a variable or an object. An *expression* is a combination of keywords, operators, variables, and constants that yields a string, number, or object. An expression can perform a calculation, manipulate characters, or test data.

If you know how to create formulas in Excel, you'll have no trouble creating expressions in VBA. With a worksheet formula, Excel displays the result in a cell. Similarly, you can assign a VBA expression to a variable or use it as a property value.

VBA uses the equal sign (=) as its assignment operator. Note the following examples of assignment statements. (The expressions are to the right of the equal sign.)

```
x = 1
x = x + 1
x = (y * 2) / (z * 2)
MultiSheets = True
```

Expressions often use functions. These can be VBA's built-in functions, Excel's worksheet functions, or custom functions that you develop in VBA. We discuss VBA's built-in functions later in this chapter.

Operators play a major role in VBA. Familiar operators describe mathematical operations, including addition (+), multiplication (*), division (/), subtraction (–), exponentiation (^), and string concatenation (&). Less familiar operators are the backslash (\) that's used in integer division and the Mod operator that's used in modulo arithmetic. The Mod operator returns the remainder of one integer divided by another. For example, the following expression returns *2:*

```
17 Mod 3
```

You may be familiar with the Excel MOD function. Note that in VBA, Mod is an operator, not a function.

VBA also supports the same comparative operators used in Excel formulas: equal to (=), greater than (>), less than (<), greater than or equal to (>=), less than or equal to (<=), and not equal to (<>). Additionally, VBA provides a full set of logical operators, as shown in Table 24-1. Refer to the Help system for additional information and examples of these operators.

Table 24-1: VBA Logical Operators

Operator	What It Does
Not	Performs a logical negation on an expression
And	Performs a logical conjunction on two expressions

Operator	What It Does
Or	Performs a logical disjunction on two expressions
Xor	Performs a logical exclusion on two expressions
Eqv	Performs a logical equivalence on two expressions
Imp	Performs a logical implication on two expressions

The order of precedence for operators in VBA exactly matches that in Excel. Of course, you can add parentheses to change the natural order of precedence.

Warning

The negation operator (a minus sign) is handled differently in VBA. In Excel, the following formula returns 25:

```
=-5^2
```

In VBA, x equals *–25* after this statement is executed:

```
x = -5 ^ 2
```

VBA performs the exponentiation operation and then applies the negation operator. The following statement returns *25:*

```
x = (-5) ^ 2
```

Error handling

In some of the macros in this book, you will see a line similar to this:

```
On Error GoTo MyError
```

This is called an error handler. Error handlers allow you to specify what happens when an error is encountered while your code runs.

Without error handlers, any error that occurs in your code prompts Excel to activate a less-than-helpful error message, which typically won't clearly convey what actually happened. However, with the aid of error handlers, you can choose to ignore the error or exit the code gracefully with your own message to the user.

There are three types of On Error statements:

- **On Error GoTo SomeLabel:** The code jumps to the specified label.
- **On Error Resume Next:** The error is ignored and the code resumes.
- **On Error GoTo 0:** VBA resets to normal error checking behavior.

On Error GoTo SomeLabel

There are times when an error in your code means you need to gracefully exit the procedure and give your users a clear message. In these situations, you can use the On Error GoTo statement to tell Excel to jump to a certain line of code.

Take this small piece of code, for example. Here, we are telling Excel to divide the value in cell A1 by the value in cell A2 and then place the answer in cell A3. Easy. What could go wrong?

```
Sub Macro1()
Range("A3").Value = Range("A1").Value / Range("A2").Value
End Sub
```

As it turns out, two major things can go wrong. If cell A2 contains a 0, we get a divide by 0 error. If cell A1 or A2 contains a nonnumeric value, we get a type mismatch error.

To avoid a nasty error message, we can tell Excel that On Error, we want the code execution to jump to the label called MyExit.

In the code that follows, you see that the MyExit label is followed by a message to the user that gives her friendly advice instead of a nasty error message. Also note the Exit Sub line before the MyExit label. This ensures that the code simply exits if no error is encountered:

```
Sub Macro1()
On Error GoTo MyExit
Range("A3").Value = Range("A1").Value / Range("A2").Value
Exit Sub

MyExit:
MsgBox "Please Use Valid Non-Zero Numbers"
End Sub
```

On Error Resume Next

Sometimes you want Excel to ignore an error and simply resume running the code. In these situations, you can use the On Error Resume Next statement.

For example, this piece of code is meant to delete a file called GhostFile.exe from the C:\Temp directory. After the file is deleted, a nice message box tells the user the file is gone:

```
Sub Macro1()
Kill "C:\Temp\GhostFile.exe"
MsgBox "File has been deleted."
End Sub
```

It works great if there is indeed a file to delete. But if for some reason the file called GhostFile.exe does not exist in the C:\Temp drive, an error is thrown.

In this case, we don't care if the file is not there. We were going to delete it anyway. So we can simply ignore the error and move on with the code.

By using the On Error Resume Next statement, the code runs its course whether or not the targeted file exists:

```
Sub Macro1()
On Error Resume Next
Kill "C:\Temp\GhostFile.exe"
MsgBox "File has been deleted."
End Sub
```

On Error GoTo 0

When you're using certain error statements, it may be necessary to reset the error-checking behavior of VBA. To understand what this means, take a look at this example.

Here, we first want to delete a file called GhostFile.exe from the C:\Temp directory. To avoid errors that may stem from the fact that the targeted file does not exist, we use the On Error Resume Next statement. After that, we are trying to do some suspect math by dividing 100/Mike:

```
Sub Macro1()
On Error Resume Next
Kill "C:\Temp\GhostFile.exe"
Range("A3").Value = 100 / "Mike"
End Sub
```

Running this piece of code should generate an error due to the fuzzy math, but it doesn't. Why? Because the last instruction we gave to the code was On Error Resume Next. Any error encountered after that line is effectively ignored.

To remedy this problem, we can use the On Error GoTo 0 statement to resume the normal error-checking behavior:

```
Sub Macro1()
On Error Resume Next
Kill "C:\Temp\GhostFile.exe"
On Error GoTo 0

Range("A3").Value = 100 / "Mike"
End Sub
```

This code ignores errors until the On Error GoTo 0 statement. After that statement, the code goes back to normal error-checking where it triggers the expected error stemming from the fuzzy math.

Using code comments

A *comment* is descriptive text embedded within your code. VBA completely ignores the text of a comment. It's a good idea to use comments liberally to describe what you do because the purpose of a particular VBA instruction is not always obvious.

You can use a complete line for your comment, or you can insert a comment after an instruction on the same line. A comment is indicated by an apostrophe. VBA ignores any text that follows an apostrophe up until the end of the line. An exception occurs when an apostrophe is contained within quotation marks. For example, the following statement does not contain a comment, even though it has an apostrophe:

```
Result = "That doesn't compute"
```

The following example shows a VBA Function procedure with three comments:

```
Function LASTSPACE(txt)
'   Returns the position of the last space character
    LASTSPACE = InStrRev(txt, Chr(32)) 'character 32 is a space
'   If no spaces, return #NA error
    If LASTSPACE = 0 Then LASTSPACE = CVErr(xlErrNA)
End Function
```

When developing a function, you may want to test it without including a particular statement or group of statements. Instead of deleting the statement, simply convert it to a comment by inserting an apostrophe at the beginning. VBA then ignores the statement(s) when the routine is executed. To convert the comment back to a statement, delete the apostrophe.

Tip

The VB Editor Edit toolbar contains two useful buttons. Select a group of instructions and then use the Comment Block button to convert the instructions to comments. The Uncomment Block button converts a group of comments back to instructions. If the Edit toolbar is not visible, choose View ➜ Toolbars ➜ Edit.

An Introductory Example Function Procedure

At this point, you should have enough working knowledge to evaluate a real-life Function procedure. This function, named REMOVESPACES, accepts a single argument and returns that argument without spaces. For example, the following worksheet formula uses the REMOVESPACES function and returns *ThisIsATest*:

```
=REMOVESPACES("This Is A Test")
```

To create this function, insert a VBA module into a project and then enter the following Function procedure into the code window of the module:

```
Function REMOVESPACES(cell) As String
'   Removes all spaces from cell
    Dim CellLength As Long
    Dim Temp As String
    Dim Character As String
    Dim i As Long
    CellLength = Len(cell)
    Temp = ""
    For i = 1 To CellLength
        Character = Mid(cell, i, 1)
        If Character <> Chr(32) Then Temp = Temp & Character
    Next i
    REMOVESPACES = Temp
End Function
```

Look closely at this function's code line by line:

- The first line of the function is called the function's *declaration line*. Notice that the procedure starts with the keyword Function, followed by the name of the function (REMOVESPACES). This function uses only one argument (cell); the argument name is enclosed in parentheses. As String defines the data type of the function's return value. The As part of the function declaration is optional.
- The second line is a comment (optional) that describes what the function does. The initial apostrophe designates this line as a comment. Comments are ignored when the function is executed.
- The next four lines use the Dim keyword to declare the four variables used in the procedure: CellLength, Temp, Character, and i. Declaring variables is not necessary, but as you'll see later, it's an excellent practice.
- The procedure's next line assigns a value to a variable named CellLength. This statement uses the VBA Len function to determine the length of the contents of the argument (cell).
- The next line creates a variable named Temp and assigns it an empty string.
- The next four lines make up a For-Next loop. The statements between the For statement and the Next statement are executed a number of times; the value of CellLength determines the number of times. For example, assume that the cell passed as the argument contains the text Bob Smith. The statements within the loop would execute nine times—one time for each character in the string.
- Within the loop, the Character variable holds a single character that is extracted using the VBA Mid function (which works just like Excel's MID function). The If statement determines whether the character is not a space. (The VBA Chr function is equivalent to Excel's CHAR function, and an argument of 32 represents a space character.) The two angle brackets (<>)

represent "not equal to." If the character is not a space, the character is appended to the string stored in the Temp variable (using an ampersand, the concatenation operator). If the character is a space, the Temp variable is unchanged, and the next character is processed. If you prefer, you can replace this statement with the following:

```
If Character <> " " Then Temp = Temp & Character
```

- When the loop finishes, the Temp variable holds all the characters that were originally passed to the function in the cell argument, except for the spaces.
- The string contained in the Temp variable is assigned to the function's name. This string is the value that the function returns.
- The Function procedure ends with an End Function statement.

The REMOVESPACES procedure uses some common VBA language elements, including

- A Function declaration statement
- A comment (the line preceded by the apostrophe)
- Variable declarations
- Three assignment statements
- Three built-in VBA functions (Len, Mid, and Chr)
- A looping structure (For-Next)
- A comparison operator (<>)
- An If-Then structure
- String concatenation (using the & operator)

Not bad for a first effort, eh? The remainder of this chapter provides more information on these (and many other) programming concepts.

Note

The REMOVESPACES function listed here is for instructional purposes only. You can accomplish the same effect by using the Excel SUBSTITUTE function, which is much more efficient than using a custom VBA function. The following formula, for example, removes all space characters from the text in cell A1:

```
=SUBSTITUTE(A1," ","")
```

Using Built-In VBA Functions

VBA has a variety of built-in functions that simplify calculations and operations. Many of VBA's functions are similar (or identical) to Excel's worksheet functions. For example, the VBA function UCase, which converts a string argument to uppercase, is equivalent to the Excel worksheet function UPPER.

To display a list of VBA functions while writing your code, type VBA followed by a period (.). The VB Editor displays a list of all functions and constants (see Figure 24-1). If this does not work for you, make sure that you select the Auto List Members option. Choose Tools ➜ Options and click the Editor tab. In addition to functions, the displayed list includes built-in constants. All the VBA functions are described in the online help. To view Excel Help, just move the cursor over a function name and press F1.

```
Sub Macro1()

VBA.
Er  Abs
    AppActivate
    Asc
    AscB
    AscW
    Atn
    Beep
```

Figure 24-1: Displaying a list of VBA functions in the VB Editor.

Here's a statement that calculates the square root of a variable by using VBA's Sqr function and then assigns the result to a variable named *x*:

```
x = Sqr(MyValue)
```

Having knowledge of VBA functions can save you lots of work. For example, consider the REMOVESPACES Function procedure presented in the previous section. That function uses a For-Next loop to examine each character in a string and builds a new string. A much simpler (and more efficient) version of that Function procedure uses the VBA Replace function. The following is a rewritten version of the Function procedure:

```
Function REMOVESPACES2(cell) As String
'   Removes all spaces from cell
    REMOVESPACES2 = Replace(cell, " ", "")
End Function
```

You can use many (but not all) of Excel's worksheet functions in your VBA code. To use a worksheet function in a VBA statement, just precede the function name with WorksheetFunction and a period.

The following code demonstrates how to use an Excel worksheet function in a VBA statement. The code snippet uses the ENCODEURL function to encode a URL:

```
URL = "http://spreadsheetpage.com"
Encoded = WorksheetFunction.ENCODEURL(URL)
```

For some reason, you can't use worksheet functions that have an equivalent VBA function. For example, VBA can't access Excel's SQRT worksheet function because VBA has its own version of that function: Sqr. Therefore, the following statement generates an error:

```
x = WorksheetFunction.SQRT(123)    'error
```

Controlling Execution

Some VBA procedures start at the top and progress line by line to the bottom. Often, however, you need to control the flow of your routines by skipping over some statements, executing some statements multiple times, and testing conditions to determine what the routine does next.

This section discusses several ways of controlling the execution of your VBA procedures:

- If-Then constructs
- Select Case constructs
- For-Next loops
- Do While loops
- Do Until loops
- On Error statements

The If-Then construct

Perhaps the most commonly used instruction grouping in VBA is the If-Then construct. This instruction is one way to endow your applications with decision-making capability. The basic syntax of the If-Then construct is as follows:

```
If condition Then true_instructions [Else false_instructions]
```

The If-Then construct executes one or more statements conditionally. The Else clause is optional. If included, it enables you to execute one or more instructions when the condition that you test is not true.

The following Function procedure demonstrates an If-Then structure without an Else clause. The example deals with time. VBA uses the same date-and-time serial number system as Excel (but with a much wider range of dates). The time of day is expressed as a fractional value—for example, noon is represented as .5. The VBA Time function returns a value that represents the time of day, as reported by the system clock. In the following example, the function starts out by assigning an empty string to GREETME. The If-Then statement checks the time of day. If the time is before noon, the Then part of the statement executes, and the function returns Good Morning:

```
Function GREETME()
    GREETME = ""
    If Time < 0.5 Then GREETME= "Good Morning"
End Function
```

The following function uses two If-Then statements. It displays either *Good Morning* or *Good Afternoon*:

```
Function GREETME()
    If Time < 0.5 Then GREETME = "Good Morning"
    If Time >= 0.5 Then GREETME = "Good Afternoon"
End Function
```

Notice that the second If-Then statement uses >= (greater than or equal to). This covers the extremely remote chance that the time is precisely 12:00 noon when the function is executed.

Another approach is to use the Else clause of the If-Then construct:

```
Function GREETME()
    If Time < 0.5 Then GREETME = "Good Morning" Else _
      GREETME = "Good Afternoon"
End Function
```

Notice that the preceding example uses the line continuation sequence (a space followed by an underscore); If-Then-Else is actually a single statement.

The following is another example that uses the If-Then construct. This Function procedure calculates a discount based on a quantity (assumed to be an integer value). It accepts one argument (quantity) and returns the appropriate discount based on that value:

```
Function DISCOUNT(quantity)
    If quantity <= 5 Then DISCOUNT = 0
    If quantity >= 6 Then DISCOUNT = 0.1
    If quantity >= 25 Then DISCOUNT = 0.15
    If quantity >= 50 Then DISCOUNT = 0.2
    If quantity >= 75 Then DISCOUNT = 0.25
End Function
```

Notice that each If-Then statement in this procedure is always executed, and the value for DISCOUNT can change as the function executes. The final value, however, is the desired value.

The preceding examples all used a single statement for the Then clause of the If-Then construct. However, you often need to execute multiple statements if a condition is *TRUE*. You can still use the If-Then construct, but you need to use an End If statement to signal the end of the statements that make up the Then clause. Here's an example that executes two statements if the If clause is *TRUE*:

```
If x > 0 Then
    y = 2
    z = 3
End If
```

You can also use multiple statements for an If-Then-Else construct. Here's an example that executes two statements if the If clause is *TRUE* and two other statements if the If clause is not *TRUE*:

```
If x > 0 Then
    y = 2
    z = 3
Else
   y = -2
   z = -3
End If
```

The Select Case construct

The Select Case construct is useful for choosing among three or more options. This construct also works with two options and is a good alternative to using If-Then-Else. The syntax for Select Case is as follows:

```
Select Case testexpression
    [Case expressionlist-n
        [instructions-n]]
    [Case Else
        [default_instructions]]
End Select
```

The following example of a Select Case construct shows another way to code the GREETME examples presented in the preceding section:

```
Function GREETME()
    Select Case Time
        Case Is < 0.5
            GREETME = "Good Morning"
        Case 0.5 To 0.75
            GREETME = "Good Afternoon"
        Case Else
            GREETME = "Good Evening"
    End Select
End Function
```

And here's a rewritten version of the DISCOUNT function from the previous section, this time using a Select Case construct:

```
Function DISCOUNT2(quantity)
    Select Case quantity
        Case Is <= 5
            DISCOUNT2 = 0
        Case 6 To 24
            DISCOUNT2 = 0.1
        Case 25 To 49
            DISCOUNT2 = 0.15
        Case 50 To 74
            DISCOUNT2 = 0.2
        Case Is >= 75
            DISCOUNT2 = 0.25
    End Select
End Function
```

Any number of instructions can be written below each Case statement; all execute if that case evaluates to *TRUE*.

Looping blocks of instructions

Looping is repeating a block of VBA instructions within a procedure. You may know the number of times to loop, or it may be determined by the values of variables in your program. VBA offers a number of looping constructs:

- For-Next loops
- Do While loops
- Do Until loops

For-Next loops

The following is the syntax for a For-Next loop:

```
For counter = start To end [Step stepval]
    [instructions]
    [Exit For]
    [instructions]
Next [counter]
```

The following listing is an example of a For-Next loop that does not use the optional Step value or the optional Exit For statement. This function accepts two arguments and returns the sum of all integers between (and including) the arguments:

```
Function SUMINTEGERS(first, last)
    total = 0
    For num = first To last
        total = total + num
    Next num
    SUMINTEGERS = total
End Function
```

The following formula, for example, returns *55*—the sum of all integers from 1 to 10:

```
=SUMINTEGERS(1,10)
```

In this example, num (the loop counter variable) starts out with the same value as the first variable and increases by 1 each time the loop repeats. The loop ends when num is equal to the last variable. The total variable simply accumulates the various values of num as it changes during the looping.

Warning

When you use For-Next loops, you should understand that the loop counter is a normal variable; it is not a special type of variable. As a result, you can change the value of the loop counter within the block of code executed between the For and Next statements. This is, however, a bad practice that can cause problems. In fact, you should take special precautions to ensure that your code does not change the loop counter.

You also can use a Step value to skip some values in the loop. Here's the same function rewritten to sum *every other* integer between the first and last arguments:

```
Function SUMINTEGERS2(first, last)
    total = 0
    For num = first To last Step 2
        total = total + num
    Next num
    SUMINTEGERS2 = Total
End Function
```

The following formula returns *25*, which is the sum of 1, 3, 5, 7, and 9:

```
=SUMINTEGERS2(1,10)
```

For-Next loops can also include one or more Exit For statements within the loop. When this statement is encountered, the loop terminates immediately, as the following example demonstrates:

```
Function ROWOFLARGEST(c)
    NumRows = Rows.Count
```

```
    MaxVal = WorksheetFunction.Max(Columns(c))
    For r = 1 To NumRows
        If Cells(r, c) = MaxVal Then
            ROWOFLARGEST = r
            Exit For
        End If
    Next r
End Function
```

The ROWOFLARGEST function accepts a column number (1–16,384) for its argument and returns the row number of the largest value in that column. It starts by getting a count of the number of rows in the worksheet. (This varies, depending on the version of Excel.) This number is assigned to the NumRows variable. The maximum value in the column is calculated by using the Excel MAX function, and this value is assigned to the MaxVal variable.

The For-Next loop checks each cell in the column. When the cell equal to MaxVal is found, the row number (variable r, the loop counter) is assigned to the function's name, and the Exit For statement ends the procedure. Without the Exit For statement, the loop continues to check all cells in the column, which can take quite a long time.

The previous examples use relatively simple loops. But you can have any number of statements in the loop, and you can even nest For-Next loops inside other For-Next loops. The following is VBA code that uses nested For-Next loops to initialize a 10 × 10 × 10 array with the value –1. When the three loops finish executing, each of the 1,000 elements in MyArray contains –1:

```
Dim MyArray(1 to 10, 1 to 10, 1 to 10)
For i = 1 To 10
    For j = 1 To 10
        For k = 1 To 10
            MyArray(i, j, k) = -1
        Next k
    Next j
Next i
```

Do While loops

A Do While loop is another type of looping structure available in VBA. Unlike a For-Next loop, a Do While loop executes while a specified condition is met. A Do While loop can have one of two syntaxes:

```
Do [While condition]
    [instructions]
    [Exit Do]
    [instructions]
Loop
```

or

```
Do
    [instructions]
    [Exit Do]
    [instructions]
Loop [While condition]
```

As you can see, VBA enables you to put the While condition at the beginning or the end of the loop. The difference between these two syntaxes involves the point in time when the condition is evaluated. In the first syntax, the contents of the loop may never be executed if the condition is met as soon as the Do statement is executed. In the second syntax, the contents of the loop are always executed at least one time.

The following example is the ROWOFLARGEST function presented in the previous section, rewritten to use a Do While loop (using the first syntax):

```
Function ROWOFLARGEST2(c)
    NumRows = Rows.Count
    MaxVal = Application.Max(Columns(c))
    r = 1
    Do While Cells(r, c) <> MaxVal
        r = r + 1
    Loop
    ROWOFLARGEST2 = r
End Function
```

The variable r starts out with a value of 1 and increments within the Do While loop. The looping continues as long as the cell being evaluated is not equal to MaxVal. When the cell is equal to MaxVal, the loop ends, and the function is assigned the value of r. Notice that if the maximum value is in row 1, the looping does not occur.

The following procedure uses the second Do While loop syntax. The loop always executes at least once:

```
Function ROWOFLARGEST(c)
    MaxVal = Application.Max(Columns(c))
    r = 0
    Do
        r = r + 1
    Loop While Cells(r, c) <> MaxVal
    ROWOFLARGEST = r
End Function
```

Do While loops can also contain one or more Exit Do statements. When an Exit Do statement is encountered, the loop ends immediately.

Do Until loops

The Do Until loop structure closely resembles the Do While structure. The difference is evident only when the condition is tested. In a Do While loop, the loop executes *while* the condition is

TRUE. In a Do Until loop, the loop executes *until* the condition is *TRUE*. Do Until also has two syntaxes:

```
Do [Until condition]
    [instructions]
    [Exit Do]
    [instructions]
Loop
```

or

```
Do
    [instructions]
    [Exit Do]
    [instructions]
Loop [Until condition]
```

The following example demonstrates the first syntax of the Do Until loop. This example makes the code a bit clearer because it avoids the negative comparison required in the Do While example:

```
Function ROWOFLARGEST4(c)
    NumRows = Rows.Count
    MaxVal = Application.Max(Columns(c))
    r = 1
    Do Until Cells(r, c) = MaxVal
        r = r + 1
    Loop
    ROWOFLARGEST4 = r
End Function
```

Finally, the following function is the same procedure but is rewritten to use the second syntax of the Do Until loop:

```
Function ROWOFLARGEST5(c)
    NumRows = Rows.Count
    MaxVal = Application.Max(Columns(c))
    r = 0
    Do
        r = r + 1
    Loop Until Cells(r, c) = MaxVal
    ROWOFLARGEST5 = r
End Function
```

Using Ranges

Most of the custom functions that you develop will work with the data contained in a cell or in a range of cells. Recognize that a range can be a single cell or a group of cells. This section describes some key concepts to make this task easier. The information in this section is intended to be practical rather than comprehensive. If you want more details, consult Excel's online help.

Cross-Ref

Chapter 26, "VBA Custom Function Examples," contains many practical examples of functions that use ranges. Studying those examples helps to clarify the information in this section.

The For Each-Next construct

Your Function procedures often need to loop through a range of cells. For example, you may write a function that accepts a range as an argument. Your code needs to examine each cell in the range and do something. The For Each-Next construct is useful for this sort of thing. The syntax of the For Each-Next construct follows:

```
For Each element In group
    [instructions]
    [Exit For]
    [instructions]
Next [element]
```

The following Function procedure accepts a range argument and returns the sum of the squared values in the range:

```
Function SUMOFSQUARES(rng as Range)
    Dim total as Double
    Dim cell as Range
    total = 0
    For Each cell In rng
        total = total + cell ^ 2
    Next cell
    SUMOFSQUARES = total
End Function
```

The following is a worksheet formula that uses the SUMOFSQUARES function:

```
=SUMOFSQUARES(A1:C100)
```

In this case, the function's argument is a range that consists of 300 cells.

Note

In the preceding example, both cell and rng are variable names. There's nothing special about either name; you can replace them with any valid variable name.

Referencing a range

VBA code can reference a range in a number of different ways:

- Using the Range property
- Using the Cells property
- Using the Offset property

The Range property

You can use the Range property to refer to a range directly by using a cell address or name. The following example assigns the value in cell A1 to a variable named Init. In this case, the statement accesses the range's Value property.

```
Init = Range("A1").Value
```

In addition to the Value property, VBA enables you to access a number of other properties of a range. For example, the following statement counts the number of cells in a range and assigns the value to the Cnt variable:

```
Cnt = Range("A1:C300").Count
```

The Range property is also useful for referencing a single cell in a multicell range. For example, you may create a function that is supposed to accept a single-cell argument. If the user specifies a multi-cell range as the argument, you can use the Range property to extract the upper-left cell in the range. The following example uses the Range property (with an argument of "A1") to return the value in the upper-left cell of the range represented by the cell argument:

```
Function SQUARE(cell as Range)
    CellValue = cell.Range("A1").Value
    SQUARE = CellValue ^ 2
End Function
```

Assume that the user enters the following formula:

```
=SQUARE(C5:C12)
```

The SQUARE function works with the upper-left cell in C5:C12 (which is C5) and returns the value squared.

Note

Many Excel worksheet functions work in this way. For example, if you specify a multicell range as the first argument for the LEFT function, Excel uses the upper-left cell in the range. However, Excel is not consistent. If you specify a multicell range as the argument for the SQRT function, Excel returns an error.

The Cells property

Another way to reference a range is to use the Cells property. The Cells property accepts two arguments (a row number and a column number) and returns a single cell. The following statement assigns the value in cell A1 to a variable named FirstCell:

```
FirstCell = Cells(1, 1).Value
```

The following statement returns the upper-left cell in the range C5:D12:

```
UpperLeft = Range("C5:D12").Cells(1,1).Value
```

Tip

If you use the Cells property without an argument, it returns a range that consists of all cells on the object of which it is a property. In the following example, the TotalCells variable contains the total number of cells in the worksheet:

```
TotalCells = Cells.Count
```

The following statement uses the Excel COUNTA function to determine the number of nonempty cells in the worksheet:

```
NonEmpty =WorksheetFunction.COUNTA(Cells)
```

The Offset property

The Offset property (like the Range and Cells properties) also returns a Range object. The Offset property is used in conjunction with a range. It takes two arguments that correspond to the relative position from the upper-left cell of the specified Range object. The arguments can be positive (down or right), negative (up or left), or zero. The following example returns the value one cell below cell A1 (that is, cell A2) and assigns it to a variable named NextCell:

```
NextCell = Range("A1").Offset(1,0).Value
```

The following Function procedure accepts a single-cell argument and returns the sum of the eight cells that surround it:

```
Function SUMSURROUNDINGCELLS(cell)
    Dim Total As Double
    Dim r As Long, c As Long
    Total = 0
    For r = -1 To 1
        For c = -1 To 1
            Total = Total + cell.Offset(r, c)
        Next c
    Next r
    SUMSURROUNDINGCELLS = Total - cell
End Function
```

This function uses a nested For-Next loop. So when the r loop counter is –1, the c loop counter goes from –1 to 1. Nine cells are summed, including the argument cell, which is Offset(0, 0). The final statement subtracts the value of the argument cell from the total. The function returns an error if the argument does not have eight surrounding cells (for example, if it's in row 1 or column 1).

To better understand how the nested loop works, following are nine statements that perform the same calculation:

```
Total = Total + cell.Offset(-1, -1) ' upper left
Total = Total + cell.Offset(-1, 0) 'left
Total = Total + cell.Offset(-1, 1) 'upper right
Total = Total + cell.Offset(0, -1) 'above
Total = Total + cell.Offset(0, 0) 'the cell itself
Total = Total + cell.Offset(0, 1) 'right
Total = Total + cell.Offset(1, -1) 'lower left
Total = Total + cell.Offset(1, 0) 'below
Total = Total + cell.Offset(1, 1) 'lower right
```

Some useful properties of ranges

Previous sections in this chapter gave you examples that used the Value property for a range. VBA gives you access to many additional range properties. Some of the more useful properties for function writers are briefly described in the following sections. For complete information on a particular property, refer to the VBA help system.

The Formula property

The Formula property returns the formula (as a string) contained in a cell. If you try to access the Formula property for a range that consists of more than one cell, you get an error. If the cell does not have a formula, this property returns a string, which is the cell's value as it appears in the Formula bar. The following function simply displays the formula for the upper-left cell in a range:

```
Function CELLFORMULA(cell)
    CELLFORMULA = cell.Range("A1").Formula
End Function
```

You can use the HasFormula property to determine whether a cell has a formula.

The Address Property

The Address property returns the address of a range as a string. By default, it returns the address as an absolute reference (for example, $A$1:$C$12). The following function, which is not all that useful, returns the address of a range:

```
Function RANGEADDRESS(rng)
    RANGEADDRESS = rng.Address
End Function
```

For example, the following formula returns the string $A$1:$C$3:

```
=RANGEADDRESS(A1:C3)
```

The formula that follows returns the address of a range named MyRange:

```
=RANGEADDRESS(MyRange)
```

The Count property

The Count property returns the number of cells in a range. The following function uses the Count property:

```
Function CELLCOUNT(rng)
    CELLCOUNT = rng.Count
End Function
```

The following formula returns *9:*

```
=CELLCOUNT(A1:C3)
```

Warning

The Count property of a Range object is not the same as the COUNT worksheet function. The Count property returns the number of cells in the range, including empty cells and cells with any kind of data. The COUNT worksheet function returns the number of cells in the range that contain numeric data.

The CountLarge property

Excel 2007 and later worksheets contain more than 17 billion cells compared with a mere 17 million in previous versions. Because of this dramatic increase, the Count property—which returns a *Long*—may return an error if there are more than 2,147,483,647 cells to be counted. You can use the CountLarge property instead of Count to be safe, but beware that CountLarge does not work in older versions of Excel. In the CELLCOUNT function, the following statement handles any size range (including all cells on a worksheet):

```
CELLCOUNT = rng.CountLarge
```

The Parent property

The Parent property returns an object that corresponds to an object's *container* object. For a Range object, the Parent property returns a Worksheet object (the worksheet that contains the range).

The following function uses the Parent property and returns the name of the worksheet of the range passed as an argument:

```
Function SHEETNAME(rng)
    SHEETNAME = rng.Parent.Name
End Function
```

The following formula, for example, returns the string Sheet1:

```
=SHEETNAME(Sheet1!A16)
```

The Name property

The Name property returns a Name object for a cell or range. To get the actual cell or range name, you need to access the Name property of the Name object. If the cell or range does not have a name, the Name property returns an error.

The following Function procedure displays the name of a range or cell passed as its argument. If the range or cell does not have a name, the function returns an empty string. Note the use of On Error Resume Next. This handles situations in which the range does not have a name:

```
Function RANGENAME(rng)
    On Error Resume Next
    RANGENAME = rng.Name.Name
    If Err.Number <> 0 Then RANGENAME = ""
End Function
```

The NumberFormat property

The NumberFormat property returns the number format (as a string) assigned to a cell or range. The following function simply returns the number format for the upper-left cell in a range:

```
Function NUMBERFORMAT(cell)
    NUMBERFORMAT = cell.Range("A1").NumberFormat
End Function
```

The Font property

The Font property returns a Font object for a range or cell. To actually do anything with this Font object, you need to access its properties. For example, a Font object has properties such as Bold, Italic, Name, Color, and so on. The following function returns *TRUE* if the upper-left cell of its argument is formatted as bold:

```
Function ISBOLD(cell)
    ISBOLD = cell.Range("A1").Font.Bold
End Function
```

The EntireRow and EntireColumn properties

The EntireRow and EntireColumn properties enable you to work with an entire row or column for a particular cell. The following function accepts a single cell argument and then uses the EntireColumn property to get a range consisting of the cell's entire column. It then uses the Excel COUNTA function to return the number of nonempty cells in the column:

```
Function NONEMPTYCELLSINCOLUMN(cell)
    NONEMPTYCELLSINCOLUMN = WorksheetFunction.CountA(cell.EntireColumn)
End Function
```

You cannot use this function in a formula that's in the same column as the cell argument. Doing so generates a circular reference.

The Hidden property

The Hidden property is used with rows or columns. It returns *TRUE* if the row or column is hidden. If you try to access this property for a range that does not consist of an entire row or column, you get an error. The following function accepts a single cell argument and returns *TRUE* if either the cell's row or the cell's column is hidden:

```
Function CELLISHIDDEN(cell)
    If cell.EntireRow.Hidden Or cell.EntireColumn.Hidden Then
        CELLISHIDDEN = True
    Else
        CELLISHIDDEN = False
    End If
End Function
```

You can also write this function without using an If-Then-Else construct. In the following function, the expression to the right of the equal sign returns either *TRUE* or *FALSE*—and this value is returned by the function:

```
Function CELLISHIDDEN(cell)
    CELLISHIDDEN = cell.EntireRow.Hidden Or cell.EntireColumn.Hidden
End Function
```

The Set keyword

An important concept in VBA is the ability to create a new Range object and assign it to a variable—more specifically, an *object variable*. You do so by using the Set keyword. The following statement creates an object variable named MyRange:

```
Set MyRange = Range("A1:A10")
```

After the statement executes, you can use the MyRange variable in your code in place of the actual range reference. Examples in subsequent sections help to clarify this concept.

Note

Creating a Range object is not the same as creating a named range. In other words, you can't use the name of a Range object in your worksheet formulas.

The Intersect function

The Intersect function returns a range that consists of the intersection of two other ranges. For example, consider the two ranges selected in Figure 24-2. These ranges, D3:D5 and B5:E5, contain one cell in common (D5). In other words, D5 is the intersection of D3:D5 and B5:E5.

	A	B	C	D	E
1					
2		NORTH	SOUTH	EAST	WEST
3		SOUT	15	13	61
4		EAST	26	2	15
5		WEST	25	18	89
6					

Figure 24-2: The intersection of two ranges.

The following Function procedure accepts two range arguments and returns the count of the number of cells that the ranges have in common:

```
Function CELLSINCOMMON(rng1, rng2)
    Dim CommonCells As Range
    On Error Resume Next
    Set CommonCells = Intersect(rng1, rng2)
```

```
    If Err.Number = 0 Then
        CELLSINCOMMON = CommonCells.CountLarge
    Else
        CELLSINCOMMON = 0
    End If
End Function
```

The CELLSINCOMMON function uses the Intersect function to create a range object named CommonCells. Note the use of On Error Resume Next. This statement is necessary because the Intersect function returns an error if the ranges have no cells in common. If the error occurs, it is ignored. The final statement checks the Number property of the Err object. If it is 0, no error occurs, and the function returns the value of the CountLarge property for the CommonCells object. If an error does occur, Err.Number has a value other than 0, and the function returns 0.

The Union function

The Union function combines two or more ranges into a single range. The following statement uses the Union function to create a range object that consists of the first and third columns of a worksheet:

```
Set TwoCols = Union(Range("A:A"), Range("C:C"))
```

The Union function takes between 2 and 30 arguments.

The UsedRange property

The UsedRange property returns a Range object that represents the used range of the worksheet. Press Ctrl+End to activate the lower-right cell of the used range. The UsedRange property can be *very useful* in making your functions more efficient.

Consider the following Function procedure. This function accepts a range argument and returns the number of formula cells in the range:

```
Function FORMULACOUNT(rng)
    cnt = 0
    For Each cell In rng
        If cell.HasFormula Then cnt = cnt + 1
    Next cell
    FORMULACOUNT = cnt
End Function
```

In many cases, the preceding function works just fine. But what if the user enters a formula like this one?

```
=FORMULACOUNT(A:C)
```

The three-column argument consists of 3,145,728 cells. With an argument that consists of one or more entire columns, the function does not work well because it loops through every cell in the range, even those that are well beyond the area of the sheet that's actually used. The following function is rewritten to make it more efficient:

```
Function FORMULACOUNT(rng)
    cnt = 0
    Set WorkRange = Intersect(rng, rng.Parent.UsedRange)
    If WorkRange Is Nothing Then
        FORMULACOUNT = 0
        Exit Function
    End If
    For Each cell In WorkRange
        If cell.HasFormula Then cnt = cnt + 1
    Next cell
    FORMULACOUNT = cnt
End Function
```

This function creates a Range object variable named WorkRange that consists of the intersection of the range passed as an argument and the used range of the worksheet. In other words, WorkRange consists of a subset of the range argument that only includes cells in the used range of the worksheet. Note the If-Then construct that checks if the WorkRange is Nothing. That will be the case if the argument for the function is outside the used range. In such a case, the function returns *0*, and execution ends.

25

Function Procedure Basics

In This Chapter

- Why you may want to create custom functions
- An introductory VBA function example
- About VBA Function procedures
- Using the Insert Function dialog box to add a function description and assign a function category
- Tips for testing and debugging functions
- Creating an add-in to hold your custom functions

Previous chapters in this book examined Excel's built-in worksheet functions and how you can use them to build more complex formulas. These functions provide a great deal of flexibility when creating formulas. However, you may encounter situations that call for custom functions. This chapter discusses why you may want to use custom functions, how you can create VBA Function procedures, and methods for testing and debugging them.

Why Create Custom Functions?

You are, of course, familiar with Excel's worksheet functions. Even novices know how to use the most common worksheet functions, such as SUM, AVERAGE, and IF. Excel 2016 includes more than 450 predefined worksheet functions—everything from ABS to ZTEST.

You can use VBA to create additional worksheet functions, which are known as *custom functions* or *user-defined functions* (UDFs). With all the functions that are available in Excel and VBA, you may wonder why you would ever need to create new functions. The answer: to simplify your work and give your formulas more power.

For example, you can create a custom function that can significantly shorten your formulas. Shorter formulas are more readable and easier to work with. However, it's important to understand that custom functions in your formulas are usually much slower than built-in functions. On a fast system, though, the speed difference often goes unnoticed.

The process of creating a custom function is not difficult. In fact, many people (these authors included) *enjoy* creating custom functions. This book provides you with the information that you need to create your own functions. In this and the next chapter, you'll find many custom function examples that you can adapt for your own use.

An Introductory VBA Function Example

Without further ado, we'll show you a simple VBA Function procedure. This function, named USER, does not accept arguments. When used in a worksheet formula, this function simply displays the user's name in uppercase characters. To create this function, follow these steps:

1. Start with a new workbook.

   This is not really necessary, but keep it simple for right now.

2. Press Alt+F11 to activate the VB Editor.
3. Click your workbook's name in the Project window.

   If the Project window is not visible, press Ctrl+R to display it.

4. Choose Insert ➜ Module to add a VBA module to the project.
5. Type the following code into the code window:

```
Function USER()
'   Returns the user's name
    USER = Application.UserName
    USER = UCase(USER)
End Function
```

Figure 25-1 shows how the function looks in a code window.

```
Function USER()
'   Returns the user's name
    USER = Application.UserName
    USER = UCase(USER)
End Function
```

Figure 25-1: A simple VBA function displayed in a code window.

To try out the USER function, activate Excel (press Alt+F11) and enter the following formula into any cell in the workbook:

```
=USER()
```

If you entered the VBA code correctly, the Function procedure executes, and your name displays (in uppercase characters) in the cell.

Note

If your formula returns an error, make sure that the VBA code for the USER function is in a VBA module (and not in a module for a Sheet or ThisWorkbook object). Also, make sure that the module is in the project associated with the workbook that contains the formula.

When Excel calculates your worksheet, it encounters the USER custom function and then goes to work following the instructions. Each instruction in the function is evaluated, and the result is returned to your worksheet. You can use this function any number of times in any number of cells.

This custom function works just like any other worksheet function. You can insert it into a formula by using the Insert Function dialog box. It also appears in the Formula AutoComplete drop-down list as you type it in a cell. In the Insert Function dialog box, custom functions appear (by default) in the User Defined category. As with any other function, you can use it in a more complex formula. For example, try this:

```
="Hello "&USER()
```

Or use this formula to display the number of characters in your name:

```
=LEN(USER())
```

If you don't like the fact that your name is in uppercase, edit the procedure as follows:

```
Function USER()
'   Returns the user's name
    USER = Application.UserName
End Function
```

After editing the function, reactivate Excel and press F9 to recalculate. Any cell that uses the USER function displays a different result.

What custom worksheet functions can't do

As you develop custom worksheet functions, you should understand a key point. A Function procedure used in a worksheet formula must be *passive*; in other words, it can't change things in the worksheet.

continued

continued

You may be tempted to try to write a custom worksheet function that changes the formatting of a cell. For example, you may want to edit the USER function (presented in this section) so that the name displays in a different color. Try as you might, a function such as this is impossible to write—everybody tries this, and no one succeeds. No matter what you do, the function always returns an error because the code attempts to change something on the worksheet. Remember that a function can return only a value. It can't perform actions with objects.

None of Excel's built-in functions are able to change a worksheet, so it makes sense that custom VBA functions cannot change a worksheet.

About Function Procedures

In this section, we discuss some of the technical details that apply to Function procedures. These are general guidelines for declaring functions, naming functions, using custom functions in formulas, and using arguments in custom functions.

Declaring a function

The official syntax for declaring a function is as follows:

```
[Public | Private][Static] Function name ([arglist]) [As type]
    [statements]
    [name = expression]
    [Exit Function]
    [statements]
    [name = expression]
End Function
```

The following list describes the elements in a Function procedure declaration:

- **Public:** Indicates that the function is accessible to all other procedures in all other modules in the workbook (optional).
- **Private:** Indicates that the function is accessible only to other procedures in the same module (optional). If you use the Private keyword, your functions don't appear in the Insert Function dialog box and are not shown in the Formula AutoComplete drop-down list.
- **Static:** Indicates that the values of variables declared in the function are preserved between calls (optional).
- **Function:** Indicates the beginning of a Function procedure (required).
- **Name:** Can be any valid variable name. When the function finishes, the result of the function is the value assigned to the function's name (required).

- **Arglist:** A list of one or more variables that represent arguments passed to the function. The arguments are enclosed in parentheses. Use a comma to separate arguments. (Arguments are optional.)
- **Type:** The data type returned by the function (optional).
- **Statements:** Valid VBA statements (optional).
- **Exit Function:** A statement that causes an immediate exit from the function (optional).
- **End Function:** A keyword that indicates the end of the function (required).

Choosing a name for your function

Each function must have a unique name, and function names must adhere to a few rules:

- **You can use alphabetic characters, numbers, and some punctuation characters.** However, the first character must be alphabetic.
- **You can use any combination of uppercase and lowercase letters.** VBA does not distinguish between cases. To make a function name more readable, you can use InterestRate rather than interestrate.
- **You can't use a name that looks like a worksheet cell's address** (such as J21 or SUM100). Actually, Excel allows you to use such a name for a function, but a worksheet formula calling the function returns a *#REF!* error.
- **You can't use spaces or periods.** Many of Excel's built-in functions include a period character, but that character is not allowed in VBA function names. To make function names more readable, you can use the underscore character (Interest_Rate).
- **You can't embed the following characters in a function's name:** #, $, %, &, or !. These are type declaration characters that have a special meaning in VBA.
- **You can use a function name with as many as 255 characters.** However, shorter names are usually more readable and easier to work with.

UPPERCASE function names?

You've probably noticed that Excel's built-in worksheet function names always use uppercase characters. Even if you enter a function using lowercase characters, Excel converts it to uppercase.

When you create custom worksheet functions, you can use uppercase, lowercase, or mixed case. It doesn't matter. When we create functions that are intended to be used in worksheet formulas, we like to make them uppercase to match Excel's style.

Sometimes, however, when we enter a formula that uses a custom function, Excel does not match the case that we used in the VBA code. For instance, assume you have a function named MYFUNC,

continued

and its function declaration uses uppercase for the name. When you type the function into a formula, though, Excel does *not* display it in uppercase. Here's how to fix it.

In Excel, choose Formulas ➜ Defined Names ➜ Define Name and create a name called MYFUNC (in uppercase letters). It doesn't matter what the name refers to.

Creating that name causes all formulas that use the MYFUNC function to display an error. That's to be expected. But you'll notice that the formula now displays MYFUNC in uppercase characters.

The final step: choose Formulas ➜ Defined Names ➜ Name Manager and *delete* the MYFUNC name. The formulas no longer display an error—and they retain the uppercase letters for the function name.

Using functions in formulas

Using a custom VBA function in a worksheet formula is like using a built-in worksheet function. However, you must ensure that Excel can locate the Function procedure. If the Function procedure is in the same workbook as the formula, you don't have to do anything special. If it's in a different workbook, you may have to tell Excel where to find it. You can do so in three ways:

- **Precede the function's name with a file reference.** For example, if you want to use a function called `CountNames` that's defined in a workbook named `Myfuncs.xlsm`, you can use a formula like the following:

  ```
  =MyFuncs.xlsm!CountNames(A1:A1000)
  ```

  If you insert the function with the Insert Function dialog box, the workbook reference is inserted automatically.

- **Set up a reference to the workbook.** You do this with the VB Editor's Tools ➜ References command (see Figure 25-2). If the function is defined in a referenced workbook, you don't need to use the worksheet name. Even when the dependent workbook is assigned as a reference, the Insert Function dialog box continues to insert the workbook reference (even though it's not necessary). Note that the referenced workbook must be open in order to use the functions defined in it.

- Function names in a referenced workbook do not appear in the Formula AutoComplete drop-down list. Formula AutoComplete works only when the formula is entered into the workbook that contains the custom function or when it is contained in an installed add-in.

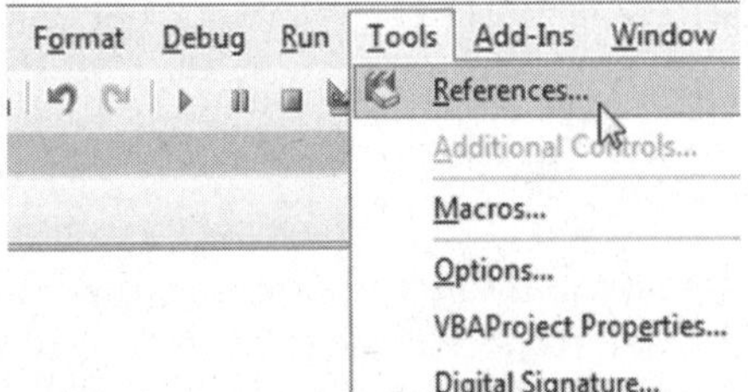

Figure 25-2: Use the References dialog box to create a reference to a project that contains a custom VBA function.

Notes

By default, all projects are named VBAProject—and that's the name that appears in the Available References list in the References dialog box. To make sure that you select the correct project in the References dialog box, keep your eye on the bottom of the dialog box, which shows the pathname and filename for the selected item. Better yet, change the name of the project to be more descriptive. To change the name, select the project, press F4 to display the Properties window, and then change the Name property to something other than VBAProject. Use a unique name because Excel does not let you create two references with the same name.

- **Create an add-in.** When you create an add-in from a workbook that has Function procedures, you don't need to use the file reference when you use one of the functions in a formula; however, the add-in must be installed. We discuss add-ins later in this chapter (see the "Creating Add-Ins for Functions" section).

Using function arguments

Custom functions, like Excel's built-in functions, vary in their use of arguments. Keep the following points in mind regarding VBA Function procedure arguments:

- A function can have no argument.
- A function can have a fixed number of required arguments (from 1 to 60).
- A function can have a combination of required and optional arguments.
- A function can have a special optional argument called a ParamArray, which allows a function to have an indefinite number of arguments.

Cross-Ref

See Chapter 26, "VBA Custom Function Examples," for examples of functions that use various types of arguments.

All cells and ranges that a function uses should be passed as arguments. In other words, a Function procedure should never contain direct references to cells or ranges.

Using the Insert Function Dialog Box

Excel's Insert Function dialog box is a handy tool that enables you to choose a particular worksheet function from a list of available functions. The Insert Function dialog box also displays a list of your custom worksheet functions and prompts you for the function's arguments.

Note

Custom Function procedures defined with the Private keyword don't appear in the Insert Function dialog box. Declaring a function as Private is useful if you create functions that are intended to be used by other VBA procedures in the same module rather than in a formula.

By default, custom functions are listed under the User Defined category, but you can have them appear under a different category. You also can add some text that describes the function.

Adding a function description

When you select one of Excel's built-in functions in the Insert Function dialog box, a brief description of the function appears (see Figure 25-3). You may want to provide such a description for the custom functions that you create.

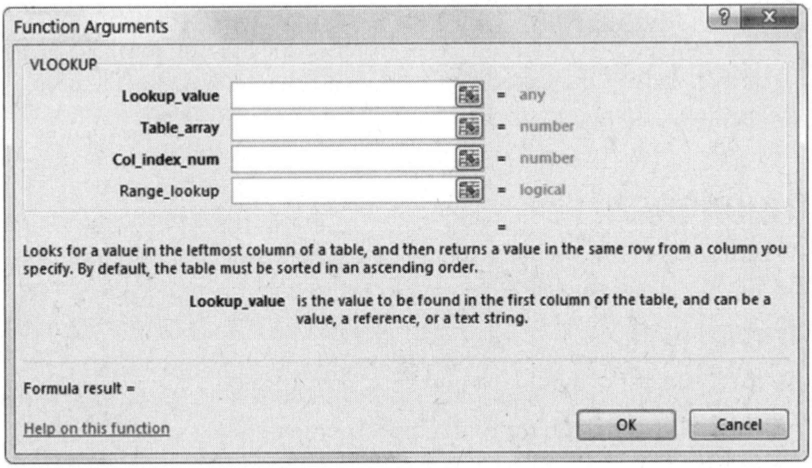

Figure 25-3: Excel's Insert Function dialog box displays a brief description of the selected function.

Note

If you don't provide a description for your custom function, the Insert Function dialog box displays the following text: No help available.

Here's a simple custom function that returns its argument, but with no spaces:

```
Function REMOVESPACES(txt)
   REMOVESPACES = Replace(txt, " ", "")
End Function
```

The following steps describe how to provide a description for a custom function:

1. Create your function in the VB Editor.
2. Activate Excel and choose Developer ➜ Code ➜ Macros (or press Alt+F8).

   The Macro dialog box lists available Sub procedures but not functions.
3. Type the name of your function in the Macro Name box.

   Make sure that you spell it correctly.

4. Click the Options button to display the Macro Options dialog box.

   If the Options button is not enabled, you probably spelled the function's name incorrectly.

5. Type the function description in the Description field (see Figure 25-4).

   The Shortcut key field is irrelevant for functions.

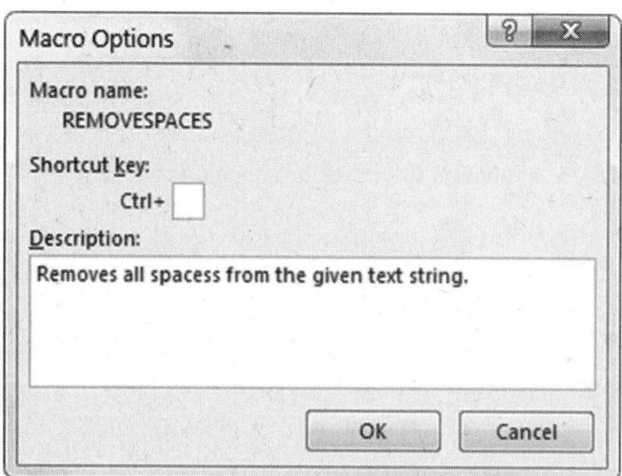

Figure 25-4: Provide a function description in the Macro Options dialog box.

6. Click OK and then click Cancel.

Specifying a function category

Oddly, Excel does not provide a direct way to assign a custom function to a particular function category. If you want your custom function to appear in a function category other than User Defined, you need to execute some VBA code. Assigning a function to a category also causes it to appear in the drop-down controls in the Formulas ➜ Function Library group.

For example, assume that you created a custom function named REMOVESPACES, and you'd like this function to appear in the Text category (that is, Category 7) in the Insert Function dialog box. To accomplish this, you need to execute the following VBA statement:

```
Application.MacroOptions Macro:="REMOVESPACES", Category:=7
```

One way to execute this statement is to use the Immediate window in the VB Editor. If the Immediate window is not visible, choose View ➜ Immediate Window (or press Ctrl+G). Figure 25-5 shows an example. Just type the statement and press Enter. Then save the workbook, and the category assignment is also stored in the workbook. Therefore, this statement needs to be executed only one time. In other words, it is not necessary to assign the function to a new category every time the workbook is opened.

```
Function REMOVESPACES(txt)
    REMOVESPACES = Replace(txt, " ", "")
End Function
```

```
Immediate
Application.MacroOptions Macro:="REMOVESPACES", Category:=7
```

Figure 25-5: Executing a VBA statement that assigns a function to a particular function category.

Alternatively, you can create a Sub procedure and then execute the procedure.

```
Sub AssignToFunctionCategory()
    Application.MacroOptions Macro:="REMOVESPACES", Category:=7
End Sub
```

After you execute the procedure, you can delete it. A function can be assigned to only one category. The last category assignment replaces the previous category assignment (if any).

You will, of course, substitute the actual name of your function, and you can specify a different function category. The AssignToFunctionCategory procedure can contain any number of statements—one for each of your functions.

Table 25-1 lists the function category numbers that you can use. Notice that a few of these categories (10–13) normally don't display in the Insert Function dialog box. If you assign your function to one of these categories, the category appears.

Table 25-1: Function Categories

Category Number	Category Name
0	All (no specific category)
1	Financial
2	Date & Time
3	Math & Trig
4	Statistical
5	Lookup & Reference
6	Database
7	Text
8	Logical
9	Information

Category Number	Category Name
10	Commands
11	Customizing
12	Macro Control
13	DDE/External
14	User Defined
15	Engineering
16	Cube
17	Compatibility*
18	Web**

**The Compatibility category was introduced in Excel 2010.*
***The Web category was introduced in Excel 2013.*

You can also create custom function categories. The statement that follows creates a new function category named My VBA Functions and assigns the REMOVESPACES function to this category:

```
Application.MacroOptions Macro:="REMOVESPACES", Category:="My VBA Functions"
```

Adding argument descriptions

When you use the Insert Function dialog box to enter a function, the Function Arguments dialog box displays after you click OK. For built-in functions, the Function Arguments dialog box displays a description for each of the function's arguments.

In Chapter 26, we present a function named EXTRACTELEMENT:

```
Function EXTRACTELEMENT(Txt, n, Separator) As String
'   Returns the nth element of a text string, where the
'   elements are separated by a specified separator character
    Dim AllElements As Variant
    AllElements = Split(Txt, Separator)
    EXTRACTELEMENT = AllElements(n - 1)
End Function
```

This function returns an element from a delimited text string and uses three arguments. For example, the following formula returns the string *fghi* (the third element in the string, which uses a dash to separate the elements):

```
=EXTRACTELEMENT("ab-cde-fghi-jkl", 3, "-")
```

Following is a VBA Sub procedure that adds argument descriptions, which appear in the Function Arguments dialog box:

```
Sub DescribeFunction()
  Dim desc(1 To 3) As String
  desc(1) = "The delimited text string"
  desc(2) = "The number of the element to extract"
  desc(3) = "The delimiter character"
  Application.MacroOptions Macro:="EXTRACTELEMENT",
  ArgumentDescriptions:=desc
End Sub
```

The argument descriptions are stored in an array, and that array is used as the ArgumentDescriptions argument for the MacroOptions method. You need to run this procedure only one time. After doing so, the argument descriptions are stored in the workbook.

Testing and Debugging Your Functions

Naturally, testing and debugging your custom function is an important step that you must take to ensure that it carries out the calculation you intend. This section describes some debugging techniques you may find helpful.

Note

If you're new to programming, the information in this section will make a lot more sense after you're familiar with the material in Chapter 24, "VBA Programming Concepts."

VBA code that you write can contain three general types of errors:

- **Syntax errors:** An error in writing the statement—for example, a misspelled keyword, a missing operator, or mismatched parentheses. The VB Editor lets you know about syntax errors by displaying a pop-up error box. You can't use the function until you correct all syntax errors.
- **Runtime errors:** Errors that occur as the function executes. For example, attempting to perform a mathematical operation on a string variable generates a runtime error. Unless you spot it beforehand, you won't be aware of a runtime error until it occurs.
- **Logical errors:** Code that runs but simply returns the wrong result.

Tip

To force the code in a VBA module to be checked for syntax errors, choose Debug ➜ Compile *xxx* (where *xxx* is the name of your project). Executing this command highlights the first syntax error, if any exists. Correct the error and issue the command again until you find all the errors.

An error in code is sometimes called a *bug*. Locating and correcting such an error is called *debugging*.

When you test a Function procedure by using a formula in a worksheet, you may have a hard time locating runtime errors because (unlike syntax errors) they don't appear in a pop-up error box. If a runtime error occurs, the formula that uses the function simply returns an error value *(#VALUE!)*. This section describes several approaches to debugging custom functions.

Tip

While you're testing and debugging a custom function, it's a good idea to use the function in only one formula in the worksheet. If you use the function in more than one formula, the code is executed for each formula, which quickly becomes annoying!

Using the VBA MsgBox statement

The MsgBox statement, when used in your VBA code, displays a pop-up dialog box. You can use MsgBox statements at strategic locations within your code to monitor the value of specific variables. The following example is a Function procedure that should reverse a text string passed as its argument. For example, passing Hello as the argument should return olleH. If you try to use this function in a formula, however, you see that it does not work—it contains a logical error:

```
Function REVERSETEXT(text) As String
'   Returns its argument, reversed
    Dim TextLen As Long, i As Long
    TextLen = Len(text)
    For i = TextLen To 1 Step -1
        REVERSETEXT = Mid(text, i, 1) & REVERSETEXT
    Next i
End Function
```

You can insert a temporary MsgBox statement to help you figure out the source of the problem. Here's the function again, with the MsgBox statement inserted within the loop:

```
Function REVERSETEXT(text) As String
'   Returns its argument, reversed
    Dim TextLen As Long, i As Long
    TextLen = Len(text)
    For i = TextLen To 1 Step -1
        REVERSETEXT = Mid(text, i, 1) & REVERSETEXT
        MsgBox REVERSETEXT
    Next i
End Function
```

When this function is evaluated, a pop-up message box appears, once for each time through the loop. The message box shows the current value of REVERSETEXT. In other words, this technique enables you to monitor the results as the function is executed. Figure 25-6 shows an example.

Four Score and Seven Years Ago

Figure 25-6: Use a MsgBox statement to monitor the value of a variable as a Function procedure executes.

The information displayed in the series of message boxes shows that the text string is being built within the loop, but the new text is being added to the beginning of the string, not the end. The corrected assignment statement is

```
REVERSETEXT = REVERSETEXT & Mid(text, i, 1)
```

When the function is working properly, make sure that you remove all the MsgBox statements.

Tip

If you get tired of seeing the message boxes, you can halt the code by pressing Ctrl+Break. Then respond to the dialog box that's presented. Clicking the End button stops the code. Clicking the Debug button enters Debug mode, in which you can step through the code line by line.

To display more than one variable in a message box, you need to concatenate the variables and insert a space character between each variable. The following statement, for example, displays the value of three variables (x, y, and z) in a message box:

```
MsgBox x & " " & y & " " & z
```

If you omit the blank space, you can't distinguish the separate values.

Alternatively, you can separate the variable with vbNewLine, which is a constant that inserts a line break. When you execute the following statement, x, y, and z each appear on a separate line in the message box:

```
MsgBox x & vbNewLine & y & vbNewLine & z
```

Using Debug.Print statements in your code

If you find that using MsgBox statements is too intrusive, another option is to insert some temporary code that writes values directly to the VB Editor Immediate window. (See the sidebar "Using the Immediate window" later in this chapter.) You use the Debug.Print statement to write the values of selected variables.

For example, if you want to monitor a value inside a loop, use a routine like the following:

```
Function VOWELCOUNT(r)
    Dim Count As Long, Ch As String
    Dim i As Long
    Count = 0
    For i = 1 To Len(r)
        Ch = UCase(Mid(r, i, 1))
        If Ch Like "[AEIOU]" Then
           Count = Count + 1
            Debug.Print Ch, i
        End If
    Next i
    VOWELCOUNT = Count
End Function
```

In this case, the value of two variables (Ch and i) prints to the Immediate window whenever the Debug.Print statement is encountered. Figure 25-7 shows the result when the function has an argument of North Carolina.

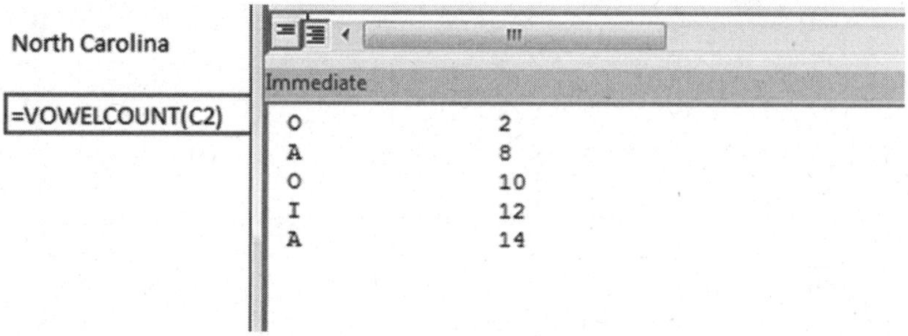

North Carolina

=VOWELCOUNT(C2)

Immediate

```
O    2
A    8
O    10
I    12
A    14
```

Figure 25-7: Using the VB Editor Immediate window to display results while a function is running.

When your function is debugged, make sure that you remove the Debug.Print statements.

Calling the function from a Sub procedure

Another way to test a Function procedure is to call the function from a Sub procedure. To do this, simply add a temporary Sub procedure to the module and insert a statement that calls your function. This is particularly useful because runtime errors display as they occur.

The following Function procedure contains a runtime error. As we noted previously, the runtime errors don't display when you are testing a function by using a worksheet formula. Rather, the function simply returns an error (*#VALUE!*):

```
Function REVERSETEXT(text) As String
'   Returns its argument, reversed
    Dim TextLen As Long, i As Long
    TextLen = Len(text)
    For i = TextLen To 1 Step -1
        REVERSETEXT = REVERSETEXT And Mid(text, i, 1)
    Next i
End Function
```

To help identify the source of the runtime error, insert the following Sub procedure:

```
Sub Test()
    x = REVERSETEXT("Hello")
    MsgBox x
End Sub
```

This Sub procedure simply calls the REVERSETEXT function and assigns the result to a variable named x. The MsgBox statement displays the result.

You can execute the Sub procedure directly from the VB Editor. Simply move the cursor anywhere within the procedure and choose Run ➜ Run Sub/UserForm (or just press F5). When you execute the Test procedure, you see the error message that is shown in Figure 25-8.

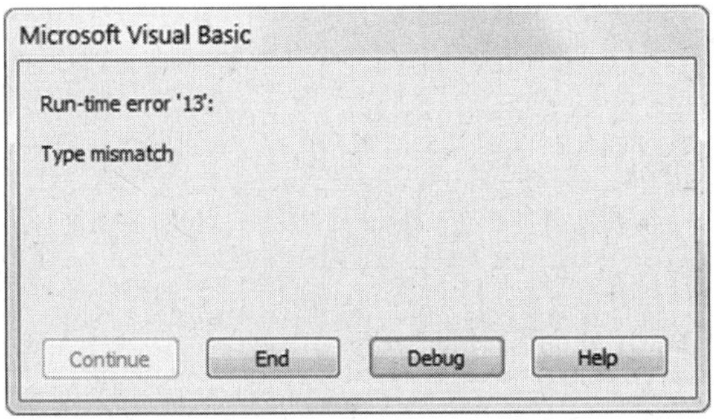

Figure 25-8: A runtime error identified by VBA.

Click the Debug button, and the VB Editor highlights the statement causing the problem (see Figure 25-9). The error message does not tell you how to correct the error, but it does narrow your choices. After you identify the statement that's causing the error, you can examine it more closely, or you can use the Immediate window. See the sidebar "Using the Immediate window" to help locate the exact problem.

```
Function REVERSETEXT(text) As String
'   Returns its argument, reversed
    Dim TextLen As Long, i As Long
    TextLen = Len(text)
    For i = TextLen To 1 Step -1
        REVERSETEXT = REVERSETEXT And Mid(text, i, 1)
    Next i
End Function
```

Figure 25-9: The highlighted statement generated a runtime error.

In this case, the problem is the use of the And operator instead of the concatenation operator (&). The correct statement is as follows:

```
REVERSETEXT = REVERSETEXT & Mid(text, i, 1)
```

Note

When you click the Debug button, the procedure is still running—it's just halted and is in break mode. After you make the correction, press F5 to continue execution, press F8 to continue execution on a line-by-line basis, or click the Reset button (on the Standard toolbar) to halt execution.

Using the Immediate window

The VB Editor Immediate window can be helpful when debugging code. To activate the Immediate window, choose View ➜ Immediate Window (or press Ctrl+G).

You can type VBA statements in the Immediate window and see the result immediately. For example, type the following code in the Immediate window and press Enter:

```
Print Sqr(1156)
```

The VB Editor prints the result of this square root operation (*34*). To save a few keystrokes, you can use a single question mark (?) in place of the Print keyword.

The Immediate window is particularly useful for debugging runtime errors when VBA is in break mode. For example, you can use the Immediate window to check the current value for variables or to check the data type of a variable.

Errors often occur because data is of the wrong type. The following statement, for example, displays the data type of a variable named Counter (which you probably think is an Integer or a Long variable):

```
? TypeName(Counter)
```

If you discover that Counter is of a data type other than Integer or Long, you may have solved your problem.

continued

continued

You can execute multiple statements in the Immediate window if you separate them with a colon. This line contains three statements:

```
x=12: y=13 : ? x+y
```

Most, but not all, statements can be executed in this way.

Setting a breakpoint in the function

Another debugging technique is to set a breakpoint in your code. Execution pauses when VBA encounters a breakpoint. You can then use the Immediate window to check the values of your variables, or you can use F8 to step through your code line by line.

To set a breakpoint, move the cursor to the statement at which you want to pause execution and choose Debug ➜ Toggle Breakpoint. Alternatively, you can press F9 or click the vertical bar to the left of the code window. Any of these actions highlights the statement to remind you that a breakpoint is in effect. (You also see a dot in the code window margin.) You can set any number of breakpoints in your code. To remove a breakpoint, move the cursor to the statement and press F9. Figure 25-10 shows a Function procedure that contains a breakpoint.

```
Function VOWELCOUNT(r)
    Dim Count As Long, Ch As String
    Dim i As Long
    Count = 0
    For i = 1 To Len(r)
        Ch = UCase(Mid(r, i, 1))
        If Ch Like "[AEIOU]" Then
           Count = Count + 1
            Debug.Print Ch, i
        End If
    Next i
    VOWELCOUNT = Count
End Function
```

Figure 25-10 The highlighted statement contains a breakpoint.

Tip

To remove all breakpoints in all open projects, choose Debug ➜ Clear All Breakpoints or press Ctrl+Shift+F9.

Creating Add-Ins for Functions

If you create some custom functions that you use frequently, you may want to store these functions in an add-in file. A primary advantage to this is that you can use the functions in formulas in any workbook without a filename qualifier.

Assume that you have a custom function named ZAPSPACES and that it's stored in Myfuncs.xlsm. To use this function in a formula in a workbook other than Myfuncs.xlsm, you need to enter the following formula:

```
=Myfuncs.xlsm!ZAPSPACES(A1:C12)
```

If you create an add-in from Myfuncs.xlsm and the add-in is loaded, you can omit the file reference and enter a formula like the following:

```
=ZAPSPACES(A1:C12)
```

A few words about passwords

Microsoft has never promoted Excel as a product that creates applications with secure source code. The password feature provided in Excel is sufficient to prevent casual users from accessing parts of your application that you want to keep hidden. However, the truth is that several password-cracking utilities are available. The security features in more recent versions of Excel are much better than those in earlier versions, but it's possible that these also can be cracked. If you must be absolutely sure that no one ever sees your code or formulas, Excel is not your best choice as a development platform.

Creating an add-in from a workbook is simple. The following steps describe how to create an add-in from a normal workbook file:

1. Develop your functions and make sure they work properly.
2. Activate the VB Editor and select the workbook in the Project window. Choose Tools ➜ *xxx* Properties and click the Protection tab (where *xxx* corresponds to the name of your project). Select the Lock Project for Viewing check box and enter a password (twice). Click OK.

   You need to do this last step only if you want to prevent others from viewing or modifying your macros or custom dialog boxes.
3. Reactivate Excel. Choose File ➜ Info ➜ Properties ➜ Show Document Panel, and Excel displays its Document Properties panel above the Formula bar. Enter a brief, descriptive title in the Title field and a longer description in the Comments field.

   This last step is not required, but it makes the add-in easier to use by displaying descriptive text in the Add-Ins dialog box.
4. Choose File ➜ Save As.
5. In the Save As dialog box, select Excel Add-In (*.xlam) from the Save as Type drop-down list.

6. If you don't want to store the add-in in the default directory, select a different directory.
7. Click Save.

   A copy of the workbook is saved (with an .xlam extension), and the original macro-enabled workbook (.xlsm) remains open.

Warning

When you use functions that are stored in an add-in, Excel creates a link to that add-in file. Therefore, if you distribute your workbook to others, they must also have a copy of the linked add-in. Furthermore, the add-in must be stored in the same directory because the links are stored with complete path references. As a result, the recipient of your workbook may need to use the Data ➜ Connections ➜ Edit Links command to change the source of the linked add-in.

After you create your add-in, you can install it by using the standard procedure:

1. Choose File ➜ Options, and click the Add-Ins tab.
2. Select Excel Add-ins from the Manage drop-down list.
3. Click Go. This shows the Add-Ins dialog box.
4. Click the Browse button in the Add-Ins dialog box.
5. Locate your *.xlam file.
6. Place a check mark next to the add-in name.

Tip

A much quicker way to display the Add-Ins dialog box is to press Alt+T+I.

26

VBA Custom Function Examples

In This Chapter

- Simple custom function examples
- A custom function to determine a cell's data type
- A custom function to make a single worksheet function act like multiple functions
- A custom function for generating random numbers and selecting cells at random
- Custom functions for calculating sales commissions
- Custom functions for manipulating text
- Custom functions for counting and summing cells
- Custom functions that deal with dates
- A custom function example for returning the last nonempty cell in a column or row
- Custom functions that work with multiple worksheets
- Advanced custom function techniques

This chapter is jam-packed with a variety of useful (or potentially useful) VBA custom worksheet functions. You can use many of the functions as they are written. You may need to modify other functions to meet your particular needs. For maximum speed and efficiency, these Function procedures declare all variables that are used.

Simple Functions

The functions in this section are relatively simple, but they can be very useful. Most of them are based on the fact that VBA can obtain helpful information that's not normally available for use in a formula.

On the Web

This book's website contains the workbook simple functions.xlsm that includes all the functions in this section.

Is the cell hidden?

The following CELLISHIDDEN function accepts a single cell argument and returns *TRUE* if the cell is hidden. A cell is considered a hidden cell if either its row or its column is hidden:

```
Function CELLISHIDDEN(cell As Range) As Boolean
'   Returns TRUE if cell is hidden
    Dim UpperLeft As Range
    Set UpperLeft = cell.Range("A1")
    CELLISHIDDEN = UpperLeft.EntireRow.Hidden Or _
       UpperLeft.EntireColumn.Hidden
End Function
```

Using the functions in this chapter

If you see a function listed in this chapter that you find useful, you can use it in your own workbook. All the Function procedures in this chapter are available at this book's website. Just open the appropriate workbook, activate the VB Editor, and copy and paste the function listing to a VBA module in your workbook. It's impossible to anticipate every function that you'll ever need. However, the examples in this chapter cover a variety of topics, so it's likely that you can locate an appropriate function and adapt the code for your own use.

Returning a worksheet name

The following SHEETNAME function accepts a single argument (a range) and returns the name of the worksheet that contains the range. It uses the Parent property of the Range object. The Parent property returns an object—the worksheet object that contains the Range object:

```
Function SHEETNAME(rng As Range) As String
'   Returns the sheet name for rng
    SHEETNAME = rng.Parent.Name
End Function
```

The following function is a variation on this theme. It does not use an argument; rather, it relies on the fact that a function can determine the cell from which it was called by using Application.Caller:

```
Function SHEETNAME2() As String
'   Returns the sheet name of the cell that contains the function
    SHEETNAME2 = Application.Caller.Parent.Name
End Function
```

In this function, the Caller property of the Application object returns a Range object that corresponds to the cell that contains the function. For example, suppose that you have the following formula in cell A1:

```
=SHEETNAME2()
```

When the SHEETNAME2 function is executed, the Application.Caller property returns a Range object corresponding to the cell that contains the function. The Parent property returns the Worksheet object, and the Name property returns the name of the worksheet.

You can use the SHEET function to return a sheet number rather than a sheet name.

Returning a workbook name

The next function, WORKBOOKNAME, returns the name of the workbook. Notice that it uses the Parent property twice. The first Parent property returns a Worksheet object, the second Parent property returns a Workbook object, and the Name property returns the name of the workbook:

```
Function WORKBOOKNAME() As String
'   Returns the workbook name of the cell that contains the function
    WORKBOOKNAME = Application.Caller.Parent.Parent.Name
End Function
```

Returning the application's name

The following function, although not very useful, carries this discussion of object parents to the next logical level by accessing the Parent property three times. This function returns the name of the Application object, which is always the string *Microsoft Excel*:

```
Function APPNAME() As String
'   Returns the application name of the cell that contains the function
    APPNAME = Application.Caller.Parent.Parent.Parent.Name
End Function
```

Understanding object parents

Objects in Excel are arranged in a hierarchy. At the top of the hierarchy is the Application object (Excel itself). Excel contains other objects; these objects contain other objects, and so on. The following hierarchy depicts the way a Range object fits into this scheme:

Application object (Excel)
  Workbook object
    Worksheet object
      Range object

In the lingo of object-oriented programming (OOP), a Range object's parent is the Worksheet object that contains it. A Worksheet object's parent is the workbook that contains the worksheet. And a Workbook object's parent is the Application object. Armed with this knowledge, you can use the Parent property to create a few useful functions.

Returning Excel's version number

The following function returns Excel's version number. For example, if you use Excel 2016, it returns the text string *16.0*:

```
Function EXCELVERSION() as String
'   Returns Excel's version number
    EXCELVERSION = Application.Version
End Function
```

Note that the EXCELVERSION function returns a string, not a value. The following function returns *TRUE* if the application is Excel 2007 or later (Excel 2007 is version 12). This function uses the VBA Val function to convert the text string to a value:

```
Function EXCEL2007ORLATER() As Boolean
    EXCEL2007ORLATER = Val(Application.Version) >= 12
End Function
```

Returning cell formatting information

This section contains a number of custom functions that return information about a cell's formatting. These functions are useful if you need to sort data based on formatting (for example, sorting all bold cells together).

Warning

The functions in this section use the following statement:

```
Application.Volatile True
```

This statement causes the function to be reevaluated when the workbook is calculated. You'll find, however, that these functions don't always return the correct value. This is because changing cell formatting, for example, does not trigger Excel's recalculation engine. To force a global recalculation (and update all the custom functions), press Ctrl+Alt +F9.

The following function returns *TRUE* if its single-cell argument has bold formatting:

```
Function ISBOLD(cell As Range) As Boolean
'   Returns TRUE if cell is bold
    Application.Volatile True
    ISBOLD = cell.Range("A1").Font.Bold
End Function
```

The following function returns *TRUE* if its single-cell argument has italic formatting:

```
Function ISITALIC(cell As Range) As Boolean
'   Returns TRUE if cell is italic
    Application.Volatile True
    ISITALIC = cell.Range("A1").Font.Italic
End Function
```

Both of the preceding functions have a slight flaw: they return an error (*#VALUE!*) if the cell has mixed formatting. For example, it's possible that only some characters in the cell are bold.

The following function returns *TRUE* only if all the characters in the cell are bold. If the Bold property of the Font object returns *Null* (indicating mixed formatting), the If statement generates an error, and the function name is never set to *TRUE*. The function name was previously set to *FALSE*, so that's the value that the function returns:

```
Function ALLBOLD(cell As Range) As Boolean
'   Returns TRUE if all characters in cell are bold
    Dim UpperLeft As Range
    Application.Volatile True
    Set UpperLeft = cell.Range("A1")
    ALLBOLD = False
    If UpperLeft.Font.Bold Then ALLBOLD = True
End Function
```

The following FILLCOLOR function returns a value that corresponds to the color of the cell's interior (the cell's fill color). If the cell's interior is not filled, the function returns *16,777,215*. The Color property values range from 0 to 16,777,215:

```
Function FILLCOLOR(cell As Range) As Long
'   Returns a value corresponding to the cell's interior color
    Application.Volatile True
    FILLCOLOR = cell.Range("A1").Interior.Color
End Function
```

Note

If a cell is part of a table that uses a style, the FILLCOLOR function does not return the correct color. Similarly, a fill color that results from conditional formatting is not returned by this function. In both cases, the function returns *16,777,215*.

The following function returns the number format string for a cell:

```
Function NUMBERFORMAT(cell As Range) As String
'   Returns a string that represents
'   the cell's number format
    Application.Volatile True
    NUMBERFORMAT = cell.Range("A1").NumberFormat
End Function
```

If the cell uses the default number format, the function returns the string *General.*

Determining a Cell's Data Type

Excel provides a number of built-in functions that can help determine the type of data contained in a cell. These include ISTEXT, ISNONTEXT, ISLOGICAL, and ISERROR. In addition, VBA includes functions such as ISEMPTY, ISDATE, and ISNUMERIC.

The following function accepts a range argument and returns a string (*Blank, Text, Logical, Error, Date, Time,* or *Value*) that describes the data type of the upper-left cell in the range:

```
Function CELLTYPE(cell As Range) As String
'   Returns the cell type of the upper-left cell in a range
    Dim UpperLeft As Range
    Application.Volatile True
    Set UpperLeft = cell.Range("A1")
    Select Case True
        Case UpperLeft.NumberFormat = "@"
            CELLTYPE = "Text"
        Case IsEmpty(UpperLeft.Value)
            CELLTYPE = "Blank"
        Case WorksheetFunction.IsText(UpperLeft)
            CELLTYPE = "Text"
        Case WorksheetFunction.IsLogical(UpperLeft.Value)
```

```
            CELLTYPE = "Logical"
        Case WorksheetFunction.IsErr(UpperLeft.Value)
            CELLTYPE = "Error"
        Case IsDate(UpperLeft.Value)
            CELLTYPE = "Date"
        Case InStr(1, UpperLeft.Text, ":") <> 0
            CELLTYPE = "Time"
        Case IsNumeric(UpperLeft.Value)
            CELLTYPE = "Value"
    End Select
End Function
```

Figure 26-1 shows the CELLTYPE function in use. Column B contains formulas that use the CELLTYPE function with an argument from column A. For example, cell B1 contains the following formula:

```
=CELLTYPE(A1)
```

B1 =CELLTYPE(A1)

	A	B	C
1	145.4	Value	*A simple value*
2	8.6	Value	*Formula that returns a value*
3	Budget Sheet	Text	*Simple text*
4	FALSE	Logical	*Logical formula*
5	TRUE	Logical	*Logical value*
6	#DIV/0!	Error	*Formula error*
7	7/27/2015	Date	*Formula that returns a date*
8	4:00 PM	Time	*A time*

Figure 26-1: The CELLTYPE function returns a string that describes the contents of a cell.

On the Web

The workbook celltype function.xlsm that demonstrates the CELLTYPE function is available at this book's website.

A Multifunctional Function

This section demonstrates a technique that may be helpful in some situations—the technique of making a single worksheet function act like multiple functions. The following VBA custom function, named STATFUNCTION, takes two arguments: the range (rng) and the operation (op). Depending on the value of op, the function returns a value computed by using any of the following worksheet functions: AVERAGE, COUNT, MAX, MEDIAN, MIN, MODE, STDEV, SUM, or VAR. For example, you can use this function in your worksheet:

```
=STATFUNCTION(B1:B24,A24)
```

The result of the formula depends on the contents of cell A24, which should be a string, such as *Average*, *Count*, *Max*, and so on. You can adapt this technique for other types of functions:

```
Function STATFUNCTION(rng As Variant, op As String) As Variant
    Select Case UCase(op)
        Case "SUM"
            STATFUNCTION = Application.Sum(rng)
        Case "AVERAGE"
            STATFUNCTION = Application.Average(rng)
        Case "MEDIAN"
            STATFUNCTION = Application.Median(rng)
        Case "MODE"
            STATFUNCTION = Application.Mode(rng)
        Case "COUNT"
            STATFUNCTION = Application.Count(rng)
        Case "MAX"
            STATFUNCTION = Application.Max(rng)
        Case "MIN"
            STATFUNCTION = Application.Min(rng)
        Case "VAR"
            STATFUNCTION = Application.Var(rng)
        Case "STDEV"
            STATFUNCTION = Application.StDev(rng)
        Case Else
            STATFUNCTION = CVErr(xlErrNA)
    End Select
End Function
```

Figure 26-2 shows the STATFUNCTION function that is used in conjunction with a drop-down list generated by Excel's Data ➜ Data Tools ➜ Data Validation command. The formula in cell C14 is as follows:

```
=STATFUNCTION(C1:C12,B14)
```

	A	B	C	D	E
1		Observation 1	135.52		
2		Observation 2	244.09		
3		Observation 3	187.33		
4		Observation 4	209.00		
5		Observation 5	200.91		
6		Observation 6	189.23		
7		Observation 7	198.22		
8		Observation 8	231.78		
9		Observation 9	189.14		
10		Observation 10	221.15		
11		Observation 11	189.05		
12		Observation 12	198.22		
13					
14		Count	12.00	<-- STATFUNCTION	
15		Average	12.00	<-- STATFUNCTION2	

Figure 26-2: Selecting an operation from the list displays the result in cell C14.

On the Web

The workbook, statfunction function.xlsm, shown in Figure 26-2, is available on this book's website.

The following STATFUNCTION2 function is a much simpler approach that works exactly like the STATFUNCTION function. It uses the Evaluate method to evaluate an expression:

```
Function STATFUNCTION2(rng As Range, op As String) As Double
    STATFUNCTION2 = Evaluate(Op & "(" & _
        rng.Address(external:=True) & ")")
End Function
```

For example, assume that the rng argument is C1:C12 and that the op argument is the string SUM. The expression that is used as an argument for the Evaluate method is this:

```
SUM(C1:C12)
```

The Evaluate method evaluates its argument and returns the result. In addition to being much shorter, a benefit of this version of STATFUNCTION is that it's not necessary to list all the possible functions.

Note

Note that the Address property has an argument: external:=True. That argument controls the way the address is returned. The default value, *FALSE*, returns a simple range address. When the external argument is *TRUE*, the address includes the workbook name and worksheet name. This allows the function to use a range that's on a different worksheet or even workbook.

Worksheet function data types

You may have noticed some differences in the data types used for functions and arguments so far. For instance, in STATFUNCTION, the variable rng was declared as a Variant, whereas the same variable was declared as a Range in STATFUNCTION2. Also, the former's return value was declared as a Variant, whereas the latter's is a Double data type.

Data types are two-edged swords. They can be used to limit the type of data that can be passed to, or returned from, a function, but they can also reduce the flexibility of the function. Using Variant data types maximizes flexibility but may slow execution speed a bit.

One of the possible return values of STATFUNCTION is an error in the Case Else section of the Select Case statement. That means that the function can return a Double data type or an Error. The most restrictive data type that can hold both an Error and a Double is a Variant (which can hold anything), so the function is typed as a Variant. On the other hand, STATFUNCTION2 does not have a provision

continued

continued

for returning an error, so it's typed as the more restrictive Double data type. Numeric data in cells is treated as a Double even if it looks like an Integer.

The rng arguments are also typed differently. In STATFUNCTION2, the Address property of the Range object is used. Because of this, you must pass a Range to the function, or it will return an error. However, there is nothing in STATFUNCTION that forces rng to be a Range. By declaring rng as a Variant, the user has the flexibility to provide inputs in other ways. Excel happily tries to convert whatever it's given into something it can use. If it can't convert it, the result is surely an error. A user can enter the following formula:

```
=STATFUNCTION({123.45,643,893.22},"Min")
```

Neither argument is a cell reference, but Excel doesn't mind. It can find the minimum of an array constant as easily as a range of values. It works the other way, too, as in the case of the second argument. If a cell reference is supplied, Excel tries to convert it to a String and has no problem doing so.

In general, you should use the most restrictive data types possible for your situation while providing for the most user flexibility.

Generating Random Numbers

This section presents functions that deal with random numbers. One generates random numbers that don't change. The other selects a cell at random from a range.

On the Web

The functions in this section are available at this book's website. The filename is random functions.xlsm.

Generating random numbers that don't change

You can use the Excel RAND function to quickly fill a range of cells with random values. But, as you may have discovered, the RAND function generates a new random number whenever the worksheet is recalculated. If you prefer to generate random numbers that don't change with each recalculation, use the following STATICRAND Function procedure:

```
Function STATICRAND() As Double
'   Returns a random number that doesn't
'   change when recalculated
    STATICRAND = Rnd
End Function
```

The STATICRAND function uses the VBA Rnd function, which, like Excel's RAND function, returns a random number between 0 and 1. When you use STATICRAND, however, the random numbers don't change when the sheet is calculated.

Note

Pressing F9 does not generate new values from the STATICRAND function, but pressing Ctrl+Alt+F9 (Excel's "global recalc" key combination) does.

Following is another version of the function that returns a random integer within a specified range of values:

```
Function STATICRANDBETWEEN(lo As Long, hi As Long) As Long
'   Returns a random integer that doesn't change when recalculated
    STATICRANDBETWEEN = Int((hi - lo + 1) * Rnd + lo)
End Function
```

For example, if you want to generate a random integer between 1 and 1,000, you can use a formula such as this:

```
=STATICRANDBETWEEN(1,1000)
```

Controlling function recalculation

When you use a custom function in a worksheet formula, when is it recalculated?

Custom functions behave like Excel's built-in worksheet functions. Normally, a custom function is recalculated only when it needs to be recalculated—that is, when you modify any of a function's arguments—but you can force functions to recalculate more frequently. Adding the following statement to a Function procedure makes the function recalculate whenever the workbook is recalculated:

```
Application.Volatile True
```

The Volatile method of the Application object has one argument (either *True* or *False*). Marking a Function procedure as "volatile" forces the function to be calculated whenever calculation occurs in *any* cell in the worksheet.

For example, the custom STATICRAND function presented in this chapter can be changed to emulate the Excel RAND() function by using the Volatile method, as follows:

```
Function NONSTATICRAND()
'   Returns a random number that
'   changes when the sheet is recalculated
    Application.Volatile True
    NONSTATICRAND = Rnd
End Function
```

Using the *False* argument of the Volatile method causes the function to be recalculated only when one or more of its arguments change. (If a function has no arguments, this method has no effect.) By default, all custom functions work as if they include an Application.Volatile False statement.

Selecting a cell at random

The following function, named DRAWONE, randomly chooses one cell from an input range and returns the cell's contents:

```
Function DRAWONE(rng As Variant) As Double
'     Chooses one cell at random from a range
      DRAWONE = rng(Int((rng.Count) * Rnd + 1))
End Function
```

If you use this function, you'll find that it is not recalculated when the worksheet is calculated. In other words, the function is not volatile. (For more information about controlling recalculation, see the previous sidebar, "Controlling function recalculation." You can make the function volatile by adding the following statement:

```
Application.Volatile True
```

After doing so, the DRAWONE function displays a new random cell value whenever the sheet is calculated.

A more general function, one that accepts array constants as well as ranges, is shown here:

```
Function DRAWONE2(rng As Variant) As Variant
'    Chooses one value at random from an array
    Dim ArrayLen As Long
    If TypeName(rng) = "Range" Then
        DRAWONE2 = rng(Int((rng.Count) * Rnd + 1)).Value
    Else
        ArrayLen = UBound(rng) - LBound(rng) + 1
        DRAWONE2 = rng(Int(ArrayLen * Rnd + 1))
    End If
End Function
```

This function uses the VBA built-in TypeName function to determine whether the argument passed is a Range. If not, it's assumed to be an array. Following is a formula that uses the DRAWONE2 function. This formula returns a text string that corresponds to a suit in a deck of cards:

```
=DRAWONE2({"Clubs","Hearts","Diamonds","Spades"})
```

Following is a formula that has the same result, written using Excel's built-in functions:

```
=CHOOSE(RANDBETWEEN(1,4),"Clubs","Hearts","Diamonds","Spades")
```

We present two additional functions that deal with randomization later in this chapter (see the "Advanced Function Techniques" section).

Calculating Sales Commissions

Sales managers often need to calculate the commissions earned by their sales forces. The calculations in the function example presented here are based on a sliding scale: employees who sell more earn a higher commission rate (see Table 26-1). For example, a salesperson with sales between $10,000 and $19,999 qualifies for a commission rate of 10.5%.

Table 26-1: Commission Rates for Monthly Sales

Monthly Sales	Commission Rate
Less than $10,000	8.0%
$10,000 to $19,999	10.5%
$20,000 to $39,999	12.0%
$40,000 or more	14.0%

You can calculate commissions for various sales amounts entered into a worksheet in several ways. You can use a complex formula with nested IF functions, such as the following:

```
=IF(A1<0,0,IF(A1<10000,A1*0.08,IF(A1<20000,A1*0.105,
IF(A1<40000,A1*0.12,A1*0.14))))
```

This may not be the best approach for a couple of reasons. First, the formula is overly complex, thus making it difficult to understand. Second, the values are hard-coded into the formula, thus making the formula difficult to modify.

A better approach is to use a lookup table function to compute the commissions. For example:

```
=VLOOKUP(A1,Table,2)*A1
```

Using VLOOKUP is a good alternative, but it may not work if the commission structure is more complex. (See the "A function for a simple commission structure" section for more information.) Yet another approach is to create a custom function.

A function for a simple commission structure

The following COMMISSION function accepts a single argument (sales) and computes the commission amount:

```
Function COMMISSION(Sales As Double) As Double
'   Calculates sales commissions
    Const Tier1 As Double = 0.08
    Const Tier2 As Double = 0.105
```

```
    Const Tier3 As Double = 0.12
    Const Tier4 As Double = 0.14
    Select Case Sales
        Case Is >= 40000
            COMMISSION = Sales * Tier4
        Case Is >= 20000
            COMMISSION = Sales * Tier3
        Case Is >= 10000
            COMMISSION = Sales * Tier2
        Case Is < 10000
            COMMISSION = Sales * Tier1
    End Select
End Function
```

The following worksheet formula, for example, returns *3,000*. (The sales amount—25,000—qualifies for a commission rate of 12%.)

```
=COMMISSION(25000)
```

This function is easy to understand and maintain. It uses constants to store the commission rates as well as a Select Case structure to determine which commission rate to use.

Note

When a Select Case structure is evaluated, program control exits the Select Case structure when the first true Case is encountered.

A function for a more complex commission structure

If the commission structure is more complex, you may need to use additional arguments for your `COMMISSION` function. Imagine that the aforementioned sales manager implements a new policy to help reduce turnover: the total commission paid increases by 1 percent for each year that a salesperson stays with the company.

The following is a modified `COMMISSION` function (named `COMMISSION2`). This function now takes two arguments: the monthly sales (sales) and the number of years employed (years):

```
Function COMMISSION2(Sales As Double, Years As Long) As Double
'   Calculates sales commissions based on
'   years in service
    Const Tier1 As Double = 0.08
    Const Tier2 As Double = 0.105
    Const Tier3 As Double = 0.12
    Const Tier4 As Double = 0.14
    Select Case Sales
        Case Is >= 40000
            COMMISSION2 = Sales * Tier4
        Case Is >= 20000
```

```
            COMMISSION2 = Sales * Tier3
        Case Is >= 10000
            COMMISSION2 = Sales * Tier2
        Case Is < 10000
            COMMISSION2 = Sales * Tier1
    End Select
    COMMISSION2 = COMMISSION2 + (COMMISSION2 * Years / 100)
End Function
```

Figure 26-3 shows the COMMISSION2 function in use. Here's the formula in cell D2:

```
=COMMISSION2(B2,C2)
```

D2 =COMMISSION2(B2,C2)

	A	B	C	D
1	Sales Rep	Amount Sold	Years Employed	Commission
2	Adams, Robert	5,010.54	1	404.85
3	Baker, Sheila	9,833.91	0	786.71
4	Clarke, Edward	12,500.32	2	1,338.78
5	Davis, Don	35,988.22	3	4,448.14
6	Elfin, Bill	41,822.99	3	6,030.88
7	Franklin, Ben	8,090.32	1	653.70
8	Gomez, Chris	11,098.32	2	1,188.63
9	Harley, Mary	48,745.23	5	7,165.55

Figure 26-3: Calculating sales commissions based on sales amount and years employed.

On the Web

The workbook, commission function.xlsm, shown in Figure 26-3, is available at this book's website.

Text Manipulation Functions

Text strings can be manipulated with functions in a variety of ways, including reversing the display of a text string, scrambling the characters in a text string, or extracting specific characters from a text string. This section offers a number of function examples that manipulate text strings.

On the Web

This book's website contains a workbook named text manipulation functions.xlsm that demonstrates all the functions in this section.

Reversing a string

The following REVERSETEXT function returns the text in a cell backward:

```
Function REVERSETEXT(text As String) As String
'   Returns its argument, reversed
    REVERSETEXT = StrReverse(text)
End Function
```

This function simply uses the VBA StrReverse function. The following formula, for example, returns *tfosorciM*:

```
=REVERSETEXT("Microsoft")
```

Scrambling text

The following function returns the contents of its argument with the characters randomized. For example, using *Microsoft* as the argument may return *oficMorts* or some other random permutation:

```
Function SCRAMBLE(text As Variant) As String
'   Scrambles its string argument
    Dim TextLen As Long
    Dim i As Long
    Dim RandPos As Long
    Dim Temp As String
    Dim Char As String * 1
    If TypeName(text) = "Range" Then
        Temp = text.Range("A1").text
    ElseIf IsArray(text) Then
        Temp = text(LBound(text))
    Else
        Temp = text
    End If
    TextLen = Len(Temp)
    For i = 1 To TextLen
        Char = Mid(Temp, i, 1)
        RandPos = WorksheetFunction.RandBetween(1, TextLen)
        Mid(Temp, i, 1) = Mid(Temp, RandPos, 1)
        Mid(Temp, RandPos, 1) = Char
    Next i
    SCRAMBLE = Temp
End Function
```

This function loops through each character and then swaps it with another character in a randomly selected position.

You may be wondering about the use of Mid. Note that when Mid is used on the right side of an assignment statement, it is a function. However, when Mid is used on the left side of the assignment statement, it is a statement. Consult the Help system for more information about Mid.

Returning an acronym

The ACRONYM function returns the first letter (in uppercase) of each word in its argument. For example, the following formula returns *IBM:*

```
=ACRONYM("International Business Machines")
```

The listing for the ACRONYM Function procedure follows:

```
Function ACRONYM(text As String) As String
'   Returns an acronym for text
    Dim TextLen As Long
    Dim i As Long
    text = Application.Trim(text)
    TextLen = Len(text)
    ACRONYM = Left(text, 1)
    For i = 2 To TextLen
        If Mid(text, i, 1) = " " Then
            ACRONYM = ACRONYM & Mid(text, i + 1, 1)
        End If
    Next i
    ACRONYM = UCase(ACRONYM)
End Function
```

This function uses the Excel TRIM function to remove any extra spaces from the argument. The first character in the argument is always the first character in the result. The For-Next loop examines each character. If the character is a space, the character *after* the space is appended to the result. Finally, the result converts to uppercase by using the VBA UCase function.

Does the text match a pattern?

The following function returns *TRUE* if a string matches a pattern composed of text and wildcard characters. The ISLIKE function is remarkably simple and is essentially a wrapper for the useful VBA Like operator:

```
Function ISLIKE(text As String, pattern As String) As Boolean
'   Returns true if the first argument is like the second
    ISLIKE = text Like pattern
End Function
```

The supported wildcard characters are as follows:

?	Matches any single character
*	Matches zero or more characters
#	Matches any single digit (0–9)
[*list*]	Matches any single character in the list
[!*list*]	Matches any single character not in the list

The following formula returns *TRUE* because the question mark (?) matches any single character. If the first argument were "Unit12", the function would return *FALSE*:

```
=ISLIKE("Unit1","Unit?")
```

The function also works with values. The following formula, for example, returns *TRUE* if cell A1 contains a value that begins with 1 and has exactly three numeric digits:

```
=ISLIKE(A1,"1##")
```

The following formula returns *TRUE* because the first argument is a single character contained in the list of characters specified in the second argument:

```
=ISLIKE("a","[aeiou]")
```

If the character list begins with an exclamation point (`!`), the comparison is made with characters *not* in the list. For example, the following formula returns *TRUE* because the first argument is a single character that does not appear in the second argument's list:

```
=ISLIKE("g","[!aeiou]")
```

To match one of the special characters from the previous table, put that character in brackets. This formula returns *TRUE* because the pattern is looking for three consecutive question marks. The question marks in the pattern are in brackets, so they no longer represent a single character:

```
=ISLIKE("???","[?][?][?]")
```

The Like operator is versatile. For complete information about the VBA Like operator, consult the Help system.

Does a cell contain a particular word?

What if you need to determine whether a particular word is contained in a string? Excel's FIND function can determine whether a text string is contained in another text string. For example, the formula that follows returns *5*, the character position of *rate* in the string *The rate has changed*:

```
=FIND("rate","The rate has changed")
```

The following formula also returns *5*:

```
=FIND("rat","The rate has changed")
```

However, Excel provides no way to determine whether a particular word is contained in a string. Here's a VBA function that returns *TRUE* if the second argument is contained in the first argument:

```
Function EXACTWORDINSTRING(Text As String, Word As String) As Boolean
  EXACTWORDINSTRING = " " & UCase(Text) & _
    " " Like "*[!A-Z]" & UCase(Word) & "[!A-Z]*"
End Function
```

Figure 26-4 shows this function in use. Column A contains the text used as the first argument, and column B contains the text used as the second argument. Cell C1 contains this formula, which was copied down the column:

```
=EXACTWORDINSTRING(A1,B1)
```

C1 =EXACTWORDINSTRING(A1,B1)

	A	B	C	D
1	The rate has changed	rate	TRUE	
2	The rate has changed	rat	FALSE	
3	The rate has changed	change	FALSE	
4	The rate has changed	The	TRUE	
5	The rate has changed	has	TRUE	
6	The rate has changed	changed	TRUE	
7	The rate has changed	The rat	FALSE	
8	The rate has changed	The rate	TRUE	

Figure 26-4: A VBA function that determines whether a particular word is contained in a string.

Note

Thanks to Rick Rothstein for suggesting this function, which is much more efficient than our original function.

On the Web

A workbook that demonstrates the EXACTWORDINSTRING function is available on this book's website. The filename is exact word.xlsm.

Does a cell contain text?

A number of Excel's worksheet functions are at times unreliable when dealing with text in a cell. For example, the ISTEXT function returns *FALSE* if its argument is a number that's formatted as Text. The following CELLHASTEXT function returns *TRUE* if the range argument contains text or contains a value formatted as Text:

```
Function CELLHASTEXT(cell As Range) As Boolean
'   Returns TRUE if cell contains a string
'   or cell is formatted as Text
    Dim UpperLeft as Range
    CELLHASTEXT = False
    Set UpperLeft = cell.Range("A1")
    If UpperLeft.NumberFormat = "@" Then
        CELLHASTEXT = True
        Exit Function
    End If
    If Not IsNumeric(UpperLeft.Value) Then
        CELLHASTEXT = True
        Exit Function
    End If
End Function
```

The following formula returns *TRUE* if cell A1 contains a text string or if the cell is formatted as Text:

```
=CELLHASTEXT(A1)
```

Extracting the *n*th element from a string

The EXTRACTELEMENT function is a custom worksheet function that extracts an element from a text string based on a specified separator character. Assume that cell A1 contains the following text:

```
123-456-789-9133-8844
```

For example, the following formula returns the string *9133,* which is the fourth element in the string. The string uses a hyphen (-) as the separator:

```
=EXTRACTELEMENT(A1,4,"-")
```

The EXTRACTELEMENT function uses three arguments:

- **txt:** The text string from which you're extracting. This can be a literal string or a cell reference.
- **n:** An integer that represents the element to extract.
- **separator:** A single character used as the separator.

Note

If you specify a space as the Separator character, multiple spaces are treated as a single space, which is almost always what you want. If n exceeds the number of elements in the string, the function returns an empty string.

The VBA code for the EXTRACTELEMENT function follows:

```
Function EXTRACTELEMENT(Txt As String, n As Long,
    Separator As String) As String
'   Returns the <i>n</i>th element of a text string, where the
'   elements are separated by a specified separator character
    Dim AllElements As Variant
    AllElements = Split(Txt, Separator)
    EXTRACTELEMENT = AllElements(n - 1)
End Function
```

This function uses the VBA Split function, which returns a variant array that contains each element of the text string. This array begins with 0 (not 1), so using n–1 references the desired element.

Spelling out a number

The SPELLDOLLARS function returns a number spelled out in text—as on a check. For example, the following formula returns the string *One hundred twenty-three and 45/100 dollars:*

```
=SPELLDOLLARS(123.45)
```

Figure 26-5 shows some additional examples of the SPELLDOLLARS function. Column C contains formulas that use the function. For example, the formula in C1 is

	A	B	C
1	32		Thirty-Two and 00/100 Dollars
2	37.56		Thirty-Seven and 56/100 Dollars
3	-32		(Thirty-Two and 00/100 Dollars)
4	-26.44		(Twenty-Six and 44/100 Dollars)
5	-4		(Four and 00/100 Dollars)
6	1.87341		One and 87/100 Dollars
7	1.56		One and 56/100 Dollars
8	1		One and 00/100 Dollars
9	6.56		Six and 56/100 Dollars
10	12.12		Twelve and 12/100 Dollars
11	1000000		One Million and 00/100 Dollars
12	10000000000		Ten Billion and 00/100 Dollars

Figure 26.5: Examples of the SPELLDOLLARS function.

```
=SPELLDOLLARS(A1)
```

Note that negative numbers are spelled out and enclosed in parentheses.

On the Web

The SPELLDOLLARS function is too lengthy to list here, but you can view the complete listing in spelldollars function.xlsm at this book's website.

Counting Functions

Chapter 7, "Counting and Summing Techniques," contains many formula examples to count cells based on various criteria. If you can't arrive at a formula-based solution for a counting problem, you can probably create a custom function. This section contains three functions that perform counting.

On the Web

This book's website contains the workbook counting functions.xlsm that demonstrates the functions in this section.

Counting pattern-matched cells

The COUNTIF function accepts limited wildcard characters in its criteria: the question mark and the asterisk, to be specific. If you need more robust pattern matching, you can use the LIKE operator in a custom function:

```
Function COUNTLIKE(rng As Range, pattern As String) As Long
'   Count the cells in a range that match a pattern
    Dim cell As Range
    Dim cnt As Long
    For Each cell In rng.Cells
        If cell.Text Like pattern Then cnt = cnt + 1
    Next cell
    COUNTLIKE = cnt
End Function
```

The following formula counts the number of cells in B4:B11 that contain the letter *e:*

```
=COUNTLIKE(B4:B11,"*[eE]*")
```

Counting sheets in a workbook

The following countsheets function accepts no arguments and returns the number of sheets in the workbook from where it's called:

```
Function COUNTSHEETS() As Long
    COUNTSHEETS = Application.Caller.Parent.Parent.Sheets.Count
End Function
```

This function uses Application.Caller to get the range where the formula was entered. Then it uses two Parent properties to go to the sheet and the workbook. Once at the workbook level, the Count property of the Sheets property is returned. The count includes worksheets and chart sheets.

Counting words in a range

The WORDCOUNT function accepts a range argument and returns the number of words in that range:

```
Function WORDCOUNT(rng As Range) As Long
'   Count the words in a range of cells
    Dim cell As Range
    Dim WdCnt As Long
    Dim tmp As String
    For Each cell In rng.Cells
        tmp = Application.Trim(cell.Value)
        If WorksheetFunction.IsText(tmp) Then
            WdCnt = WdCnt + (Len(tmp) - _
                Len(Replace(tmp, " ", "")) + 1)
        End If
    Next cell
    WORDCOUNT = WdCnt
End Function
```

We use a variable, tmp, to store the cell contents with extra spaces removed. Looping through the cells in the supplied range, the ISTEXT worksheet function is used to determine whether the cell has text. If it does, the number of spaces are counted and added to the total. Then one more space is added because a sentence with three spaces has four words. Spaces are counted by comparing the length of the text string with the length after the spaces have been removed with the VBA Replace function.

Date Functions

Chapter 6, "Working with Dates and Times," presents a number of useful Excel functions and formulas for calculating dates, times, and time periods by manipulating date and time serial values. This section presents additional functions that deal with dates.

On the Web

This book's website contains a workbook, date functions.xlsm, that demonstrates the functions presented in this section.

Calculating the next Monday

The following NEXTMONDAY function accepts a date argument and returns the date of the following Monday:

```
Function NEXTMONDAY(d As Date) As Date
    NEXTMONDAY = d + 8 - WeekDay(d, vbMonday)
End Function
```

This function uses the VBA WeekDay function, which returns an integer that represents the day of the week for a date (1 = Sunday, 2 = Monday, and so on). It also uses a predefined constant, vbMonday.

The following formula returns *12/28/2015*, which is the first Monday after Christmas Day, 2015 (which is a Friday):

```
=NEXTMONDAY(DATE(2015,12,25))
```

Note

The function returns a date serial number. You need to change the number format of the cell to display this serial number as an actual date.

If the argument passed to the NEXTMONDAY function is a Monday, the function returns the *following* Monday. If you prefer the function to return the same Monday, use this modified version:

```
Function NEXTMONDAY2(d As Date) As Date
    If WeekDay(d) = vbMonday Then
        NEXTMONDAY2 = d
    Else
        NEXTMONDAY2 = d + 8 - WeekDay(d, vbMonday)
    End If
End Function
```

Calculating the next day of the week

The following NEXTDAY function is a variation on the NEXTMONDAY function. This function accepts two arguments: a date and an integer between 1 and 7 that represents a day of the week (1 = Sunday, 2 = Monday, and so on). The NEXTDAY function returns the date for the next specified day of the week:

```
Function NEXTDAY(d As Date, day As Integer) As Variant
'   Returns the next specified day
'   Make sure day is between 1 and 7
    If day < 1 Or day > 7 Then
        NEXTDAY = CVErr(xlErrNA)
```

```
    Else
        NEXTDAY = d + 8 - WeekDay(d, day)
    End If
End Function
```

The NEXTDAY function uses an If statement to ensure that the day argument is valid (that is, between 1 and 7). If the day argument is not valid, the function returns *#N/A*. Because the function can return a value other than a date, it is declared as type Variant.

Which week of the month?

The following MONTHWEEK function returns an integer that corresponds to the week of the month for a date:

```
Function MONTHWEEK(d As Date) As Variant
'   Returns the week of the month for a date
    Dim FirstDay As Integer

'   Check for valid date argument
    If Not IsDate(d) Then
        MONTHWEEK = CVErr(xlErrNA)
        Exit Function
    End If

'   Get first day of the month
    FirstDay = WeekDay(DateSerial(Year(d), Month(d), 1))

'   Calculate the week number
    MONTHWEEK = Application.RoundUp((FirstDay + day(d) - 1) / 7, 0)
End Function
```

Working with dates before 1900

Many users are surprised to discover that Excel can't work with dates prior to the year 1900. To correct this deficiency, we created a series of extended date functions. These functions enable you to work with dates in the years 0100 through 9999.

The extended date functions follow:

- **XDATE(y,m,d,fmt):** Returns a date for a given year, month, and day. As an option, you can provide a date formatting string.
- **XDATEADD(xdate1,days,fmt):** Adds a specified number of days to a date. As an option, you can provide a date formatting string.
- **XDATEDIF(xdate1,xdate2):** Returns the number of days between two dates.

- **XDATEYEARDIF(xdate1,xdate2):** Returns the number of full years between two dates (useful for calculating ages).
- **XDATEYEAR(xdate1):** Returns the year of a date.
- **XDATEMONTH(xdate1):** Returns the month of a date.
- **XDATEDAY(xdate1):** Returns the day of a date.
- **XDATEDOW(xdate1):** Returns the day of the week of a date (as an integer between 1 and 7).

Figure 26-6 shows a workbook that uses a few of these functions.

4	**Examples: President Birthdays**							
5								
6	**President**	**Year**	**Month**	**Day**	**XDATE**	**XDATEDIF**	**XDATEYEARDIF**	**XDATEDOW**
7	George Washington	1732	2	22	February 22, 1732	103,519	283	Friday
8	John Adams	1735	10	30	October 30, 1735	102,173	279	Sunday
9	Thomas Jefferson	1743	4	13	April 13, 1743	99,451	272	Saturday
10	James Madison	1751	3	16	March 16, 1751	96,557	264	Tuesday
11	James Monroe	1758	4	28	April 28, 1758	93,957	257	Friday
12	John Quincy Adams	1767	7	11	July 11, 1767	90,596	248	Saturday
13	Andrew Jackson	1767	3	15	March 15, 1767	90,714	248	Sunday
14	Martin Van Buren	1782	12	5	December 5, 1782	84,970	232	Thursday
15	William Henry Harrison	1773	2	9	February 9, 1773	88,556	242	Tuesday
16	John Tyler	1790	3	29	March 29, 1790	82,299	225	Monday

Figure 26-6: Examples of the extended date function.

On the Web

These functions are available on this book's website, in a file named extended date functions.xlsm. The website also contains a PDF file (extended date functions help.pdf) that describes these functions. The functions are assigned to the Date & Time function category.

Warning

The extended date functions don't make adjustments for changes made to the calendar in 1582. Consequently, working with dates prior to October 15, 1582, may not yield correct results.

Returning the Last Nonempty Cell in a Column or Row

This section presents two useful functions: LASTINCOLUMN, which returns the contents of the last nonempty cell in a column, and LASTINROW, which returns the contents of the last nonempty cell in a row. Chapter 15, "Performing Magic with Array Formulas," presents standard formulas for this task, but you may prefer to use a custom function.

On the Web

This book's website contains last nonempty cell.xlsm, a workbook that demonstrates the functions presented in this section.

Each of these functions accepts a range as its single argument. The range argument can be a column reference (for LASTINCOLUMN) or a row reference (for LASTINROW). If the supplied argument is not a complete column or row reference (such as 3:3 or D:D), the function uses the column or row of the upper-left cell in the range. For example, the following formula returns the contents of the last non-empty cell in column B:

```
=LASTINCOLUMN(B5)
```

The following formula returns the contents of the last nonempty cell in row 7:

```
=LASTINROW(C7:D9)
```

The LASTINCOLUMN function

The following is the LASTINCOLUMN function:

```
Function LASTINCOLUMN(rng As Range) As Variant
'   Returns the contents of the last nonempty cell in a column
    Dim LastCell As Range
    With rng.Parent
        With .Cells(.Rows.Count, rng.Column)
            If Not IsEmpty(.Value) Then
                LASTINCOLUMN = .Value
            ElseIf IsEmpty(.End(xlUp).Value) Then
                LASTINCOLUMN = ""
            Else
                LASTINCOLUMN = .End(xlUp).Value
            End If
        End With
    End With
End Function
```

Notice the references to the Parent of the range. This is done to make the function work with arguments that refer to a different worksheet or workbook.

The LASTINROW function

The following is the LASTINROW function:

```
Function LASTINROW(rng As Range) As Variant
'   Returns the contents of the last nonempty cell in a row
    With rng.Parent
        With .Cells(rng.Row, .Columns.Count)
            If Not IsEmpty(.Value) Then
                LASTINROW = .Value
            ElseIf IsEmpty(.End(xlToLeft).Value) Then
                LASTINROW = ""
            Else
                LASTINROW = .End(xlToLeft).Value
            End If
        End With
    End With
End Function
```

Cross-Ref

In Chapter 15, we describe array formulas that return the last cell in a column or row.

Multisheet Functions

You may need to create a function that works with data contained in more than one worksheet within a workbook. This section contains two VBA custom functions that enable you to work with data across multiple sheets, including a function that overcomes an Excel limitation when copying formulas to other sheets.

On the Web

This book's website contains the workbook multisheet functions.xlsm that demonstrates the multisheet functions presented in this section.

Returning the maximum value across all worksheets

If you need to determine the maximum value in a cell (for example, B1) across a number of worksheets, use a formula like this one:

```
=MAX(Sheet1:Sheet4!B1)
```

This formula returns the maximum value in cell B1 for Sheet1, Sheet4, and all sheets in between. But what if you add a new sheet (Sheet5) after Sheet4? Your formula does not adjust automatically, so you need to edit it to include the new sheet reference:

```
=MAX(Sheet1:Sheet5!B1)
```

The following function accepts a single-cell argument and returns the maximum value in that cell across all worksheets in the workbook. For example, the following formula returns the maximum value in cell B1 for all sheets in the workbook:

```
=MAXALLSHEETS(B1)
```

If you add a new sheet, you don't need to edit the formula:

```
Function MAXALLSHEETS(cell as Range) As Variant
    Dim MaxVal As Double
    Dim Addr As String
    Dim Wksht As Object
    Application.Volatile
    Addr = cell.Range("A1").Address
    MaxVal = -9.9E+307
    For Each Wksht In cell.Parent.Parent.Worksheets
        If Not Wksht.Name = cell.Parent.Name Or _
          Not Addr = Application.Caller.Address Then
            If IsNumeric(Wksht.Range(Addr)) Then
                If Wksht.Range(Addr) > MaxVal Then _
                  MaxVal = Wksht.Range(Addr).Value
            End If
        End If
    Next Wksht
    If MaxVal = -9.9E+307 Then MaxVal = CVErr(xlErrValue)
    MAXALLSHEETS = MaxVal
End Function
```

The For Each statement uses the following expression to access the workbook:

```
cell.Parent.Parent.Worksheets
```

The parent of the cell is a worksheet, and the parent of the worksheet is the workbook. Therefore, the For Each-Next loop cycles among all worksheets in the workbook. The first If statement inside the loop checks whether the cell being checked is the cell that contains the function. If so, that cell is ignored to avoid a circular reference error.

Note

You can easily modify the MAXALLSHEETS function to perform other cross-worksheet calculations: Minimum, Average, Sum, and so on.

The SHEETOFFSET function

A recurring complaint about Excel (including Excel 2016) is its poor support for relative sheet references. For example, suppose that you have a multisheet workbook, and you enter a formula like the following on Sheet2:

```
=Sheet1!A1+1
```

This formula works fine. However, if you copy the formula to the next sheet (Sheet3), the formula continues to refer to Sheet1. Or if you insert a sheet between Sheet1 and Sheet2, the formula continues to refer to Sheet1, when most likely, you want it to refer to the newly inserted sheet. In fact, you can't create formulas that refer to worksheets in a relative manner. However, you can use the SHEETOFFSET function to overcome this limitation.

Following is a VBA Function procedure named SHEETOFFSET:

```
Function SHEETOFFSET(Offset As Long, Optional cell As Variant)
'   Returns cell contents at Ref, in sheet offset
    Dim WksIndex As Long, WksNum As Long
    Dim wks As Worksheet
    Application.Volatile
    If IsMissing(cell) Then Set cell = Application.Caller
    WksNum = 1
    For Each wks In Application.Caller.Parent.Parent.Worksheets
        If Application.Caller.Parent.Name = wks.Name Then
            SHEETOFFSET = Worksheets(WksNum + Offset)_</p><p>
  .Range(cell(1).Address).Value
            Exit Function
        Else
            WksNum = WksNum + 1
        End If
    Next wks
End Function
```

The SHEETOFFSET function accepts two arguments:

- **offset:** The sheet offset, which can be positive, negative, or 0.
- **cell:** (Optional) A single-cell reference. If this argument is omitted, the function uses the same cell reference as the cell that contains the formula.

For more information about optional arguments, see the section "Using optional arguments," later in this chapter.

The following formula returns the value in cell A1 of the sheet before the sheet that contains the formula:

```
=SHEETOFFSET(-1,A1)
```

The following formula returns the value in cell A1 of the sheet after the sheet that contains the formula:

```
=SHEETOFFSET(1,A1)
```

Advanced Function Techniques

In this section, we explore some even more advanced functions. The examples in this section demonstrate some special techniques that you can use with your custom functions.

Returning an error value

In some cases, you may want your custom function to return a particular error value. Consider the simple REVERSETEXT function, which we presented earlier in this chapter:

```
Function REVERSETEXT(text As String) As String
'   Returns its argument, reversed
    REVERSETEXT = StrReverse(text)
End Function
```

This function reverses the contents of its single-cell argument (which can be text or a value). If the argument is a multicell range, the function returns *#VALUE*!

Assume that you want this function to work only with strings. If the argument does not contain a string, you want the function to return an error value (*#N/A*). You may be tempted to simply assign a string that *looks* like an Excel formula error value. For example:

```
REVERSETEXT = "#N/A"
```

Although the string *looks* like an error value, it is not treated as such by other formulas that may reference it. To return a *real* error value from a function, use the VBA CVErr function, which converts an error number to a real error.

Fortunately, VBA has built-in constants for the errors that you want to return from a custom function. These constants are listed here:

- xlErrDiv0
- xlErrNA
- xlErrName
- xlErrNull
- xlErrNum

- xlErrRef
- xlErrValue

The following is the revised REVERSETEXT function:

```
Function REVERSETEXT(text As Variant) As Variant
'   Returns its argument, reversed
    If WorksheetFunction.ISNONTEXT(text) Then
        REVERSETEXT = CVErr(xlErrNA)
    Else
        REVERSETEXT = StrReverse(text)
    End If
End Function
```

First, change the argument from a String data type to a Variant. If the argument's data type is String, Excel tries to convert whatever it gets (for example, number, Boolean value) to a String and usually succeeds. Next, the Excel ISNONTEXT function is used to determine whether the argument is not a text string. If the argument is not a text string, the function returns the *#N/A* error. Otherwise, it returns the characters in reverse order.

Note

The data type for the return value of the original REVERSETEXT function was String because the function always returned a text string. In this revised version, the function is declared as a Variant because it can now return something other than a string.

Returning an array from a function

Most functions that you develop with VBA return a single value. It's possible, however, to write a function that returns multiple values in an array.

Cross-Ref

Part IV, "Array Formulas," deals with arrays and array formulas. Specifically, these chapters provide examples of a single formula that returns multiple values in separate cells. As you'll see, you can also create custom functions that return arrays.

VBA includes a useful function called Array. The Array function returns a variant that contains an array. It's important to understand that the array returned is not the same as a normal array composed of elements of the variant type. In other words, a variant array is not the same as an array of variants.

If you're familiar with using array formulas in Excel, you have a head start understanding the VBA Array function. You enter an array formula into a cell by pressing Ctrl+Shift+Enter. Excel inserts brackets around the formula to indicate that it's an array formula. See Chapter 14, "Introducing Arrays," and Chapter 15 for more details on array formulas.

Note

The lower bound of an array created by using the Array function is, by default, 0. However, the lower bound can be changed if you use an Option Base statement.

The following MONTHNAMES function demonstrates how to return an array from a Function procedure:

```
Function MONTHNAMES() As Variant
    MONTHNAMES = Array( _
       "Jan", "Feb", "Mar", "Apr", _
       "May", "Jun", "Jul", "Aug", _
       "Sep", "Oct", "Nov", "Dec")
End Function
```

Figure 26-7 shows a worksheet that uses the MONTHNAMES function. You enter the function by selecting A4:L4 and then entering the following formula:

```
{=MONTHNAMES()}
```

Figure 26-7: The MONTHNAMES function entered as an array formula.

Note

As with any array formula, you must press Ctrl+Shift+Enter to enter the formula. Don't enter the brackets—Excel inserts the brackets for you.

The MONTHNAMES function, as written, returns a horizontal array in a single row. To display the array in a vertical range in a single column, select the range and enter the following formula:

```
{=TRANSPOSE(MONTHNAMES())}
```

Alternatively, you can modify the function to do the transposition. The following function uses the Excel TRANSPOSE function to return a vertical array:

```
Function VMONTHNAMES() As Variant
    VMONTHNAMES = Application.Transpose(Array( _
       "Jan", "Feb", "Mar", "Apr", _
```

```
        "May", "Jun", "Jul", "Aug", _
        "Sep", "Oct", "Nov", "Dec"))
End Function
```

On the Web

The workbook monthnames.xlsm that demonstrates MONTHNAMES and VMONTHNAMES is available at this book's website.

Returning an array of nonduplicated random integers

The RANDOMINTEGERS function returns an array of nonduplicated integers. This function is intended for use in a multicell array formula. Figure 26-8 shows a worksheet that uses the following formula in the range A3:D12:

```
{=RANDOMINTEGERS()}
```

A3 {=RANDOMINTEGERS()}

	A	B	C	D	E	F
2						
3	4	5	7	8		
4	10	11	12	14		
5	16	17	18	20		
6	21	23	26	31		
7	32	33	34	37		
8	38	39	1	24		
9	25	15	27	28		
10	29	30	9	2		
11	6	19	35	36		
12	3	13	22	40		
13						

Figure 26-8: An array formula generates nonduplicated consecutive integers, arranged randomly.

This formula was entered into the entire range by using Ctrl+Shift+Enter. The formula returns an array of nonduplicated integers, arranged randomly. Because 40 cells contain the formula, the integers range from 1 to 40. The following is the code for RANDOMINTEGERS:

```
Function RANDOMINTEGERS()
    Dim FuncRange As Range

    Dim V() As Integer, ValArray() As Integer
    Dim CellCount As Double
    Dim i As Integer, j As Integer
    Dim r As Integer, c As Integer
```

```
    Dim Temp1 As Variant, Temp2 As Variant
    Dim RCount As Integer, CCount As Integer
    Randomize
'   Create Range object
    Set FuncRange = Application.Caller

'   Return an error if FuncRange is too large
    CellCount = FuncRange.Count
    If CellCount > 1000 Then
        RANDOMINTEGERS = CVErr(xlErrNA)
        Exit Function
    End If

'   Assign variables
    RCount = FuncRange.Rows.Count
    CCount = FuncRange.Columns.Count
    ReDim V(1 To RCount, 1 To CCount)
    ReDim ValArray(1 To 2, 1 To CellCount)

'   Fill array with random numbers
'   and consecutive integers
    For i = 1 To CellCount
        ValArray(1, i) = Rnd
        ValArray(2, i) = i
    Next i

'   Sort ValArray by the random number dimension
    For i = 1 To CellCount
        For j = i + 1 To CellCount
            If ValArray(1, i) > ValArray(1, j) Then
                Temp1 = ValArray(1, j)
                Temp2 = ValArray(2, j)
                ValArray(1, j) = ValArray(1, i)
                ValArray(2, j) = ValArray(2, i)
                ValArray(1, i) = Temp1
                ValArray(2, i) = Temp2
            End If
        Next j
    Next i

'   Put the randomized values into the V array
    i = 0
    For r = 1 To RCount
        For c = 1 To CCount
            i = i + 1
            V(r, c) = ValArray(2, i)
        Next c
    Next r
    RANDOMINTEGERS = V
End Function
```

On the Web

The workbook random integers function.xlsm containing the RANDOMINTEGERS function is available at this book's website.

Randomizing a range

The following RANGERANDOMIZE function accepts a range argument and returns an array that consists of the input range in random order:

```
Function RANGERANDOMIZE(rng)
    Dim V() As Variant, ValArray() As Variant
    Dim CellCount As Double
    Dim i As Integer, j As Integer
    Dim r As Integer, c As Integer
    Dim Temp1 As Variant, Temp2 As Variant
    Dim RCount As Integer, CCount As Integer
    Randomize

'   Return an error if rng is too large
    CellCount = rng.Count
    If CellCount > 1000 Then
        RANGERANDOMIZE = CVErr(xlErrNA)
        Exit Function
    End If

'   Assign variables
    RCount = rng.Rows.Count
    CCount = rng.Columns.Count
    ReDim V(1 To RCount, 1 To CCount)
    ReDim ValArray(1 To 2, 1 To CellCount)

'   Fill ValArray with random numbers
'   and values from rng
    For i = 1 To CellCount
        ValArray(1, i) = Rnd
        ValArray(2, i) = rng(i)
    Next i

'   Sort ValArray by the random number dimension
    For i = 1 To CellCount
        For j = i + 1 To CellCount
            If ValArray(1, i) > ValArray(1, j) Then
                Temp1 = ValArray(1, j)
                Temp2 = ValArray(2, j)
                ValArray(1, j) = ValArray(1, i)
                ValArray(2, j) = ValArray(2, i)
                ValArray(1, i) = Temp1
                ValArray(2, i) = Temp2
```

```
            End If
        Next j
    Next i

'   Put the randomized values into the V array
    i = 0
    For r = 1 To RCount
        For c = 1 To CCount
            i = i + 1
            V(r, c) = ValArray(2, i)
        Next c
    Next r
    RANGERANDOMIZE = V
End Function
```

The code closely resembles the code for the RANDOMINTEGERS function. Figure 26-9 shows the function in use. The following array formula, which is in E15:F27, returns the contents of B15:C27 in a random order:

```
{=RANGERANDOMIZE(B15:C27)}
```

E15 {=RANGERANDOMIZE(B15:C27)}

	A	B	C	D	E	F	G
13							
14		Original			Randomized		
15		A	N		L	T	
16		B	O		Z	E	
17		C	P		C	V	
18		D	Q		J	Y	
19		E	R		U	B	
20		F	S		I	F	
21		G	T		R	P	
22		H	U		M	Q	
23		I	V		H	X	
24		J	W		D	W	
25		K	X		G	A	
26		L	Y		S	O	
27		M	Z		N	K	

Figure 26-9: The `RANGERANDOMIZE` function returns the contents of a range, but in a randomized order.

On the Web

The workbook range randomize function.xlsm, which contains the RANGERANDOMIZE function, is available at this book's website.

Using optional arguments

Many of the built-in Excel worksheet functions use optional arguments. For example, the LEFT function returns characters from the left side of a string. Its official syntax is as follows:

```
LEFT(text,<i>num_chars</i>)
```

The first argument is required, but the second is optional. If you omit the optional argument, Excel assumes a value of 1.

Custom functions that you develop in VBA can also have optional arguments. You specify an optional argument by preceding the argument's name with the keyword Optional. The following is a simple function that returns the user's name:

```
Function USER()
    USER = Application.UserName
End Function
```

Suppose that in some cases, you want the user's name to be returned in uppercase letters. The following function uses an optional argument:

```
Function USER(Optional UpperCase As Variant) As String
    If IsMissing(UpperCase) Then UpperCase = False
    If UpperCase = True Then
        USER = Ucase(Application.UserName)
    Else
        USER = Application.UserName
    End If
End Function
```

Note

If you need to determine whether an optional argument was passed to a function, you must declare the optional argument as a variant data type. Then you can use the IsMissing function within the procedure, as demonstrated in this example.

If the argument is *FALSE* or omitted, the user's name is returned without changes. If the argument is *TRUE*, the user's name converts to uppercase (using the VBA Ucase function) before it is returned. Notice that the first statement in the procedure uses the VBA IsMissing function to determine whether the argument was supplied. If the argument is missing, the statement sets the UpperCase variable to *FALSE* (the default value).

Optional arguments also allow you to specify a default value in the declaration, rather than testing it with the IsMissing function. The preceding function can be rewritten in this alternate syntax as follows:

```
Function USER(Optional UpperCase As Boolean = False) As String
    If UpperCase = True Then
        USER = UCase(Application.UserName)
    Else
        USER = Application.UserName
    End If
End Function
```

If no argument is supplied, UpperCase is automatically assigned a value of *FALSE*. This allows you to type the argument appropriately instead of with the generic Variant data type. If you use this method, however, there is no way to tell whether the user omitted the argument or supplied the default argument. Also, the argument will be tagged as optional in the Insert Function dialog.

All the following formulas are valid in either syntax (and the first two have the same effect):

```
=USER()
=USER(False)
=USER(True)
```

Using an indefinite number of arguments

Some of the Excel worksheet functions take an indefinite number of arguments. A familiar example is the SUM function, which has the following syntax:

```
SUM(number1,number2...)
```

The first argument is required, but you can have as many as 254 additional arguments. Here's an example of a formula that uses the SUM function with four range arguments:

```
=SUM(A1:A5,C1:C5,E1:E5,G1:G5)
```

You can mix and match the argument types. For example, the following example uses three arguments—a range, followed by a value, and finally an expression:

```
=SUM(A1:A5,12,24*3)
```

You can create Function procedures that have an indefinite number of arguments. The trick is to use an array as the last (or only) argument, preceded by the keyword ParamArray.

Note

ParamArray can apply only to the *last* argument in the procedure. It is always a variant data type, and it is always an optional argument (although you don't use the Optional keyword).

A simple example of arguments

The following is a Function procedure that can have any number of single-value arguments. It simply returns the sum of the arguments:

```
Function SIMPLESUM(ParamArray arglist() As Variant) As Double
    Dim arg as Variant
    For Each arg In arglist
        SIMPLESUM = SIMPLESUM + arg
    Next arg
End Function
```

The following formula returns the sum of the single-cell arguments:

```
=SIMPLESUM(A1,A5,12)
```

The most serious limitation of the SIMPLESUM function is that it does not handle multicell ranges. This improved version does:

```
Function SIMPLESUM(ParamArray arglist() As Variant) As Double
    Dim arg as Variant
    Dim cell as Range
    For Each arg In arglist
        If TypeName(arg) = "Range" Then
            For Each cell In arg
                SIMPLESUM = SIMPLESUM + cell.Value
            Next cell
        Else
            SIMPLESUM = SIMPLESUM + arg
        End If
    Next arg
End Function
```

This function checks each entry in the Arglist array. If the entry is a range, the code uses a For Each-Next loop to sum the cells in the range.

Even this improved version is certainly no substitute for the Excel SUM function. Try it by using various types of arguments, and you'll see that it fails unless each argument is a value or a range reference. Also, if an argument consists of an entire column, you'll find that the function is *very* slow because it evaluates every cell—even the empty ones.

Emulating the Excel SUM function

This section presents a Function procedure called MYSUM. Unlike the SIMPLESUM function listed in the previous section, MYSUM emulates the Excel SUM function perfectly.

Before you look at the code for the MYSUM function, take a minute to think about the Excel SUM function. This versatile function can have any number of arguments (even missing arguments), and the arguments can be numerical values, cells, ranges, text representations of numbers, logical values, and even embedded functions. For example, consider the following formula:

```
=SUM(A1,5,"6",,TRUE,SQRT(4),B1:B5,{1,3,5})
```

This formula—which is valid—contains all the following types of arguments, listed here in the order of their presentation:

- A single cell reference (A1)
- A literal value (5)
- A string that looks like a value ("6")
- A missing argument
- A logical value (*TRUE*)
- An expression that uses another function (SQRT)
- A range reference (B1:B5)
- An array ({1,3,5})

The following is the listing for the MYSUM function that handles all these argument types:

```
Function MySum(ParamArray args() As Variant) As Variant
' Emulates Excel's SUM function
' Variable declarations
  Dim i As Variant
  Dim TempRange As Range, cell As Range
  Dim ECode As String
  Dim m, n
  MySum = 0

' Process each argument
  For i = 0 To UBound(args)
```

```
'   Skip missing arguments
    If Not IsMissing(args(i)) Then
'     What type of argument is it?
      Select Case TypeName(args(i))
        Case "Range"
'         Create temp range to handle full row or column ranges
          Set TempRange = Intersect(args(i).Parent.UsedRange, args(i))
          For Each cell In TempRange
            If IsError(cell) Then
              MySum = cell ' return the error
              Exit Function
            End If
            If cell = True Or cell = False Then
              MySum = MySum + 0
            Else
              If IsNumeric(cell) Or IsDate(cell) Then _
                 MySum = MySum + cell
              End If
          Next cell
        Case "Variant()"
            n = args(i)
            For m = LBound(n) To UBound(n)
               MySum = MySum(MySum, n(m)) 'recursive call
            Next m
        Case "Null"  'ignore it
        Case "Error" 'return the error
          MySum = args(i)
          Exit Function
        Case "Boolean"
'         Check for literal TRUE and compensate
          If args(i) = "True" Then MySum = MySum + 1
        Case "Date"
          MySum = MySum + args(i)
        Case Else
          MySum = MySum + args(i)
      End Select
    End If
  Next i
End Function
```

On the Web

The workbook sum function emulation.xlsm containing the MYSUM function is available at this book's website.

Figure 26-10 shows a workbook with various formulas that use SUM (column E) and MYSUM (column G). As you can see, the functions return identical results.

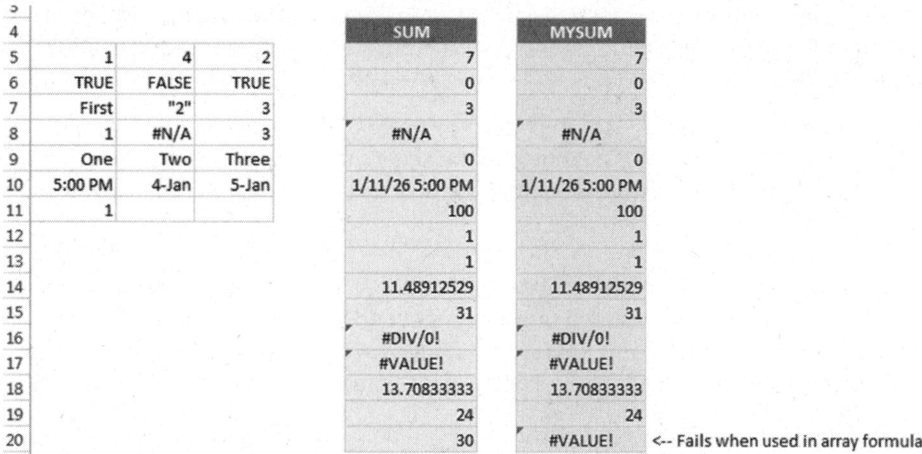

				SUM	MYSUM	
4				SUM	MYSUM	
5	1	4	2	7	7	
6	TRUE	FALSE	TRUE	0	0	
7	First	"2"	3	3	3	
8	1	#N/A	3	#N/A	#N/A	
9	One	Two	Three	0	0	
10	5:00 PM	4-Jan	5-Jan	1/11/26 5:00 PM	1/11/26 5:00 PM	
11	1			100	100	
12				1	1	
13				1	1	
14				11.48912529	11.48912529	
15				31	31	
16				#DIV/0!	#DIV/0!	
17				#VALUE!	#VALUE!	
18				13.70833333	13.70833333	
19				24	24	
20				30	#VALUE!	<-- Fails when used in array formula

Figure 26-10: Comparing Excel's SUM function with a custom function.

MYSUM is a close emulation of the SUM function, but it's not perfect. It cannot handle operations on arrays. For example, this array formula returns the sum of the squared values in range A1:A4:

```
{=SUM(A:A4^2)}
```

This formula returns a *#VALUE!* error:

```
{=MYSUM(A1:A4^2)}
```

As you study the code for MYSUM, keep the following points in mind:

- Missing arguments (determined by the IsMissing function) are simply ignored.
- The procedure uses the VBA TypeName function to determine the type of argument (Range, Error, or something else). Each argument type is handled differently.
- For a range argument, the function loops through each cell in the range and adds its value to a running total.
- The data type for the function is Variant because the function needs to return an error if any of its arguments is an error value.
- If an argument contains an error (for example, #DIV0!), the MYSUM function simply returns the error—just like the Excel SUM function.
- The Excel SUM function considers a text string to have a value of 0 unless it appears as a literal argument (that is, as an actual value, not a variable). Therefore, MYSUM adds the cell's value only if it can be evaluated as a number (VBA's IsNumeric function is used for this).

- Dealing with Boolean arguments is tricky. For MYSUM to emulate SUM exactly, it needs to test for a literal TRUE in the argument list and compensate for the difference (that is, add 2 to –1 to get 1).
- For range arguments, the function uses the Intersect method to create a temporary range that consists of the intersection of the range and the sheet's used range. This handles cases in which a range argument consists of a complete row or column, which would take forever to evaluate.

You may be curious about the relative speeds of SUM and MYSUM. MYSUM, of course, is much slower, but just how much slower depends on the speed of your system and the formulas themselves. On our system, a worksheet with 5,000 SUM formulas recalculated instantly. After we replaced the SUM functions with MYSUM functions, it took about 8 seconds. MYSUM may be improved a bit, but it can never come close to SUM's speed.

By the way, we hope you understand that the point of this example is not to create a new SUM function. Rather, it demonstrates how to create custom worksheet functions that look and work like those built into Excel.

Appendixes

A

Excel Function Reference

This appendix contains a complete listing of the Excel worksheet functions. The functions are arranged alphabetically in tables by categories used by the Insert Function dialog box.

For more information about a particular function, including its arguments, select the function in the Insert Function dialog box and click Help on This Function.

On the Web

An interactive workbook that contains this information is available at this book's website. The filename is worksheet functions.xlsx.

Table A-1: Compatibility Category Functions

Function	What It Does
BETADIST	Returns the cumulative beta probability density function.
BETAINV	Returns the inverse of the cumulative beta probability density function.
BINOMDIST	Returns the individual term binomial distribution probability.
CEILING	Rounds a number to the nearest integer or to the nearest multiple of significance.
CHIDIST	Returns the right-tailed probability of the chi-squared distribution.
CHIINV	Returns the inverse of the right-tailed probability of the chi-squared distribution.
CHITEST	Returns the test for independence.
CONFIDENCE	Returns the confidence interval for a population mean.
COVAR	Returns *covariance,* the average of the products of paired deviations.
CRITBINOM	Returns the smallest value for which the cumulative binomial distribution is less than or equal to a criterion value.
EXPONDIST	Returns the exponential distribution.
FDIST	Returns the F probability distribution.
FINV	Returns the inverse of the F probability distribution.
FLOOR	Rounds a number down, toward zero.

continued

Table A-1: Compatibility Category Functions *(continued)*

Function	What It Does
FORECAST	Predicts a future value along a linear trend.
FTEST	Returns the result of an F-test.
GAMMADIST	Returns the gamma distribution.
GAMMAINV	Returns the inverse of the gamma cumulative distribution.
HYPGEOMDIST	Returns the hypergeometric distribution.
LOGINV	Returns the inverse of the lognormal distribution.
LOGNORMDIST	Returns the cumulative lognormal distribution.
MODE	Returns the most common value in a data set.
NEGBINOMDIST	Returns the negative binomial distribution.
NORMDIST	Returns the normal cumulative distribution.
NORMINV	Returns the inverse of the normal cumulative distribution.
NORMSDIST	Returns the standard normal cumulative distribution.
NORMSINV	Returns the inverse of the standard normal cumulative distribution.
PERCENTILE	Returns the *k*th percentile of values in a range.
PERCENTRANK	Returns the percentage rank of a value in a data set.
POISSON	Returns the Poisson distribution.
QUARTILE	Returns the quartile of a data set.
RANK	Returns the rank of a number in a list of numbers.
STDEV	Estimates standard deviation based on a sample, ignoring text and logical values.
STDEVP	Calculates standard deviation based on the entire population, ignoring text and logical values.
TDIST	Returns the Student's t-distribution.
TINV	Returns the inverse of the Student's t-distribution.
TTEST	Returns the probability associated with a Student's t-test.
VAR	Estimates variance based on a sample, ignoring logical values and text.
VARP	Calculates variance based on the entire population, ignoring logical values and text.
WEIBULL	Returns the Weibull distribution.
ZTEST	Returns the one-tailed p-value of a z-test.

The functions in the Compatibility category all have new versions that were introduced in Excel 2010 or later. The old versions are still available for compatibility.

Table A-2: Cube Category Functions

Function	What It Does
CUBEKPIMEMBER	Returns a key performance indicator property and displays the name and property in the cell.
CUBEMEMBER	Returns a member or tuple in a cube hierarchy.

Function	What It Does
CUBEMEMBERPROPERTY	Returns the value of a member property in the cube.
CUBERANKEDMEMBER	Returns the *n*th, or ranked, member in a set.
CUBESET	Defines a calculated set of members or tuples by sending a set expression to the cube on the server.
CUBESETCOUNT	Returns the number of items in a set.
CUBEVALUE	Returns an aggregated value from a cube.

Table A-3: Database Category Functions

Function	What It Does
DAVERAGE	Averages the values in a column of a list or database that match conditions you specify.
DCOUNT	Counts the cells that contain numbers in a column of a list or database that match conditions you specify.
DCOUNTA	Counts the nonblank cells in a column of a list or database that match conditions you specify.
DGET	Extracts a single value from a column of a list or database that matches conditions you specify.
DMAX	Returns the largest number in a column of a list or database that matches conditions you specify.
DMIN	Returns the smallest number in a column of a list or database that matches conditions you specify.
DPRODUCT	Multiplies the values in a column of a list or database that match conditions you specify.
DSTDEV	Estimates the standard deviation of a population based on a sample by using the numbers in a column of a list or database that match conditions you specify.
DSTDEVP	Calculates the standard deviation of a population based on the entire population, using the numbers in a column of a list or database that match conditions you specify.
DSUM	Adds the numbers in a column of a list or database that match conditions you specify.
DVAR	Estimates the variance of a population based on a sample by using the numbers in a column of a list or database that match conditions you specify.
DVARP	Calculates the variance of a population based on the entire population by using the numbers in a column of a list or database that match conditions you specify.

Table A-4: Date & Time Category Functions

Function	What It Does
DATE	Returns the serial number of a particular date.
DATEVALUE	Converts a date in the form of text to a serial number.
DAY	Converts a serial number to a day of the month.
DAYS**	Returns the number of days between two dates.
DAYS360	Calculates the number of days between two dates, based on a 360-day year.
EDATE	Returns the serial number of the date that is the indicated number of months before or after the start date.

continued

Table A-4: Date & Time Category Functions *(continued)*

Function	What It Does
EOMONTH	Returns the serial number of the last day of the month before or after a specified number of months.
HOUR	Converts a serial number to an hour.
ISOWEEKNUM**	Returns the ISO week number in the year for a given date.
MINUTE	Converts a serial number to a minute.
MONTH	Converts a serial number to a month.
NETWORKDAYS	Returns the number of whole workdays between two dates.
NETWORKDAYS.INTL*	Returns the number of whole workdays between two dates (international version).
NOW	Returns the serial number of the current date and time.
SECOND	Converts a serial number to a second.
TIME	Returns the serial number of a particular time.
TIMEVALUE	Converts a time in the form of text to a serial number.
TODAY	Returns the serial number of today's date.
WEEKDAY	Converts a serial number to a day of the week.
WEEKNUM	Returns the week number in the year.
WORKDAY	Returns the serial number of the date before or after a specified number of workdays.
WORKDAY.INTL*	Returns the serial number of the date before or after a specified number of work-days (international version).
YEAR	Converts a serial number to a year.
YEARFRAC	Returns the year fraction representing the number of whole days between two dates.

* *Indicates a function introduced in Excel 2010.*
** *Indicates a function introduced in Excel 2013.*

Table A-5: Engineering Category Functions

Function	What It Does
BESSELI	Returns the modified Bessel function In(x).
BESSELJ	Returns the Bessel function Jn(x).
BESSELK	Returns the modified Bessel function Kn(x).
BESSELY	Returns the Bessel function Yn(x).
BIN2DEC	Converts a binary number to decimal.
BIN2HEX	Converts a binary number to hexadecimal.
BIN2OCT	Converts a binary number to octal.
BITAND**	Returns a bitwise AND of two numbers.
BITLSHIFT**	Returns a value number shifted left by a specified number of bits.

Function	What It Does
BITOR**	Returns a bitwise OR of two numbers.
BITRSHIFT**	Returns a value number shifted right by a specified number of bits.
BITXOR**	Returns a bitwise Exclusive OR of two numbers.
COMPLEX	Converts real and imaginary coefficients into a complex number.
CONVERT	Converts a number from one measurement system to another.
DEC2BIN	Converts a decimal number to binary.
DEC2HEX	Converts a decimal number to hexadecimal.
DEC2OCT	Converts a decimal number to octal.
DELTA	Tests whether two values are equal.
ERF	Returns the error function.
ERF.PRECISE*	Returns the error function.
ERFC	Returns the complementary error function.
ERFC. PRECISE*	Returns the complementary error function.
GESTEP	Tests whether a number is greater than a threshold value.
HEX2BIN	Converts a hexadecimal number to binary.
HEX2DEC	Converts a hexadecimal number to decimal.
HEX2OCT	Converts a hexadecimal number to octal.
IMABS	Returns the absolute value (modulus) of a complex number.
IMAGINARY	Returns the imaginary coefficient of a complex number.
IMARGUMENT	Returns the argument *theta,* an angle expressed in radians.
IMCONJUGATE	Returns the complex conjugate of a complex number.
IMCOS	Returns the cosine of a complex number.
IMCOSH**	Returns the hyperbolic cosine of a complex number.
IMCOT**	Returns the cotangent of a complex number.
IMCSC**	Returns the cosecant of a complex number.
IMCSCH**	Returns the hyperbolic cosecant of a complex number.
IMDIV	Returns the quotient of two complex numbers.
IMEXP	Returns the exponential of a complex number.
IMLN	Returns the natural logarithm of a complex number.
IMLOG10	Returns the base 10 logarithm of a complex number.
IMLOG2	Returns the base 2 logarithm of a complex number.
IMPOWER	Returns a complex number raised to an integer power.
IMPRODUCT	Returns the product of complex numbers.
IMREAL	Returns the real coefficient of a complex number.
IMSEC**	Returns the secant of a complex number.

continued

Table A-5: Engineering Category Functions *(continued)*

Function	What It Does
IMSECH**	Returns the hyperbolic secant of a complex number.
IMSIN	Returns the sine of a complex number.
IMSINH**	Returns the hyperbolic sine of a complex number.
IMSQRT	Returns the square root of a complex number.
IMSUB	Returns the difference of two complex numbers.
IMSUM	Returns the sum of complex numbers.
IMTAN**	Returns the tangent of a complex number.
OCT2BIN	Converts an octal number to binary.
OCT2DEC	Converts an octal number to decimal.
OCT2HEX	Converts an octal number to hexadecimal.

* *Indicates a function introduced in Excel 2010.*
** *Indicates a function introduced in Excel 2013.*

Table A-6: Financial Category Functions

Function	What It Does
ACCRINT	Returns the accrued interest for a security that pays periodic interest.
ACCRINTM	Returns the accrued interest for a security that pays interest at maturity.
AMORDEGRC	Returns the depreciation for each accounting period.
AMORLINC	Returns the depreciation for each accounting period.
COUPDAYBS	Returns the number of days from the beginning of the coupon period to the settlement date.
COUPDAYS	Returns the number of days in the coupon period that contains the settlement date.
COUPDAYSNC	Returns the number of days from the settlement date to the next coupon date.
COUPNCD	Returns the next coupon date after the settlement date.
COUPNUM	Returns the number of coupons payable between the settlement date and maturity date.
COUPPCD	Returns the previous coupon date before the settlement date.
CUMIPMT	Returns the cumulative interest paid between two periods.
CUMPRINC	Returns the cumulative principal paid on a loan between two periods.
DB	Returns the depreciation of an asset for a specified period, using the fixed declining-balance method.
DDB	Returns the depreciation of an asset for a specified period, using the double declining-balance method or some other method that you specify.
DISC	Returns the discount rate for a security.
DOLLARDE	Converts a dollar price, expressed as a fraction, into a dollar price expressed as a decimal number.

Function	What It Does
DOLLARFR	Converts a dollar price, expressed as a decimal number, into a dollar price expressed as a fraction.
DURATION	Returns the annual duration of a security with periodic interest payments.
EFFECT	Returns the effective annual interest rate.
FV	Returns the future value of an investment.
FVSCHEDULE	Returns the future value of an initial principal after applying a series of compound interest rates.
INTRATE	Returns the interest rate for a fully invested security.
IPMT	Returns the interest payment for an investment for a given period.
IRR	Returns the internal rate of return for a series of cash flows.
ISPMT	Returns the interest paid during a specific period.
MDURATION	Returns the Macauley modified duration for a security with an assumed par value of $100.
MIRR	Returns the internal rate of return where positive and negative cash flows are financed at different rates.
NOMINAL	Returns the annual nominal interest rate.
NPER	Returns the number of periods for an investment.
NPV	Returns the net present value of an investment based on a series of periodic cash flows and a discount rate.
ODDFPRICE	Returns the price per $100 face value of a security with an odd first period.
ODDFYIELD	Returns the yield of a security with an odd first period.
ODDLPRICE	Returns the price per $100 face value of a security with an odd last period.
ODDLYIELD	Returns the yield of a security with an odd last period.
PDURATION*	Returns the number of periods required by an investment to reach a specified value.
PMT	Returns the periodic payment for an annuity.
PPMT	Returns the payment on the principal for an investment for a given period.
PRICE	Returns the price per $100 face value of a security that pays periodic interest.
PRICEDISC	Returns the price per $100 face value of a discounted security.
PRICEMAT	Returns the price per $100 face value of a security that pays interest at maturity.
PV	Returns the present value of an investment.
RATE	Returns the interest rate per period of an annuity.
RECEIVED	Returns the amount received at maturity for a fully invested security.
RRI*	Returns an equivalent interest rate for the growth of an investment.
SLN	Returns the straight-line depreciation of an asset for one period.
SYD	Returns the sum-of-years' digits depreciation of an asset for a specified period.
TBILLEQ	Returns the bond-equivalent yield for a Treasury bill.
TBILLPRICE	Returns the price per $100 face value for a Treasury bill.

continued

Table A-6: Financial Category Functions *(continued)*

Function	What It Does
TBILLYIELD	Returns the yield for a Treasury bill.
VDB	Returns the depreciation of an asset for a specified or partial period using a double declining-balance method.
XIRR	Returns the internal rate of return for a schedule of cash flows that is not necessarily periodic.
XNPV	Returns the net present value for a schedule of cash flows that is not necessarily periodic.
YIELD	Returns the yield on a security that pays periodic interest.
YIELDDISC	Returns the annual yield for a discounted security, for example, a Treasury bill.
YIELDMAT	Returns the annual yield of a security that pays interest at maturity.

** Indicates a function introduced in Excel 2013.*

Table A-7: Information Category Functions

Function	What It Does
CELL	Returns information about the formatting, location, or contents of a cell.
ERROR.TYPE	Returns a number matching an error value.
INFO	Returns information about the current operating environment.
ISBLANK	Returns TRUE if the cell is empty.
ISERR	Returns TRUE if the value is any error value except #N/A.
ISERROR	Returns TRUE if the value is any error value.
ISEVEN	Returns TRUE if the number is even.
ISFORMULA*	Returns TRUE if there is a reference to a cell that contains a formula.
ISLOGICAL	Returns TRUE if the value is a logical value.
ISNA	Returns TRUE if the value is the #N/A error value.
ISNONTEXT	Returns TRUE if the value is not text.
ISNUMBER	Returns TRUE if the value is a number.
ISODD	Returns TRUE if the number is odd.
ISREF	Returns TRUE if the value is a reference.
ISTEXT	Returns TRUE if the value is text.
N	Converts a non-number value to a number, a date to a serial number, TRUE to 1, and anything else to 0.
NA	Returns the error value #N/A.
SHEET*	Returns the sheet number of the referenced sheet.
SHEETS*	Returns the number of sheets in a reference.
TYPE	Returns a number indicating the data type of a value.

** Indicates a function introduced in Excel 2013.*

Table A-8: Logical Category Functions

Function	What It Does
AND	Returns TRUE if all its arguments are TRUE.
FALSE	Returns the logical value FALSE.
IF	Specifies a logical test to perform.
IFERROR	Returns an alternate result if the first argument evaluates to an error.
IFNA*	Returns an alternate result if the first argument evaluates to #N/A.
NOT	Changes FALSE to TRUE and TRUE to FALSE.
OR	Returns TRUE if any argument is TRUE.
TRUE	Returns the logical value TRUE.
XOR*	Returns a logical Exclusive OR of all arguments.

** Indicates a function introduced in Excel 2013.*

Table A-9: Lookup & Reference Category Functions

Function	What It Does
ADDRESS	Returns a reference as text to a single cell in a worksheet.
AREAS	Returns the number of areas in a reference.
CHOOSE	Chooses a value from a list of values based on an index number.
COLUMN	Returns the column number of a reference.
COLUMNS	Returns the number of columns in a reference.
FORMULATEXT*	Returns the formula at the given reference as text.
GETPIVOTDATA	Returns data stored in a pivot table.
HLOOKUP	Searches for a value in the top row of a table and then returns a value in the same column from a row you specify.
HYPERLINK	Creates a shortcut that opens a document on your hard drive, a server, or the Internet.
INDEX	Uses an index to choose a value from a reference or array.
INDIRECT	Returns a reference indicated by a text string.
LOOKUP	Returns a value from either a one-row or one-column range or from an array.
MATCH	Returns the relative position of an item in an array.
OFFSET	Returns a reference offset from a given reference.
ROW	Returns the row number of a reference.
ROWS	Returns the number of rows in a reference.
RTD	Returns real-time data from a program that supports COM automation.
TRANSPOSE	Returns the transpose of an array.
VLOOKUP	Searches for a value in the leftmost column of a table and then returns a value in the same row from a column you specify in the table.

** Indicates a function introduced in Excel 2013.*

Table A-10: Math & Trig Category Functions

Function	What It Does
ABS	Returns the absolute value of a number.
ACOS	Returns the arccosine of a number.
ACOSH	Returns the inverse hyperbolic cosine of a number.
ACOT**	Returns the arccotangent of a number.
ACOTH**	Returns the hyperbolic arccotangent of a number.
AGGREGATE*	Returns an aggregate in a list or database.
ARABIC**	Converts a Roman number to Arabic, as a number.
ASIN	Returns the arcsine of a number.
ASINH	Returns the inverse hyperbolic sine of a number.
ATAN	Returns the arctangent of a number.
ATAN2	Returns the arctangent from *x* and *y* coordinates.
ATANH	Returns the inverse hyperbolic tangent of a number.
BASE**	Converts a number into a text representation with the given radix (base).
CEILING.MATH**	Rounds a number up, to the nearest integer or to the nearest multiple of significance.
COMBIN	Returns the number of combinations for a given number of objects.
COMBINA**	Returns the number of combinations with repetitions for a given number of items.
COS	Returns the cosine of a number.
COSH	Returns the hyperbolic cosine of a number.
COT**	Returns the cotangent of an angle.
COTH**	Returns the hyperbolic cotangent of a number.
CSC**	Returns the cosecant of an angle.
CSCH**	Returns the hyperbolic cosecant of an angle.
DECIMAL**	Converts a text representation of a number in a given base into a decimal number.
DEGREES	Converts radians to degrees.
EVEN	Rounds a number up to the nearest even integer.
EXP	Returns *e* raised to the power of a given number.
FACT	Returns the factorial of a number.
FACTDOUBLE	Returns the double factorial of a number.
FLOOR.MATH**	Rounds a number down, to the nearest integer or to the nearest multiple of significance.
GCD	Returns the greatest common divisor.
INT	Rounds a number down to the nearest integer.
LCM	Returns the least common multiple.
LN	Returns the natural logarithm of a number.
LOG	Returns the logarithm of a number to a specified base.
LOG10	Returns the base 10 logarithm of a number.

Function	What It Does
MDETERM	Returns the matrix determinant of an array.
MINVERSE	Returns the matrix inverse of an array.
MMULT	Returns the matrix product of two arrays.
MOD	Returns the remainder from division.
MROUND	Returns a number rounded to the desired multiple.
MULTINOMIAL	Returns the multinomial of a set of numbers.
MUNIT**	Returns the unit matrix or the specified dimension.
ODD	Rounds a number to the nearest odd integer away from zero.
PI	Returns the value of pi.
POWER	Returns the result of a number raised to a power.
PRODUCT	Multiplies its arguments.
QUOTIENT	Returns the integer portion of a division.
RADIANS	Converts degrees to radians.
RAND	Returns a random number between 0 and 1.
RANDBETWEEN	Returns a random number between the numbers that you specify.
ROMAN	Converts an Arabic numeral to Roman, as text.
ROUND	Rounds a number to a specified number of digits.
ROUNDDOWN	Rounds a number down, toward zero.
ROUNDUP	Rounds a number up, away from zero.
SEC**	Returns the secant of an angle.
SECH**	Returns the hyperbolic secant of an angle.
SERIESSUM	Returns the sum of a power series based on the formula.
SIGN	Returns the sign of a number.
SIN	Returns the sine of the given angle.
SINH	Returns the hyperbolic sine of a number.
SQRT	Returns the square root of a number.
SQRTPI	Returns the square root of a number multiplied by pi.
SUBTOTAL	Returns a subtotal in a list or database.
SUM	Adds its arguments.
SUMIF	Adds the cells specified by a given criteria.
SUMIFS	Adds the cells specified by a multiple criteria.
SUMPRODUCT	Returns the sum of the products of corresponding array components.
SUMSQ	Returns the sum of the squares of the arguments.
SUMX2MY2*	Returns the sum of the difference of squares of corresponding values in two arrays.
SUMX2PY2*	Returns the sum of the sum of squares of corresponding values in two arrays.

continued

Table A-10: Math & Trig Category Functions *(continued)*

Function	What It Does
SUMXMY2*	Returns the sum of squares of differences of corresponding values in two arrays.
TAN	Returns the tangent of a number.
TANH	Returns the hyperbolic tangent of a number.
TRUNC	Truncates a number to a specified precision.

* *Indicates a function introduced in Excel 2010.*
** *Indicates a function introduced in Excel 2013.*

Table A-11: Statistical Category Functions

Function	What It Does
AVEDEV	Returns the average of the absolute deviations of data points from their mean.
AVERAGE	Returns the arithmetic mean of its arguments.
AVERAGEA	Returns the arithmetic mean of its arguments and includes evaluation of text and logical values.
AVERAGEIF	Returns the arithmetic mean for the cells specified by a given criterion.
AVERAGEIFS	Returns the arithmetic mean for the cells specified by multiple criteria.
BETA.DIST*	Returns the beta cumulative distribution function.
BETA.INV*	Returns the inverse of the cumulative distribution function for a specified beta distribution.
BINOM.DIST*	Returns the individual term binomial distribution probability.
BINOM.DIST.RANGE**	Returns the probability of a trial result using a binomial distribution.
BINOM.INV*	Returns the smallest value for which the cumulative binomial distribution is less than or equal to a criterion value.
CHISQ.DIST*	Returns the chi-squared distribution.
CHISQ.DIST.RT*	Returns the right-tailed probability of the chi-squared distribution.
CHISQ.INV*	Returns the inverse of the left-tailed probability of the chi-squared distribution.
CHISQ.INV.RT*	Returns the inverse of the right-tailed probability of the chi-squared distribution.
CHISQ.TEST*	Returns the test for independence.
CONFIDENCE.NORM*	Returns the confidence interval for a population mean.
CONFIDENCE.T*	Returns the confidence interval for a population mean, using a Student's t-distribution.
CORREL	Returns the correlation coefficient between two data sets.

Function	What It Does
COUNT	Counts how many numbers are in the list of arguments.
COUNTA	Counts how many values are in the list of arguments.
COUNTBLANK	Counts the number of blank cells in the argument range.
COUNTIF	Counts the number of cells that meet the criteria you specify in the argument.
COUNTIFS	Counts the number of cells that meet multiple criteria.
COVARIANCE.P*	Returns covariance, the average of the products of paired deviations.
COVARIANCE.S*	Returns the sample covariance, the average of the products' deviations for each data point pair in two data sets.
DEVSQ	Returns the sum of squares of deviations.
EXPON.DIST*	Returns the exponential distribution.
F.DIST*	Returns the F probability distribution.
F.DIST.RT*	Returns the F probability distribution.
F.INV*	Returns the inverse of the F probability distribution.
F.INV.RT*	Returns the inverse of the F probability distribution.
F.TEST*	Returns the result of an F-test.
FISHER	Returns the Fisher transformation.
FISHERINV	Returns the inverse of the Fisher transformation.
FORECAST.ETS***	Returns the forecasted value for a specific future target date using exponential smoothing method.
FORECAST.ETS.CONFINT***	Returns a confidence interval for the forecast value at the specified target date.
FORECAST.ETS.SEASONALITY***	Returns the length of the repetitive pattern detected for the specified time series.
FORECAST.ETS.STAT***	Returns the requested statistic for the forecast.
FORECAST.LINEAR***	Predicts a future value along a linear trend by using existing values.
FREQUENCY	Returns a frequency distribution as a vertical array.
GAMMA**	Returns the gamma function value.
GAMMA.DIST*	Returns the gamma distribution.
GAMMA.INV*	Returns the inverse of the gamma cumulative distribution.
GAMMALN	Returns the natural logarithm of the gamma function.
GAMMALN.PRECISE*	Returns the natural logarithm of the gamma function.
GAUSS**	Returns 0.5 less than the standard normal cumulative distribution.
GEOMEAN	Returns the geometric mean.

continued

Table A-11: Statistical Category Functions *(continued)*

Function	What It Does
GROWTH	Returns values along an exponential trend.
HARMEAN	Returns the harmonic mean.
HYPGEOM.DIST*	Returns the hypergeometric distribution.
INTERCEPT	Returns the intercept of the linear regression line.
KURT	Returns the kurtosis of a data set.
LARGE	Returns the *k*th largest value in a data set.
LINEST	Returns the parameters of a linear trend.
LOGEST	Returns the parameters of an exponential trend.
LOGNORM.DIST*	Returns the cumulative lognormal distribution.
LOGNORM.INV*	Returns the inverse of the lognormal cumulative distribution.
MAX	Returns the maximum value in a list of arguments, ignoring logical values and text.
MAXA	Returns the maximum value in a list of arguments, including logical values and text.
MEDIAN	Returns the median of the given numbers.
MIN	Returns the minimum value in a list of arguments, ignoring logical values and text.
MINA	Returns the minimum value in a list of arguments, including logical values and text.
MODE.MULT*	Returns a vertical array of the most frequently occurring or repetitive values in an array or range of data.
MODE.SNGL*	Returns the most common value in a data set.
NEGBINOM.DIST*	Returns the negative binomial distribution.
NORM.DIST*	Returns the normal cumulative distribution.
NORM.INV*	Returns the inverse of the normal cumulative distribution.
NORM.S.DIST*	Returns the standard normal cumulative distribution.
NORM.S.INV*	Returns the inverse of the standard normal cumulative distribution.
PEARSON	Returns the Pearson product moment correlation coefficient.
PERCENTILE.EXC*	Returns the *k*th percentile of values in a range, where *k* is in the range 0 through 1, exclusive.
PERCENTILE.INC*	Returns the *k*th percentile of values in a range, where *k* is in the range 0 through 1, inclusive.
PERCENTRANK.EXC*	Returns the rank of a value in a data set as a percentage (0 through 1, exclusive) of the data set.
PERCENTRANK.INC*	Returns the rank of a value in a data set as a percentage (0 through 1, inclusive) of the data set.

Function	What It Does
PERMUT	Returns the number of permutations for a given number of objects.
PERMUTATIONA**	Returns the number of permutations for a given number of objects (with repetitions) that can be selected from the total objects.
PHI**	Returns the value of the density function for a standard normal distribution.
POISSON.DIST*	Returns the Poisson distribution.
PROB	Returns the probability that values in a range are between two limits.
QUARTILE.EXC*	Returns the quartile of the data set, based on percentile values from 0 through1, exclusive.
QUARTILE.INC*	Returns the quartile of a data set.
RANK.AVG*	Returns the rank of a number in a list of numbers.
RANK.EQ*	Returns the rank of a number in a list of numbers.
RSQ	Returns the square of the Pearson product moment correlation coefficient.
SKEW	Returns the skewness of a distribution.
SKEW.P**	Returns the skewness of a distribution based on a population.
SLOPE	Returns the slope of the linear regression line.
SMALL	Returns the *k*th smallest value in a data set.
STANDARDIZE	Returns a normalized value.
STDEV.P*	Calculates standard deviation based on the entire population.
STDEV.S*	Estimates standard deviation based on a sample.
STDEVA	Estimates standard deviation based on a sample, including text and logical values.
STDEVPA	Calculates standard deviation based on the entire population, including text and logical values.
STEYX	Returns the standard error of the predicted *y*-value for each *x* in the regression.
T.DIST	Returns the left-tailed Student's t-distribution.
T.DIST.2T*	Returns the the two-tailed Student's t-distribution.
T.DIST.RT*	Returns the right-tailed Student's t-distribution.
T.INV*	Returns the left-tailed inverse of the Student's t-distribution.
T.INV.2T*	Returns the two-tailed inverse of the Student's t-distribution.
T.TEST*	Returns the probability associated with a Student's t-test.
TREND	Returns values along a linear trend.
TRIMMEAN	Returns the mean of the interior of a data set.

continued

Table A-11: Statistical Category Functions *(continued)*

Function	What It Does
`VAR.P*`	Calculates variance based on the entire population.
`VAR.S*`	Estimates variance based on a sample.
`VARA`	Estimates variance based on a sample, including logical values and text.
`VARPA`	Calculates variance based on the entire population, including logical values and text.
`WEIBULL.DIST*`	Returns the Weibull distribution.
`Z.TEST*`	Returns the one-tailed probability-value of a z-test.

* *Indicates a function introduced in Excel 2010.*
** *Indicates a function introduced in Excel 2013.*
*** *Indicates a function introduced in Excel 2016.*

Table A-12: Text Category Functions

Function	What It Does
`BAHTTEXT`	Converts a number to Baht text.
`CHAR`	Returns the character specified by the code number.
`CLEAN`	Removes all nonprintable characters from text.
`CODE`	Returns a numeric code for the first character in a text string.
`CONCATENATE`	Joins several text strings into one text string.
`DOLLAR`	Converts a number to text, using currency format.
`EXACT`	Returns `TRUE` if two text strings are identical.
`FIND`	Returns the starting position of one text string within another (case sensitive).
`FIXED`	Formats a number as text with a fixed number of decimals.
`LEFT`	Returns the specified number of characters from the start of a text string.
`LEN`	Returns the number of characters in a text string.
`LOWER`	Converts text to lowercase.
`MID`	Returns a specific number of characters from a text string, starting at the position you specify.
`NUMBERVALUE*`	Converts text to number in a locale-independent manner.
`PROPER`	Capitalizes the first letter in each word of a text string.
`REPLACE`	Replaces part of a text string with a different text string.
`REPT`	Repeats text a given number of times.
`RIGHT`	Returns the specified number of characters from the end of a text string.
`SEARCH`	Returns the starting position of one text string within another (not case sensitive).
`SUBSTITUTE`	Substitutes new text for old text in a text string.
`T`	Returns the text argument or an empty string for a non-text argument.

Function	What It Does
TEXT	Formats a number and converts it to text.
TRIM	Removes excess spaces from text.
UNICHAR*	Returns the Unicode character that is referenced by the given numeric value.
UNICODE*	Returns the number (code point) that corresponds to the first character of the text.
UPPER	Converts text to uppercase.
VALUE	Converts a text argument to a number.

** Indicates a function introduced in Excel 2013.*

Table A-13: Web Category Functions

Function	What It Does
ENCODEURL*	Returns a URL-encoded string.
FILTERXML*	Returns specific data from the XML content by using the specified XPath.
WEBSERVICE*	Returns data from a web service.

** Indicates a function introduced in Excel 2013.*

Using Custom Number Formats

Although Excel provides a good variety of built-in number formats, you may find that none of these suits your needs. This appendix describes how to create custom number formats and provides many examples.

About Number Formatting

By default, all cells use the General number format. This is basically a "what you type is what you get" format. If the cell is not wide enough to show the entire number, the General format rounds numbers with decimals and uses scientific notation for large numbers. In many cases, you may want to format a cell with something other than the General number format.

The key thing to remember about number formatting is that it affects only how a value is displayed. The actual number remains intact, and any formulas that use a formatted number use the actual number.

Note

An exception to this rule occurs if you specify the Precision as Displayed option on the Advanced tab of the Excel Options dialog box. If that option is in effect, formulas will use the values that are actually displayed in the cells as a result of a number format applied to the cells. In general, using this option is not a good idea because it changes the underlying values in your worksheet.

One more thing to keep in mind: if you use Excel's Find and Replace dialog box (choose Home ➜ Editing ➜ Find & Select ➜ Find), characters that are displayed are a result of number formatting (for example, a currency symbol) and are not searchable by default. To locate information based on formatting, use the Search in Value option in the Find and Replace dialog box.

Automatic number formatting

Excel is smart enough to perform some formatting for you automatically. For example, if you enter **12.3%** into a cell, Excel knows that you want to use a percentage format and applies it automatically. If you use commas to separate thousands (such as 123,456), Excel applies comma formatting for you. And if you precede your value with a currency symbol, Excel formats the cell for currency.

Note

You have an option when it comes to entering values into cells formatted as a percentage. Access the Excel Options dialog box and click the Advanced tab. If the check box labeled Enable Automatic Percent Entry is checked (the default setting), you can simply enter a normal value into a cell formatted to display as a percent (for example, enter 12.5 for 12.5%). If this check box isn't selected, you must enter the value as a decimal (for example, .125 for 12.5%).

Excel automatically applies a built-in number format to a cell based on the following criteria:

- If a number contains a slash (/), it may be converted to a date format or a fraction format.
- If a number contains a hyphen (-), it may be converted to a date format.
- If a number contains a colon (:), or is followed by a space and the letter A or P (uppercase or lowercase), it may be converted to a time format.
- If a number contains the letter E (uppercase or lowercase), it may be converted to scientific notation (also known as *exponential format*). If the number doesn't fit into the column width, it may also be converted to this format.

Tip

Automatic number formatting can be very frustrating. For example, if you enter a part number 10-12 into a cell, Excel will convert it to a date. Even worse, there is no way to convert it back to your original entry! To avoid automatic number formatting when you enter a value, pre-format the data input range with the desired number format or precede your entry with an apostrophe. (The apostrophe makes the entry text, so number formatting is not applied to the cell.)

Formatting numbers by using the Ribbon

The Number group on the Home tab of the Ribbon contains several controls that enable you to apply common number formats quickly. The Number Format drop-down control gives you quick access to 11 common number formats. In addition, the Number group contains some buttons. When you click one of these buttons, the selected cells take on the specified number format. Table B-1 summarizes the formats that these buttons perform in the U.S. English version of Excel.

Note

Some of these buttons actually apply predefined styles to the selected cells. Access Excel's styles by using the Style gallery, from the Styles group of the Home tab. You can modify the styles by right-clicking the style name and choosing Modify from the shortcut menu.

Table B-1: Number-Formatting Buttons on the Ribbon

Button Name	Formatting Applied
Accounting Number Format	Adds a dollar sign to the left, separates thousands with a comma, and displays the value with two digits to the right of the decimal point. This is a drop-down control, so you can select other common currency symbols.

Button Name	**Formatting Applied**
Percent Style	Displays the value as a percentage, with no decimal places. This button applies a style to the cell.
Comma Style	Separates thousands with a comma and displays the value with two digits to the right of the decimal place. This button applies a style to the cell.
Increase Decimal	Increases the number of digits to the right of the decimal point by one.
Decrease Decimal	Decreases the number of digits to the right of the decimal point by one.

Using shortcut keys to format numbers

Another way to apply number formatting is to use shortcut keys. Table B-2 summarizes the shortcut key combinations that you can use to apply common number formatting to the selected cells or range. Notice that these are the shifted versions of the number keys along the top of a typical keyboard.

Table B-2: Number-Formatting Keyboard Shortcuts

Key Combination	**Formatting Applied**
Ctrl+Shift+~	General number format (that is, unformatted values).
Ctrl+Shift+!	Two decimal places, thousands separator, and a hyphen for negative values.
Ctrl+Shift+@	Time format with the hour, minute, and AM or PM.
Ctrl+Shift+#	Date format with the day, month, and year.
Ctrl+Shift+$	Currency format with two decimal places. (Negative numbers appear in parentheses.)
Ctrl+Shift+%	Percentage format with no decimal places.
Ctrl+Shift+^	Scientific notation number format with two decimal places.

Using the format cells dialog box to format numbers

For maximum control of number formatting, use the Number tab of the Format Cells dialog box. To access this dialog box

- Click the dialog box selector in the Home ➜ Number group.
- Choose Home ➜ Number ➜ Number Format ➜ More Number Formats.
- Press Ctrl+1.

The Number tab of the Format Cells dialog box contains 12 categories of number formats from which to choose. When you select a category from the list box, the right side of the dialog box changes to display appropriate options.

Following is a list of the number-format categories along with some general comments:

- **General:** The default format; it displays numbers as integers, as decimals, or in scientific notation if the value is too wide to fit into the cell.

- **Number:** Enables you to specify the number of decimal places, whether to use your system thousands separator (for example, a comma) to separate thousands, and how to display negative numbers.
- **Currency:** Enables you to specify the number of decimal places, to choose a currency symbol, and to display negative numbers. This format always uses the system thousands separator symbol (for example, a comma) to separate thousands.
- **Accounting:** Differs from the Currency format in that the currency symbols always line up vertically, regardless of the number of digits displayed in the value.
- **Date:** Enables you to choose from a variety of date formats and select the locale for your date formats.
- **Time:** Enables you to choose from a number of time formats and select the locale for your time formats.
- **Percentage:** Enables you to choose the number of decimal places; always displays a percent sign.
- **Fraction:** Enables you to choose from among nine fraction formats.
- **Scientific:** Displays numbers in exponential notation (with an E): 2.00E+05 = 200,000. You can choose the number of decimal places to display to the left of E.
- **Text:** When applied to a value, causes Excel to treat the value as text (even if it looks like a value). This feature is useful for such items as numerical part numbers and credit card numbers.
- **Special:** Contains additional number formats. The list varies, depending on the locale you choose. For the English (United States) locale, the formatting options are Zip Code, Zip Code +4, Phone Number, and Social Security Number.
- **Custom:** Enables you to define custom number formats not included in any of the other categories.

Note

If the cell displays a series of hash marks after you apply a number format (such as #########), it usually means that the column isn't wide enough to display the value with the number format that you selected. Either make the column wider (by dragging the right border of the column header) or change the number format. A series of hash marks also can mean that the cell contains an invalid date or time.

Creating a Custom Number Format

The Custom category on the Number tab of the Format Cells dialog box (see Figure B-1) enables you to create number formats not included in any of the other categories. Excel gives you a great deal of flexibility in creating custom number formats. When you create a custom number format, it can be used to format any cells in the workbook. You can create as many custom number formats as you need.

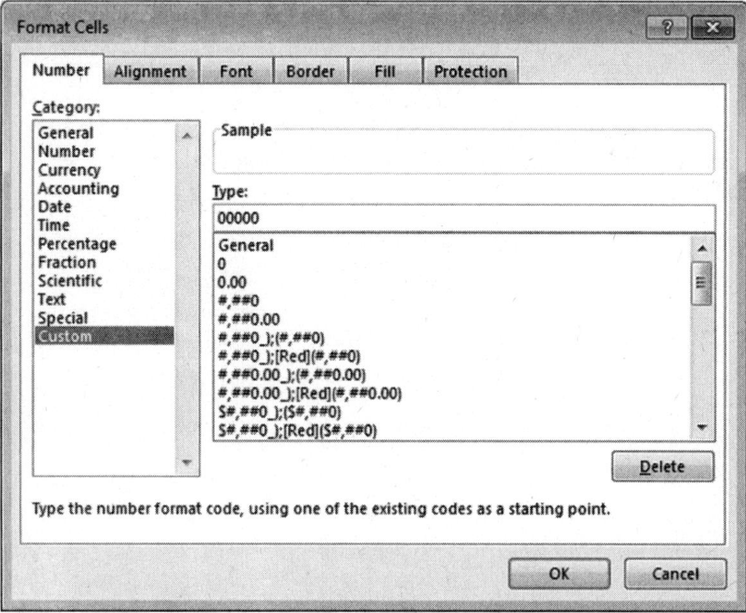

Figure B-1: The Number tab of the Format Cells dialog box.

Tip

Custom number formats are stored with the workbook in which they are defined. To make the custom format available in a different workbook, you can just copy a cell that uses the custom format to the other workbook.

You construct a number format by specifying a series of codes as a number format string. You enter this code sequence in the Type field after you select the Custom category on the Number tab of the Format Cells dialog box. Here's an example of a simple number format code:

```
0.000
```

This code consists of placeholders and a decimal point; it tells Excel to display the value with three digits to the right of the decimal place. Here's another example:

```
00000
```

This custom number format has five placeholders and displays the value with five digits (no decimal point). This format is good to use when the cell holds a five-digit ZIP code. (In fact, this is the code actually used by the Zip Code format in the Special category.) When you format the cell with this number format and then enter a ZIP code, such as 06604 (Bridgeport, CT), the value is displayed with the leading zero. If you enter this number into a cell with the General number format, it displays 6604 (no leading zero).

Scroll through the list of number formats in the Custom category of the Format Cells dialog box to see many more examples. In many cases, you can use one of these codes as a starting point, and you'll need to customize it only slightly.

On the Web

This book's website contains a workbook with many custom number format examples. The file is named number formats.xlsx.

Parts of a number format string

A custom format string can have up to four sections, which enables you to specify different format codes for positive numbers, negative numbers, zero values, and text. You do so by separating the codes with a semicolon. The codes are arranged in the following order:

```
Positive format; Negative format; Zero format; Text format
```

If you don't use all four sections of a format string, Excel interprets the format string as follows:

- **If you use only one section:** The format string applies to all numeric types of entries.
- **If you use two sections:** The first section applies to positive values and zeros, and the second section applies to negative values.
- **If you use three sections:** The first section applies to positive values, the second section applies to negative values, and the third section applies to zeros.
- **If you use all four sections:** The last section applies to text stored in the cell.

The following is an example of a custom number format that specifies a different format for each of these types:

```
[Green]General;[Red]General;[Black]General;[Blue]General
```

This custom number format example takes advantage of the fact that colors have special codes. A cell formatted with this custom number format displays its contents in a different color, depending on the value. When a cell is formatted with this custom number format, a positive number is green, a negative number is red, a zero is black, and text is blue.

Cross-Ref

If you want to apply cell formatting automatically (such as text or background color) based on the cell's contents, a much better solution is to use Excel's Conditional Formatting feature (covered in Chapter 19, "Conditional Formatting").

Pre-formatting cells

Usually, you'll apply number formats to cells that already contain values. You also can format cells with a specific number format before you make an entry. Then, when you enter information, it takes on the format that you specified. You can pre-format specific cells, entire rows or columns, or even the entire worksheet.

Rather than pre-format an entire worksheet, however, you can change the number format for the Normal style. (Unless you specify otherwise, all cells use the Normal style.) Change the Normal style by displaying the Style gallery (choose Home ➜ Styles). Right-click the Normal style icon and then choose Modify to display the Style dialog box. In the Style dialog box, click the Format button and then choose the new number format that you want to use for the Normal style.

Custom number format codes

Table B-3 lists the formatting codes available for custom formats, along with brief descriptions.

Table B-3: Codes Used to Create Custom Number Formats

Code	Comments
General	Displays the number in General format.
#	Digit placeholder. Displays only significant digits and does not display insignificant zeros.
0 (zero)	Digit placeholder. Displays insignificant zeros if a number has fewer digits than there are zeros in the format.
?	Digit placeholder. Adds spaces for insignificant zeros on either side of the decimal point so that decimal points align when formatted with a fixed-width font. You can also use ? for fractions that have varying numbers of digits.
.	Decimal point.
%	Percentage.
,	Thousands separator.
E- E+ e- e+	Scientific notation.
$ - + / ( ) : space	Displays this character.
\	Displays the next character in the format.
*	Repeats the next character, to fill the column width.
_ (underscore)	Leaves a space equal to the width of the next character.

continued

Table B-3: Codes Used to Create Custom Number Formats *(continued)*

Code	Comments
"text"	Displays the text inside the double quotation marks.
@	Text placeholder.
[*color*]	Displays the characters in the color specified. Can be any of the following text strings (not case sensitive): Black, Blue, Cyan, Green, Magenta, Red, White, or Yellow.
[Color *n*]	Displays the corresponding color in the color palette, where *n* is a number from 0 to 56.
[condition value]	Enables you to set your own criterion for each section of a number format.

Table B-4 lists the codes used to create custom formats for dates and times.

Table B-4: Codes Used in Creating Custom Formats for Dates and Times

Code	Comments
m	Displays the month as a number without leading zeros (1–12).
mm	Displays the month as a number with leading zeros (01–12).
mmm	Displays the month as an abbreviation (Jan–Dec).
mmmm	Displays the month as a full name (January–December).
mmmmm	Displays the first letter of the month (J–D).
d	Displays the day as a number without leading zeros (1–31).
dd	Displays the day as a number with leading zeros (01–31).
ddd	Displays the day as an abbreviation (Sun–Sat).
dddd	Displays the day as a full name (Sunday–Saturday).
yy or yyyy	Displays the year as a two-digit number (00–99) or as a four-digit number (1900–9999).
h or hh	Displays the hour as a number without leading zeros (0–23) or as a number with leading zeros (00–23).
m or mm	When used with a colon in a time format, displays the minute as a number without leading zeros (0–59) or as a number with leading zeros (00–59).
s or ss	Displays the second as a number without leading zeros (0-59) or as a number with leading zeros (00–59).
[ ]	Displays hours greater than 24, or minutes or seconds greater than 60.
AM/PM	Displays the hour using a 12-hour clock. If no AM/PM indicator is used, the hour uses a 24-hour clock.

Where did those number formats come from?

Excel may create custom number formats without you realizing it. When you use the Increase Decimal or Decrease Decimal button on the Home ➜ Number group of the Ribbon (or in the Mini Toolbar), Excel creates new custom number formats, which appear on the Number tab of the Format

Cells dialog box. For example, if you click the Increase Decimal button five times, the following custom number formats are created:

```
0.0
0.000
0.0000
0.000000
```

A format string for two decimal places is not created because that format string is built in.

Custom Number Format Examples

The remainder of this appendix consists of useful examples of custom number formats. You can use most of these format codes as-is. Others may require slight modification to meet your needs.

Scaling values

You can use a custom number format to scale a number. For example, if you work with very large numbers, you may want to display the numbers in thousands (that is, displaying 1,000,000 as 1,000). The actual number, of course, will be used in calculations that involve that cell. The formatting affects only how it displays.

Displaying values in thousands

The following format string displays values without the last three digits to the left of the decimal place, and no decimal places. In other words, the value appears as if it's divided by 1,000 and rounded to no decimal places.

```
#,###,
```

A variation of this format string follows. A value with this number format appears as if it's divided by 1,000 and rounded to two decimal places.

```
#,###.00,
```

Table B-5 shows examples of these number formats.

Table B-5: Examples of Displaying Values in Thousands

Value	Number Format	Display
123456	#,###,	123
1234565	#,###,	1,235

continued

Table B-5: Examples of Displaying Values in Thousands *(continued)*

Value	Number Format	Display
-323434	#,###,	-323
123123.123	#,###,	123
499	#,###,	(blank)
500	#,###,	1
123456	#,###.00,	123.46
1234565	#,###.00,	1,234.57
-323434	#,###.00,	-323.43
123123.123	#,###.00,	123.12
499	#,###.00,	.50
500	#,###.00,	.50

Displaying values in hundreds

The following format string displays values in hundreds, with two decimal places. A value with this number format appears as if it's divided by 100 and rounded to two decimal places.

```
0"."00
```

Table B-6 shows examples of these number formats.

Table B-6: Examples of Displaying Values in Hundreds

Value	Number Format	Display
546	0"."00	5.46
100	0"."00	1.00
9890	0"."00	98.90
500	0"."00	5.00
-500	0"."00	-5.00
0	0"."00	0.00

Displaying values in millions

The following format string displays values in millions, with no decimal places. A value with this number appears as if it's divided by 1,000,000 and rounded to no decimal places.

```
#,###,,
```

A variation of this format string follows. A value with this number appears as if it's divided by 1,000,000 and rounded to two decimal places.

```
#,###.00,,
```

Here's another variation. This format string adds the letter M to the end of the value.

```
#,###,,"M"
```

The following format string is a bit more complex. It adds the letter M to the end of the value — and also displays negative values in parentheses as well as displaying zeros.

```
#,###.0,,"M"_);(#,###.0,,"M)";0.0"M"_)
```

Table B-7 shows examples of these format strings.

Table B-7: Examples of Displaying Values in Millions

Value	Number Format	Display
123456789	#,###,,	123
1.23457E+11	#,###,,	123,457
1000000	#,###,,	1
5000000	#,###,,	5
-5000000	#,###,,	-5
0	#,###,,	(blank)
123456789	#,###.00,,	123.46
1.23457E+11	#,###.00,,	123,457.00
1000000	#,###.00,,	1.00
5000000	#,###.00,,	5.00
-5000000	#,###.00,,	-5.00
0	#,###.00,,	.00
123456789	#,###,,"M"	123M
1.23457E+11	#,###,,"M"	123,457M
1000000	#,###,,"M"	1M
5000000	#,###,,"M"	5M
-5000000	#,###,,"M"	-5M
0	#,###,,"M"	M
123456789	#,###.0,,"M"_);(#,###.0,,"M)";0.0"M"_)	123.5M
1.23457E+11	#,###.0,,"M"_);(#,###.0,,"M)";0.0"M"_)	123,456.8M
1000000	#,###.0,,"M"_);(#,###.0,,"M)";0.0"M"_)	1.0M
5000000	#,###.0,,"M"_);(#,###.0,,"M)";0.0"M"_)	5.0M
-5000000	#,###.0,,"M"_);(#,###.0,,"M)";0.0"M"_)	(5.0M)
0	#,###.0,,"M"_);(#,###.0,,"M)";0.0"M"_)	0.0M

Appending zeros to a value

The following format string displays a value with three additional zeros and no decimal places. A value with this number format appears as if it's rounded to no decimal places and then multiplied by 1,000.

```
#",000"
```

Examples of this format string, plus a variation that adds six zeros, are shown in Table B-8.

Table B-8: Examples of Displaying a Value with Extra Zeros

Value	Number Format	Display
1	#",000"	1,000
1.5	#",000"	2,000
43	#",000"	43,000
-54	#",000"	-54,000
5.5	#",000"	6,000
0.5	#",000,000"	1,000,000
0	#",000,000"	,000,000
1	#",000,000"	1,000,000
1.5	#",000,000"	2,000,000
43	#",000,000"	43,000,000
-54	#",000,000"	-54,000,000
5.5	#",000,000"	6,000,000
0.5	#",000,000"	1,000,000

Hiding zeros

In the following format string, the third element of the string is empty, which causes zero-value cells to display as blank:

```
General;-General;
```

This format string uses the General format for positive and negative values. You can, of course, substitute any other format codes for the positive and negative parts of the format string.

Displaying leading zeros

To display leading zeros, create a custom number format that uses the 0 character. For example, if you want all numbers to display with ten digits, use the number format string that follows. Values with fewer than ten digits will display with leading zeros.

```
0000000000
```

You also can force all numbers to display with a fixed number of leading zeros. The format string that follows, for example, prepends three zeros to each number:

```
"000"#
```

Displaying fractions

Excel supports quite a few built-in fraction number formats. (Select the Fraction category from the Number tab of the Format Cells dialog box.) For example, to display the value .125 as a fraction with 8 as the denominator, select As Eighths (4/8) from the Type list.

You can use a custom format string to create other fractional formats. For example, the following format string displays a value in 50ths:

```
# ??/50
```

To display the fraction reduced to its lowest terms, use a question mark after the slash symbol. For example, the value 0.125 can be expressed as 2/16, and 2/16 can be reduced to 1/8. Here's an example of a number format that displays the value as a fraction reduced to its simplest terms:

```
# ?/?
```

If you omit the leading hash mark, the value displays without a leading value. For example, the value 2.5 would display as *5/2* using this number format code:

```
?/?
```

The following format string displays a value in terms of fractional dollars. For example, the value 154.87 displays as *154 and 87/100 Dollars.*

```
0 "and "??/100 "Dollars"
```

The following example displays the value in 16ths, with an appended double quotation mark. This format string is useful when you deal with inches (for example, 2/16).

```
# ??/16\"
```

Displaying N/A for text

The following number format string uses General formatting for all cell entries except text. Text entries appear as N/A.

```
0.0;0.0;0.0;"N/A"
```

You can, of course, modify the format string to display specific formats for values. The following variation displays values with one decimal place:

```
0.0;0.0;0.0;"N/A"
```

Displaying text in quotes

The following format string displays numbers normally but surrounds text with double quotation marks:

```
General;General;General;\"@\"
```

Repeating a cell entry

The following number format is perhaps best suited as an April Fool's gag played on an office mate. It displays the contents of the cell three times. For example, if the cell contains the text Budget, the cell displays Budget Budget Budget. If the cell contains the number 12, it displays as 12 12 12.

```
@ @ @
```

Testing custom number formats

When you create a custom number format, don't overlook the Sample box in the Number tab of the Format Cells dialog box. This box displays the value in the active cell using the format string in the Type box.

It's a good idea to test your custom number formats by using the following data: a positive value, a negative value, a zero value, and text. Often, creating a custom number format takes several attempts. Each time you edit a format string, it is added to the list. When you finally get the correct format string, access the Format Cells dialog box one more time and delete your previous attempts.

Displaying a negative sign on the right

The following format string displays negative values with the negative sign to the right of the number. Positive values have an additional space on the right, so both positive and negative numbers align properly on the right.

```
0.00_-;0.00-
```

To make the negative numbers more prominent, you can add a color code to the negative part of the number format string:

```
0.00_-;[Red]0.00-
```

Conditional number formatting

Conditional formatting refers to formatting that is applied based on the contents of a cell. Excel's Conditional Formatting feature provides the most efficient way to perform conditional formatting of numbers, but you also can use custom number formats.

Note

A conditional number formatting string is limited to three conditions: two of them are explicit, and the third one is implied (that is, everything else). The conditions are enclosed in square brackets and must be simple numeric comparisons.

The following format string displays different text (no value), depending on the value in the cell. This format string essentially separates the numbers into three groups: less than or equal to 4, greater than or equal to 8, and other.

```
[<=4]"Low"* 0;[>=8]"High"* 0;"Medium"* 0
```

The following number format is useful for telephone numbers. Values greater than 9999999 (that is, numbers with area codes) are displayed as (xxx) xxx-xxxx. Other values (numbers without area codes) are displayed as xxx-xxxx.

```
[>9999999](000) 000-0000;000-0000
```

For U.S. ZIP codes, you might want to use the format string that follows. This displays ZIP codes using five digits. If the number is greater than 99999, it uses the ZIP-plus-four format (xxxxx-xxxx).

```
[>99999]00000-0000;00000
```

Coloring values

Custom number format strings can display the cell contents in various colors. The following format string, for example, displays positive numbers in red, negative numbers in green, zero values in black, and text in blue:

```
[Red]General;[Green]-General;[Black]General;[Blue]General
```

Following is another example of a format string that uses colors. Positive values display normally; negative numbers and text cause Error! to display in red.

```
General;[Red]"Error!";0;[Red]"Error!"
```

Using the following format string, values that are less than 2 display in red. Values greater than 4 display in green. Everything else (text, or values between 2 and 4) displays in black.

```
[Red][<2]General;[Green][>4]General;[Black]General
```

As seen in the preceding examples, Excel recognizes color names such as [Red] and [Blue]. It also can use other colors from the color palette, indexed by a number. The following format string, for example, displays the cell contents using the 16th color in the color palette:

```
[Color16]General
```

Note

Excel's conditional formatting is a much better way to color text in a cell based on the cell's value.

Formatting dates and times

When you enter a date into a cell, Excel formats the date using the system short date format. You can change this format using the Windows Control Panel (Regional and Language options).

Excel provides many useful built-in date and time formats. Table B-9 shows some other custom date and time formats that you may find useful. The first column of the table shows the date/time serial number.

Table B-9: Useful Custom Date and Time Formats

Value	Number Format	Display
41456	mmmm d, yyyy (dddd)	July 1, 2013 (Monday)
41456	"It's" dddd!	It's Monday!
41456	dddd, mm/dd/yyyy	Monday, 07/01/2013
41456	"Month: "mmm	Month: July
41456	General (m/d/yyyy)	41456 (7/4/2013)
0.345	h "Hours"	8 Hours
0.345	h:mm "o'clock"	8:16 o'clock
0.345	h:mm a/p"m"	8:16 am
0.78	h:mm a/p".m."	6:43 p.m.

Cross-Ref

See Chapter 6, "Working with Dates and Times," for more information about Excel's date and time serial number system.

Displaying text with numbers

The ability to display text with a value is one of the most useful benefits of using a custom number format. To add text, just create the number format string as usual (or use a built-in number format as a starting point) and put the text within quotation marks. The following number format string, for example, displays a value with the text (US Dollars) added to the end:

```
#,##0.00 "(US Dollars)"
```

Here's another example that displays text before the number:

```
"Average: "0.00
```

If you use the preceding number format, you'll find that the negative sign appears before the text for negative values. To display number signs properly, use this variation:

```
"Average: "0.00;"Average: "-0.00
```

The following format string displays a value with the words Dollars and Cents. For example, the number 123.45 displays as *123 Dollars and .45 Cents.*

```
0 "Dollars and" .00 "Cents"
```

Displaying a zero with dashes

The following number format string displays zero values as a series of dashes:

```
#,##0.0;-###0.0;------
```

You can, of course, create lots of variations. For example, you can replace the six hyphens with any of the following:

```
<0>
-0-
~~
"<NULL>"
" [NULL] "
```

Note

When using angle brackets or square brackets, you must place them within quotation marks.

Formatting numbers using the TEXT function

Excel's TEXT function accepts a number format string as its second argument. For example, the following formula displays the contents of cell A1 using a custom number format that displays a fraction:

```
=TEXT(A1,"# ??/50")
```

However, not all formatting codes work when used in this manner. For example, colors and repeating characters are ignored. The following formula does not display the contents of cell A1 in red:

```
=TEXT(A1,"[Red]General")
```

Using special symbols

Your number format strings can use special symbols, such as the copyright symbol, degree symbol, and so on.

The easiest way to insert a symbol into a number format string is to enter it into a cell. Copy the character and then paste it into your custom number format string (using Ctrl+V). Use the Insert ➜ Text ➜ Symbol command, which displays the Insert Symbol dialog box, to enter a special character into a cell.

Suppressing certain types of entries

You can use number formatting to hide certain types of entries. For example, the following format string displays text but not values:

```
;;
```

This format string displays values (with one decimal place) but not text or zeros:

```
0.0;-0.0;;
```

This format string displays everything except zeros (values display with one decimal place):

```
0.0;-0.0;;@
```

You can use the following format string to completely hide the contents of a cell:

```
;;;
```

Note that when the cell is activated, however, the cell's contents are visible on the Formula bar.

Displaying a number format string in a cell

Excel doesn't have a worksheet function that displays the number format for a specified cell. You can, however, create your own function using VBA. Insert the following function procedure into a VBA module:

```
Function NUMBERFORMAT(cell) As String
'   Returns the number format string for a cell
    Application.Volatile True
    NUMBERFORMAT = cell.Range("A1").NumberFormat
End Function
```

Then you can create a formula such as the following:

```
=NUMBERFORMAT(C4)
```

This formula returns the number format for cell C4. If you change a number format, use Ctrl+Alt+F9 to force the function to be reevaluated.

Cross-Ref

Refer to Part VI, "Developing Custom Worksheet Functions," for more information about creating custom worksheet functions using VBA.

Filling a cell with a repeating character

The asterisk (*) symbol specifies a repeating character in a number format string. The repeating character completely fills the cell and adjusts if the column width changes. The following format string, for example, displays the contents of a cell padded on the right with dashes:

```
General*-;-General*-;General*-;General*-
```

Displaying leading dots

The following custom number format is a variation on the accounting format. Using this number format displays the dollar sign on the left and the value on the right. The space in between is filled with dots.

```
($*.#,##0.00_);_($*.(#,##0.00);_($* "-"??_);_(@_)
```

Index

D

E

F

M

Q

R

U

V

W

X-Y-Z